Advanced Management Accounting

Advanced Management Accounting

Tom Groot

Frank Selto

PEARSON

Harlow, England • London • New York • Boston • San Francisco • Toronto • Sydney
Auckland • Singapore • Hong Kong • Tokyo • Seoul • Taipei • New Delhi
Cape Town • São Paulo • Mexico City • Madrid • Amsterdam • Munich • Paris • Milan

PEARSON EDUCATION LIMITED
Edinburgh Gate
Harlow CM20 2JE
Tel: +44 (0)1279 623623
Website: www.pearson.com/uk

First published 2013 (print and electronic)

ISBN: 978-0-273-73018-7 (print)
978-0-273-73021-7 (PDF)
978-0-273-78070-0 (eText)

British Library Cataloguing-in-Publication Data
A catalogue record for the print edition is available from the British Library

Library of Congress Cataloging-in-Publication Data
Selto, Frank H.
Advanced management accounting/Frank Selto, Tom Groot.
p. cm.
Includes bibliographical references.
ISBN 978-0-273-73018-7 (print) – ISBN 978-0-273-73021-7 (PDF) – ISBN 978-0-273-78070-0 (eTest) 1. Managerial accounting. I. Groot, Tom. II. Title.
HF5657.4.S426 2013
658.15'11–dc23
2012044309

ARP impression 98

Front cover image: © Getty Images

Print edition typeset in 9.5/12.5 pt Charter ITC Std by 71
Print edition printed and bound in Great Britain by Ashford Colour Press Ltd

NOTE THAT ANY PAGE CROSS REFERENCES REFER TO THE PRINT EDITION

To my parents, Loes and Lou, who taught me to learn and grow. To my wife Geske and my daughters Susanne and Wieteke for their enduring support and love. And to my students who inspire me to continue in teaching and research. – Tom Groot

To my students at all levels who have challenged me and have helped me sustain my curiosity and devotion to learning and teaching. I hope this text delivers value to all readers. – Frank Selto

Contents

Preface

Purpose of the text

Welcome to *Advanced Management Accounting,* which has been a multi-year effort to serve instructors and students of upper level management accounting courses. Our intent is to provide in one place many of the most salient discussions of research and practice that the stakeholders of these courses have had to gather and integrate on their own. From our own efforts and from helpful reviews by our peers, we know that no textbook of reasonable size can serve all users and cover all of the relevant areas of management accounting knowledge and research. Nonetheless, and with apologies if we have omitted your favorite topic, we have crafted a text that we believe will provide the chapter texts and end of chapter items that most of us will use successfully. We welcome your recommendations for improvements.

Pedagogical approach

As authors (please see our short biographies), we are active management accounting researchers and teachers. We are eager to bring high quality research into our classrooms that challenges and extends current practices. Fortunately, the world community of management accounting is active and always evolving. However, this does make it difficult to keep a traditional textbook at the cutting edge, which might explain why some management accounting texts appear unchanged from decades ago when we also were students. We want to push the envelope to include valid research and useful practice, but we know that we, too, will always supplement this text with the latest developments. Despite evolving research and practice, we believe that fundamentals endure within changing contexts and technologies. We acknowledge our debts to our mentors, and we are loath to rush to the latest fad, whatever its source. Although we are somewhat conservative in this regard, we want to recognise important developments and point toward areas of potential innovations that will enrich our understanding and teaching of management accounting. Our pedagogy relies on five principles that are explained next.

1. *Integration of research and practice.* Our view of research and practice is that they are entwined, and they are mutually beneficial. Research innovates and validates practice. Practice might lag research because of costs of education and application, but practice might also lead research by venturing into uncharted territory in search of solutions to new problems or opportunities. Each of our chapters seeks to reflect vibrant interactions between research and practice. The numerous citations provide the authority for our writing and provide sources for interested readers to begin their own explorations.
2. *Examples grounded in current practice, guided by theory.* Each of our chapters is grounded in the observed practices of real (but disguised) organisations. With few exceptions, we do not create hypothetical Company A selling Product X, because the real world is replete with

compelling examples that we have observed and from which we have learned. Because not every organisation has applied all of the research and tools that we wish to describe, we take some liberties with the experiences of actual organisations, which is why we often fictionalise their names and elaborate the breadth and depth of their applications of management accounting knowledge. This creative licence allows us to fully explore and reflect in a realistic way on the interactions of management accounting research and practice.

3. *Hands on analysis, with extensive uses of Excel®.* We believe that learning while doing is the most effective pedagogical approach. Indeed, this is how we have learned what we share in this text. In each chapter we apply the guidance of research to solving the problems raised by our grounded example organisations. We invite readers to work with us as we develop and apply solution methods that we believe are generalisable to other organisations in similar contexts. We insist on using Excel® throughout the text because this is the business tool of choice for most management accounting professionals. It is also a tool that is most widely available and accessible. We strongly believe that every one of our students must be proficient with this ubiquitous tool or one of its close competitors.
4. *End of chapter (EOC) items that reflect and extend chapter text.* Most of our EOC items are also drawn from the experiences of real organisations. These are identified by name when the pertinent information has been publicly reported or disclosed. Otherwise, they too have fictionalised names. Although an instructor might gather basic research and practice readings to form the backbone of an upper level management accounting course, many find it difficult to craft enough EOC items properly to exercise and extend their students' critical thinking and applications of key concepts and tools. We have worked hard to supply adequate EOC items for our readers.
5. *Short, data intensive cases that also require critical thinking.* Many instructors choose to supplement their courses with commercially available cases, such as the many Harvard Business School type cases. We think this is a legitimate and valuable addition to any upper level course. However, we have decided to provide our own, shorter cases that require manipulation and analyses of data in contexts similar to the chapter text. We have successfully taught these short cases ourselves, so we know that they 'work.' This is an overt cost saving decision that puts all the materials needed for most courses in a single package. Instructors should feel free to use these cases or to supplement the text with favourite commercial cases.

Performance measurement and reward management

We believe that we should briefly describe our views of several very important meta-topics related to performance measurement and reward management. These views condition our expositions of the text chapters and may be a useful introduction to those who are new to the theory and practice of these concepts.

Most traditional management accounting topics were developed in the manufacturing settings of many decades ago, and we teach and use many of them still today in both manufacturing and service contexts. However, the globalisation of business has had profound impacts on management practice and the demand for efficient management accounting tools and methods. For example, almost no one still yearns for the days when an organisation (or even a centrally controlled economy) could be managed as a linear program. Life might have been simpler then, or at least we imagined it so. We mused that, if only we could enumerate all the constraints and measure the parameters of the linear program more accurately, management accountants could serve the greater good of efficient management. However, the world of global business did not stand still long enough to allow us to complete our model specifications–and it never will.

We believe that mathematical programming continues to be a useful mental framework and finds great practical application at small scales of management. However, the most important keys to successful management in our rapidly changing global economy appear to be decentralisation and goal congruence. Managers at the local level must have both the authority and responsibility for operating decisions. To do so effectively requires that local managers have ready access to measures of performance relevant to the organisation's goals and that they are accountable for their decisions. These decision making tasks create demands for measures of relevant costs, contribution margins, profits, sustainability and compatible incentives. Apart from sustainability issues, none of this is new (as we acknowledge at the appropriate times throughout the text), but command and control mentalities linger, perhaps as a response to fear of risk (exposure to loss). Yet, the opportunity costs of maintaining centralised decision making may far exceed the losses from mistaken decisions that might only be recognised as mistakes *ex post.* Most of this text is devoted to understanding the alternative measures and methods that organisations can use to improve local decision making. Because of our exciting, dynamic economic reality, this text must forever be a work in process.

Behavioural and rational economic perspectives of management accounting

Another meta-topic that underlies our text chapters is the tension between classical, rational economic views of management accounting and alternative explanations of observed behaviour.

The previously described linear programming approach to decision making and management control was derived directly from the normative position that managers should behave as rational economic beings and maximise profits (or the like). Now that vast computing power is available at low cost, one might have difficulty explaining today's decentralised organisations and economies. Why not scale up the size of the linear program? Transaction costs related to obtaining current information about products, processes and markets probably explain why even centralised economies that now could use supercomputers to quickly run even a mammoth linear program, instead are decentralising decision making (perhaps with some cultural reluctance).

It is now controversial whether management accounting should provide integrated decision support for intendedly (or 'boundedly') rational, local managers or whether management accounting should instead strive for more accurate measures of performance that managers should integrate and act upon. After all, if complex performance measures can be integrated accurately, why rely on fallible or untrustworthy managers?

Not many of us are capable, intuitive linear programmers, as much as we might try. Thus, linear programs (or other mathematical and qualitative descriptions of the firm) may continue to serve as useful decision aids to those of us who intend to be rational in our local decision making, but need some help. This need for integrated relevant information might explain the popularity of balanced scorecards, which some proponents attempt to mould into linear programming clones. Perhaps this can be successful, and command and control types can regain centralised control. In contrast, we believe (and hope) that the problems of management require decentralisation and many capable managers, who demand accurate, relevant, timely management accounting information.

If we are correct, we still need to understand whether managers are intendedly rational or, in a more complex view, are 'predictably irrational,' which is a compelling but somewhat uncomfortable 'behavioral' view of decision making by even highly educated individuals. If the latter view is descriptive, we management accountants could prepare accurate and relevant information for our supposed rational managers, only to see the information misused, if it is used at all. Would we be swimming upstream to try to force rationality, or would we be better advised to learn how to better communicate decision making information to human managers? This might be the next challenge for management accounting, and we hope that our coverage of these issues motivates the next generation of researchers and professionals to seek effective solutions.

Major themes achieved by inter-related chapters *(with brief descriptions)*

The text major sections and chapters are inter-related, as is the entire field of Management Accounting. Although instructors are free to cover the chapters as they wish, we believe that a good order is to cover them in numerical sequence.However, any of the chapters may be skipped if the material is covered elsewhere in the curriculum. The section and chapter coverage is as follows:

Section 1–Management Accounting for decision making

Chapter 1–Foundations of Management Accounting. The origins of management accounting are venerable, and its evolution has been steady. Chapter 1 traces the development of management accounting from the early history of civilized society, through two industrial revolutions, to the modern day. Readers may be surprised both by management accounting's durability and adaptability. We consider this first chapter to be essential reading.

Chapter 2–Planning and decision making under risk. Chapter 2 develops, compares, contrasts and applies rational-economic and behavioural-economic models of decision making. This chapter demonstrates the enduring strength of the rational approach, but also its limitations. Behavioural approaches are appealing but are no simpler to apply, at least at this time. How decisions should be and are made is of paramount importance to management accountants whose task is to provide decision relevant information to managers.

Chapter 3–Management control. This chapter on management control is devoted to developing and using management instruments to ensure goal congruence and performance. Management control theorists and professionals have developed numerous ways to describe and apply the many types of management controls available. Chapter 3 synthesises these multiple approaches to management control into a single model and applies the model to multiple organisational contexts.

Chapter 4–Financial modelling. Chapter 4 develops and applies the spreadsheet skills that every management accountant should master. These spreadsheet skills are focused on problems of estimating performance and performance risk through sensitivity, scenario and Monte Carlo analysis. Subsequent chapters rely on this and other chapters' tools.

Section 2–Profitability analysis

Chapter 5–Budgeting and beyond. Chapter 5 confronts the behavioural 'problems' of budgeting and explores whether and how two recent remedies (abandon budgeting or reform it) can result in more effective budgeting practice. Most of the numerical examples in Chapter 5 apply an activity based approach to budgeting (the most salient remedy) and budget variance analysis. This chapter extends budgeting practice far beyond the typical textbook treatment of this important topic.

Chapter 6–Cost analysis and estimation. Chapter 6 develops estimates of cost functions based on the amount and quality of historical data that are available. The chapter thoroughly develops cost function estimation through multiple regression analysis, non-linear learning curve analysis, and an engineering method that is data intensive, but not so dependent on historical data. In rapidly changing contexts, this last method might be the most valuable.

Chapter 7–Investment analysis. This chapter covers common and emerging methods to analyse long-term decisions, where opportunity costs of funds are materially important. Chapter 7 briefly reviews the theory of interest, the cost of capital, and then proceeds to develop and apply discounted cash flow methods that include net present value, internal rate of return and real options.

Chapter 8–Management of operational performance. Chapter 8 develops and applies optimal production models that progress from simple linear programmes to more complex models, including Theory of Constraints, which features manipulation of production constraints and opportunities. The chapter has special emphasis on managing productive capacity and product quality through such methods as quality control, TQM and Six Sigma.

Section 3–Management Control systems

Chapter 9–Transfer pricing in decentralised organisations. Chapter 9 develops the economics of transfer pricing and applies the wisdom of this rational approach to the difficult settings of limited information and differences in international tax regimes. In these settings, simple market based transfer prices might not be available or even applicable. The chapter develops and applies alternative methods used for international transfer pricing.

Chapter 10–Integrated financial and non-financial measures. Of course, Chapter 10 describes and critiques the Balanced Scorecard, but this chapter also describes what probably are its predecessors, including the Tableau de Bord and the Performance Pyramid. This chapter explores the opportunities and difficulties of relating financial and non-financial measures of performance into a coherent framework to support improved planning and control.

Chapter 11–Inter-organisational control. Chapter 11 presents the emerging issues of contracting and management control across organisational and international boundaries. The chapter develops a model of inter-organisational management control that reflects current theory, including transaction cost theory and the resource based view of the firm. The chapter confronts this theory with examples from current practice.

Chapter 12–Reward systems in organisations. The final chapter builds theoretical foundations of motivation and incentives to support designing reward systems in nearly any organisation. The chapter contrasts the shareholder and the stakeholder perspectives of organisational goals and concludes hopefully that they can be complementary. The chapter describes and explores the many performance and reward dyads and points the way to future research and applications in this compelling application of management accounting knowledge and methods.

Lecturer Resources

For password-protected online resources tailored to support the use of this textbook in teaching, please visit **www.pearsoned.co.uk/grootselto**

About the authors

Tom Groot is Professor of Management Accounting at the VU University in Amsterdam, The Netherlands, since 1995. He is chair of the Department of Accounting and director of the Amsterdam Research Center in Accounting (ARCA). He learned his teaching skills while he practiced problem based learning at Maastricht University. He has co-authored several books nationally and internationally on management accounting and financial management. He has published widely in academic and professional journals and served on various editorial review boards. He is actively involved in advising and supervising profit seeking and non-profit organisations.

Frank Selto is Professor of Accounting at the University of Colorado, Boulder, where he has taught management accounting at all levels since 1985. His teaching always includes a heavy use of spreadsheet modelling and analysis. He is a co-author of an intermediate level cost management text that has been adopted internationally. He has published widely in areas of management accounting in leading international academic and professional journals. He has served on several editorial review boards. He earned BSME, MSME, MBA and PhD degrees–before the availability of personal computers. His first computer was an Apple II, and he still prefers Apple products.

Publisher's acknowledgements

We are grateful to the following for permission to reproduce copyright materia

Figures

Figure 1.1 adapted from Management accounting in an early multidivisional organization: General Motors in the 1920s, *Business History Review*, 52(4), pp. 490–517 (Johnson, H.T. 1978), reproduced with permission; Figure 1.1 from Microsoft Corporation, Microsoft product screenshot(s) reprinted with permission from Microsoft Corporation; Figure 2.7 from Prospect theory: an analysis of decision under risk, *Econometrica*, 47(2), pp. 263–291 (Kahneman, D. and Tversky., A 1979), reproduced with permission; Figure 2.8 adapted from Earnings management to avoid earnings decreases and losses, *Journal of Accounting and Economics*, 24, pp. 99–126 (Burgstahler, D., & Dichev, I. 1997), Copyright 1997. With permission from Elsevier; Figure 3.5 adapted from Choice and change of measures in performance measurement models, *Management Accounting Research*, 15 (4), pp. 441–69 (Malina, M. and F. Selto 2004), Copyright 2004. With permission from Elsevier; Figure 10.2 from *The Balanced Scorecard*, Harvard Business Press (Kaplan, R.S., & Norton, D.P. 1996) Reprinted by permission of Harvard Business School Press. Copyright ©1996 by the Harvard Business School Publishing Corporation; all rights reserved; Figure on page 405 adapted from Supervisory control of a multi-echelon supply chain: A modular petrinet approach for inter organisational control *Robotics and Computer-Integrated Manufacturing*, 24 (6), pp. 728–734 (Dryzmalski, J. and Odrey, N. G. 2008), Copyright 2008. With permission from Elsevier; Figure 11.1 from Control of international joint ventures, *Accounting, Organizations and Society* 25, pp. 579–607 (Groot, T. and K. Merchant 2000), Copyright 2000. With permission from Elsevier; Figure 11.4 from Control of inter-organizational relationships: evidence on appropriation concerns and coordination requirements, *Accounting, Organizations and Society*, 29 (1), pp. 27–49 (Dekker,H. 2004), Copyright 2004. With permission from Elsevier.

Tables

Table on pages 181–182 adapted from Edmunds.com, Data provided by Edmunds.com, Inc. True Market Value® is a registered trademark of that company; Table 8.6 from *Implementing Six Sigma: Smarter Solutions Using Statistical Methods*, John Wiley & Sons (Breyfogle, F. W., III 2003) Copyright ©2012 John Wiley & Sons. Reproduced with permission of John Wiley & Sons Inc.

Text

Case Study 3.4 adapted from Strategic planning, ABC, and high technology, *Management Accounting Quarterly*, March, pp. 37–40 (Selto, F. and Jasinski, D. 1996), Management accounting quarterly by Institute of Management Accountants Copyright 1996 Reproduced with permission of INSTITUTE OF MANAGEMENT ACCOUNTANTS in the format Republish in a textbook/'other' book via Copyright Clearance Center.; Case Study 3.5 adapted from

Choice and change of measures in performance measurement models, *Management Accounting Research*, 15 (4), pp. 441–69 (Malina, M. and F. Selto 2004), Copyright 2004, With permission from Elsevier; Boxs 11.1, 11.3 from Control of international joint ventures, *Accounting, Organizations and Society* 25, pp. 579–607 (Groot, T. and K. Merchant 2000), Copyright 2000. With permission from Elsevier.

Photographs

Alamy Images: © Everett Collection Historical 11, © Pictorial Press Ltd 6; Corbis: © Bettmann 8; GM Media Archive: 9.

In some instances we have been unable to trace the owners of copyright material, and we would appreciate any information that would enable us to do so.

SECTION 1

Management accounting for decision making

Chapter 1

Foundations of management accounting

1.1 The role of management accounting information

Management accounting is concerned with the generation, communication and use of financial and non-financial information for managerial decision making and control activities. Management accounting information can take many forms, like accounting information derived directly from the accounting system, financial information taken from external financial data sources, quantitative information from production departments or qualitative information from human resource or customer satisfaction enquiries. Management accounting information does not have to follow standard rules or regulations that are commonly used for external financial reporting. Each organisation can freely choose how to organise the management accounting function and how to generate and use management accounting information. The absence of regulation allows managers to generate information that best fits their needs. It also creates the condition for many different management accounting approaches and information to emerge: some better equipped for supporting management decisions and control systems than others. The differences may also in the end appear to become sources of competitive advantage: companies using more adequate management accounting information may reach better decisions and may also more effectively motivate and control their units and employees.

Most of our current management accounting systems and techniques have been developed in practice. Managers developed each of the new planning and control techniques to solve specific challenges. In this chapter we want to reconstruct management accounting history and trace back in time to answer the question of why management accounting planning and control information and methods of production (or 'instruments') commonly known to us have evolved and why new ones are emerging. As this chapter will show, we can distinguish three main reasons why new management accounting techniques are developed. **First,** a major driver of management accounting development is the way economic activity is organised. Managers active in fully transparent and efficient markets appear to rely more on market information and price signals. When markets become less efficient, firms try to integrate business functions and replace market price information by internal information about resource consumption that mimic and partly replace price information. A **second** major driver of management accounting developments is the way organisations are structured. Fully centralised organisations require a different internal management accounting system than decentralised organisations. Similarly, specialised firms require different management accounting information compared to diversified corporations. And **third,** the type of productive activities performed in organisations may lead to differences in management accounting information used.

Reconstructing the reason why specific management accounting practices have been developed may also allow us to pose the same questions again, when reconsidering the needs of contemporary business organisations. Management accounting solutions that worked well for past problems may not be necessarily the best solution for current problems, and we can expect new solutions to evolve.

1.2 Early developments in trade and production

1.2.1 Merchants and artisans

It is generally believed that the market economy as we know it today originated among Mediterranean and Baltic societies around 1000 A.D. Independent institutions for production and trade were allowed to accumulate private property, thus incentivising individuals to search for productive opportunities. The information that guided market exchanges was provided by market prices. Prices also led to the development of extensive trading networks. Traders active in these networks used market prices to search for and select economic opportunities. However, they rarely used currencies, but they used elaborate claims and counter-claims to settle their transactions. These claims were registered in double-entry accounts, which facilitated the exact registration of what was owing and owed. This seems to have been the main purpose of double-entry accounting systems in those days (Johnson, 1983).[1] Most transactions were market transactions between merchant-entrepreneurs and self-employed artisans. This changed when individuals discovered large profit opportunities, provided by an increase in market demand for textiles in Western Europe in the early eighteenth century (Landes, 1969). However, when merchants tried to substantially increase supply, they discovered that this was costly and inconvenient. An option was to contract more artisans, but this required more travelling to supervise more workers. An alternative was to offer higher prices, but this approach frequently motivated artisans to relax more and produce less. A viable alternative for the decentralised putting-out, piece-rate contract that allowed each artisan to decide independently how much to produce, is to replace this contract by a wage contract. Merchants thus became employers, gaining control over the artisans' productive activities by administering their production tasks (Johnson, 1983).

1.2.2 The small sized, functionally unspecialised firm

The merchant-employers, who replaced the market based contracts with their suppliers by labour contracts, organised productive activities in centralised work places specialised in mainly one activity, that of transforming raw materials into finished products. They relied on wholesale suppliers for the provision of raw materials and commissioned merchants for selling finished goods to customers. In this system, the impersonal forces of supply and demand governed the flow of inputs to the factories and the flow of goods from the factory to customers (Chandler, 1966b, 1977). While merchant-employers solved the productivity problem with individual artisans by placing them in an organisation and by offering a wage contract instead of a transaction contract, they also encountered a new problem. The market-determined

[1] Moreover, some authors claim that double-entry account keeping might not have been used if the transactions had always been done in cash.

piece-rate prices they previously used for evaluating productivity were no longer provided within the firm. Employers needed to replicate this information by using 'cost accounting' information about labour and other conversion costs[2] per unit of output for each worker and every process in the firm. It is commonly viewed that this information anticipated management accounting information as we know it today (Johnson, 1981). The 'invisible hand' of market forces steering decision making of merchants was gradually being replaced by the 'visible hand' of cost accounting information guiding the internal planning and coordination decisions of merchant-employers. The new cost accounting information was used for the evaluation of worker productivity and for steering the search for better production technologies. It was also used to define property claims of different stakeholder groups.

1.2.3 The large scale, functionally specialised firm

Companies in the 1800s grew both in size and in geographic dispersion. This was especially true for railroad companies since 1850 and companies in steel, chemical and metal working industries since 1870. These companies used complex production processes, which were organised in **functionally specialised organisational forms.** At the same time, these organisations grew in size and operated in oligopolistic markets. All these conditions required reliable cost data to manage business processes from a remote corporate unit, to evaluate unit performance, and to determine final product selling prices (Chandler, 1966b). The earliest factory cost records known to historians are from integrated, multi-process textile mills, like Charlton Mills (England around 1800), Boston Manufacturing Company (US, 1820s) and Lyman Mills (New England, established around 1855). Lyman Mills used an elaborate cost accounting system to control the receipt and use of raw materials like cotton, and to monitor the cost of finished goods, the productivity of workers and to predict the financial effects of changes in plant layout. Most textile companies used records of wages paid to workers and records of pounds of cotton converted in different processes, like picking, carding, roving, spinning, warping and weaving, and dyeing and finishing. Most of the data came from the double-entry bookkeeping system that was used to record the payment of liabilities. By combining both sets of records, textile companies could determine the direct labour cost per unit of output for each process. Most companies also recorded direct overhead cost per unit of output for each process. Overhead items generally included repairs, maintenance, bleach, dyes, fuel and teaming (Johnson, 1981).[3] Factory managers used the direct labour and conversion cost per output unit to steer internal operations and evaluate unit and individual worker performance (Chandler, 1977).[4] They also used contribution margin information (selling prices minus variable costs) for short-term decisions about special-order pricing and equipment modifications (Johnson, 1972).

Railroad companies were the first organisations with a wide geographic dispersion: most organisational units were located at a large distance from each other and from headquarters. Management needed more **summary financial information** about subunit performance in measures like cost per ton-mile and the **operating ratio,** which equalled the operating

[2] Conversion costs = Direct labour + manufacturing overhead.

[3] Interestingly, the factory did not use depreciation in the accounts. Expenditures for plant, equipment and major renovations were generally charged to profit and loss in the year they were incurred. Ordinary repair costs were included in the overhead expense total and allocated to each mill account (each production site within the Lyman Mills organisation).

[4] Not all costs were charged to inventory: manufacturing payroll and factory overhead was charged to the mill accounts, although part of these expenses could have been allocated to work in process according to modern standards (Johnson, 1972, p. 470).

income divided by sales (Kaplan, 1984). The industrial revolution in the mid 1800s led to the rise of mass production and distribution companies, adapting the US railroad cost accounting systems to their own needs. Many companies in this era introduced production processes that were increasingly capital intensive. This development, however, did not immediately motivate entrepreneurs to use their accounting systems to account for long lived (fixed) assets. Most of them gave only slight attention to asset depreciation or to full-absorption product costing. A well-documented example of management accounting practice is Andrew Carnegie, one of the most successful entrepreneurs of his time who managed his giant steel company from 1872 to 1902. His cost accounting system almost exclusively focused on prime or direct cost, and little attention was paid to overhead and capital costs. Carnegie and his general manager Shinn continuously gathered data on all direct costs in every process and produced weekly data on direct material and conversion costs for each process in his mills. Carnegie also gathered information about his competitors' direct production costs. His strategy was to produce at lower direct costs than those of all competitors in order to set lower prices for his products, which would enable him to run his factory at full capacity and outperform competitors on the market place, even in times of economic recession.

Andrew Carnegie (1835-1919) in 1905

Source: © Pictorial Press Ltd / Alamy

Carnegie did not manage his company by looking at costs alone: he had intimate knowledge of production processes. He insisted on high quality standards for his products and understood his customers' needs very well from personal connections with his clients (Johnson, 1992, p. 27). Continuous improvement of production technology was important, and Carnegie had a group of experts travelling extensively in the US and Europe in search of new investment opportunities. The basic rule Carnegie used for investment decisions was to invest only in new capacity or production technology when it would result in lower direct production costs (Johnson, 1981). This approach proved to be very successful at the time, but we should keep in mind that this can only work when prices set in this way will always meet sufficient demand in the market place and that the dominant strategy among all companies is to assess investment opportunities on their capability to reduce costs instead of on their potential to add value that would open up new markets for innovated products at premium prices.

The large scale, highly mechanised and functionally specialised firms gave engineers the opportunity to analyse parts of the production process by time and motion studies of elementary production activities. These studies allowed the engineers to drive slack out of the production process. They first optimised elementary production activities and then, by recombining optimised essential parts, also optimised the entire manufacturing process. The 'Scientific Management Movement' advocated this approach to the optimisation of production processes, which was particularly powerful between 1880 and 1914. It provided a major impetus to the development of cost accounting practices by improving standard cost accounting calculations. **Standard costing** techniques defined the allowed amount of labour and materials required for a unit of output, and were used for setting operational budgets. **Variance analysis** was developed to monitor and evaluate variances between standard and actual costs. Standard costing and variance analysis were jointly used for improving efficiency and managing reward systems that paid workers on a piece-rate basis (Epstein, 1978). The Scientific Management Movement also led to a new form of organisation in which the traditional line functions were supplemented by staff functions. They were designed not to accomplish work, but to set standards and ideals so that the line may work more efficiently. Consequently, the Scientific Management Movement also caused organisations to develop ways to measure and allocate overhead costs to products (Kaplan, 1984). These ideas were not introduced in firms overnight but it appears that the acceptance of Scientific Management ideas as well as the design of appropriate management and accounting systems have taken quite some time in the first half of the 20th century to be widely adopted and used by American companies(Fleischman & Tyson, 2007)

1.3 Increasing complexity of operations

1.3.1 The vertically integrated firm

At the turn of the 20th century, the US economy was driven by large, mass-producing manufacturing firms that were capable of achieving unprecedented speeds of throughput by the use of sophisticated, mass-production techniques. These techniques allowed corporate management substantially to curtail slack in production activities. However, similar benefits could not be captured in the supply of inputs and in the distribution of finished products. Traditional wholesale networks were reaching fewer customers and selling less products, while raw material suppliers did not realise or pass on sufficient benefits that could be gained by ordering larger input quantities. The gain-sharing contracts that were used at the time to coordinate procurement contracts and sales activities were apparently not capable of motivating agents elsewhere in the value chain to capture and pass on the gains that could be realised by the effective techniques developed in the manufacturing firms. During the merger wave of 1897-1903, large firms integrated backward with suppliers and forward with distributors and thus combined their production activities with new activities such as purchasing, marketing and transportation. The integrated companies now controlled internally many transactions across the value chain that had been mediated in the past by market exchanges (Chandler, 1977).

It is generally believed that inefficient markets may have caused the merger wave of 1897-1903. Some studies show that the UK market system was much more sophisticated and more efficient than America's. The UK system had low industrial concentration and almost no monopoly positions, competitive pressures were strong and the market was free for international entrants. UK firms remained much longer (until the 1920s) un-integrated, relying on market prices for exchanges among firms (Hannah, 1980; Johnson & Kaplan, 1987). The more complex US integrated organisations also needed a new organisational structure to control their diverse set of activities. Most organisations changed to the **unitary form of organisation**, which is comprised of independent units and one central office to manage both the units and the entire firm (Chandler, 1966a).

Traditional management accounting information like product level conversion costs and sales turnover did not suffice in the more complex organisations and were supplemented by budgeting information for the entire enterprise, as well as for each of its constituent units. These budgets expressed the corporate financial objectives and defined each department's required contribution to the firm's total financial performance. Common denominators to measure and compare the inherently very different department's contributions to the success of the entire company were **cash flow** (expressed in cash budgets) and **return on investment.** The E.I. DuPont de Nemours Powder Company (generally abbreviated to DuPont Powder Company) developed this approach in the years between 1903 and 1912. This was shortly after three DuPont cousins (Alfred, Coleman and Pierre) acquired E.I. DuPont de Nemours and Company, an explosives manufacturer in America since 1804. At the time they acquired the company, the explosives industry was organised around several explosives firms who coordinated output quotas and prices through the Gun Powder Trade Association, a loosely structured black blasting powder cartel. After 1903, the DuPont cousins rescinded almost all trade agreements, incorporated trade activities in the firm and restructured the organisation into three main departments: manufacturing, sales and purchasing.

Pierre S. Dupont, president GM 1920-1923
Source: © Bettman / Corbis

The DuPont accounting system[5] supported two central management functions: planning (the allocation of investments, including working capital and financing new capital requirements) and control (coordination and management of the horizontal flow of operations). The investment decisions were guided by the principle that the expenditures for additions to the earning equipment should be applied to those activities that generate the most additional value to the company(Johnson, 1975). The criterion used to evaluate investment projects was **Return on Investment:** net earnings (minus depreciation and before deduction of interest on long-term debt) divided by net assets (total assets minus goodwill and other intangibles, current liabilities, and reserves for depreciation).

Pierre du Pont opposed the then widely used measure of profits or earnings as a percentage of sales or costs (as was illustrated by the Carnegie Steel Company). In his view, the ultimate test is not the percentage of profit on cost, but the rate of return on the money invested in the business. In order to calculate the denominator, DuPont made a complete record of investment in plant and equipment in an 'asset accounting system'. This was a major innovation, sharply contrasting with the conservative accounting practice around 1903, which stimulated charging off capital expenditures to retained earnings as quickly as possible (Johnson, 1972). It took until about 1912 when one of DuPont's financial officers, Donaldson Brown, decomposed the ROI measure further into the product of the **sales turnover ratio** (sales divided by total investment) and the **operating ratio** (earnings to sales) and further down into other elementary components. This disaggregation was helpful in detecting the reasons for ROI outcomes to deviate from ROI targets in a given period. The second planning issue was the financing decision. A general rule was not to use debt financing: all investments were financed out of retained earnings and sales of company shares. The projection of future net earnings was, thus, used to

Donaldson Brown (1885-1965)

Source: GM Media Archive

[5] The accounting system is generally viewed as the most important part of DuPont's revolutionary new management system. It was developed by Pierre DuPont, Arthur Moxham, and Russell Dunham. They had all previously worked in several firms in Pennsylvania and Ohio, which used Frederick Taylor's manufacturing cost accounting system following Scientific Management principles.

determine the maximum amount of funds available for future investments. Total net earnings were projected by multiplying the quantity of explosives to be sold by the estimated net profit per unit for each product, added to the non-operating income from land sales and earnings from financial investments. Comparing this number with the investment appropriations led to the projection of the firm's cash position and thus to the estimation of additional financing needed (Chandler & Salsbury, 1971).

The management control function at DuPont was supported by detailed management accounting information systems as they were already fully developed by earlier non-integrated firms. The DuPont accounting information system was tailored to each of the three major departments: manufacturing, sales and procurement. Monthly manufacturing cost information about material usage and the dollar costs of all other inputs (except administrative overhead) in every production stage of each product in each mill was sent to the mill superintendents of the more than forty geographically dispersed mills. This information was intended to support the superintendents in their primary responsibility of improving production efficiency. The product and process costs were compared with predetermined standards and with cost information from other mills. The corporate management team (the Executive Committee) received a second set of information displaying the financial costs of goods manufactured, net earnings, and return on investment for each product and each mill.

The sales function was managed by a Sales Board, a committee of sales department executives from each of the three product branches (high explosives, smokeless gunpowder, and black blasting powder). They determined minimum sales prices by adding a given return to the costs per output, calculated by the accounting department. Sales managers could not sell at prices below the minimum price level. Additionally, the Sales Board determined a 'base sales' monetary amount per salesman, which was calculated by multiplying a 'normal' volume (an average expected volume) with a 'base' price (which was higher than a minimum price). The salesmanager's salary increased proportionally with the amount he exceeded the base price. He could independently determine the combination of price and volume, as long as he did not set a price below the minimum price level. The branch managers were also monitored on how they controlled their inventories and sales costs. The sales department estimated a 'normal' ratio of sales costs to gross sales for each branch office. Sales costs included general office expenses, plus 5% of the average accounts receivable and 5% of the average inventory balance (Johnson, 1975).

Until 1908, most DuPont purchases were done with independent agents who used terms that were easily comparable with market prices. As DuPont started integrating purchasing, it also employed its own agents, for instance in Chile to buy nitrates. In 1907, however, the backward integration process almost caused a working capital crisis. The procurement department kept buying large stocks at predetermined prices, while at the same time declining orders for explosives, which severely reduced DuPont's working capital. In order to lower the risk from oversupply, DuPont decided to make the purchasing department responsible for buying at the lowest prices only up to a certain stock level that was determined by each month's end product sales projections. DuPont also recognised the risks of undersupply, and decided to acquire (parts of) the ownership of supply sources, like nitrate and glycerin producers. DuPont's stake in these companies secured uninterrupted supply of quality inputs.

1.3.2 The multi-divisional firm

After World War I, some larger companies started to diversify their activities, mostly in an attempt to capture economies of scope and to diversify business risks. However, diversification also introduced new management problems. Diversifying companies such as Du Pont,

Sears Roebuck (a chain of retail stores) and General Motors (GM, an automotive company) discovered that their centralised structures and detailed management accounting information did not suffice for the management of diverse product lines or sales areas (Chandler, 1966). A good example is GM, which was founded by William Durant in 1912. GM was different, because it consisted of several diversified units, each manufacturing and selling a unique line of autos or parts. Each unit performed all operating functions, from purchasing, manufacturing to marketing and sales. Durant managed the entire company, using the same management systems that had been successfully developed by vertically integrated firms since the early 1900s. The detailed management accounting information and centralised control immersed Durant in the particular activities of each unit. However, the large variety and complexity of the firm did not allow him effectively to manage each unit, and it also made it impossible to generate sufficient economies of scope for the whole company.

When GM encountered a great crisis in 1920 (which was known as the 'inventory crisis') the chairman of the board, Pierre Du Pont[6], decided to replace Durant as company president and asked Alfred P. Sloan to work with him in restructuring the firm. They invited Donaldson Brown, the architect of the DuPont management accounting system, to join their team as chief financial officer. The new team installed a new management system that aimed at accomplishing **'centralised control with decentralised responsibility'.** This new approach differs greatly from the management systems used in integrated firms in that it **decentralised operational decision making and control,** while at the same time it **centralised corporate strategy making and firm wide coordination of diversified units.**

Donaldson Brown, the architect of GM's new system, placed the owners' interest at the forefront. The most important objective of the firm was to earn the highest long-term return on investment 'consistent with a sound growth of the business' (Sloan, 1963). Corporate

Alfred Sloan (1875-1966)

Source: © Everett Collection Historical/Alamy

[6] During the mid-1910s, the DuPont family was buying shares of GM stock which made them one of the larger shareholders of the company.

management implemented this general policy by stating that the firm in the long run should earn an average after-tax profit equal to 20% of investment while operating on average at 80% of 'standard volume' capacity. The standard volume was set at 80% of full capacity (Johnson, 1978). This required rate of return worked as a long-term planning objective against which annual operating plans of the divisions were evaluated.

Each division prepared an annual 'price study' in which division managers proposed selling prices for their products, based on sales estimates for the coming year in units and in dollars, costs, profits, capital requirements and return on investment, both at 'standard volume' and at the forecast volume, based on estimations provided by central office. If the proposed price for any model fell below the dollar equivalent of the standard price ratio and, if the gap between these two prices could not be attributed to short-term competitive pressures, then top management requested a division manager to reduce the proposed operating cost (Johnson, 1978, p. 500). During the execution of the plan, GM developed several sophisticated ways of controlling operations. Special attention was given to coordination problems between manufacturing and sales functions and to coordination between production divisions. Also the evaluation and reward functions of management were significantly improved. We will have a short look at each of these domains.

In coordinating operations, two major issues are of importance: shortening reaction time in production when sales numbers and inventory levels change, and facilitating the exchange of products and services between divisions. The shortening of reaction time was needed as a result of the inventory crisis, during which the division production schedules were not compared with timely sales and inventory data from car dealers. The Ten-day Sales Report was a summary that each dealer was required to send to the division every ten days of cars delivered to customers, the number of new orders taken, the total orders on hand, and the inventory numbers of new and used cars. Division managers compared the sales report to the estimate and, if the estimate was too high, production was immediately reduced. If the estimate was too low, the production programme was increased, within the plant capacity. If the sales reports showed an upward sales trend, also price and production capacity could be adjusted to meet market demands.

Most divisions did not only produce finished products, but also parts to be used in other divisions. GM's management devised a 'transfer pricing' system that allowed parts and products to be exchanged at cost-plus transfer prices. The general approach of transfer prices was to set internal prices at such a level as would also be used in transactions with external, independent business partners. This would also guarantee an undisturbed image of value transfers that had taken place within the company.

For the evaluation of production efficiency at different output levels, GM used 'flexible budgets' to restate the budget at different output levels. In this way the corporate level was able to distinguish actual income differences caused by unplanned and uncontrollable sales volume variations from controllable operating efficiency variations.[7] The improved forecasts from the Ten-day Sales Reports and the flexible budget variance analysis led to significant improvements in efficiency and in the use of working capital. As a result, the company managed to raise its average annual turnover of total inventories from 1.5 times in 1921 to 6.3 times in 1925.

The reward plan for senior managers of the corporation did not make the reward solely dependent on divisional performance, because GM's management feared that this would lead to behaviour that would optimise divisional performance without taking much care of the impact it might have on the welfare of the whole corporation. Bonuses were based on

[7] Other companies at the time also used flexible budgets, like Gillette Safety Razor Company (1927) and the Westinghouse Electric Corporation (late 1930s)(Johnson, 1978, p. 504).

divisional performance records, with possibilities for considering special divisional circumstances, and they were given in the form of rights to GM common stock. These rights only became vested if the manager stayed with GM for an additional period of time, usually five years. The reward package was intended in such a way that it focused the orientation of senior managers to the welfare of the entire corporation and to the performance of the company in the longer term. The significant growth of GM's common stock in the 1920s was not only an incentive for senior management to comply with the company's performance goals, but also convinced them to stay with the company for a longer time period (Johnson, 1978).

1.3.3 Twentieth century developments in management accounting

Our historic overview stops around 1925, and it is surprising to notice that a large portion of the management accounting methods and techniques currently taught in management accounting textbooks had already been developed by then. Most of these innovations were developed by engineers and industrialists working in organisations, rather than by academic researchers. Some additional innovations have been developed since 1925, mostly designed to improve existing management accounting techniques. For instance, Joel Dean, managing partner of Joel Dean Associates, a consulting firm specialising in investment decisions, advocated discounting cash flows for capital budgeting purposes (Dean, 1954). The discounting of cash flows from new investments should replace the older systems, based on payback period or the non-discounted return on investment ratio.[8] This improvement was intended to include the time value of money in the calculations of expenses and benefits of future investment opportunities.

Another innovation, aimed at improving already existing practice, was the development of residual income (RI) as an alternative for the ROI measure. It is generally believed that the General Electric Company developed RI in the 1950s. The residual income measure is defined as the difference between net operating income after taxes (NOPAT) and the cost of invested capital (total assets minus non-interest-bearing current liabilities). However, RI has never been widely used: a survey by Reece and Cool (1978) showed that only 2% of the companies surveyed used RI and 28% used both ROI and RI to measure investment centre performance. The popularity of RI type measures was greatly increased when the Stern Stewart & Company consulting firm advocated the economic value added *(EVA)* concept in the 1990s. The idea behind the EVA concept was to promote a measure of economic performance that correlates best with the shareholder's economic evaluation of company performance. To this end, the basic building blocks of RI, net operating profit and capital employed, are corrected for accounting 'distortions' to convert the accrual accounting figures into cash accounting information, which is supposed to better represent economic value (Stewart, 1991; Stern, et al., 1995). After a short period of great interest in EVA type measures in the 1990s, many companies stopped using EVA, mostly because of the numerous corrections (over 150 possible adjustments) on the accounting data that were needed. These made use of EVA complex and the EVA scores for most users difficult to understand and to interpret.

In the 1980s, Robin Cooper and Robert Kaplan proposed improvements in the allocation of indirect costs to cost objects (products, regions, functions or other objects) known as activity based costing (ABC). The basic idea of ABC was to follow resource consumption patterns for the attribution of indirect costs to cost objects (Cooper, 1988a, 1988b, 1988c, 1989b, 1989a, 1992). This development has been mainly motivated by observations of increased proportion

[8] In an earlier writing, Dean proposed to discount the stream of earnings instead of cash flows from an investment project, and concluded that discounting 'frequently may not be worth the cost' (Kaplan, 1984, p. 402).

of indirect costs of total production cost and the need reliably to estimate total product costs for pricing, planning and control decisions. The availability of computerised information systems helped companies in generating overhead consumption information needed for allocating overhead costs to cost objects. Perhaps upwards of 30% of firms use some form of ABC today.

In this period, also, new ideas about cost control and pricing were developed, which did not only come from the US, but also from other countries such as Germany and Japan. New costing methods like target costing and strategic costing show that labour based standard costing should be replaced by cost management procedures more attuned to strategic issues and with the cost structure of automated manufacturing (Kato, 1993; Shank & Govindarajan, 1993). Interestingly, in countries such as Germany, Austria, Switzerland and the Nordic countries, which have been highly influenced by German accounting ideas, financial accounting and management accounting have always been considered two separate systems. The German *Grenzplankostenrechnung* makes a distinction between variable (called 'proportional') and fixed costs and uses variable cost figures to optimise production plans within given production possibilities (linear programming techniques are widely used for this purpose). Cost analysis and cost control systems use hierarchies of cost centres to attribute cost elements (fixed and variable) to cost objects using cost drivers *(Bezugsgrößen)*.[9] This system was developed almost 40 years before Cooper and Kaplan's writings about Activity-based Costing (Ewert & Wagenhofer, 2007).

Old ideas like budgeting and standard costing, which were developed in large hierarchical and bureaucratic organisations in the beginning of the 20th century, became widely questioned. Some authors fear that management accounting techniques intended to control costs may virtually defeat themselves because they help to create feelings of confusion, frustration, suspicion and hostility, especially in organisations that prioritise team building, group decision making and worker empowerment (Caplan, 1966; Fleischman & Tyson, 2007).

In the 1990s, markets become more dynamic as a result of governments reducing trade barriers, combined with information technology facilitating the generation and distribution of product information to a wide audience of customers. Competitive advantage is not only about outperforming competitors on price, but also on product characteristics like quality, functionality, timeliness of service, customer friendliness and customer support. Most performance dimensions are not accounting, and mostly not even tangible. Competitive success generally lies in outperformance on difficult-to-measure product and service characteristics and is greatly dependent on the timing of competitive actions. Corporate management, therefore, needs to be proactive, and looks for information that can be used to prepare timely for future developments. Accounting information is inherently backward looking information, which is good for corporate reporting purposes, but which is not well-suited for preparing the company for future challenges. Robert Kaplan and David Norton proposed the construction of a more complete dashboard of performance indicators that may complement the existing accounting information, which they have coined the 'Balanced Scorecard' (Kaplan & Norton, 1992; Kaplan & Norton, 1993, 1996b; Kaplan & Norton, 1996a). The idea of constructing an extended scorecard containing a diverse set of accounting and non-accounting performance indicators is, however, not new. French companies already used a dashboard of mostly quantitative performance measures and they call it the *'Tableau de Bord',* which means something like 'dashboard' in French (Bourguignon, et al., 2004).

An important driver of management accounting innovation since the year 2000 is the availability of more business related data than ever before. The wide spread implementation

[9] These systems can become quite extensive: Deutsche Telekom uses 20,000 cost centres and cost assignments (Krumwiede, 2005).

of enterprise resource systems (ERP), point-of-sale systems (POS), and web sites, led to an unprecedented production of data about market performance, transactions and internal business processes. The set of technologies and processes that use data to understand and analyse business performance is also known as 'business intelligence'. It comprises data access, data analysis and data reporting activities for decision making and control. Recent improvements in hardware computer technology brought desktop computers into the board room with large data storage capabilities and fast processors for data analysis purposes. Software developers have dramatically expanded the functionality of products for data handling and analysis. Companies increasingly use 'analytics' to gain competitive advantages. The term 'analytics' means the extensive use of data, statistical and quantitative analysis, explanatory and predictive models, and fact based management to drive decisions and actions (Davenport & Harris, 2007). The use of analytic approaches to business problems is not new, but started in the 1960s when 'decision support systems' were developed for rather narrow activities like production planning, investment portfolio management and transportation routing. In later years 'executive support systems' have tried to bring analytics to the executive level, but these systems have been largely used for monitoring and reporting performance data, and not so much for analytical decision making. Today's companies increasingly compete on the extensive and systematic use of analytics to reach better decisions and superior performance. In our view, this is also changing the management accounting function. For better decision making, management accounting needs to bring together a larger variety of data from different business functions, like from marketing, sales, production, R&D, technology and finance. More analyses will be based on managing and analysing large databases, to better understand and manage important business processes. This will also enable management accountants to expand retrospective analyses with prospective planning. New analytical procedures and data availability will provide the opportunity not only to analyse costs and cost drivers, but also value creation and profit drivers. They will also enable a better understanding of how intangibles, like knowledge, product quality and customer loyalty, contribute to corporate performance. See 'The use of analytics' for some examples.

The use of analytics

UK's largest food retailer Tesco uses a loyalty card program called 'The Clubcard'. This card is used by individual customers who earn rewards for shopping at Tesco. The cards also collect information for Tesco on shopping behaviour, which helps the company to target specific customer groups, to increase the effectiveness of direct mail campaigns and to detect changes in customer tastes in an early stage (Humby, et al., 2007).

A medium sized internet company selling low priced airline tickets searched in 2010 for reasons why sales are always low in the months February to April. It appeared that a large proportion of the customers in that period were high income seniors flying to golf resorts in Mediterranean countries. The company could offer additional arrangements at premium prices for this customer group to compensate partly for sales losses in this period.

The US hotel chain Marriott has been known as an industry leader in revenue management. It uses the 'One Yield' program to optimise pricing for hotel rooms. The computerised system proposes optimal prices based on historical data on past bookings for a particular day, reservations that are currently on the books, and rates that were turned down by potential customers. Optimal prices for a specific hotel are the highest prices that will still lead to full occupancy (Overby, 2007).

Table 1.1 Overview of practical management accounting innovations

Economic system	Organisational form	Main objective	Management accounting system	Management control application
Market coordination	Small business	Efficient spot market transactions	Double-entry bookkeeping	Market transactions
Hierarchical instead of market coordination	Small sized, functionally unspecialised firm	Productivity improvements	Direct labor and conversion cost	Productivity Production innovation Definition of property claims
Functional specialisation in large firms operating in oligopolistic markets	Large scale, functionally specialised and capital intensive firm	Low cost, volume and high quality by specialisation	Product and overhead cost Contribution margin Efficiency Capital cost	Operational control Pricing Equipment modifications Investments
Integrating value chains within organisational structures	Vertically integrated firm	Capturing benefits generated in buying and selling organisations	Budgeting information Cash Flow Return on Investment	Coordination across the value chain Detailed operational control
Expansion of hierarchical coordination to multiple products	Multi-divisional firm	Economies of scope Diversification of business risk	Model based ROI budgets Revisions of sales forecasts Transfer pricing	Connecting short-term and long-term planning Optimising capacity use Coordination of internal transactions
More dynamic markets More competitive markets	Flat organisations Self empowered teams Business alliances	Economies of scale and scope Risk management Proactive management	RI, EVA ABC/ABM BSC Business analytics	Optimise economic value Better decisions about cost and price Proactive strategic decisions

1.3.4 Drivers of management accounting practice

Management accounting is a discipline, which has largely developed through practice. Engineers and industrialists have tried to improve management accounting information with the aim of finding concrete answers to practical managerial problems. New managerial problems arose when the economic system that guided entrepreneurial and managerial work changed and when new organisational forms were created. Both changes in economic system and in organisational form posed new challenges for management in planning and controlling organisational activities. New economic realities needed to be captured in accounting terms and management had to invent new ways to communicate accounting information to participants in and around the firm. A schematic summary of the most important developments in management accounting practice and their respective drivers is presented in Table 1.1.

1.4 Management accounting theory

1.4.1 Dominance of financial accounting thought

Most of the 19th and early 20th century cost accounting practices were developed by engineer-managers for internal use within the company. They used cost accounting information to decide how resources could best be employed in optimising corporate gain and to control internal processes and activities that generated those gains (Johnson & Kaplan, 1987). In this period, only very few manufacturing firms issued financial reports. Andrew Carnegie's steel company did not issue public reports. New England textile and American railroads companies issued semi-annual and annual reports to their non-managing directors in their early years, and published annual reports to stockholders by the 1850s (Previts & Merino, 1979). Virtually none of these companies had their reports audited by independent public accountants. The need for financial reporting rose after 1900 because a growing number of US companies needed to raise funds from widespread and detached suppliers of capital. The providers of capital, in their, turn required financial reports to be audited by independent public accountants.

In order to facilitate the auditors' work, the public accountants established well-defined methods and procedures for corporate financial reporting. The rule making work of public accountants has influenced greatly the development of management accounting theory and practice since the early 1920s. A classic example can be found in 'inventory costing' procedures. Textile companies valued their inventories at approximations of market price, and did not use cost information for that purpose. Cost information was mainly used to steer production activities, to evaluate performance and to support production improvement decisions. Public accountants, however, started to develop rules for financial reporting, which required that all information in financial statements were traceable to historical costs and financial accounts of transactions recorded in the double-entry books. For inventory costing this meant that rules were developed to attach total manufacturing costs to the total number of equivalent units of products produced. This 'accounted cost' is used to value inventories of finished and in-process inventories to report on the balance sheet, and to value the cost of products sold to match against revenues on the income statement. The purpose was no longer to support internal decision making and control, but to report the impact of costs on reported profits following objective, auditable and conservative accounting rules (Johnson & Kaplan, 1987).

1.4.2 In search of accounting information that is relevant for managers

The early academic writers on cost accounting in the early 1900s emphasised that the main task of the management accountant was to make sure that the operational data and financial reports are connected in one single objective and verifiable accounting image of corporate performance and wealth. William Paton, one of the most influential educators of his time, described the essential basis for the work as cost accountant as 'the postulate that the value of any commodity, service, or condition, utilised in production *passes over into* the object or product for which the original item was expended and *attaches to* the result, giving it its value.' (Patton, 1922). Attaching material, labour and indirect costs to products as they travel through the factory may lead to an objective and auditable, albeit arbitrary, allocation of period expenditures between products sold and products in inventory. However, the different stages in which input costs are aggregated in product costs make it difficult to identify, let alone manage, the different cost components.

An important academic writer was John Maurice Clark from the University of Chicago in the 1920s. He tried to relate cost accounting information to the managerial decision making, using microeconomic analysis of marginal cost and marginal revenues. He was one of the earliest writers who advised to make a distinction between 'fixed and variable costs': fixed costs are not affected by variations in production volumes within a certain range of output, while variable costs do vary in direct proportion to output volumes. Statistical studies of long run variable costs in the railroad industry have been particularly influential (Johnson & Kaplan, 1987, p. 154). Clark also noted that the distinction between fixed and variable costs is time dependent: a longer decision horizon makes costs variable that appear fixed in the short term, and the reverse for a shorter decision horizon. However, decisions may also have other different relations to costs. Clark also used the term 'differential costs' for cost items that will change as a consequence of a given decision, and he also coined the term 'sunk costs' for costs already incurred that will not change no matter what decision will be taken. His idea that cost information is not uniform and that it should be tailored to the decision problem at hand is best captured by his frequently cited expression 'different costs for different purposes' (Clark, 1923). He also contended that the accounting system should not be the only source of information but 'there must be studies and analyses of cost which are not part of the books of account and need not be bound by any of their standards of procedure' (Clark, 1923, pp. 256-257, as cited by Johnson & Kaplan, 1987, p. 1155).

In the 1930s and independently of the writings of Clark, some authors at the London School of Economics (LSE) also criticised the irrelevance of data from the books of accounts for managerial decision making (Buchanan & Thirlby, 1973). The aggregation of fixed cost allocations throughout the production function made it difficult to identify the variable costs of products, services and functions. This makes it difficult to compare financial consequences of alternative decisions. One of the most prominent LSE writers, Ronald Coase, related cost information to specific decision problems by introducing the 'opportunity cost' concept in economic thinking in 1938.[10] Cost accountants take from the books of accounts the historic costs of decisions made and match these costs against the associated revenues. Decision makers, however, do not look backwards at decisions already taken, but forward to new opportunities. The cost of the decision at hand should, therefore, be compared with costs of the next best option not taken as a consequence of the preferred decision. The opportunity cost of the preferred option equals the costs incurred or revenues foregone as a result of the next best option, which could also include the option of doing nothing.[11]

These authors did not have a major influence on mainstream textbooks in cost accounting in the 1940s, of which 73% of the chapters were devoted to inventory valuation, 21% to cost control and only 6% to management decision making (Foster, 1971 as cited in Horngren, 1989). University of Chicago professor William Vatter took a clearly and significantly different approach when he published a textbook of which the title already signaleed the importance of accounting for management. His textbook Managerial Accounting (1950) originated from a final chapter of John Neuner's *Cost Accounting* (1944) textbook and emphasised the managerial, as opposed to the external, use of financial information. He stressed the importance of having frequent and timely information (at least more frequent than the quarterly financial statements) and information that is relevant for managerial planning and control decisions. From 1950 onwards, management accounting had re-assumed its own specific role in managing organisations. The clear positioning and focus on management decisions also inspired scholars to use theoretical advancements in behavioural sciences of economics, psychology and sociology. These theories, combined with analytic tools like operations research and statistics, have advanced our knowledge in a wide array of management accounting topics like cost analysis, budgeting, capital budgeting, profitability analysis, transfer pricing and performance evaluation.

---

[10] This was done in a series of twelve articles published in *Accountant* in the period 1 October to 17 December 1938. The term was first introduced byeconomist Friedrich van Wieser, a member of the Austrian School of economics, in his book *'Theorie der gesellschaftlichen Wirtschaft'* (1914).

[11] Suppose a manager needs to take a production decision and his production system is capable of producing one thousand hectoliters of premium beer and two thousand hectoliters of common beer. The decision to produce one hectoliter of premium beer equals two hectoliters of common beer foregone, assuming a linear production possibilities function. Thus, the opportunity cost of producing premium beer is the foregone profit from producing twice as much common beer, and vice versa.

1.4.3 Analytic approaches to decision problems

Since 1960, newly developed disciplines like operations research (O. R) and mathematical economics, were used by academics to solve decision problems in which cost information was involved. Operations researchers introduced linear, non-linear and integer programming models, queuing theory, inventory theory and game theory to solve complex managerial problems (Koopmans, 1951; Churchman, et al., 1957). The problem-solving heuristics that O. R specialists used were greatly advanced by the calculative power that became available from the rapidly emerging computer technology in the 1960s. Mathematical programming techniques, for instance, are used now for optimising product mix decisions under production and sales constraints, for determining when to investigate variances, and for allocating overhead costs, service department costs, joint and by-product costs. Statistical and simulation methods are applied for the analysis of 'cost-volume-profit' decisions under uncertainty, and the analysis of cost behaviour. During the 1960s to 1980s, these applications were mainly developed and used in academic research. However, when computer capacity became cheaper and more accessible for users outside academic and other research institutes, the more advanced analytical techniques became also more widely used in practice. We will discuss some of the more commonly used techniques in this book.

In most economic models, the person that is supposed to be supported by management accounting information is assumed to be a rational decision maker. This person lives in an uncertain but well-defined world and is well-informed about all future possible states of nature and about costs and benefits of each future condition. They also know all the choice options available to them, while a clearly defined utility function allows them to put all choice options in an absolute order, ranging from the most preferred to least preferred outcome. In other words, economic-rational decision makers are capable of reaching an optimal decision outcome. However, most decision makers are boundedly rational decision makers: they do not know every option, they are not capable of expressing and ranking their preferences very well, and they have limited knowledge about future conditions (Simon, 1976). New models of decision making used 'information economics' to model the condition of uncertainty. Additional (accounting) information can reduce uncertainty; however, this additional information is costly. Information economics is also viewed as a fundamental discipline in accounting research, because it addresses directly the added value of accounting information to decision making.

1.4.4 Management control

The early scholarly work in management control is Herbert Simon's research of the controllership function in organisations. Simons' research team conducted over 400 interviews at seven major U.S. companies (Simon, et al., 1954). The study reported that accounting information was to serve three different functions of controllership within an organisation:

- *scorecard keeping;*
- *attention directing;*
- *problem solving.*

Scorecard keeping relates to how the firm performs (mostly captured in financial terms like financial statements and cost summaries), attention directing arises when actual-to-budget line items are compared (line items showing significant deviations from the norm stand out and call for attention), and problem solving involves studies to evaluate special decisions such as detailed cost analyses for loss making products, make-or-buy comparisons, product pricing alternatives and the analysis of investment opportunities.

Robert Anthony of the Harvard Business School started writing textbooks about management control systems, starting with a generic framework that uses a cybernetic model of organisational control. The model includes different control functions, like monitoring, evaluation and intervention. He also proposed a hierarchical framework of planning and control activities for which a completely different set of accounting principles are used than those needed for financial reporting purposes (Anthony, 1965).

In practice, since the 1950s companies have grown rapidly and expanded internationally at an ever growing pace. Although the multi-divisional organisational structure already originated in the 1920s, with notable examples like DuPont and General Motors, the multi-divisional organisational form did not proliferate until after 1950 (Chandler, 1966b). Accounting numbers were increasingly used to manage these large companies, operating in multiple, different business segments and producing very different products. Business failures in the 1970s and 1980s called attention to management control problems caused by managers being almost exclusively focused on achieving accounting scorecard results. The failures showed that effective management control requires a combination of accounting information, knowledge of production processes (including quality issues), and a deep understanding of customer needs (Johnson, 1992). Organisations have also gradually changed organisational form from hierarchical bureaucratic organisations with controlled top down information flows to flatter organisational structures and information flows needed at all organisational levels (Ashton, et al., 1995). Management control developed into a discipline in which accounting numbers have become gradually detached from their original financial reporting purpose, as was already proposed by Robert Anthony. Nowadays, accounting numbers are increasingly also combined with knowledge and experience in other areas, like production and logistic technology, human behaviour, strategy and marketing.

Many scholars have contributed to the management control area since Anthony's first textbook was published. Also a wide variety of theoretical orientations and empirical approaches have been used. Notable are the contributions of Kenneth Merchant, who followed an empirical approach in studying management control. He built a management control framework based on a large number of field studies. The resulting management control framework provides not only the most common tools used by managers in controlling internal activities, but it also analyses the functional and disfunctional behaviour they may cause (Merchant, 1985, 1990, 1998; Merchant & van der Stede, 2011). Merchant's colleague at the Harvard Business School, Robert Simons, provided another control framework based on field studies that tries to capture a more dynamic image of management control change and adaptation (Simons, 1990, 1991, 1994, 1995, 2000).

1.5 Conclusion

Management accounting is a discipline that is primarily developed within companies by managers and entrepreneurs who respond to changing economic systems and dramatic changes in organisational structures. The most visible and startling innovations have been introduced when corporate organisations underwent dramatic structural changes in the 19th and early 20th century. The most recent developments in management accounting are inspired by the applications of more advanced analytical techniques and the use of advanced production and information technologies.

Management accounting as an academic discipline had been dominated by financial accounting ideas and methods before it became a separate discipline around 1950. It is only in the second half of the 20th century that management accounting and management control theory emerged. These theories consider accounting information mainly in their role of supporting internal decision making and control. It has become increasingly clear that both managerial activities require specific accounting information that may be different from accounting information for financial reporting purposes. At the same time, however, it becomes also evidently clear that decision making and controlling activities also require additional insights from economic, psychological, and organisational theories to provide a more complete understanding of human behaviour in management decision making. The numerous empirical studies conducted since the 1970s have broadened our understanding of the use of accounting information in decision making and control, and the behavioural consequences of their use. They also show that these managerial tasks are complicated activities that can only be well understood and executed if accounting knowledge is combined with insights that other disciplines can offer. The productive combination of different disciplines will undoubtedly be one of the major opportunities for future management accounting practitioners and academics to advance the field.

The purpose of this book is to collect, analyse and evaluate salient features of current management accounting practice and research. This foundation can be the starting point for those who will be foremost in the development of new management accounting practice and research. That is, this text is intended to build your knowledge and support your future innovations in the field of management accounting.

EXERCISES

Exercise 1.1 Current management accounting practice

Review a current issue of a professional management accounting magazine such as *CMA Magazine, Strategic Finance, CFO Magazine, . . .*

a. As well as you can, by reading at least the article abstracts, relate the topics covered in this magazine to the historical developments of management accounting described in this chapter.
b. By your analysis of management accounting practice, how have business management and management accounting information evolved in recent times?

Exercise 1.2 Current management accounting research

Review a current issue of an academic management accounting journal such as *Management Accounting Research, The Journal of Management Accounting Research, . . .*

a. As well as you can, by reading at least the article abstracts, relate the topics covered in this journal to the historical developments of management accounting described in this chapter.
b. By your analysis of current management accounting research, how have business management and management accounting information evolved in recent times?

Exercise 1.3 Lyman Mills cost accounting practices

The Lyman Mills cost accounting practice dates back to mid 19th century. The factory general ledger included two 'mill accounts': one for coarse goods production and one for fine goods production. Both resembled modern work-in-process control accounts, each of which was charged with its share of cotton, factory labour, and factory overhead expense every month. The cost of cotton (based on the contract price including freight and insurance charges) that was purchased but not yet used in production (which is normally referred to as 'unexpired costs') was charged to inventory and not to current manufacturing expenses. The entire amount expended each period on manufacturing payroll and factory overhead was charged to the mill accounts. Production of cotton is a continuous process that does not vary much in volume over time. The cost of cotton is by far the largest cost component in total manufacturing cost.

a. Comment on this accounting practice. Does it match current accounting practice?
b. What was the impact of the Lyman Mills accounting treatment on reported period profits?
c. If we compare annual profits based on the Lyman Mills accounting method with profits based on modern accounting procedures, how large do you estimate the difference would be?

Exercise 1.4 Markets versus hierarchies

Before early 18th century, most transactions between merchants and artisans (producers of goods like cotton and other hand made products) were done at the market place and guided by price information, and supply and demand. Early 1800 merchants started to employ artisans and, by doing so, they replaced market based contracts by labour contracts.

a. What were the main reasons for merchants to bring their contractual market relations into a hierarchical organisation?
b. Are the reasons mentioned under the previous question similar to what economic theory used to call 'market failures'? Explain your answer.
c. If market based transactional relations are replaced by hierarchical coordination based on labour contracts, could this lead to a more effective coordination? Motivate your answer.
d. Ronald Coase and Oliver Williams have developed 'transaction cost theory' to analysed the difference between market coordination and coordination within organisational hierarchies. Use transaction cost theoretical insights to explain the developments around 1800.

Exercise 1.5

The industrial revolution since 1850 has made most industrial processes more capital intensive. Surprisingly, however, the accounting systems in the early capital intensive factories did not immediately account for long lived fixed assets. A good example is the Carnegie Steel Company.

a. What were the main reasons for Carnegie not accounting for long lived fixed assets?
b. By not accounting for fixed assets, did Carnegie miss out on crucial business opportunities? Explain.

Somewhat later on, the Scientific Management Movement stimulated the development of new accounting methods, like 'standard costing' and 'variance analysis'.

a. Explain why the Scientific Management Movement stimulated the creation of the two management accounting methods.

Exercise 1.6

Relatively unknown is the way in which Pierre du Pont connected the old practice of using financial ratios related to sales with the new practice of relating financial measures to the money invested in the business. An example is the following pro forma profit and loss statement based on sales at normal capacity of 40 000 units (see Figure 1.1).

a. How can we calculate the ROI numbers directly from return on sales (ROS) figures? Use the standard volumes.
b. The division turned in their financial report and it appears that they have realised sales of 30 000 units, which is 10 000 below standard (see Figure 1.1, the two righthand columns). State the reasons why some ROS figures have changed, while other remained the same.

In order to directly calculate the impact of several ROS measures, DuPont had invented the following equation:

$$x = \frac{b + a\left(\frac{m-1}{m}\right)}{c + \frac{d}{m}}$$

In which:

x = return on investment
b = the ratio of net profit to sales
a = the ratio of fixed factory and commercial costs to sales
c = the ratio of working capital to sales
d = the ratio of fixed investment to sales
m = the ratio of proposed or realised volume to standard volume

c. Explain the working of DuPont's equation.
d. Suppose the division continues to operate on 30 000 units (10 000 below standard volume) and needs to produce a ROI of 20%, what would be a reasonable strategy if we know that fixed costs and capital investments (both in working capital and fixed investments) cannot be changed.

		Standard volume (a)			Below standard sales	
		Amounts	Ratio to Sales		Amounts	Ratio to Sales
Annual sales in units		40,000	--		30,000	--
Price per unit	€	1,250	--	€	1,250	--
Profit and Loss Statement:						
Annual sales	€	50,000,000	1.000	€	37,500,000	1.000
Factory cost of sales						
Variable portion		35,000,000	0.700		26,250,000	0.700
Fixed portion at $125 per unit		5,000,000	0.100		3,750,000	0.100
Gross factory profit		10,000,000	0.200		7,500,000	0.200
Add overabsorbed factory burden						
Deduct unabsorbed factory burden					1,250,000	0.033
Commercial Expense, variable		1,200,000	0.024		900,000	0.0240
Commercial Expense, fixed		2,300,000	0.046		2,300,000	0.0613
Net profit from operations	€	6,500,000	0.130	€	3,050,000	0.0813
Capital investment statement:						
Working capital	€	17,500,000	0.350	€	13,125,000	0.350
Fixed investment		15,000,000	0.300		15,000,000	0.400
Total investment	€	32,500,000	0.650	€	28,125,000	0.750
Return on investment, annual percent		20.00%			10.84%	

a): The division's rated annual capacity is 50,000 units
Standard capacity is 80% of rated capacity

Figure 1.1 Du Pont's Divisional ROS and ROI scheme
Source: Adapted with minor changes from Johnson (1978).

Exercise 1.7 DuPont based variance analysis

The DuPont variance analysis scheme is built on the following basic equation:

$$\text{Return on investment} = \text{Return on sales} \times \text{Investment turnover}$$

Consider two divisions A and B, each generating the same return on investment (see Figure 1.2).

a. Use the DuPont variance analysis scheme (and perhaps also the basic equation) to detect the fundamental differences between the two divisions.
b. Which three basic areas of performance could be considered to improve performance to a ROI of 25%?

		Division A		Division B
Annual sales in units		40,000		50,000
Price per unit	€	1,250	€	1,000
Profit and Loss Statement:				
Annual sales	€	50,000,000	€	50,000,000
Factory cost of sales				
Variable costs		35,000,000		32,000,000
Fixed costs		5,000,000		3,000,000
Gross factory profit		10,000,000		15,000,000
Commercial Expense, variable		1,200,000		1,000,000
Commercial Expense, fixed		2,300,000		2,000,000
Net profit from operations	€	6,500,000	€	12,000,000
Assets and Liabilities:				
Cash		6,000,000		12,000,000
Receivables		3,000,000		8,000,000
Payables		7,000,000		5,000,000
Inventories		18,000,000		30,000,000
Fixed assets		12,500,000		15,000,000

Figure 1.2 DuPont based variance analysis

Exercise 1.8 Different costs for different purposes

The couturier of Fashion House wants to add a new evening dress to his assortment. He already paid for a market study to see whether his potential clients would favour yet another product in the evening dress category. The study outcome was favourable. The market research costs were € 20 000. He had his staff develop three new designs, for which the development team used a new computer system that was especially bought for this project at a cost of € 14 000. The first design Purple Star was a further development of an old idea that was declined a year ago. The design costs for the old idea were € 18 000 and the additional costs to develop the new design were € 32 000. The design costs for the second dress Green Delight were € 44 000 and, for the third design Blue Elegance, the design costs were € 60 000. The selling prices are already set: Purple Star will be priced € 300, Green Delight € 400 and Blue Elegance € 600. Giving these prices, sales are forecasted to be 140, 120 and 110 respectively.

1. What are the financial consequences of each design to be taken into production?
2. Which costs play a role in this decision and which costs do not? Explain your opinion.
3. What are the opportunity costs of each alternative?
4. What is the opportunity cost of doing nothing, i.e. not introducing a new model?
5. Which design should be chosen when Fashion House wants to optimise the financial outcome of the decision?

Exercise 1.9 Management control models

Robert Anthony proposed in his writings the following basic management control model (Figure 1.3).

This model is a so called 'cybernetic control model'. It is a measurement and control device that resembles the workings of a thermostat. It has influenced many practitioners and scholars in their thinking about management control systems.

a. What are the strong points of this system? Why has it been so influential?
b. Could you also think of some weaker points in the way management control is portrayed in Figure 1.3?

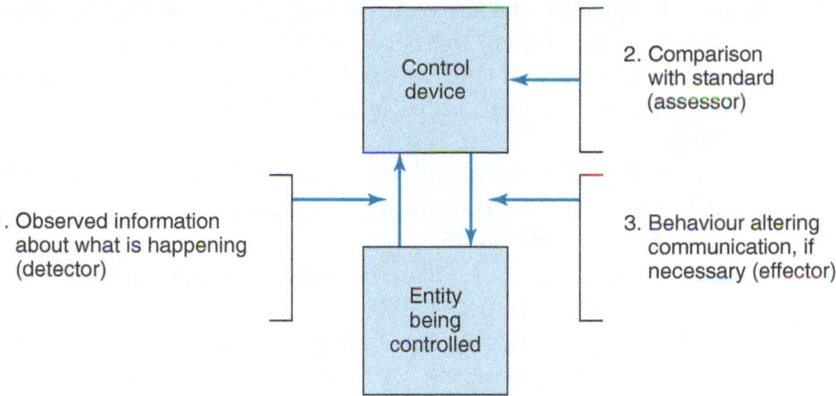

Figure 1.3 Management Control System according to Anthony (Anthony, 1965; 1992)

References

Anthony, R. (1965). *Planning and Control Systems: A Framework for Analysis.* Boston: Harvard Business School Press.

Anthony, R., Dearden, J., and Govindarajan, V. (1992). *Management Control Systems* (7th ed.). Homewood, Ill., Boston, USA: Irwin.

Ashton, D., Hopper, T., and Scapens, R.W. (1995). The Changing Nature of Issues in Management Accounting. In D. Ashton, T. Hopper & R.W. Scapens (Eds.), *Issues in Management Accounting* (2 ed., pp. 1-20). London: Prentice Hall.

Bourguignon, A., Malleret, V., and Nørreklit, H. (2004). The American balanced scorecard versus the French tableau de bord: the ideological dimension. *Management Accounting Research, 15*(2, June), 107-134.

Buchanan, J.M., and Thirlby, G.F. (Eds.). (1973). *L.S.E. Essays on Cost.* London: London School of Economics and Political Science.

Caplan, E.H. (1966). Behavioral assumptions of management accounting. *The Accounting Review, 41,* 496-509.

Chandler, A.D., Jr. (1966a). *Strategy and Structure.* New York: Garden City.

Chandler, A.D., Jr. (1966b). *Strategy and Structure: Chapters in the History of the Industrial Enterprise.* Boston: M.I.T. Press.

Chandler, A.D., Jr. (1977). *The Visible Hand: The Managerial Revolution in American Business.* Boston: Harvard University Press.

Chandler, A.D., Jr., and Salsbury, S. (1971). *Pierre S. duPont and the Making of the Modern Corporation.* New York.

Churchman, G.W., Ackoff, R.L., and Arnoff, E.L. (1957). *Introduction to Operations Research.* New York: Wiley.

Clark, J.M. (1923). *Studies in the Economics of Overhead Costs:* University of Chicago Press, Chicago.

Cooper, R. (1988a). The Rise of Activity-Based Costing - Part One: What is an Activity-based Cost System? *Journal of Cost Management for the Manufacturing Industry, summer,* 45-54.

Cooper, R. (1988b). The Rise of Activity-Based Costing - Part Two: When do I need an Activity-Based Cost System? *Journal of Cost Management, fall,* 41-48.

Cooper, R. (1989a). The Rise of Activity-Based Costing - Part Four: What do Activity-based Cost Systems look like? *Journal of Cost Management for the Manufacturing Industry, spring,* 38-49.

Cooper, R. (1989b). The Rise of Activity-Based Costing - Part Three: How many cost drivers do you need and how do you select them? *Journal of Cost Management for the Manufacturing Industry, winter,* 34-46.

Cooper, R., Kaplan, R.S. (1988c). Measure costs right: make the right decisions. *Harvard Business Review, sept/oct,* 96-103.

Cooper, R., Kaplan, R.S. (1992). Activity-Based Systems: Measuring the Cost of Resource Usage. *Accounting Horizons, Vol. 6, Nr. 3, September,* 1-13.

Davenport, T.H., and Harris, J.G. (2007). *Competing on Analytics, The New Science of Winning.* Boston: Harvard Business School Press.

Dean, J. (1954). Measuring the Productivity of Capital. *Harvard Business Review, Jan/Febr.,* 120-130.

Epstein, M.J. (1978). *The Effect of Scientific Management on the Development of the Standard Cost System:* Arno Press.

Ewert, R., and Wagenhofer, A. (2007). Management Accounting Theory and Practice in German-Speaking Countries. In C.S. Chapman, A.G. Hopwood & M.D. Shields (Eds.), *Handbook of Management Accounting Research* (Vol. 2, pp. 1035-1069). Amsterdam: Elsevier.

Fleischman, R., and Tyson, T. (2007). The History of Management Accounting in the U.S. In C.S. Chapman, A.G. Hopwood & M.D. Shields (Eds.), *Handbook of Management Accounting Research* (Vol. 2, pp. 1071-1089). Amsterdam: Elsevier.

Foster, G. (1971). *The Decision Making Theme in Expositions of Accounting.* Sidney: University of Sidney.

Horngren, C.T. (1989). *Cost and Management Accounting: Yesterday and Today.* In M. A. Hopwood, Bromwich (Eds), Research and Current Issues in Management (pp. 31-43): Pitman Publishing, London.

Hannah, L. (1980). Great Britain. In A.D. Chandler, Jr. and H. Daems (Eds.), *Managerial Hierarchies: Comparative Perspectives on the Rise of the Modern Industrial Enterprise* (pp. 41-76). Cambridge, Mass.: Harvard University Press.

Humby, C., Hunt, T., and Philips, T. (2007). *Scoring Points; How Tesco continous to win customer loyalty.* London: Kogan Page.

Johnson, H.T. (1972). Early Cost Accounting for Internal Management Control: Lyman Mills in the 1850's. *Business History Review*(Winter), 466-474.

Johnson, H.T. (1975). Management Accounting in an Early Integrated Industrial: E.I. dePont de Nemours Powder Company, 1903-1912. *Business History Review, 49*(Summer), 184-204.

Johnson, H.T. (1978). Management Accounting in an Early Multidivisional Organization: General Motors in the 1920s. *Business History Review, Winter,* 490-517.

Johnson, H.T. (1981). Toward a new understanding of nenteenth-centure cost accounting. *The Accounting Review, 56*(3), 510-518.

Johnson, H.T. (1983). The search for gain in markets and firms: a review of the historical emergence of management accounting systems. *Accounting, Organizations and Society, 8*(2/3), 139-146.

Johnson, H.T. (1992). *Relevance Regained.* New York: The Free Press.

Johnson, H.T., and Kaplan, R.S. (1987). *Relevance Lost.* Boston, Masachussettes: Harvard Business School Press.

Kaplan, R.S. (1984). The evolution of management accounting. *The Accounting Review, 59*(3), 390-418.

Kaplan, R.S., and Norton, D.P. (1992). The Balanced Scorecard - Measures that drive performance. *Harvard Business Review*(January-February), 71-79.

Kaplan, R.S., and Norton, D.P. (1993). Putting the balanced scorecard to work. *Harvard Business Review*(September/October), 134-147.

Kaplan, R.S., and Norton, D.P. (1996a). *The Balanced Scorecard.* Boston: Harvard Business Press.

Kaplan, R.S., and Norton, D.P. (1996b). Using the Balanced Scorecard as a strategic management system. *Harvard Business Review*(January-February), 75-85.

Kato, Y. (1993). Target costing support systems: lessons from leading Japanese companies. *Management Accounting Research, 4*(1), 33-47.

Koopmans, T.C. (Ed.). (1951). *Activity Analysis of Production and Allocation.* New York: John Wiley.

Krumwiede, K.R. (2005). Rewards and realities of German cost accounting. *Strategic Finance*(April), 27-34.

Landes, D.S. (1969). *The Unboud Prometheus: Technological Change and Industrial Development in Western Europe from 1750 to the Present.* Cambridge: Cambridge University Press.

Merchant, K.A. (1985). *Control in Business Organizations.* USA: Ballinger.

Merchant, K.A. (1990). Controls in Business Organizations. In C. Emmanuel, D. Otley & K. Merchant (Eds.), *Accounting for Management Control* (2 ed., pp. 109-123). London: Chapman & Hall.

Merchant, K.A. (1998). *Modern Management Control Systems: Text & Cases.* London: Prentice-Hall International.

Merchant, K.A., & van der Stede, W.A. (2011). *Management Control Systems* (3 ed.). Harlow: Financial Times, Prentice Hall.

NZa (2010). *Uitvoeringstoets Budgettering honoraria medisch specialisten.* Utrecht: Nederlandse Zorgautoriteit.

Overby, S. (2007). The Price is always Right. *CIO*(June 13), 1-5.

Patton, W.A. (1922). *Accounting Theory* (Vol. reprinted in 1973). Houston, Tex.: Scholars Book Co.

Previts, G.J., and Merino, B.D. (1979). *A History of Accounting in America.* New York: John Wiley.

Reece, J., and Cool, W. (1978). Measuring Investment Center Performance. *Harvard Business Review, 56*(3), 28-37.

Shank, J.K., and Govindarajan, V. (1993). *Strategic Cost Management: The New Tool for Competitive Advantage.* New York: The Free Press.

Simon, H.A. (1976). *Administrative Behavior: A Study of Decision-Making Processes in Administrative Organization.* New York: Wiley.

Simon, H.A., Guetzkov, H., Kozmetsky, G., and Tyndall, G. (1954). *Centralization versus Decentralization in Organizing the Controller's Department.* New York: Controllership Foundation Inc.

Simons, R. (1990). The role of management control systems in creating competitive advantage: new perspectives. *Accounting, Organizations and Society, 15,* 127-143.

Simons, R. (1991). Strategic orientation and top management attention to control systems. *Strategic Management Journal, 12,* 49-62.

Simons, R. (1994). How new top managers use control systems as levers of strategic renewal. *Strategic Management Journal, 15,* 169-189.

Simons, R. (1995). *Levers of Control: How managers use innovative control systems to drive strategic renewal.* Boston: Harvard Business School Press.

Simons, R. (2000). *Performance Measurement & Control Systems for Implementing Strategy.* Upper Saddle River, New Jersey: Prentice Hall.

Sloan, A.P. (1963). *My Years with General Motors:* The Library of Management Classics, London.

Stern, J., Stewart, G., and Chew, D. (1995). The EVA® Financial Management System. *Journal of Applied Corporate Finance* (Summer), 32-46.

Stewart, G.B., III (1991). *The Quest for Value.* New York: Harper Business.

Vatter, W.J. (1950). *Managerial Accounting:* Prentice-Hall, New York.

Chapter 2

Planning and decision making

2.1 Decision making

2.1.1 Information and the individual

In everyday life, individuals make many decisions. In fact, it seems as if this is an almost continuous activity. Most decisions do not take much time and are made unconsciously. We seem to use many routines and 'rules-of-thumb' to guide our decision making behaviour. Examples are how to cook our meals, where people sit around the table and how we behave in traffic. However, some decisions are different: they appear only rarely and they may have enormous consequences. For instance, consider the acquisition of a house or the decision to change jobs. In general, fewer ready-to-apply established guidelines apply to these situations and more time is needed to oversee possible consequences of the decision.

A similar situation exists in organisations: most routine jobs in the workplace seem to be taken also instantaneously without much consideration. Most of them are guided by work manuals, rules and regulations, and by practical experience. The more complex decisions are those that do not occur on a frequent basis, and that have unique characteristics each time they appear. These elements call for new information and full consideration of which decision is most appropriate. In this chapter we look at non-routine decisions that have far reaching consequences in both place (having impact on more people and organisational entities) and time (producing notable consequences for a longer period of time into the future). Our main focus is on decision making for strategic planning, organisational planning and budgeting purposes. Since strategic decision making is focused on a longer time horizon and it also introduces the important element of uncertainty and risk. The more far reaching the decision's consequences in place and time, the more uncertainty generally surrounds the decision.

2.1.2 Models of decision making behaviour

Traditional economic theory portrays the decision maker as a **rational** human being who has complete information about all decision consequences and a clear preference ordering of alternatives. This enables reaching an optimal decision in which utility will be maximised, which is known as 'optimising behaviour'. In most real life situations this is not a very realistic representation of the information quality and completeness and of the decision maker's cognitive capabilities. In most cases, decision makers **strive** to be rational decision makers but they are not able fully to comply with the requirements of economic rationality. Most decision makers do not fully oversee all possible alternative choices, they do not have full information about each and every alternative and they do not have a completely defined preference scheme that helps them to produce a clear ordering of alternatives from most preferred to least preferred. Economic actors are thus seen as 'limitedly rational' they are not able to reach 'optimal; decisions, but 'satisficing solutions' at best. As soon as an acceptable solution has been reached, satisficing decision makers stop searching for even better solutions. This is also influenced by the decision situation: more strategic decisions are inherently less structured and provide fewer opportunities for optimising behaviour. In this chapter, we will have a look at some strategic decisions and we will increasingly complicate the decision situation so that we can see how rational decision making procedures are followed by approaches in which subjective judgment becomes more likely and more important.

Decision makers may deal with bounded (which means 'limited') rationality by using an **incremental** decision making process. In this approach, the decision maker focuses on a few most important decision areas and implements solutions in an incremental manner. This involves a step-by-step implementation process provides opportunities to learn along the way, and which enables a quick change in plans when the incremental implementation does produce the desired results. This approach is also known as **muddling through:** the changes implemented are not drastic and build on previous experiences. The resulting changes are incremental, providing opportunities to learn. In the event that it turns out that wrong decisions have been made, the incremental changes can be reversed relatively easily without causing too much damage and without disrupting operations too much.

2.1.3 Decision making practices in organisations

The rationality of decision making can be influenced by the following three conditions:

1. The ability of decision makers to define a clear, coherent and limited set of **decision objectives.**
2. The **knowledge** available to analyse a decision situation and to reach a reasoned conclusion. In most cases this will be influenced by the knowledge about production technologies.
3. The **time and attention** decision makers devote to a specific decision problem.

If none of these conditions is met in practice, then the decision situation is characterised as **an organised anarchy.** Complex organisations like state agencies, universities and R&D institutes have been inspiring examples of the organised anarchy model but essentially in every organisation we can find decision situations that meet the conditions of organised anarchies. Under these conditions, decision makers have diffuse, and often conflicting ideas about the most important objectives in the organisation. There is little objective, undisputed knowledge about how decisions impact on the organisation. This is because there is no clear idea how the basic production processes in organised anarchies actually work and how these processes may be improved. Each decision maker may have their own ideas about them, but these ideas are generally not shared among all participants. In most organisations, decision makers frequently come and go. The replacement of individuals also implies that different ideas are introduced, which makes the outcome of decision making processes less predictable.

Improving strategic decisions requires improvements in at least one or several of the above mentioned conditions: more clear and articulated decision objectives, a better insight in the working of relevant parts of the organisation and more time and attention of decision makers to the decision process.

In this chapter, we will look at techniques and approaches that make strategic decision making more transparent and effective. Special attention will be given to the impact of risk and uncertainty because they can be seen as dominant and distinctive features of strategic decision making processes. In Section 2.2.1 we look at a decision situation without risk and uncertainty. In Section 2.2.2 we start introducing uncertainty for some of the decision variables. Section 2.2.4 discusses how much effort we should make to reduce the level of uncertainty. Section 2.3 presents alternative decision making strategies under conditions of complete uncertainty. We conclude this chapter by looking at the behaviour of decision makers under conditions of uncertainty. Uncertainty levels under different conditions appear to influence the decision maker's utility function and, thus, also the decisions made.

2.2 Decision making under risk and uncertainty

2.2.1 Conditions of certainty: the use of deterministic CVP models

Many managerial decisions are focused on the implications alternative decisions in markets, customers, sales, price, costs or other factors may have for total revenues, costs and net profit. Costs and revenues may react differently to the decision variables, like sales volume, price, production technology and procurement decisions. A simple model that demonstrates the impact of these decision variables on profitability is the cost-volume-profit (CVP) model. The basic single product CVP model forms the basis for an intuitive understanding of the cost structure of the firm and how decision variables, like production volume, price, cost of inputs and revenues, influence profits. We start by defining a **deterministic** model. The variables of this model can *ex ante* be estimated and, thus, the model will generate point estimates of expected profits.

The basic CVP model is represented by the following equation:

$$\begin{aligned}\text{After tax profit} &= (\text{Revenues} - \text{Cost})(1 - \text{tax rate}) = \\ &= [(\text{price} - \text{variable cost})\text{quantity} - \text{fixed cost}](1 - \text{tax rate})\end{aligned}$$

Or more formally:

$$P = [(p - v)x - f](1 - t)$$

P = after-tax profit

p = selling price

v = variable cost

x = production volume (which we expect to be sold in the same period)

f = fixed costs of the period

t = tax rate (the (1-t) term determines what is left from profit once the taxes are paid)

The difference between the price and the variable cost per unit $(p - v)$ is the **contribution margin per unit.** If we multiply this term by the total number of products sold, which is represented by the term $(p - v)x$, we get the **contribution margin.**

In most basic CVP analysis, selling price, cost figures and tax rate are given. The focal decision variable then becomes the production volume. In order to make this variable explicit, we need to rework the basic CVP equation:

$$P = [(p - v)x - f](1 - t)$$

$$\frac{P}{(1 - t)} = (p - v)x - f$$

$$(p - v)x = f + \frac{P}{(1 - t)}$$

$$x = \frac{f + \dfrac{P}{(1 - t)}}{(p - v)}$$

The last equation determines the level of products sold that is needed to generate a required profit level P. A special point in case is the **break-even point** or **break-even quantity.** This is the number of products produced and sold at which the contribution margin just covers the fixed costs. That is also the output level x_{be} at which profits are zero. The above equation then converts into the *break-even equation* as follows:

$$x_{be} = \frac{f}{(p - v)}$$

where x_{be} is the break-even quantity.

This equation shows the relationship between fixed costs, selling price and variable costs on the one hand and required number of units sold on the other hand. A higher number of units sold is required when fixed costs and variable costs increase, and a lower number of units is required when selling prices can be set higher.

An important part of the CVP analysis is the determination of the relevant variables, like selling price, attainable sales numbers and costs. CVP analysis requires a separation of fixed and variable costs. **Fixed costs** are costs that remain unchanged in a given period despite variation in activity levels or number of units produced. **Variable cost** change in proportion to changes in the related level of activity or production volume. Whether a cost item is fixed or variable depends on the characteristic of the cost item and on the time period considered. We should first have a closer look at these cost classifications, because in most cases they cannot be defined easily. This is especially important, because in most CVP models the way in which costs are classified influences to a great extent the outcome of the model.

Let us have a look at the cost item characteristic first. Some direct cost items, like energy costs, labour costs and maintenance costs, are generally considered variable. In practice, however, the level of variability also depends on the specific contracts that are used to acquire these resources. Energy costs will have fixed cost elements when the contract with the energy provider contains fixed terms, defined by a guaranteed number of energy units or a fixed rate. Similarly, labour costs are not always variable. Most employees have a fixed labour contract, which makes the related costs fixed in the short term. The cost of flexible workers flexible work however, who are paid on an hourly basis or for the number of products they produce, are more variable. Management may decide to make the workforce more flexible, which may lead to a higher wage per hour but also to more flexibility in adjusting the costs to changes in production volume. Another way of making labour costs more variable is to introduce more performance based bonus elements in the labour contracts. Maintenance costs are mostly considered to relate directly to the activity levels of the firm: a higher production volume requires more machine hours, which will increase the level of maintenance required. Companies may also have leased the equipment they use. Most lease contracts also include a fixed payment for maintenance, irrespective of the actual production volumes. The use of lease contracts reduces the variability of maintenance costs.

Costs can also be classified in two different types: 'committed costs' and 'discretionary costs'. Committed costs are fixed costs for the installed production capacity resources, like plant installations, buildings and equipment. The related cost items are depreciation, interest payments and property taxes. These costs are mostly committed in the capital budgeting process (see also Chapter 8) and are not avoidable or controllable in the short term.

Discretionary costs arise from specific decisions made during the planning period, when the execution of the plan or budget takes place. Examples of discretionary costs are costs for marketing campaigns, advertisement, research and development, reorganisations, unscheduled maintenance and factory support. These decisions do not relate directly to the activity levels, but are mostly based on the informed judgment of experienced decision makers. Discretionary costs can, and this is in stark contrast with committed costs, be influenced in the short term. A marketing campaign can be cancelled or reduced, the decision to hire *ad interim* managers can be postponed and the organisation of a business event can be rescheduled. The drivers of costs are not always clearly visible. Complexity of production systems and control efforts in complex organisations generate additional fixed and variable costs. The decision to simplify systems may also lead to a considerable cost reduction. Some costs are direct, which means they can be attributed directly to a cost object, like a product, service, function, region or organisational unit. Other costs are indirect costs. Indirect costs are costs that cannot be traced to a cost object in an economically feasible (cost effective) way. Some indirect costs are technically not traceable to products, like factory insurance cost and cost of senior management. However, most indirect costs may, perhaps, be traced to cost objects, if we have the adequate and cost effective tools to do so. The use of computer based high technology production equipment (robotics) in, for instance, the automotive industry allows, at low marginal costs, for the generation of an additional flow of data enabling indirect costs to be traced directly to the specific products or types of cars produced. Computerised cost data systems may also provide a low cost possibility to apply activity based costing (ABC) techniques for the identification and assignment of (parts of) indirect costs to specific products. Both conditions may, in the end, change a part of the indirect fixed costs to become (semi-) variable and directly related to variation in production numbers. Direct fixed costs may also be changed by using different contractual arrangements. Outsourcing of parts of the business to external service providers generally has the effect that fixed costs become more variable, when the outsourcing agreement is based on a price per unit serviced.

The second important element in the cost classification work for our CVP analysis is the timeframe we use. If we make a CVP analysis for a longer time period into the future, for instance for the next five to ten years, more fixed cost items become variable and avoidable. Within this timeframe, equipment may be replaced, buildings can be sold and the organisation structure of the company may be changed. If we, for instance, foresee that a lower number of products will be demanded by the market, we could try to streamline the company by reducing the number of managerial positions or overhead functions. By doing this in the coming four years, we reduce the short-term fixed costs in year five. These decisions impact on the short-term fixed costs, which make them more variable in the longer term. The reverse is also true:

for a sufficient short time period, for instance a day or hour or minute, virtually all costs will be fixed. Materials are acquired, employees have been contracted and utilities are already turned on. If we made a CVP analysis for the coming six months we would have to use a different classification of fixed and variable costs than when we make the analysis for five years from now.

Let us consider Marseille Mass Storage Company (MMS), a French firm producing USB sticks. This mass storage device is the only product MMS produces. MMS expects to sell 90 000 USB sticks at a price of €9.00 in the coming year. The variable costs are €5.80 for each unit and the fixed costs are €200 000 a year. The corporate tax rate is 25%. All basic data can be found in Figure 2.1.

A good way to set up a CVP analysis in Excel® is to make a distinction between a DATA panel and a MODEL panel. The data panel displays the basic data for the CVP model. The model panel uses the relationships between the data elements in order to predict the company's net profit. Organising the spreadsheet in this way allows the user to change input data relatively easily and see their immediate effect on predicted net profit. In the model panel, different ways of presenting the data can be chosen. We have included two different forms: the 'Pro forma Income Statement' and the 'Contribution Statement' (see Figure 1). Both statements lead to the same result (net income), but present a different overview of data elements.

CVP analysis.xlsx - Microsoft Excel

	A–C	D	E	F	G	H–I	J	K	L
1	Marseille Mass Storage Company								
2									
3	Data section								
4									
5	Quantity	90,000	units						
6									
7	Price	€ 9.00							
8									
9	Variable costs					Fixed costs			
10	Material	€ 2.30				Manufacturing	€ 100,000		
11	Labor	€ 1.50				Sales	60,000		
12	Overhead	€ 1.10				Administrative	40,000		
13	Commissions	€ 0.90	(10% of sales)			Total fixed costs	€ 200,000		
14	Total variable costs	€ 5.80							
15						Tax rate	25%		
16	Contribution margin	€ 3.20							
17									
18									
19	Pro forma Income Statement					Contribution Statement			
20									
21	Revenues		€ 810,000	=D5*D7		Revenues		€ 810,000	=D5*D7
22	Cost of Goods Sold					Variable costs			
23	Materials	€ 207,000		=D5*D10		Material	€ 207,000		=D5*D10
24	Direct labor	135,000		=D5*D11		Labor	135,000		=D5*D11
25	Variable overhead	99,000		=D5*D12		Overhead	99,000		=D5*D12
26	Fixed costs	100,000		=J10		Commissions	81,000		=D5*D13
27			541,000	=SUM(D23:D26)				522,000	=SUM(J23:J26)
28	Gross profit		269,000	=E21-E27		Contribution margin		288,000	=K21-K27
29	Other expenses					Fixed costs			
30	Variable sales costs	€ 81,000		=D5*D13		Manufacturing	€ 100,000		=J10
31	Fixed sales costs	60,000		=J11		Sales	60,000		=J11
32	Fixed administrative	40,000		=J12		Administrative	40,000		=J12
33			181,000	=SUM(D30:D32)		Total fixed costs		200,000	=SUM(J30:J32)
34	Income before taxes		88,000	=E28-E33		Income before taxes		88,000	=K28-K33
35	Taxes at 25%		22,000	=J15*E34		Taxes at 25%		22,000	=J15*K34
36	Net Income		€ 66,000	=E34-E35		Net Income		€ 66,000	=K34-K35
37									

Blad1 | Stochastic | Volume & Price | Strategy Choice | Blad3

Figure 2.1. CVP analysis Marseille Mass Storage (MMS) Company

The Pro forma Income Statement makes a distinction between Cost of Goods sold (in which also the beginning and ending inventories of finished goods could be included) and Other expenses, not directly related to product costs. The Contribution Statement presents a different view and makes a distinction between variable costs and fixed costs. It more closely follows the CVP model discussed earlier.

The break-even point for MMS can be determined as follows:

$$\frac{f}{(p - v)} = \frac{200\,000}{9 - 5.80} = \frac{200\,000}{3.20} = 62\,500 \text{ units}$$

Suppose MMS shareholders want MMS to generate a net income of at least €90 000, the minimum required production volume needs to be:

$$\frac{f + \dfrac{P}{(1 - t)}}{(p - v)} = \frac{200\,000 + \dfrac{90\,000}{0.75}}{3.20} = \frac{320\,000}{3.20} = 100\,000 \text{ units}$$

Suppose MMS has the possibility to determine the selling price, while the production capacity for the next period has already been established at 80 000 units. What price is necessary for the required net income level of €90 000?

In order to focus on the contribution margin, the breakeven equation needs to be rewritten as follows:

$$(p - v) = \frac{f + \dfrac{P}{(1 - t)}}{x} = \frac{200\,000 + \dfrac{90\,000}{0.75}}{80\,000} = \frac{320\,000}{80\,000} = 4$$

The minimum price MMS needs to set is $4 + 5.80 = €9.80$.

All these analyses focus on one decision variable at a time, considering that none of the other variables will change (using the so-called *ceteris paribus* condition).

CVP models also allow for simultaneous changes in multiple variables at the same time. Changing several variables in the Data section of the CVP model instantaneously generates different outcomes in the Pro forma Income Statement and Contribution Statement. Some simultaneous changes belong to a certain **scenario.** For example, when management decides to follow a low cost strategy, price will be reduced, and direct cost elements may also become lower. Excel's scenario tool (which can be found in the *what-if analyses* menu) may help in generating and documenting different scenarios and their respective effects on key decision variables, like gross profit, contribution margin and net income.

2.2.2 Stochastic models: the introduction of risk

In real life, most of the variables in a CVP model are not deterministic, but are approximations of expected future conditions. The values of these variables are influenced by underlying distribution functions, which make these variables 'stochastic variables' instead of deterministic. A variable's distribution function can be defined by the mean and dispersion of the observations around the mean. This dispersion may have different forms, of which the bell shaped form, represented by the Gauss-curve, is the most frequently used. The bell shaped form depicts the 'normal distribution', in which positive and negative deviations from the mean have equal possibilities to occur. Under the normal distribution condition, the mean has the same value as the median. The median value is the middle value of a variable when all values are ordered from low to high. The standard normal distribution is a normal distribution function with a mean of 0 and a standard deviation of 1. We use the standard normal distribution to calculate probabilities for any normally distributed variable.

Suppose MMS has documented the number of products sold in recent years. A well-known indicator of the level of risk is the 'variance': it represents the average squared differences between each year's sales numbers and the mean sales numbers, calculated as follows:

$$variance = \frac{\sum_{i=1}^{n}(x_i - \bar{x})^2}{n}$$

The standard deviation is the square root of the variance. Suppose MMS had sold the following numbers during the last twenty years (see Figure 2.2). The standard deviation of the sales numbers is 10 907, the numbers are normally distributed (see the corresponding histogram in Figure 2.2).

The historical average sales number is 95 735 and the standard deviation is 10 907. Sales are $n(95\,735,\ 10\,907)$. Given this level of uncertainty, what is the probability for MMS to break even in the next year, provided that the break-even sales numbers are 80 000 units?

In order to use the standard normal distribution, we first need to standardise the empirical distribution. This means, bringing the average sales numbers to zero and the current standard deviation to one. This can be done by the following equation:

$$z = \frac{x - \bar{x}}{s.d.}$$

Where x is the test variable, and $\bar{x}$ and $s.d.$ are the average and the standard deviation of the actual sales numbers. The value z indicates the number of standard deviations at which the actual number of sales is positioned from the mean in the standard normal distribution function. z-tables give the surface under the normal distribution function between the mean and the test variable[1], indicating the probability of attaining the required number of sales (see Appendix A). The z-value for MMS is:

Year	Sales numbers
1	91 000
2	83 500
3	110 000
4	106 700
5	95 000
6	100 000
7	92 000
8	79 000
9	75 000
10	97 000
11	109 500
12	96 000
13	90 000
14	94 000
15	85 000
16	111 000
17	97 000
18	112 000
19	86 000
20	105 000

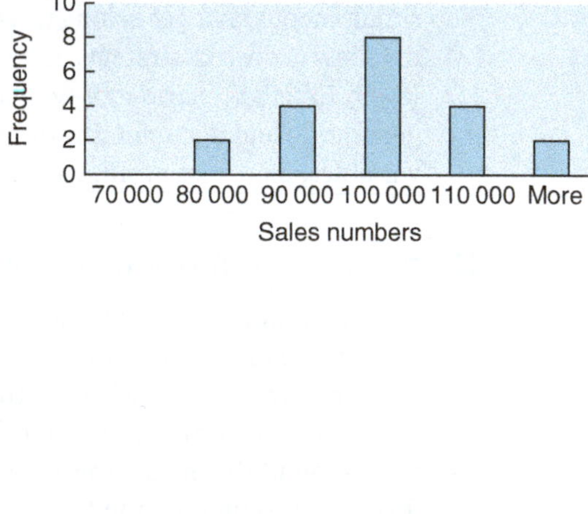

Figure 2.2. MMS Sales figures

[1] Be aware that some z-tables use different definitions of the area under the normal curve.

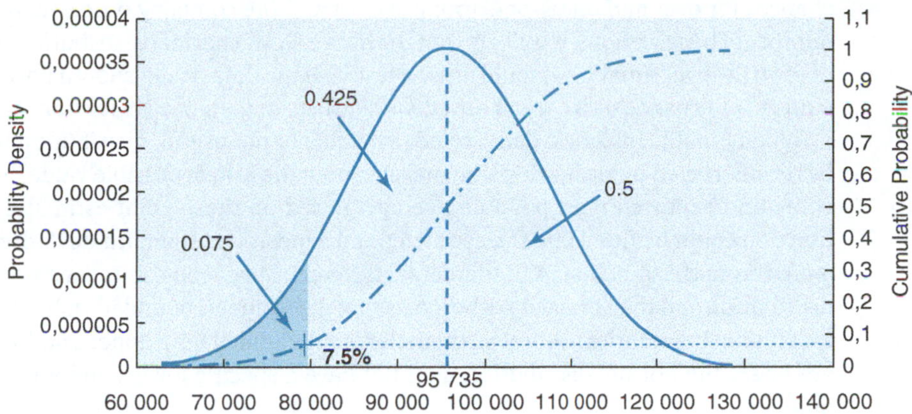

Figure 2.3 Probability of breaking even at MMS

$$z_{MMS} = \frac{80000 - 95735}{10907} = -1.44$$

The z-table gives us the value 0.42507, which corresponds with the area under the normal distribution curve between 80 000 and the mean of 95 735, as depicted in Figure 2.3. To get the total probability of selling 80 000 units or more, we also need to add the probability area of the distribution higher than 95 735. This area is exactly 50% of the total area (due to the perfectly symmetrical shape of the normal distribution), which leads to a total probability of 0.42507 + 0.5 = 0.92507, or (rounded) 92.5%. The shaded area in Figure 2.3 is the remaining probability of 7.5% (which means the risk that MMS will not reach the break-even sales numbers). This value can be found at the right hand axis, which contains the cumulative probabilities represented by the red coloured curve.

When we consider the MMS shareholder requirement for a profit of at least €37 500 for which MMS needs to sell at least 100 000 units, the probability of selling the required numbers, given the past experiences of MMS, can similarly be determined:

$$z_{100000} = \frac{100000 - 95735}{10907} = 0.391$$

The target sales number of 100 000 is 0.391 standard deviations above the mean. According to the z-table, the z-value of 0.391 corresponds with the area between 95 735 and 100 000, representing 0.15173 of the total probability. The probability of reaching 100 000 units or higher is therefore: 1 − (0.5 + 0.15173) = 1 − 0.65173 = 0.34827, or (rounded) 34.8%. The inverse (65.2%) is the probability of not reaching the target, which is indicated in the right hand axis (cumulative probability). Excel's NORM.DIST function can be used to calculate the probabilities discussed in this paragraph.[2]

2.2.3 Stochastic models: some extensions

The use of dispersion measures, like variance and standard deviation, as approximations of risk is useful when the company has sufficient data available about past performance and when these historic data are still representative for the decision situation. When equal

[2] Use the term TRUE to get cumulative probabilities (from all values up to the target value), and UNTRUE for the probability density information.

chances for over and under-performance exist and the company possesses a sufficient high number of observations, it is likely that the data follow a normal distribution. Whether this is really true in all situations should also be tested. If the data do not show a normal distribution pattern, alternative distribution functions, like beta or gamma distributions can also be used.

When reliable historical data are not available or not useful, distribution functions could be reconstructed by asking decision makers about the lowest possible value, highest possible value and expected most possible average. Based on these point estimates, a continuous function could be fitted into the estimates and a mean and standard deviation could be estimated from this function. A fundamental difference between this reconstructed probability distribution and the normal distribution is that the former is bounded (it has lowest and highest volume boundaries), whereas the latter is unbounded (the upper and lower boundaries are open: the normal distribution does not have a specific lowest and and highest volume number).

So far, we have only looked at the distribution of single line items. A further analysis of the distribution properties is to disentangle volume and price. If we look at revenues, the company is mostly in the position to fix a price, making price a deterministic variable, while demand is uncertain, which makes volume a stochastic variable. Similarly, in most cases the volume of resource consumption is well-known to the company, but the price to be paid for resources is often uncertain. Suppose we have the following price data and standard deviations for MMS (see Table 2.1).

In Table 2.1 we see that price, variable material costs and variable labour costs are uncertain. Consequently, variable overhead and commission fees are certain. The expected value of Total Contribution Margin (TCM) can be calculated as follows:

$$\text{TCM} = 90000^*(9 - 3.80) = €468000$$

The linear combination of variances of combined variables is:

$$var(ax + by) = a^2var(x) + b^2var(y)$$

If we know all other variables with certainty and if all prices are independent of each other, we can determine the standard deviation of Income before Taxes as follows:

$$Var(TCM) = (90000^2)(0.5^2) + (90000^2)(0.2^2) + (90000^2)(0.1^2) = 2430000000$$

The standard deviation is €49,295, which is large, compared to the expected value of TCM of €468 000. It is mainly due to the multiple sources of uncertainty that have a compounding effect on TCM. The possibility of a lower than expected TCM has increased (the negative side of uncertainty), but also the possibility of reaching a higher expected TCM (the positive side of uncertainty).

We could also consider both volume and price uncertain. However, multiplying two normally distributed variables will generate a variable that does not have a normal distribution. A way out of this dilemma is to fix one variable first and then analyse the influence of

Table 2.1. MMS price uncertainties

Revenues:		Variable costs:	
Quantity	90000 units	Price materials	€2.30
		S.d. material price	€0.20
Price	€9.00		
Standard deviation	€0.50	Labour wages	€1.50
		S.d. labor wages	€0.10

uncertainty on the second (the price) variable. If prices are known with relative certainty, the reverse can also be done. Another alternative is to use Monte Carlo simulations for each of the decision variables. This approach will be discussed in Chapter 4.

Information on uncertainty, as represented by variance and standard deviations, may be difficult to obtain in practice. In order to have reliable data on variation which are relevant for the decision problem, processes need to be repetitive and they should not have undergone major restructuring or innovation. Most processes in practice are influenced by changing conditions and may be subject to alterations and improvements, which make historical data on variation and mean performance less representative for the current decision problem. An alternative may be to ask local managers or specialists to reconstruct expected variation by estimating different expected outcomes under different conditions, classified into, for instance, adverse, normal and optimal conditions.

2.2.4 Making decisions under uncertainty

In our MMS example we considered risk in a passive way: we measured its impact on certain variables and its eventual (combined) impact on profit. In most cases, however, decision makers also want to see if and how they can actively influence risk and uncertainty. Uncertainty is generally a reason to see how things can be done differently. Alternative decisions may not only impact on profit but may also change the firm's risk profile. Let us have a new look at MMS. One of the most important line items is revenues, which is mostly driven by sales numbers. Decision makers in organisations generally look at market uncertainties and try to make sensible marketing and sales decisions that maximise firm profit while holding the company's risk levels within acceptable limits.

MMS considers an improvement of its USB product to make it more acceptable for the business traveller. Two alternative improvements are considered: one is a low cost improvement by just making the USB appearance somewhat more 'representative'. The other is a high value improvement by which the USB's storage capacity will be doubled and some additional handy standard software for business applications will be installed on the product. MMS does not know how price sensitive the business travellers are: are they willing to pay a higher price for the high value improvement or is a low cost solution more optimal?

The decision on how the USB product will be improved therefore depends primarily on the appreciation of the business traveller market. Suppose the MMS marketing department thinks there is a 40% chance that the business market is price sensitive (making a low cost solution the preferred option) and 60% that the market is price insensitive (making the high value solution more attractive). The sales department has, thus, defined the different states of nature[3]:

$$p(\text{price sensitive market}) = 0.40$$
$$p(\text{price insensitive market}) = 0.60$$

MMS has sufficient data to calculate the expected sales and resulting net income for each alternative decision. The different decision options, states of nature and corresponding results can easily be represented by a **decision tree** or by a **decision matrix** (see Figure 2.4).

[3] We only look at two states of nature and two decision possibilities here, but these numbers can be increased without altering the approach.

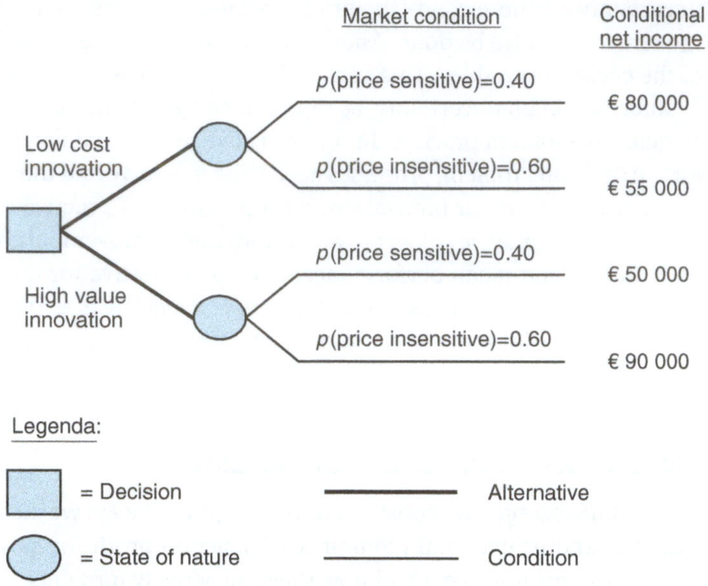

Figure 2.4 MMS product innovation decision tree

A decision tree is composed of **decision** nodes where all decision **alternatives** originate, and **state of nature** nodes with which all possible future **conditions** are connected. The corresponding decision matrix looks like the one in Table 2.2.

Table 2.2 MMS product innovation decision matrix

Alternative decisions	States of nature	
	Price sensitive p = 0.40	Price insensitive p = 0.60
Low cost innovation	80 000	55 000
High value innovation	50 000	90 000

If MMS management know with certainty that the market is price sensitive, the best alternative would then be the low cost innovation strategy. High price sensitivity of customers would lead to higher sales numbers and, therefore, to higher net income. If MMS know with certainty that the customers are price insensitive, the best alternative would be to follow the high value innovation strategy. Under this strategy, the higher price and a larger product gross margin would yield a higher net income.

The probabilities p can be used to calculate a weighted average value (cast in a result variable like gross margin or net income) for each alternative, using the probabilities as weights. The weighted average is the expected value (EV) of each alternative:

$$\text{EV(low cost innovation)}: (0.4 * €80\,000) + (0.6 * €55\,000) = €65\,000$$
$$\text{EV(high value innovation)}: (0.4 * €50\,000) + (0.6 * €90\,000) = €74\,000$$

Thus, based on the expected values, managers would choose the high value innovation strategy. This strategy generates €9 000 more expected value than the low cost innovation strategy.

2.2.5 Expected value of additional information

If the high value innovation in a price sensitive market would yield at least €80 000, a calculation would not be necessary: under all conditions the high value innovation alternative is the best decision to make. All information about future states of nature and possible financial consequences would not be valuable, because they will not change the strategy selection decision. Information only has a certain value when it is capable of changing decisions.

Here the question becomes: can we improve our decision if we have additional or more certain information about the future states of nature? We can estimate the additional value by looking backwards: if we knew the future state of nature would be a price sensitive market, we would have choosen the low cost innovation. If we knew the market would be price insensitive, we would opt for the high value innovation. Given these perfect choices, the highest expected value of given information (EVGI) can be determined as follows:

$$\text{EVGI} = (0.4 * €80000) + (0.6 * €90000) = €86000$$

We still use the weighted average function here, because we cannot predict the future market at this stage with certainty. The only thing we know is what we should do, if we had perfect information in each future market condition. The difference between the expected value of given information and our current expected value with no additional information is the **expected value of perfect information** (EVPI):

$$\text{EVPI} = \text{EVGI} - \text{EV}$$

In our example:

$$\text{EVPI} = €86000 - €74000 = €12000$$

The amount of €12 000 represents the maximum price MMS management is willing to pay for perfect information. Suppose a consulting firm would offer to do a market study for a price of €10 000, the expected value would be reduced by the consultancy cost of €10 000 to €76 000, but this amount is still €2 000 higher than the highest attainable expected value of €74 000. Thus the cost of additional information is lower than the marginal value of improved decision making.

However, the idea of getting perfect information is not very realistic. Predictions of future states of nature are always imperfect, because they are inherently uncertain to a higher or lower degree. This does not mean that it is not possible to do a better job in predicting. In the current decision situation, MMS could decide to interview a sample of prospective customers, asking them what they would do if MMS launched new low cost or new high value products. This information could add credibility to the prediction on how the future market will react. The better MMS does the job of additional market research, for instance by interviewing more customers, by using more additional information, by using more experienced researchers or by applying more sophisticated analysis techniques, the more valuable MMS' market study will be. We call this the value of 'sample information': it is information that is added to our current estimation of future events and that is aimed at making the initial estimations less uncertain.

The Bayes' Theorem, or Bayesian revision of existing information, is used to assess the additional value of sample information. We start with 'prior probabilities', which is our own, original assessment of the market, before any new information is examined. Let us use the variable n_i to denote the states of nature i: n_1 is a price sensitive market and n_2 is a price insensitive market. Our prior probabilities are:

$$p(\mathrm{n}_1) = 0.40$$
$$p(\mathrm{n}_2) = 0.60$$

Suppose MMS invites the consulting firm Market Demand to conduct a market survey. The main task for Market Demand is to see whether the market is price sensitive or price insensitive. How convincing the market research report will be depends on the quality of Market Demand's survey. In most cases, some information will be available on the consulting firm's past performance. Suppose Market Demand was in 90% of the cases successful in predicting a price sensitive market and in 80% successful in predicting a price insensitive market. This means that Market Demand has a higher accuracy in predicting price sensitive markets than price insensitive markets. These quality assessments of additional information are called 'conditional probabilities' since they are conditional on the market actually being price sensitive or not. The sample information coming from the consultants' report is represented by s_i, where the subscript i represent to the i different states of nature that are predicted by *Market Demand*. So now we have four possible combinations: the consultants' predictions and the actual states of nature, which can be expressed as follows:

$$\begin{aligned}
p(\mathrm{s}_1 \mid \mathrm{n}_1) &= p(\text{survey shows a price sensitive market when the market is price sensitive}) \\
&= 0.90 \\
p(\mathrm{s}_2 \mid \mathrm{n}_1) &= p(\text{survey shows a price insensitive market when the market is price sensitive}) \\
&= 0.10 \\
p(\mathrm{s}_2 \mid \mathrm{n}_2) &= p(\text{survey shows a price insensitive market when the market is price insensitive}) \\
&= 0.80 \\
p(\mathrm{s}_1 \mid \mathrm{n}_2) &= p(\text{survey shows a price sensitive market when the market is price insensitive}) \\
&= 0.20
\end{aligned}$$

The information between brackets should be read in a reversed order: given the actual future condition $\mathrm{n_i}$ that is the probability that the consultants have predicted a future state of nature $\mathrm{s_i}$. As we can see, two combinations represent the possibility that the predictions are correct, and two combinations represent incorrect predictions. We now want to know what the possibilities of a price sensitive or price insensitive market are **once we have received** a certain prediction of the consultants. These possibilities are called the **posterior probabilities** and can be determined by using the prior and conditional probabilities in the following way:

$$p(n_i \mid s_i) = \frac{p(n_i)p(s_i \mid n_i)}{\sum_{n(i)=1}^{n(i)=m} p(n_i)p(s_i \mid n_i)}$$

Please note that in this equation $p(n_i \mid s_i)$ of posterior probabilities, the positions of sample information and state of nature have switched places compared to the conditional probabilities $p(s_i \mid n_i)$. Now we determine the probability that, given a certain prediction of the market demand, a given actual market condition will actually present itself.

The posterior probabilities can be determined as follows:

$$p(n_1 \mid s_1) = \frac{p(n_1)p(s_1 \mid n_1)}{p(n_1)p(s_1 \mid n_1) + p(n_2)p(s_1 \mid n_2)} = \frac{0.4 * 0.9}{(0.4 * 0.9) + (0.2 * 0.6)} = 0.75$$

$$p(n_2 \mid s_1) = \frac{p(n_2)p(s_1 \mid n_2)}{p(n_1)p(s_1 \mid n_1) + p(n_2)p(s_1 \mid n_2)} = \frac{0.2 * 0.6}{(0.4 * 0.9) + (0.2 * 0.6)} = 0.25$$

$$p(n_2 \mid s_2) = \frac{p(n_2)p(s_2 \mid n_2)}{p(n_2)p(s_2 \mid n_2) + p(n_1)p(s_2 \mid n_1)} = \frac{0.6 * 0.8}{(0.6 * 0.8) + (0.4 * 0.1)} = 0.93$$

$$p(n_1 \mid s_2) = \frac{p(n_1)p(s_2 \mid n_1)}{p(n_2)p(s_2 \mid n_2) + p(n_1)p(s_2 \mid n_1)} = \frac{0.4 * 0.1}{(0.6 * 0.8) + (0.4 * 0.1)} = 0.07$$

The working of Bayes' Theorem can be demonstrated by using Table 2.3:

Table 2.3 Bayes' Theorem explained

		States of nature		
		n_1	n_2	Total
Reports	s_1	**0.90** 0.4*0.9 = 0.36 0.36/0.48 = 0.75	**0.20** 0.2*0.6 = 0.12 0.12/0.48 = 0.25	0.48
	s_2	**0.10** 0.4*0.1 = 0.04 0.04/0.52 = 0.07	**0.80** 0.6*0.8 = 0.48 0.48/0.52 = 0.93	0.52
		0.40	**0.60**	**1.0**

The figures in bold are given data: they represent the prior probabilities (bottom row) and the conditional probabilities (in each of the four cells). For instance, in the upper left cell we find the conditional probabilities for receiving a report that correctly predicts a price sensitive market. The probability to end up in this cell, taking also into account the possibilities of having a price insensitive market, is 0.4*0.9 = 0.36. This is done for each of the cells. Now we can use the symmetry of the table by changing our column-wise view into a row oriented view. Adding the probabilities for each row gives us the probability of receiving a report that either predicts a price sensitive or a price insensitive market. When we divide the probability of the occurrence of cel (s_1, n_1) by the probability of receiving report s_1 (which is 0.48) we obtain the probability of getting a price sensitive market once we receive a report which predicts a price sensitive market (see the calculations put in italic numbers). And here we have the reversal of $p(s_1 \mid n_1)$ into $p(n_1 \mid s_1)$.

When we receive Market Demand's survey report, it will change our estimations of the future states of nature, and it will, therefore, also change our expected values. The difference between our original expected values and the revised expected values based on Market Demand's reports is called the 'expected value of sample information' (EVSI). The EVSI represents the added value because of the revision of original probabilities. Suppose we receive a report that indicates a price sensitive market, the expected values of the two product innovation strategies would become the following:

EV(low cost innovation, price sensitive market report)
= (0.75 * €80000) + (0.25 * €55000) = €73750
EV(high value innovation, price sensitive market report)
= (0.75 * €50000) + (0.25 * €90000) = €60000

Under the condition that we receive a report predicting a price insensitive market, the revised expected values of the different strategies become the following:

EV(low cost innovation, price insensitive market report)
= (0.07 * €80000) + (0.93 * €55000) = €56923
EV(high value innovation, price insensitive market report)
= (0.07 * €50000) + (0.93 * €90000) = €86923

The results show that when we receive a report predicting a price sensitive market, we should choose the low cost innovation (with expected value of €73 750), and when we receive a report predicting a price insensitive market, we should select the high value innovation strategy (with expected value of €86 923). In order to be able to compare these values with the original predictions, we need to know the probabilities of receiving the reports. These probabilities are determined by the denominators of the posterior probabilities:

$$p(\text{price sensitive market report}) = (0.9 * 0.4) + (0.2 * 0.6) = 0.48$$
$$p(\text{price insensitive market report}) = (0.1 * 0.4) + (0.8 * 0.6) = 0.52$$

The total expected value of requesting a survey report becomes:

$$(0.48 * €73750) + (0.52 * €86923) = €80600$$

The original expected value with no marketing report was €74000. The sample report is able to raise the expected value to €80600. The expected value of sample information equals the difference between the two values:

The expected value of optimal choices based on the predictions given by sample information (in this case: *Market Demand's* survey report) *minus* the expected value of the optimal strategy without the sample information: €80 600 − €74 000 = €6600.

The economic interpretation of this amount is that MMS is willing to pay Market Demand the maximum of €6600 for their market survey report. If MMS a higher price than €6600 our calculations show that MMS would have a higher cost of additional information than it expects to earn on the basis of the survey report it would receive. Paying a lower amount means that acquiring the report adds more to the expected value of the strategy choice than the cost of the sample information.

In general, the expected value of sample information EVSI is lower than the expected value of perfect information EVPI, simply because the quality of sample information is not certain and will, therefore, increase uncertainty, which is expressed in the expected values.

2.3 Decision making under complete uncertainty

2.3.1 The role of information

Most of the decisions managers deal with uncertainty because they are oriented towards the future: they prepare the organisation for future states of nature or they are meant to make a future state happen. The more the decisions influence organisational processes into the future (the 'time' dimension), or the more entities will be affected by the decisions taken (the 'place' dimension), the more strategic the decisions are. In general, the more strategic the decision is, the more uncertainty will be involved.

A sensible way of coping with uncertainty is to identify its causes, to measure the probability of occurrence and to assess its influence on future outcomes. In the previous section we have done all three in one decision problem. We identified the cause of uncertainty by grouping the market into two possible customer preferences. We attached probabilities of occurrence to each of the customer preference groups and assessed the influence of each group on the possible outcomes of alternative product innovation strategies. The information for these assessments may come from objective data sources, like archival data about market performance and customer surveys, and from subjective assessments provided by well-informed managers, professionals or external experts. Objective assessments have the advantage that they cannot easily be influenced or distorted by individuals. Sometimes, participants may have interests at stake, or they work under incentive schemes that motivate them to bias the estimates they provide in the decision making process. In most cases there is thin line between objective and subjective assessments: objective data can be interpreted subjectively, or subjective expert opinions are needed to select, analyse and interpret objective data. Both approaches may lead to more or less meaningful information: sometimes objective data are not interpretable and subjective assessments may generate distorted information.

This leads us to a situation where we do not have much additional information about possible future conditions or states of nature, and how they impact on company performance. Nevertheless, decision makers need to make a decision, also under conditions of complete uncertainty. A situation of complete uncertainty means that we do not have probability estimations any more. In our MMS example, this would mean that we do not know how high the probability is that certain states of nature will occur. There can be good reasons for not having probability estimations available: companies may enter markets that are unknown, they may introduce completely new and innovative products or they encounter unprecedented business conditions about which no knowledge or experience is available. Let us return to our decision matrix. We now still have the decision we need to make, we also have some ideas of how different market reactions will impact our performance, but we are completely ignorant about the possibilities of occurrence of the different market reactions. As you can appreciate, Table 2.4 is identical to Table 2.3, except for the probabilities: Table 2.4 does not have any probability estimations any more.

Table 2.4 MMS decision making under uncertainty

Alternative decisions	States of Nature	
	Price sensitive	Price insensitive
Low cost innovation	80 000	55 000
High value innovation	50 000	90 000

This decision matrix does not give us much opportunity for making calculations about expected outcomes. And yet MMS needs to make a decision. It looks as if nothing more can be done than just throwing up a coin and having Lady Fortuna decide. But that is not the case here. The less information about future probabilities decision makers have, the more important their attitudes towards risk become in the decision making process. It is exactly the decision maker's risk attitude that can be used to reach a decision. They can lead to alternative decision rules, which we will see in the next paragraphs.

2.3.2 Maxi-max and maxi-min utility rule

The maxi-max decision rule applies to optimistic decision makers who expect that the best possible condition will be the most likely and that the decision maker should seize the opportunity it provides. Stated more formally, the decision maker aims at selecting the highest possible outcome under most ideal conditions:

$$\max_{i} \max_{j} [r_{ij}]$$

This formula states that first we look at each column and select the row containing the maximum value. Then we evaluate all maximum values across rows and select the strategy that is related to the highest value of the column outcomes. In our example, we therefore first identify for each condition separately the best possible outcome across rows i in the results matrix (Table 2.4). We obtain €80 000 for the price sensitive market condition and €90000 for the price insensitive market condition. The price insensitive condition contains the highest net income of €90 000. In order to reach this highest outcome across columns j, the high value innovation option should be selected.

The maxi-min decision rule was developed by Abraham Wald. This selection approach is based on a pessimistic decision maker's attitude. He expects that most things would not work out as intended: once a strategy is selected, the most adverse state of nature will occur. Here we start by looking for the lowest outcomes for each strategy. Low cost innovation has a minimal outcome of €55 000 and high value innovation of €50 000. We then select the best alternative available, which is low cost innovation. This is the strategy that at least generates an outcome of €55 000, which is still €5000 higher than the worst possible outcome for the high value innovation strategy. The decision maker avoids an even lower profit by making the right choice among adverse conditions. This procedure can be formally described as follows:

$$\max_{i}\min_{j}[r_{ij}]$$

Another, more complicated approach is to look at the opportunity costs. The opportunity cost of a chosen strategy is the net income generated by the best alternative that has not been chosen. This requires that the decision makers first imagine what would happen if the decision about to be made will turn out to be a good or bad decision. They try to predict the consequences of making the wrong decision by constructing a 'regret matrix.' For each state of nature, we look at the outcome of each decision alternative. If we have chosen the best alternative under given conditions, the amount of regret is zero. If an alternative decision gives a higher outcome, the difference between the current outcome and the opportunity cost is the amount of regret attached to the decision. See Table 2.5 for the results that correspond to the MMS decision problem depicted in Table 2.4.

Table 2.5 MMS regret matrix

Alternative decisions	States of nature	
	Price sensitive	Price insensitive
Low cost innovation	0	35 000
High value innovation	30 000	0

In each column we now look at the maximum level of regret, which are the positive numbers in this example. For example, the €35 000 regret for the low cost innovation in a price insensitive market is the difference between the corresponding profit of €55 000 and the potential profit of €90 000 if the high value innovation strategy would have been chosen. Then we choose the alternative with the lowest maximum regret. In our example, this is the high value innovation option (with corresponding €30 000 regret). This approach tries to prepare the decision maker for liability discussions after the decision is made. The decision maker can show that the high value innovation option does not incur maximum losses, since there is always a higher loss situation (the low cost innovation under price insensitive market conditions). More formally:

$$\min_{i}\max_{j}[regret_{ij}]$$

Until now we have worked with discretionary categories of optimistic and pessimistic decision makers, each having its own decision rule. We can also work with a continuous scale of optimism using the Hurwicz-scale (developed by Leonard Hurwizc). Of each alternative, the highest value corresponds with optimism (because it relates to the best possible condition under which the strategy can be executed) and the lowest with pessimism (there is no worse condition to execute the corresponding strategy). The level of optimism is represented by the Hurwicz α, a variable between 0 and 1. The value of 1 means that the decision maker is fully optimistic, while the value of 0 means that the decision maker is pessimistic. The level of pessimism is, thus, the complement of optimism and is determined by (1-α). For each decision alternative α_i we can determine a function based on the level of optimism, using the following equation:

$$H(\alpha_i) = \alpha \max_j[r_{ij}] + (1 - \alpha) \min_j[r_{ij}]$$

We can now restate the MMS decision problem in terms of optimism and pessimism, as follows:

$$H(\alpha_1) = \alpha.80000 + (1\text{-}\alpha).55000 = 55000 + 25000\alpha$$
$$H(\alpha_2) = \alpha.90000 + (1\text{-}\alpha).50000 = 50000 + 40000\alpha$$

Both equations are shown graphically in Figure 2.5.

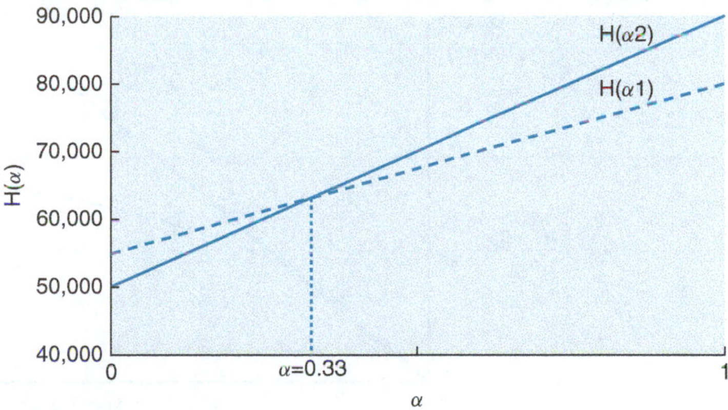

Figure 2.5 MMS choice preferences using the Hurwicz criterium

Decision makers are indifferent about the alternatives when both choices lead to the same Hurwicz value, which is when $H(\alpha_1) = H(\alpha_2)$:

$$55000 + 25000\alpha = 50000 + 40000\alpha$$
$$5000 = 15000\alpha$$
$$\alpha = 0.33$$

As we can see from Figure 2.5, more pessimistic people than $\alpha = 0.33$ should choose the low cost innovation, whereas relatively optimistic people should favour the high value innovation option. The final choice between alternatives is basically determined by the level of optimism of the decision maker.

2.4 Risk, uncertainty and the decision maker

2.4.1 The appreciation of risk

In the expected utilities calculations we made in the previous sections, we expected that decision makers value relative differences in probabilities equally to the same relative differences in outcomes. For instance, in our MMS example we calculated an expected value of the low cost alternative under a price sensitive market condition of 0.4 * 80000 = €32000. Suppose the possibility of encountering a price sensitive market would increase by 10%, the expected outcome would then become 0.44 * 80000 = €35200. This same result could also have emerged from an increase of the expected profit under a 40% probability: 0.4 * 88000 = €35200. The question now is, would a decision maker under real-life circumstances value these two outcomes as identical results? In the first situation, the possibility of earning €80,000 has increased, while in the second situation the possibility has not changed, but the pay-out has. Many empirical studies have demonstrated that most people favour a reduction of risk more than the same increase in profit. In other words: decision makers are generally risk averse. Figure 2.6 portrays different risk attitudes by iso-utility curves. An iso-utility curve contains all different combinations of risk and expected returns that represent the same utility for the decision maker.

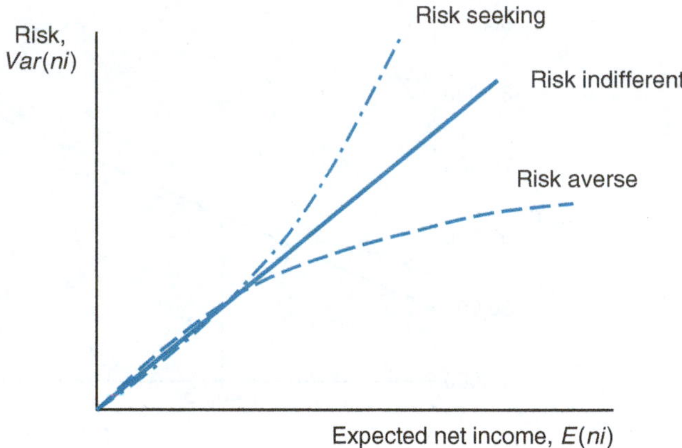

Figure 2.6 **Iso-utility curves for different risk attitudes**

Risk averse decision makers require a higher expected net income for the same levels of risk than risk indifferent or risk seeking decision makers. Or, put it differently, they accept lower levels of risk at the same levels of expected net income. Their iso-utility curve is concave because the second derivative of the Utility function to risk is smaller than 0 (written more formally: $U''(ni) < 0$).

Kahneman and Tversky have studied the sensitivities of decision makers to different levels of risk under different circumstances. They developed a set of propositions about decision-making behaviour that has become known as 'prospect theory'.[4] It explains how

[4] The psychologist Daniel Kahneman received the Nobel memorial prize in economic science for his work in this area in 2002.

decision makers deal with different outlooks (prospects) of the future. The utility function does not seem to be a continuous decreasing function of risk, but at the extremes there seem to be some irregularities. People in general seem to favour certain outcomes much more than uncertain outcomes: they prefer an option with a certain outcome over an alternative option with an uncertain outcome, even when the expected value of the uncertain alternative is higher than the expected value of the certain option. You can check this yourself by looking at the following decision problem[5]:

What would you prefer?

A. An 80% chance of gaining €4000; (and 20% chance of getting nothing)

B. A certain gain of €3000

Option A can also be expressed in the following way: (4000, .80) which means: a gain of €4000 with a probability of 80%. Option B can be written as (3000): a certain gain of €3000. Most people (not all) are inclined to prefer Option B: they value the certainty of receiving the gain higher than the expected value of Option A. If we use the expected value approach, Option A would be the preferred option (0.8 * €4000 = €3200), which is €200 higher than the expected value of option B (1.0 * €3000 = €3000). This phenomena is called the 'certainty effect': decision makers attach disproportionately more additional value to a certain alternative over an uncertain alternative.

Also at the low end of the risk spectrum we find anomalies. When decision makers are confronted with substantial probabilities, like the ones we used in our MMS example of 0.40 and 0.60, risk averse managers appear to favour the higher probabilities if the expected value of the alternatives are the same. However, if the possibilities used are very low, for instance of 0.001 and 0.002, the same decision makers turn out to choose the alternative that offers the larger gain, even if it is the higher risk alternative.

Consider the following two decision situations, which option would you prefer?

Decision problem 1:		
A: (6000, .45)	or	B: (3000, .90)
Decision problem 2:		
C: (6000, .001)	or	D: (3000, .002)

While the expected values of the options in both situations are the same, most decision makers prefer Option B in the first case, and Option C in the second. In the first decision problem, people seem to prefer more certainty over less certainty, while in the second problem they already know that the possibility of gaining is very low and they then prefer the higher gain and lower possibility of receiving the gain (in fact, only half the possibility of option D!). This finding contradicts the 'substitution axiom' of expected utility theory, which expects that when an alternative (y,pq) is equivalent to (x,p), the alternative (y,pqr) will also be equivalent to (x,pr) (we expect p, q and r to be between 0 and 1). In the above

[5] Most examples are taken from Kahneman, D., Tversky, A. (1979). Prospect Theory: an analysis of decision under risk. *Econometrica,* Vol. 47, No. 2, 263-291.:

example: B(x, p)>A(y, 0.5p) while D(x, 0.022p)<C(y, 0.5*0.022p). Expected outcome and possibility are clearly not perfectly substitutable.

Until now we have only looked at decision situation where we had a possibility to **gain** something. We could also look at situations where we have the possibility to **lose.** In reality, risk management is designed to look at possible adverse conditions, to predict the likelihood of occurrence and to estimate the potential impact on outcomes (mostly stated in terms of expected losses). It turns out that most decision makers appreciate risk differently when they are in the domain of positive results (like profits) than when they make their decisions in the negative domain (losses). The negative value of losses seems to cause a higher 'disutility' (negative utility) for the decision maker than the same value in the positive domain generates a utility. Apparently, a loss causes a larger disutility than a gain of the same amount causes a utility. Please consider the following two options:

What would you prefer?

A. An 80% chance of loosing €4000 (and 20% chance of zero loss)

B. A certain loss of €3000.

Most people (again, not all) prefer Option A over Option B, because Option A still has the possibility of not loosing anything. Here we see that decision makers become more risk seeking because they prefer a risky alternative over a certain outcome. Compare your choice to this problem with the answer you gave to the first problem on the previous page. As you can see: the numbers are identical, while the only difference is the change from a positive into a negative domain. Most people have choosen a different solution; Option B in the positive domain problem and Option A in the negative domain problem. This is called the **reflection effect;** the preference between positive prospects is the mirror image of the preference between negative prospects.

The fundamental drive behind this 'irrational' behaviour is the difference in appreciation of gains and losses. Most people value the loss of money higher than the pleasure of gaining the same amount. We then get the following value function for gains and losses (see figure 2.7).

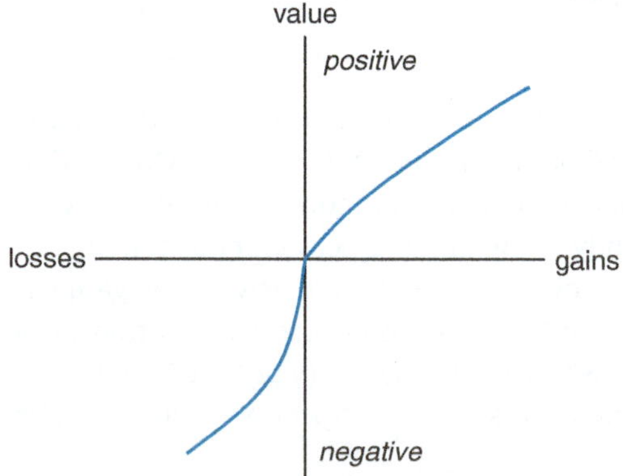

Figure 2.7 The value function (Kahnemann & Tverski, 1976)

The value function is steeper for losses than for gains, which means an increase in losses is considered to cause more aggravation than the same amount of increase in gains will cause pleasure. The form of the function is also different across domains: concave for gains and convex for losses, causing the greatest differences around the zero.

In practice, when the earnings are expected to fall just below the zero earnings point, managers appear to engage in earnings manipulations in order to help them cross the 'red line' for the year (Hayn, 1995). This can be demonstrated by looking at 75 999 US firm-year observations in the period 1977-1994 of net earnings scaled by the beginning-of-the-year market value. The distribution appears to follow a bell shaped distribution, but with a remarkable irregularity around zero earnings. Earnings slightly less than zero occur much less frequently and earnings slightly larger than zero occur much more frequently than would be expected given the smoothness of the remainder of the distribution (see Figure 2.8).

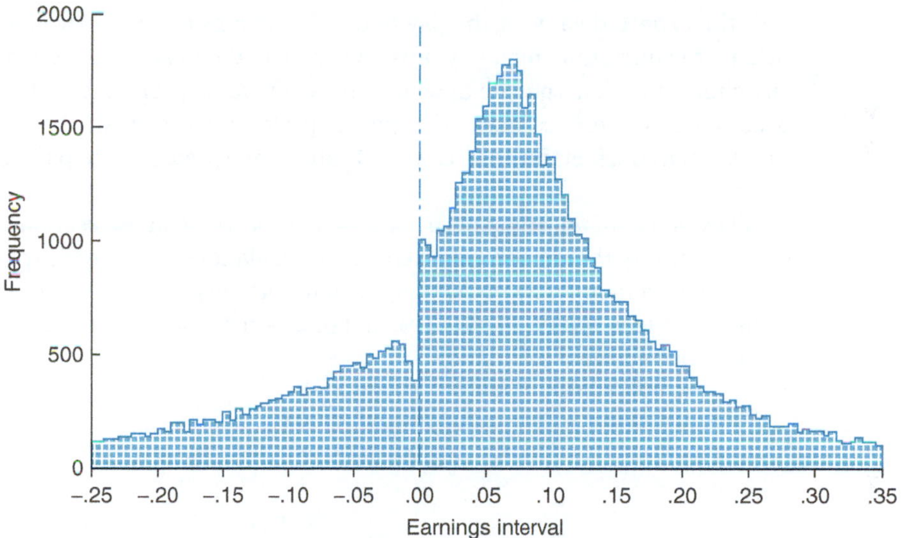

Figure 2.8 The distribution of annual net income (Burgstahler & Dichev, 1997)

A similar pattern is apparent when managers try to avoid earning decreases. The longer the period of previous run of earnings increases, the more managers try to avoid a decrease in earnings (Burgstahler & Dichev, 1997).

This means that decision makers may be sensitive for where the zero-value exactly is. It works like a **reference point:** either you are on the 'good' side (in the positive domain) or in the 'bad' side (the negative domain) of this point. In our little experiments, the zero is supposed to mean not losing and not gaining any money. However, in practical situations, like in budgeting or long term planning processes, the reference point may also be the target budget levels or target profit required by higher management or by shareholders. Just reconsider MMS shareholders requiring a net income of at least €37 500 in the break-even section of this chapter. Shareholders are now **framing** management: falling short of the required €37 500 net income may be considered a loss, while surpassing the target will be considered a gain. Management may engage in more risk seeking behaviour when they foresee that the target profit level will not be reached. They may also engage in operational and administrative manipulations to improve short-term performance data. Some of the administrative manipulations are known as 'earnings management': these entail efforts to present an image of performance that will contribute to a positive assessment of the company or the organisational unit. Some earnings management practices are allowed, others may be more debatable, while some may also be outright fraudulent.

We also see some strange effects when we combine high positive and negative payoffs with low probabilities. Consider the following problem:

What would you prefer?

A: a 0.1% chance of winning €5000 or B: a certain gain of €5.

What would you prefer?

C: a 0.1% chance of loosing €5000 or D: a certain loss of €5.

Most subjects prefer A over B, which expresses their preference for uncertain high pay-outs over the expected value of the pay-out. This explains the attractiveness of buying lottery tickets: the uncertain, high pay-outs add value to the ticket over its expected value. In the last choice problem, people appear to have a reverse preference. Most people choose D over C. This preference shows that people prefer to pay a small amount in order to avoid the risk of a considerable loss. Option D can be interpreted as the payment of an insurance premium.

All examples of uncertain decision situations provided in this section violate the tenets of expected utility theory and expected value calculations. Although expected value calculations can be a rational way of dealing with uncertainty, it is also important to note that the decision maker's appreciation of risk and return may not behave in the same linear fashion as the expected value calculations.

Appendix A

Area under the Normal Curve Between the Mean and Successive Values of z

Example: If $z = 1.87$, the area between the mean and 1.87 standard deviations is .46926 and the area to the right of z is .03074 (.50000 − .46926).

z	.00	.01	.02	.03	.04	.05	.06	.07	.08	.09
.0	.00000	.00399	.00798	.01197	.01595	.01994	.02392	.02790	.03188	.03586
.1	.03983	.04380	.04776	.05172	.05567	.05962	.06356	.06749	.07142	.07535
.2	.07926	.08317	.08706	.09095	.09483	.09871	.10257	.10642	.11026	.11409
.3	.11791	.12172	.12552	.12930	.13307	.13683	.14058	.14431	.14803	.15173
.4	.15542	.15910	.16276	.16640	.17003	.17364	.17724	.18082	.18439	.18793
.5	.19146	.19497	.19847	.20194	.20540	.20884	.21226	.21566	.21904	.22240
.6	.22575	.22907	.23237	.23565	.23891	.24215	.24537	.24857	.25175	.25490
.7	.25804	.26115	.26424	.26730	.27035	.27337	.27637	.27935	.28230	.28524
.8	.28814	.29103	.29389	.29673	.29955	.30234	.30511	.30785	.31057	.31327
.9	.31594	.31859	.32121	.32381	.32639	.32894	:33147	.33398	.33646	.33891
1.0	.34134	.34375	.34614	.34849	.35083	.35314	.35543	.35769	.35993	.36214
1.1	.36433	.36650	.36864	.37076	.37286	.37493	.37698	.37900	.38100	.38298
1.2	.38493	.38686	.38877	.39065	.39251	.39435	.39617	.39796	.39973	.40147
1.3	.40320	.40490	.40658	.40824	.40988	.41149	.41309	.41466	.41621	.41774
1.4	.41924	.42073	.42220	.42364	.42507	.42647	.42785	.42922	.43056	.43189
1.5	.43319	.43448	.43574	.43699	.43822	.43943	.44062	.44179	.44295	.44408
1.6	.44520	.44630	.44738	.44845	.44950	.45053	.45154	.45254	.45352	.45449
1.7	.45543	.45637	.45728	.45818	.45907	.45994	.46080	.46164	.46246	.46327
1.8	.46407	.46485	.46562	.46638	.46712	.46784	.46856	.46926	.46995	.47062
1.9	.47128	.47193	.47257	.47320	.47381	.47441	.47500	.47558	.47615	.47670
2.0	.47725	.47778	.47831	,47882	.47932	.47982	.48030	.48077	.48124	.48169
2.1	.48214	.48257	.48300	.48341	.48382	.48422	.48461	.48500	.48537	.48574
2.2	.48610	.48645	.48679	.48713	.48745	.48778	.48809	.48840	.48870	.48899
2.3	.48928	.48956	.48983	.49010	.49036	.49061	.49086	.49111	.49134	.49158
2.4	.49180	.49202	.49224	.49245	.49266	.49286	.49305	.49324	.49343	.49361
2.5	.49379	.49396	.49413	.49430	.49446	.49461	.49477	.49492	.49506	.49520
2.6	.49534	.49547	.49560	.49573	.49585	.49598	.49609	.49621	.49632	.49643
2.7	.49653	.49664	.49674	.49683	.49693	.49702	.49711	.49720	.49728	.49736
2.8	.49744	.49752	.49760	.49767	.49774	.49781	.49788	.49795	.49801	.49807
2.9	.49813	.49819	.49825	.49831	.49836	.49841	.49846	.49851	.49856	.49861
3.0	.49865									
4.0	.49997									

EXERCISES

Exercise 2.1 Amsterdam Digitizers

Amsterdam Digitizers (AD) is a relatively new Dutch firm in the telecommunication industry. It produces memory cards for end user products, like cameras and GPS systems. The current financial position is not bad, but AD management wants to improve it considerably. It has developed three alternative strategic scenarios.

The first scenario is called 'Product Quality'. AD aims at improving quality by putting additional effort of production personnel in producing the products, leading to a 20% increase in direct labour costs. It is also planning to make the production equipment more up to date by investing extra in manufacturing equipment, which leads to a yearly increase in fixed production costs of €25 000. Higher quality should cost more to the customer, hence AD wants to increase selling price by €0.50. AD expects this scenario to lead to 10% higher sales quantity.

An alternative approach is to start a 'Marketing Campaign' by lowering the selling price to €6.40 and by motivating the sales force to put extra effort in approaching customers. To this end, AD will increase the sales persons' commissions to 15% of sales. It also wants to invest in additional publicity by adding €10 000 to the fixed sales expenses. This scenario should generate 15% additional sales quantity.

The third alternative strategy is labelled 'Product Innovation'. AD has the option to introduce a renewed memory card, using more expensive materials and innovated production processes. The machinery needs replacement, which will lead to an annual additional amount of €40 000 fixed manufacturing costs. The material costs will double, while the variable overhead costs will be four times higher, at €2 per piece. Labour is not yet familiar with the new production process, which means that direct labour costs are estimated at €1.25 per piece. Since it will be a new product, AD does not expect a large impact on sales quantity: only a 5% increase for next year.

Current sales numbers are 80 000 units, price is €7. Material variable costs is €2 per unit, fixed manufacturing costs are €100 000. Direct labour costs are €1 per unit and variable overhead is €0.50 per unit. Fixed overhead costs is €50 000 for sales and €30 000 for administration. AD has sales people taking care of customer relations and direct sales. Each sales person receives a 10% commission on sales revenues. Tax rate is 35%.

Required:

1. Make a pro forma income statement in Excel based on the current situation for Amsterdam Digitizers. Make a distinction between a Data Section (in which the most relevant given data are stored) and a Pro Forma Income Statement. What is AD's current net income?
2. Produce a systematic overview of the financial implications of each of the alternative strategies proposed by AD. Make use of Excel's scenario feature. You can find this feature under \Extra.

After having reviewed all options, AD's management decides **not** to change the strategy. They prefer to capitalise on the market strengths the company already posesses. The following market information may be relevant:

Mean sales for last five years:	80 000 units
Standard deviation of sales volume:	6000 units
Last year's sales:	84 000 units
Goal for next year:	90 000 units

Recapitulation of additional information:

Price:	€7 per unit
Variable costs:	€4.20 per unit
Fixed costs:	€180 000

3. What is the probability of at least breaking even?
4. What is the probability of achieving next year's sales goal?
5. Suppose AD's management has reviewed the statistical information and it comes to the conclusion that the standard deviation is 12 000. How does this change your answer to questions 4 and 5?

Exercise 2.2 **Choosing the right franchise contract**

Up and Running is a successful coffee corner chain operating in public places, like train stations, airports and musea. *Up and Running's* headquarters is planning to expand internationally and is considering extending a franchise contract to Mr. Lacroix, a Belgian entrepreneur. Sales in Belgium are very uncertain and expectations run from a low of €600 000 to a high of €1 800 000 a year.

The basic problem now is what kind of contract should be given to Mr. Lacroix? In the past, three different franchise contracts have already been used:

- Contract 1: a flat fee of €80 000 a year and an additional €20 for each €1000 sales
- Contract 2: a flat fee of €60 000 a year and an additional €40 for each €1000 sales
- Contract 3: a flat fee of €10 000 a year and an additional €70 for each €1000 sales

Required:

1. Management of *Up and Running* is thinking of three possible future sales in Belgium: €600 000, €1 200 000 or €1 800 000. Suppose management is pessimistic, which alternative would then be chosen?
2. Suppose *Up and Running's* management wants to avoid the regret of having chosen the wrong contract. Or put it differently: it wants to minimise opportunity costs. Which contract should then be selected?
3. The management team of *Up and Running* is known for not taking too many risks, and for not being too risk averse. What contract suits this management team best? (Hint: use the Hurwicz-scale to depict the level of optimism.)
4. Based on previous experiences in Luxemburg and France, the marketing manager of *Up and Running* estimates the possibilities of generating the different levels of sales as follows:
   - sales of €600 000 (60% probability)
   - Sales of €1 200 000 (30% probability)
   - sales of €1 800 000 (10% probability).

Given these probabilities, which contract is most attractive?

5. What is the value of perfect information? What does this value mean?
6. As we have seen, it really matters how you look at the decision situation. It would be most helpful if *Up and Running* could get more certainty about expected sales in Belgium. The marketing manager decides to ask a market research firm to survey prospective clients in Belgium. The marketing firm is known for being reasonably accurate in predicting high sales numbers, but less accurate in predicting low numbers. The following table is drawn from earlier marketing studies by the research firm:

- When predicting €600 000 sales it is 80% right, in 15% it is €1 200 000 and in 5% it is €1 800 000.
- When predicting €1 200 000 sales it is 80% right, in 15% it is €600 000 and in 5% it is €1 800 000.
- When predicting €1 800 000 sales it is 90% right, in 5% it is €600 000 and in 5% it is €1 200 000.

The marketing research bureau is willing to do the market research project for €500 000. Given the accuracy information provided, should *Up and Running* ask the marketing bureau to do the research?

Exercise 2.3 **Amsterdam Gardens Hotel**

Amsterdam Gardens Hotel has 125 hotel rooms. This cozy family hotel has always been a very profitable hotel, due to its nice location on the outskirts of Amsterdam near the beautiful Amstel river, its spacious gardens, and its fine dining opportunities. This historically successful track record, however, stopped two years ago where its occupancy rate was only approximately 57% (26 006 hotel rooms a year). To calculate a profit and loss statement, and to make projections for next year, the hotel controller prepared the following figures for the hotel revenues, variable and fixed costs. Two years ago, the hotel had the following figures:

Revenues	881 500
-Rooms	1 025 375
-Food and beverage	95 000
-Additional	
Costs	56 425
Variable costs	415 425
-rooms	27 128
-food and beverage	
-additional	
Fixed costs	1 031 306

Required:

1. Compute the contribution margin (total and per hotel room) and the net income before tax using the data given.

Although demand for hotel rooms already decreased last year, next year especially will be a very uncertain year for Amsterdam Gardens. In answering the following questions assume that the costs above are similar to the costs next year.

2. How many rooms should the hotel rent next year to break even?

Since it is unclear how long the current crisis will prolong, a lot of uncertainty exists around the number of hotel rooms that can be rented. When the crisis deepens, occupancy rates will decrease even further, but when the crisis ends the hotel management assumes that the number of rooms rented will go up. Based on this information it expects that the rooms rented follows a normal distribution with an average of 26 006 (last years sales) and a standard deviation of 3000 rooms.

3. What is the probability that the hotel indeed will break even this year?
4. To satisfy its wealthy family members that invest in the hotel, net income needs to go up to €500 000. What is the probability that this income level will be reached?

In explaining to the investors what the probabilities are that the hotel makes a profit of €500 000, one of the investors is arguing that the calculations are overly optimistic because the level of uncertainty is much higher. He orders the management to come up with the same computations but with a standard deviation for the expected number of hotel rooms rented of 4000 instead of 3000.

5. What is the new probability of the profit of €500 000 when the standard deviation increases?

In the computations above, hotel management is assuming that uncertainty in demand will be normally distributed. It therefore assumes that the level of uncertainty is symmetric for decreases and increases in future rooms rented.

6. Do you think this is a realistic assumption? What could be an alternative for this normal distribution (no computations required)?

At the start of the year, the hotel owners considered the plan to outsource the restaurant facility to a third party. This would make the hotel less dependent on the variation in demand. This strategy would severely change the revenue and cost structure. By outsourcing the restaurant facility it would receive €500 000 from the third party, the restaurant would have no variable costs for food and beverage, and be able reduce the fixed costs by €200 000.

7. What is the impact on the probability to break even and to gain a profit of €500 000? Assume the standard deviation is still €3000.
8. In general, what is the impact of reducing fixed costs in the face of uncertainty?

Exercise 2.4 The Daily Financial Times

The *Lowlands* publishing company has decided to launch a new magazine for financial specialists with the brand new title *The Daily Financial Times.* The problem is that this has not been done before. The *Lowlands* management does not have a clue how many copies will be sold and they think it will be somewhere between 60 000 and 120 000 copies.

The magazine sells for €4 and the variable cost to print is €1.20. Unsold magazines are destroyed.

Required:

1. Prepare a results matrix (or pay-off table) for different levels of demand: 60 000, 80 000, 100 000 and 120 000.
2. Suppose *Lowlands* management wants to avoid being blamed afterwards for having selected the wrong production plan, what production level should they then choose?

One of *Lowlands*' marketing specialists has looked at sales numbers of similar magazines in the past. This leads to the following information about demand:

Demand	p(Demand)
60 000	0.20
80 000	0.30
100 000	0.30
120 000	0.20

3. What strategy should be chosen if management wants to maximise the expected value of future strategies?
4. What is the Expected Value of Perfect Information?

Management has decided to invite a consultancy firm to do a market study. The aim of this study is to make a reliable estimate of future demand. The consultancy firm is relatively good in predicting small sized markets and not so good in predicting larger and more mature markets. The conditional probabilities are the following:

	n(60 000)	n(80 000)	n(100 000)	n(120 000)
s(60 000)	0.7	0.1	0.1	0.1
s(80 000)	0.1	0.7	0.1	0.1
s(100 000)	0.1	0.1	0.5	0.3
s(120 000)	0.1	0.1	0.3	0.5

The above table means that the consultant will predict in 70% of the cases of 60 000 sales the right number, but in 30% of the cases the prediction is wrong. The wrong predicted values here equal chance of occurrence (10% each) when the actual sales number turns out to be 60 000.

5. What is the best strategy when the consultant has produced the report? Make a prediction for each of the outcomes the consultant may produce.
6. Suppose the consultant offers to do the market study for €6500. Should we hire the consultant?

Exercise 2.5 Amsterdam Zuid Properties

Brinkman, the chairman of the Amsterdam Zuid Properties development company, has been offered two rental contracts at the Zuid-as in Amsterdam for the same prospective lessee. Each contract is for a year and the lessee would be responsible for all occupancy costs including utilities, building insurance and property taxes.

The first contract is for €60 000 per year plus €30 per unit of product sold by the lessee. The other contract is for €5000 per year and €70 per unit sold. This prospect seems to be the only one interested in the space available. Recent overbuilding in the area has cut demand drastically for at least a year. For the sake of this analysis, assume that the sale of units in this one year is independent of sales in any other year.

Required:

1. Brinkman knows that two states of nature may occur: a demand of 1000 units or a demand of 2000 units. But he has no information about the probability of occurrence. He knows one thing for sure: he does not want to get blamed afterwards too badly for having made a bad decision. With this in mind, which contract should Brinkman choose?
2. Suppose Brinkman is neither pessimistic nor optimistic, but exactly 'in the middle', which contract should he prefer?
3. Suppose Brinkman has information about the probabilities of demand. There is 40% chance the demand will be 1000 offices, and 60% that the demand will be 2000 offices. Which alternative should Brinkman choose, if he wants to maximise the expected value?
4. What is the expected value of perfect information?
5. Find the expected value of sample information given the following facts. A consultant with a track record of being correct 85% of the time when predicting a low market and 90% of the time correct when predicting a strong market offers to do some market research for Brinkman at a cost of €800. Sampling will result in one of two reports:

a. A pessimistic report – demand will be 1000 offices
b. An optimtistic report – demand will be 2000 offices

Will it be worthwile paying the consultant €800 for the information?

Exercise 2.6 Hightech Electronics Company

The Hightech Electronics Company produces consumer electronics products. One of its production plants produces a product at a selling price of €10 at the current quantity of 100 000 units. Variable material costs are €1.50, variable labor costs are €1.80 and variable overhead costs are €0.50 per product. Fixed manufacturing costs are €200 000 per year, and general and administrative (G&A) costs are €150 000 a year. Sales costs are composed of sales commissions (10% of sales) and annual fixed sales costs of €100 000. The corporate tax rate is 35%.

Required:

1. Prepare an Excel sheet, consisting of a Data section and a Pro Forma Income Statement section. Show in the Pro Forma Income Statement at least Gross profit, Income before taxes and Net income.

The Hightech Electronics shareholders are not satisfied with current financial performance and require at least €100 000 annual net income. The Hightech Electronics management team has developed three alternative scenarios to improve the financial performance of the company, labelled Marketing, Cost control and Quality.

The Marketing scenario is focused on additional sales based on an intensified marketing campaign. A brand new commercial will be launched (which leads to fixed sales costs of €160 000), sales managers will be paid a higher commission of 15% of sales, both of which will lead to higher annual sales of 120 000 pieces.

The Cost control scenario is targeted at lowering the sales prices to €8 per product. This will generate sales of 140 000 products. Variable material and labour costs will both be reduced by €0.20, and G&A fixed costs will be lowered to €100 000.

The Quality scenario is designed to premium-price the product upwards to €12. Additional features and higher quality finishing require variable material and labor cost to be €2 each per product. The variable overhead costs will need to be set at €0.80 per product, because of a new quality control system. Fixed manufacturing cost will be €250 000, fixed sales cost €110 000 and G&A costs €180 000. Sales numbers are expected to rise, despite the higher sales price, to a total number of 120 000.

2. Evaluate the financial effects of the three scenarios using Excel's What-If Analyses tool. Try to make an informative 'Scenario Summary.'
3. Which scenario(s) turn out to comply with Hightech Electronics' shareholder demands?

Exercise 2.7 Hightech Electronics Company, part B

The Hightech Electronics Company has recently gone through a strategic planning session for all of its sales personnel. Based on past experience and on the goals and strategies set for the upcoming year, the following information is available about sales:

Mean sales for last five years:	100 000 units
Standard deviation of sales volume:	8000 units
Last year's sales:	106 000 units
Goal for next year:	111 300 units (5% increase)

Other information regarding the company is already given in exercise 2.6 (the existing situation, not one of the senarios).

Required:

1. What is the probability of at least breaking even?
2. What is the probability of achieving next year's sales goal?
3. What additional information do you want to be more confident about your probability assessments in the previous two parts?
4. How are your answers in questions 1 and 2 affected by a shift of the mean sales from 100000 to 106000?
5. Independent from your response to question 4, how are your answers to questions 1 and 2 affected by a reduction of the standard deviation to 4000 units? And by an increase in the standard deviation to 12000 units?

References

Burgstahler, D., and Dichev, I. (1997). Earnings management to avoid earnings decreases and losses. *Journal of Accounting and Economics, 24,* 99-126.

Hayn, C. (1995). The information content of losses. *Journal of Accounting and Economics, 20,* 125-153.

Chapter 3

Management control

3.1 Management issue

Modern organisations are complex and dynamic; they have many parts that are all moving and changing. The concept of 'the firm' as a 'black box' from neoclassical microeconomics stops being descriptive or useful for actually managing real firms once one begins to peer inside the box. To organisational theorists' delight, fascinating questions about the nature of the firm and its internal organisation and operations are abundant – if one is brave enough to open the box. Managers are inside, and they have no choice but to immerse themselves in the firm's organisation and activities. They are faced with many difficult choices for which the venerable economic truth, 'maximise value by making improvements (or producing) up to the point where marginal value equals marginal cost,' needs some assistance.

Fortunately, we have many valuable insights from decades of theoretical and empirical research on such basic questions as:

- **'Why are there firms?'** Ronald Coase answered in the 1930s that organisations exist because they minimise the costs of some transactions that would be more costly to conduct in markets.[1] Otherwise, we would have only a myriad of sole proprietorships buying every resource and activity that the proprietors did not own or could not do themselves. Coase's answer might not be the entire answer, but it seems undeniably important and has spawned innumerable studies on what is known today as Transaction Cost Economics, or TCE.
- **'What are the boundaries of the firm?'** Oliver Williamson has refined TCE since the 1970s and received the Nobel prize in economic science in 2009 for his contributions.[2] We now know many of the markers of the boundaries of firms' internal activities or those obtained externally by a market transaction. A key insight from TCE is that legal and market forces control the quality, price, etc. of externally contracted transactions. Within the firm, however, managers use bureaucratic or hierarchical tools to control internal activities' quality, cost and so on.
- **'How are firms organised internally?'** Starting in the 1940s and 1950s Herbert Simon, a 1978 Nobel prize winner, inquired about the origins and effects of centralised versus

[1] Coase, R. H. (1937). (full citations are at the end of the chapter)

[2] Williamson, O.E. (1985).

decentralised operations.[3] We have since gained insights about the limits of rationality, ownership of knowledge, and incentives that can motivate individuals to share their knowledge with the firm.

- **'How do managers of firms execute the tasks of planning, risk management and control of operations?'** Robert Anthony advanced Chester Barnard's 1938/1968 investigation of how managers of organisations assist members to do their jobs effectively.[4] Most recently we are learning that organisations can use tools originally designed for internal use to complement market forces that regulate market based transactions (this is the topic of Chapter 11).

Although we still do not know all of the answers to the many questions regarding the management and control of organisations' internal activities, we have made interesting progress. Researchers around the globe are pushing back these frontiers of knowledge about internal management.

It is difficult to overstate the importance of effective control of complex organisations. It is likely not an accident or merely good luck when an organisation consistently runs smoothly and efficiently–one can be reasonably sure that effective controls are at work. Because they work, effective controls are not always obvious and visible. Control failures, however, provide clear and sometimes catastrophic examples of the damage that ineffective controls can cause or allow. A particularly poignant example (to accountants, at least) is the failure of Arthur Andersen LLC, once one of the world's largest and most respected public accounting firms. The firm did not control the actions of its employees responsible for the audits of Enron Corporation and WorldCom (and several other troubled audits). Although Arthur Andersen eventually was cleared of criminal charges, the firm's severe loss of reputation led to its demise.[5]

3.2 Governance and control of strategic management

We often idealise that organisations follow an orderly process of **strategic management,** which is the set of activities that managers perform to answer two questions: Where do we want to go with this organisation? How will we get there? Ideally, we think, an organisation follows these steps:

1. **Goal formulation** Managers of the organisation answer the 'Where?' question when they formalise the goals of the organisation's stakeholders, who are represented by a board of directors. Interestingly, stakeholders' goals can be competing (for example: stockholders want more profits, but employees want higher wages and benefits and citizens want less pollution). To be actionable by managers, goals are translated into observable objectives or targets.
2. **Action identification** Managers identify the alternative courses of action that could answer the 'How?' question and meet the targeted goals.These actions may come from

[3] Simon, H.A.,(1997).
[4] Chester I. Barnard (1968), R. N. Anthony and V. Govindarajan(2007).
[5] See the summary at **http://en.wikipedia.org/wiki/Arthur_Andersen**

past experience, analysis of competitors and 'best in class' firms, or pure discovery. One thing for sure is that most goals and objectives might be achieved by any of a multitude of actions. The management task is to choose the best actions from among the possible. This choice is especially difficult when competing goals exist.

3. **Action choice** Managers translate the best course(s) of action into business plans, which are plans for future resources and processes. These first three steps to specify stakeholders' goals and targets, alternative actions and the best action often constitute the 'strategic plan,' but thorough strategic plans also address the next two steps. Remember the five Ps of management: Prior Planning Prevents Poor Performance.
4. **Implementation** Managers execute the business plan(s) by setting operational targets and by the management of operations. This step features the most obvious uses of controls. Many tools and measures of performance have been designed to facilitate effective operations, management. Management of operations is the major focus of Chapter 8, and is also important to this chapter.
5. **Evaluation** Managers observe, measure and learn from results. This learning provides feedback to the preceding strategic management steps. So called business plan autopsies can provide invaluable feedback to each step that should lead to improved strategic management (if this step is followed faithfully and honestly). These reflective analyses should take place frequently or no later than at major milestones in the implementation of the plan. Unfortunately, many strategic failures can be traced afterwards to poor implementation. When plans fail, either the plans did not identify all the important contingencies, or managers were unable or incapable of implementing an otherwise good plan.

Probably no one would object to this rational approach to strategic management, in theory. However, all individuals at best are 'boundedly rational'. That is, although individuals may intend to behave rationally, their cognitive limitations often result in either 'satisficing' choices, which are just 'good enough,' or the wrong choices given the complexity of the task (as discussed in Chapter 2). Furthermore, some individuals in an organisation might wish to pursue private goals (for example, personal enrichment or extra leisure) at the expense of the goals of the organisation. These sub-optimal behaviours can subvert or frustrate all of the idealised strategic management steps.

Managers try to prevent or mitigate unwanted behaviour at all steps of strategic management by choosing the most efficient organisational structure and controls.[6] Organisational structure defines the oversight of operational and reporting responsibilities, which are the topics of Chapter 8. **Management controls** are all of the many methods managers can use to help and encourage employees to design, communicate and implement all the steps of strategic and operational planning. Management controls promote managers' **accountability,** which is their ownership of and responsibility for planning, decisions and outcomes. The purpose of this chapter is to describe and apply the current state of knowledge regarding the question of how managers can best control internal operations. Formally, this is the domain of the academic and professional topic of Management Control.

[6] Jerold Zimmerman (2009) calls the combination of structure and controls a firm's *organisational architecture*.

EXAMPLE FROM PRACTICE

The case of Scandinavian Forest Products

Scandinavian Forest Products, or SFP, is a large producer of wood and wood fibre products.[7] SFP is a publicly traded enterprise that embraces sustainability. SFP competes financially in global woodproduct markets but also has strategic goals to improve the sustainability of its business practices. SFP has definite financial targets, and also has non-financial targets for its other dimensions of sustainability. We will use SFP's targets and measures for its wide range of subunits' and managers' goals and accountability throughout this chapter.

Critics of corporate culture sometimes argue that financial goals dominate the non-financial environmental and social goals, which, when mentioned at all, appear to be for public relations or 'greenwashing.' The counter argument can be that none of the non-financial goals are feasible unless the firm is sufficiently profitable to afford them or unless an outside party, such as a government, subsidises them. Both of these arguments support the notion that non-financial goals are residuals attainable after sufficient profit or cash flow have been made (somewhere by someone). A third argument that supports sustainability is that, in the long-run, organisations that achieve both financial and non-financial goals will ultimately be more successful than those that focus only on financial goals. Which argument is correct is an empirical issue that is playing out before our eyes in the second decade of the 21st century, currently during a persistent, global recession. This is a challenging time to be making the sustainability argument, yet that is SFP's approach (and that of other firms).

SFP's overarching financial goal of capital efficiency is reflected in its choices of financial performance measures.These measures reflect four slightly different measures of financial returns and two measures of financial risks that are important to SFP's stockholders and creditors. Contributors of capital to SFP expect competitive returns at acceptable risks. SFP's recent financial performance surpasses many of its targets and surpasses the performance some of SFP's global competitors on the same targets.

- **Yield** (a measure of realised operating return on all invested capital) The target is a minimum of 6.0%. *Measure:* Operating profit before unrealised change in forest value (*see the research discussion below*), divided by average total assets.
- **Return on total assets** (the earned operating return on all invested capital) The target is a minimum of 7.0%. *Measure:* Operating profit divided by average total assets.
- **Return on equity** (the net return on stockholders' invested capital) The target is a minimum of 10.0%. *Measure:* Profit after tax divided by average stockholders' equity.
- **Dividend** (the distributed return to stockholders) The ordinary dividend should be at least 60% of profit after tax. *Measure:* Dividend divided by profit after tax, excluding unrealised change in value of forest assets.

[7] SFP is a fictional company that is based on a composite of publicly available information from four actual companies: Bergvik Skog, SCA, Stora Enso and Sveaskog. Using a composite is necessary because almost no companies disclose complete information about internal targets.

- **Interest cover** (a measure of short-term liquidity risk) The long-term target is 2.0. *Measure:* Operating profit before unrealised change in value of forest assets divided by interest expense.
- **Debt to equity ratio** (a measure of long-term solvency risk) The maximum is 0.7 but planned levels down to 0.3 are permitted. *Measure:* Interest-bearing debt divided by equity.

This chapter will use SFP to illustrate how it uses measures of performance as management controls to help managers keep the company on track to meet its financial and sustainability goals.

EXAMPLE FROM RESEARCH

Accounting researchers are very interested in the effects of financial reporting rules on managers' motivation, behaviour and compensation. Many countries have adopted International Financial Reporting Standards (IFRS) to replace local accounting rules. IFRS changes can have dramatic impacts on reported profit and equity accounts. Some researchers argue that managers will be biased against operating decisions that worsen reported earnings (and *vice-versa*) because of bonus compensation plans that are based on those earnings. Others argue to the contrary that companies will revise compensation plans, which are affected by IFRS changes, to retain desired incentives. For example, some argue that adopting IFRS will change U.S. managers' incentives to invest in R&D costs that are currently expensed in the U.S. but that are capitalised under IFRS. But this assumes that U.S. firms based their bonus calculations blindly on reported earnings when they could have based the bonus on a measure of profit before R&D expense. Similarly, IFRS can revise greatly the reported earnings of companies like SFP that have forest assets of uneven age that will be held to maturity. These previously were valued at historical cost, but must be valued at fair value under IFRS. As we have just seen, SFP chooses to define many of its financial targets **before** fairvalue changes in forest value. There is every reason to believe that other firms behave similarly to keep financial targets consistent across financial reporting changes, but this is an active area for research.

The following working papers are examples of current work in this new area of research: A. Haelstrom and W. Schuster (2008) and J.S. Wu and I. Zhang (2010)

3.3 Management control concepts and frameworks

3.3.1 The cybernetic model

One might hear descriptions of management controls that use analogies to electro mechanical controls, such as speed controllers on vehicles and thermostats in buildings. These devices act to keep a system in the desirable state of being 'in control.' For example, 'in control' can describe a vehicle on the highway travelling at the desired speed or a building at the desired temperature. Thus by **cybernetic control** analogy, management controls should continuously measure the state of the organisation (e.g. speed or temperature) and make needed corrections (e.g. release the accelerator or turn on the air conditioning) to keep the organisation on target (e.g. maintaining its interest cover ratio). These analogies are helpful only inasmuch as they indicate the intent of using management controls in complex organisations that face uncertain conditions.

The uncertain nature of the state of an organisation can be illustrated with a slight complication of the mechanical control analogy. Assume that an organisation (or sub-unit) can be in only one of two states: 'in control' or 'out of control,' which we can define at the strategic or operational level. Furthermore, a manager can measure the state of the organisation at an inspection cost, I (we will put numbers on these concepts shortly). Historically, when the manager has measured the state of the organisation, it has been found to be 'in control' p% of the time, and "out of control" 1-p% of the time. The true state of the organisation is unknown until its state is measured. If the organisation is found to be 'out of control,' the cost of returning to the in control state (e.g. the correction) is c. Without an inspection, the manager cannot know whether the organisation is truly 'out of control,' which if it continued undetected would inflict a much higher cost, C. For example, a pharmaceutical company can test the quality of its production process randomly, regularly or at the slightest indication of poor quality. The tests might be costly, but far less costly than allowing fatally poor quality drugs to reach the market undetected.

Consider a model of this management control decision in Table 3.1 where the symbolic amounts in the cells are the known costs that would be incurred with the four combinations of the management control decision and the uncertain state of the organisation.

Table 3.1 Control model

	True state of the organisation	
Management control decision	In control	Out of control
Measure state	I	$I + c$
Do not measure state	0	C
Probability of the true state	p	1-p

$I =$ the inspection cost to measure the state of the organisation
$c =$ the cost to correct an out of control organisation after the inspection
$C =$ the cost to correct an out of control organisation after customers have received faulty products

The question posed by this model is: When should the manager measure the true state of the organisation, if at all? The answer is generally stated as, "Measure when the expected cost of the 'Measure' decision is less than the expected cost of 'Do not Measure'."

$$\textit{Expected Cost of 'Measure'} < \textit{Expected Cost of 'Do not Measure'}$$

We can solve for an indifference or inflection point algebraically after asserting that one of the two states of the organisation must be true, whether the manager measures or not. The expected value is the sum of the probability weighted costs of each decision.

$$E[\textit{Cost of 'Measure'}] = (p)(I) + (1 - p)(I + c)$$

$$E[\textit{Cost of 'Do not Measure'}] = (p)(0) + (1 - p)I$$

$$= (1 - p)C$$

Therefore, the manager should measure the true state of the organisation when

$$pI + (1 - p)(I + c) < (1 - p)C$$

Expanding the terms on both sides of the inequality and simplifying yields,

$$pI + I + c - pI - pc < C - pC$$
$$I + c - pc < C - pC$$

Collecting terms with p on the left further yields,

$$p(C - c) < C - c - I$$
$$p < (C - c - I)/(C - c)$$
$$p < 1 - I/(C - c)$$

In other words, the **management control solution** has two parts:

a. Inform the manager that they should measure the true state of the organisation if they find that the probability of the organisation's being in control is less than the inflection point, $1 - I/(C - c)$.

b. Direct the manager to intervene and apply the correction, if the true state is found to be 'out of control.'

The 'optimal' management control decision depends on the manager's assessment of the probability of the organisation's true state, 'in control' or 'out of control.' To illustrate numerically, assume the following costs of I, c, and C in Table 3.2:

Table 3.2 Example control model

	True state of the organisation	
Management control decision	In control	Out of control
Measure state	I = €100	c = €500 $I + c$ = €600
Do not measure state	0	C = €5000
Probability of the true state	p	$1 - p$

$$p < 1 - €100/(€5000 - €500)$$
$$p < 97.78\%$$

According to this model, the manager should measure the true state if the assessment is that the probability that the organisation is **in control** is less than 97.78%.

This **optimal** solution begs the question of how the managers know the current, in control probability that they should compare to the critical value of 97.78%. The theoretical answer is that the organisation employs an 'information system' (or management control) that 'signals' whether the probability of the organisation's true state has changed. Thus, in this conceptual framework, which is known as information economics, the role of a management control is to permit the manager to re-assess the probability that the organisation (or a sub-unit) is either 'in control' or 'out of control.' Addressing variations of this decision model and its information system has been the focus of the academic field of information economics for decades.

Quite a number of organisational realities complicate an application to real organisations of the information economic adaptation of the cybernetic model of control.[8] While we do not wish to raise a 'straw man' argument, it is instructive to gauge the magnitude of the management control problem by judging whether the basic cybernetic model and its parameters can be descriptive:

1. **True state of the organisation.** It is not difficult to imagine more than the two states of in or out of control, which would be multiplied by the number of independent sub-units of the organisation and by the number of dimensions of organisational performance that,

[8] See G. Hofstede, (1978) for a thorough discussion of the alternative conceptions of the organisation and appropriate management control frameworks.

in the aggregate, describe the state of the organisation. This numerical complexity could easily become overwhelming to describe and to monitor.

2. **Measure the true state**. The model assumes that managers have valid measures of the true state of the organisation. That is, managers must use measurements that are relevant, reliable, stable, accurate, timely and faithful reflections of the true state. These are worthy attributes of measures, but they are very difficult to obtain and maintain.
3. **Accurate costs of measuring, correcting or not correcting**. Each cause of being 'out of control' might have different and unknown costs of detection, correction and unchecked control lapses. It is difficult to know how a manager would compute an inflection point to investigate the unknown state of the organisation if the relevant costs are unknown. The unknown errors can compound, resulting in serious over or under estimates of relevant costs.
4. **Reliable signal to investigate**. Whether the organisation's information system reliably reports the right signals at the right time to the right managers can be problematic. Uncertainty over the reliability of the signals might lead to over-investigation of potential problems, which could lead to inefficiencies or disregard (e.g., the U.S. government finally realised that no one listened to airport security warnings that were continuously announced at U.S. airports).
5. **Manager's decision to investigate**. The cybernetic model assumes that investigations are automatic upon receipt of the critical signal and also that corrections are made if an out of control state is detected. In real organisations, managers might not fully understand the signal, or they might misinterpret it.
6. **Manager's discretion**. Managers can choose to measure the state and can choose to apply a correction. Because the information is imperfect, they might not trust the signal. However, they might cover up an out of control state or decline to intervene for private reasons. Similarly, managers might knowingly trade off performance dimensions to favour those that are deemed more important or easier to manage.[9]

In response to these complications, observers of organisational management have formulated a variety of alternative management control models that seek to guide or describe practice. We will synthesise some of the more prominent models and illustrate the result with SFP's practices.

EXAMPLE FROM PRACTICE

SFP's financial performance

SFP uses its set of performance measures that were presented earlier as indications of whether the company and its business units are in control of their financial performance. That is, managers at all levels evaluate performance to gauge whether SFP is meeting its strategic goals and whether SFP is competitive with other firms in its industry. For all the reasons just enumerated, this is not a strict application of the cybernetic model of management control. However, the intention is that departures from targets should signal whether SFP is in control.

[9] See Feltham & Xie (1994) and Banker & Datar (1989) for important theoretical work on this difficult problem, which surely exists in practice. For example, the authors of this text have worked with a well-known company that specified more than 70 targeted dimensions of performance for each of its hundreds of global operations sites – and these were only for Human Resource services!

The practice of comparing internal performance over time to internal targets and performance relative to peers is known as **benchmarking.** Many firms belong to industry associations that share anonymous operating performance data from its members. In some cases the performance data is in publicly available sources, such as annual financial and sustainability reports. Benchmarking is not confined to financial targets. Furthermore, benchmarking may be employed by any organisation with access to historical data about its and similar organisations' performance.

Consider the financial ratios in Figure 3.3, which are computed from data from SFP's annual reports. Figures that meet or beat the targets are in bold font. Figure 3.4 graphically displays SFP's five-year Yield performance against its target of 6.0%. Figure 3.5 presents SFP's 2009 financial performance compared to its competitors (highest values are bold font). Figure 3.6 graphically displays the comparative Yield performance, where SFP has the highest performance relative to the group.[10]

SFP financial performance and targets	2009	2008	2007	2006	2005
Yield: Operating profit before change in forest value/ average total assets	**6.28%**	5.36%	**6.81%**	**6.57%**	4.07%
yield target ≥	6.00%	6.00%	6.00%	6.00%	6.00%
ROA: Operating profit/ average total assets	6.60%	5.76%	**10.27%**	6.81%	4.30%
ROA target ≥	7.00%	7.00%	7.00%	7.00%	7.00%
ROE: Profit after tax/ average equity	9.23%	7.52%	**17.93%**	**10.74%**	4.03%
ROE target ≥	10.00%	10.00%	10.00%	10.00%	10.00%
Interest cover: Operating profit before change in forest value/ interest expense	**4.71**	**2.99**	**3.97**	**4.15**	**2.66**
interest cover target ≥	2.00	2.00	2.00	2.00	2.00
Debt/ equity: Interest bearing debt/ equity	**0.66**	0.83	**0.68**	**0.70**	0.77
debt/ equity target ≤	0.70	0.70	0.70	0.70	0.70
Dividend: Percent of profit after tax, excluding change in forest value	44.54%	**74.64%**	50.23%	34.00%	**64.77%**
dividend target =	60.00%	60.00%	60.00%	60.00%	60.00%

Figure 3.3 SFP financial targets and performance over time

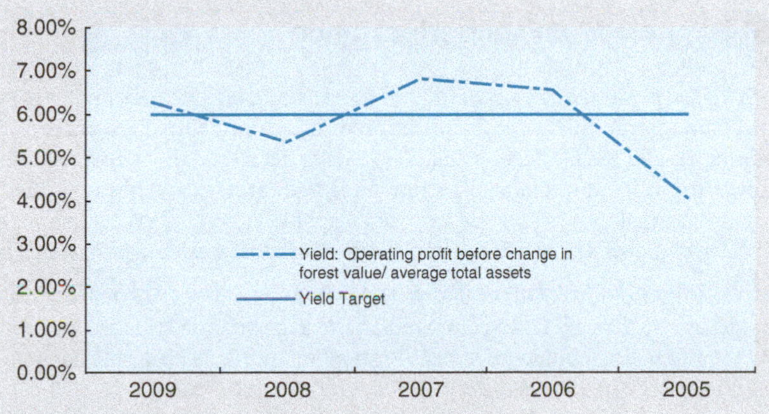

Figure 3.4 SFP yield performance over time

[10] Exercises 3.1–3.5 extend the analyses of Figure 3.1 and 3.2.

Comparative financial performance	SFP	Sveaskog	Stora Enso	SCA
	2009	2009	2009	2009
Yield: Operating profit before change in forest value/ average total assets	**6.28%**	3.53%	–5.07%	5.74%
ROA: Operating profit/ average total assets	6.60%	**8.64%**	–5.10%	5.30%
ROE: Profit after tax/ average equity	9.23%	**11.33%**	–16.21%	7.23%
Interest cover: Operating profit before change in forest value/ interest expense	4.71	4.4	–1.24	**4.92**
Debt/ equity: Interest bearing debt/ equity	66.3%	36.5%	**75.7%**	66.7%
Dividend: Percent of profit after tax, excluding change in forest value	44.5%	44.3%	–18.1%	**45.4%**

Figure 3.5 SFP competitive financial benchmarking

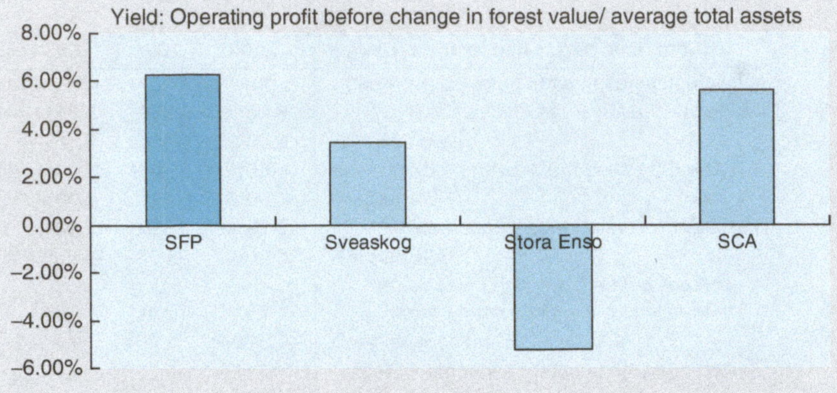

Figure 3.6 Comparative yield performance

EXAMPLE FROM PRACTICE

SFP's non-financial performance

SFP has expressed a strong commitment to sustainable business practices (as have many of its competitors). SFP identified three areas of sustainability performance: Financial, Environment, and Social Responsibility. We have described SFP's financial performance and now turn to its non-financial performance and targets. SFP has identified four summary environmental targets and one for social responsibility. While these are not numerous, each is quite complex and has broad implications for SFP's business practices. They are:

- **Carbon dioxide (CO2) emission reduction:** Reduce CO2 (and equivalent greenhouse gases) by 20% by 2020 compared to the base year of 2004. Achieving this target will require major modifications of SFP's manufacturing, heating and cooling, transportation, and energy use. Nearly every SFP activity will be affected.
- **Wood fibre sourcing:** Obtain 100% wood fibre from non-controversial sources by 2010. Controversial sources include illegal logging, logging from endangered biological areas, logging from areas that adversely affect indigenous peoples.

- **Water consumption:** Reduce overall water consumption by 15% by 2010 by improved efficiency and re-use of water.
- **Water quality:** Reduce the organic content of waste water by 30% by 2010 with improved chemical processes and treatment of used water.
- **Code of conduct:** Adopt and implement a consistent code of conduct worldwide by 2010. This code of conduct details acceptable business and human rights practices, consistent with the UN's Global Compact and emerging ISO 26000 standards. It will apply to SFP's global employees and business partners, but differences in politics and culture complicate the code's implementation.

SFP benchmarks its non-financial performance over time and relative to its competitors. Unlike financial measures, which are reasonably similar across firms, non-financial performance measures can vary widely to meet specific firms' strategic needs. It is difficult for outsiders and even the firms to assess the relevance and accuracy of these environmental and social disclosures. At the present time, many firms that disclose sustainability performance contract with consulting and auditing firms which express their opinions about the reliability of the disclosures. The current lack of sustainability standards that are comparable to IFRS makes assurance of sustainability performance uneven and risky. Our uses of sustainability performance data are dependent on the emerging reputations of the new assurance service firms and on environmental and human rights watchdogs.

Figure 3.7 reports SFP's five-year performance against its sustainability targets, and Figure 3.8 graphically shows its CO2 emission reductions against the target of 20% reduction by 2020. Note that most of the firms have sourced wood fibre according to goal, but only one has implemented its code of conduct completely. Figure 3.9 presents SFP's sustainability performance relative to its competitors, and Figure 3.10 has CO2 reduction relative performance.[11]

Do these financial and non-financial data indicate that SFP is in control of its strategic performance? The picture is unclear. 'Interest Cover' performance consistently beats its financial target, but other financial and non-financial performance achievements are noisy because of the many other factors that affect performance. Based on historical and relative current performance, should SFP investigate whether the company is out of control? To be honest, we cannot answer this question from aggregate, company level data. Although SFP executives have ultimate responsibility, the company delegates' responsibility for financial

SFP sustainability performance and targets	2009	2008	2007	2006	2005
Reduction of CO2	–12%	–9%	–7%	–3%	–1%
CO2 reduction target by 2020 =	–20%	–20%	–20%	–20%	–20%
Fiber from non-controversial sources	**100%**	98%	95%	89%	81%
fiber source target by 2010 =	100%	100%	100%	100%	100%
Water consumption reduction	–7%	–5%	–2%	–1%	–1%
water consumption target by 2010 =	–15%	–15%	–15%	–15%	–15%
Organic content of waste water reduction	–25%	–20%	–14%	–11%	–5%
waste water target by 2010 =	–30%	–30%	–30%	–30%	–30%
Universal code of conduct implemented	In process	In process	under development	under development	under development
code of conduct target by 2010 =	100%	100%	100%	100%	100%

Figure 3.7 SFP's sustainability performance over time

[11] Exercises 3.6 – 3.8 extend the analyses of SFP's and its competitors' sustainability performance.

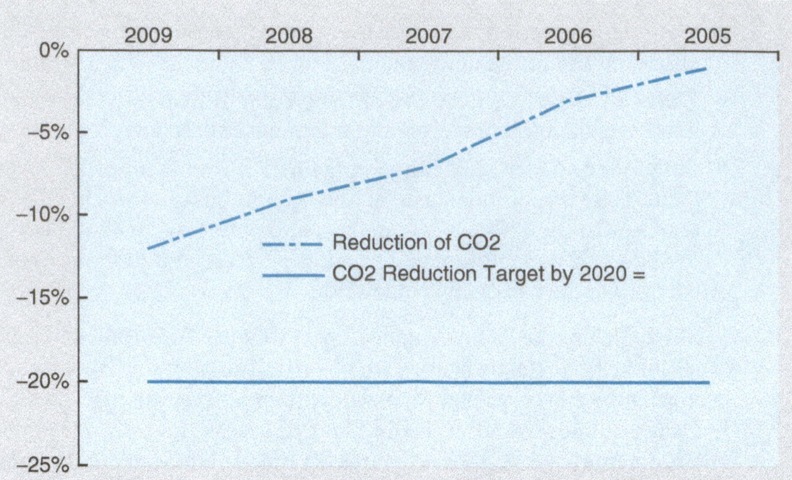

Figure 3.8 SFP's CO2 emission reductions over time

Sustainability performance	SFP	Sveaskog	Stora Enso	SCA
	2009	**2009**	**2009**	**2009**
Reduction of CO2 emissions	–12%	**–23%**	–18%	–2.2%
Fiber from non-controversial sources	**100%**	**100%**	99%	**100.0%**
Reduce water consumption	–7%	**–10%**	–3%	–4.9%
Reduce organic content of waste water	–25%	–35%	–1%	**–40.0%**
Universal code of conduct implemented 100%	In process	**100%**	In process	In process

Figure 3.9 SFP's relative sustainability performance

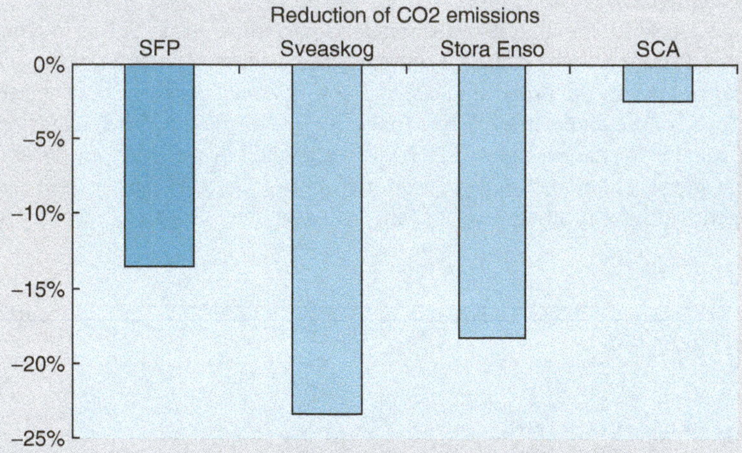

Figure 3.10 SFP's Relative CO2 emission reductions

and sustainability performance to its product line based business units (Personal Care, Tissue, Packaging and Forest Products). SFP relies on a'decentralisation' theory, which we will elaborate in the next section, that managers who are closest to operating decisions are best able to monitor, detect and correct out of control states. Furthermore, proper incentives might increase the likelihood that they will do so.

3.3.2 Economic models of management control

Economic theories of management control are derived from the cybernetic model, which we believe is a useful conceptual framework, but which might not be fully descriptive of real managers or organisations. For example, Zimmerman (2009) builds a conceptual framework based on economic agency theory, which assumes that individuals are rational but also self-interested and averse to work.[12] In this framework some management controls serve to apportion **decision rights,** which specify the scope of individuals' decision making. Other management controls serve as incentives to motivate individuals to work hard and to create **goal congruence,** which is the alignment of personal goals with the organisation's goals. This framework assumes that measures of performance clearly signal the state of the organisation, and economic incentives are sufficient to induce managers to seek and take corrective actions to correct an out of control state.

Williamson's (1985) economic view uses Coase's (1937) transaction cost perspective to reason that management controls regulate internal activities, whereas market forces manage external (e.g. outsourced) activities. Williamson departs from the cybernetic model's assumption of rational decision making. In this view, managers are indeed self-interested but are constrained by **bounded rationality,** which means that even if managers intend to make the right choices, they are cognitively limited. The additional role of management controls, therefore, is to assist managers by providing relevant information about actions and likely outcomes of these actions.[13] Robert Simons' (1995) view of bureaucratic controls is consistent with Williamson. Simons has observed that managers design and use management controls to 'lever' individuals to accept and achieve an organisation's strategy. His two categories based on control use are **diagnostic controls,** which detect the state of an organisation, and **interactive controls,** which provide real time information about the effectiveness of managers' actions to direct the organisation or correct an out of control state.

3.3.3 Organisational theory models of management control

Other prominent models of management control are implicitly based on the cybernetic model, but they benefit from observations of actual practice and depart more dramatically from the cybernetic notion that management controls are simply regulating devices similar to speed controllers or thermostats. For example, Barnard (1938/1968) observed that successful executives use incentives, but also manage organisations with clear and authoritative communications. Ouchi (1979) observed firms that use **clan controls,** which use social or professional norms of behaviour to control performance, can attract like-minded individuals or mould employees to fit with the 'clan' norms. This is similar to Hofstede's (2003) explanation of controls that create or maintain **organisational culture,** which is the set of an organisation's preferred practices and procedures. Burns and Stalker (1961) had observed at least two types of firms, mechanistic and organic, that have very different business contexts and management styles. Mechanistic firms are predictable and hierarchical and might be somewhat well suited for cybernetic controls. However, firms that are more successful in

[12] Please review Chapter 2 for models of rational choice. Zimmerman builds on the work of Jensen and Meckling (1976) and, for the importance of organisation structure, on H. Simon (1947).

[13] Williamson's 'bureaucratic controls' also capture Anthony's (1965) and Merchant and van der Stede's (2007) views that management controls are all of the devices that organisations use to align employees' goals and to make it possible for them to do their jobs effectively. Note also that Williamson's bounded rationality is not identical to H. Simon's observation of managers' satisficing behaviour, which is intentionally 'just good enough.'

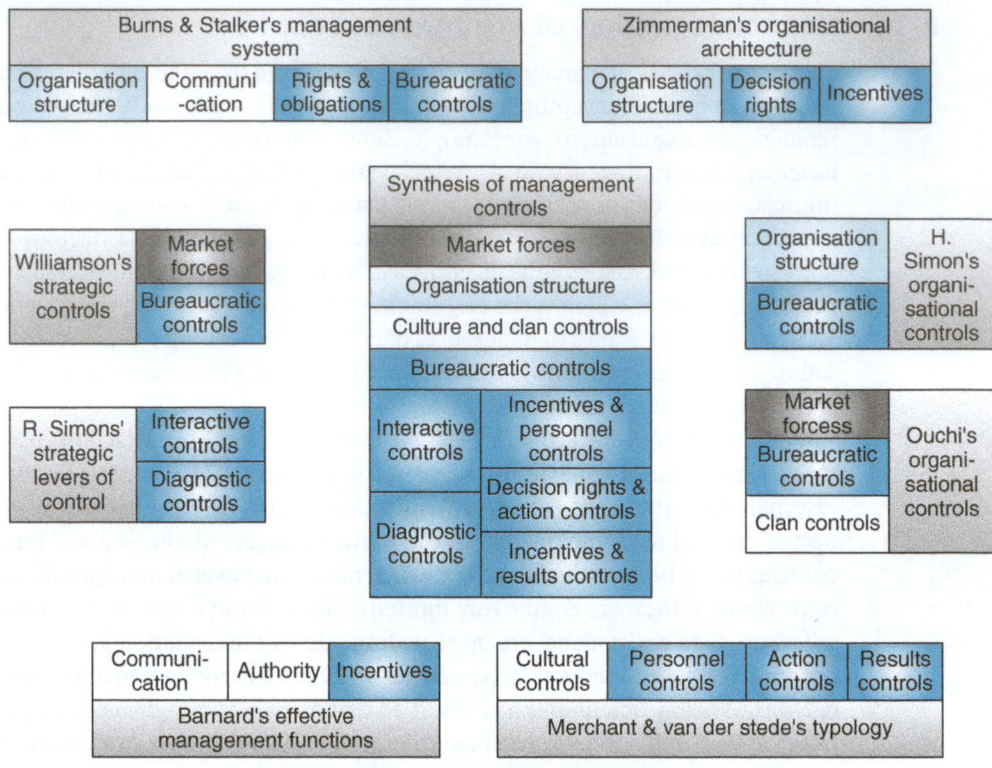

Figure 3.11 Synthesis of management control frameworks

dynamic, uncertain context exhibit an organic style that is less formal and more adaptive in its set of controls. Hofstede (1978) extended Burns and Stalker and observed that the cybernetic model of management control is insufficient to serve real firms that are complex, dynamic social organisations.

We cannot exhaust the extensive management-control literature here, but we conclude this discussion with Merchant and van der Stede's (2007) very useful typology of the types of management controls that they have observed in use. These categories overlap many of the elements of management control theories and observed practice. They include:

1. **Cultural controls,** which managers use to create or maintain an organisation's preferred practices and procedures.
2. **Personnel controls,** which managers use to select, train and motivate employees.
3. **Action controls,** which constrain or direct employees' decisions and action choices.
4. **Results controls,** which monitor and report the state(s) of an organisation and its outcomes.

3.3.4 Synthesis of management control frameworks

We see tremendously interesting overlaps in the many models of management control. We summarise these models in Figure 3.11. The centre of this figure is our synthesis, which demonstrates the compatibility of the set of 'rival' management control models reviewed here. Each complementary model contributes to the synthesis and reinforces other models. What is not illustrated in this synthesis (for clarity) is the feedback that each element should provide to each other element. For example, the outcomes reported by 'results controls' can inform managers about the successes or failures of the decision to manage outsourced activities via 'market forces' – and every other control decision in between. Also note, that although each element is not a prominent feature of or even mentioned in every framework, all frameworks implicitly contain all elements. However, some appear to be of secondary importance or are not elaborated by their authors.

The synthesis in the centre of Figure 3.11 permits us to describe a reasonably exhaustive portfolio of management control design elements. Not every organisation will use all of the design elements, and every organisation may implement its management control elements differently. Mastering the design and use of management controls, perhaps, is as much art as it is science, and those who become masters are able to contribute immense value to their organisations. This synthesised theory of management control and its elements is not sufficiently advanced to permit predictions of how a particular organisation will apply the synthesised management control framework. The framework, however is useful for **describing** an organisation's management controls. In the next section, we will walk through the synthesis from top to bottom, using examples from SFP, other companies and relevant research.

3.4 Management control system design

We define a **management control system** to be the portfolio of management controls that support all of the steps of strategic decision making. The term 'system' strongly implies that the portfolio is deliberately designed and is not a random collection of controls. That is, all management control elements in Figure 3.11 can and should work in concert to help an organisation meet its strategic and operational goals.

3.4.1 Control through markets or firms

At its inception and throughout the life of an organisation, managers should consider which activities internal employees and technologies will conduct and which to obtain from external suppliers. This basic decision is also described as the vertical integration, 'make or buy,' or outsourcing decision. This decision is a primary feature of Williamson's and Ouchi's management control frameworks and is the first element of our framework. Market forces, such as enforceable contracts and supplier reputation, control the quality and price of externally obtained activities. These market forces reward or punish suppliers according to their performance. However, if market forces are insufficient to protect the interests of the purchaser, certain activities will be internalised instead. Likewise, the organisation will internalise activities that can be performed more cheaply. For example, SFP grows its own wood products for the European market but contracts for wood and wood fibre with certified suppliers in Asia, North and South America. Some of its competitors, such as Stora Enso, have developed forest plantations in these areas, which might cut direct costs, but exposes the firms to political and social risks.[14]

[14] An either-or framework might be oversimplified for inter-organisational control. The bases and dynamics of the decision to 'make or buy' and the specifics of management control of outsourced activities is the topic of Chapter 11. For purposes of this chapter, we will focus on the management control of currently internalised activities.

CAUTIONARY EXAMPLE FROM PRACTICE

Boeing Co.'s decision to outsource the 787 Dreamliner

The Boeing Co. historically has designed, developed and manufactured its aircraft internally. In 2003 Boeing decided to contract with a global team of suppliers to design and build many parts of the new, largely carbon fibre 787 aircraft. The decision was based on a desire to lower development costs and to encourage international sales. The new plane was originally scheduled for delivery in 2007, but at this writing (Sep 2012), relatively few planes have been delivered. As reported by the *Wall St. Journal,* the delays are the results of relying too much on the market reputations of suppliers while seriously underestimating the costs and difficulties of contracting and coordinating the complex external activities for which no market then existed. Boeing even internalised the activities of a key, troubled supplier by purchasing the company.[15]

3.4.2 Control through organisation structure

Organisation structure describes the form of the relationships and responsibilities for internal activities. A completely **centralised organisation** controls all strategic management steps from a central authority. Sub-units of a centralised organisation have defined operational targets, and little discretion in how to achieve them. A completely **decentralised organisation** delegates some or all parts of strategic management to sub-units. For example, SFP delegates the responsibilities for financial and non-financial performance to its four business units, which in turn delegate responsibilities to department heads.

A **networked organisation** structure links resources across the organisation to accomplish specific projects. A networked organisation creates project based sub-units that may have some or all responsibility for strategic management. Many organisations properly can be described as hybrid organisations, where some strategic steps are centralised, others are decentralised and some are networked. Organisational structure is a key feature of the control frameworks of Burns & Stalker, Zimmerman and H.Simon. In any case, the types and uses of management controls may vary according to an organisation's structure.

EXAMPLE FROM RESEARCH

Centralised or decentralised controllership?

H. Simon's (1954) investigation of centralised or decentralised finance and accounting functions is a classic field study.[16] Simon and colleagues described the intents and impacts of the decision whether to operate the controller's function as an extension of central management or as a member of a decentralised management team. The primary intent of employing a 'controller' resource is to improve the organisation's financial and non-financial operating information. In the economic model of management control this improved information will lead to improved organisational performance. Simon found that, except for routine report generation, a decentralised controller who is perceived as an integral part of the local management team and who provides information directly to local managers best serves that organisation.

[15] J. Lynn Lunsford. Dec 7, 2007, p. 1; March 28, 2008,
[16] Herbert Simon, et al. 1954.

3.4.3 Culture and clan controls

Many authors have described the effects of national culture and organisational culture on the design and use of management controls. Hofstede (1983, 1991) defines **national culture** as the set of characteristics on five dimensions that tend to be shared by persons of a specific nationality.[17] Of course, and as Hofstede cautions, these are average characteristics and should not be attributed to individuals simply because of their passports. Hofstede (1998) also distinguishes 'organisational culture' from national culture as shared acceptance of 'organisational' practices. Ouchi's (1979) notion of 'clan control' is an informal socialisation process that eliminates goal incongruence among individuals, and may substitute for organisation structure or bureaucratic controls. The general argument is that controls to achieve common culture can be a more efficient way to achieve goal congruence than using structural or bureaucratic controls at higher cost. Current research still seeks to understand how these individual characteristics can influence management control practices and effectiveness.

EXAMPLE FROM RESEARCH

The case of a global airline

We have investigated the importance of national and organisational culture to management control of a global airline (GA). Although GA operated on six continents, it was not terribly concerned with managing different national cultures. GA instead hired local nationals who could navigate the complexities of local cultures and regulations. Far more important to GA were their employees' shared attitudes toward GA's organisational culture, which stressed open, frequent, honest and clear communications. GA sought out future employees who exhibited these communication skills and values and who also understood specific national cultures.

3.4.4 Bureaucratic controls

Every model of management control prominently features **bureaucratic controls,** which are the formal practices that an organisation uses to communicate, plan, monitor and evaluate important dimensions of performance. Formal management controls are documented in policies and procedures and are frequently reported internally and sometimes publicly. **Formal controls** inform, prepare and motivate individuals and sub-units to achieve financial or non-financial targets. Organisations may tie performance evaluations, compensation and other incentives to achievement of the targets. For example, SFP's Code of Conduct attempts to strengthen its competitiveness by informing, preparing and motivating its global employees to attract new customers, reduce long run environmental costs, develop internal talent, attract ethical investors, and reduce environmental and social risks.

[17] The original four dimensions: power distance, uncertainty avoidance, individualism *versus* collectivism, and masculinity versus femininity, have been augmented by a fifth: long *versus* short-run outlook. Geert Hofstede,1983, 1991 and 1998.

EXAMPLE FROM RESEARCH

Budget targets: Easy or difficult?

Ken Merchant and Jean-Francois Manzoni studied whether firms set budget targets tightly or loosely.[18] The prevailing theory had been that optimum performance is achieved when budget targets are difficult but attainable with strong effort. In contrast, their study of 54 decentralised business units in 12 companies found that most targets were set at easily achievable levels. This interesting finding has many implications for the descriptiveness of economic theories of management control and for the roles of management controls for communication and planning. For example: are managers at all levels maximisers, as assumed by economic theory, or satisficers, as described by Simon? Does setting targets loosely conserve resources that otherwise would have been used to investigate whether the organisation is in or out of control?

3.5 Evaluating the effectiveness of management controls

We observe that most organisations have implemented extensive management control systems that employ many of the elements that we have just described. A common question one can and should pose to the designers of management control systems is: 'How do you know that the chosen management control system is effective or efficient for the organisation's strategic decision making?' This is a quite difficult question to answer, in part because:

1. Organisations do not line up conveniently on dichotomous dimensions (such as, Burns & Stalker's organic *versus* mechanistic) that otherwise would permit prediction of controls. Furthermore, many different dimensions of organisations and their environments might simultaneously affect control choice (e.g. environmental risk, ownership), but we do not know how these dimensions interact. Looking at only one dimension at a time runs the risk of ignoring the impacts of all the others.
2. Every organisation appears to design and use its portfolio of management controls differently. Furthermore, the designs might reflect practical issues of measurement and verifiability, as much as issues of theory.
3. One cannot easily use stock price or financial performance as a simple, *post hoc* guide to identifying efficient management control systems. An organisation with an *ex ante*, well-designed system cannot be guaranteed numerous attempts to overcome momentary bad luck. Furthermore, as Nassim Taleb (2005) argues, even a long run of good financial performance could be the result of random good luck.

Our framework for improving management control effectiveness follows this chapter's model of strategic decision making and recommendations by David Otley (1999). Otley argues that a well-designed and executed management control system is likely to be effective, and perhaps efficient. This is not an infallible approach because good or bad luck can always intervene. That is, a well-designed and executed system can fail, and a badly designed and

[18] Kenneth A. Merchant and Jean-François Manzoni. 1989.

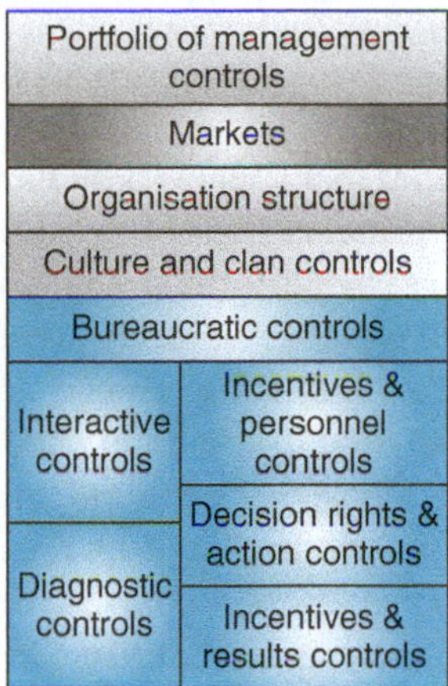

Figure 3.12 Synthesis of management controls = portfolio of choices

executed system can persist. We trust, however, that good design and execution of the management control system improves the odds of organisational success. Otherwise, we should put down this text and buy lottery tickets![19]

Figure 3.12 presents the synthesis of management controls as the 'portfolio' of available management controls that an organisation may apply to each step of the strategic decision making process. We will proceed through the strategic planning process presented at the beginning of this chapter and identify how the portfolio may be applied.

3.5.1 Goal formulation

Goal formulation is the task of translating the organisation's values and strategy into observable targets. It seems deficient to design a management control system without clearly set and observable goals. For example, we have seen that SFP has set measurable and verifiable targets for its financial and non-financial goals. The relevant management control questions to ask at this first step are: *How does the organisation insure that it has chosen the right dimensions of performance, the right measures of performance, and the right targets?* If we were advising the organisation, we would walk down the portfolio of management control choices.[20]

The first choice is whether to use market or bureaucratic (organisational) means to control the performance measurement and target setting tasks. For example, SFP might outsource the tasks to a consulting firm via a **market** mediated contract. The contract would specify deliverables and responsibilities for both parties (and fees, of course). Instead SFP chose to

[19] Ferreira & Otley 2010 extend Otley 1999 to urge the use of empirical testing to verify whether appealing designs actually work as intended. We do not disagree, but observe that empirical testing of management control effectiveness is extraordinarily difficult for at least the reasons listed at the beginning of this section.

[20] Here we take strategy as a 'given,' but we recognise that this process can begin with developing a strategy. We will work through the management-control portfolio for this first, goal setting step, but give only brief examples for the other steps. Exercises at the end of the chapter ask the reader to proceed more completely through the management control portfolio for the other steps in the process.

develop its performance dimensions, measures and targets (described earlier) internally by collaboration among the key players in its **organisational structure:** its board of directors, top executives and the managers of its four decentralised business units. These key players share common values that support both financial and sustainability performance.They also share the **organisational culture** of measuring performance and holding responsible parties accountable for meeting performance targets.

As we have seen with SFP, internal and external benchmarking is an important tool for target setting. By benchmarking competitors who face similar market pressures and opportunities, SFP found good information about others' choices of financial and non-financial performance dimensions, measures and targets. Although SFP and its competitors are independently interested in controlling both financial and non-financial performance, it is certain that they have learned what is important from each other and from contributors of capital. It is, therefore, not surprising that firms in the same industry often choose similar performance dimensions, measures and targets.[21]

3.5.2 Action identification

Action identification is the development of the alternative choices to achieve the organisation's goals – alternative products, locations, technologies and so on. Choice development includes estimating the efforts, outcomes and risks of each alternative action. **Risk** is the exposure to loss. Common risks to the choices of strategic actions are either external or internal in origin. External risks that affect the feasibility of actions (such as changes in the political, macroeconomic and technology environments) usually cannot be controlled. However, external risks can be at least partially ensured by diversification of actions(or hedging) and by professional, informational activities. For example, political lobbying is a costly activity that seeks to influence political changes and to gain early warning of impending changes.[22] Participating in economic and technology forums may have similar benefits.

Organisations use *cultural* and *personnel controls* to insure against the internal risks to good action identification (and risks to the next step, choice). These controls ensure that the people who are engaged in the action-identification step have the competency and motivation[23] to select the best set of alternatives that fit the organisation's values, risk tolerance, financial and technology capabilities. For example, many firms such as SFP have 'codes of conduct' that guide individuals to choose acceptable behaviour and actions. The promise of accountability for the outcomes of possible choices also can serve as an incentive to identify the best alternatives. For example, a manager at SFP will think very carefully about a project with a high financial return but a low probability of success if they are also responsible for the outcomes of that project.

---

[21] If organisations are unable to learn industry 'best practices' for control of performance, they may employ knowledgeable consultants for this step. Similarly, organisations may use consultants at every strategic planning step. A key issue is whether an organisation that uses consultants heavily can learn to develop its own strategic management capability.

[22] It is important to distinguish between lobbying, which generally is a legal, informational activity, and bribery, which nearly always is illegal, but might be accepted in some cultures. For example, Hui Chen, David Parsley and Ya-Wen Yang, 2009.

[23] These risks are also known as adverse selection and shirking, respectively.

3.5.3 Action choice

Action choice is the step where managers commit the organisation's scarce resources to specific actions.[24] Organisations delegate 'decision rights' to individuals or groups who make and manage these commitments. This is the essence of the decentralisation issue for organisational structure. Organisations often pair decision accountability with these decision rights, which serves as a powerful incentive to choose feasible actions. Organisations also use 'action controls', such as procedures manuals, to constrain or encourage choices of actions. For example, SFP has procedures that help managers to select equipment replacements that offer lower energy use and longer useful lives, which will improve operating costs and reduce CO2 emissions.

3.5.4 Implementation

Implementation is the step where managers (who should be capable and motivated – via personnel and culture controls) actually deploy resources and see results. Organisations typically create 'results controls' for the performance dimensions, measures and targets for chosen alternatives. Results controls are designed to create accountability and provide the types of outcome feedback that signal whether the implemented action is in control. For example, SFP monitors CO_2 emissions at all of its installations to hold managers accountable for progress on the emission reduction goal. Information on CO_2 emissions also signals whether the company is in control of its emission-creating processes (transportation, manufacturing, energy consumption, and so on).

One key to successful use of results controls is the frequency and scope of monitoring results. In other words, how often and at what levels of the organisation should results be monitored? Some managers complain about spending so much time reporting on results that they do not have sufficient time to deliver improved results. Yet infrequent monitoring of results and only at divisional levels (for example) may miss some out-of-control situations at local installations for too long, permitting a lot of damage. Finding the right frequency and depths of results reporting are important to whether management controls support the implementation step or impede it.

Alternatively (or in concert with results controls), an organisation may rely on **trust** in managers' integrity, competence and benevolence to implement strategy and to manage risks. Because continuous monitoring would be intolerable in many job situations (nuclear power plants and casinos may be notable exceptions), organisations must rely somewhat on trust for every employment relationship. Human nature, however, dictates that some results controls are prudent, but trust versus control is also a matter of finding the right balance. Even highly trustworthy managers can benefit from results controls that provide valuable feedback on the control state of operations. These results, which might not be reported up the management hierarchy, are essential to detecting and quickly correcting out of control states.

[24] These commitments may be irreversible (except at great cost), or they may be structured as 'real options.' Real options are actions that are designed to allow changes as more information about the state of the environment is received. Chapter 7 covers real options in more detail.

3.5.5 Evaluation

Evaluation of the entire strategic decision making process is the step when managers assess performance against targets and possibly assign rewards or penalties for accomplishments. This step is necessary for effective management. The full portfolio of management controls is available for this purpose. Performance evaluation provides feedback for:

- learning and process improvement;
- reporting to stakeholders;
- employee motivation, advancement and compensation.

The last item typically generates the most attention because all of us are evaluated for how well we perform our responsibilities. If we have targets, did we meet or beat them? Did we do so on time, without errors? Chapter 12 extends the discussion of motivation and incentives.

Target levels are not necessarily constrained by past achievements, because the organisation may choose to set either 'stretch' targets that are difficult or loose targets that are easily reached. This choice can have significant motivational effects and, as reported earlier, firms are not uniform in their practice. Decades of laboratory research shows that individuals perform at the highest levels when they:

- perceive that targets are specific, difficult but attainable; that is targets are neither vague nor easy;
- believe that their performance affects the performance measure; that is the performance measure is 'actionable';
- believe that achieving targets will result in promised rewards.

Internal benchmarking (over time) is important for setting attainable targets. For example, SFP chose a difficult CO_2 reduction target (20% reduction by 2020). As shown previously in Figure 3.3, SFP's CO_2 reduction efforts are resulting in progress toward its 2020 goal, but future progress might be more costly per unit of reduction. All the while, SFP must sustain its competitive financial performance targets. Often financial and non-financial goals appear to be contradictory in the short run, but SFP's strategy clearly expresses the belief that meeting both types of goals is necessary for long run competitiveness.

Rewards or incentives may themselves be financial or non-financial, and they may or may not be tied to achieving specific performance targets. For example, one of SFP's competitors, Sveaskog, sets performance targets that are similar to SFP, and similarly evaluates performance against the targets. But unlike SFP, which has a strong pay for performance culture, Sveaskog does not use these evaluations for managers' bonuses. This reflects a difference in organisational culture that might be rooted in ownership differences: Sveaskog is state owned, whereas SFP is privately owned and publicly traded. We observe many different applications of performance targets and incentives that probably reflect organisations'different cultures and contexts.

The stylised, black box firm has only one objective: maximise profits.[25] As we have seen, opening the black box and managing a complex firm can benefit from extensive management controls, even if it were to only maximise profits. However, the operational complexity of managing a real firm is apparent when multiple results controls are used for performance evaluations. For example, SFP has results controls for a) its financial return and risk targets

[25] The stylised socially responsible firm maximises profits while obeying the laws and regulations of its society.

and b) its sustainability targets and uses these results controls for evaluating business units and managers at various levels within business units.[26]

Consider yourself to be the manager of SFP's Packaging Products business unit. You and your business unit are evaluated on the results of four financial return measures, two financial risk measures and five sustainability measures – eleven measures in all. If you are new to this position, you might reasonably ask:

1. *Are these measures equally important to SFP and to my evaluation?* In other words, what is the weighting of each of these measures? It is possible but unlikely that the measures are weighted equally; that is, each of the 11 measures may or may not contribute 9.09% of your evaluation. Some measures may be weighted higher, some lower. Observed differences in the weightings of multiple performance measures may be because of differences of importance to strategic goals or differences of verifiability, ease and accuracy of measurement.[27] Even very important measures may be weighted lightly if the organisation is not confident that the measures are valid representations of performance.
2. *Can my performance affect each of these measures equally?* In other words, are some targets easier to achieve than others? Even if the measures are equally weighted, you may choose to exert more effort on meeting targets that are easier for you to achieve than others as a way to maximise your overall performance. Similarly, but possibly less beneficially to the firm, you might choose to manage the performance measures by choosing the magnitudes and timing of activities that are favourable for periodic evaluations.[28]
3. *Will my evaluation be based solely on these objective results controls or on other, subjective factors?* Perhaps there is no such thing as purely objective performance evaluation, because at a minimum the choices of targets and performance measures are subjective and value based. It is likely, however, that organisations that have 'objective' performance measures also evaluate performance subjectively, even for bonus compensation. Normally this flexibility is beneficial to all parties, but it can be harmful and might be discriminatory if organisations espouse objective performance measurement but clandestinely evaluate on subjective criteria (e.g., evaluate males differently than females, and so on).

EXAMPLE FROM PRACTICE

McGraw-Hill Corporation's 2009 Proxy statement indicated subjective use of an objective performance measure:

'We use both subjective and objective measures of performance in setting compensation levels. The primary objective measure that we use is growth in earnings per share. . . .'

[26] Chapter 8 has more details on performance measures for decentralised business units.

[27] Chapter 10 focuses on the integrated design and use of multiple financial and non-financial performance measures.

[28] This approach to performance management is called 'earnings management' when recognition of revenues and expenses are moved to time periods that benefit evaluations (earlier or later), and 'real earnings management' when activities themselves are moved to time periods that improve reported results. Both are on the edge of ethical behaviour but are fundamentally different than fraudulent reporting.

> 'Approximately 81% of our CEO's 2008 compensation opportunity was variable with the payment or value of the awards subject to the achievement of an annual double-digit earnings per share growth goal for the cash bonus opportunity. . . .'
>
> 'Further, we made fine-tuning adjustments to an otherwise strong program for 2009 by adopting EPS targets that were reasonable and realistic in the difficult and volatile economic climate we face in 2009. . . .'

3.6 Summary

Management controls are the devices that organisations use to ensure that employees work diligently and well to meet the organisation's strategic goals. Management controls (at least conceptually) signal whether an organisation is 'in control' of its strategy. An organisation has a complete portfolio of management controls (i.e., Figure 3.6) that is available to build a management control system. We observe that apparently successful firms use different systems; that is, there are many management control paths to strategic success. However, firms within the same industry and economic environment often have similar management control systems. These similarities likely reflect economic and social forces that influence the implementation of strategies. Internal and external benchmarking are valuable tools for assessing the composition and effectiveness of management control systems. Because environments and strategies are dynamic, we should expect that management control systems also are dynamic. Therefore, keeping a management control system effective is an ongoing, very important task.

EXERCISES

Exercise 3.1 SFP's financial return performance

Use the data in Figure 3.1 in the text to analyse SFP's four financial return measures against targets, over time. Prepare a graph similar to Figure3.1 and a brief statement about each measure. Is SFP in control of its financial return performance?

Exercise 3.2 SFP's financial risk performance

Use the data in Figure 3.1 in the text to analyse SFP's two financial risk measures against targets, over time. Prepare a graph similar to Figure3.1 and a brief statement about each measure. Is SFP in control of its financial risk performance?

Exercise 3.2 SFP's relative financial return performance.

Use the data in Figure 3.2 in the text to analyse SFP's four financial return measures against its competitors' performance. Prepare a graph similar to Figure3.2 and a brief statement about each measure. Is SFP in control of its financial return performance?

Exercise 3.4 SFP relative financial risk performance.

Use the data in Figure 3.2 in the text to analyse SFP's two financial risk measures against its competitors' performance. Prepare a graph similar to Figure3.2 and a brief statement about each measure. Is SFP in control of its financial risk performance?

Exercise 3.5 SFP's financial performance.

If you have completed Exercises 3.4–3.5, write a one-page report that describes SFP's financial performance.

Exercise 3.6. SFP's Sustainability Performance.

Use the data in Figure 3.3 in the text to analyse SFP's five sustainability measures against targets, over time. Prepare a graph similar to Figure3.3 and a brief statement about each measure. Is SFP in control of its sustainability performance?

Exercise 3.7 SFP's relative sustainability performance.

Use the data in Figure 3.4 in the text to analyse SFP's five sustainability measures against its competitors' performance. Prepare a graph similar to Figure 3.4 and a brief statement about each measure. Is SFP in control of its sustainability performance?

Exercise 3.8 SFP's sustainability performance.

If you have completed Exercises 3.6–3.7, write a one-page report that describes SFP's sustainability performance.

Exercise 3.9. In or out of control?

Refer to Figures 3.1 and 3.2. Assume the following costs:

Control Model Element	A	B	C
Inspection cost, I	€400	€800	€1600
Cost to correct out of control state, c	€1500	€1500	€1500
Cost of uncorrected out of control state, C	€5000	€5000	€5000

a. Compute the critical probability level, p, for each combination of costs, A, B, and C. Explain how p is related to different levels of I.

b. Explain how the inspection cost, I, represents a management control device.

Exercise 3.10. In or Out of Control?

Refer to Figures 3.1 and 3.2. Assume the following costs:

Control Model Element	D	E	F
Inspection cost, I	€800	€800	€800
Cost to correct out of control state, c	€1000	€1500	€2500
Cost of uncorrected out of control state, C	€5000	€5000	€5000

a. Compute the critical probability level, p, for each combination of costs, D, E and F. Explain how p is related to different levels of c.

b. Explain how the cost to correct an out of control state, c, might be incurred.

Exercise 3.11 In or out of control? Refer to Figures 3.1 and 3.2. Assume the following costs:

Control Model Element	G	H	J
Inspection cost, I	€800	€800	€800
Cost to correct out of control state, c	€1500	€1500	€1500
Cost of uncorrected out of control state, C	€5000	€7500	€10000

a. Compute the critical probability level, *p*, for each combination of costs, G, H, and J. Explain how *p* is related to different levels of *C*.
b. Explain difficulties that might preclude accurate measures of *C*.

Exercise 3.12 In or out of control?

What would one need to know to actually apply the 'cybernetic' model of management control in Figures 3.1 and 3.2 to strategic or operational management?

CASES

Case 3.1 Airline Benchmarking

Consider the following actual performance information from Southwest Airlines and Jet Blue Airways when completing the requirements of this exercise.

RPMs are the number of scheduled miles flown by revenue passengers.

Operating statistics (unaudited):	Year ended December 31,				
Jet Blue Airways	**2010**	**2009**	**2008**	**2007**	**2006**
Reveue passengerts (000)	24,254	22,450	21,920	21,387	18,565
Revenue passenger miles (RPMs) (000)	28,279	25,955	26,071	25,737	23.320
Available seat miles (ASMs)(000)	34,744	32,558	32,442	31,904	28,594
Load factor (1)	81.40%	79.70%	80.40%	80.70%	81.60%
Aircraft utilisation (hours per day)	11.6	11.5	12.1	12.8	12.7
Average fare	140.69	130.67	139.56	123.28	119.75
Yield per passenger mile (cents, $.01)	12.07	11.3	11.73	10.24	9.53
Passenger revenue per ASM (cents)	9.82	9.01	9.43	8.26	7.77
Operating, revenue per ASM (cents)	10.88	10.11	10.45	8.91	8.27
Operating expense per ASM (cents)	9.92	9.24	10.11	8.38	7.82
Operating expense per ASM, excluding fuel (cents)	6.71	6.33	5.8	5.34	5.07
Airline operating expense per ASM (cents)	9.71	8.99	9.87	8.27	7.76
Departures	225,501	215,526	205,389	196,594	159,152
Average stage length (miles)	1,100	1,076	1,120	1,129	1,186
Average number of operating aircraft during period	153.5	148	139.5	127.8	106.5
Average fuel cost per gallon, including fuel taxes	2.29	2.08	3.08	2.18	2.08
Fuel gallons consumed (millions)	486	455	453	444	377
Full-time equivalent employees at period end	11,121	10,704	9,895	9,909	9,265

Operating data:	Year ended December 31,				
Southwest Airlines	**2010**	**2009**	**2008**	**2007**	**2006**
Revenue passengers carried (000)	88,191	86,310	88,529	88,713	83,815
Revenue passenger miles (RPMs) (000s)	78,047	74,457	73,492	72,319	67,691
Available seat miles (ASMs) (000s)	98,437	98,002	103,271	99,636	92,663
Load factor (1)	79.30%	76.00%	71.20%	72.60%	73.10%
Average length of passenger haul (miles)	885	863	830	815	808
Average aircraft stage length (miles)	648	639	636	629	622
Trips flown	1,114,451	1,125,111	1,191,151	1,160,699	1,092,331
Average passenger fare, $	130.27	114.61	119.16	106.6	104.4
Passenger revenue yield per RPM (cents)	14.72	13.29	14.35	13.08	12.93
Operating revenue yield per ASM (cents)	12.3	10.56	10.67	9.9	9.81
Operating expenses per ASM (cents)	11.29	10.29	10.24	9.1	8.8
Fuel costs per gallon, including taxes (average), $/gal	2.51	2.12	2.44	1.80	1.64
Fuel consumed, in gallons (millions)	1,437	1,428	1,511	1,489	1,389
Fulltime equivalent Employees at period-end	34,901	34,726	35,499	34.378	32,664
Aircraft in service at period-end	548	537	537	520	481

ASMs are the number of seats available for passengers multiplied by the number of miles those seats are flown.

Passenger load factor is derived by dividing RPMs by ASMs.

Operating revenue yield is a measure of average price paid per passenger mile, which is calculated by dividing passenger revenues by RPMs.

Required:

1. Assume you are a consultant to Jet Blue Airways. Analyse and describe the competitive situation that is revealed by these benchmark data. You should use supplemental analyses of these data, such as combined calculations and clearly labelled charts to illustrate your analysis. Use at least three existing ratios, and create at least one new ratio for this analysis.
2. Based on your response above and using only the data shown here, make recommendations to the management of Jet Blue Airways for two performance measures that are especially important to advance Jet Blue's competitive position. Be sure to explain why these measures are important.

Case 3.2 University benchmarking

Burlington University is a small, private university located in the US Midwest. The president of Burlington University, Dr. Frederick Coughlin, is concerned about the university's viability and its ability to sustain its mission of humanities education in the face of stagnant enrolment. The recent loss of a community training program that was profitable, but outside of the university's mission, has adversely affected funds available to support other operations. The board of trustees will not allow borrowing to cover operating losses, and past deficits have been covered by sales of currently unused properties owned by the university. President Coughlin has engaged you to inject a dose of 'financial reality' to the strategic planning efforts of the school's senior staff and to suggest opportunities for increased operating efficiencies. He wants your 'outsider's view' because the senior staff appears to be focused on internal politics and exhibits signs of unwillingness or inability to change. He is hoping that your analysis will motivate the senior staff to appreciate the need to look more closely at internal opportunities for sustainable growth and improved productivity. This could involve improving or cutting academic programmes, a future task in which you might also participate.

Burlington University belongs to an association of private universities, which reports annual financial and operational statistics for member universities. Selected recent data for Burlington University's peer group are contained in the 'Peer Group' worksheet. Historical data for Burlington U is at the 'Historical' worksheet.

The National Association of College and University Business Officers (NACUBO, **http://www.nacubo.org)** and the US Department of Education (**http://nces.ed.gov/ipeds**) are sources of advice and benchmarking data. Other resources include:

Financial Ratio Analysis Comes to Nonprofits. Author: Kent John Chabotar, *The Journal of Higher Education,* Vol. 60, No. 2, (Mar. - Apr., 1989), pp. 188-208

The small college guide to financial health: Beating the odds. Author: Michael K. Townsley, NACUBO, 2002, Chapter 5.

Required:

1. Review the recommended information sources, the data available on the case's supporting worksheets and your own understanding of university performance indicators. Develop a set of benchmarking ratios to evaluate Burlington University's financial and operating performance (a) relative to the peer group of schools and (b) over time.
2. Prepare a brief report that explains your chosen ratios and computes, displays and evaluates Burlington University's performance on each.
3. Based on the available information, make recommendations to President Coughlin for improving Burlington University's performance.
4. Make recommendations for information that you would use to evaluate the performance of individual academic programmes.

Peer Group Data

FINANCIAL & OPERATING STATISTICS, FISCAL YEAR 2007 (July 1, 2007 to June 30, 2008)	Burlington University	University 2	University 3	University 4	University 5	University 6	University 7	University 8	University 9	University 10	University 11	University 12
TUITION & FEES REVENUES												
Total revenue charged (tuition & fees)	$ 17,334,000	$ 21,300,000	$ 12,600,000	$ 30,600,000	$ 19,700,000	$ 30,900,000	$ 20,200,000	$ 12,100,000	$ 14,600,000	$ 14,900,000	$ 23,500,000	$ 25,100,000
Institutional tuition grants (discounts) funded	105,930	210,000	-	93,000	590,000	30,000	18,000	530,000	22,000	210,000	100,000	160,000
Institutional tuition grants (discounts) unfunded	2,696,400	5,400,000	340,000	2,300,000	-	-	3,500,000	-	990,000	1,900,000	2,600,000	5,800,000
External tuition grants received	597,060	1,500,000	1,100,000	6,640,000	180,000	6,400,000	2,830,000	710,000	1,300,000	1,800,000	4,900,000	3,200,000
Net tuition revenue	$ 15,128,730	$ 17,190,000	$ 13,360,000	$ 34,847,000	$ 19,290,000	$ 37,270,000	$ 19,512,000	$ 12,280,000	$ 14,888,000	$ 14,590,000	$ 25,700,000	$ 22,340,000
AUXILIARY FUNDS												
Sales and services of auxiliary enterprises	$ 394,830	$ 2,200,000	$ -	$ 1,700,000	$ -	$ -	$ 1,800,000	$ -	$ 464,000	$ -	$ 2,200,000	$ 4,300,000
ENDOWMENT												
Value of endowment assets at end of fiscal year	$ 4,237,200	$ 6,600,000	$ 1,400,000	$ 1,800,000	$ 1,400,000	$ 390,000	$ 9,900,000	$ 7,900,000	$ 620,000	$ 10,000,000	$ 7,100,000	$ 3,600,000
Endowment return	211,860	300,000	65,000	133,000	99,000	30,000	450,000	440,000	27,000	620,000	480,000	191,000
UNRESTRICTED GIFTS AND GRANTS												
Private gifts	$ 1,155,600	$ 2,500,000	$ 130,000	$ 240,000	$ 330,000	$ 7,200,000	$ 801,000	$ 1,100,000	$ 450,000	$ 380,000	$ 1,200,000	$ 760,000
Research grants and contracts	240,750	470,000	45,000	48,000	46,000	610,000	670,000	98,000	40,000	130,000	640,000	140,000
Total gifts, grants and contracts	$ 1,396,350	$ 2,970,000	$ 175,000	$ 288,000	$ 376,000	$ 7,810,000	$ 1,471,000	$ 1,198,000	$ 490,000	$ 510,000	$ 1,840,000	$ 900,000
TOTAL REVENUES	$ 17,131,770	$ 22,660,000	$ 13,600,000	$ 36,968,000	$ 19,765,000	$ 45,110,000	$ 23,233,000	$ 13,918,000	$ 15,869,000	$ 15,720,000	$ 30,220,000	$ 27,731,000
EXPENSES												
Instruction	$ 9,437,400	$ 8,600,000	$ 3,200,000	$ 9,200,000	$ 6,600,000	$ 8,200,000	$ 8,900,000	$ 6,400,000	$ 6,100,000	$ 5,400,000	$ 8,900,000	$ 6,500,000
Academic support	88,596	350,000	1,800,000	1,800,000	5,200,000	4,800,000	1,500,000	1,050,000	2,250,000	1,400,000	440,000	490,000
Student services	1,733,400	3,900,000	2,100,000	5,800,000	1,100,000	6,000,000	2,200,000	1,600,000	1,800,000	2,500,000	1,700,000	3,000,000
Institutional support	5,874,300	4,800,000	5,100,000	7,000,000	4,600,000	9,800,000	5,200,000	3,200,000	2,400,000	3,100,000	7,500,000	8,000,000
Interest	510,390	310,000	510,000	1,100,000	1,300,000	140,000	320,000	-	190,000	100,000	580,000	640,000
Auxiliary enterprises	385,200	1,600,000	-	2,200,000	-	-	1,400,000	-	760,000	-	480,000	2,900,000

(continued)

Peer Group Data, Continued

FINANCIAL & OPERATING STATISTICS, FISCAL YEAR 2007 (July 1, 2007 to June 30, 2008)	Burlington University	University 2	University 3	University 4	University 5	University 6	University 7	University 8	University 9	University 10	University 11	University 12
TOTAL EXPENSES	$ 18,029,286	$ 19,560,000	$ 12,710,000	$ 27,100,000	$ 18,800,000	$ 28,940,000	$ 19,520,000	$ 12,250,000	$ 13,500,000	$ 12,500,000	$ 19,600,000	$ 21,530,000
SURPLUS OR (LOSS)	$ (897,516)	$ 3,100,000	$ 890,000	$ 9,868,000	$ 965,000	$ 16,170,000	$ 3,713,000	$ 1,668,000	$ 2,369,000	$ 3,220,000	$ 10,620,000	$ 6,201,000
FACULTY SALARY												
Average fulltime faculty annual salary	$ 43,624	$ 54,000	$ 43,500	$ 68,400	$ 50,400	$ 66,400	$ 67,000	$ 53,000	$ 60,000	$ 52,000	$ 57,000	$ 47,000
GRADUATION RATES												
6-year undergrad graduation rate	33.7%	38.0%	93.0%	36.0%	55.0%	41.0%	44.0%	62.0%	36.0%	71.0%	29.0%	34.0%
ENROLLMENTS					+							
Undergraduate enrollment	530	1,400	630	1,630	530	1,600	1,800	310	1,100	1,300	1,100	1,500
Graduate enrollment	780	830	1,200	290	1,620	650	470	1,020	350	250	930	550
Total enrollment	1,310	2,230	1,830	1,920	2,150	2,250	2,270	1,330	1,450	1,550	2,030	2,050
DEGREES AWARDED	356	360	410	380	420	590	290	270	470	410	480	440
CLASS SIZE & TEACHING LOAD												
Average class size	10.6	15.0	19.0	15.0	12.0	11.0	16.0	11.0	14.0	15.0	14.0	18.0
Faculty FTE teaching load (3-hour semester classes)	5.6	6.1	6.3	6.2	7.1	7.1	6.3	5.9	6.4	6.3	6.1	5.1

Note: These are disguised data

Burlington University historical data

Financial & operating statistics	FY 2003	FY 2004	FY 2005	FY 2006	FY 2007
Tuition & fees revenues					
Total revenue charged (tuition & fees)	$ 15,369,480	$ 15,600,600	$ 16,361,370	16,852,500	$ 17,334,000
Institutional tuition grants (discounts) funded	46,224	202,230	241,713	74,151	105,930
Institutional tuition grants (discounts) unfunded	1,357,830	2,407,500	1,495,539	1,733,400	2,696,400
External tuition grants received	423,720	221,490	327,420	452,610	597,060
Net tuition revenue	14,389,146	$ 13,212,360	$ 14,951,538	$ 15,497,559	$ 15,128,730
AUXILIARY FUNDS					
Sales and services of auxiliary enterprises	$ 1,348,200	$ 1,396,350	$ 1,463,760	$ 1,540,800	$ 394,830
ENDOWMENT					
Value of endowment assets at end of fiscal year	$ 1,588,950	$ 2,407,500	$ 2,985,300	$ 3,659,400	$ 4,237,200
Endowment return	98,226	97,263	144,450	250,380	211,860
UNRESTRICTED GIFTS AND GRANTS					
Private gifts	$ 1,155,600	$ 1,040,040	$ 1,251,900	$ 1,059,300	$ 1,155,600
Research grants and contracts	250,380	847,440	770,400	885,960	240,750
Total gifts, grants and contracts	$ 1,405,980	$ 1,887,480	$ 2,022,300	$ 1,945,260	$ 1,396,350
TOTAL REVENUES	$ 17,241,552	$ 16,593,453	$ 18,582,048	$ 19,233,999	$ 17,131,770
EXPENSES					
Instruction	$ 9,726,300	$ 9,591,480	$ 9,341,100	$ 9,533,700	$ 9,437,400
Academic support	134,820	221,490	89,559	235,935	88,596
Student services	722,250	954,333	1,184,490	1,637,100	1,733,400
Institutional support	5,200,200	5,681,700	6,548,400	5,296,500	5,874,300
Interest	154,080	288,900	452,610	500,760	510,390
Auxiliary enterprises	539,280	433,350	385,200	375,570	385,200
Total expenses	$ 16,476,930	$ 17,171,253	$ 18,001,359	$ 17,579,565	$ 18,029,286
SURPLUS OR (LOSS)	$ 764,622	$ (577,800)	$ 580,689	$ 1,654,434	$ (897,516)
FACULTY SALARY					
Average fulltime faculty annual salary	$ 41,602	$ 41,891	$ 39,868	$ 41,409	$ 43,624
GRADUATION RATES					
6-year undergrad graduation rate	52%	47%	96%	32%	34%
ENROLLMENTS					
Undergraduate enrollment	472	501	491	530	530
Graduate enrollment	636	713	819	828	780
Total enrollment	1,108	1,214	1,310	1,358	1,310
DEGREES AWARDED	270	270	299	318	356
CLASS SIZE & TEACHING LOAD					
Average class size	9	14	13	13	11
Faculty FTE teaching load (3-hour semester classes)	6	5	5	5	6

Note: These are disguised data

Case 3.3 New Product Development

The New Product Development Division

(NPD) is a business unit of a large U.S. high technology company. NPD's goal is to contribute to the continued growth and profitability of the company. The primary objectives of NPD are to generate the company's future products and services and to motivate development of new technology by the company's basic research division. NPD combines marketing research on customers' emerging needs with the company's basic and applied research activities to generate new product concepts and introductions. The company measures the success of NPD by the number of new products brought to market, the speed with which they are developed, new technologies developed for NPD, and new product market success.

In the past year, the company's top management has observed that NPD has not introduced as many successful new products as either large competitors or new entrants to the industry. The company has obtained many new products in recent years by acquiring smaller companies; top management feels that this approach is quite costly in both the short and long run. The company must pay a premium for the new products, and this diverts resources from internal new product development. In the long run, this reliance on purchasing new products might cripple the company's ability to fund basic research that has been responsible for generations of new technology, and which historically has been one of the company's comparative advantages.

Top management believed that NPD's exclusive reliance on project management practices, which often do not link project development processes with customer value and market success, partly caused its lagging new product introductions. In contrast, key competitors have brought more new products to the market and more quickly.

Introduction to project management

NPD for years has applied engineering principles of project management[29] to its development process. Project management resembles organisational management in that it relies on planning, implementation, and control of activities and processes. However, it differs from organisational management in several respects. Critical differences are the temporary nature of a project, its defined objectives, and limited resources – including time. Another distinguishing feature is the use of cross-functional teams, which are created for an annual period, are attached for the duration of a project and reassigned or disbanded at its termination or completion. A typical NPD team will consist of a team leader, several hardware and software engineers, and specialists from marketing, finance and customer service.

These project management characteristics have influenced the nature of project controls, which rely heavily on process stages, decision checkpoints (or milestones), and measurements of process performance. The case's exhibit illustrates NPD's development process with its major stages and checkpoints. Moving from one completed stage to the next stage requires NPD management approval at a 'go – no go' decision checkpoint.

Interviews with Team Leaders

Your assistant has interviewed five current team leaders and five experienced team members. A summary of her notes is at Appendix 3.1.

Case Analysis and Requirements

1. Read carefully several original readings referenced in this chapter:
2. Prepare a report based on both the case and **your** selected readings. Answer the questions:

a. What management control(s) should NPD use?
b. Why and with what support from your readings?

[29] The industry's basic reference is *A Guide to the Project Management Body of Knowledge* (PMBOK). Copies are available from the Project Management Institute, **www.pmi.org**. *PMBOK* chapters 1 – 3 introduce the major features of project management. Later chapters provide extensive details.

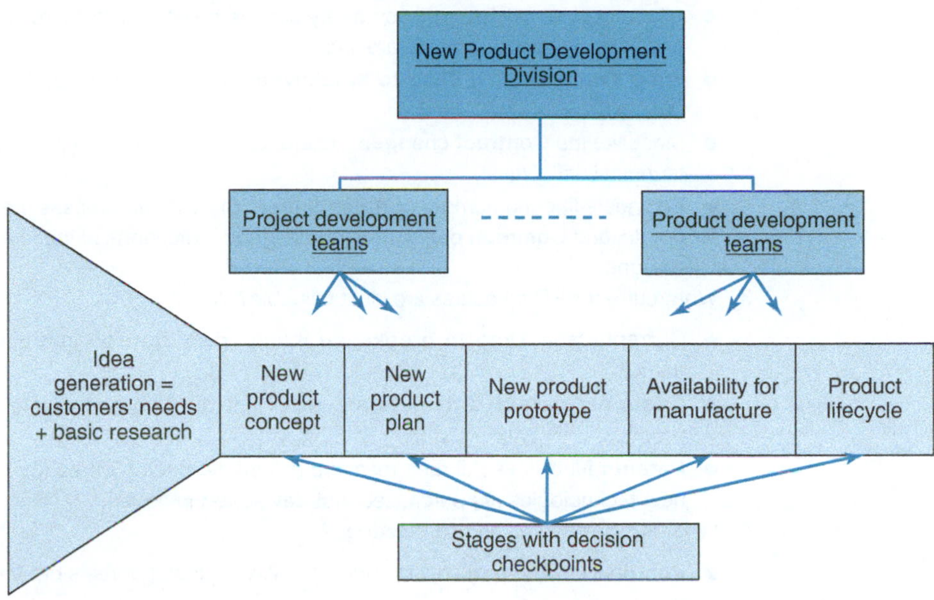

Case exhibit: new product development process

NPD process stage	Stages and checkpoint description
Idea generation	NPD generates ideas and also receives them from customers, company researchers, marketing, sales and technical customer support personnel. NPD teams screen batches of project ideas for acceptance or deletion from the process. Acceptance rate to the concept phase has been 5 – 10%.
New product concept	Product concept prepared by an NPD team approved by NPD management – justifies further investment in process and development of new technology, if required. Acceptance rate to the new product plan phase has been 40 – 50%.
New product plan	Product plan prepared by the team, approved by NPD management – includes approval of product technical attributes, schedule, and budget. Acceptance rate to the prototype phase has been 70 – 90%.
New product prototype	Verification by the team to NPD management that the prototype (working model) meets functional, quality, and marketing requirements. Acceptance rate to availability phase has been more than 90%.
Availability for manufacture	NPD, manufacturing, finance, and marketing departments document that the product is ready for manufacturing, sale, and delivery to customers.
Product life cycle	Product division manages the product during market life from initial manufacture to end of life.

Appendix 3.1: Summary of interviews with NPD team employees

1. Could you describe your current position and work?
   - The first question was used as an icebreaker and to establish context for other answers. The five interviewees were NPD team leaders, all with engineering backgrounds, and five were key team members from various company functions, such as marketing, finance, quality assurance and technical customer service.
2. What current NPD measures are most valuable? Why?
   - **Time to availability for manufacturing** is very important to a number of people – a key indicator of process efficiency.

- All budget and schedule measures are seen to be vital – project resources are limited and windows of opportunity are short.
- **Time to market** and **Time to breakeven** are valued by all as important process outcomes.
- Most like the **Contract changes** – useful to track changes in project objectives and technical difficulties.
- Engineers like the number of **Patents filed**, the various process stages and check-points, and **Common parts utilisation** – good indications of innovative, economical designs.

3. What current NPD measures are least valuable? Why?
   - Currently, the **Time to breakeven** is important but too imprecise to be really useful.
   - **Customer detected defects** are important but known too late to improve the product.
   - **Patents filed** is useful as a measure of new technology breakthroughs, but many new technologies are purchased, not developed in house.
4. What NPD measures should be added?
   - Real time quality measures to improve ability to detect defects before customers find them.
   - Matching of product changes and their costs; consider next time in developing new products.
   - Customer feedback on function and usability, not just defects (e.g. ease of use and recommendations on missing functionality).
   - Reused software modules (analogous to common parts use in hardware).
   - Costs and use of purchased technology *versus.* technology developed in-house.
   - Customer loyalty and repeat purchases.
   - Projected versus. actual sales, returns and pricing.
   - Post-availability financial performance at 6 & 12 months.
   - Product profitability, annual and lifecycle.
   - Return on investments in new products.
   - Measurement of the NPV of the new product development process.
   - More complete and accurate reporting on all projects.
5. What drives new product revenues?
   - Meeting customers' current and projected needs.
   - Quality of products and company's reputation for customer service.
   - Annuities from long term maintenance and service contracts.
6. What drives new product costs?
   - Purchasing technology from other sources.
   - Project complexity.
   - Common parts utilisation (negative relation expected).
   - Product defects.
   - Contract changes.
   - Team abilities and experience (negative relation expected)
7. What does the company do to improve employees' ability to develop new products?
   - Requires employee development plans to help employees improve their skills.

- Uses new and current technologies to aid developers.
- Sends employees to industry trade shows and technology forums.
- Encourages employees to update skills through internally offered courses.

8. What does the company do to improve new product development processes?
   - Encourages people to think outside the box.
   - Uses new processes.
   - Keeps skill base current.
   - Makes existing development processes flexible.
   - Corrects previous implementation errors
9. What does the company do to improve new products and services?
   - **Most important—most frequently cited by interviewees:** The company works with the customer and gets the products right. Knows what the customers wants, what problems they have, what needs they want filled. Provides a high quality product that meets those needs.
   - Stays in touch with the industry; encourages employees to read current industry magazines and attend trade shows.
   - Monitors competitors.
   - Assesses the skills of employees and teams.
   - Uses a solid budgeting plan.
10. What does the company do to improve financial performance of new products?
    - Develops a good product and markets the heck out of it. Develops good products by knowing what the customer wants.
    - Uses good marketing for effective product launch.
    - Gets sales employees who know a lot about products out into the market and selling.
    - Tracks costs, minimises costs using solid budget.
11. Do you have any general comments or recommendations for improving NPD processes?
    - Transform the process measures from a pure reporting tool to a planning device.
    - Create more interaction between NPD and the basic research division.
    - Integrate measures more with daily activities.
    - Correlate measures such as schedule and spending variances to time to market and financial outcomes.

Case 3.4 Datacom case[30]

Datacom is a young, privately held, high technology firm, that was formed to design, assemble and sell computer data communication products. Datacom had experienced highly volatile changes in its industry, product line, sales and organisational form. It had transformed from a completely functional organisation (Finance and Accounting or F&A, Engineering, Marketing, etc.) to one with three business units, each dedicated to a separate technology, product line and business strategy. A relatively large group of employees comprised a functional core that provided business and technical services to the business units. The CEO acknowledged the critical importance of professional management, 'reality in finance and accounting,' and strategic marketing as the company's most critical management needs. He was confident that

[30] Adapted from Selto, F. and D. Jasinski. 1996. 'Strategic planning, ABC, and high technology.' *Management Accounting,* March: 37-40.

the founders and technical employees would keep abreast or ahead of technology, but was not as sure that their technological breakthroughs could translate to business success without superior management talent.

One of the new business units, Data Centre Network (DCN), focused on fibre optic data communication within large data centres and with network systems. Success hinged on the unit's ability to forecast and lead significant development of communications technology. This unit faced the highest technological and business risk, but, if successful, it had the potential to launch the company far beyond previous levels of sales and profitability. A second unit, Open Systems, focused on copper cable solutions to connecting mainframe computers with industry standard networks (e.g. solutions to the 'open systems' problem). This unit would apply known technology to the significant problems of coordinating different computing platforms within computer networks. Technological risk was only moderate, but business risk was relatively high due to the large number of competent competitors and the high cost of product development. The third business unit (Mainframe Peripheral Controllers - MPC) maintained and extended the company's original communication product line (connecting mainframe computers to terminals). The executive board hoped the MPC unit would generate sufficient cash flow to fund basic R&D in Data Centre Network and product development in Open Systems.

Datacom's top managment came to realise that its earlier success with MPC products had been no fluke. After analysing its history and capabilities, top executives and technical personnel believed Datacom's comparative advantages were to predict correctly data communication technology change, quickly develop superior products, and build strong original equipment manufacturing (OEM) customer relationships to ensure sales for the life of the products. Datacom, they reasoned, was not a superior, low cost manufacturer or distributor. Datacom determined on the basis of its technology and marketing forecasts to pursue new Data Centre Network products with an emphasis on software and to jettison MPC and Open Systems as soon as possible.

F&A had previously provided reliable cost control data for monitoring the profitability of MPC and Open Systems products. In response to charges of inaccuracy of measuring new business unit profitability, they laboured for over a year to improve tracking of all activities to business units and their products. In most employees' opinions a year later, F&A had greatly improved measurement of the new business unit's profitability. Business unit and F&A personnel were frustrated that the increasingly accurate tracking of resources was consuming their valuable time, but executives did not use measures of business unit profitability. Executives did not feel this information was useful for strategy formulation because it was focused on current products and manufacturing processes. They knew Data Centre Network was unprofitable because of its relatively large R&D expenses and very low sales. It was more important to top managers to discover the most promising new products to develop. Engineering and marketing personnel provided input for those decisions.

Required:

1. Discuss how the roles and responsibilities of F&A staff to support strategic decision making might change when a company like Datacom restructures into decentralised business units.
2. What changes in management controls would you recommend for a company like Datacom that has changed its focus from functional to product-line based business units? Would these management controls differ between the MPC and DCN business units? Explain.

Case 3.5 Performance targets.[31]

An international manufacturing company (IMC) provides parts and repair services to the transportation industry through geographically diverse distributorships. Distributors must exclusively sell IMC products and services within defined sales territories (e.g. Great Britain, Scandinavia, New South Wales, Western US and so on). IMC has defined ten important financial and non-financial performance measures and targets for its distributors. IMC rates each distributor quarterly on each performance dimension as 'light blue' if it performs better than target, 'white' if it performs within target limits, and 'dark blue' if it performs worse than target. Furthermore, IMC allocates 100 points unequally across the 10 performance measures. A light blue rating earns all of a measure's points; white earns half of the points and dark blue earns no points. IMC makes annual evaluations, bonus compensation and job tenure contingent on whether distributorships are ranked by total points within the upper, middle or lower third of all distributorships.

The case exhibit presents the IMC financial and non-financial performance measures, points, and recent ratings and scores of the highest and lowest rated distributorships (D1 and D2).

Performance measure	Definition	Points	D1	D2
Customer order parts fill rate	Percentage of customer orders filled from current stock	12	6	6
Service diagnosis and completion	Average time to diagnose and complete repair services (within service class targets)	12	12	6
Productive hour ratio	Ratio of billed technician hours to total hours	15	15	7.5
Safety record	Number of lost-time accidents	8	8	8
Personnel performance reviews	Percentage of personnel performance reviews completed	6	3	3
Community involvement	Percentage of management personnel active in local business and charitable organisations	6	6	6
Training	Percentage of technical personnel certified at correct levels	10	10	5
Automotive market share	Regional market share for automotive (truck) parts and service	25	25	0
Other market share	Regional market share for parts and service applied to other uses (power generation, marine applications, natural gas drilling)	6	0	6
Total		100	85	47.5

Case exhibit: distributor performance measures

Consider excerpts from an interview with the manager of D1, whose sales territory mostly includes long distance trucking customers. (D2 is located in a densely populated, mostly urban area.)

A. What do you think of the performance evaluations based on these measures? "This approach at least gives some quantitative basis to evaluation process. Overall it is more objective. The ratings are black and white on key areas. So far everyone has a little bit of

[31] Adapted from Malina and Selto 2004.

fear that the system may be used as a punishment tool but I haven't personally experienced that. The initial attempt was minimally collaborative, but lately we have had no more input since the first version that had too many measures. I like all A's on my report card so I want all them green. I agree with almost all the measures. Some of the measures we report, and others are given to us by IMC. I worry about whether all distributors report their performance as objectively as I do, without gaming or shading the truth.

"I grew up working for a CPA and he ingrained in me that "if you can't measure it, you can't improve it." So I like this system because it takes some of the guessing out of how IMC views me. I just like knowing my grades. I assume that if I have an "A", IMC is happy. This helps me think that high grades will take the stress away from my next annual review."

B. Are you satisfied with the quality of the measurements that you think are important?*"Customer order parts fill rate* is a critical measure but one that is in disastrous shape. We can build no customer loyalty without parts for ourselves and for customers to perform service repairs in the field. This really is a joint measure of how well both IMC resupply from the factory and we as a distributor are serving our customers. I'm white because IMC's supply to me is only 50%, and I can't be at 90% to customers (that is, light blue) if IMC is only 50% to me. We've done terrible damage to the customer base. The only way I might be light blue is to maintain very large inventories, and that is only if I guess correctly about future customer needs.

"Service diagnosis and completion is a great tool. I was not an advocate at the start, but now I am. It tells us how quickly we can make an intelligent statement to the customer. We have been able to flow more work through our shop by getting the quick easy stuff through the shop first. The difficulty in this measure is that we are not able to do it automatically as with other measures. Everyone is doing this manually and there is no standardisation. For example, when does a job start? I think it should be when the customer places an order, but I know that others don't start the clock until parts are in and the work is begun.

"Productive hour ratio is a very important measure, but we don't do it quite the way IMC defines it. It wasn't done collaboratively, and we like our measure better. Besides, the trend is important, not the absolute number. I did not get a response when I reported how I measure the productive hour ratio, so I am doing it my way.

"Safety record is a totally ludicrous target, but a great measure. I have 100 technicians, and if they have more than one accident in a year, I'm in the dark blue. We are not working in a factory clean room. My guys are lying in mud, with a flashlight strapped to their ass trying to fix this equipment. We are safety conscious, but someone is going to cut his hand and be out for a day. Just one of those, and I'm dark blue. Any distributor who is green is a liar.

"Automotive market share measurement is a great indicator, and we have measured it the same way as IMC does now. This market has been IMC's and our primary market for decades.

"Othermarket share (e.g., power generation) is not too important to us, given our location and market, but I understand that several of the distributors in cities with lots of high-rise buildings that now need back-up power generation or with major ports or offshore drilling that offer new marine applications are not happy with the point allocation."

Required:

1. From the information in the case, critique the set of performance measures and targets that IMC uses to evaluate its distributors.
2. Make recommendations for improvement of the selection and uses of IMC's performance measures and targets.

References

Anthony, R. N. and V. Govindarajan (2007) *Management Control Systems,* 12th ed. Boston: McGraw-Hill/Irwin.

Banker, R. and S. Datar (1989). Sensitivity, Precision, and Linear Aggregation of Signals for Performance Evaluation, *Journal of Accounting Research,* Vol. 27, No. 1 (Spring), pp. 21-39.

Barnard, Chester I.. (1968) *The Functions of the Executive,* Harvard University Press.

Burns and Stalker (1961) *The Management of Innovation,* London: Tavistock.

Chen, Hui, David Parsley and Ya-Wen Yang, (2009) "Corporate Lobbying and Financial, University of Colorado working paper.

Coase, R. H. (1937). "The Nature of the Firm." Econometrica 4(16): 386-405.

Feltham, G. and J. Xie (1994), 'Performance measure congruity and diversity in multi-task principal/agent relations'. *The AccountingReview* **69**, 429-452.

Ferreira and Otley (2010) The design and use of performance management systems: An extended framework for analysis. *Management Accounting Research* 20: 263–282.

Haelstrom, A. and W. Schuster (2008) "Standards, management incentives and accounting practice – lessons from the IFRS transition in Sweden" Stockholm School of Economics.

Hofstede, G. (1983) National Cultures in Four Dimensions: A Research-based Theory of Cultural Differences among Nations. *Jn[. Siudies of Man.& Org..* Vol. Xlll. No. 1-2, pp. 46-74.

Hofstede, G. (1991) *Cultures and organizations: Softwareof the mind.* London: McGraw-Hill UK.

Hofstede, G. (1998) Attitudes, values and organizational culture: Disentangling the concepts. *Organization Studies,* 19/3, 477-92

Hofstede, G. (1978). The poverty of management control philosophy, *The Academy of Management Review,* Vol. 3, No. 3, pp. 450-461.

Jensen, M and Meckling, W.H. (1976) Theory of the firm: Managerial behavior, agency costs and ownership structure, *Journal of Financial Economics.*

Kenneth, A. Merchant and Jean-François Manzoni. (1989). The Achievability of Budget Targets in Profit Centers: A Field Study. *The Accounting Review,* Vol. 64, No. 3, pp. 539-558.

Lunsford, J. Lynn. (2007) Boeing Scrambles to Repair Problems with New Plane. *The Wall Street Journal.* Dec 7, p. 1.

Lunsford, J. Lynn. (2008) Boeing to Buy Stake in Plant Doing Dreamliner Assembly. *The Wall Street Journal Online.* March 28.

Malina, M. and F. Selto. (2004). "Choice and change of measures in performance measurement models." Management Accounting Research 15(4): 441-69.

Merchant, KA and WA van der Stede (2007) *Management control systems: performance measurement, evaluation and incentives,* Upper Saddle River, NJ: Prentice Hall.

Nassim Taleb, (2005). Fooled by Randomness: The Hidden Role of Chance in Life and *in the Markets.* New York: Random House and Penguin. ISBN 0-8129-7521-9.

Otley, D. (1999) Performance management: a framework for management control systems research, *Management Accounting Research.*

Ouchi (1979) A Conceptual Framework for the Design of Organizational Control Mechanisms. *Management Science,* Vol. 25, No. 9, pp. 833-848.

Simon, H.A., (1997) *Administrative Behavior: A Study of Decision-Making Processes in Administrative Organizations-* 4th ed. in, The Free Press.

Simon, Herbert, George Kozmetsky, Harold Guetzkow, Gordon Tyndall. (1954). *Centralization vs Decentralization of the Controller's Department.* Controllership Foundation, Inc., reprinted (1978) by Scholars Book Co, Houston TX.

Simons. R. (1995) Levers of control: How managers use innovative control systems to drive strategic renewal. Harvard Business School Press: Boston, MA.

Williamson, O.E. (1985). *Markets and Hierarchies: Analysis and Antitrust Implications.* New York: Free Press.

Wu, J.S. and I. Zhang, (2010) "Accounting integration and comparability: Evidence from relative performance evaluation around IFRS adoption" Wm E. Simon Graduate School of Business Administration, University of Rochester.

Zimmerman, J. (2009). *Accounting for Decision Making and Control.* McGraw-Hill.

Chapter 4

Financial modelling

4.1 Introduction

4.1.1 Management issue

All of us face life's decisions similarly – we must decide now and hope that we have accounted for the future's unknowns as well as possible. Managers' decisions necessarily address the future when general business conditions, organisational capabilities, process quality, and individuals' talents and efforts are unknown. They, too, must decide now, facing alternative decisions and conditions of the unknown future. This is the essence of managerial decision making, and professional judgment is required. Else why would organisations need operating managers? Many managers use a **financial model,** which is a set of cost and revenue relations that simulate, organise, analyse and report the likely impacts of the future's unknowns on financial outcomes. Financial models cannot replace the manager, but an effective model can complement and improve professional judgment. The purpose of this chapter is to describe the development of financial models that can range from simple 'back of the envelope' calculations to complex interactive sets of mathematical relations. These models might become part of your daily professional life, as either a developer or user of financial models.

4.1.2 Overview

Any model is a representation of reality, but cost effective models of complex phenomena, such as business organisations, abstract away from myriad complexities and focus on key indicators of performance and relations among them. As technology and knowledge of business processes improve, developers of financial models are inclined to increase the complexity of their models. It is unclear in practice whether the benefits of very complex financial models exceed their development and maintenance costs. Starting simply and then adding complexity may be a prudent approach to building effective financial models. This also is the approach of this chapter.

One may judge the effectiveness of a financial model by how well it simulates cost and revenue relations for its various purposes. This sounds easier than it really is, but consider the objectives of financial modelling and example indicators of effectiveness in Table 4.1.

Table 4.1 Objectives and effectiveness of financial modelling

Objectives of financial modelling	Indicators of effectiveness
Improved decision making	**Widespread and continued use of the model.** Why measure 'use' of the model and not a direct measure of improved decisions? Many organisations have defaulted to measures of use because identifying and measuring 'improved' decision making in decentralised organisations is hampered by a) the unobservability of alternatives not chosen or the efforts of managers to analyse alternatives, b) a necessarily incomplete or somewhat inaccurate model, and c) the role of luck, good or bad. **Perceived ease of use.** Models that are intuitive and that reflect the form of business decisions should result in better decisions.
Improved response to business changes	**Model flexibility.** Models with built in ease of changing cost and revenue assumptions can be adapted quickly without extensive revisions. **Response time.** Financial models that can be used quickly to meet changed business conditions (such as changed customer orders) may result in quicker decisions about pricing, costs, delivery times, etc.
Improved communications	**Perceived communication clarity and reliability.** Managers may use financial models to communicate expected impacts of strategies and alternative decisions. Communications that are perceived to be clear, reliable and trustworthy should improve employee understanding and motivation. **Reduced or more effective meeting time.** Improved communications with financial models should reduce meeting times or make those meetings more effective by quickly and easily displaying alternatives or changes.
Better understanding about the drivers of revenues and costs and insights to complex business problems	**Predictive ability.** Financial models that reliably predict future financial outcomes can improve managers' understanding of the drivers of costs and revenues and how changes to those drivers can affect financial outcomes. **Process improvements.** A major lession of activity based costing is different financial outcomes can occur by changing the quantities of the drivers employed or by changing processes to consume less or to use a less costly driver.
Better training of employees	**Employee knowledge.** Organisations may use reliable financial models as low cost training simulators, similar to flight simulators used to train pilots. **Employee suggestions for improvement.** Employees who use and understand financial models may be more likely to suggest improvements in models and processes that can lead to improved decision making and financial outcomes.

RESEARCH EXAMPLE

Decades of research have addressed whether 'models or man' are superior decision makers. Findings often are that 'models' outperform 'man' in many tasks, even such complex tasks as the game of chess [see **http://en.wikipedia.org/wiki/Deep_Blue_(chess_computer)**]. While this can be a distressing outcome, human judgment, often aided by models, is the norm in most business decision making contexts. Researchers have long studied whether and how these models affect business decision making. Jay Bourgeois' and Kathleen Eisenhardt's classic 1988 study found that top managers in fast changing environments, where reliable models might be most useful, were most effective when they used models as incremental supplements to their own judgment. More recent research has not indicated that models are likely to replace managers altogether anytime soon; this remains an active area of inquiry.

"Strategic Decision Processes in High Velocity Environments: Four Cases in the Microcomputer Industry" by L. J. Bourgeois, III and Kathleen M. Eisenhardt.

4.2 Models for business decision making

Business decision making models typically reflect pro forma or forecasted financial statements (or parts thereof), such as the income statement (e.g. sales revenues less operating expenses), statements of cash flow (e.g. operating cash flow), and the balance sheet (e.g. selected balances that are inputs to key ratios). A model of the complete suite of pro forma financial statements for an organisation is often called a **business model,** a business plan model, or a master budget model. Small portions of financial statements may be tailored to examine a specific business decision, such as adding or dropping a product, without explicit references to the impacts on the entire business model. A piecemeal approach to modelleing business decisions certainly is simpler than revising an entire business model for every business decision. However, a piecemeal approach that models only profitability, for example, can overlook impacts on cash flows or key balance sheet accounts. When possible, managers prudently should test the financial impacts of major business decisions on a complete business model.

4.2.1 Profit planning models

A **profit planning model** mimics the entire income statement (or parts of it, such as revenues less some or all categories of expenses) for an individual unit of product **or** for a period's total output. Building a profit planning model requires that one understands, measures and models the key business activities that will generate or 'drive' revenues and expenses. First consider activities that drive revenues in the simplest case, which is the sale of a single product in a stable, competitive market. Here sales revenue is the product of the sales price, P, and sales volume, Q. The basic model assumes that the sales price is given by the competitive market, and the firm's sales volume is determined by its use of its productive capacity. Thus, in this simplest case, the only driver of total revenues is production volume ($P \times Q$, Price multiplied by volume).[1] Similarly in this case, the production volume is the only driver of costs and expenses, but the behaviour between production volume and total cost can be more complex because of multiple dimensions of productive activity.[2] These may be modelled by including additional cost drivers.

4.2.2 Cost behaviour

Financial models usually reflect the ways that costs are expected to change as business activity changes. Chapter 6 covers the topic of cost estimation in detail, so we will consider only basic cost behaviour here. We distinguish between two types of cost behaviour, which are caused by differences in scale of productive activity. **Fixed costs,** F, are incurred to enable the firm's desired total productive capacity. These costs may be set contractually or at the discretion of management on a periodic basis. However, managers may change fixed cost levels by changing decisions about scale, technology and location. Fixed costs in the simplest case do not vary within the designed scale of operations, and may reflect the occupancy costs of facilities, leases of equipment, and salaries of managers. **Variable costs** are incurred for each unit produced or sold, and include measures of the use of direct materials, direct labour, and variable overhead and sales costs. These are typically modelled as fixed amounts, V, per unit produced or sold,

[1] Because we want to describe basic concepts first, we will defer discussions of the challenges that forecasting actually presents for financial modelling.

[2] Complications of multiple cost drivers are covered in Chapter 6.

and total variable costs vary directly with production quantities (i.e. V × Q). In the simplest case, total costs are linear with the quantity of output, with an intercept equal to total fixed costs and a slope equal to total variable cost per unit produced or sold (i.e. TC = F + V × Q).

Costing methods can complicate the modelling of profit. Firstly, profit planning models match costs and revenues of products that are expected to be sold. The costs of unsold units remain as inventories, and units sold from prior inventories (i.e. FIFO costs) may differ from current or expected production costs. Thus, total costs incurred in a particular period might not model total costs expensed in that period if inventories are non-zero. Secondly, per unit costs may contain only variable costs, which is called **variable costing,** wherein variable costs are either expensed with units sold or remain as inventory of unsold goods. Total fixed costs are expensed in the period. This costing method mirrors the basic cost behaviour and simplifies the accounting for production costs in financial models. However, variable costing is not commonly used for financial reporting. Models can closely mimic income for financial reports that use **absorption costing,** which measures product cost as variable costs plus 'normal' allocations of fixed production costs.[3] The two costing methods measure income identically if inventories are either zero or production equals sales and product costs are not expected to change. Large deviations from conditions of non-zero inventories and changing costs can induce large FIFO differences in the timing of reported income between variable and absorption costing.

EXAMPLE OF BASIC FINANCIAL MODELLING

We illustrate features of financial modelling throughout this chapter with a model of revenue and costs that we modify for each specific modelling purpose. We begin with the context of the modelling situation.

In 2009, fewer than 20% percent of India's 72 million households had a refrigerator.[4] An Indian appliance manufacturer (IAM) saw a large, untapped market, which if served successfully could restore the company's market position that was threatened by European and Chinese competition. Serving this untapped refrigerator market, however, would require a significantly lower sales price. The price reduction in turn would not be economically feasible without significant innovations in design, manufacturing and distribution. Before addressing this strategic analysis, let us first build a basic financial model that IAM could have used to support its strategic planning. The financial model has two separate sections, data input and results, which isolate (uncertain) input variables from financial relationships that normally are never changed.

Consider the relations among the sales price and costs per unit in ten rows of Figure 4.1 for the smallest conventional, home refrigerator currently sold for the Indian market.[5] These

[3] By the IAS 2 requirement of per unit product costs should contain allocated fixed product costs based on normal production levels. Cost accounting texts provide detailed coverage of absorption costing.

[4] This example is adapted from an article by Bellman, E. 2009. "Indian Firms Shift Focus to the Poor." *Wall Street Journal,* October 20, 2009. IAM is loosely based on an actual manufacturer, but none of the financial modelling is taken from the real company's experience. Specific prices and costs are estimates modified for the purpose of this example and are not actual prices and costs. The Excel models used in this chapter are available to classroom adopters of the text.

[5] Several formatting conventions are used throughout this chapter. Data that are supplied from other sources are in shaded cells; whereas calculated figures are unshaded.

data support a straightforward profitability analysis for a specific product (described here by its capacity and number of parts). As shown in Figure 4.2 and if used in a spreadsheet program such as Microsoft's Excel, the profit model is an improvement over simply using a calculator. Because outcomes of interest are computed by formulas (repeated for convenience) in column C, changing the shaded inputs changes the financial outcomes. This simple financial model, in spreadsheet form, is the foundation of this chapter's illustrations of financial modelling.

Observe that the example's profit-planning model constructs variable-costing profit. This model computes the product's **contribution margin** (sales revenue less total variable costs), operating profit, and the **profit margin ratio**(also known as the **return on sales**) at the normal level of sales and production activity, which is operating profit divided by sales revenue. This ratio can be a useful tool for comparing the profitability of alternative products. The total annual fixed cost, 100,500,000 Rupees,[6] is a normal level of fixed overhead cost and fixed sales and distribution costs that are expensed each year. Operating above the normal level might require additional productive capacity, which could incur additional fixed costs of both types.

4.2.3 Basic CVP model: break-even and target profit

The basic profitability model shown in Figure 4.1 is also known as a Cost-Volume-Profit (CVP) model because given a competitive sales price, product costs and volumes drive profits. A usual feature of CVP models is that revenues and costs are modelled as linear relations without time lags. These simplifications typically are justified when the firm is producing within the normal or 'relevant' range of activity when revenue and cost functions might be approximately linear. Break-even analysis computes the volume or quantity of sales and production activity that will generate a contribution margin exactly equal to fixed costs (**break-even**) or fixed costs plus a profit target (**target break-even**). One may use the following symbols to create an algebraic model that can be solved for the desired quantity, Q_{BE}:

Q_{BE} = (zero-profit) break-even or target break-even quantity

P = sales price per unit

V = total variable costs per unit

F = total fixed costs per period

T = target profit (which is zero at break-even or positive at target break-even)

$$Q_{BE} = \frac{F + T}{P - V}$$

The **time to break-even**, or the payback period, is the time needed to recoup an initial outlay from periodic income or cash flow.[7]

[6] In October 2012, 1 USD = 57.9 Rs and 1 Euro = 67.6 Rs.

[7] Chapter 7 considers multiple models of the opportunity cost of investments.

	A	B	C
1	**Conventional Refrigerator Profitability Analysis**		
2	Refrigerator capacity	100	litres
3	Number of parts	200	parts
4	Normal production and sales per annum, Q_N	50,000	units
5	Sales price per unit, P	6,000.00	Rs (Rupees)
6	Direct materials cost per unit, V_{DM}	1,360.00	Rs
7	Direct labor cost per unit, V_{DL}	630.00	Rs
8	Variable manufacturing overhead, V_{OH}	1,100.00	Rs
9	Variable sales and distribution, V_S	300.00	Rs
10	Fixed manufacturing overhead cost per annum, F_M	60,500,000	Rs
11	Fixed sales and distribution cost per annum, F_S	40,000,000	Rs
12	**Annual profit at normal production and sales**		
13	Sales revenue, P x Q_N	300,000,000	= B4*B5
14	Variable cost of sales, $V_{DM}+V_{DL}+V_{OH}+V_S$	169,500,000	= SUM(B6:B9)
15	Contribution margin	130,500,000	= B13-B14
16	Total fixed costs, F_M+F_S	100,500,000	= B10 + B11
17	Operating profit	30,000,000	= B15-B16
18	Profit margin ratio	10.0%	= B17/B13

Figure 4.1 Refrigerator profitability analysis

At normal capacity, the Refrigerator Division generates an operating profit of 30 million Rs. If IAM had invested a total of 135 million Rs to establish the Division, its time to break-even is:

$$\textbf{Time to break-even} = \frac{135{,}000{,}000\ RS}{30{,}000{,}000\ RS \text{ per year}} = 4.5 \text{ years}$$

IAM may adapt a basic profitability analysis, such as that from the conventional refrigerator example, to compute the desired quantity, as shown in Figure 4.2. Achieving a zero profit target (i.e. just enough contribution margin to cover fixed costs) requires a sales and production break-even quantity of 38 506 units (rounded up). Replacing the zero in cell B30 with a target profit computes the **target break-even** quantity in cell B35. For example, to achieve a profit target of 60 000 000 Rs (double the normal profit), IAM would have to produce and sell 61 494 of the smallest conventional refrigerators. This also may be solved algebraically, as follows:[8]

$$Q_{BE} = \frac{100500000 + 60000000}{6000 - 3390} = 61494 \text{ units}$$

4.2.4 Target costing

Constraints on productive or sales capacity might make increasing output of a particular product an infeasible approach to achieving desired profits. An alternative to target break-even analysis is **target costing,** which computes the desired profit margin (or return on sales), given a competitive price and sales quantity, and the total cost reduction required to

[8] One may use Excel's Solver to find the sales and production activity, QBE, that results in zero total profit. Solver is a very powerful tool that is found within Excel's Data toolbar, but might be an 'add-in' if it has not been used previously.

	A	B	C
20	Conventional refrigerator breakeven analysis		
21	Refrigerator capacity	100	litres
22	Number of parts	200	parts
23	Normal production and sales per annum, Q_N	50,000	units
24	Sales price per unit, P	6,000.00	Rs (Rupees)
25	Direct materials cost per unit, V_{DM}	1,360.00	Rs
26	Direct labor cost per unit, V_{DL}	630.00	Rs
27	Variable manufacturing overhead, V_{OH}	1,100.00	Rs
28	Variable sales and distribution, V_S	300.00	Rs
29	Fixed manufacturing overhead cost per annum, F_M	60,500,000	Rs
30	Fixed sales and distribution cost per annum, F_S	40,000,000	Rs
31	Target profit, T	0	Rs
32	Annual breakeven analysis within normal range of activity		
33	Total fixed costs, F_M+F_S	100,500,000	= B29+B30
34	Target profit, T	-	= B31
35	Divide by contribution margin per unit	2,610	= B24-SUM(B25:B28)
36	Breakeven sales and production activity, units, Q_{BE}	38,506	= (B33+B34)/B35
37	Profit margin ratio at breakeven activity	0.0%	= B34/(B36*B24)

Figure 4.2 Break-even analysis

achieve that profit.[9] Using the example data in Figures 4.1 or 4.2, consider the cost reduction required if the appliance manufacturer wished to earn a 20-percent return on sales (at the normal sales volume) of its smallest conventional refrigerator:

Target sales revenue.....	300 000 000 Rs
Target return on sales at 20%.....	60 000 000 Rs
Target total cost.....	240 000 000 Rs
Minus current total variable and fixed cost	270 000 000 Rs
Required cost reduction.....	(30 000 000) Rs

The total **target cost** is the target sales revenue minus the targeted return. If the manufacturer could reduce annual total variable and fixed costs by 30 million Rupees, and maintain the target sales volume and price, this product would generate a return on sales (profit margin ratio) of 20%.

Although target costing appears to be only a slight modification of the CVP model, target costing places great emphasis on designing inputs and processes to reduce costs sufficiently for the desired profitability, without compromising customer value and price. Research shows that target costing does control costs, but it can induce high levels of stress and can have adverse consequences on individuals and firm efficiency.[10] Research has also shown that significant cost savings are most achievable at the design stage, before inputs and processes are set. Let us adapt the basic financial model to the appliance manufacturer's target costing analysis of the proposed smaller and more efficient refrigerator for the Indian market (nicknamed the 'Nano').

[9] Target costing is discussed more thoroughly in Chapter 4.
[10] Yutaka Kato 1993.

After extensive marketing research, IAM determined that characteristics of a successful 'Nano' refrigerator include:

- small size and portability;
- sales price that was no more than one-third of its currently smallest unit;
- improved insulation to withstand frequent power outages;
- at least a 50% reduction in electricity consumption per unit of capacity;
- reduced repair frequency and cost.

Marketing research further indicated that a successful 'Nano' should sell 1.1 m units over a five-year period. After this time period, the product may require significant re-design to maintain marketability.

Design engineers and cost analysts responded with a prototype design with the following features and expected costs:

- 43 litre capacity, which would decrease energy consumption proportionately.
- Reduction from 200 conventional parts to 20 higher technology parts, which would reduce direct materials by 25% and direct labour by 60% (after reaching an efficient scale of production) and would reduce repair frequency and cost by at least 50%.
- 4-hour cooling retention without power by using innovative insulation that would increase direct materials cost by 5%. When combined with the parts effect the Nano would have $(1 + .05) \times (1 - .25) = 78.75\%$ of the conventional direct materials cost, or a 21.25% reduction.
- Variable manufacturing overhead would decrease by 80%.
- Fixed manufacturing overhead would drop by 60%.

Finance and Marketing personnel collaborated to develop a village oriented sales and distribution system that promised a 50% reduction in fixed and variable sales and distribution costs compared to usual distribution channels. This approach would create a system of individual distributors, supported by micro-finance institutions.

The question facing top management is whether this combination of features and design innovations lead to a profitable product. Consider the target costing analysis in Figure 4.3, which assumes that the company desires the Nano to be at least as profitable as the smallest conventional refrigerator; that is, earning a 10% profit margin or return on sales.

The profitability analysis in Figure 4.3 uses Nano revenue and cost estimates that are derived from expected changes from an existing conventional product. This analysis forecasts that the Nano could be profitable, although at only a 4.3% profit margin (cell B56). This is a 'razor thin' margin, which likely is quite sensitive to price and cost estimates. These fluctuations could occur in pricing, manufacturing, distribution and coordination with external, micro-finance entities.

IAM might believe that the very large, untapped market justifies launching a product with such a low margin. The company could point to significant environmental and social benefits from this product that might enhance its standing in the market and demonstrate its good citizenship. These include health benefits to those who could not afford refrigeration, reduced energy consumption and creation of micro-distribution entrepreneurs. IAM might also find new export markets for this reliable, low energy product.

However, and because the company's competitive position has eroded, it is risky for IAM to introduce another marginally profitable product, especially when competitors might respond with a similar product. The target costing analysis does show that the product can achieve conventional profitability, if the marketing and design personnel create a 114 million Rs cost reduction (cell B63) over the five-year period (22.8 million Rs per year). If this level of cost reduction (or more) is not possible, the product may not be feasible, and a market opportunity would be lost.

	A	B	C	D	E
39	"Nano" Refrigerator Target Costing Analysis				
40		Conventional	Cost Changes	"Nano" Estimates	
41	Refrigerator capacity	100		43	
42	Number of parts	200		20	
43	Target sales price per unit, P_T	6,000	-66.67%	2,000	=B43*(1+C43)
44	Direct materials cost per unit, V_{DM}	1,360	-21.25%	1,071	=B44*(1+C44)
45	Direct labor cost per unit, V_{DL}	630	-60.00%	252	=B45*(1+C45)
46	Variable manufacturing overhead, V_{OH}	1,100	-80.00%	220	=B46*(1+C46)
47	Variable sales and distribution, V_S	300	-50.00%	150	=B47*(1+C47)
48	Fixed manufacturing overhead cost per annum, F_M	60,500,000	-60.00%	24,200,000	=B48*(1+C48)
49	Fixed sales and distribution cost per annum, F_S	40,000,000	-50.00%	20,000,000	=B49*(1+C49)
50	"Nano" Profitability Analysis	Nano Forecast			
51	Analysis period, years	5			
52	Target sales volume over the analysis period, units, Q_T	1,000,000			
53	Target sales revenue, $P_T \times Q_T$	2,000,000,000	=B52*D43		
54	Variable cost of sales, $(V_{DM}+V_{DL}+V_{OH}+V_S) \times QT$	1,693,000,000	=B52*SUM(D44:D47)		
55	Contribution margin	307,000,000	=B53-B54		
56	Total fixed costs, F_M+F_S	221,000,000	=B51*(D48+D49)		
57	Operating profit	86,000,000	=B55-B56		
58	Forecast profit margin ratio (return on sales)	4.3%	=B57/B53		
59	"Nano" Target Cost Analysis	Nano Target			
60	Target sales revenue, $P_T \times Q_T$	2,000,000,000	=B53		
61	Target profit margin (return on sales) percentage	10%			
62	Target profit	200,000,000	=B60*B61		
63	Target total cost (variable and fixed)	1,800,000,000	=B60-B62		
64	Forecasted total cost (variable and fixed)	1,914,000,000	=B54+B56		
65	Required cost reduction	**(114,000,000)**	=B63-B64		

Figure 4.3 Target costing analysis

4.2.5 Alternative cost and revenue drivers

Production and sales activities are the most commonly used drivers of costs and revenues in financial models. However, production and sales activities can include more dimensions than merely product quantity produced or sold. The chapter's example indicates several additional dimensions that affect the Nano refrigerator's revenues and costs. The Nano is designed to serve a particular customer base that has specific needs that translate into processes, prices and costs that differ from the company's current customer base. One should expect additional dimensions of revenue and cost drivers whenever serving customer needs require product or customer service differences. Likewise, employing different technologies or distribution channels most likely indicate revenue and cost driver dimensions beyond mere product quantities. Table 4.2 presents just a few examples of modelling additional dimensions of revenue and cost drivers.[11]

[11] Chapter 6 discusses details of cost estimation and modelling the effects of multiple cost drivers.

Table 4.2 Model dimensions

Drivers of	Drivers beyond product quantity	Modeled by
Revenue	Product features	Price and analysis for each product (feature)
	Customer type (taste, risk)	Price and analysis for each customer type
	Customer	Analysis for each customer
	Season or location	Season and location
Cost	Product complexity	Cost per part
	Product innovation	Cost of development (amortised)
	Product customisation	Cost of customised features
	Process technology	Cost per process batch, step or unit of time
	Distribution channels	Cost and analysis per channel
	Customer (type)	Cost and analysis for each customer (type)
	Scales of operation	Costs outside the relevant range
	Season or location	Season and location
	...	...

Modelling the drivers could be done with separate analyses for each dimension. Alternatively, one could create a model with alternative data entries (e.g. selected from lists), and choice of each alternative driver results in different financial outcomes. Clearly models that can account for all of these differences (and more) can be large, complex and costly to maintain with up to date information. Nonetheless, more complex models can be built by replicating or extending the basic models used so far in this chapter.

4.2.6 Modelling pro-forma financial statements

The financial outputs of a complete business model include forecasted or pro-forma financial statements. The full set of statements can be necessary to assure that all expected revenues, costs, cash and accrual transactions are properly anticipated. While modelling the profitability of a new product, it is possible to overlook working capital needs (especially cash), for example, that could strain the organisation's financial position. The chapter's example of profitability analysis of the new Nano refrigerator indicated that the product can be profitable over a five-year period, particularly if cost reductions are achieved. However, nowhere does that basic analysis account for cash, inventory, and process investments required to produce and deliver the expected quantity of product. Even a relatively simple business model shows linkages between expected transactions and the set of financial statements. The linked inputs and outcomes can alert managers to inadequacies in key resources, such as cash, that could impair the success of an otherwise profitable business alternative.

4.2.7 Financial ratio analyses

Another justification for building a comprehensive business model is its ability to forecast financial ratios based on financial statement outcomes. Many organisations, either by policy or because of contracts with external parties such as lenders, seek to maintain certain levels of key financial ratios. For example, many debt agreements contain covenants that obligate the maintenance of liquidity and leverage ratios at specified levels throughout the duration of an agreement. Although no one should believe that pro forma financial statements are completely accurate predictions, these statements can be good sources for the assessment of the risks that a firm might violate its financial ratio policies or contractual obligations. Note that actual business models can be large and complex, but they are constructed and function by mimicking a budget process to do the following: [12]

1. Forecast future activity levels (e.g. sales and production quantities), prices and costs.
2. Starting with an initial financial position (beginning balance sheet), prepare supporting schedules that forecast cash and accrual transactions to support activity levels.
3. Forecast the resulting financial statements for the first period (balance sheet, statement of cash flows, income statement, ending balance sheet).
4. Compute key financial ratios from financial statement outcomes.
5. Repeat for subsequent periods.

We return to the Nano refrigerator example to illustrate the concepts of modelling pro-forma financial statements and several key financial ratios.

IAM is organised internally into several profit centres,[13] including the Refrigerator Division that planned to introduce the Nano refrigerator to its line of conventional refrigerators. Although each profit centre operated independently, the company monitors plans and results closely to insure that each division contributes to profitability and operates within the company's financial constraints.

The Division uses a five-year business model for budgeting and planning purposes that was built and revised according to the five budget process steps outlined previously. The business model's first step, forecasting future activity levels, includes the addition of the Nano sales, cost and revenue data to the business model. This step includes extending the first year input data to the five-year modelling window. Figure 4.4 presents the Division's model-input data that projects 3% growth in sales, prices and costs following the first year (blue-filled cells).[14] One of the great advantages to using spreadsheet software is that one may copy and paste formulas from the first year to all subsequent years. These projected data include all the variables needed (in this simplified case) to model the planned cash and accrual transactions that drive expected changes in financial position necessary to organise resources and execute productive activities to fulfil the periodic sales forecasts.[15]

---

[12] See Chapter 5 for discussions of budget processes.

[13] Chapters 8 and 11 addresses issues of organisational design and responsibility.

[14] One might reasonably ask whether the data input estimates are accurate, and 'what if' they are not? Inaccurate input data and incorrect structure of the model's relations comprise 'modelling risk.' We defer the very important discussions of modelling dimensions of risk to the next section.

[15] The reader may wish to refer to the chapter's electronic supplement and work through the details of these and other Figures and tables that are prepared from the example's business model.

ProForma Financial Statements - Refrigerator Division					
1. Activity, Cost, and Revenue Data	Year 1	Year 2	Year 3	Year 4	Year 5
Refrigerator Division Costs and Policies					
Annual sales and price/cost growth	0%	3%	3%	3%	3%
General and administrative costs, G&A (000 Rs)	2,500,000	2,575,000	2,652,250	2,731,818	2,813,772
Minimum cash balance (000 Rs)	1,500,000	1,545,000	1,591,350	1,639,091	1,688,263
Minimum direct materials balance (000 Rs)	750,000	772,500	795,675	819,545	844,132
Sales collections within a specific year					
Cash sales percentage	90%				
Credit sales percentage	10%				
Payments for inventory within a specific year					
Cash purchases percentage	60%				
Credit purchases percentage	40%				
Borrowing rate (annual)	8%				
Conventional Refrigerators (000 Rs, except per unit)					
Sales volume, units per annum	2,000	2,060	2,122	2,185	2,251
Average sales price per unit, P	13,200	13,596	14,004	14,424	14,857
Average direct materials cost per unit, V_{DM}	4,080	4,202	4,328	4,458	4,592
Average direct labor cost per unit, V_{DL}	1,890	1,947	2,005	2,065	2,127
Variable manufacturing overhead per unit, V_{OH}	3,300	3,399	3,501	3,606	3,714
Variable sales and distribution per unit, V_S	900	927	955	983	1,013
Fixed manufacturing overhead cost per annum, F_M	1,815,000	1,869,450	1,925,534	1,983,300	2,042,798
Fixed sales and distribution cost per annum, F_S	1,200,000	1,236,000	1,273,080	1,311,272	1,350,611
Nano Refrigerator (000 Rs, except per unit)					
Sales volume, units per annum	100	150	250	300	200
Target sales price per unit, P_T	2,000	2,060	2,122	2,185	2,251
Direct materials cost per unit, V_{DM}	1,071	1,103	1,136	1,170	1,205
Direct labor cost per unit, V_{DL}	252	260	267	275	284
Variable manufacturing overhead per unit, V_{OH}	220	227	233	240	248
Variable sales and distribution per unit, V_S	150	155	159	164	169
Fixed manufacturing overhead cost per annum, F_M	24,200	24,926	25,674	26,444	27,237
Fixed sales and distribution cost per annum, F_S	20,000	20,600	21,218	21,855	22,510

Figure 4.4 Refrigerator Division's data

A	B	C	D	E	F
	3. Forecasted Financial Statements				
Refrigerator Division Beginning Balance Sheet (000 Rs)	Beg. of Year 1	Beg. of Year 2	Beg. of Year 3	Beg. of Year 4	Beg. of Year 5
Assets					
Cash	1,500,000				
Accounts receivable	3,000,000				
Inventories	1,000,000				
Plant, property & equipment (net)	12,500,000				
Total assets	18,000,000				
Liabilities and Equities					
Accounts payable	4,000,000				
Notes payable	5,000,000				
Interest payable	400,000				
Stockholders equity	8,600,000				
Total equities	18,000,000				

Figure 4.5 Refrigerator Division beginning balance sheet

Step 2 uses the input data from Figure 4.4 and the beginning balance sheet (Figure 4.5) to prepare prospective cash collections, disbursements and accruals to move to the next financial position. Because this type of plan is almost always prepared in advance, the beginning balance sheet itself is usually budgeted or estimated (also known as 'pro forma'). The balance sheet positions for any subsequent year cannot be known until after modelling the prior year's ending financial position (which becomes the subsequent year's beginning balance sheet).

A	B	C	D	E	F
2. Supporting Cash and Accrual Transactions	Year 1	Year 2	Year 3	Year 4	Year 5
Sales forecast (000 Rs)	26,600,000	28,316,760	30,243,883	32,178,617	33,892,934
Schedule of Cash Collections (000 Rs):	Year 1	Year 2	Year 3	Year 4	Year 5
Current cash sales	23,940,000	25,485,084	27,219,494	28,960,755	30,503,640
Collections on account	3,000,000	2,660,000	2,831,676	3,024,388	3,217,862
Total Collections	26,940,000	28,145,084	30,051,170	31,985,143	33,721,502
Direct Material Purchases Budget (000 Rs)	Year 1	Year 2	Year 3	Year 4	Year 5
Direct material for production	8,267,100	8,822,414	9,468,208	10,094,560	10,577,928
Add: Minimum direct materials balance	750,000	772,500	795,675	819,545	844,132
Total Required	9,017,100	9,594,914	10,263,883	10,914,105	11,422,059
Deduct: Beginning direct materials balance	1,000,000	750,000	772,500	795,675	819,545
Required Purchases	8,017,100	8,844,914	9,491,383	10,118,430	10,602,514
Schedule of Payments for Direct Mat'l Purchases (000 Rs)	Year 1	Year 2	Year 3	Year 4	Year 5
Payments on account	4,000,000	3,206,840	3,537,965	3,796,553	4,047,372
Current payments	4,810,260	5,306,948	5,694,830	6,071,058	6,361,509
Total direct material purchase payments	8,810,260	8,513,788	9,232,795	9,867,611	10,408,881
Schedule of Payments for Periodic Costs (000 Rs)	Year 1	Year 2	Year 3	Year 4	Year 5
Direct labor cost	3,805,200	4,049,136	4,321,260	4,596,128	4,845,117
Variable manufacturing overhead cost	6,622,000	7,035,930	7,486,708	7,952,865	8,410,205
Fixed manuracturing overhead cost	1,839,200	1,894,376	1,951,207	2,009,743	2,070,036
Variable sales and distribution cost	1,815,000	1,932,795	2,065,700	2,198,467	2,313,951
Fixed sales and distribution costs	1,220,000	1,256,600	1,294,298	1,333,127	1,373,121
General and administrative costs	2,500,000	2,575,000	2,652,250	2,731,818	2,813,772
Total periodic cost payments	17,801,400	18,743,837	19,771,423	20,822,148	21,826,201

Figure 4.6 Supporting cash and accrual transactions

For simplicity, all transactions in these schedules are cash and the only driver is each year's sales forecast (row 35 in Figure 4.6). For example, the Year 1 cash collections are computed as follows from the sales forecast:

Sales forecast (000 Rs)	26 600 000 Rs
Current cash sales = 26,000,000 × 0.8 =	23 940 000
Collections on account = prev. Acct Rec =	3 000 000
Total Collections =	26 940 000 Rs

Step 3 of the business model combines the supporting schedules with the beginning balance sheet to prepare a pro forma statement of cash flows and an income statement for the first year. These statements are the changes in financial position that result in the year's ending pro forma balance sheet.[16] Each year's ending balance sheet becomes the next year's beginning balance sheet, and the modelling cycle begins for each subsequent year. The suite of financial statements in Figure 4.7 and 4.8 complete the example's business model for the five-year period.

The beginning balance sheets (Figure 4.5) commence for the first year from the data input section. Subsequent balance sheets are the same as the prior year's ending balance sheet (Figure 4.8). The statement of cash flows focuses on changes in cash position, which are derived from schedules in the previous figures.

The financing section demonstrates how the firm might manage its cash position with short term borrowing and repayments. This section assumes that borrowing takes place at the beginning of the year and any repayments are at the end of the year. Thus, any borrowed short term funds accrue interest for an entire year. Note that monthly operating

[16] This balance sheet lists liabilities from short-term to long-term.

A	B	C	D	E	F
	3. Forecasted Financial Statements				
Refrigerator Division Beginning Balance Sheet (000 Rs)	Beg. of Year 1	Beg. of Year 2	Beg. of Year 3	Beg. of Year 4	Beg. of Year 5
Assets					
Cash	1,500,000	1,500,000	1,545,000	1,591,350	1,639,091
Accounts receivable	3,000,000	2,660,000	2,831,676	3,024,388	3,217,862
Inventories	1,000,000	750,000	772,500	795,675	819,545
Plant, property & equipment (net)	12,500,000	12,500,000	12,500,000	12,500,000	12,500,000
Total assets	18,000,000	17,410,000	17,649,176	17,911,413	18,176,497
Liabilities and Equities					
Accounts payable	4,000,000	3,206,840	3,537,965	3,796,553	4,047,372
Notes payable	5,000,000	5,071,660	4,634,934	4,040,064	3,163,215
Interest payable	400,000	405,733	405,733	370,795	323,205
Stockholders equity	8,600,000	8,725,767	9,070,544	9,704,001	10,642,705
Total equities	18,000,000	17,410,000	17,649,176	17,911,413	18,176,497
A	B	C	D	E	F
Pro Forma Statement of Cash Flows (000 Rs)	Year 1	Year 2	Year 3	Year 4	Year 5
Sources of Cash					
Beginning Cash Balance	1,500,000	1,500,000	1,545,000	1,591,350	1,639,091
Cash Collections	26,940,000	28,145,084	30,051,170	31,985,143	33,721,502
Total Cash Available	28,440,000	29,645,084	31,596,170	33,576,493	35,360,592
Uses of Cash					
For Inventory Purchases	8,810,260	8,513,788	9,232,795	9,867,611	10,408,881
For Operating Expenses	17,801,400	18,743,837	19,771,423	20,822,148	21,826,201
For Interest	400,000	405,733	405,733	370,795	323,205
Total Payments	27,011,660	27,663,358	29,409,950	31,060,554	32,558,287
Required Cash Balance	1,500,000	1,545,000	1,591,350	1,639,091	1,688,263
Total Cash Required	28,511,660	29,208,358	31,001,300	32,699,644	34,246,550
Cash Excess(deficit)	(71,660)	436,726	594,870	876,849	1,114,042
Financing:					
Short-term borrowing	71,660	-	-	-	-
Repayments on debt	-	436,726	594,870	876,849	1,114,042
Ending cash Balance	1,500,000	1,545,000	1,591,350	1,639,091	1,688,263
Net cash flow	-	45,000	46,350	47,741	49,173
Net cash flow from operations	(71,660)	481,726	641,220	924,590	1,163,215

Figure 4.7 Forecasted financial statements

A	B	C	D	E	F
Pro Forma Income Statement (000 Rs)	**Year 1**	**Year 2**	**Year 3**	**Year 4**	**Year 5**
Sales	26,600,000	28,316,760	30,243,883	32,178,617	33,892,934
Variable cost of sales	20,509,300	21,840,275	23,341,875	24,842,020	26,147,201
Contribution Margin	6,090,700	6,476,486	6,902,007	7,336,597	7,745,733
Fixed expenses:					
Fixed manufacturing overhead	1,839,200	1,894,376	1,951,207	2,009,743	2,070,036
Fixed sales and distribution costs	1,220,000	1,256,600	1,294,298	1,333,127	1,373,121
General and administrative costs	2,500,000	2,575,000	2,652,250	2,731,818	2,813,772
Interest expense	405,733	405,733	370,795	323,205	253,057
Total Expense	5,964,933	6,131,709	6,268,550	6,397,893	6,509,986
Net Operating Income	125,767	344,777	633,457	938,704	1,235,747
A	B	C	D	E	F
Pro Forma (ending) Balance Sheet (000 Rs)	**Year 1**	**Year 2**	**Year 3**	**Year 4**	**Year 5**
Assets					
Cash	1,500,000	1,545,000	1,591,350	1,639,091	1,688,263
Accounts receivable	2,660,000	2,831,676	3,024,388	3,217,862	3,389,293
Inventory	750,000	772,500	795,675	819,545	844,132
Plant, property & equipment(net)	12,500,000	12,500,000	12,500,000	12,500,000	12,500,000
Total assets	17,410,000	17,649,176	17,911,413	18,176,497	18,421,688
Liabilities and Equities					
Accounts payable	3,206,840	3,537,965	3,796,553	4,047,372	4,241,006
Interest payable	405,733	405,733	370,795	323,205	253,057
Notes payable	5,071,660	4,634,934	4,040,064	3,163,215	2,049,173
Stockholders' equity	8,725,767	9,070,544	9,704,001	10,642,705	11,878,453
Total liabilities & equities	17,410,000	17,649,176	17,911,413	18,176,497	18,421,688

Figure 4.8 Pro forma financial statement

budgets typically make similar simplifying assumptions. The short term borrowing that is modelled in the rows titled "financing" is of particular interest because a) the Division will need to pre-arrange the availability of funds for the first year, and b) the forecasted sales growth drives eventual repayments of the borrowing from positive net cash flows from operations. It appears that the introduction of the Nano does not impair the division's financial position.

Finally, the Refrigerator Division has the modelling tools for a business case to IAM for the introduction of the Nano refrigerator. The Division and IAM can use the financial model to judge how the Division contributes to meeting the company's financial objectives and constraints. One of the most important financial constraints is a debt covenant that stipulated the maintenance of an overall current ratio of at least 2.0, an interest coverage ratio of at least 2.0, and a debt to value ratio of no more than 0.50. The ratios were defined as follows:

$$\text{Current ratio} = \text{current assets} \div \text{current liabilities}$$

$$\text{Interest coverage ratio} = \text{earnings before interest and tax (EBIT)} \div \text{interest expense}$$

$$\text{Debt to value ratio} = \text{total liabilities} \div \text{total assets}$$

Figure 4.9 compares pro forma calculations of the Refrigerator Division's key financial ratios, with and without the introduction of the Nano.[17] Two things stand out from this comparison. First, the Refrigerator Division does not meet all of IAM's financial-ratio targets.[18] The Division's current and interest coverage ratios initially fall below the targets of 2.0. The current ratio deteriorates, but the interest coverage ratio is projected to improve steeply over time. The debt to value ratio initially is barely below the limit of 0.50 but shows consistent improvement over time. Second, the planned introduction of the Nano over the five-year horizon appears to worsen the current ratio, but improves the interest coverage ratio and debt to value ratio. This appears to be a favourable product, but the margins of improvement clearly depend on inputs to the model. It is prudent to investigate the risks to I AM posed by the Refrigerator Division.

A	B	C	D	E	F
4. Key Financial Ratios, Refrigerator Division	**Year 1**	**Year 2**	**Year 3**	**Year 4**	**Year 5**
Current ratio - Target	2.000	2.000	2.000	2.000	2.000
Current ratio - Pro Forma with Nano	1.359	1.306	1.299	1.299	1.318
Current ratio - Pro Forma without Nano	1.370	1.320	1.321	1.324	1.333
Interest coverage ratio - Target	2.000	2.000	2.000	2.000	2.000
Interest coverage ratio - Pro Forma with Nano	1.310	1.850	2.708	3.904	5.883
Interest coverage ratio - Pro Forma without Nano	1.341	1.842	2.602	3.665	5.538
Debt to value ratio - Target	0.500	0.500	0.500	0.500	0.500
Debt to value ratio - Pro Forma with Nano	0.499	0.486	0.458	0.414	0.355
Debt to value ratio - Pro Forma without Nano	0.497	0.485	0.458	0.417	0.360

Figure 4.9 Key financial ratios

[17] Financial ratios without Nano are computed by setting Nano sales forecasts and fixed costs to zero (entire model not tabulated).

[18] Cells with no shading denote performance better than the goal, and cells with shading denote performance worse than the goal.

4.3 Modelling risk and uncertainty

The preceding discussions imply that the inputs and their mathematical manipulations are known to be correct, and decision making is simply choosing the alternative with the highest beneficial outcome. That is, the implied assumption is that financial models are 'deterministic', but this is not the case. Business decision making is never made under conditions of certainty about the correctness of the model or knowing for certain the future outcomes of current actions. That is, business decision making is risky. **Risk** is a source of danger or loss, or the exposure to, or chance of, a loss or misfortune. Many dimensions of risk exist, such as health, reputation, legal and so on. This chapter focuses on modelling **financial risk,** which is the quantified likelihood of loss or less than expected returns. It is a natural extension of financial models to describe and quantify an organisation's exposure to uncertainty, ambiguity and financial risk.[19]

4.3.1 Uncertainty and ambiguity

Uncertainty is the state of not knowing future conditions or outcomes (and being exposed to risk), but being able to model future economic conditions and decision outcomes as probability distributions over the possibilities. The sources of knowledge of the parameters of these probability distributions (e.g. means, variances and so on) are hotly debated. The Classical or objective view is that probability distributions must be derived from historical data. The Bayesian or subjective view is that a probability distribution may be derived as a degree of belief from one's experience and judgment. Wherever one sides on this debate, the intended result is that the probabilities of future conditions and outcomes can be quantified and used in turn to quantify financial risk.

Ambiguity, is the state of not knowing future conditions or outcomes, but being **unable** to describe or model future conditions or outcomes as probability distributions. That is, one has neither historical data nor the informed judgment on which to base distribution parameters or degrees of belief over possible future outcomes. This can be a precarious decision making context. Nassim Taleb argues that we often do not know what the possibilities are. Therefore, the risk of an unforeseeable, calamitous financial outcome (also known as a 'Black Swan') cannot be modelled with conventional statistical analysis that assumes knowable, stable probability distributions for possible outcomes. So we should approach the task of modelling financial risk itself with caution.

4.3.2 Modelling financial risk

Modelling financial risk entails modelling the sources of risk, which are the inputs to the model, such as revenue and cost functions and uncontrollable economic conditions. It is abundantly clear from the events of 2008 onward, that many financial managers either did not understand the importance of modelling financial risk or did not sufficiently question

[19] Chapter 2 discusses details and challenges of risky business decision making.

the assumptions of their financial models. Key assumptions that are often outside the boundaries of a financial model, which by necessity is a simplification of reality, can expose the organisation to risks of capability, liquidity, funding, regulatory change, credit and competition that cannot be easily modelled at this time. Yet it would be a mistake not to address these sources of risk that can greatly affect the typically modelled relations of price, cost and quantity. Although researchers are pushing the boundaries of the sources of risk, the risks can emanate from assumptions about the organisation's resources, decision rights and business processes, and customer/supplier relations should at least be challenged and established qualitatively.[20]

Typically, financial models quantify the impacts of a) specific levels of inputs within b) linear cost and revenue functions (i.e. the CVP model). One cannot know for certain what future input values such as sales forecasts will be, but one may assess the financial risk from any or all of the inputs' varying singly or together, and either randomly or by reasonably likely amounts. The basic methods covered in this section of the chapter are outlined in Table 4.3

Table 4.3 Basic methods

Model of financial risk	Single or multiple changes to inputs	Fixed or random amounts
Deterministic (no risk analysis)	None	None
Sensitivity analysis	Single changes	Fixed amounts
Scenario analysis	Multiple changes (also known as scenario)	Fixed amounts
Monte Carlo analysis	Single or multiple changes	Random amounts

The quantified financial risk would be the change in a financial outcome of interest, driven by a change or scenario. For example, a variation in an input, such as unit sales, might drive a key financial ratio below the level required by a debt covenant, putting the firm at risk of default and higher costs of capital. The basic methods to model financial risk may offer different assessments of the risk of loss or misfortune. The ability to conduct quantified risk analysis perhaps the most powerful attribute of financial modelling.

4.3.3 Sensitivity analysis

Sensitivity analysis measures the impacts on financial outcomes from changing a single input to an alternative value. Sensitivity analysis queries the financial model: 'What if one of the model inputs is a different value than expected? Higher or lower?' Often these higher or lower values correspond to best case or worst case situations, but one may model the financial risk of as many different values of a single input as seem likely.[21] Because the proper financial

[20] For example, see J.R. Segerstrom, 'Are financial models really to blame?' and Y. Shi and T. Manning, 'Understanding business models and business model risks.'

[21] If one is able to place an objective or subjective probability on each likely realisation of a single input, one can compute an 'expected value' of a financial outcome, but Monte Carlo analysis, which is discussed later, would be a more efficient method.

model is built entirely from formulas (apart from data input, perhaps), changing an input value cascades the change through the entire model to each financial outcome. A useful measure of the impact on a financial outcome is its elasticity to the input change. The **financial elasticity** is measured as the percentage change in the financial outcome divided by the percentage change in the model input.

$$\text{Financial elasticity} = \frac{\%\ \text{Change in financial outcome}}{\%\ \text{Change in model input}}$$

Financial elasticity with an absolute value greater than 1.0 (or a lower value if desired) indicates high sensitivity to the input change. A full sensitivity analysis evaluates the impact and elasticity of every model input. The inputs causing the highest elasticities may be the greatest sources of risk and deserve special scrutiny for accuracy or improvement. These are often the primary cost and revenue drivers in the financial model, and also where model relations might not be linear (e.g. out of the range of normal operations).

The IAM Refrigerator Division's business model may be queried with sensitivity analysis on each of the model's inputs shaded cells in Figures 4.1 to 4.4). One could test the sensitivity of each of the important financial outcomes to each of the inputs, but the method is identical for each query. For economy of presentation, but with no loss of generality, let us query the model for the sensitivity of its three key financial ratios in Figure 4.9 to possible changes in Nano unit sales in the first year, which makes this an incomplete analysis. One of IAM's market researchers determined that it is equally likely that first-year Nano unit sales could be 40, 100 or 160 thousand units, which the Refrigerator Division considers worst, most likely and best case sales conditions. Without changing any other inputs, a financial analyst adapted the business model for the sensitivity analysis as shown in Figure 4.10. Each of the inputs listed under the 'Worst' and 'Best' columns could be changed to worst and best case values to assess the impact of each change on each of the model's first-year outcomes.[22]

If the different Nano unit sales are equally likely (probability of each = 1/3 and no better or worse than the estimated values), IAM appears to face little additional financial risk from the Nano introduction. In the case of 100 000 Nano units sold in the first year, the division contributes favourably to meeting only IAM's debt to value ratio constraint, but this contribution improves in subsequent years as per Figure 4.9. Unsurprisingly, the best case generally promises relatively better first-year results; however, the current ratio decreases slightly because of increased accounts payable for purchases of materials for production. In the worst case of 40,000 units sold, the Division's financial ratio performance is generally slightly worse. The new product appears to be benign but not the dramatic improvement that the Division appears to need.

[22] The basic model was rearranged for presentation of financial ratio outcomes. Several approaches to sensitivity analysis in Excel are: a) create data lists for each input with Excel's Data Validation and Copy-Paste Special-Values the outcomes or b) use Scenario Manager to change inputs and collect outcome information. See Excel's 'data Lists'

ProForma Financial Statements - Refrigerator Division - Sensitivity Analysis			
1. Activity, Cost, and Revenue Data, Year 1	**Most Likely**	**Worst**	**Best**
Refrigerator Division Costs and Policies			
Annual sales and price/cost growth	0%	0%	0%
General and administrative costs, G&A (000 Rs)	2,500,000	2,500,000	2,500,000
Minimum cash balance (000 Rs)	1,500,000	1,500,000	1,500,000
Minimum direct materials balance (000 Rs)	750,000	750,000	750,000
Sales collections within a specific year			
Cash sales percentage	90%	90%	90%
Credit sales percentage	10%	10%	10%
Payments for inventory within a specific year			
Cash purchases percentage	60%	60%	60%
Credit purchases percentage			
Borrowing rate (annual)	8%	8%	8%
ProForma Financial Ratios - Refrigerator Division - Sensitivity Analysis			
Conventional Refrigerators (000 Rs, except per unit)			
Sales volume, units per annum	2,000	2,000	2,000
Average sales price per unit, P	13,200	13,200	13,200
Average direct materials cost per unit, V_{DM}	4,080	4,080	4,080
Average direct labor cost per unit, V_{DL}	1,890	1,890	1,890
Variable manufacturing overhead per unit, V_{OH}	3,300	3,300	3,300
Variable sales and distribution per unit, V_S	900	900	900
Fixed manufacturing overhead cost per annum, F_M	1,815,000	1,815,000	1,815,000
Fixed sales and distribution cost per annum, F_S	1,200,000	1,200,000	1,200,000
Nano Refrigerator (000 Rs, except per unit)	**Most Likely**	**Worst**	**Best**
Sales volume, units per annum	100	40	160
Target sales price per unit, P_T	2,000	1,400	2,400
Direct materials cost per unit, V_{DM}	1,071	1,071	1,071
Direct labor cost per unit, V_{DL}	252	252	252
Variable manufacturing overhead per unit, V_{OH}	220	220	220
Variable sales and distribution per unit, V_S	150	150	150
Fixed manufacturing overhead cost per annum, F_M	24,200	24,200	24,200
Fixed sales and distribution cost per annum, F_S	20,000	20,000	20,000
Key Financial Ratios, Refrigerator Division	**Most Likely**	**Worst**	**Best**
Nano unit sales	**100**	**40**	**160**
Current ratio - Target	**2.000**	**2.000**	**2.000**
Current ratio - Pro Forma	**1.359**	**1.363**	**1.357**
Interest coverage ratio - Target	**2.000**	**2.000**	**2.000**
Interest coverage ratio - Pro Forma	**1.310**	**1.193**	**1.535**
Debt to value ratio - Target	**0.500**	**0.500**	**0.500**
Debt to value ratio - Pro Forma	**0.499**	**0.501**	**0.494**

Figure 4.10 Sensitivity of financial ratios

EXAMPLE FROM PRACTICE

The Bureau of Taiwan High Speed Rail built a business model that it could use to test the feasibility of private contractors' proposals and bids and the sensitivity of the model's financial statement predictions of key financial ratios to variability in many key data inputs such as construction costs, maintenance costs and tax rates.[23]

[23] Chang, LM and PH Chen. 2001. BOT Financial Model: Taiwan High Speed Rail Case."

4.3.4 Scenario analysis

It would be the rare situation if the realisation of only one input varied from all of the inputs that make up the most likely case. It is far more likely that the future will unfold as a **scenario,** which is a set of multiple changes of model inputs that together tell a credible story of the future. **Scenario analysis** considers alternative sets of credible changes in inputs that describe alternative unfoldings of the future. Scenario analysis is an improvement in realism over sensitivity analysis, which focuses attention on the impacts of only one input change at a time. For example, a favourable set of changes could include the higher than expected sales volumes and prices that accompany a better than expected reception for a new product. A poor reception would most likely result in reduced sales volumes and prices. Of course, every input to the financial model is likely to be different than expected in the planning or model building stage.

Getting the inputs of diverse managers and customers can be essential in developing alternative scenarios. At a minimum, one should consider at least the most likely, worst case and best case scenarios, but there is practically no limit to the number of alternative scenarios one can present in a properly constructed financial model. Risk is modelled similarly to sensitivity analysis by comparing key financial outcomes driven by alternative scenarios to goals or constraints. If likely scenarios indicate unacceptable levels of risk and, if the scenarios cannot be improved, managers may decide against proceeding. As well, if likely scenarios predict significant gains or improvement, managers may decide to move quickly or to a greater degree.

IAM's financial model for the Refrigerator Division is well suited to the application of scenario analysis.[24] The Division's financial analyst combined information from multiple managers from the Division and from IAM's finance and accounting department. Together they created three scenarios for the Division's five-year planning horizon: Most likely case, Best case, and Worst case scenarios. The financial analyst entered each of the scenarios into the Division's financial model via Excel's Scenario Manager and communicated the summary results to the management team in Figures 4.11 to 4.13. Note that the figures show only the rows with scenarios and resulting financial ratios. All other parts of the financial model are used to generate these results.

ProForma Financial Statements - Refrigerator Division Scenario Analysis					
Scenarios	Annual Growth	Conventional 1st Yr Sales	Conventional 1st Yr Price	Nano 1st Yr Sales	Nano 1st Yr Price
Most likely scenario	3%	2,000	13,200	100	2,000
Best case scenario	4%	2,200	13,400	160	2,400
Worst case scenario	1%	1,700	12,900	40	1,400
Key Financial Ratios, Refrigerator Division	**Year 1**	**Year 2**	**Year 3**	**Year 4**	**Year 5**
Current ratio - Target	2.000	2.000	2.000	2.000	2.000
Current ratio - Pro Forma	1.359	1.306	1.299	1.299	1.318
Interest coverage ratio - Target	2.000	2.000	2.000	2.000	2.000
Interest coverage ratio - Pro Forma	1.310	1.850	2.708	3.904	5.883
Debt to value ratio - Target	0.500	0.500	0.500	0.500	0.500
Debt to value ratio - Pro Forma	0.499	0.486	0.458	0.414	0.355

Figure 4.11 Most likely scenario

[24] Scenario analysis may be implemented with Excel's data list Validation or the Scenario Manager, both found under the Data menu. As noted above, one may create and use as many scenarios, involving as many inputs as one can justify from effort and feasibility perspectives.

The most likely scenario results are in Figure 4.11 and are identical to the earlier results shown in Figure 4.9 (pro forma with Nano). This case shows that the Division always violates the current ratio constraint and always meets the debt to value ratio constraint. The Division gradually improves on its interest coverage ratio performance, and bests it comfortably by the end of the horizon. Whether the Division can be allowed to violate the current ratio constraint depends on how its financial position consolidates with other divisions.

The best case scenario results are in Figure 4.12. The Division projects easily meeting both the current ratio and interest coverage ratio constraints. By the fifth year, the Division also meets the interest coverage ratio constraint, which is undefined (#DIV/0) because the interest expense in the denominator is zero in the 5th year. This might not reflect IAM's desire to maintain a certain debt level; that is, perhaps not all excess cash would be used to repay debt. Nonetheless, this is a rosy scenario indeed.

ProForma Financial Statements - Refrigerator Division Scenario Analysis					
Scenarios	Annual Growth	Conventional 1st Yr Sales	Conventional 1st Yr Price	Nano 1st Yr Sales	Nano 1st Yr Price
Most likely scenario	3%	2,000	13,200	100	2,000
Best case scenario	4%	2,200	13,400	160	2,400
Worst case scenario	1%	1,700	12,900	40	1,400
Key Financial Ratios, Refrigerator Division	**Year 1**	**Year 2**	**Year 3**	**Year 4**	**Year 5**
Current ratio - Target	2.000	2.000	2.000	2.000	2.000
Current ratio - Pro Forma	1.323	1.302	1.320	1.923	2.538
Interest coverage ratio - Target	2.000	2.000	2.000	2.000	2.000
Interest coverage ratio - Pro Forma	4.150	6.428	13.969	561.946	#DIV/0!
Debt to value ratio - Target	0.500	0.500	0.500	0.500	0.500
Debt to value ratio - Pro Forma	0.444	0.360	0.248	0.218	0.199

Figure 4.12 Best case scenario

The worst case scenario in Figure 4.13 is something of a disaster, and all ratios steadily worsen against the constraints. IAM and its Division managers might not want to acknowledge these possible outcomes, but it is far better to be alerted early than late. If this scenario is realised, IAM would face a decision whether to subsidise or drop the Division.

ProForma Financial Statements - Refrigerator Division Scenario Analysis					
Scenarios	Annual Growth	Conventional 1st Yr Sales	Conventional 1st Yr Price	Nano 1st Yr Sales	Nano 1st Yr Price
Most likely scenario	3%	2,000	13,200	100	2,000
Best case scenario	4%	2,200	13,400	160	2,400
Worst case scenario	1%	1,700	12,900	40	1,400
Key Financial Ratios, Refrigerator Division	**Year 1**	**Year 2**	**Year 3**	**Year 4**	**Year 5**
Current ratio - Target	2.000	2.000	2.000	2.000	2.000
Current ratio - Pro Forma	1.382	1.283	1.229	1.182	1.151
Interest coverage ratio - Target	2.000	2.000	2.000	2.000	2.000
Interest coverage ratio - Pro Forma	(1.765)	(1.461)	(1.213)	(1.005)	(0.799)
Debt to value ratio - Target	0.500	0.500	0.500	0.500	0.500
Debt to value ratio - Pro Forma	0.579	0.672	0.771	0.876	0.983

Figure 4.13 Worst case scenario

Because two scenarios are mostly favourable, one might predict that managers will choose to introduce the Nano to the Division's product line. However, the management team would be prudent to have an exit plan and to monitor sales growth and prices carefully, early and often. If the worst case scenario is indeed likely, especially given increased foreign competition in the refrigerator market, IAM may choose to rethink the viability of the entire Refrigerator Division.

4.3.5 Monte Carlo analysis

The previous methods of modelling financial risk (sensitivity and scenario analyses) create alternative financial outcomes based upon specific changes to various model inputs. These approaches may be quite useful to describe ranges of key financial outcomes when conditions and inputs are relatively well known and stable. However, using either method to incorporate all of the possible combinations of inputs, and changes to those inputs, is cumbersome when knowledge of the inputs is limited or conditions change rapidly and unexpectedly. **Monte Carlo analysis** simulates distributions of financial outcomes by selecting random values of uncertain model inputs thousands of times. Monte Carlo analysis expresses uncertainty as probability distributions over inputs and quantifies risk by creating simulated distributions of financial outcomes. Monte Carlo analysis has been used in numerous fields, but seems especially well suited for modelling financial risk. Monte Carlo analysis requires 'only' a financial model such as used in this chapter and probability distributions of possible values of model inputs. Combining these elements into spreadsheet software such as Microsoft Excel on a mid capacity or better personal computer creates an incredibly powerful risk analysis tool.

The critical element to create a useful Monte Carlo model for quantifying risk is developing credible probability distributions for model inputs. As mentioned earlier, classical statisticians require historical evidence from which one can 'objectively' measure means, standard deviations and other probability distributions. Conditions under which one can confidently extrapolate distribution information from past experience might be limited, however, especially if one wants to model the financial risk of new products, markets or organisations. Others (i.e. Bayesians) trust professional judgment to extrapolate degrees of belief (surely based on past experiences) into subjective measures of distribution means and so forth. It seems reasonable to use past information when it is available but to quantify degrees of belief when necessary (with full disclosure in both cases).

Whether objectively or subjectively measured, the most commonly used probability distribution in financial analysis is the Normal distribution that is represented by the well known bell shaped curve.[25] The Normal distribution is specified by its mean and standard deviation (or variance). In addition to being well known and well behaved, the Normal distribution has the very desirable (exponential) property that when several Normal distributions (say, price and quantity) are combined the resulting product might also be indistinguishable from a Normal distribution (i.e. sales revenue).[26] However, actual distributions of financial inputs and their combinations might not be Normal. This means that the mathematics of financial modelling is usually intractable, and one cannot find a purely mathematical solution to the question, for example 'What is the probability of violating financial constraints?'

Monte Carlo analysis breaks down the statistical problem into individual distributions for each financial model input of interest. Some of these distributions might be derived from historical evidence and others from degrees of belief. They may be Normal or non-Normal distributions; Monte Carlo analysis handles all of them with ease. The analysis selects and

[25] The Uniform distribution is commonly used, too, wherein values between two limits are equally likely. Using this distribution poses no particular problem for implementing Monte Carlo analysis.

[26] See Kottas, J., & Lau, H. 1978.

combines random values of each model input to randomise the financial model relations. This randomisation transforms a deterministic financial model, where risk must be teased out and may be never fully described, into a stochastic financial model which measures financial risk directly and perhaps fully.[27]

The Monte Carlo model can 'bootstrap' or repeatedly sample from the randomised variables thousands of times to create empirical outcome distributions that can answer such questions as, what is the probability of violating financial constraints? One can use the simulated distribution of outcomes to create confidence intervals or measure the probability of reaching (or failing) a targeted result. One also can observe the frequency and magnitude of extreme results (i.e. in the tails of the outcome distributions) that could be catastrophic if realised.

IAM's financial analyst developed a Monte Carlo risk analysis of the Refrigerator Division by adapting the Division's business model to include randomised drivers of the costs and revenues that drive all of the modelled financial outcomes. The first step is to specify the probability distributions for the randomised drivers. Sufficient reliable evidence exists to measure the historical means and standard deviations of 'annual growth' in unit sales and sales prices, 'first-year conventional unit sales' and 'sales price'. The analyst has determined that the historical distributions were indistinguishable from Normal distributions. The marketing research team has drawn on past new product introductions to estimate subjectively the means and standard deviations of Nano's 'first-year unit sales' and 'sales price'. The team assumes that these, too, are 'Normally' distributed and conservatively assumed that Nano sales would grow at the same rate as conventional products. The estimated distribution parameters are in rows 3 and 4 of Figure 4.14.[28] The Monte Carlo analysis randomly selects values from these five probability distributions for each occurrence of these inputs in the Division's financial model.[29] Thus, every calculation and subsequent outcome in the model that uses these inputs directly or indirectly is randomised, too.

ProForma Financial Statements - Refrigerator Division Monte Carlo Analysis					
Randomised Variables	Annual Growth	Conventional 1st Yr Sales	Conventional 1st Yr Price	Nano 1st Yr Sales	Nano 1st Yr Price
Mean input values	3.0%	2,000	13,200	100	2,000
Estimated Standard Errors	1.1%	365	611	20	100
Simulated Key Financial Ratios, Refrigerator Division	**Year 1**	**Year 2**	**Year 3**	**Year 4**	**Year 5**
Current ratio - Target	**2.000**	**2.000**	**2.000**	**2.000**	**2.000**
Current ratio - Pro Forma	**1.299**	**1.297**	**1.735**	**2.393**	**3.074**
Interest coverage ratio - Target	**2.000**	**2.000**	**2.000**	**2.000**	**2.000**
Interest coverage ratio - Pro Forma	**5.901**	**10.328**	**40.996**	**#DIV/0!**	**#DIV/0!**
Debt to value ratio - Target	**0.500**	**0.500**	**0.500**	**0.500**	**0.500**
Debt to value ratio - Pro Forma	**0.412**	**0.289**	**0.217**	**0.201**	**0.184**

Figure 4.14 Monte Carlo analysis

[27] Observe that this shifts the concerns of sensitivity analysis from the values of the model inputs to the values of the distribution parameters (means, standard deviations) of the model inputs.

[28] For economy of presentation, we do not present the fully randomised Monte Carlo model that uses probability distributions for all of the financial model's uncertain inputs.

[29] The values in the model are replaced by the Excel function NORMINV(RAND(),mean, standard deviation). The nested RAND() function creates a random variable between 0 and 1, so each calculation of the input value is random and distributed with the input's mean and standard deviation. Excel has other probability distribution functions that could be used, as appropriate.

The simulated financial ratios in rows 7 to 12 are similar to those presented in Figures 4.11 to 4.13. The key difference is that the previous Figures were computed with deliberately chosen input values that represented managers' beliefs about most likely, best and worst case scenarios. These three scenarios do not exhaust the possible input sets, and they might reflect limited or biased knowledge about future inputs. Monte Carlo analysis expresses managers' knowledge of future inputs as probability distributions from which input values are selected randomly, without bias. However, a single draw of randomised inputs is just that, a single draw. There is no reason to believe that the financial ratio outcomes in Figures 4.14 from a single, random draw reflects future financial ratio outcomes any more reliably than one of the earlier scenarios. One could argue that the outcomes of a single random draw are less reliable that a manager's judgment of a likely scenario. The real power of Monte Carlo analysis comes from its ability to make thousands of random, simultaneous draws from the input probability distributions. What results is a simulated probability distribution of future outcomes, and it can have as many observations as one's computer can produce.

IAM's financial analyst followed these steps and used Microsoft Excel on a PC to adapt the Division's financial model for Monte Carlo analysis and to create a series of simulated outcomes:

1. Type 'Simulations' in a blank cell.
2. Type 1 in the cell below it; fill in as many numbers below it as the number of desired simulation runs (use Editing/Fill/Series/Column as a shortcut).
3. To the right of the number 1 type the cell reference(s) to the results you wish to simulate (e.g. sales units, annual growth, debt to value ratio,. . .).
4. In the 'Formula' menu select 'manual' under 'Calculation Options'.
5. Select the area to hold your simulated results, including **all** numbered rows (e.g. 1000 or more rows)
6. Under the Data bar select What-If Analysis/Data Table and choose the blank cell below the numbered column for the 'Column input cell' (nothing for the 'Row input cell').
7. Hit the F9 key to generate a new set of simulated results (Table 4.4) – only the first several simulations are shown.

Table 4.4 Year 1 simulation results

	Conventional sales units	Nano sales units	Annual growth	Debt to value Ratio
Maximum	3,227	105	4.538%	0.810
Minimum	741	96	−4.157%	0.246
Percent that exceed ratio constraint			0.500	53.4%
Percent that mark insolvency			1.000	0.0%
Simulations	**Conventional sales Units**	**Nano sales units**	**Annual growth**	**Debt to value Ratio**
1	**2,235**	**101**	**1.132%**	**0.358**
2	1,911	98	−1.539%	0.619
3	2,434	101	0.885%	0.333

(Note that Excel for Macintosh computers works slightly differently. Also note that commercial Monte Carlo simulation add-ins for Excel, which greatly simplify this procedure, may be available at student pricing.)

The excerpt from the simulated series for the first year results is repeated for each of the five years of the analysis horizon. For this example, the drivers and the debt to value ratio have been simulated 1000 times for each of the five years. Maximums and minimums are recorded for each. Importantly, the analysis provides a simulated probability of violating the debt to value ratio constraint (must be less than 0.500) and the probability of insolvency (debt exceeding book value of total assets, or negative stockholders' equity). These are important considerations, especially as they unfold in the simulated five-year horizon. Consider the summary of these two statistics in Figure 4.15, which displays answers to the questions: What is the probability of the Division's violating the debt to value constraint? What is the probability of the Division's becoming insolvent?

The probability of violating the debt to value constraint declines over time, but still seems quite high. More alarming perhaps is the probability of insolvency, which rises steadily and quickly during this horizon. The uncertainty about future growth and profitability grows and

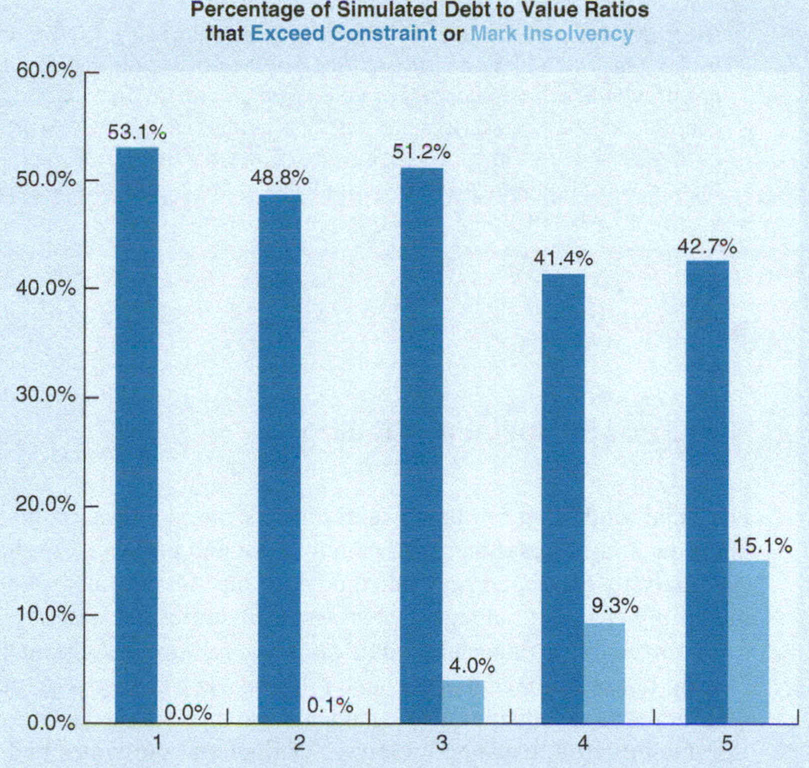

Figure 4.15 Summary of statistics

surfaces ultimately as a rather high probability of insolvency, which begins to look more like the 'worst case' scenario of the previous sections than the 'most likely case.'

Whether these concerns are worthy of attention can be traced directly to the estimated probability distributions for the drivers of costs and revenues. Surely if these are unreliable, the simulated financial outcomes are unreliable. One might anticipate that disparagers of these uncomfortable results will challenge the probability distributions, but if these are shown to be reliable, IAM needs to pay attention to the simulated results. Perhaps adverse outcomes are likely and deserve management attention, perhaps even to the point of divesting this division. If the inputs are reliable, this Monte Carlo analysis should trigger investigations of the long term viability of the Refrigerator Division and its new products. These investigations should focus on refining estimates of the probability distributions of model inputs.

EXAMPLE FROM PRACTICE

Actuaries are common users of 'dynamic financial analysis' (DFA) models that simulate investment and underwriting risks. Actuaries stress the key insight that DFA models might not predict absolute outcomes precisely (i.e. a specific financial ratio level) but they are useful to assess relative risks. That is, DFA models can be used to predict whether a company will be better or worse off by accepting a particular risky endeavour. Another key insight is that actuaries can communicate relative risks to investment managers more effectively when using a DFA that mimics projected financial results.[30]

4.4 Recap of financial modelling

Financial modelling can be a useful aid to strategic decision making and operational planning. Many cross functional management and project teams have (or need) a financial analyst who creates financial models of business problems and solutions. Financial modelling is a key component of strategic planning risk assessment, and project management. Reliable financial models can serve as important management training tools. The methods presented in this chapter describe key elements of financial modelling that offer benefits to individuals who gain and use this knowledge and to their organisations that benefit from expanded analyses of financial outcomes and risks of not meeting financial goals.

[30] Sclafane, S. 2000. 'Dynamic Financial Analysis.'

Key recommendations for successful financial modelling include:

1. Design financial models to reflect the context and drivers of management decisions.
2. Spend the time necessary to refine estimates of input values and their distributions.
3. Build financial models to the point that they can be used as reliable Monte Carlo simulations that inform and assess value and financial risk

EXERCISES

Exercise 4.1 CVP model and time to break-even

Larsen Building Co. owns land in an urban area that is zoned for commercial use. Larsen plans to construct and rent a 50 000 square foot commercial building on the site. Larsen is considering whether to design a building that meets criteria for LEED platinum certification (**http://www.usgbc.org**), which has marketing and sustainability advantages in the current commercial real estate market. Larsen expects normal construction to meet local needs and buildings codes will cost $275 per square foot. Because of the urban location, meeting the LEED platinum certification is expected to add 8% to construction costs. However, if the commercial building is successfully certified, Larsen can qualify for a one time, combined federal and state 'green' tax credit of $2.20 per square foot. Uncertified commercial property in the vicinity rents typically for $20 per square foot per month, but, because renters can market their 'green-ness' and more easily pay for utilities, the occupancy rate for LEED certified properties can increase from 70% to 85%, despite rents that are 10% higher.

Annual maintenance costs for non-certified buildings in the area average $3.00 per square foot, while the cost to maintain LEED buildings can be 1/3 less costly. Larsen's effective tax rate is 30%. The building 's expected life is 40 years with no salvage value. Ignore other expenses and the time value of money.

Required:

1. What qualitative factors should Larsen Building Co. consider before deciding whether to seek LEED certification?
2. Prepare a financial model to answer the question whether it is worthwhile building to the LEED certification or not.

Data input	Non-LEED	LEED certified		
Building size	50 000		50,000	square feet
Construction cost	$275.00	8%	$297.00	per square foot
Green tax credit	—		$2.20	per square foot
Rent	$20.00	10%	$22.00	per square foot
Occupancy rate	70%		85%	
Maintenance	$3.00	−0.333333333	$2.00	per square foot
Tax rate	30%		30%	
Building expected life	40		40	years

Exercise 4.2 Profit planning model

Flying-A Ranch is a former cattle ranch that the owners have converted to an exclusive guest ranch. The ranch offers daily horseback riding, hiking, fishing and just relaxing to a maximum of 14 guests per week. The weekly fee covers costs of all meals, horseback riding and unguided fishing and hiking. A few other ranch activities are offered at modest cost, and guests may contract with other tourist entities for off ranch tours. The table below contains data concerning a typical four month ranch season. Because of its remote location and severe winters, the ranch is closed to guests for the remainder of the year.

Required:.Use the data input to prepare a profit planning model for a typical season.

Data input				
Weeks per month	4			
Meals provided per week per guest	21			
Double occupancy, rate per week per guest	$ 2000			
Single occupancy, rate per week per guest	$ 3000			
Guest ranch season	**June**	**July**	**August**	**September**
Double occupancy, guests per week	8	12	12	10
Single occupancy, guests per week	2	1	1	2
Other activities per guest, per week	**Charge**	**CM ratio**	**Proportion of guests**	
Souvenirs	$ 40.00	50%	80%	
Flyfishing	10.00	80%	50%	
Skeet and trap shooting	25.00	40%	20%	
Off-ranch tours (offered by other entities)	300.00	20%	10%	
Costs per guest				
Cabin maintenance per week	50.00			
Food cost per meal	10.00			
Monthly facility costs				
Wranglers (3)	6000			
Kitchen staff (3)	5000			
Cabin maintenance staff (1)	1500			
Horses and tack	12 000			
Maintenance of equipment and vehicles	2500			
Utilities	2000			
Insurance	3000			
Legal and accounting services	2000			
Depreciation of buildings, equip. and veh.	5000			
Income tax rate	30%			

Exercise 4.3 CVP model

Refer to the narrative and data input for Exercise 4.2. The owners have been offered $12m for the ranch. They expect to operate the ranch for ten more years, before retirement.

Required:

Use the results of Exercise 4.2 and quantify the implications of refusing the offer.

Exercise 4.4 Profit planning model and CVP

The City of Rock Ridge is considering building and operating a small event centre that can host second and third level professional sporting events and music concerts. Rock Ridge must balance its budget each year and cannot subsidise activities like this; that is, the event centre must be self-sustaining. Although the city can borrow funds to finance the construction of an event centre, the centre must be profitable enough to retire its associated debt in no more than 20 years. The table below presents planned operating data presented by a citizen group that represents both advocates and opponents of the proposal. The design of the centre will provide flexible seating and staging to accommodate both athletic and concert events with no loss of seating capacity. The city council has required that the event centre caters to the needs of elderly residents, who otherwise would not be able to attend events, for a minimum of 6 events per annum. This will involve providing prime seats, transportation, and refreshments for at least 50 elderly citizens for each event.

		Range	
Input data	**Most likely**	**High**	**Low**
Arena seating capacity per event	3,000	3,100	2,900
Athletic events per annum	50	60	40
Concerts per annum	12	16	-
Average percentage of seats sold per event	80%	90%	70%
Sales price per ticket - Prime seats	$ 25.00	$ 30.00	$ 20.00
General admission seats	10.00	12.00	6.00
Sales mix assumption - Prime seats	10%	20%	5%
General admission seats	90%	80%	95%
Printing and administrative cost per ticket	$ 2.00	$ 3.00	$ 1.00
Cost per event - Athletic event	3000	5000	2500
- Concert (additional)	25 000	30 000	20 000
Administrative cost per annum - Athletic events	80 000	95 000	60 000
- Concerts	28 000	32 000	20,000
Elderly customer - friendly events	12	16	6
Elderly customers	60	80	50
Cost per elderly customer	95	110	80
Costs per annum - Building	$ 200 000	225 000	185 000
- General administration	250 000	280 000	200 000

Required:

1. Prepare a profit planning model for the city's proposed event centre using the 'Most likely' input values.
2. Use the model to compute the annual break-even percentage of seats sold.

Exercise 4.5 Sensitivity analysis

Refer to the narrative and data for Exercise 4.2 to complete this exercise.

Required:

1. Prepare a sensitivity analysis of the ranch profitability to 20% changes in each of the drivers of revenue and cost.
2. Compute the financial elasticity of profit to each parameter. Explain the importance of the elasticity calculations to the ranch owners.

Exercise 4.6 Sensitivity analysis

Refer to the narrative and data for Exercise 4.4 to complete this exercise.

Required:

1. Prepare a sensitivity analysis of the event centre profitability for at least six drivers of revenue and cost. Be prepared to explain your choice of inputs to analyse.
2. Compute the financial elasticity of profit to each parameter. Explain the importance of the elasticity calculations to the city's managers.

Exercise 4.7 Scenario analysis

Refer to the narrative and data for Exercise 4.4 to complete this exercise.

Required:

1. Prepare best case, worst case, and most likely case scenario analyses from the data input. What do these analyses imply about the viability of the proposed event centre?
2. Given the most likely case scenario, what is the most that the City of Rock Ridge can spend to acquire the land and build the event centre? What advice can you give the city council?

Exercise 4.8 Scenario analysis

Road Equipment Company (REC) manufactures and distributes heavy construction equipment worldwide. REC's assistant controller, Alberta King, is aware that one of its primary competitors, Caterpillar, has implemented a re-manufacturing process, which refinishes recycled engine parts to new part specifications and performance. Caterpillar encourages its customers (equipment repair companies) to recycle these parts by selling remanufactured parts with new-part warranties at a price much less than new parts, if the customer returns an old part prior to purchasing a replacement. King believes that REC must meet the competitive challenge posed by Caterpillar's new programme and also sees an opportunity to improve the company's financial and environmental performance.

King has asked you, as a new financial analyst at REC, to analyse alternative processes for new and remanufactured parts. You have gathered the following information related to the remanufacture of an engine's fuel injection case, a part commonly discarded and replaced during a major engine repair.

Data input	New	Re manufactured
Current sales volume per year, units	1 000 000	?
Sales price per unit	$ 6.00	$ 4.00
Direct material cost used per unit	$ 1.00	$ 0.12
Direct labor cost used per unit	$ 1.00	$ 0.20
Fixed manufacturing overhead per year	$1 200 000	$ 400 000
Fixed labor cost per year	$1 400 000	$ 260 000

Required:

1. Prepare profit planning models for sales of new and remanufactured parts.
2. Use this model to analyse four alternative scenarios:
   a. REC sells only new parts but loses 20% of its unit sales to Caterpillar, which expands its share of the market by selling increased quantities of remanufactured parts
   b. REC sells 80% new and 20% remanufactured parts and maintains its level of unit sales.

c. REC sells only new parts, loses 20% of its unit sales (as in part a) but an economic downturn reduces market demand for heavy construction equipment by 25%.

d. REC sells 80% new and 20% remanufactured parts and maintains its market share (as in part b), but an economic downturn reduces market demand for heavy construction equipment by 25%.

Exercise 4.9 Monte Carlo analysis

This is an exercise to develop basic Monte Carlo modelling skills.

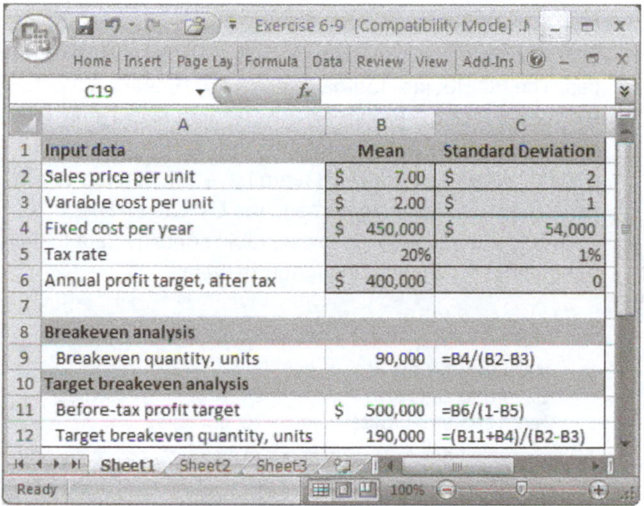

Exercise 6-9 [Compatibility Mode]

C19

	A	B	C
1	**Input data**	**Mean**	**Standard Deviation**
2	Sales price per unit	$ 7.00	$ 2
3	Variable cost per unit	$ 2.00	$ 1
4	Fixed cost per year	$ 450,000	$ 54,000
5	Tax rate	20%	1%
6	Annual profit target, after tax	$ 400,000	0
7			
8	**Breakeven analysis**		
9	Breakeven quantity, units	90,000	=B4/(B2-B3)
10	**Target breakeven analysis**		
11	Before-tax profit target	$ 500,000	=B6/(1-B5)
12	Target breakeven quantity, units	190,000	=(B11+B4)/(B2-B3)

Sheet1 Sheet2 Sheet3

Ready 100%

Required:

1. Replicate the simple CVP model shown above.
2. Assume that the input data are Normally distributed. Prepare a Monte Carlo analysis that prepares and describes a simulated distribution of a) breakeven quantity and b) target breakeven quantity.

Exercise 4.10 Monte Carlo analysis

This is an exercise to develop basic Monte Carlo modelling skills.

Data input	Most likely	High	Low
Sales price per unit	$ 12.00	$ 13.50	$ 10.65
Variable cost per unit	6.50	8.48	1.50
Fixed cost per year	675 000	720 000	547 000
Profit target per year, before tax	400 000	400 000	400 000
Target breakeven analysis			
Fixed costs plus profit target		$ 1 075 000	per period
Contribution margin		5.50	per unit
Breakeven or target quantity		195 455	units per period

Required:

1. Build a simple CVP model from the data shown above.
2. Assume that the input data are distributed uniformly between the high and low values. Prepare a Monte Carlo analysis that prepares and describes a simulated distribution of breakeven quantity. Compute mean, standard deviation, minimum and maximum values of this simulated distribution.

CASES

Case 4.1 Profit planning model

Part A: Amateur sports teams for school aged children are often supported by volunteer activities. The FC Boulder football (soccer) U-16 team will participate in an early summer, two-day tournament for age groups U12 - U16. Apart from entry fees, which pay for field rental, referees and trophies, the U-16 team generates revenues from the sale of drinks, ice and tournament t-shirts. Parents of the U-16 team have volunteered to organise the supply and sale of these items. Per the league agreement, the U-16 team keeps 70% of the profit and pays 30% to the FC Boulder league. The following table contains data that are relevant to the beverage, ice and t-shirt sales for the upcoming tournament.

Data input, Part A

Beverage case size	24	bottles
Team share of profits	70%	

Tournament items	Sales price per unit	Cost per T-shirt, cup, bag, or case	Expected sales quantity*	
T-shirt, short-sleeved, each	$12.00	$4.00	200	t-shirts
T-shirt, long-sleeved, each	$24.00	$8.00	40	t-shirts
Coffee	$2.00	$0.60	80	cups
Ice, per bag	$2.00	$0.70	100	bags
Sport drink	$2.00	$12.00	20	cases
Coke products	$1.00	$6.00	10	cases
Pepsi products	$1.00	$6.00	20	cases
Eldorado Springs water	$1.00	$5.00	15	cases

* sales expectations are based on fine weather, which is typical at this time of year.

Required:

Prepare a profit planning model for the sale of tournament items.

Part B: The parents of the U-16 soccer team believe they should be prepared for inclement weather, which will reduce demand for ice and cold drinks but will increase demand for coffee and long sleeved t-shirts. The probability for fine (normal) weather at this time of year is 60%, with a 40% chance of cold, inclement weather. Because items are generally purchased in advance, the parents wonder how to optimise purchase of items to account for the changeable weather. Although all t-shirts must be ordered in advance, for a prepaid fee a local supplier will deliver any quanitity of the beverage items and ice (at the advance cost) with a one-hour notice. Alternatively, a parent can purchase beverage items and ice at 'spot' prices, which are double, at a nearby grocery store. Only whole cases of beverages can be purchased. Unsold items have no sales value. The following table presents weather and demand data relevant for modelling the impacts of changeable weather.

Data input	Inclement weather
Probability	40%
Changes in demand for:	
T-shirts, short-sleeved (SS)	−20%
T-shirts, long-sleeved (LS)	50%
Coffee	100%
Ice	−75%
Sport drinks	0%
Coke products	−10%
Pepsi products	−10%
Eldorado Springs water	−10%
Prepaid delivery fee, per day	$ 100
Spot price differential	100%

Required:

Analyse the weather related decisions and make purchasing recommendations. Hint: display the alternative decisions and conditions with a decision tree (Chapter 2).

Case 4.2 Business model

'Debt covenants at risk for Overlevered Corp'

Posted 13 October 2010 @ 04:05 pm EST

An analyst said Monday Overlevered Corp is in danger of violating debt covenants as sales in the industry sink amid the global economic slowdown.

"Based on our revised forecasts, we estimate that could trip debt covenants in the December quarter," ABC Capital Markets analyst Aaron Burr told investors in a research note. "We expect that the company will be able to manage through these issues, but the risk profile has certainly changed in the past few months."

Burr cut his price target on Overlevered to $7 from $13, citing the manufacturer's "deteriorating earnings outlook and growing balance sheet stress. The primary risk to our price target is that Overlevered is not successful in negotiating with its lenders to ensure sufficient liquidity."

From Overlevered Corporation's 2009 Form 10-K

"The Company has a $650.0 million long-term revolving credit facility (Facility) with a group of banks.... Under the terms of the Facility, Overlevered is subject to a leverage test, as well as restrictions on secured debt. The Company was in compliance with these covenants at December 31, 2009."

Assume that the leverage constraint is the debt to equity ratio, total debt divided by stockholders' equity, which cannot exceed 40% at year's end.

Required:

1. Prepare input model estimates of the financial parameters in the shaded boxes on the following business model. Explain your method(s) for making these estimates. **Note:** Not all variables should be forecasted; some variables should be computed from forecasted values using accounting logic.

Overlevered Corporation - Business Model

For the periods ending December 31

Note: Shaded cells should be forecasts; white cells should be accounting logic)

Annual Income Statement	2005	2006	2007	2008	2009	Estimated 2010	Estimated 2011
Revenue (*Estimates from = FORECAST()*)	4,128.7	5,229.3	5,923.8	5,665.0	5,671.2	5,500.7	5,374.4
Costs of goods sold	3,131.6	3,915.1	4,499.2	4,439.3	4,528.1		
Gross profit	997.1	1,314.2	1,424.6	1,225.7	1,143.1		
Gross profit margin	***24.20%***	***25.10%***	***24.00%***	***21.60%***	***20.20%***		
SG&A expense	625.1	756.0	783.8	717.2	855.8		
Depreciation & amortisation	150.6	157.5	162.2	167.3	180.1		
Operating income	221.4	400.7	478.6	341.2	107.2		
Nonoperating income	20.7	23.0	70.4	14.1	16.5		
Nonoperating expenses	41.0	45.2	53.2	60.5	52.3		
Income before taxes	201.1	378.5	495.8	294.8	71.4		
Income taxes	65.9	108.7	110.4	46.5	13.1		
Effective tax rate	***32.8%***	***28.7%***	***22.3%***	***15.8%***	***18.3%***		
Net income after taxes	135.2	269.8	385.4	248.3	58.3		
Annual cash flow statement	**2005**	**2006**	**2007**	**2008**	**2009**	**Estimated 2010**	
Net operating cash flow	395.1	415.2	432.9	315.3	314.3		
Net investing cash flow	−371.9	−439.9	−322.8	−283.9	−98.5		
Net financing cash flow	−28.7	178.6	−122.2	−235.7	−167.8		
Net change in cash (**2010 by the indirect method**)	−5.5	153.9	−12.1	−204.3	48.0		
Cash dividends paid	−45.9	−58.1	−57.3	−55.0	−52.6		
Annual balance sheet	**2005**	**2006**	**2007**	**2008**	**2009**	**Estimated 2010**	
Cash	345.9	499.8	487.7	283.4	331.4		
Net receivables	374.4	755.9	797.2	742.2	822.3		
As a % of sales	***9.1%***	***14.5%***	***13.5%***	***13.1%***	***14.5%***		
Inventories	623.8	786.8	874.6	861.9	906.7		
As a % of next year's sales	***11.9%***	***13.3%***	***15.4%***	***15.2%***	***16.5%***		
Other current assets	371.1	56.2	75.5	190.9	53.9		
Total Current Assets	1,715.2	2,098.7	2,235.0	2,078.4	2,114.3		
Net fixed assets	827.1	876.4	970.2	1,047.7	1,052.8		
Other non-current assets	1,060.2	1,371.3	1,416.3	1,324.2	1,198.5		
Total assets	3,602.5	4,346.4	4,621.5	4,450.3	4,365.6		
Accounts payable	1,078.0	1,243.1	1,304.1	1,197.5	1,295.4		
As a % of next year's sales	***20.6%***	***21.0%***	***23.0%***	***21.1%***	***23.5%***		
Short-term debt	23.8	10.7	1.1	0.7	0.8		
Other current liabilities	0.0	0.0	0.0	95.0	0.0		
Total current liabilities	1,101.8	1,253.8	1,305.2	1,293.2	1,296.2		
Long-term debt	583.8	728.4	723.7	725.7	727.4		
Other non-current liabilities	593.9	651.9	613.8	559.6	449.1		
Total liabilities	2,279.5	2,634.1	2,642.7	2,578.5	2,472.7		
Common stock equity	1,323.0	1,712.3	1,978.8	1,871.8	1,892.9		
Total liabilities and equity	3,602.5	4,346.4	4,621.5	4,450.3	4,365.6		
	2005	**2006**	**2007**	**2008**	**2009**	**2010**	
Debt to equity ratio	44.1%	42.5%	36.6%	38.8%	38.4%		

Case 4.3 Business model and scenario analysis

Use the data and business model from Case 4.2.

Required:

1. Adapt the Overlevered business model for three scenarios of Overlevered's business activities: most likely, best, and worst cases. Explain how you derived these scenarios.
2. Explain the implications of each of these scenarios for Overlevered's risk of violating its debt covenant.

Case 4.4 Business model and Monte Carlo analysis

Use the data and business model from Case 4.2.

Required:

1. Adapt the Overlevered business model for Monte Carlo analysis to create a simulated distribution of Overlevered's 2010 debt to equity ratio. Clearly describe which variables you have chosen to vary randomly and how you have done so.
2. Based on your analysis, what is the probability of Overlevered's violating its debt covenant?
3. Evaluate the risks in the tails of the distribution.

Case 4.5 Business model and scenario analysis

AbbaDabba Company has a debt to value ratio covenant attached to its line of credit (i.e. notes payable). AbbaDabba may not exceed a debt to value ratio of more than 30% at the end of any year or it faces cancellation or restructuring of the terms of its line of credit. Use the following input data to create a business model similar to the chapter's example model that reflects the most likely case for the coming year.

Data input	Most likely
Covenant ratio limit	30%
Beginning balance sheet	Assets
Cash	$3 000
Accounts receivable	$1 000
Inventory	$2 000
Plant, property & equipment(net)	$10 000
Total assets	$16 000
Accounts payable	$3 000
Notes payable	$1 000
Interest payable	-
Owners equity	$12 000
Total equities	$16 000
Budgeted sales	$18 000
Cash sales rate	80%
Credit sales rate	20%
Budgeted expenses	
Salaries and wages	$4 000
Advertising	$500
Depreciation	800
Minimum cash balance	$1 500
Minimum inventory	$1 000
Payments for inventory	
Cash purchases	75%
Credit purchases	25%
Gross margin ratio	30%
Borrowing rate (annual)	8%

Required:

1. Modify this model for each of the following scenarios (other parameters are at the base levels):

   Scenario 1: Budgeted sales = \$15000, Cash sales rate = 70%, Gross margin ratio = 25%, Borrowing rate = 8%.

   Scenario 2: Budgeted sales = \$20000, Cash sales rate = 90%, Gross margin ratio = 40%, Borrowing rate = 6%.

   Scenario 3: Cash sales rate = 70%, Budgeted salaries and wages \$5000, Advertising = \$700, Minimum cash balance = \$2000, Minimum inventory = \$1500.

2. Discuss the risks associated with each scenario.

Case 4.6 Profit planning and Monte Carlo analysis

Pendant Corporation is a local financial services firm that sells home mortgages to home owners. The company has focused on growing its regional market share and managing its profitability. You are a consultant to Pendant, and your current assignment is to build a profitability model of the company that is driven by key environmental and policy variables. The company identifies interest rate variability as the largest source of financial risk but is also concerned about other possible sources of risk. Accordingly, you have also agreed to analyse the financial risk of the model via Monte Carlo analysis. NOTE: This obviously is a simplified depiction of the mortgage banking business.

Required:

1. Prepare a mortgage sales forecasting model from the following time series annual sales data. Hint: Use multiple regression analysis. The indicator (0,1) variables may pick up shifts in the home lending market. The rate is the annual average 30-year mortgage rate. Mortgage sales is the dollar value of mortgages sold. Use the forecasting model to estimate 2010 mortgage sales.

Historical sales data

Year	1980-86	After 1986	Mortgage lending rate (%)	Pendant mortgage sales \$
1972	0	0	7.38	9560000
1973	0	0	8.04	9440000
1974	0	0	9.19	9470000
1975	0	0	9.04	9507000
1976	0	0	8.86	9625000
1977	0	0	8.84	9757000
1978	0	0	9.63	9850000
1979	0	0	11.19	9846000
1980	1	0	13.77	8400000
1981	1	0	16.63	7950000
1982	1	0	16.08	8200000
1983	1	0	13.23	8920000
1984	1	0	13.87	8580000
1985	1	0	12.42	9320000
1986	1	0	10.18	9570000
1987	0	1	10.20	11350000
1988	0	1	10.34	11260000

Historical sales data				
Year	**1980-86**	**After 1986**	**Mortgage lending rate (%)**	**Pendant mortgage sales $**
1989	0	1	10.32	11 350 000
1990	0	1	10.13	11 160 000
1991	0	1	9.25	11 160 000
1992	0	1	8.40	11 320 000
1993	0	1	7.33	11 470 000
1994	0	1	8.35	11 470 000
1995	0	1	7.95	11 630 000
1996	0	1	7.80	11 790 000
1997	0	1	7.60	12 130 000
1998	0	1	6.94	12 220 000
1999	0	1	7.43	12 470 000
2000	0	1	8.06	12 570 000
2001	0	1	6.97	12 720 000
2002	0	1	6.54	12 600 000
2003	0	1	5.82	12 570 000
2004	0	1	5.84	10 330 000
2005	0	1	5.86	11 660 000
2006	0	1	6.41	13 200 000
2007	0	1	6.34	13 090 000
2008	0	1	6.03	12 700 000
2009	0	1	5.04	12 520 000
2010*	0	1	4.90	unknown

*Forecast

2. Use the results from your regression analysis and the following input data to build a 2009 profit planning model for Pendant Corporation. Pendant earns the difference between its cost of borrowed money to finance the mortgages and the mortgage lending rate it charges homeowners (the 'spread') on these dollar amounts. For example, if the spread was 2%, Pendant earned on its average 1972 mortgage sales $(.0738) \times (\$9560000/2)$ as revenue in 1972 and paid $(.0738 - .02) \times (\$9560000/2)$ as interest expense. Pendant also earns the lending rate on its mortgage assets.

Data input	
Beginning balance sheet	**12/31/2008**
Cash	$1 500 000
Accounts receivable (net)	6 000 000
Plant, property & equipment (net)	12 000 000
Mortgage assets	8 000 000
Total assets	$27 500 000
Accounts payable	$ 400 000
Interest payable	1 200 000
Short-term debt	1 300 000
Long-term debt	4 000 000
Stockholders' equity	20 600 000
Total equities	$27 500 000
2009 Annual sales and costs	**2009**
Fees per new mortgage (closing costs)	1.75%
Interest spread on mortgages*	2.00%
Uncollectible sales	5.00%

Data input	
Mortgage resale rate**	90.00%
Mortgage resale earnings rate**	1.00%
Cash sales collection rate (applies to all sales)	92.00%
Budgeted expenses:Expected inflation rate	3%
Salaries and wages	$ 6200000
Advertising	1300000
Depreciation	600000
General administrative	3000000
Outsourced services	1200000
Cash payment rate (applies to cash expenses)	90%
Minimum cash balance	500000
Plant, property and equip purchases***	300000
PPE assumed life, years	20

* The mortgage interest spread is the targeted difference between the cost of borrowed money and the mortgage lending rate (e.g. the gross profit rate).
** Approximately 90% of mortgages are resold to other mortgage companies after one year, with net proceeds to Pendant of 1% of the mortgage value.
*** Increases in depreciation expense reflect purchases of 20 year equipment, paid with cash.

3. Modify your profit planning model to perform Monte Carlo analysis on expected 2010 profits. Randomise annual mortgage sales using the results of your sales analysis in question 1.

Case 4.7 Comprehensive case

Franklin Bank Corp was founded in 2001 with the purpose of providing community banking services outside the major metropolitan areas of Texas. From its Houston headquarters, Franklin Bank managed approximately 40 community banks in Texas and commercial lending and mortgage origination offices in many Western states. Franklin Bank Corp was headed by Lewis Ranieri, who has been credited with inventing structured mortgage securities, which are derivative securities based on mortgages or other loans. Despite managements' credentials and previously glowing recommendations by financial analysts, Franklin's stock price plummeted over the past year from over $20 per share to under $1, and the company has been threatened with delisting by NASDAQ. Behind the fall is the bursting of the real estate bubble, beginning in 2007, and the consequent increases in loan defaults, foreclosures and distress sales of properties. In recent years, more than 80% of Franklin Bank's total assets have been 'loans held for investment,' which are mostly home mortgages. The causes of the burst bubble are legion, but many observers cite low savings rates by individuals, lax lending practices by banks, lax government oversight of those practices, initially low interest rates, excessive debt carried by individuals and unrealistic expectations about uninterrupted growth in property market values.

Franklin Bank Corp's auditors discovered accounting irregularities related to the recognition of the allowance for loan losses and write offs of uncollectible loans. Whether these were willful attempts to mislead investors and prop up the bank's faltering stock price or rather were the results of mismanagement is not known at this time, but is the subject of an SEC investigation. For purposes of this case, assume that Franklin Bank underestimated its allowance by not recognising the bursting of the real estate bubble and its exposure to increased default risk.

Required:

1. Read the article, 'Mortgage-bond guru hit by loan bust,' Friday May 23, 2008 12:49 pm ET , By Rachel Beck, AP Business Writer ALL BUSINESS: 'No quick end to credit crisis when mortgage-bond inventor gets hit by loan bust.' NEW YORK (AP).

2. Build a spreadsheet model to estimate Franklin Bank's 'allowance for credit losses.' Use the excepts from Franklin Bank's 2007 10-Q report, plus other relevant information that you can gather regarding likely ranges of key variables that plausibly affect defaults on the types of loans owned by Franklin Bank. Clearly cite sources of information obtained outside this case. Clearly state all assumptions that underlie your allowance for the loan loss model. Also clearly describe limitations to your model that presumably could be relieved with more detailed, inside information. For this case, ignore other sources of business risk to Franklin Bank, such as losses on securities held for trading.
3. Evaluate the sensitivity of your model to individually significant sources of variation in your allowance for credit losses model.
4. Create and evaluate multiple scenarios, including at least the best case, worst case and most likely case scenarios.
5. Use Monte Carlo analysis to estimate business risk, as reflected in this case in the allowance for credit losses.

References

Bellman, E. (2009). "Indian Firms Shift Focus to the Poor." *Wall Street Journal,* October 20.

Bourgeois, L. J. III and Kathleen M. Eisenhardt "Strategic Decision Processes in High Velocity Environments: Four Cases in the Microcomputer Industry."*Management Science,* Vol. 34, No. 7 (Jul., 1988), pp. 814-835. Stable URL: http://www.jstor.org/stable/2632297 Accessed: 18/05/2010 12:56.

Chang, LM and PH Chen. (2001). BOT Financial Model: Taiwan High Speed Rail Case." *Journal of Construction Engineering and Management* 127 (3): 214-222.

Hindo, B. (2006). Everything old is new again. *BusinessWeek,* pp. 64-70.

http://en.wikipedia.org/wiki/Deep_Blue_(chess_computer)

Kato, Yutaka (1993). Target costing support systems: Lessons from leading Japanese companies. *Management Accounting Research* 4(1): 33-47.

Kottas, J., & Lau, H. (1978). A General Approach to Stochastic Management Planning Models: An Overview. *The Accounting Review,* pp. 389-401.

Sclafane, S. (2000). "Dynamic Financial Analysis" *National Underwriter.* pp. 28, 30, 50.

Segerstrom, J.R. (2009) "Are financial models really to blame?" *Bank Accounting & Finance,* pp. 39-42.

Shi, Y. and T. Manning, (2009) "Understanding business models and business model risks," *The Journal of Private Equity,* pp. 49-59.

Taleb, Nassim (2004). *Fooled by Randomness*. New York: Random House.

Taleb, Nassim (2007). *The Black Swan*. New York: Random House.

SECTION 2

Profitability analysis

Chapter 5

Budgeting and beyond

5.1 Introduction

A **Budget** is a quantitative expression of planned money inflows and outflows driven by projected business activities that are guided by short term and long term organisational objectives. **Budgeting** is the process of preparing, using and evaluating budgets. Budgeting is widely used in business, non-profit organisations and government to plan and control organisational activities. The word 'budget' dates back to the roman word 'bulga' which related to the leather bag or pouch merchants attached to their horse when they went out trading. They were responsible for its content and for the future revenues that it was expected to generate (Hofstede, 1967). Since the beginning of the 19th century, European states have extensively used budgets to manage state revenues and expenditure. In some European countries, like the UK, the Netherlands and France, the word 'budget' (or '*bougette*' in French) is used for the little suitcase in which the Minister of Finance carries the annual government budget proposals to parliament. In the US, budgeting became popular in companies in the 1920s when they were primarily used for cost control purposes.

Budgets for short term operations have become an important, if controversial, management instrument in contemporary businesses and non-business organisations. A reason for this is the fact that budgeting plays multiple goals in organisations, covering all areas of organisational activity (D. T. Otley, 1999). However, many are concerned with adverse side effects of 'traditional' budgeting. **Traditional budgeting** is a centrally coordinated activity (often the only one) in organisations supporting the basic management functions of 'planning' and 'control'.[1] Traditional budgeting is used for central management's purposes such as allocating resources, coordinating activities, motivating and evaluating employees and guiding decentralised decision making (Covaleski, Evans, Luft, & Shields, 2003). The multiplicity of goals and applications makes budgeting attractive, often deemed as essential, for management and it has, therefore, in many organisations become deeply ingrained in the organisation's fabric (Scapens & Roberts, 1993). We first look at the roles budgeting plays in planning and control activities.

[1] Traditional budgeting for operations is commonly discussed in detail in introductory and intermediate level management accounting textbooks. We do not repeat these discussions here. Budgeting for operations is distinguished from long term capital budgeting, which is the topic of Chapter 7.

5.1.1 Budgeting as a planning device

Budget preparation or **planning** is the process of developing financial and non-financial aspects of future plans of action by management. This process mainly relates to the planning function of budgeting. In this phase, central management decides about the amount of resources available for the planning period and about the resource allocation to different parts of the organisation. Budget preparation may be top down or bottom up, depending on the culture and structure of the organisation, but traditionally budgeting is predominantly top down. The organisational parts that receive budgets may be sub-units, geographic regions, product-market combinations, functions, programmes, projects or activities. In the budget preparation phase, setting up budgets also helps to anticipate potential problems and to prepare solutions for them. Budgets demonstrate the financial consequences for the statements of income, financial position, cash flow covering and key financial ratios (e.g. that may be essential to contracts) in future periods. The relationships between budgets for different business functions and organisational entities also visualise potential coordination problems. In this way, budgets also may support organisational and operational planning.

5.1.2 Budgeting as a management control device

Budget control starts when budgets communicate organisational objectives and planned activities to budget holders, who have the responsibility and authority to implement the budget. Budgets as controls further specify objectives, targets and processes. The intent is to create a better understanding of, and adherence to, organisational goals, which helps budget holders in the coordination of their activities with other related organisational entities. During the execution period, budgets provide guidelines for operations, and the budget also controls by setting limitations for organisational resource use in the attainment of budget targets.

As the budget period progresses, budgets may be used for the basis of performance evaluation, as passed or as revised to reflect current market conditions. **Variance analysis** compares actual performance to planned performance (e.g. for the period or to date) for the purpose of understanding the magnitude of, and causes for, the differences between planned and realised performance, related costs and revenues. The variance analysis can be used for learning, corrective actions, performance assessment and reward decisions. Figure 5.1 displays the flow of traditional budgeting process and activities.

5.2 Different approaches to budgeting

Completed budgets have had a similar appearance in organisations for generations: pro forma financial statements derived from sales, production and cost objectives or targets. What is not consistent, however, is **how** budgets are defined and **how** they should be used in controlling budget execution. Here is where practice may deviate greatly. Both practitioners as well as academics have expressed their concerns about the possible disadvantages and dysfunctions of traditional budgeting.

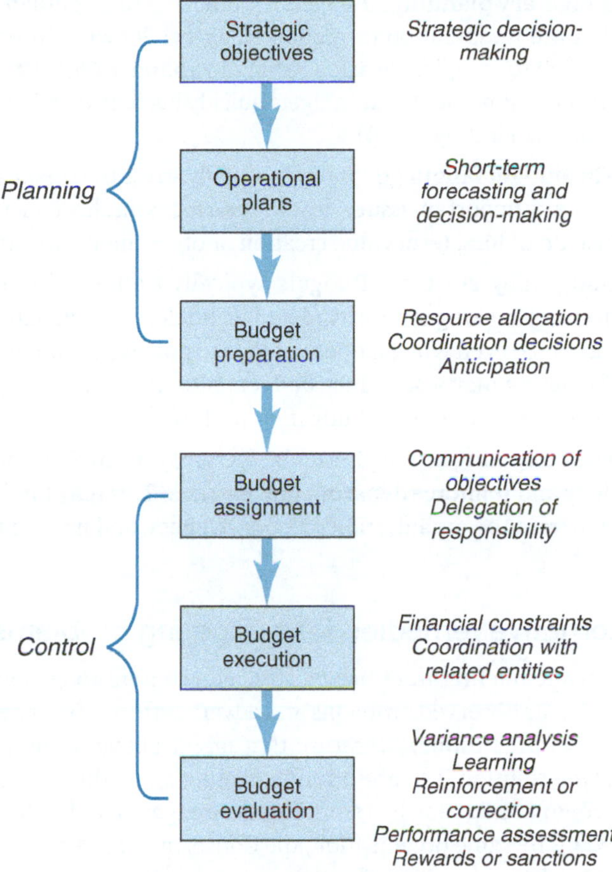

Figure 5.1 Planning and control activities of budgeting

5.2.1 Common budgeting problems

Budgets are abstractions of reality: they do not fully represent the complexities and dynamics of corporate strategy, nor do they portray all relevant dimensions of the production processes. These shortcomings may eventually lead to problems with budgeting in practice (Stephen C. Hansen, Otley, & van der Stede, 2003; Merchant & van der Stede, 2011; Neely, Sutcliff, & Heyns, 2001). Depending on the severity of budgeting problems, managers may not find the effort put into budgeting to generate sufficient value. For example, only 27% of Dutch companies report to be satisfied with their current budgeting system. Similarly, only 25% of Finnish managers surveyed wants to retain the existing budgeting process, but a majority of 61% wants to improve budgeting, while 14% want to go further and to at least consider abandoning budgeting altogether (Ekholm & Wallin, 2000). To elaborate, common budgeting problems include:

1. **Budgeting effort:** Budgeting processes consume a large portion of managers' time at all levels. Budgeting may absorb up to 30% of management time, that is 14 weeks a year (J. Hope & Fraser, 2003). A majority of Dutch managers think that their budgeting processes take too much time (de Waal, San, & Zwanenburg, 2005).

2. **Budgetary planning:** Budgets are often based on outdated and unsupported assumptions that are updated too infrequently, especially when used in uncertain environments or applied to complex decision settings. Around 40% of US and Canadian managers agreed with the statement that budgets quickly become obsolete or outdated as the year goes by (Libby & Lindsay, 2010).
3. **The budget language:** Budgets usually stress the financial dimension and not other strategically important issues, leading to a focus on short term profitability and cost reduction instead of long term value creation or other important strategic issues.
4. **Budgetary control:** Budgets typically define a limited set of responsibilities and decision-making authority to budget holders, which may lead them to optimise local performance even when it does not lead to positive economic outcomes for the organisation. Budgeting may also induce budget holders to engage in gaming and perverse behaviour to maximise their own budgetary performance (Libby & Lindsay, 2010).
5. **The budgeting atmosphere:** Budgets may strengthen vertical command and control relations and reinforce departmental barriers. This may hinder the exchange of information, constrain the organisation's responsiveness, and impose barriers to change.

5.2.2 Alternative remedies for budgeting problems

The academic literature has mostly been content to critique traditional budgeting and to examine its observed problems and adverse effects. Two alternative solutions have emerged from the practitioner literature that might alleviate the problems of traditional budgeting. One solution is to **abandon** budgeting altogether, whereas the other solution suggests **improving** budgeting by reforming the budget model. Interestingly, both suggestions originated in the same organisation, the Consortium for Advanced Manufacturing-International (CAM-I). This is a non-profit organisation in which members from manufacturing and service companies, government organisations, consultancy agencies, and academic and professional bodies collectively study management problems and critical business issues.

The European based CAM-I *Beyond Budgeting Round Table* (BB) group takes a radical approach and recommends abandoning budgeting, as we know it. Instead of budgeting, **Beyond Budgeting** recommends introducing a system of decentralised decision making in the hands of empowered local managers while replacing budget based performance evaluation by relative performance contracts with hindsight. This approach is consistent with strong clan control, decentralisation, and pay for performance. BB provides an alternative for budgeting that relies on managers to make more strategy-focused planning and control decisions, without the constraints of an imposed budget.

The US based CAM-I *Activity-Based Planning and Budgeting* (ABB) *Group* advocates improving budgeting by relating budgetary planning, the budget language and budgetary control more to the activities and work in the firm. The **ABB** approach is to use the analytical approach of activity based costing to elaborate an operational plan that drives a financial budget (Brimson & Antos, 2002; Stephen C. Hansen, et al., 2003; Stephan C. Hansen & Torok, 2004).

Whereas the ABB Group intends to make budgeting more meaningful to operations managers, the BB group takes a different route by suggesting alternative control methods to build relations between strategy and decentralised managers' decisions (J. Hope & Fraser, 1999, 2003; J. H. Hope, Fraser, & Robin, 2003; Jensen, 2001). We will now compare and contrast these rival replacements to traditional budgeting.

5.2.3 Beyond budgeting

The beyond budgeting (BB) model is presented as 'a new coherent management model.' (J. H. Hope, et al., 2003, p. 29). This model originates from the experiences of the Swedish bank *Svenska Handelsbanken.* In the 1970's, this bank was in financial difficulties and lost customers to a smaller rival run by Dr. Jan Wallander. The *SvenskaHandelsbank* invited him to become CEO and shortly after his arrival, Wallander started a reform process. These reforms transformed the bank into a successful enterprise, outperforming its Nordic rivals. The first measure he took was radically to **decentralise decision making** in autonomous units led by empowered managers not being constrained by a specific budget or management agreement. This enabled managers to adapt quickly to changing circumstances.

Budgets are abandoned for target setting to local managers because they are considered counterproductive under changing conditions, since they constrain local managers to predetermined budget standards (Wallander, 1999). Centralised planning and results control, both cornerstones of traditional budgeting, were replaced by centrally defined business principles and constraints, and by personnel and clan based controls like employee selection, training and shared values.

How decentralised managers plan, budget, and execute plans is left to the decentralised managers. Of course, they may choose to decentralise their responsibilities further, or to employ traditional or ABB budgeting models when further decentralisation is not feasible.

Performance evaluation of decentralised business units is based on a system of 'relative performance assessment with hindsight' (Hansen, et al., 2003). The relative performance is measured by means of benchmarking the local units' achievements with other internal units from the same organisation or external units from comparable organisations in the market. Benchmarked performance targets have two advantages:

- Benchmarked targets are arguably attainable (if others can do it, so can we),
- They adjust for uncontrollable factors that are common to all benchmarked units (like developments in product markets and regions).

The hindsight component means that the target performance level is not set inflexibly in advance, but will be established when the evaluation takes place and is equal to the benchmarked performance. The task local managers receive at the start of the planning period is simply to outperform the benchmarked business units. A wide range of financial and non-financial performance measures, which are aligned with the organisation's strategic objectives, were used to measure the performance of local managers.

The outcomes of the performance evaluation of the sub-units are represented in a 'league table'. The best performers on top of the list receive recognition for their achievements and they are invited to explain to the units on the bottom of the list how they may improve their position. Financial compensation is not attached to the units' relative position, but to the company's overall financial results only. This system of organisation based-rewards is meant to make local managers feel responsible for the joint performance of all units, discouraging internal rivalry among units, while promoting the exchange of information and mutual cooperation.

The most important BB principles are the following (Gurton, 1999; J. Hope & Fraser, 1999; de Waal, Bilstra, & Ottens, 2004):

1. decentralisation of decision making to empowered units;
2. corporate management based on business principles and clan based controls;

3. relative performance assessment with hindsight;
4. organisation based financial rewards and unit based non-financial rewards.

Since the *Svenska Handelsbanken* paved the way for BB, its supporters claim that the BB principles form a coherent management model that must be implemented fully to attain optimal benefits. Yet, others question whether BB is necessary or feasible in all organisations. Not all companies may benefit from decentralisation, especially when clan control is weak, knowledge is concentrated in some units, but internal cooperation is required among operational units. In some companies it may be difficult finding comparable benchmark units to make relative performance evaluation systems work. And finally, most companies may prefer to coordinate their organisational units by setting clear targets at the beginning of the budget period. This may give more certainty about, and direction to, possible future local managers' actions. Certainly setting ambitious targets is consistent with the extensive target setting literature that is discussed in Chapter 12. Setting that body of knowledge aside for vague, 'do your best' targets might require special circumstances.

5.2.4 Activity based budgeting (ABB)

Traditional budgeting creates budgets for often hierarchical organisational units and functional 'silos', such as production, marketing and administration departments. Traditional budgeting then allocates (or 'pushes') functional budgets to products. This is the budgeting model that is typically described in introductory or intermediate level management accounting textbooks and that is implemented in many organisations. Although traditional budgeting is important because of its widespread use, this text focuses on an alternative budgeting model that promises improved planning and evaluation of performance.

The alternative budgeting model is ABB, which focuses instead on the major activities performed by an organisation in response to (or 'pulled' by) sales orders or forecasted future sales. ABB reflects an organisation's activities that describe how the organisation performs and balances its work across functional silos:

1. Budgeting by activity reflects how the organisation's work is to be performed, not by organisational chart hierarchies.
2. Major activities often draw resources from multiple functions. For example, new product development typically uses personnel and other resources from the functions of marketing, engineering, finance and manufacturing.
3. Comparing ABB resources supplied to actual resources used gives useful analysis of capacity planning and capacity use.

ABB modifies the traditional budgeting process to better reflect the operational processes in the organisation. Planning to meet forecasted sales identifies the needed productive activities, and the needed activities determine the needed resource capabilities. Figure 5.2 displays the intended process of the ABB budgeting model for a firm that operates in a competitive market.

The **operational plan** is the result of the first ABB budgeting phase (i.e. the operational budget loop at the left hand side of Figure 5.2), which begins with forecasting future market demand for the firm's final goods and services. The sales forecast drives the product quantity/mix decision, which then drives the expected production activities. Activity based drivers help operational planners to estimate the resources that are needed to fulfil the product

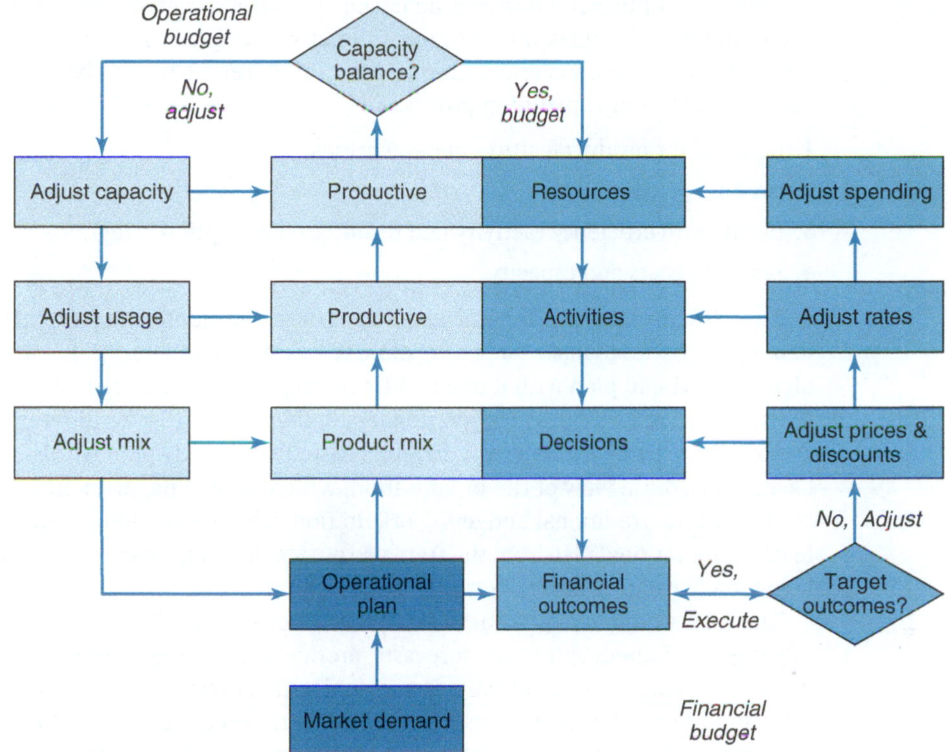

Figure 5.2 Activity-based budgeting model (adapted from the CAM-I ABB group and Hansen et al., 2003)

demand requirements. **Activity rates** define the type and number of activities needed to produce the expected product/service mix. **Resource consumption rates** define the resources needed to execute the productive activities required.

Budgetary unit managers analyse **resource capacity**, which is the capability of the system to conduct activities, by comparing the necessary resources with the resources available to see if the activity plan is feasible in the short term. If not, the operating budget loop may be adjusted in order to reach a capacity balance between resources required and resources available. In case of unbalance, three short term adaptations may be feasible:

1. Adjust the capacity (e.g. seasonal hiring, outsourcing).
2. Adjust productive activity use (e.g. modify scheduling).
3. Adjust the product mix to fit resources available.

Short term adjustments to resources that appear likely to recur may prompt requests for capital investment. Note that a traditional budgeting system rebalances by changing the product mix or resources available (capacity). ABB adds a broader perspective by recognising changes to productive activities and production capacity as well.

After reaching operational balance, the second stage (the financial budget loop) is the **financial plan**, which is the aggregation of pro forma accounting transactions that result in the pro forma financial results. The financial plan is typically broken down into information by resources, activities, products or other cost objects (Stephen C. Hansen, et al., 2003).

The **financial budget balance** is achieved when the targeted financial results are met. If the initial financial plan does not meet the target, the ABB system again reviews product decisions, activity costs and resource costs. They represent the basic budget issues that comprise the budget planning process:

1. demand for product features and quantities;
2. product prices;
3. production efficiency (activity and resource consumption rates);
4. resource costs and capacity.

The ABB approach has several advantages over traditional budgeting. The ABB approach to budgeting tries to make budgeting more relevant for managers by combining a more complete operational plan with a detailed financial plan. The detailed activity based planning in the first loop facilitates an operational plan that is sensitive for differences in unit, batch, customer and facility related cost drivers. The activity-based approach also leads to a process-based, horizontal view of the organisation, which crosses departmental borders. This contrasts with the traditional budgeting orientation, which is predominantly vertical. Having a feasible operational plan from the start also avoids that unnecessary financial projections are being made for unrealistic plans.

The ABB system also provides a complete set of tools for balancing the financial budget, looking simultaneously at sales forecasts, production efficiency, procurement prices, capacity decisions and product pricing. Having a detailed operational plan ready also makes the resulting financial budget more relevant for operational managers. The resulting transparency may reduce budget holder's gaming behaviour, and it may also facilitate a better coordination and adaptation within the firm. The ABB model requires more detailed operational and financial information than traditional budgeting systems, however. It is still an open question whether the higher complexity costs of the ABB approach can be sufficiently earned back by improved corporate performance. We present an extended example that illustrates and might encourage readers to consider the ABB reforms to traditional budgeting.

5.3 Activity based budgeting application

Most organisations prepare more than one budget for a particular period. Each budget relates to a specific function, area or activity that is assigned to a manager who holds responsibility for that particular budgetary unit. The aggregation of all budgets together gives a complete description of the budgeted operations (sales, products, activities, resources), budgeted capital investments and financial performance of the entire organisation. This aggregation of ABB operating and capital budgets is also called the 'master budget', which is illustrated in Figure 5.3.

The **ABB operating budget** implements the organisation's strategy by forecasting the expected levels of activities, such as sales, purchasing, production, maintenance, marketing and distribution (and other 'overhead' activities). Sales forecasts lead to product mix decisions, which then determine the necessary production activities. The production budget prompts plans for the purchase and supply of raw materials, components, and minimum required inventories of materials inputs, as well as direct labour and manufacturing overheads. The production budget may signal the need for permanent changes to capacities, which is modelled in the 'capital investment budget'. The effects of all operating and capital investment activities result in sales revenue, expenses and cash flows that directly affect the

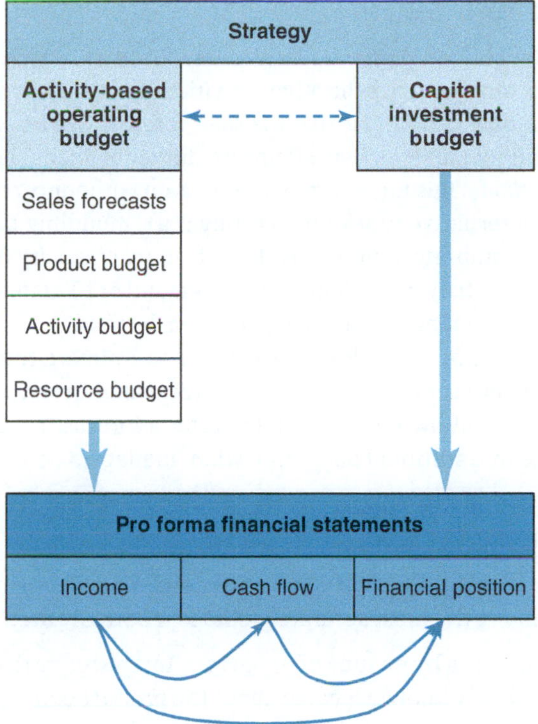

Figure 5.3 Master budget components

firm's financial position. Thus, the ABB budgets culminate (as does traditional budgeting) in pro forma financial statements, which managers analyse for suitability with strategic and operational plans. Adjustments in the capacity to produce may be effected by the capital investment budget,[2] or by temporary adjustments captured in the operating budget.

Note that *all* budgeted spending in the ABB operating budget is related to budgeted levels of sales and productive activity, including administrative support activities. If one cannot justify 'discretionary' activities, such as legal and human resource activities, promotions, advertising, training and so on, by current or planned productive activity, then these areas of spending have escaped scrutiny for too long. Indeed, many companies in recent years noticed that administrative spending was growing uncontrollably. Closer looks revealed that this spending was not closely related to productive activity. These companies either have greatly reduced this spending or have outsourced the support activities.

The precedence of budgeting sales (or desired service levels or donations) perhaps should be true for government agencies and non-profit organisations, as well. Historically, however, the starting point for non-commercial enterprises has been the budget allocated by the government, the organisation's board of directors, or the general assembly of constituents. As budgets tighten in all organisations, the past practices of incremental budgeting (e.g. use last year's budget amount plus inflation) or spending whatever is granted appear to be disappearing. ABB may permit non-commercial enterprises to provide sustainably valued services to constituents, even in difficult times.

[2] We regard research and development as similar to capital investment activity, although required financial reporting may differ.

5.3.1 Sales forecasting

The first budget to prepare is the **sales forecast**, which predicts future sales levels and the product mix that drive the other activities for the budget period. Sales forecasting is not easy,[3] and the only certainty is that the sales forecast will be wrong. However, good management is intentional and, as Henri Poincaré, father of chaos theory, stated in a 1903 essay *Science and Method*, "It is far better to foresee even without certainty than to not foresee at all."[4]

The alternative to sales forecasting is a) "muddling through" by purposely forgoing sales or by maintaining a sufficiently large resource capacity (production, logistics, and inventory stocks) to satisfy more than average demand or b) maintaining outsourcing-option relationships that hopefully will react quickly on demand.

Thus, the aim of sales forecasting is to estimate future sales as accurately as possible. The danger seems not in realising forecasting errors, which are inevitable, but having no recourse or allowing no flexibility after a forecast is made. This appears to be a common mistake in traditional budgeting when managers do not flexibly adjust to new conditions.

5.3.2 Methods for sales forecasting

Armstrong and Green (2011) describe and evaluate many alternative sales forecasting methods. Among the most accurate methods reportedly are:

- **Judgments by groups of experts.** Interestingly the 'experts' need not be, individually, completely knowledgeable about the product market to be forecasted. However, using a group of reasonably knowledgeable and experienced judges to forecast sales has been shown to be more accurate than other judgment based forecasting methods. We refer the reader to Armstrong and Kesten (2011) for elaboration and related references.
- **Econometric models built on historical data.** Many methods use historical data, including data mining and neural network analysis. However, a well-specified and estimated econometric (linear regression) model tends to be the most accurate. This method is similar to methods used in this text's Chapter 6, and will be illustrated here. The same cautions from Chapter 6 apply. If sufficient reliable data are not available, one should consider using a group of experts instead to forecast sales.

5.3.3 Forecasting sales from historical data

As Chapter 6 cautions, one should use historical data prudently to estimate linear regression models of sales or costs. Because the sales forecast is so important to the budgeting process, one should be especially conservative. One particularly should be beware of factors that appear to reduce unexplained variance by discarding sources of variance. For example, most

[3] 'It is very difficult to make an accurate prediction, especially about the future.' Niels Bohr, Nobel laureate in physics (http://en.wikipedia.org/wiki/Niels_Bohr).

[4] Poincaré also cautioned 'If we knew exactly the laws of nature and the situation of the universe at the initial moment, we could predict exactly the situation of that same universe at a succeeding moment. But even if it were the case that the natural laws had no longer any secret for us, we could still only know the initial situation *approximately*. If that enabled us to predict the succeeding situation with *the same approximation*, that is all we require, and we should say that the phenomenon had been predicted, that it is governed by laws. But it is not always so; it may happen that small differences in the initial conditions produce very great ones in the final phenomena. A small error in the former will produce an enormous error in the latter. Prediction becomes impossible, and we have the fortuitous phenomenon' (http://www-chaos.umd.edu/misc/poincare.html#NewtonClock)

historical datasets contain data from only successful, surviving firms, business units or product lines. Failed or merged sub-units tend to be purged from the record, but this is misleading to forecasting, because future failures or restructurings are possibilities. Another common data censoring method eliminates so-called 'outlier' data because they seem to be highly unusual. Unless one can verify that apparently outlying data are data entry errors, do not discard them simply to improve the model's apparent ability to explain sales variability – the appearance was gained by eliminating variability. This practice is a disservice to the forecasting effort because, if an unusual event happened before, it can happen again. One does no service to decision makers by censoring variability that is part of the process being modelled.

Even if an unusual event has not occurred in the historical record, this does not mean one might not happen in the future. Nassim Taleb (2009) cautions,' Rare events cannot be estimated from empirical observation since they are rare. . . Real life is not a casino with simple bets. This is the error that helps the banking system go bust with an astonishing regularity.' One should try to insure against catastrophic, unseen events by retaining enough resources to survive such an event and by having an exit plan if, for example, sales completely collapse.

Less dramatically but importantly, one should analyse past data for clues about important, regular influences on sales, such as seasonal buying patterns, discounts and competitor promotions.

5.3.4 Assessing the accuracy and variability of sales forecasts

One can assess the accuracy of a sales forecasting model before the budget period commences if sufficient data exist to hold out a sub-sample of data for a test of predictive ability.[5] A **hold out sample** could be a randomly held out sample of cross-sectional data or a sub-sample of the most recent time series data. The **estimation sample** is used to create the regression model of historical sales, which is then used to predict actual sales in the hold out sample. The resulting sales prediction errors (actual – predicted) are an indication but perhaps an understatement of the likely sales forecast errors for the budget period.

The sales variability of the prediction errors and the standard error of the forecast from the regression model can be used in sensitivity, scenario and Monte Carlo simulation analyses, as introduced in Chapter 4. We now proceed with an example of sales forecasting driven, activity based budgeting.

5.3.5 Sales forecasting and activity based budgeting example

Cell-Phone Company Ltd is a small, speciality producer of three types of mobile phones: Basic, Handy and Excel, which have increasingly more features, higher prices and larger profit margins. These speciality phones are especially durable and are purchased mostly by law enforcement agencies. Because of competition and technological advances, all mobile phone products have short product lives, generally no more than three years.[6] The short product lives, rapid technological change and growing competition make the task of sales forecasting difficult but also very important. Cell-Phone managers forecast sales with a linear regression model built on historical

[5] Some suggest holding out 30% of the sample for testing predictive ability. This might be difficult if available data are scarce.

[6] For this example, we assume that product generations do not overlap. The new generation is phased in after the old model is phased out.

sales data. Because historical data lags the most current market conditions, Cell-Phone managers may modify the statistical sales forecasts (up or down) to reflect their expert judgments.

Table 5.1 Phone-Cell Company historical sales data

Quarterly sales data				
Quarter	Second year of generation	Year	Intention to buy	Sales units
1	0	1	12.6%	2791
2	0	1	12.9%	3045
3	0	1	13.6%	3299
4	0	1	15.0%	3553
1	1	2	12.3%	3264
2	1	2	13.3%	3561
3	1	2	14.8%	3857
4	1	2	14.9%	4154
1	0	3	12.6%	3019
2	0	3	12.7%	3294
3	0	3	14.6%	3568
4	0	3	14.6%	3843
1	0	4	12.7%	3103
2	0	4	13.8%	3386
3	0	4	14.6%	3668
4	0	4	14.9%	3950
1	1	5	12.0%	3537
2	1	5	12.5%	3859
3	1	5	13.4%	4180
4	1	5	15.3%	4502
1	0	6	12.9%	3269
2	0	6	13.3%	3566
3	0	6	14.4%	3863
4	0	6	14.3%	4160
1	0	7	11.9%	3282
2	0	7	13.8%	3580
3	0	7	13.7%	3878
4	0	7	15.7%	4177
1	1	8	13.0%	3725
2	1	8	13.7%	4064
3	1	8	14.9%	4402
4	1	8	14.4%	4741
1	0	9	11.2%	3538
2	0	9	12.3%	3859
3	0	9	14.8%	4181
4	0	9	15.0%	4503

Historical data

The company is about to begin its 10th year of operations and its fourth generation phones. The available historical, quarterly sales data are shown in Table 5.1. These data are minimal for the task of sales forecasting, yet managers will hold out Year 9's sales data to test the predictive ability of a regression model based on the first eight years. This test will allow Cell-Phone to anticipate Year 10's likely forecasting errors.

The variable, 'Second Year of Generation,' identifies the middle year of a phone's lifecycle, when sales historically have been highest. The variable, 'Year,' is the sequential year of Cell-Phone's operations. The variable, 'Intention to buy,' is a measure designed by Cell-Phone's Director of Marketing that gauges how likely is the company's target customer group to buy its mobile phones during a particular quarter.[7]

[7] 'Intention to buy' is one of several measures of consumer choice that marketers can use to predict near term customer purchases. It may be measured by surveys of potential customers and by their browsing of product websites.

Estimation and predictive ability

Cell-Phone managers used the first eight years of data to explain historical sales with a linear regression model. They then used this regression model to predict actual unit sales in Year 9. The predictions underestimated actual sales by about 6%, as shown in Figure 5.4.

Predictive Ability Test of Year 9 using estimation dataset							
	Estimation coefficients						
	Second year	Year	Intention to buy	Intercept			
	415.21	81.98	28,346.9	-720.94			
Quarter	Second year	Year	Intention to buy	Predicted sales	Actual sales	Percentage errors
1	0	9	11.2%	3192	3538	-9.8%
2	0	9	12.3%	3501	3859	-9.3%
3	0	9	14.8%	4218	4181	0.9%
4	0	9	15.0%	4258	4503	-5.4%
Total Year 9				15168.06	16081	-5.7%

Figure 5.4 Predictive ability test.

Example: Quarter 1's predicted sales, $3192 = 415.21 \times 0 + 81.98 \times 9 + 28346.9 \times 11.2\% - 720.94$

Forecasting model

The amount of error in Figure 5.4 was judged to be tolerable, and managers proceeded to use the entire dataset to forecast Year 10's unknown unit sales. This model is shown as an Excel output in Figure 5.5.[8]

Full dataset linear regression

Regression Statistics		
R	0.93	
R Square	0.86	
Adjusted R Square	0.85	
S	179.88	Used to compute the standard error of the forecast
Total number of observations	36	

Sales Units =- 439.7921 + 378.0902 * Second Year + 97.0863 * Year + 26014.2367 * Intention to buy

ANOVA	*d.f.*	*SS*	*MS*	*F*	*p-level*
Regression	3.	6,451,752.95	2,150,584.32	66.47	7.7E-14
Residual	32.	1,035,360.79	32,355.02		
Total	35.	7,487,113.74			

	Coefficients	*Standard Error*	*LCL*	*UCL*	*t Stat*	*p-level*	*H0 (5%)?*
Intercept	-439.79	373.5	-1,200.58	321.	-1.18	0.2477	*No*
Second Year	378.09	63.6	248.53	507.65	5.94	0.0012	*Rejected*
Year	97.09	11.61	73.43	120.74	8.36	0.0001	*Rejected*
Intention to buy	26,014.24	2,683.02	20,549.11	31,479.37	9.7	0.0001	*Rejected*
T (5%)	2.04						

Figure 5.5 Cell-Phone company sales forecasting model

The estimated regression coefficients create the regression model that is highlighted in the middle of Figure 5.5. Observe that 'S', the standard error of the **estimate** is highlighted for later

[8] Observe that this is an unusually good statistical model as shown by its high Adjusted-R^2, large F-statistic, and high t-statistics.

use in this chapter when we estimate the standard error of the **forecast**. The **standard error of the forecast** reflects increased variability that can be expected when predicting beyond the bounds of historical data.

Sales forecast

Cell-Phone managers used the model in Figure 5.5 to forecast Year 10's quarterly and annual unit sales. They used the relatively stable averages of the quarterly 'Intention to buy' data to make the forecasts that are shown in Figure 5.6. The managers' next step was to apply their professional judgment to modify the statistical sales forecasts.

Managers observed that in prediction tests the statistical model underestimated actual sales, and reasoned that the forecasts for Year 10 might also be underestimates. Cell-Phone Company had implemented a vigorous sales campaign that reinforced the need for reliable mobile communications in troubled times, and initial feedback from the target customer population was quite favourable. Ultimately, managers decided to adjust subjectively the annual sales forecast upwards to 17000 units for Year 10.

A further step is to apply the company's expected sales mix to total unit sales. Across the phone generations the sales mix has settled on a mix of 58.8% Basic, 29.4% Handy and 11.8% Excel. However, the sales mix has varied by quarter for each of the three products. The historical, quarterly sales mix is shown in Figure 5.7, which the Cell-Phone managers applied to the sales forecast in Figure 5.7 to prepare the projected sales for Year 10 in Figure 5.9, after the subjective adjustment to total sales units by the company's managers. The arrows indicate the order by which the total sales forecast (17,000 units) is populated to the revenue budget by product and by quarter. For example, the 3,700 units of all products forecasted in Quarter 1 are 21.8% × 17,000 units. Of these, 67.6 per cent are forecasted to be Basic IV, or $67.6\% \times 3{,}700 = 2{,}500$ units of Basic IV in Quarter 1. Other sales forecasts are computed similarly.

Sales forecast using full dataset				
	Forecasting coefficients			
	Second year	Year	Intention to buy	Intercept
	378.09	97.09	26,014.24	-439.79
Quarter	Second year	Year	Intention to buy	Forecasted Sales
1	0	10	12.4%	3,745
2	0	10	13.1%	3,948
3	0	10	14.3%	4,257
4	0	10	14.9%	4,402
Total Year 10				16,351

Figure 5.6 Cell-Phone Company's Year 10 sales forecast
Example: Quarter 1's forecasted sales,
$3393 = 378.09 \times 0 + 97.09 \times 10 + 26014.24 \times 11.0\% - 720.94$

Historical/Expected Sales Mix	Quarter				Year as
Years 1 - 8	1	2	3	4	a whole
Basic I, II, III	67.6%	61.0%	55.6%	53.2%	58.8%
Handy I, II, III	27.0%	29.3%	31.1%	29.8%	29.4%
Excel I, II, III	5.4%	9.8%	13.3%	17.0%	11.8%
Quarterly sales distribution	21.8%	24.1%	26.5%	27.6%	**100.0%**

Figure 5.7 Cell-Phone company historical sales mix

Revenue Budget Detail Year 10	Quarter 1	Quarter 2	Quarter 3	Quarter 4	Year as a whole
Projected Sales units					
Basic IV	2,500	2,500	2,500	2,500	10,000
Handy IV	1,000	1,200	1,400	1,400	5,000
Excel IV	200	400	600	800	2,000
Total projected sales units	3,700	4,100	4,500	4,700	**17,000**
Selling prices					
Basic IV	€ 200	€ 200	€ 200	€ 200	
Handy IV	300	300	300	300	
Excel IV	450	450	450	450	
Projected revenues					
Basic IV	€ 500,000	€ 500,000	€ 500,000	€ 500,000	€ 2,000,000
Handy IV	300,000	360,000	420,000	420,000	1,500,000
Excel IV	90,000	180,000	270,000	360,000	900,000
Total revenues	€ 890,000	€ 1,040,000	€ 1,190,000	€ 1,280,000	€ 4,400,000

Figure 5.8 Year 10 projected sales units and revenue budget

5.3.6 Activity based production budgets

After approving the sales forecast, budget analysts follow Figures 5.2 and 5.3 to prepare Production and Activity Budgets, which are shown in Figures 5.9, 5.10, and 5.11 (one for each product). The **production budgets** estimate the quantities and timing of product requirements; these are shown in the top section of each of these figures. The expected sales unit quantity needs to be available in the coming budget period, but in some cases production activities

Product and production activity budgets Year 10: Basic IV		Quarter 1	Quarter 2	Quarter 3	Quarter 4	Year as a whole
Product budget						
Budgeted sales, units		2,500	2,500	2,500	2,500	10,000
+ Target closing inventory		**1,000**	1,000	1,000	1,000	
= Total requirements		3,500	3,500	3,500	3,500	
- Opening inventory		**200**	1,000	1,000	1,000	
Units to produce		3,300	2,500	2,500	2,500	10,800
Activity budget	Activity rates per unit of activity					
Unit-level activities						
Parts & components used	€ 20	€ 66,000	€ 50,000	€ 50,000	€ 50,000	€ 216,000
Assembly & testing labor used	€ 30	99,000	75,000	75,000	75,000	324,000
Packaging & stocking labor use	€ 10	33,000	25,000	25,000	25,000	108,000
Batch-level activities						
Materials handling/order*	€ 500	2,000	1,500	1,500	1,500	6,500
EOQ, units	1,000					
Product-level activities						
Production supervision/ qtr	€ 40,000	40,000	40,000	40,000	40,000	160,000
Depreciation/qtr	€ 15,000	15,000	15,000	15,000	15,000	60,000
Customer-level activities						
Customisation used/qtr	€ 2,500	0	0	0	0	0
Facility-level activities assigned**						
Central management used/qtr	€ 10,000	10,000	10,000	10,000	10,000	40,000
Business services used/qtr	€ 2,000	6,000	6,000	6,000	6,000	24,000
Engineering services used/qtr	€ 5,000	0	0	0	0	0
Space occupancy used/qtr	€ 30,000	30,000	30,000	30,000	30,000	120,000
Selling & distribution used/qtr	€ 24,000	24,000	24,000	24,000	24,000	96,000
Total activity cost		€ 325,000	€ 276,500	€ 276,500	€ 276,500	€ 1,154,500

* Even a partial order consumes the same resources as a full 1,000 unit order

** Units of business service reflect the size of product-line operations. Other facility level activities are budgeted as needed.

Figure 5.9 Basic IV product and activity budgets

are already undertaken in the previous period, and inventory stocks have been built up. Then, at the end of the current budget period, a target quantity of new stock needs to be ready for sale in the next period. Units of each product to produce in each period are derived from the following balancing equation:

Units to produce = Budgeted sales units + Target closing inventory − Opening inventory

The **activity budgets** estimate the types and quantities of production activities that are needed to implement the operational plan. These budgets are based on typical activity based costing categories of activities and resources used and are the second sections of Figures 5.9, 5.10, and 5.11. In brief, these activities consume resources in expected amounts, which are known 'activity rates', and include:[9]

Product and activity budgets Year 10: Handy IV		Quarter 1	Quarter 2	Quarter 3	Quarter 4	Year as a whole
Product budget						
Budgeted sales, units		1,000	1,200	1,400	1,400	5,000
+ Target closing inventory		500	500	500	500	
= Total requirements		1,500	1,700	1,900	1,900	
- Opening inventory		**0**	500	500	500	
Units to produce		1,500	1,200	1,400	1,400	5,500
Activity budget	Activity rates per unit of activity					
Unit-level activities						
Parts & components used	€ 40	€ 60,000	€ 48,000	€ 56,000	€ 56,000	€ 220,000
Assembly & testing labor used	€ 50	75,000	60,000	70,000	70,000	275,000
Packaging & stocking labor used	€ 10	15,000	12,000	14,000	14,000	55,000
Batch-level activities						
Materials handling/order	€ 500	1,000	1,000	1,000	1,000	4,000
EOQ, units	1,000					
Product-level activities						
Production supervision/ qtr	€ 30,000	30,000	30,000	30,000	30,000	120,000
Depreciation/qtr	€ 20,000	20,000	20,000	20,000	20,000	80,000
Customer-level activities						
Customisation used/qtr	€ 2,500	0	0	0	0	0
Facility-level activities						
Central management used/qtr	€ 20,000	20,000	20,000	20,000	20,000	80,000
Business services used/qtr	€ 2,000	4,000	4,000	4,000	4,000	16,000
Engineering services used/qtr	€ 5,000	5,000	0	0	0	5,000
Space occupancy used/qtr	€ 20,000	20,000	20,000	20,000	20,000	80,000
Selling & distribution used/qtr	€ 25,000	25,000	25,000	25,000	25,000	100,000
Total activity cost		€ 275,000	€ 240,000	€ 260,000	€ 260,000	€ 1,035,000

Figure 5.10 Handy IV product and activity budgets

- **Unit level activities** – performed for each *unit* of product (e.g. direct materials and direct labour used to build each product).
- **Batch level activities** – performed for each *batch* of products (e.g. materials ordered in batches per economic order quantity (EOQ) optimisation).

[9] The reader is referred to nearly any intermediate level cost accounting or cost management text for descriptions of activity based costing (ABC). This discussion assumes that the organisation has at least a rudimentary implementation of ABC. It may be possible to reconfigure traditional accounts into an ABC like scheme, especially if the organisation uses an enterprise resource planning (ERP) system.

Product and activity budgets Year 10: Excel IV			Quarter 1	Quarter 2	Quarter 3	Quarter 4	Year as a whole
Product budget							
Budgeted sales, units			200	400	600	800	2,000
+ Target closing inventory			200	200	200	200	
= Total requirements			400	600	800	1,000	
- Opening inventory			**400**	200	200	200	
Units to produce			0	400	600	800	1,800
Activity budget	Activity rates per unit of activity						
Unit-level activities							
Parts & components used	€	80	€ -	€ 32,000	€ 48,000	€ 64,000	€ 144,000
Assembly & testing labor used	€	75	0	30,000	45,000	60,000	135,000
Packaging & stocking labor used	€	25	0	10,000	15,000	20,000	45,000
Batch-level activities							
Materials handling/order	€	500	0	500	500	500	1,500
EOQ, units		1,000					
Product-level activities							
Production supervision/ qtr	€	40,000	40,000	40,000	40,000	40,000	160,000
Depreciation/qtr	€	25,000	25,000	25,000	25,000	25,000	100,000
Customer-level activities							
Customisation used/qtr	€	2,500	5,000	0	5,000	0	10,000
Facility-level activities							
Central management used/qtr	€	30,000	30,000	30,000	30,000	30,000	120,000
Business services used/qtr	€	2,000	6,000	6,000	6,000	6,000	24,000
Engineering services used/qtr	€	5,000	10,000	0	0	0	10,000
Space occupancy used/qtr	€	20,000	20,000	20,000	20,000	20,000	80,000
Selling & distribution used/qtr	€	25,000	25,000	25,000	25,000	25,000	100,000
Total activity cost			€ 161,000	€ 218,500	€ 259,500	€ 290,500	€ 929,500

Figure 5.11 Excel IV product and activity budgets

- **Product level activities** – performed to sustain each *product line* (e.g. dedicated production supervision, depreciation of equipment dedicated to the product line).
- **Customer level activities** – performed for each or each type of *customer* (e.g. customised production, or pre- and post-sale services).
- **Facility level activities** – performed for each product line from general company resources (e.g. allocations of executive time, business services and so on).

The Activity Budget estimates the costs of each of the activities employed to build each product in each period by multiplying the appropriate activity rate by the units of activity used. The activity budget sums these activity costs for each period and the entire year. These budgets feed into Product Margin Budgets and the pro forma Statement of Income.

5.3.7 Product margin budget

The **Product Margin Budget** in Figure 5.12 displays each product's budgeted sales revenues from Figure 5.9 and matched activity costs of sales. Figure 5.13 also computes product margin ratios for each product, each period. This Figure shows that Basic IV is expected to consistently add to profits for all periods. Cell-Phone Company expects Handy IV to steadily increase its contributions to profit. Excel IV, the company's most expensive and feature-laden product, however, contributes losses early in the budget timeframe but begins to contribute to profits later. These losses are the results of forecasted low sales volumes and relatively heavy consumption of resources. This may be cause for concern if this behavior is atypical of the previous generations of the Excel product line.

Product margin budget basic IV, Year 10	Quarter 1	2	3	4	Year as a whole
Sales revenue	€ 500,000	€ 500,000	€ 500,000	€ 500,000	2,000,000
Activity costs of sales					
Unit level - materials	50,000	50,000	50,000	50,000	200,000
Unit level - labor	100,000	100,000	100,000	100,000	400,000
Batch level	2,000	1,500	1,500	1,500	6,500
Product level	55,000	55,000	55,000	55,000	220,000
Customer level	-	-	-	-	-
Facility level	70,000	70,000	70,000	70,000	280,000
Total activity costs	277,000	276,500	276,500	276,500	1,106,500
Product margin	€ 223,000	€ 223,500	€ 223,500	€ 223,500	€ 893,500
Product margin ratio	44.6%	44.7%	44.7%	44.7%	44.7%

Product margin budget handy IV, Year 10	Quarter 1	2	3	4	Year as a whole
Sales revenue	€ 300,000	€ 360,000	€ 420,000	€ 420,000	1,500,000
Activity costs of sales					
Unit level - materials	40,000	48,000	56,000	56,000	200,000
Unit level - labor	60,000	72,000	84,000	84,000	300,000
Batch level	1,000	1,000	1,000	1,000	
Product level	50,000	50,000	50,000	50,000	200,000
Customer level	-	-	-	-	-
Facility level	74,000	69,000	69,000	69,000	281,000
Total activity costs	225,000	240,000	260,000	260,000	985,000
Product margin	€ 75,000	€ 120,000	€ 160,000	€ 160,000	€ 515,000
Product margin ratio	25.0%	33.3%	38.1%	38.1%	34.3%

Product margin budget excel IV, Year 10	Quarter 1	2	3	4	Year as a whole
Sales revenue	€ 90,000	€ 180,000	€ 270,000	€ 360,000	900,000
Activity costs of sales					
Unit level - materials	16,000	32,000	48,000	64,000	160,000
Unit level - labor	20,000	40,000	60,000	80,000	200,000
Batch level	-	500	500	500	
Product level	65,000	65,000	65,000	65,000	260,000
Customer level	5,000	-	5,000	-	10,000
Facility level	91,000	81,000	81,000	81,000	334,000
Total activity costs	197,000	218,500	259,500	290,500	965,500
Product margin	€ 107,000-	€ 38,500-	€ 10,500	€ 69,500	€ 65,500-
Product margin ratio	-119%	-21.4%	3.9%	19.3%	-7.3%

Figure 5.12 Product margin budget

Capacity cost budget Year 10	Quarter 1	2	3	4	Year as a whole
Unit-level activities					
Direct labor	€ 240,000	€ 240,000	€ 240,000	€ 240,000	€ 960,000
Batch-level activities					
Materials handling	5,000	5,000	5,000	5,000	20,000
Product-level activities					
Production supervision	110,000	110,000	110,000	110,000	440,000
Depreciation of equipment	60,000	60,000	60,000	60,000	240,000
Customer-level activities					
Product customisation	5,000	5,000	5,000	5,000	20,000
Facility-level activities					
Central management	60,000	60,000	60,000	60,000	240,000
Business services	20,000	20,000	20,000	25,000	85,000
Engineering services	15,000	15,000	15,000	15,000	60,000
Space occupancy	80,000	80,000	80,000	80,000	320,000
Selling & distribution	74,000	74,000	74,000	74,000	296,000
Total capacity costs	€ 669,000	€ 669,000	€ 669,000	€ 674,000	€ 2,681,000

Figure 5.13 Capacity cost budget

5.3.8 Capacity cost budget and statement of income, pro forma

The budgeting flow of Figure 5.2 directs managers to balance the resource needs that are budgeted in Figure 5.12 with the Phone Cell Company's budgeted resource costs, which are displayed in Figure 5.13. The **Capacity Cost Budget** presents the annual plan to supply resources for productive activities. For example, the company plans to supply €240,000 each quarter of the budget year, and similarly for most of the other resources supplied.[10] Although production activities are expected to vary somewhat by quarter, the company prefers to budget relatively constant resources, perhaps because the costs of flexibility are excessive. Still, the company must balance its budgeted needs against its budgeted supply of resources.

The final budget that we consider in this chapter is the pro forma Statement of Income,[11] Figure 5.14, which consolidates the product margins and balances the activity costs assigned to products against the supply of resources. The latter important comparison is shown in the section labelled, **unassigned activity costs**, which are the costs of unused activity capacity that are charged as period expenses.

Statement of income, *pro forma* year 10	Quarter 1	Quarter 2	Quarter 3	Quarter 4	Year as a whole
Sales revenue	€ 890,000	€ 1,040,000	€ 1,190,000	€ 1,280,000	€ 4,400,000
Activity costs of sales (see detail)					
Basic IV	277,000	276,500	276,500	276,500	1,106,500
Handy IV	225,000	240,000	260,000	260,000	985,000
Excel IV	197,000	218,500	259,500	290,500	965,500
Total cost of sales	699,000	735,000	796,000	827,000	3,057,000
Gross activity margin	191,000	305,000	394,000	453,000	€ 1,343,000
Gross activity margin ratio	21.5%	29.3%	33.1%	35.4%	30.5%
Unassigned activity costs					
Unit-level costs (direct labor)	€ 18,000	€ 28,000	€ (4,000)	€ (24,000)	€ 18,000
Batch level costs (mat'ls handling)	2,000	2,000	2,000	2,000	8,000
Product-level costs (super., depr.)	-	-	-	-	-
Customer-level costs (customisation)	-	5,000	-	5,000	10,000
Facility-level costs					
Central management	-	-	-	-	-
Business services	4,000	4,000	4,000	9,000	21,000
Engineering services	-	15,000	15,000	15,000	45,000
Space occupancy	10,000	10,000	10,000	10,000	40,000
Selling & distribution	-	-	-	-	-
Total unassigned costs	34,000	64,000	27,000	17,000	€ 142,000
Operating profit	157,000	241,000	367,000	436,000	1,201,000
Provision for income taxes @20%	31,400	48,200	73,400	87,200	240,200
Net profit	€ 125,600	€ 192,800	€ 293,600	€ 348,800	€ 960,800
Net profit margin ratio	14.11%	18.54%	24.67%	27.25%	21.84%

Figure 5.14 Statement of income, pro forma

[10] The company budgets additional business service resources in the fourth quarter for outsourced tax services.

[11] A complete, Master Budget also budgets pro forma statements of cash flow and financial position. ABB budgets these two statements similarly to traditional budgeting. See Exercises 5.2 and 5.3 for a combination of sales forecasting and a master budget.

Consider the first quarter's unassigned, unit level cost of €18,000 for direct labor (blue font).[12] This is computed as follows.

Unassigned direct labour cost = Cost of direct labour supplied (Figure 5.13)
− Cost of direct labour assigned to products (Figure 5.12)
€18,000 = €240,000 − €132,000 (Basic) − €90,000 (Handy) − €0 (Excel)

Other costs of unassigned resources are computed similarly. Note that direct labour resources supplied for Quarters 3 and 4 are insufficient for budgeted needs, but supplies of direct labour are unused in Quarters 1 and 2. If direct labour cannot be rescheduled across the quarters of the year, Phone-Cell Company must contract for additional labour resources in Quarters 3 and 4 (€4000 + €24000), while incurring unused labour costs in Quarters 1 and 2. Perhaps seasonal employees are available, or the company might offer overtime work to existing employees (at higher rates and with likely impacts on other resources). Alternatively, the company might choose to build products in excess of sales needs in Quarters 1 and 2, storing them for sale in Quarters 3 and 4. This would reduce unused labour costs but exposes the company to some risks of excess inventory, such as holding costs and obsolescence.

Other resources are budgeted either exactly for use as supplied or in excess of budgeted needs. The company may see the total of unassigned costs, €142 000 for the year as not excessive compared to the budgeted total cost of €2 681 000 (5.3%, excluding direct materials). Alternatively, the company might be budgeting some resources too closely if realised demand is more than forecasted. The company might find it useful to explore what are the possible and likely financial and resource implications of variations of actual sales from budgeted sales. For an exploration of budget risk, we turn to Monte Carlo simulation analysis.

5.4 Monte Carlo budget simulations

Cell-Phone Company's budgets are 'pulled' by sales forecasts that drive all of the budget elements. Of course, sales forecasts are probabilistic statements about future events, and the only certainty is that the aggregate forecast will be in error–but by how much? As discussed in Chapter 4, firms may use sensitivity, scenario and Monte Carlo analyses to assess the impacts of possible changes in a financial model's parameters. Monte Carlo analysis is uniquely designed to answer questions of the type, 'What is the probability that (any critical outcome: resource use, profitability, . . .) will be realised?' For example, managers at Cell-Phone Company might well ask of their budget model, **'What is the probability that the product margin of the Excel IV model phone will be greater than zero for the year?'** Let us consider the information needed to answer this question (and similar others) using a Monte Carlo simulation.

First, we need a model that links the sales forecast to the Excel IV product margin. The linked budget elements from Figure 5.2 to Figure 5.12 comprise such a model.

Second, we need a probability distribution of the uncertain product sales, which is obtained from the Figures 5.5 and 5.6. Therein, we have the forecasting model, which produces a mean

[12] Cell Phone Company orders raw materials as needed for production, and incurs no unassigned costs for this resource.

forecast of annual unit sales of 16351 units, and the information to compute the **standard error of the forecast**, which is an estimate of the standard error of future sales estimated outside of the historical data set. The standard error of the forecast is computed with the following formula:

$$SE(Forecast) = SE(Regression) \times \left\{1 + \frac{1}{n} + \sum_{i=1}^{k}[(X_i - X_i bar)/(n^{.5} \times SD(X_i))]^2\right\}^{.5}$$

Where:

- SE(regression) = standard error of the forecasting model regression, 179.88 units
- n = number of observations used to estimate the forecasting model regression, 36
- X_i = value of each of the independent variables for each quarter, which also must be forecasted if they are uncertain
- X_i-bar = historical mean of each of the independent variables used to estimate the regression
- SD(X_i) = historical standard deviation of each of the independent variables used to estimate the regression

It is true, of course, that the future quarterly sales variable is not the only uncertainty in the linked budget models. Sales mix, sales prices, and activity cost rates and supplies are also uncertain and easily could be additional probabilistic elements of a Monte Carlo budget simulation. For simplicity of this example, we will restrict uncertainty to the sales forecast.[13]

Third, we need to implement the Monte Carlo method, which simulates thousands of budget outcomes quickly and summarises the outcomes in useful ways that support answers to probabilistic questions.[14]

Fourth, we interpret the simulation results. Consider Figure 5.15's (a) histogram and (b) cumulative probability plot of the Excel IV annual product margins from 1,000 random simulations of Figure 5.13.

The simulated results are 'well behaved,' which follows from this example's probabilistic sales forecast as a random, normally distributed variable. From the simulation, the empirical answer to the question, **'What is the probability that the product margin of the Excel IV model phone will be greater than zero for the year?'** is **'zero.'** This product has no chance to be profitable for the entire year. That sales are expected to increase steadily over the course of the year might be reassuring that the product will be profitable over its 3-year life cycle, but the Excel IV is the company's riskiest product.[15]

[13] The random sales forecast can be computed with the Excel formula, = NORMINV(RAND(), 16351, 179.88)

[14] One can 'force' Microsoft Excel to perform Monte Carlo simulations using 'Data Tables' and the 'Histogram' function. Search the Excel 'Help' menu for 'Monte Carlo simulation.' Equivalently and far easier is to use a commercial product (Excel add-in or stand-alone product) for the simulation. Some online vendors offer 'student' pricing for their add-in risk simulators, which are inexpensive and work quite well.

[15] Other summary information of this simulation of Excel IV's product margin include:

Mean	€(91028)
St. Dev.	€12728
Mean St. Error	€402
Minimum	€(137683)
First Quartile	€(99496)
Median	€(90830)
Third Quartile	€(82667)
Maximum	€(48064)

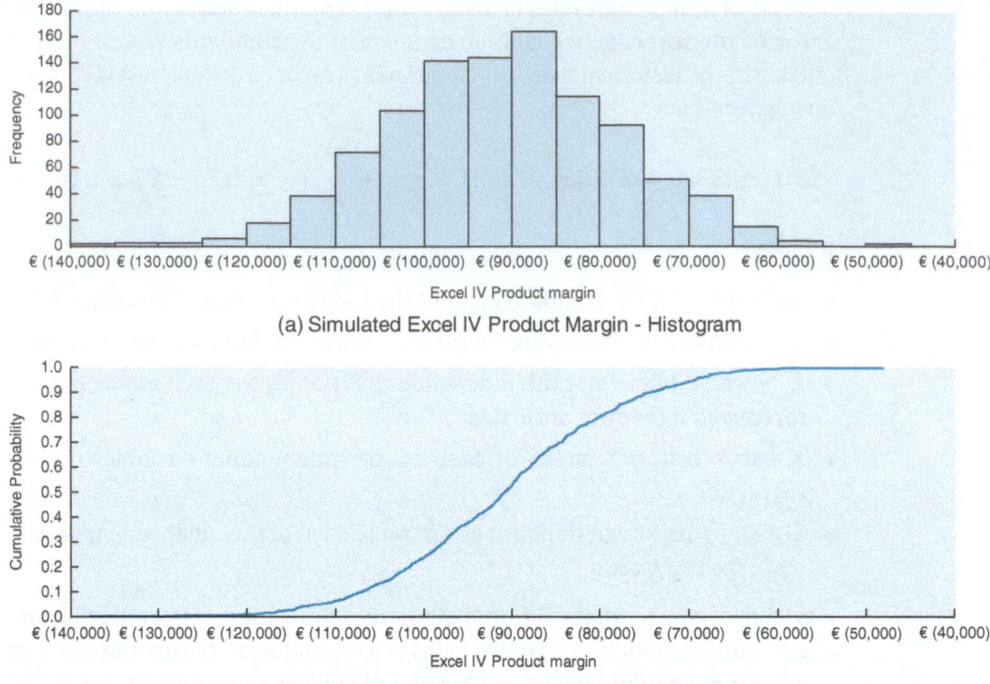

(a) Simulated Excel IV Product Margin - Histogram

(b) Simulated Excel IV Product Margin - Cumulative Chart

Figure 5.15 Monte Carlo simulation summary: Excel IV product margin

The beauty of the Monte Carlo simulation method is that any budget outcome can be simulated and queried probabilistically. The only constraint is quality of information about input variables' probability distributions.[16]

5.5 The hazardous game of aggregating budgets

In practice, an organisation's budget is often an aggregation of subsidiary budgets. A company's overall production budget may be composed of a larger set of production budgets, one for each responsible production manager. These budgets may be set in such a way that they guide the production manager to produce an optimal amount and quality of products for the firm. While setting the budget, company management may set challenging, yet attainable targets that should motivate managers to put additional effort into their jobs.

The budget holder faces a dilemma: accepting a higher target may lead to more resources and better career prospects, but it may also lead to a higher risk of failing to reach the proposed budget targets. Setting challenging targets also introduces an additional dilemma at

[16] A clear strength of Monte Carlo simulation is its ability to 'empirically' combine disparate probability distributions that could not be combined mathematically. Of course, one must describe the random variable thoughtfully.

the company level: what will happen to the risk of failing to reach the budget targets at the company level when all risky budgets are accumulated to the master budget?

An alternative to Monte Carlo simulation analytically assesses budget risk by aggregating standard errors of independent business units' profit. Assume a simple case in which four decentralised profit centre managers produce a single product under identical (but dispersed) conditions and report to a single superior (see Table 5.2)[17]. Each manager has an expected profit of €800, which is normally distributed with standard deviation of €200.[18] Suppose the firm would like to make budget attainment somewhat more challenging and decides to raise the profit target from €800 to €934. The target reduces the chance that managers attain their budget from 50% to 25%. This can be seen by using the normal z-value: $(934 - 800)/200 = 0.67$; the z-table gives the corresponding probability of $(1 - (0.5 + 0.25)) = 0.25$. If we would raise the budget difficulty for all managers in the same way, the total projected corporate profit would rise from €3200 to €3736. This is the good news: we are aiming for more profit. However, at the same time, the risk of not attaining that profit also rises. The square root of the variances aggregates the standard deviations of all managers as follows:

$$\sqrt{[n \times \text{var}(x)]} = \sqrt{(4 \times 200^2)} = €400$$

Table 5.2 Aggregation of decentralised profit centre budgets

	Profit centre		Optimistic scenario		Pessimistic scenario	
Unit	Expected profit	Standard deviation	Proposed budget	Attainability	Proposed budget	Attainability
A	800	200	934	25%	666	75%
B	800	200	934	25%	666	75%
C	800	200	934	25%	666	75%
D	800	200	934	25%	666	75%
Aggregate	3200	400	3736	9%	2664	91%

The z-value for the company becomes 1.34, which represents a corresponding probability of success of only 9%. This means that aggregating (independent) profit centre managers' budgets with moderate levels of risk aggregates to an corporate budget with a high, perhaps even unacceptably high, level of risk.

A symmetrical effect results from aggregating individual budgets that are easy to attain: The resulting corporate budget goal will be very easy to attain. Figure 5.16 therefore shows that budget estimates, which are initially submitted as mildly optimistic forecasts, become grossly optimistic when aggregated. And conversely, budget proposals, which are initially pessimistic, aggregate into grossly pessimistic estimates. This amplifying effect becomes larger when the degree of initial optimism or pessimism is larger and when more units are aggregated. Sometimes, organisational units use intermediate products from other units or are supported by services from other units. In these cases,

[17] This example is taken from Otley & Berry (1979).

[18] The class of probability distributions that can be combined as illustrated here is limited to exponential functions such as the normal distribution.

the output of a certain unit becomes dependent on the performance of other units. Generally, greater dependencies between units also amplify risks when these units' budgets are aggregated.

We could correct the overly optimistic and pessimistic scenarios at the central level by fixing the master budget targets at a level that corresponds with 25% budget attainability for the optimistic scenario and 75% attainability for the pessimistic scenario. These target amounts can be found by solving the following equation:

$$(X\text{-}\mu)/\sigma = 0.67 \text{ (z-value corresponding with 25\% attainability)}$$

Solving this equation leads to €3736 target profit under the optimistic scenario and using the same value for 75% profit attainability leads to the corporate target profit of €2932. We will divide the difference between the corporate initial budget estimate and the revised budget evenly among the business units. This leads to more attainable budget levels under the optimistic scenario and somewhat more challenging targets with lower attainability chances under the pessimistic scenario (see Table 5.3).

Table 5.3 Budget revisions to correct overly optimistic and pessimistic master budgets

Unit	Profit centre		Optimistic scenario		Pessimistic scenario	
	Expected profit	Standard deviation	Revised budget	Attainability	Revised budget	Attainability
A	800	200	867	37%	733	63%
B	800	200	867	37%	733	63%
C	800	200	867	37%	733	63%
D	800	200	867	37%	733	63%
Aggregate	3200	400	3468	25%	2932	75%

Organisations usually consist of business units of different size and of different risk profile. Table 5.3 presents the same corporate target profit level, but aggregated across units of different expected profit size and standard deviations. One adjustment strategy is to reduce each unit's target profit level by an equal amount. Table 5.4 redistributes the master budget reduction in equal parts over the units, which now leads to significantly different chances for unit managers of attaining their budget targets. These differences range from 32% budget

Table 5.4 Budget revision by equal redistribution of budget targets

Unit	Expected profit	Standard deviation	Proposed budget	Attainability	Revision by equal adjustments	
					Budget	Attainability
A	200	100	267	25%	209	46%
B	600	140	694	25%	636	40%
C	1000	220	1147	25%	1090	34%
D	1,400	280	1,588	25%	1530	32%
Aggregate	3200	395	3696	10%	3465	25%

attainability for the largest unit to 46% of the smallest unit. Although it may seem fair to relax the budget target for each unit with the same amount, it eventually leads to marked differences in budget attainability between units.

An alternative way to revise the budget proposal, which is also frequently used in practice, is to redistribute the target difference based on relative size of the units, giving large units a higher target reduction and smaller units a lower target reduction. Table 5.5 shows that this approach leads to a reduction of the variation in attainability scores, but it does not lead to the elimination of differences in attainability between units. Only when the master budget revision amount is distributed to the units based on relative risk (measured by its standard deviation, compared to the standard deviation of other units), will the units' budgets lead to unit budgets that provide equal attainability opportunities for all unit managers involved. This result calls attention to the concept of **budget fairness**. Many budget processes aspire to be fair to all managers involved. Budget fairness in this context means having equal opportunities to reach the budget target. As we can see from this example, looking at fairness does not only mean looking at budget targets, but also at the risk of not being able to meet the budget target. Concerns for budget risk surface when managers in a budget discussion try to answer the question: 'What are my chances of making this budget proposal, and what are the odds for me of not reaching the budget target?'

Table 5.5 Budget revisions that are proportional to size and risk

			Proportional to size		Proportional to risk	
Unit	**Expected profit**	**Standard deviation**	**Budget**	**Attainability**	**Budget**	**Attainability**
A	200	100	250	31%	236	36%
B	600	140	650	36%	650	36%
C	1000	220	1076	37%	1079	36%
D	1400	280	1488	38%	1500	36%
Aggregate	3200	395	3465	25%	3465	25%

5.6 Budget variance analysis

Recall that budgeting serves the important management function of **budgetary control**, which is accomplished by **budget variance analysis** that compares actual performance against the plan or budget. The main purposes of **budgetary control** are to a) analyse the causes of the variance between plan and performance and b) to indicate corrective action to ensure that future targets are achieved. Variance analysis is also helpful in identifying who may be held responsible for positive and negative budget variances. Sometimes budget variances are beyond the control of budget holders, because they are caused by external conditions like market price movements or quality problems in semi-finished products acquired. In such cases, 'flexing' the budget model for updated conditions may be informative about managers' performance, given that conditions have changed since the original budget was set.

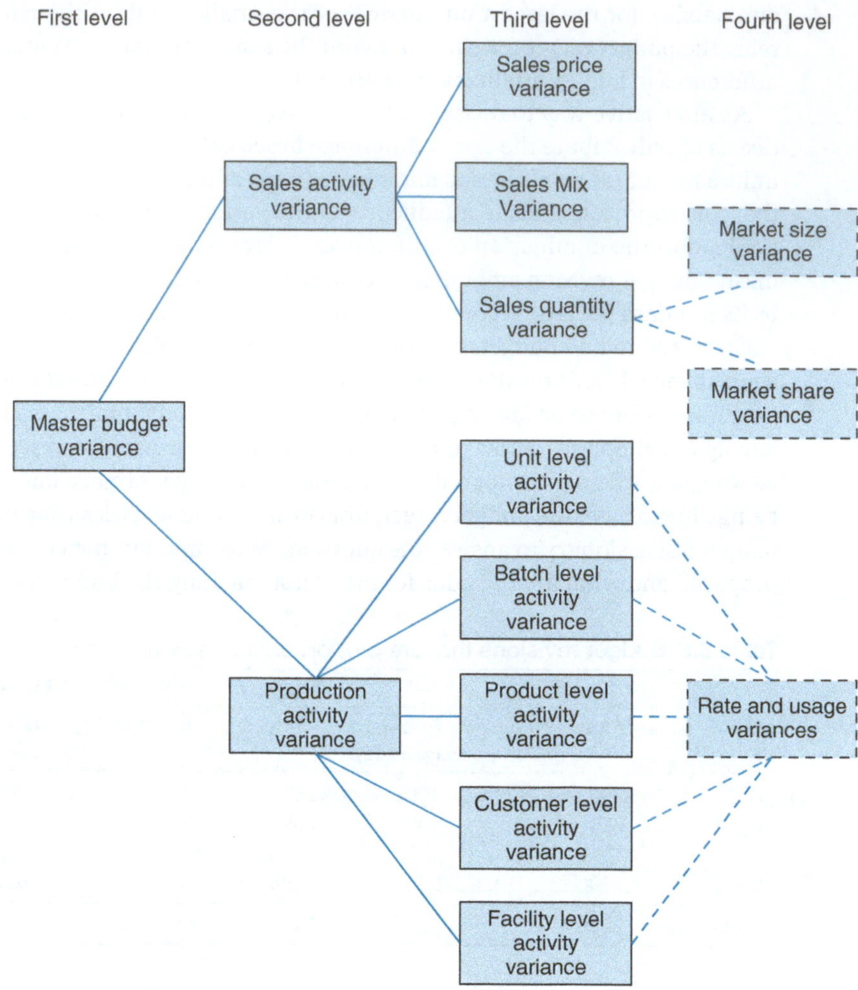

Figure 5.16 ABB variance framework

5.6.1 Activity based budget variance framework

This section of the chapter presents an overview of budget variance analysis in the context of activity based budgeting from our previous Phone-Cell Company example.[19] An ABB variance framework is shown in Figure 5.16, which resembles traditional budget variance analysis with multiple levels of computed variances. However, the objects of ABB and its related variances are sales and productive activities that range from unit level to facility level activities for each product.

The ABB framework decomposes the aggregate, master budget variance (*first level*) that is created by differences in sales and production activities (*second level*). The variance due to sales activity differences can be explained by variances from differences in sales

[19] A fuller coverage of variance analysis would require an entire chapter, which is common in most intermediate level cost or management accounting texts. Another framework that we particularly like was first formulated by Banker, Datar and Kaplan (1989) and further elaborated in Kaplan and Atkinson's 1998 *Advanced Management Accounting* textbook (Kaplan & Atkinson, 1998).

quantities and sales mix (*third level*). The sales quantity variance is decomposed into variances caused by changes in market size and market share (*fourth level*), if that information is available.

The second level variance caused by production activity differences is decomposed into variances caused by differences in each of the activity levels (*third level*), which can be further decomposed into input price (rate) and usage (efficiency) variances (*fourth level*). For economy of presentation, we present representative computations of three levels of variances.

5.6.2 Computation of ABB variances

This section focuses on computations and explanations of Phone-Cell Company's first quarter results, compared to the budget. We compute **sales activity variances** as differences of unit level margins (comparable to contribution margins) at budgeted production costs. We compute production activity variances as differences in costs driven by production activities, which may differ in volume from sales activity because of opening and closing inventory quantities. This treatment of variances assumes that all production activity variances are expensed as annual, period costs, and that inventories are not carried at actual cost. This is standard practice in standard costing systems, but may be allowed for in an ABC system (per IAS 2) if actual and budgeted costs are not 'materially' different. A summary of budgeted and actual activities for Quarter 1 is in Figure 5.17. The company had rebalanced

Sales and production activity summary					
Year 10, Quarter 1	Quarter 1 Budget	Quarter 1 Actual	Variance		
Sales Units					
Basic IV	2500	2400		100-	Unfavorable
Handy IV	1000	1100		100	Favorable
Excel IV	200	180		20-	Unfavorable
Total sales units	3700	3680		20-	Unfavorable
Sales Mix					
Basic IV	67.57%	65.22%		-2.35%	Unfavorable
Handy IV	27.03%	29.89%		2.86%	Favorable
Excel IV	5.41%	4.89%		-0.51%	Unfavorable
Total sales mix	100.00%	100.00%		0.00%	
Selling Prices					
Basic IV	200.00	200.00	€	-	Favorable
Handy IV	300.00	310.00		10.00	Favorable
Excel IV	450.00	450.00		-	Favorable
Production Units					
Basic IV	3,300	3400		100	units
Handy IV	1,500	1500		-	units
Excel IV	150	160		10	units
Total units produced	4950	5060		110	units
Unit-Level Costs					
Basic IV	60.00	61.10	€	1.10	Unfavorable
Handy IV	100.00	97.30		2.70-	Favorable
Excel IV	180.00	184.80		4.80	Unfavorable

Figure 5.17 Sales and production activities

its production budget to economise on the usage of direct labour by shifting production of 150 units of Excel IV to the first quarter. The shift eliminated the need to consider either overtime or seasonal labour, with minimal impacts on other productive activities (i.e. an additional €500 for materials handling in the first quarter to accommodate the increased production). A variance is labelled 'Unfavourable' if it has an adverse effect on quarterly income, and *vice versa*.

5.6.2.1 Sales activity variances

The total variance of the unit level margin variance to be explained by sales activity, €11,600 F, is computed in panel (a) of figure 5.18, and is decomposed into the (b) sales price and (c) sales activity variances, €11,000 F and €600 F, respectively. The sales activity variance is further decomposed into the (d) sales mix and (e) sales volume variances, €3,865 F and €3,265 U, respectively. The largest favorable impacts on the total margin are the higher sales

(a) Total unit-Level margin variance (at budgeted unit-level costs)

Unit-level margin variance budgeted Year 10, Quarter 1	Unit-level margin	Actual unit-level margin at budgeted costs	Unit-level variance	
Basic IV	€ 350,000	€ 336,000	€ 14,000-	Unfavorable
Handy IV	200,000	231,000	31,000	Favorable
Excel IV	54,000	48,600	5,400-	Unfavorable
Total	€ 604,000	€ 615,600	€ 11,600	Favorable

(b) Sales price variance (at budgeted unit-level costs)

Product	Budgeted unit margin	Actual unit margin	Actual sales units	Sales price variance	
Basic IV	€ 140.00	€ 140.00	2,400	€ -	Favorable
Handy IV	200.00	210.00	1,100	€ 11,000	Favorable
Excel IV	270.00	270.00	180	€ -	Favorable
Total				€ 11,000	Favorable

(c) Sales activity variance (at budgeted sales prices and unit-level costs)

Product	Budgeted unit margin	Budgeted sales units	Actual sales units	Sales activity variance	
Basic IV	€ 140.00	2,500	2,400	€ 14,000-	Unfavorable
Handy IV	200.00	1,000	1,100	20,000	Favorable
Excel IV	270.00	200	180	5,400-	Unfavorable
Total		3,700	3,680	€ 600	Favorable

(d) Sales mix variance (at actual sales volume, budgeted prices & costs)

Product	Budgeted unit margin	Sales mix difference	Actual sales units	Sales mix variance	
Basic IV	€ 140.00	-2.35%	3,680	€ 12,108-	Unfavorable
Handy IV	200.00	2.86%	3,680	21,081	Favorable
Excel IV	270.00	-0.51%	3,680	5,108-	Unfavorable
Total				€ 3,865	Favorable

(e) Sales volume variance (at budgeted sales mix, prices & costs)

Product	Budgeted unit margin	Budgeted sales units	Budgeted sales at actual quantity	Sales volume variance	
Basic IV	€ 140.00	2,500	2,486	€ 1,892-	Unfavorable
Handy IV	200.00	1,000	995	1,081-	Unfavorable
Excel IV	270.00	200	199	292-	Unfavorable
Total		3,700	3,680	€ 3,265-	Unfavorable

Figure 5.18 Decomposition of the total unit level margin variance

Basic IV, Unit-level Production Costs Year 10, Quarter 1	Original budget at budgeted quantity Per unit	 Total	Flexible budget variance	Flexible budget at actual quantity Per unit	 Total	Actual costs at actual quantity Per unit	 Total	Production activity variance	
Unit-level activities	3,300 units		100	3,400 units		3,400 units			
Parts & components used	€ 20.00	€ 66,000	€ 2,000	€ 20.00	€ 68,000	€ 20.50	€ 69,700	€ 1,700	Unfavorable
Assembly & testing labor used	30.00	99,000	3,000	30.00	102,000	31.00	105,400	3,400	Unfavorable
Packaging & stocking labor used	10.00	33,000	1,000	10.00	34,000	9.60	32,640	1,360-	Favorable
Sub-total	€ 60.00	€ 198,000	€ 6,000	€ 60.00	€ 204,000	€ 61.10	€ 207,740	3,740	Unfavorable
Batch-level activities									
Materials handling		€ 2,000	€ -		€ 2,000		2,000	-	Favorable
Product-level activities									
Production supervision		40,000	-		40,000		40,000	-	Favorable
Depreciation of equipment		15,000	-		15,000		15,000	-	Favorable
Customer-level activities									
Product customisation		-	-		-		2,000	2,000	Unfavorable
Facility-level activities									
Central management		10,000	-		10,000		10,000	-	Favorable
Business services		6,000	-		6,000		6,500	500	Unfavorable
Engineering services		-	-		-		-	-	Favorable
Space occupancy		30,000	-		30,000		30,000	-	Favorable
Selling & distribution		24,000	-		24,000		24,500	500	Unfavorable
Total Activity costs		€ 325,000	€ 6,000		€ 331,000		€ 337,740	€ 6,740	Unfavorable

Figure 5.19 Basic IV production activity variances

and prices commanded by the Handy IV product. Other products performed less well by contributing unfavorable impacts on unit-level margins.

5.6.2.2 Production activity variances

For economy of presentation, we present production activity variances for the Basic IV product in Figure 5.22. Other products' variances are computed similarly (see Exercises 5.9 and 5.10 to perform these calculations).

The originally budgeted, total activity cost, €325,000, is adjusted for the 1000 unit increase in production to €331,000. This middle column of costs is the **flexible activity budget**, which is the sum of budgeted activity costs at the actual production quantity. The total flexible budget variance of €6,000 is wholly attributable to budgeted unit level costs of the actual production quantity. Sufficiently higher actual production would also affect other activity costs. The flexible budget at the actual production quantity is compared to actual costs to create production activity variances that might be diagnostic of cost control problems.

If any of these production activity variances in the final column is deemed 'material' (no pun intended), the production manager would investigate the sources of the variances and take corrective actions. Of course, an alert manager would not wait until the close of a quarter to investigate material variances, but the manager should be prepared to explain at the next budget meeting the solutions the department has implemented to prevent future occurrences.

For example, a plausible story to explain the first quarter's Basic IV sales and production variances was that the sales manager took a special order to customise 200 units of Basic IV for a customer who would take delivery in Quarter 2. One hundred of these customised units will be extra Quarter 2's sales, and Quarter 1 sales of 100 units were deferred for the special order. Was the special order worth it? The analysis in table 5.6 of incremental sales and production activities, which span two quarters, demonstrate the value of the special order (and possibly a new market for customised low end phones), despite apparently adverse effects in the first quarter from lower sales and higher costs. (See Table 5.6.)

Table 5.6 Phone-Cell Company historical sales data

Analysis of special order	
Special order increment	100 units
Unit-level margin	€60.00 per unit
Incremental unit-level margin	6000
Customisation	2000
Contract services	500
Selling & distribution	500
Net margin	€3,000

If the Basic IV department instead had clung to its original budget and missed the profitable sales opportunity, this would reinforce BB critics who decry the dysfunctions of traditional budgeting. Perhaps the ABB approach illustrated here permitted transparent calculations of the costs of activities to support the special order analysis.

5.7 The future of budgeting

Although ABB and BB are presented as radically different solutions to documented budgeting problems (i.e. using more sophisticated budgeting methods or abandoning budgeting as we know it) they may in fact be complementary solutions. Most organisations do not seem restricted to only one of the two approaches, but select elements from each model that seem to work best. Some European companies, like *Rhodia* and *Borealis*, have centralised strategic decision making in order to solve strategic uncertainties first, and then communicate their strategic priorities to the operating units. These companies use clearly articulated targets, which are set at the start of the budgeting period. Other firms, like *Svenska Handelsbanken* and *Ahlsell*, have chosen to decentralise both strategic and operational decision making to lower organisational units. They do not issue specific target levels set *ex ante*, but use relative performance assessment with hindsight after the budget period has ended (Groot, 2007; Hope, et al., 2003).

Common improvement attempts in a sample of US and Canadian firms are to better align budgeting with strategic planning, to prepare less detailed budgets initially and update them regularly using ongoing (rolling) forecasts. Some problems however, still remain like the occurrence of budgetary gaming. The most frequently occurring games are deferring necessary expenditures to future periods, spending money at year end to avoid losing it, accelerating sales near year end to make the budget, taking a 'big bath', and negotiating easier targets by 'sandbagging.'[20] (Libby & Lindsay, 2010).

The examples from both sides of the Atlantic show that budgeting is not abandoned, but it is being reconstructed in most cases. This shows both its strengths and weaknesses: it is virtually impossible for most companies to operate without budgets, but the way they are applied requires continuous rethinking and reshaping of the budgeting system. For the better we think, budgets are here to stay, but they, too, must evolve with other business practices.

---

[20] Sandbagging means that budget holders are deliberately performing at a lower level than they are capable of. The reason for this behaviour is to avoid a challenging target in the future.

EXERCISES[21]

Exercise 5.1 Sales forecasting

Nordic-Is is Norway's largest ice cream maker, and is steadily increasing its market share in Norway, Sweden and Denmark.

Required:

Prepare a seasonal sales forecasting model from the following historical sales data. *Hint*: use multiple regression analysis. Predict the next year's sales and compute standard errors of the forecasts.

Historical Sales Data

Sales, millions of liters	Year	Calendar month
4400	1	1
4490	1	2
4669	1	3
4754	1	4
4930	1	5
5150	1	6
5270	1	7
5090	1	8
4930	1	9
4770	1	10
4610	1	11
4540	1	12
4690	2	13
4989	2	14
5081	2	15
5330	2	16
5520	2	17
5630	2	18
5550	2	19
5353	2	20
5300	2	21
5140	2	22
5040	2	23
5000	2	24
5090	3	25
5287	3	26
5412	3	27
5720	3	28
5970	3	29
6050	3	30
5980	3	31
5825	3	32
5650	3	33
5600	3	34
5540	3	35
5410	3	36

[21] Excel files for Exercises and Cases are available to text adopters.

Exercise 5.2 Sales forecasting

Pendant Corporation is a (disguised) U.S. financial services firm that sells home mortgages to homeowners. The company has focused on growing its regional market share and managing its profitability. You are a consultant to Pendant, and your current assignment is to build a sales forecasting model of the company that is driven by key environmental and policy variables. The company identifies interest rate variability as the largest source of financial risk but also is concerned about other possible sources of risk.

Required:

Prepare and critically discuss a mortgage sales forecasting model from the following time series, annual sales data. Predict the mortgage lending rate and mortgage sales for the next two years. *Hint*: Use multiple regression analysis.

Historical sales data		
Year	30-yr fixed lending rate (%)	Mortgage sales $
1	7.38%	$9 560 000
2	8.04%	9 440 000
3	9.19%	9 470 000
4	9.04%	9 507 000
5	8.86%	9 625 000
6	8.84%	9 757 000
7	9.63%	9 850 000
8	11.19%	9 846 000
9	13.77%	8 400 000
10	16.63%	7 950 000
11	16.08%	8 200 000
12	13.23%	8 920 000
13	13.87%	8 580 000
14	12.42%	9 320 000
15	10.18%	9 570 000
16	10.20%	11 350 000
17	10.34%	11 260 000
18	10.32%	11 350 000
19	10.13%	11 160 000
20	9.25%	11 160 000
21	8.40%	11 320 000
22	7.33%	11 470 000
23	8.35%	11 470 000
24	7.95%	11 630 000
25	7.80%	11 790 000
26	7.60%	12 130 000
27	6.94%	12 220 000
28	7.43%	12 470 000
29	8.06%	12 570 000
30	6.97%	12 720 000
31	6.54%	12 600 000
32	5.82%	12 570 000
33	5.84%	10 330 000
34	5.86%	11 660 000
35	6.41%	13 200 000
36	6.34%	13 090 000
37	?	?
38	?	?

Exercise 5.3 Sales forecasting and budgeted operating income

Refer to the data and analysis from Exercise 5.2. Pendant Corporation earns the difference (the 'spread') between its cost of borrowed money to finance the mortgages and the mortgage lending rate that it charges homeowners on these dollar amounts. For example if the spread was 2% Pendant earned (.02) × $9560000 as sales revenue in Year 1. The spread also is earned on the 10% of mortgages held for investment; 90% of mortgages are resold to other institutions during the year. Consider the following additional operating activity data.

Pendant Corp Data	
Opening statement of financial position	**End of Year 36**
Cash	$1 500 000
Accounts receivable (net)	6 000 000
Plant, property & equipment (net)	12 000 000
Mortgage assets	8 000 000
Total assets	$27 500 000
Accounts payable	$400 000
Interest payable	1 200 000
Short-term debt	1 300 000
Long-term debt	4 000 000
Owners equity	20 600 000
Total equities	$27 500 000

Estimated annual sales activities and costs	Year 37
Fees per new mortgage (closing costs)	1.75%
Interest spread on mortgages*	2.00%
Uncollectible sales	5.00%
Mortgage resale rate**	90.00%
Mortgage resale earnings rate**	1.00%
Cash sales collection rate (applies to all)	92.00%
Budgeted expenses, expected inflation rate	
Salaries and wages	$6 200 000
Advertising	1 300 000
Depreciation	600 000
General administrative	3 000 000
Outsourced services	1 200 000
Cash payment rate (applies to cash expenses)	90%
Minimum cash balance	500 000
Plant, property and equip purchases+	300 000
PPE expected life, years	20
Forecasts (from previous exercise):	
Annual mortgage lending rate, %	?
Annual mortgage sales	?

* The mortgage interest spread is the targeted difference between the cost of borrowed money and the mortgage lending rate (e.g., the gross profit rate). The spread is earned on the average amounts of both new and existing (held) mortgage assets.

** Approximately 90% of mortgages are resold to other mortgage companies after one year, with net proceeds to Pendant of 1% of the mortgage value.

+ Purchases of 20 year equipment, paid with cash.

Required:

Prepare Pendant's pro forma statement of income for Year 37.

Statement of income, pro forma	Year 37
Sales revenues	
Mortgage interest earned (net)	
Mortgage closing costs	
Mortgage resales	
Total sales revenues	
Expenses	
Interest expense	
Salaries and wages	
Advertising	
Depreciation	
General administrative	
Outsourced services	
Total expenses	
Operating income before tax	

Exercise 5.4 Sales forecasting, budgeting and Monte Carlo budget simulation

Refer to the analyses for Exercises 5.2 and 5.3.

Required:

1. Use the sales forecast for Year 37 as the mean of sales, and compute the standard error of the forecast for Year 37. *Hint*: You might also have to forecast one or more independent variables first.
2. Use Monte Carlo analysis to simulate Pendant's net profit margin before tax.
3. Discuss the simulated risk that Pendant might be unprofitable in Year 37.

Exercise 5.5 Budgeted leverage ratio and scenario analysis

AbbaDabba Company has a leverage ratio covenant attached to its line of credit (e.g. notes payable). For this contract, the leverage ratio is defined as total debt divided by total assets. AbbaDabba's leverage ratio may not exceed 30% at the end of any year or it faces cancellation or restructuring of the terms of its line of credit. The following annual budget model reflects the most likely case for the coming year.

Budgeted leverage ratio analysis	Most likely case	Scenario 1	Scenario 2	Scenario 3
Leverage ratio covenant limit =	**30%**			
Budgeted leverage ratio (computed)	**20.96%**			
Assets				
Cash	€3 000			
Accounts receivable	1 000			
Inventory	2 000			
Plant, property & equipment (net)	10 000			
Total assets	€16 000			
Liabilities and Equities	-			
Accounts payable	€3 000			
Notes payable	1 000			
Interest payable	-			
Owners equity	12 000			

Budgeted leverage ratio analysis	Most likely case	Scenario 1	Scenario 2	Scenario 3
Total equities	€16 000			
Budgeted sales	€18 000			
Cash sales rate	80%			
Credit sales rate	20%			
Budgeted expenses				
Salaries and wages	€4 000			
Advertising	500			
Depreciation	800			
Minimum cash balance	1 500			
Minimum inventory	1 000			
Payments for inventory				
Cash purchases	75%			
Credit purchases	25%			
Gross margin ratio	30%			
Borrowing rate (annual)	8%			
Schedule of cash collections:				
Current cash sales	€14 400			
Past credit sales	1 000			
Total Collections	€15 400			
Inventory purchases budget				
Budgeted CGS	€12 600			
Add: Closing Inv.	1 000			
Total Required	13 600			
Deduct Opening Inv.	2 000			
Required Purchases	€11 600			
Schedule of cash payments for inventory purchases				
For last month	€3 000			
For this month	8700			
Total purchase payments	€11 700			
Schedule of cash payments for expenses:				
Salaries	€4 000			
Advertising	500			
Total expense payments	€4 500			
Cash budget				
Sources of cash				
Beg Cash Balance	€3 000			
Cash Collections	15 400			
Total Cash Available	18 400			
Uses of cash				
For inventory purch	11 700			
For operating expenses	4 500			
For interest	-			
Total payments	16 200			
Req'd cash balance	1 500			
Total cash required	17 700			
Cash excess(deficit)	700			
Financing:				
Borrowing	-			
Repayments	700			
Cash balance ending	€1 500			
Budgeted statement of income				
Sales	€18 000			
Cost of goods sold	12 600			
Gross margin	5 400			

(continued)

Budgeted leverage ratio analysis	Most likely case	Scenario 1	Scenario 2	Scenario 3
Expenses:				
Salaries	4 000			
Advertising	500			
Interest expense	7			
Depreciation	800			
Total expense	5 307			
Net operating income	€93			
Budgeted statement of financial position				
Cash	€1 500			
Accounts receivable	3 600			
Inventory	1 000			
Plant, property & equipment (net)	9 200			
Total assets	€15 300			
Accounts payable	$2 900			
Notes payable	300			
Interest payable	7			
Owners equity	12 093			
Total liabilities & equities	€15,300			
Leverage ratio (total debt/total assets)	**20.96%**			

Required:

1. Modify AbbaDabba's budget model for each of the following scenarios (keep other parameters at the most likely levels):

   Scenario 1:Budgeted sales = €15,000, Cash sales rate = 70%, Gross margin ratio = 25%, Borrowing rate = 8%.
   Scenario 2:Budgeted sales = €20,000, Cash sales rate = 90%, Gross margin ratio = 40%, Borrowing rate = 6%.
   Scenario 3:Cash sales rate = 70%, Budgeted salaries and wages €5,000, Advertising = €700, Minimum cash balance = €2,000, Minimum inventory = €1,500.

2. Comment on the scenario analysis evidence for the risks of AbbaDabba's violating the leverage ratio covenant.

Exercise 5.6 Budget model simulation

Required:

1. Review the budget model in Exercise 5.5 and its accompanying Excel file.
2. Randomise the variables chosen for scenario analysis with reasonable descriptions of the variables' probability distributions. Clearly label and describe your randomised variables.
3. Simulate AbbaDabba's leverage ratio computed by the budget model using Monte Carlo analysis.
4. Interpret the evidence in histogram and cumulative probability charts as the probability that AbbaDabba will violate its debt covenant.

Exercise 5.7 Activity based budgeting

Review Figures 5.12, 5.14 and 5.15 in the chapter.

Required:

1. Explain why direct labour resources are out of balance in Figure 5.15.
2. Explain with a numerical example how adjusting quarterly production units of Excel IV balances direct labour resources for the year.
3. Describe the impacts on other activities and resources from this rebalancing.

Exercise 5.8 ABB variance analysis

Required:

Consider the following actual activity cost data for the Handy IV phone for the first quarter of Year 10. Prepare a variance analysis similar to Figure 5.19 for this product's first quarter production results. Explain how these variances might have arisen.

Unit level activities	**Actual**
Parts & components used	€39.20
Assembly & testing labor used	48.70
Packaging & stocking labor used	9.40
Other production activities	**Actual**
Batch level activities	
Materials handling	€1000
Product level activities	
Production supervision	35,000
Depreciation of equipment	24,000
Customer level activities	
Product customisation	-
Facility-level activities	
Central management	22,000
Business services	6,000
Engineering services	5,000
Space occupancy	20,000
Selling & distribution	25,000

Exercise 5.9 ABB variance analysis

Required:

Consider the following actual activity cost data for the Excel IV phone for the first quarter of Year 10. Prepare a variance analysis similar to Figure 5.19 for this product's first quarter production results. Explain how these variances might have arisen.

Unit level activities	**Actual**
Parts & components used	€81.20
Assembly & testing labor used	76.60
Packaging & stocking labor used	27.00
Other production activities	**Actual**
Batch level activities	
Materials handling	€500
Product level activities	
Production supervision	35,000
Depreciation of equipment	25,000
Customer-level activities	
Product customisation	5,000

(continued)

Facility level activities	
Central management	28,000
Business services	4,000
Engineering services	15,000
Space occupancy	20,000
Selling & distribution	20,000

Exercise 5.10 Sales activity variances

Review Figures 5.17 and 5.18. Assume the following results for Year 11. Analyse sales activity variances as in Figure 5.19.

Sales and production activity summary				
Year 11, Quarter 1	Quarter 1 budget	Quarter 1 actual	Variance	
Sales units				
Basic IV	4122	4030	92-	Unfavorable
Handy IV	1649	1900	251	Favorable
Excel IV	330	340	10	Favorable
Total sales units	6100	6270	170	Favorable
Sales mix				
Basic IV	67.57%	64.27%	-3.29%	Unfavorable
Handy IV	27.03%	30.30%	3.28%	Favorable
Excel IV	5.41%	5.42%	0.02%	Favorable
Total sales mix	100.00%	100.00%	0.00%	
Selling prices				
Basic IV	$ 200.00	$ 200.00	€ -	Favorable
Handy IV	300.00	290.00	€ 10.00-	Unfavorable
Excel IV	450.00	450.00	€ -	Favorable
Production units				
Basic IV	4200	4100	(100)	units
Handy IV	1700	2100	400	units
Excel IV	400	360	(40)	units
Total units produced	6300	6560	260	units
Unit-level costs				
Basic IV	$ 60.00	$ 60.05	€ 1.10	Unfavorable
Handy IV	100.00	98.10	2.70-	Favorable
Excel IV	180.00	176.00	4.80	Unfavorable

CASES

Case 5.1 Sales forecasting, budgeting and Monte Carlo simulation

The purpose of this case is to build and explain a sales forecasting model for North American monthly sales of three major Japanese auto manufacturers that can be used as input to a simulated budget model for each company. You are commissioned to build the aforementioned models and to provide an interpretation of the riskiness of sales and gross margin forecasts for these three companies.

Edmunds.com's *"Consumer Vehicle Purchase Intent by Manufacturer" for a specified period is the percentage of visitors to* www.edmunds.com *who perform activities on that website that are highly correlated with a purchase of that model within the following three months (as determined by Edmunds' statistical analysis of visitor activities), as a share of visitors who perform similar activities for all models that are in the same manufacturer segment.* Edmunds.com *believes that "purchase intent" is a metric for measuring a model's share of consumer demand. While actual model sales are affected by several factors other than consumer demand (including model supply, configuration availability, incentive changes, dealer marketing strategies and fleet sales), purchase intent is a good predictor of near-term consumer sales. The Discount Percentage data is the sales-weighted average percentage difference between the MSRP and the "True Market Value®" of all available trim levels sold in the months indicated.*

Required:

1. Build the sales forecasting model only from the data in the 'Edmunds Data' table. You may transform the data as you wish, but clearly document any transformations that are not obvious. Clearly label all analysis outputs.
2. Complete the gross margin budgets for each company for month 27.
3. Use Monte Carlo simulation to measure the riskiness of gross margin forecasts for each company. Make a meaningful evaluation of these simulations (i.e. in the context of the case).

Manufacturer	Year	Month	Sequential month	Purchase intent	Discount percentage	Sales, units
Honda	2009	12	1	14.2%	10.5%	107 143
Honda	2010	1	2	13.8%	10.3%	67 479
Honda	2010	2	3	14.0%	11.3%	80 671
Honda	2010	3	4	13.9%	12.5%	108 262
Honda	2010	4	5	14.4%	12.7%	113 697
Honda	2010	5	6	13.8%	11.9%	117 173
Honda	2010	6	7	13.7%	12.0%	106 627
Honda	2010	7	8	14.1%	12.8%	112 437
Honda	2010	8	9	13.8%	12.7%	108 729
Honda	2010	9	10	14.0%	12.9%	97 361
Honda	2010	10	11	14.1%	10.7%	98 811
Honda	2010	11	12	13.4%	10.9%	89 617
Honda	2010	12	13	11.7%	12.2%	129 616
Honda	2011	1	14	10.0%	12.7%	76 268
Honda	2011	2	15	11.4%	12.6%	98 059
Honda	2011	3	16	11.7%	13.3%	133 650
Honda	2011	4	17	11.8%	12.1%	124 799
Honda	2011	5	18	11.8%	8.3%	90 773
Honda	2011	6	19	11.4%	8.2%	83 892
Honda	2011	7	20	10.9%	9.7%	80 502
Honda	2011	8	21	10.5%	9.3%	82 321
Honda	2011	9	22	10.5%	8.5%	89 532
Honda	2011	10	23	10.9%	6.8%	98 333
Honda	2011	11	24	10.3%	7.8%	83 925
Honda	2011	12	25	11.0%	8.5%	105 230
Honda	2012	1	26	11.4%	7.7%	83 009
Nissan	2009	12	1	8.1%	10.9%	73 404
Nissan	2010	1	2	8.3%	12.7%	62 572
Nissan	2010	2	3	9.1%	13.5%	70 189
Nissan	2010	3	4	9.2%	13.3%	95 468
Nissan	2010	4	5	8.8%	13.7%	63 769
Nissan	2010	5	6	8.6%	14.6%	83 764
Nissan	2010	6	7	8.5%	14.1%	64 570
Nissan	2010	7	8	8.7%	15.5%	82 337
Nissan	2010	8	9	8.7%	15.5%	76 827
Nissan	2010	9	10	8.4%	15.5%	74 205
Nissan	2010	10	11	9.0%	13.3%	69 773
Nissan	2010	11	12	8.6%	12.2%	71 366

(continued)

Manufacturer	Year	Month	Sequential month	Purchase intent	Discount percentage	Sales, units
Nissan	2010	12	13	7.6%	13.3%	93 730
Nissan	2011	1	14	7.4%	15.0%	71 847
Nissan	2011	2	15	7.6%	16.8%	92 370
Nissan	2011	3	16	7.7%	15.4%	121 141
Nissan	2011	4	17	7.0%	13.0%	71 526
Nissan	2011	5	18	7.1%	14.1%	76 148
Nissan	2011	6	19	7.0%	11.9%	71 941
Nissan	2011	7	20	7.3%	12.9%	84 601
Nissan	2011	8	21	7.7%	12.6%	91 541
Nissan	2011	9	22	7.5%	12.3%	92 964
Nissan	2011	10	23	7.0%	12.1%	81 877
Nissan	2011	11	24	6.9%	11.9%	85 182
Nissan	2011	12	25	6.7%	12.5%	100 927
Nissan	2012	1	26	6.4%	13.2%	79 313
Toyota	2009	12	1	18.6%	11.4%	187 860
Toyota	2010	1	2	17.2%	11.0%	98 796
Toyota	2010	2	3	15.4%	13.1%	100 027
Toyota	2010	3	4	18.6%	15.9%	186 863
Toyota	2010	4	5	17.0%	13.4%	157 439
Toyota	2010	5	6	16.0%	13.1%	162 813
Toyota	2010	6	7	15.7%	12.7%	140 604
Toyota	2010	7	8	15.4%	13.2%	169 224
Toyota	2010	8	9	15.3%	12.9%	148 388
Toyota	2010	9	10	15.8%	13.0%	147 162
Toyota	2010	10	11	16.0%	12.0%	145 474
Toyota	2010	11	12	16.0%	12.0%	129 317
Toyota	2010	12	13	14.4%	13.0%	177 488
Toyota	2011	1	14	14.2%	13.1%	115 856
Toyota	2011	2	15	14.0%	13.8%	141 846
Toyota	2011	3	16	14.8%	12.9%	176 222
Toyota	2011	4	17	14.1%	11.0%	159 540
Toyota	2011	5	18	12.7%	8.8%	108 387
Toyota	2011	6	19	12.7%	10.0%	110 937
Toyota	2011	7	20	13.3%	10.9%	130 802
Toyota	2011	8	21	13.5%	11.1%	129 482
Toyota	2011	9	22	14.1%	10.0%	121 451
Toyota	2011	10	23	15.2%	7.2%	134 046
Toyota	2011	11	24	15.5%	7.9%	137 960
Toyota	2011	12	25	15.3%	8.9%	178 131
Toyota	2012	1	26	15.5%	9.2%	124 540

Source: adapted from Edmunds.com, Inc. True Market Value® is a registered trademark of that company.

Honda sales	Mean/Median	Std Dev/Range
Monthly sales forecast, 000 units		
Average retail sales price, $ per unit*		
Discount forecast		
Average gross margin ratio, %**		
Budget simulation, month	**27**	
Randomised variables		
Sales units		
Sales price		
Discount		
Gross margin ratio		

Sales revenue, net ($ 000)		
Cost of goods sold		
Gross margin		
Nissan sales	**Mean/Median**	**Std Dev/Range**
Monthly sales forecast, 000 units		
Average retail sales price, $ per unit		
Discount forecast		
Average gross margin ratio, %		
Budget simulation, month	**27**	
Randomised variables		
Sales units		
Sales price		
Discount		
Gross margin ratio		
Sales revenue, net ($ 000)		
Cost of goods sold		
Gross margin		
Toyota sales	**Mean/Median**	**Std Dev/Range**
Monthly sales forecast, 000 units		
Average retail sales price, $ per unit		
Discount forecast		
Average gross margin ratio, %		
Budget simulation, month	**27**	
Randomised variables		
Sales units		
Sales price		
Discount		
Gross margin ratio		
Sales revenue, net ($ 000)		
Cost of goods sold		
Gross margin		

- * Estimate from www.buyingadvice.com/template-car-types/ or another source
- ** Estimate from Hoover's online or another source

Case 5.2 Activity based budgeting

The Mystic River Flyfishing Company designs, manufactures and retails fly rods to fishing enthusiasts around the world via its website. Mystic River is known for its advanced materials, innovative designs, and lifetime warranties against breakage. Mystic River produces three fly-rod designs that are targeted to fly fishers of different abilities: beginning (Smooth 100), intermediate (Crisp 200) and advanced (Rapid 300).

Part A

Mystic River wishes to develop an activity based budgeting approach to budgetary planning and control, and has engaged you as a consultant to prepare initial budgeting models and analyses. Your first step was to identify the major activities performed in the manufacture of fly rods. You have identified the following major activities performed for all products:

1. Procurement and handling of fly rod materials (e.g., graphite) and components (e.g., line guides, handles, reel seats).
2. Use of assembly labour (e.g., forming the fly rod, assembling the components, finishing).
3. Use of testing and packaging labour.
4. Use of selling and distribution services.
5. Production supervision.

6. Periodic use of equipment.
7. Customising fly rods for fishing club promotions.
8. Central management planning and control.
9. Use of business services (e.g. human resources, finance & accounting, legal, security, product design and so on).
10. Use of factory space.

Your next step was to estimate the costs of these activities and their appropriate cost-drivers.

Required:

Describe how you ideally would estimate activity costs and their cost drivers. What practical problems do you foresee?

Part B

Assume that Mystic River's Director of Sales and Marketing has provided a quarterly sales forecast for the next year. This forecast is shown in Table A. Mystic River's production policy is to manufacture the next quarter's expected sales in the preceding quarter.

Table A

Mystic River Flyfishing Company Revenue Budget Detail	Quarter 1	 2	 3	 4	Year as a whole
Projected sales units					
Smooth 100	1,200	2,100	900	1,800	6,000
Crisp 200	2,000	3,500	1,500	3,000	10,000
Rapid 300	800	1,400	600	1,200	4,000
Total projected sales units	4,000	7,000	3,000	6,000	20,000
Selling prices					
Smooth 100	€ 175	€ 175	€ 175	€ 175	
Crisp 200	350	350	350	350	
Rapid 300	750	750	750	750	
Projected revenues					
Smooth 100	€ 210,000	€ 367,500	€ 157,500	€ 315,000	€ 1,050,000
Crisp 200	700,000	1,225,000	525,000	1,050,000	3,500,000
Rapid 300	600,000	1,050,000	450,000	900,000	3,000,000
Total revenues	€ 1,510,000	€ 2,642,500	€ 1,132,500	€ 2,265,000	€ 7,550,000

Assume that you have estimated current annual spending on activities. Further assume that you have estimated activity cost drivers and consumption rates. The results of these time consuming and somewhat uncertain tasks are shown in Tables B and C.

Required:

Use the information in Tables A, B and C to prepare production activity budgets for each product for the next year. *Hint*: Use the format of Figures 5.9, 10 & 11.

Part C

Activity-based budgeting requires balancing of resources used and resources supplied (e.g., Figure 5.2).

Required:

1. Using the results of the previous parts of this case, construct an activity based statement of income that recognises under or over assigned resources. *Hint*: Follow the format of Figure 5.15.
2. Discuss how Mystic River might use this capacity balance information to improve its production efficiency for future years.

Table B

Mystic River Flyfishing Company capacity cost budget	Quarter 1	2	3	4	Year as a whole
Unit-level activities					
Direct labor	€ 200,000	€ 200,000	€ 200,000	€ 200,000	€ 800,000
Batch-level activities					
Materials handling	5,000	5,000	5,000	5,000	20,000
Product-level activities					
Production supervision	55,000	55,000	55,000	55,000	220,000
Depreciation of equipment	60,000	60,000	60,000	60,000	240,000
Customer-level activities					
Product customization	5,000	5,000	5,000	5,000	20,000
Facility-level activities					
Central management	60,000	60,000	60,000	60,000	240,000
Business & design services	35,000	35,000	35,000	35,000	140,000
Space occupancy	60,000	60,000	60,000	60,000	240,000
Selling & distribution	60,000	60,000	60,000	60,000	240,000
Total capacity costs	€ 540,000	€ 540,000	€ 540,000	€ 540,000	€ 2,160,000

Table C

Mystic River Flyfishing Company production activity budgets	Cost rates per unit of activity Smooth 100	Crisp 200	Rapid 300
Unit-level activities			
Materials & components used	€ 75	€ 110	€ 185
Assembly labor used	€ 20	€ 30	€ 65
Packaging & stocking labor used	€ 5	€ 5	€ 15
Batch-level activities			
Materials handling/order*	€ 200	€ 200	€ 300
EOQ, units	400	400	500
Product-level activities			
Production supervision/ qtr	€ 20,000	€ 20,000	€ 30,000
Depreciation/qtr	€ 10,000	€ 15,000	€ 20,000
Customer-level activities			
Customization used/qtr	€ 2,500	€ 1,250	€ 2,000
Facility-level activities assigned			
Central management used/qtr	€ 12,000	€ 15,000	€ 20,000
Business services used/qtr	€ 3,000	€ 4,000	€ 1,000
Space occupancy used/qtr	€ 24,000	€ 17,000	€ 16,000
Selling & distribution used/qtr	€ 18,000	€ 23,000	€ 20,000

Case 5.3 Activity based university budgeting

Columbo College is a small, independent college that has a small income producing endowment and a low rate and level of annual gifts. The college is almost entirely dependent on tuition revenue. Columbo is facing a financial crisis that has been worsened by its traditional budgeting practices. Each year's budget has been an incremental change to the prior year's budget that is roughly based on forecasted changes in enrolment and expected changes in cost of living. In reality, Columbo College has not been able to accurately forecast enrolment one year out and only knows its enrolment for the autumn term when students arrive. Thus, the first few weeks of the autumn term are chaotic as the college tries to align its largely fixed resources to meet student enrolment demands. Typically, enrolment change has not been an effective driver of the budget, and the budget has been adjusted solely by the expected changes in the government's cost of living index.

Nearly every year, Columbo College struggles to keep spending within its budget, and it has no budget slack to absorb unexpected spending. For the past five years, the college has paid for nearly $1M annual budget deficits by cancelling planned salary adjustments, deferring property upgrades, maintenance and repairs, and selling non-essential properties. These 'escape hatches' are closing rapidly, and the college's new president envisions an improved budgeting system that will abandon the incremental practices of the past and focus on essential activities and the resources to sustain them. She recently announced her plans to secure the college's financial sustainability in an open letter to stakeholders (faculty, students, alumni and trustees). Part of that letter follows.

"The fact is that Columbo's budget is not sustainable. While recent budgets have been technically balanced, this has only been possible by making choices that delayed meeting important needs, thereby accumulating what might be described as a 'structural deficit.' Bills are paid, paychecks are issued and the lights are on, but each year, the senior management has in essence employed financial sleight of hand to bring forward a balanced budget. Balanced is true in the accounting sense but the ethical deficit results in higher than desirable tuition, flat salaries, and weakened benefits.

'In our recent meeting with the Board of Trustees, we sought to balance all priorities from the implementation of the strategic plan. The worldwide economic outlook tells us that we cannot justify only adjustments of the current budget to compensate for our current and foreseeable budgetary shortfalls. We must take a prudent and responsible approach to these economic realities.

'Unfortunately, these realities require that we make some substantial budget cuts, with a target of reducing our annual spending by at least $1 million this academic year and beyond. I have asked our CFO and our Vice-President of Academic Affairs to work with the budget committee to address this urgent issue. While we may all ask how these decisions will affect us personally, the truth is that we do not know yet.

"We do not anticipate that this process will be easy, and I believe that it is important that I be as transparent as possible at the very beginning of this process. It is likely that this undertaking will reduce the number of fulltime positions at the University and may result in layoffs, although we would far prefer to reach our targeted budget reductions without having to make such drastic moves. Our goal will be not just to cut our costs, but to improve the way we operate Columbo College in the pursuit of our mission."

You have been engaged to help Columbo College design an improved budgeting process and system. Your experience with higher education has led you to prepare the following activity-based budget 'map.'

Required:

1. Explain how this budget map describes the ways that resources would be supplied and used at Columbo College, in the spirit of activity based budgeting.
2. How does this ABB approach differ from Columbo's traditional, incremental budgeting practice?
3. Describe a strategy to develop the information you would need to translate this budget map into a functioning, ABB budget process.
4. What obstacles should you anticipate that might impede implementation of this ABB approach?

5. Develop a numerical ABB example from the Psychology Department, which has the following operating characteristics. Note that the full time faculty teach most course sections, but some are taught by a part-time faculty who teach one or two course sections per year.

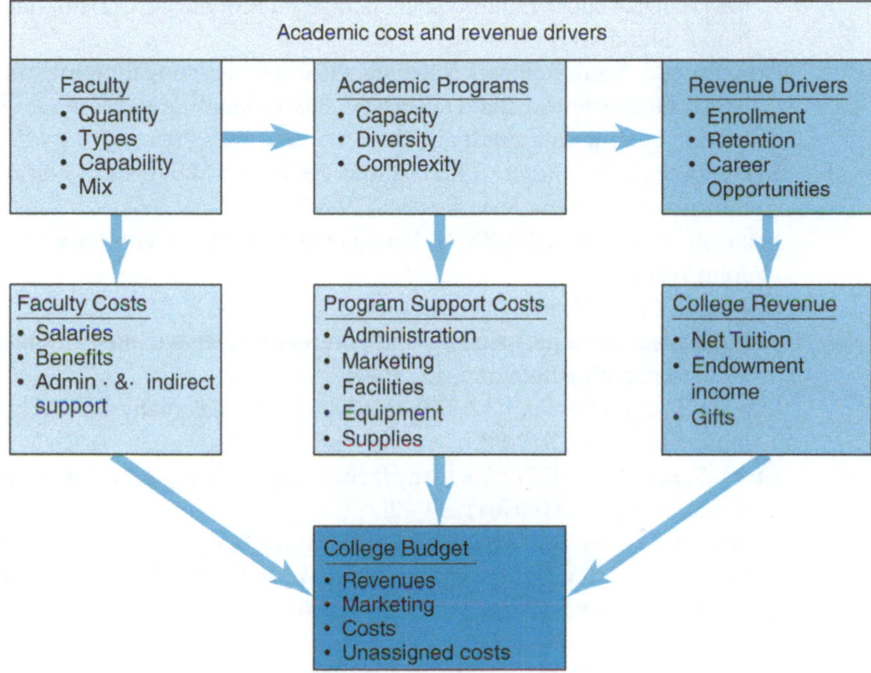

Case 5.3 Budget Map

Psychology Department			
Full-time (FT) faculty		10.00	
FT faculty, available to teach		9.50	
FT teaching load, sections		6	per year
FT capacity, sections		57	per year
Average salary, FT		$34,000	per year
Benefits		17%	
FT faculty rate		?	per section
Part-time (PT) rate		$ 2,500	per section
Average enrollment		12	per section
Course sections planned	Undergrad.	Graduate	
Taught by full-time	23	5	per year
Taught by part-time	7	6	per year
Tuition rate	$ 2,100	$ 2,400	per section
Departmental overhead			
Department chair (.5 FT)		$17,000	per year
Department administration		$10,000	per year

References

Armstrong, J. Scott and K. C. Green. (2011). DEMAND FORECASTING: EVIDENCE-BASED METHODS. Oxford Handbook in Managerial Economics. Christopher R. Thomas and William F. Shughart II (Eds.).

Armstrong, J. Scott, Roderick J. Brodie. (1999) Forecasting for Marketing. Published in Graham J. Hooley and Michael K. Hussey (Eds.), Quantitative Methods in Marketing, Second Edition.London: International Thompson Business Press, pp. 92-119.

Berg, Joyce E., Thomas A. Rietz. (2003) Prediction Markets as Decision Support Systems. Information Systems Frontiers 5:1, 79–93.

Brimson, J., & Antos, J. (2002). Driving value using Activity-Based Budgeting. New York: John Wiley.

Covaleski, M. A., Evans, J. H., III, Luft, J. L., & Shields, M. D. (2003). Budgeting research: three theoretical perspectives and criteria for selective integration. Journal of Management Accounting Research, 15, 3-49.

Ekholm, B.-G., & Wallin, J. (2000). Is the annual budget really dead? The European Accounting Review, 9(4), 519-539.

Groot, T. L. C. M. (2007). The many faces of beyond budgeting. MCA (Management Control & Accounting), 11(maart), 34-42.

Gurton, A. (1999). Bye bye budget ... the annual budget is dead. Accountancy(March), 60.

Hansen, S. C., Otley, D. T., & van der Stede, W. A. (2003). Practice Developments in Budgeting: An overview and research perspective. Journal of Management Accounting Research, 15, 95-116.

Hansen, S. C., & Torok, R. (2004). The Closed Loop: Implementing Activity-Based Planning and Budgeting. Bedford, TX: CAM-I.

Hofstede, G. H. (1967). The Game of Budget Control: Van Gorcum, Assen.

Hope, J., & Fraser, R. (1999). Beyond budgeting. Building a new management model for the information age. Management Accounting(January), 16-21.

Hope, J., & Fraser, R. (2003). Who needs Budgets? Harvard Business Review, 81(2, February), 108-115.

Hope, J. H., Fraser, J., & Robin, T. (2003). Beyond Budgeting: How Managers Can Break Free from the Annual Performance Trap. Boston: Harvard Business School Press.

Jensen, M. C. (2001). Corporate Budgeting is broken - Let's fix it. Harvard Business Review, 79(10, November), 95-101.

Libby, T., & Lindsay, R. M. (2010). Beyond budgeting or budgeting reconsidered? A survey of North-American budgeting practice. Management Accounting Research, 21(1), 56-75.

Merchant, K. A., & van der Stede, W. A. (2011). Management Control Systems (3 ed.). Harlow: Financial Times, Prentice Hall.

Neely, A., Sutcliff, M. R., & Heyns, H. R. (2001). Driving value through strategic planning and budgeting. New York, NY: Accenture.

Otley, D., & Berry, A. (1979). Risk distribution in the budgetary process. Accounting and Business Research, 9(36), 325-337.

Otley, D. T. (1999). Performance management: a framework for management control systems research. Management Accounting Research, 10(4), 363-382.

Scapens, R. W., & Roberts, J. (1993). Accounting and control: a case study of resistance to accounting change. Management Accounting Research, 4(1), 1-32.

Shan, Jerry Z., Hsiu-Khuern Tang, Ren Wu, Fereydoon Safai. Dynamic Modeling and Forecasting on Enterprise Revenue with Derived Granularities. Intelligent Enterprise Technologies Laboratory, HP Laboratories Palo Alto, HPL-2005-90, May 12, (2005).

Taleb, N. N. , (2009). Common Errors in Interpreting the Ideas of The Black Swan and Associated Papers NYU Poly Institute .

Trueman, Brett , M. H. Franco Wong, Xiao-Jun Zhang. Back to Basics: Forecasting the Revenues of Internet Firms. Review of Accounting Studies, 6, 305–329, (2001).

de Waal, A. A., Bilstra, E. P., & Ottens, P. H. J. (2004). Beyond Budgeting; Het praktische alternatief voor budgetteren (Vol. 62). Deventer: Kluwer.

de Waal, A. A., San, R. J. T., & Zwanenburg, E. (2005). Budgettering in Nederland. Chief Financial Magazine.

http://ssrn.com/abstract=1490769Wallander, J. (1999). Budgeting - an unnecessary evil. Scandinavian Journal of Management, 15, 405-421.

Chapter 6

Cost analysis and estimation

6.1 Introduction

Costs are resources that are consumed by the organisation to produce products and services. Managers need to control costs to maximise efficiency of resource use and to balance costs with the revenues that the products are expected to generate. In non-profit and government organisations cost control is equally important, because here managers are obliged to optimise the use of resources within the (cost) budget constraints. In order to understand how to manage costs effectively, it is necessary to understand how costs behave. **Cost behaviour** describes how internal conditions and the activities of an organisation affect costs. Any condition or activity that influences, causes or changes costs is called a **cost driver.** Some common examples of cost drivers are number of labour hours, quantities of materials consumed, machine hours, and number of products or services produced (as is also discussed in Chapter 4). More use of a cost driver is expected to result in higher total costs for the organisation. The exact relationship between cost drivers and costs may differ: some may be linearly variable while others may be non-linear, fixed or stepwise. A better understanding of the actual cost behaviour is important for managers, because they can use this information in important management decision situations:

1. Knowing how costs behave makes it possible for managers to make predictions of cost levels into the future, knowing that some cost drivers (like production volume or machine use) will change in the future. For instance, predictions can be made of how much total costs will vary when production numbers are changed. This information is necessary for making **planning** and **financial modelling** decisions (see also Chapters 2 and 4). Knowledge of cost behaviour helps managers in making cost predictions for activity levels that are different from the current levels of operation.
2. Cost behaviour information is also useful in **budgeting.** In most cases, managers first define the required type and level of activities, for instance the number of each type of product to produce. For each product, the specific cost function can be used to reliably define the budget required.
3. More insight in cost behaviour also helps in **cost control.** The comparison of actual costs with predetermined costs, based on cost models, helps in identifying the causes of cost deviations and the measures that may help control costs more effectively.

The purpose of this chapter is to present and use effective methods for defining cost behaviour and estimating costs by establishing reliable **cost functions.**

6.2 Cost functions

A **cost function** is a mathematical or statistical relation between a cost and one or more cost drivers. The steps to establish a cost function are informed choices of:

- cost driver(s);
- functional form;
- relevant data;
- analysis method;
- tests of reliability.

Note that rarely does the establishment of a cost function proceed only once through these steps. Most often, the process is iterative; that is, based on the observed results at any step, one may decide to back up to and repeat a previous step.

6.2.1 Choice of cost drivers

The choice of cost drivers (or explanatory variables) relates directly to the question of what variables reliably influence cost behaviour. The most frequently used cost drivers, such as number of products, labour hours and machine hours, are tangible and operational cost drivers. However, this is only a small sub-set of possible cost drivers. Under current market conditions, competitive advantage is not only dependent on tangible cost drivers, but is increasingly dependent on intangible drivers like product quality, timeliness of service, employee morale and location of facilities. Some are operational drivers, which can be adjusted in the short term, others are more strategic and it will take more time, effort and the contribution of more organisation members to change them. Table 6.1 presents examples of possible cost drivers in a two dimensional scheme, depicting the nature of different cost drivers.

Table 6.1 Different types of cost drivers

	Operational	Strategic
Tangible	Number of products Number of product lines Labor hours Machine hours Energy consumption Number of product parts	Product functionality Plant layout Product innovation Market development Product offerings Strategic alliances
Intangible	Quality of operations Employee capabilities Absenteeism Labor turnover Labor morale Production technology	Plant location Product image Competitive positioning Sustainability profile Company image Local community's loyalty

Most cost drivers not only play a role in the total cost function, but also influence the revenue function by making the product offering or the company profile more attractive to customers and other stakeholders. Some cost drivers, therefore, also appear as **revenue drivers:** they also play a role in the generation of additional value of the firm by improving its competitive position. This can be achieved by adding value to the product, by attracting more competent employees, and by gaining more public support for the company as a whole.

6.2.2 Functional form

A **functional form** describes the relationship between cost and cost drivers. The functional form may be different for the different cost drivers considered. If we take the cumulative total costs over a product's total life cycle, most economists expect to find a non-linear relationship for revenues and for total costs as depicted in Figure 6.1.

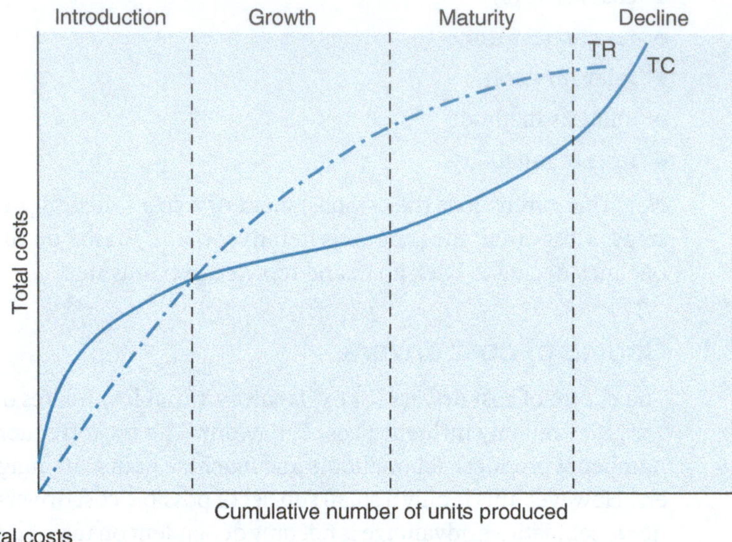

Figure 6.1 Costs and revenues over a product's lifecycle

The lifecycle total cost in Figure 6.1 is a stylised example how costs might behave, and is frequently used to describe the different life cycle phases (it is however not a pattern that each product in every industry should go through in their lifecycle–each life cycle may be different). In the stylised life cycle of Figure 6.1 we find different cost behaviour patterns in one cost function that may be classified piece-wise in different **functional forms.** The entire function could be expressed as an exponential function. In the **introduction phase** sales are relatively low, prices are high and costs are relatively high with **increasing** productivity. The functional form for this relation may be described as a polynomial with decreasing marginal costs:

$$TC_I = a_I + b_I x - c_I x_I^2$$

(subscript I denotes *Introduction phase*: this function's relevant part of the lifecycle)

In the **growth phase,** revenues are rising, while marginal costs are constant. Production systems are more optimised and more stable, leading to a linear relationship between units produced and total costs. As depicted in Figure 6.1, the functional relationship between number of products and costs can be represented by a positive linear function:

$$TC_G = a_G + b_G x_G,$$

in which a_G is the total fixed cost, b_G the unit variable cost, and x_G the cumulative total number of units produced during the growth phase.

In the **maturity and decline phases,** peak sales are generated at relatively low costs while costs start to increase due to intensive use of production capacity, aging equipment and additional costs of repairs. The functional form is best described by decreasing productivity, which is represented by a polynomial form with increasing marginal costs:

$$TC_M = a_M + b_M x_M + c_M x_M^2$$

As can be appreciated from Figure 6.1, in the longer run cost functions appear to be non-linear. In many cases of normal operations, however, cost analysis is done by using linear cost functions. This may be a feasible solution when the variation in the cost driver is reduced to a linear 'relevant range' in which the actual cost curve can be reliably estimated by a linear cost function. When non-linearity is dominant, as in the introduction and decline phases, linear relevant ranges can still be determined, but the ranges will be significantly smaller than in the growth phase.

6.3 Cost estimation techniques

6.3.1 Cost benefit concerns

Cost estimation is, first, the measurement of a cost function's parameters and, second, the use of the cost function to predict costs. Costs can be estimated in many different ways, depending on the availability of cost information, the required accuracy and reliability of cost estimations, and on the time and resources available for estimating costs.

Figure 6.2 displays alternative cost estimating techniques in the order of cost benefit considerations. The account classification method has the least data requirements and can be the least accurate, with the engineering method at the other end of the scale. In between we find different statistical techniques. In the choice of statistical techniques, we may still want to find the appropriate balance between the analysis outcome of reliability and input requirements. We will have a closer look at each of the cost estimation techniques to see how they function and how the quality of the resulting cost estimation outcomes can be evaluated.

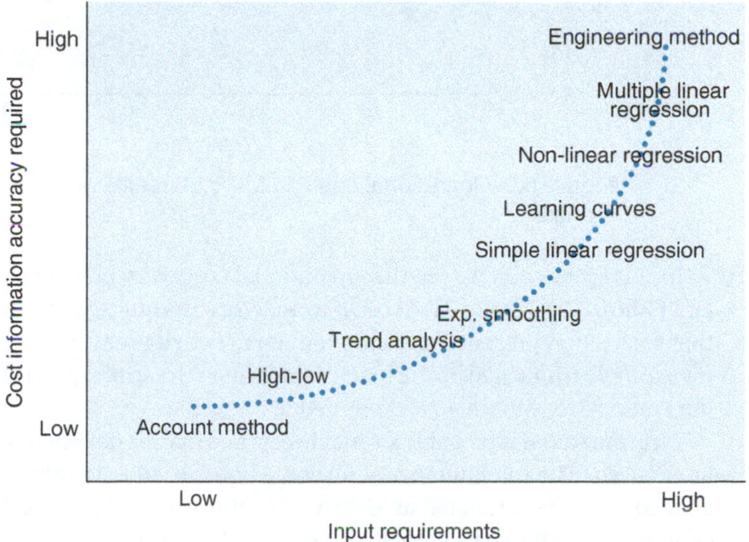

Figure 6.2 Cost estimation techniques

6.3.2 Account classification method

When all of the cost benefit conditions are low (which means not much cost information is available, accuracy requirements are not very high and the resources for estimation are restricted) the **account classification method** is frequently used. The basis of this method is the cost items (the 'accounts') as they appear in the company's bookkeeping system, budget or financial statements. The method aims at classifying each of these accounts as being fixed, variable or mixed, which is a combination of fixed and variable components. The account classification method does not require much additional analysis and relies to a great extent on experience and knowledge of costs analysts.

The account classification method starts by looking at the accounting information, generated by the bookkeeping system. For each of the line items the relationship between costs and business activity needs to be defined. This is generally done by judgment, which is based on experience, detailed analysis of specific accounts, or joint decision making by a group of well-informed specialists or decision makers.

Let us have a look at the cost data of *Micropower Computers (MC)*, a French firm that assembles, packages and sells microcomputers. One of the major production plants in Marseille has generated an overview of monthly cost data during a 4 year period. The operational costs are taken from the accounting system and a chronological representation is depicted in Figure 6.3.

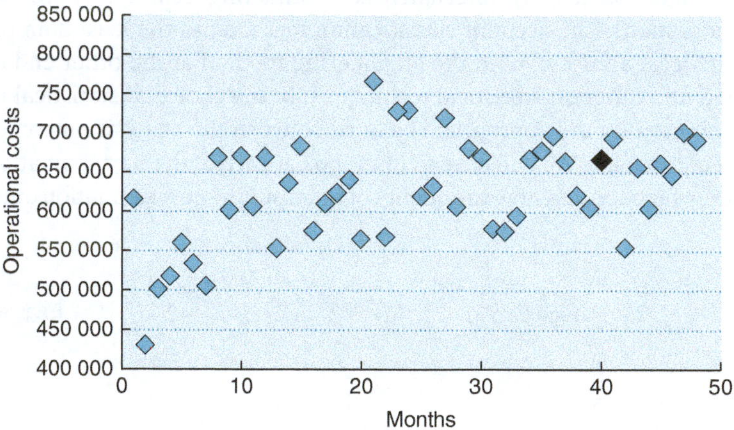

Figure 6.3 Operational costs in MC's Marseille plant in 48 consecutive months

In this scatterplot we see that operational costs vary between a low €430 958 in Month 2 and €766 022 in Month 21. In order to analyse costs quickly, we could decide to take a month that seems to represent costs and production activity reasonably well. Let us take Month 40 for example (indicated by the black datapoint in the scatterplot). The underlying accounting information for Month 40 is presented in Table 6.2.

Direct material is probably a variable cost and may be dependent on the number of machine hours used. The total number of machine hours used is 10 000, which means that the variable cost can be estimated as €100 000/10 000 = €10 per machine hour. We also expect energy costs to fluctuate with machine hours, leading to an estimated €40 000/10 000 = €4 per machine hour. Some accounts can be classified as completely fixed, like housing and

Table 6.2 Micropower Computers accounting information for Month 40

Accounts	Total cost
Direct material	€100 000
Direct labour	€240 000
Payroll taxes	€80 000
Depreciation	€20 000
Energy	€40 000
Indirect costs	€90 000
Housing	€50 000
Miscellaneous	€40 000
	€660 000

miscellaneous. Other accounts may be mixed, like direct labour and payroll taxes. A large portion of the labour force (some 75%) is on a permanent contract and execute maintenance and service labour on the highly automated production processes. The labour costs incurred for these employees will therefore not vary with fluctuations in activity levels, like number of products, labour hours or machine hours. This is different however for operational personnel that are on short term contracts, which count for 25% of the salary costs in our example. The total number of flexible labour hours contracted is 8000 in Month 40. The variable labour costs is thus (0.25 * €240 000)/8000 = €7.50 per flexible labour hour. The corresponding payroll taxes are estimated at (0.25 * 80 000)/8000 = €2.50 per flexible labour hour. Half of the indirect costs are fixed, like insurance, R&D and management costs, for an amount of €45 000. The other half of the indirect costs varies with production. Of this part, around two thirds (being €30 000) are costs for HRM services (salary registration, personnel advise and HR services) and management fees, which can be related to labour hours for an amount of (€30 000/8000 = €3.75). The remaining variable indirect costs (in our example €15 000) represent procurement and maintenance costs: they may be considered to fluctuate with machine hours at a rate of (€15 000/10 000 = €1.50). A complete overview of the account classification exercise is given in Table 6.3.

The account classification procedure yields the following cost estimation result for Micropower Computers:

Annual total costs = €395 000 + €15.50 * (machine hours) + €13.75 * (labor hours)

Table 6.3 Micropower Computers account classification scheme

Accounts	Total cost	Fixed cost	Variable cost	Variable cost/ Machine-hour	Variable cost/Labor hour
Direct material	€100 000		€100 000	€10,0	
Direct labor	€240 000	€180 000	€60 000		€7.50
Payroll taxes	€80 000	€60 000	€20 000		€2.50
Depreciation	€20 000	€20 000			
Energy	€40 000		€40 000	€4.00	
Indirect costs	€90 000	€45 000	€45 000	€1.50	€3.75
Housing	€50 000	€50 000			
Miscellaneous	€40 000	€40 000			
	€660 000	€395 000	€265 000	€15.50	€13.75

The account classification procedure is relatively simple, inexpensive and quick: it does not require much empirical analysis and can be done in a relatively short timeframe. However, the results may not be very reliable, because of the following conditions:

1. The analysis mostly relies on a single observation: in our example we only estimate a cost function based on accounting information in Month 40, looking at 10000 machine hours and 8000 labour hours. We do not know how actual costs will change under different machine and labour use. Expanding the window by looking at a whole year would probably provide more stable results, but then you still need to answer the question of whether the whole year was representative. Expanding the observations over time may also introduce more extreme values and disturbances (so called 'noise') in the data.
2. In determining whether costs are fixed or variable, analysts rely on a large variety of evidence: from detailed engineering studies to estimations based on experience and group decision making procedures. Hence, the validity of the evidence may vary much as well: some may be reliable sources of information, but others may be very unreliable due to arbitrary judgments.
3. In analysing cost functions using the account classification method, analysts often use easy to understand and, therefore, sometimes simplified representations of cost relations. The analyses are mostly restricted to the most recent data (due to the memory effect: recent events are remembered better than older events), the cost drivers are mostly tangible, operational variables, which are easily visible and measurable, and the relationships are mostly expected to be linear.

6.3.3 Engineering method

When a high level of accuracy is required, an alternative approach is the **engineering method.** This approach is in strong contrast with accounting classification methods, because engineering studies require direct observations of production activities and their relation to costs. These studies try to understand the input-output relationships in production systems in order to build cost functions. This approach originates from the late 19th century in the era of the industrial revolution when the **Scientific Management Movement** tried to optimise production systems by decomposing them into basic production activities. Each of the production activities were studied and optimised, and a relation to costs was found. It was generally expected that by recomposing all optimised basic production activities, the resulting entire production system would also be optimised.

The engineering approach is applicable for production processes that are stable and repetitive. Cost analysis outcomes may be used to set more appropriate budget levels and to improve cost control, productivity and efficiency. Generally, engineering studies provide more reliable cost information, but it will take more time and resources to carry out the studies. Although the results may be more reliable, it is not always certain that the additional information costs will be sufficiently earned back by improved decision making. When the company is in turbulent times, where conditions change frequently, the company may not get sufficient time to earn back the costs of expensive engineering studies.

The engineering method can also be applied when no historic cost data exist, for instance when new or innovated products are taken into production. Cost data may then be taken from product blueprints or prototypes, or from similar products and production systems. Japanese companies use **cost tables** to store cost information for making product design decisions (so called **design cost tables,** with varying degree of cost detail for basic to detailed design decisions), designing manufacturing processes (by using **manufacturing process design cost tables** showing cost effects of alternative methods of production), and setting cost control targets for production activities (Yoshikawa, Innes, & Mitchell, 1990; Yoshikawa, et al., 1993). Setting production cost targets for new or innovated products or production systems also requires knowledge about how fast employees learn to master the new or innovated production activities. This knowledge may come from similar learning experiences elsewhere and may be used effectively to control production costs. We will discuss the estimation of learning effects later in this chapter.

6.3.4 High-low method

When more historical information is available than for the account classification method, for instance an array of production numbers and operating costs, the 'high-low method' is a simple method to find a linear-cost function. Let us have a second look at Micropower Computers' operational cost data. Given the highly automated nature of the production processes, we expect to find a relationship between operational costs and number of machine hours. In order to make this relationship visible, we rearrange the data in the scatterplot of Figure 6.3 by replacing the time order on the *x*-axis by the number of machine hours. Now we do not get a longitudinal view of the data anymore, but we have rearranged the cost data in order of increasing number of machine hours (see Figure 6.4).

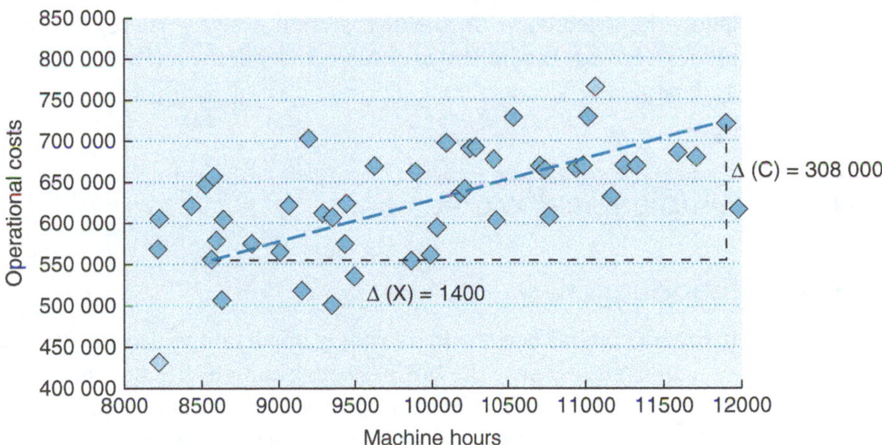

Figure 6.4 Micropower computers' operational costs against machine hours

The high-low method uses the highest and lowest activity datapoints representative for normal operations to calculate the marginal cost factor. We know that two datapoints may not be fully representative for normal operations: the lowest operational cost is due to a strike, so machines have been working on low capacity and only some workers were present at the time. The highest costs were incurred because of a lot of unanticipated rework caused by unusual low quality of inputs.

From the remaining data points, the highest and lowest that best seem to fit the data points are (8 568, 554 799) and (11 904, 720 142). The variation in operational costs caused by the variation in machine hours can be estimated by using the discrete differences in operational costs divided by the related discrete differences in machine hours:

$$\frac{\Delta(C)}{\Delta(X)} = \frac{720142 - 554799}{11904 - 8568} = €49.56 \textit{ per machine hour}$$

Fixed costs are estimated by substituting the product cost for one of the two extreme activity levels:

$$\begin{aligned}\text{At low-activity level: Fixed costs} &= \text{Total cost} - \text{variable costs}\\ &= 554799 - (8568 * 49.56)\\ &= 554799 - 424657 = €130142\\ \text{At high-activity level: Fixed costs} &= 720142 - (11904 * 49.56)\\ &= 720142 - 590000 = €130142\end{aligned}$$

Micropower Computer's operational cost function is therefore:

$$C = €130142 + 49.56 * \text{number of machine hours.}$$

As we can see, the high-low method is simple and subjective. Most subjectivity is in the selection of the lowest and highest datapoints. The high-low method is heavily influenced by visual line fitting: one tries to select both datapoints in such a way that the cost curve cuts nicely through the cloud of datapoints, leaving equal numbers of observations above and below the fitted curve. In the next section, we will use regression techniques. These techniques decrease the influence of subjectivity in the analysis, but are more demanding as far as data quality is concerned.

6.4 Simple linear regression

6.4.1 Introduction

In practice, it has become increasingly important to use statistical techniques, like regression analysis, because the business environment has become very information intensive. Many large databases offer the opportunity to use statistical techniques. The large amount of data they possess make it also necessary to use statistical techniques structure and analyse the data. Statistical analysis also needs to be done on a frequent basis, as archival data can age quickly because of rapid changes in the business. The availability of inexpensive computer hardware and software brings statistical techniques within reach of business analysts and management accountants. But like other methods explained in this chapter, statistical techniques should also be applied with the use of sufficient expert judgment. It is important to understand regression results and to know what the limitations of regression analysis are. In this section we will cover the basic ideas and workings of regression techniques such that the reader can apply these with the required expert judgment. More detailed and technical treatments of regression analysis can be found in statistics and econometrics books.

6.4.2 The basic linear regression model

The regression method is a statistical estimation technique that determines relationships between one **dependent variable** (or endogeneous variable: the variable which needs to be explained or estimated, like costs or revenues) and one or more **independent variables** (or exogeneous variables: the ones that are supposed to independently explain or drive the variation in the dependent variable). Let's return to our example of Micropower Computers and look at the 4 year monthly cost data sheet from the Maseille plant, one of MC's major production plants. The operational costs are taken from the accounting system and represented according to machine hours (see Figure 6.5).

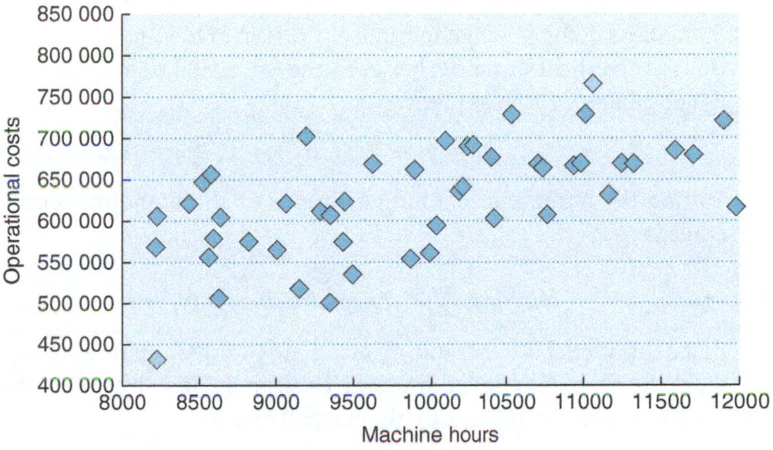

Figure 6.5 **Operational costs in MC's Marseille plant by machine hours**

In this scatterplot we see that operational costs vary between a low €430 958 and €766 022 (we have not removed these datapoints from the database, but this would have been an option). Suppose we did not know anything else about the conditions under which production takes place. What would be a sensible guess for the level of operational costs? If we think that every data point in this scatterplot is equally important for our prediction, a good starting point would be to use the unweighted average: €626 180. This is the starting point of linear regression analysis.

In its simplest form, the **simple linear regression method,** relates one dependent variable to an independent variable. This may be a time dependent variable or another type of variable, like number of units produced, machine hours, labour hours or any plausible activity or condition that is expected to influence operational costs. In the more complex form of the **multiple regression method,** regression analysis relates one dependent variable to more than one independent variable.

Simple regression analysis assumes a linear relationship between the dependent variable (in our example: costs) and independent variable(s). In our example of the computer manufacturer, most production systems are heavily automated. We, therefore, expect operational costs to be dependent on the number of machine hours Let:

$$y_t = \text{operational costs in month t}$$
$$x_t = \text{number of machine hours in month t}$$

we assume the following linear cost model:

$$y_t = a + bx_t + e_t$$

The coefficients a and b are not yet known to us and will be estimated by the regression analysis, which usually is more objective than the earlier methods described in this chapter. The coefficient e is a random variation attributed to unknown factors. It is the unexplained residual that remains because the estimated model will not be able to capture all variation. Generally speaking, the error term may contain non-linear effects (if they exist) and the effects of 'omitted independent variables': these are variables that might influence operational costs, which are not included in the model.

The mathematical technique that is most commonly used to find coefficients a and b is called the 'ordinary least squares (OLS)' method: it determines a linear curve through the datapoints in the plot that minimises the sum of the squared deviations (Σe_t^2). These deviations are vertical distances between the estimated regression curve and the observations, which can be written as follows:

$$e_t = y_t - (a + bx_t) = y_t - a - bx_t$$

To find the minimum squared deviations of all datapoints requires solving the following equation:

$$\textit{Minimise} \sum_{t=1}^{n} e_t^2, \textit{ by minimising} \sum_{t=1}^{n} (y_t - a - bx_t)^2$$

Since this model is quadratic, all terms are positive and finding the lowest value for Σe^2 will yield the absolute minimum value. This can be done by taking the partial derivatives with respect to a and b and setting them equal to zero:

$$\frac{\partial}{\partial a}\sum e_i^2 = \frac{\partial}{\partial a}\sum (Y_i - a - bX_i)^2 = -2\sum (Y_i - a - bX_i)$$

$$\frac{\partial}{\partial b}\sum e_i^2 = \frac{\partial}{\partial b}\sum (Y_i - a - bX_i)^2 = -2\sum X_i(Y_i - a - bX_i)$$

Setting these equations equal to zero and taking care of the summations produce two equations with two unknowns a and b:

$$\sum Y_i = na + b\sum X_i$$

$$\sum X_iY_i = a\sum X_i + b\sum X_i^2$$

Since all other variables X and Y are known, we can easily solve the two equations for a and b so that the sum of squared errors will be minimised.[1]

The estimation of the coefficients can be obtained in Excel by arranging the dependent and independent variables in columns in a datasheet and by using **Data-analysis** and then **Regression.**[2] The results are represented in Figure 6.6.

The Excel output shows that the predicted equation for operational costs is (y'_t denotes the predicted value, which may be different from the actual value of y_t):

$$y'_t = 250566 + 37.93\, x_t$$

[1] Multiple regressions, handling more than one independent variable, use matrix calculations to solve a series of multiple equations: one for each independent variable and one for the intercept.

[2] The option Data-analysis might not be active and needs to be installed using the Excel options and add-in menus.

Micropower Computers						
Regression Statistics						
Mulitple R	0.606004024					
R Square	0.367240877					
Adjusted R Square	0.353485244					
Standard Error	54227.96971					
Observations	48					
ANOVA						
	df	*SS*	*MS*	*F*	*Significance F*	
Regression	1	78508579855	78508579855	26.69748996	5.00927E-06	
Residual	46	1.35271E+11	2940672699			
Total	47	2.1378E+11				
	Coefficients	*Standard Error*	*t Stat*	*P-value*	*Lower 95%*	*Upper 95%*
Intercept	250566.2391	73115.44092	3.426994845	0.001295652	103392.4922	397739.986
Machine hours	37.93926115	7.34266396	5.166961385	5.00927E-06	23.15924541	52.71927688

Figure 6.6 Regression results for operational costs

The intercept of 250 566 is sometimes interpreted as the fixed cost part of the total cost function. An intercept is the value of y when x_t is zero. However, as we have seen before, when values of x_t fall outside the range of normal activity, or outside the 'relevant range', the linear relationships in the model may no longer hold. This means that other elements of the equation may also change, which may lead to completely different fixed costs when the number of machine hours approaches very low numbers. Therefore, separate analyses are often required to estimate costs outside the relevant range, but sufficient historical data might not be available to support the use of OLS regression. One of the earlier, less data intensive methods might be used instead.

6.4.3 Assessing the goodness of fit of a regression equation

How well does this equation fit our data? Let us have a look at the scatterplot again (see Figure 6.7).

If all the datapoints were exactly on the regression line, then all the variation in costs would have been explained by the regression equation. As we can see in Figure 6.7, being on the regression line is more the exception: the equation found fits the datapoints better than

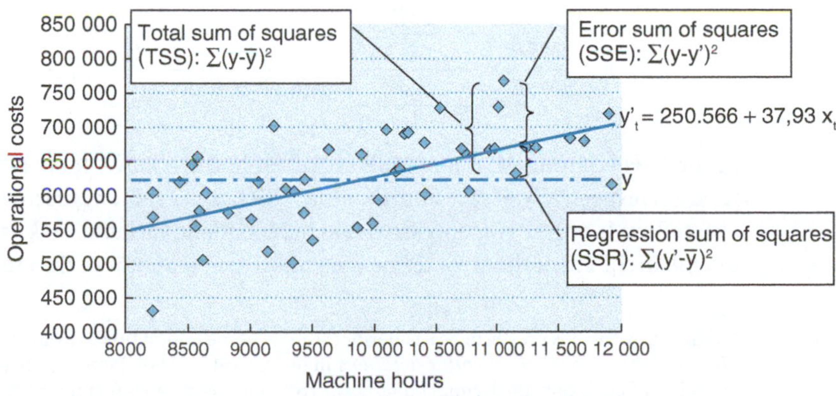

Figure 6.7 Explained and unexplained variance

the unweighted average $\bar{y}$, but is not a perfect fit. So how well does our equation fit the datapoints? The total variation in costs that needs to be explained is the sum of all the squared prediction errors of y-values around their mean: $\Sigma(y\text{-}\bar{y})^2$. The total of the squared errors has a relation with the **variance** of y, which is the average or mean squared error per observation.[3]

Let us take a closer look at the datapoint (11 086; 766 022), which is coloured red. The error that needs to be explained is the vertical difference between this point and the unweighted average: $(y\text{-}\bar{y})$. The sum of all such squared errors is also known as the 'total sum of squares' (TSS). We see that the regression line has reduced the variation by the variation $(y'\text{-}\bar{y})$, which when squared and summed across all datapoints is called the 'regression sum of squares' (SSR). The remaining, still unexplained, variation is (y-y'), which after squaring and summing is referred to as the 'sum of squares of the error term' (SSE). From Figure 6.7 it is easy to see that the total sum of squares is divided in two parts: the regression sum of squares (the portion of total variation explained by the regression equation) and the error sum of squares:

$$SST = SSR + SSE$$

One of the 'goodness of fit' measures used to assess how well the model explains the variation in the dependent variable is the 'coefficient of determination', or r^2. This coefficient measures the proportion of variation in costs that is explained by the regression equation. Thus:

$$r^2 = \frac{SSR}{TSS} = \frac{1 - SSE}{TSS} = \frac{78\,508\,579\,855}{213\,780\,000\,000} = 0.3672$$

You find the numbers in the equation in the Excel output under ANOVA (analysis of variance).[4] The r^2 indicates the percentage of variation in costs that is explained by variation in machine hours. This is in our example 36.72%. Whether this is a good or bad result is a subjective matter.

A more formal way of testing the coefficient of determination is by testing whether the r^2 is statistically different from zero. The F statistic is designed to test the ratio of two variables, which are here the 'mean square of the regression' (MSR) and the 'mean square of the error' term (MSE). They are also known as the 'variance' of the regression and the error term, which are calculated by dividing each sum of squares by its appropriate 'degrees of freedom' (df). The degrees of freedom of the regression is the number of estimated coefficients (apart from the intercept), whereas the degrees of freedom of the error term is the sample size minus the number of estimated coefficients (besides the intercept) minus 1:

$$F = \frac{MSR}{MSE} = \frac{\frac{SSR}{k}}{\frac{SSE}{n-k-1}} = \frac{SSR}{(SST - SSR)} * \frac{(n-k-1)}{k}$$

In the Excel output, MSR and MSE are given in the ANOVA table by MS regression and MS residual respectively. Please note that the MSR has the same value as SSR because the degrees of freedom is only 1 (we only used one independent variable, so $k = 1$). The square root of the mean square of the error terms is an unbiased estimator of the **standard deviation** of the

[3] Dividing by (n-1) is proven to be a superior estimate of the population's variance for relatively small samples.

[4] E-notations in Excel are *scientific notations* in order to abbreviate large numbers. The letter E indicates the number of positions the decimal point needs to be moved to the left (for a negative number) or to the right (for a positive number).

error term and this is reported in the Excel sheet under **regression statistics** as **Standard Error.** The SSE term is divided by *(n-k-1)* because if we have a number of observations that equals $(k + 1)$ (1 is for the intercept), the line would be perfectly fitted to the observations. We need more observations than $(k + 1)$ to estimate effectively the equation's standard error. The F-value is calculated as follows:

$$F - value = \frac{78\,508\,579\,855}{2\,940\,672\,699} = 26.6974$$

The F value follows an F distribution with *k* and *n-k-1* degrees of freedom. The resulting significance level is represented as **Significance F.** In our example in Figure 6.7 the significance is 0.0005%, which means that there is more than 99.9995% chance that this model's r^2 is not equal to zero. The higher the explained variation compared to the unexplained variation, the higher the F-value and thus the more significant the r^2. When SSR approaches SST, the more the regression equation explains the total variability in the dependent variable. As can be appreciated from the F-value formula, the F-value will increase and the F-test will become highly significant.

Assessing the **goodness of fit** of a regression equation starts by looking at the F-value: does the regression equation as a whole lead to a significant prediction of the variation in the dependent variable, in other words does it generate an r^2 that is significantly different from zero (which is no relationship between dependent and independent variable(s)). The second step is to look at the level of fit of the model by looking at the r^2. Only when these tests have proven that the model as a whole has a sufficient fit with the observations, is it worthwhile to look at the confidence levels of the different coefficients within the model. To put this point differently, if the **goodness of fit** tests would indicate that the model as a whole does not fit well with the data (indicated by a low F-value and high probability of r^2 not being significantly different from 0), then the significant levels of the individual coefficients in the model do not contribute to meaningful estimations of the dependent variable.

6.4.4 Assessing the confidence of a regression equation

In our example, we see that our model's **goodness of fit** is good enough to have a closer look at the independent variables. The central question here is: does each of them contribute sufficiently well to the prediction of the dependent variables? In order to answer this question we need to assess the **confidence levels** of each of the independent variables. The confidence level is a test to see whether a specific variable's corresponding coefficient is statistically significant from zero. If the coefficient is not statistically different from zero, then it does not contribute to the explanation of the dependent variable's variation. Since we do not test a ratio but a single variable, we can use the student's t-test. The t-variable is calculated as the difference between the sample coefficient and the hypothesised value (which is zero in our case) divided by the standard error of the sample coefficient:

$$t = \frac{b_i - 0}{s_{b_i}}$$

The standard error of the coefficient is the relation between the squared root of the sum of the squared deviations of s_i about its mean[5] and the regression standard error,

[5] This factor is the same as the independent variable's standard deviation multiplied by $(n - 1)$.

which is an unbiased estimator of its standard deviation. The standard error of the regression is:

$$s_{b_i} = \frac{s_e}{\sqrt{ss_{b_i}}} = \frac{\sqrt{\dfrac{SSE}{(n - k - 1)}}}{\sqrt{\sum(b_{in} - \bar{b}_i)^2}}$$

If we compute the t-value for the machine hours in our example, this would give us the following results:

$$t_{b_1} = \frac{37.93926115}{\dfrac{\sqrt{2940672699}}{\sqrt{54543045}}} = \frac{37.93926115}{\dfrac{54227}{7385}} = \frac{37.93926115}{7.34266396} = 5.16696$$

Please note that almost all elements of the computation are given by Excel (try to locate them in the output sheet) except for the sum of squared deviations of b_1. The t-values can be found in a table of the Student's t distribution [6] to determine the maximum probability that the coefficients found by Excel are in fact zero. As we can appreciate from Figure 6.6, both coefficients have a low probability of 0.1% and 0.0005% of being zero, respectively.

Excel also provides a confidence interval for each coefficient, using 95% confidence levels which correspond with a t-value of 1.96 when there are a large number of observations (which causes many degrees of freedom). In our example, the degrees of freedom are (n-k-1) = 46 and this corresponds with a t-value of 2.013. Excel uses the following equation:

Estimated coefficient value $\pm$ t * standard error of the coefficient

In our example, the confidence interval for the machine hours coefficient is calculated as follows:

$$(37.9392 \pm 2.013) * 7.3426 = 23.15 \text{ to } 52.71$$

As you can appreciate, the value 0 does not fall within the range given by the 95% confidence interval. This also counts for the confidence interval for the intercept.

Once we have ensured that the model has a good fit and the coefficients are reliable, we should first have a closer look at the model and see if the model is **plausible.** Does the model make sense? Do we believe the relationships that are estimated in the model have technical, logical, economic or behavioural meaning? In some instances, especially when a large number of datapoints is used, regression analysis may produce a good fit and reliable parameters which have been largely caused by chance and coincidence (so-called 'nonsense' or 'spurious' 'correlations'). Statistical tests will not detect this, only the interpretation of the meaning of the regression outcome may identify inappropriate models.

6.4.5 Specification tests

Until now we have mainly looked at the performance of the current model by assessing the model's goodness of fit to the observed data and the confidence levels of the individual model coefficients. The goodness of fit measures, like F-value and (adjusted) r^2, show us how well the model explains the behavior of the dependent variable. The confidence measures, like the F-values and confidence intervals, help us determining the reliability of each of the

[6] This can be done in Excel by using the TDIST() function.

model's coefficients. These tests can only be confidently applied, if we know that the data behave according to the assumptions underlying the regression analysis. The most critical assumptions are the following:

1. **Linearity.** Linear regression expects the existence of a linear relationship between the independent and dependent variables. This means that the effect of changes in the independent variables on the dependent variable is not influenced by the level of any of the independent variables. If the relationships between the dependent and independent variables are indeed non-linear, this may be detected by looking at the error terms (also called 'residuals'). Recall that the error terms are found when the estimated data are subtracted from the observed datapoints: $y_e = y - y'$. When the actual relationship is non-linear and the model expects a linear relationship, the scatterplot of the residuals will show the remaining non-linear effects.
2. **The observations are independent of one another.** Data that are taken from the same object over time are called 'longitudinal data' or 'time series'. Longitudinal observations need to be independent from each other. Sometimes, observations are not independent, because they may partly be influenced by preceding observations. Price inflation or deflation are among the main causes in time series data, but also learning effects and systematic build up of production capacities over time may influence successive datapoints. The resulting effect is called 'serial correlation': a series of datapoints are partly dependent on previous observations. The net effect of serial correlation is that the independent variables do not only influence one, but a number of datapoints at the same time, which will lead to underestimation of the standard errors. In fact, the serial dependence of the observations takes away part the separate variation of each datapoint. Serial correlation can be detected by the Durbin-Watson statistic, which provides a measure of association between the successive values of the error terms.[7] An alternative way is to have a visual inspection of the error terms. Serial correlation will show as a positive or negative trend in the error terms when they are printed along the time axis.[8]
3. **Constant variance.** When the reliability of the coefficients is measured, OLS expects every observation to have the same variance as all other observations. This means that the variance of the error terms is not dependent on time, the size of independent variables and the size of the dependent variable. When these conditions are met, the condition of 'homoscedasticity' exists. We can check for homoscedasticity by looking at a scatterplot of (standardised) residuals and see whether the vertical variation of the data cloud is equal for all values of the horizontal axis (this axis can represent the passage of time, one of the independent variables or the dependent variable). If the equal-variance conditions are not met, the data are called 'heteroscedastic' and the usual estimates of variance are understated. For instance, larger cost variance at higher levels of activity may be caused by control difficulties in busy conditions. Heteroscedasticity shows itself as non-constant variances in the error terms (either becoming larger or smaller for higher values on the horizontal axis; the data cloud takes a conic shape).

[7] The Durbin-Watson statistic is not included in the Excel software, but can be installed using add-ins. A DW-statistic around 2 suggests no serial correlation, less than 1,5 indicates positive serial correlation, and higher than 2.5 is usually evidence of negative serial correlation.

[8] Excel does not automatically generate this scatterplot. It needs to be made by hand, using the residuals or standard residuals produced by Excel (the residuals need to be requested by checking the corresponding option in the regression menu).

4. **Normal distribution of the error terms.** All the statistical test procedures applied in OLS assume that all variables are normally distributed. If all variables are normally distributed, so must the error terms be distributed as well. Normal distribution means bell shaped distribution of error terms around the average of 0. The zero average is no coincidence, because the OLS procedure aims at fitting a line exactly through the centre of a data cloud, which leads to a precise balance between positive and negative residuals. Plotting these residuals results in a scatterplot around $y_e = 0$. The residual scatterplot can be arranged in different ways: across a time axis, across one of the independent variables or across the values of the dependent variable. If the resulting residual scatterplot provides a non-random distribution that contains 'patterns' in the residuals, this may indicate that variables are not normally distributed, or it may indicate that a systematic effect has not been taken care of in the model (the so called 'omitted variable' problem). This may motivate model builders to look for additional variables that capture the omitted systematic influence(s) on the dependent variable.

Let us return to our example and analyse the error terms. Error terms can be plotted against machine hours, operational costs or time. In Figure 6.8 you find a scatterplot of the standardised error terms[9] against time.

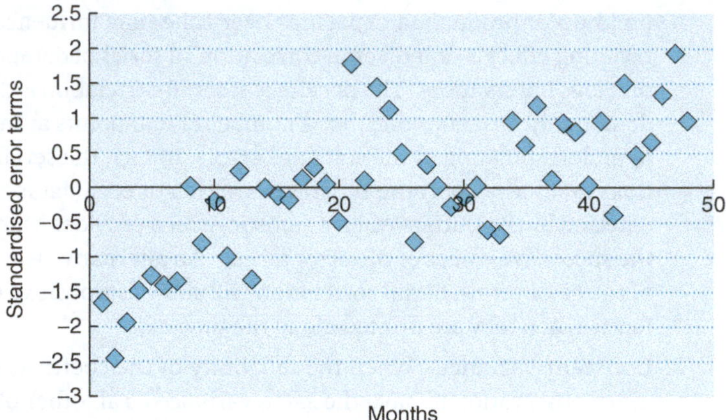

Figure 6.8 Scatterplot of the regression's standardised error terms

The error terms do not appear to be randomly scattered across this plot's area. We do not see convincing proof of violations of the linearity assumption: the general shape of the data cloud seems to represent a straight line relationship between time and error terms. Also the constant variance assumption (Assumption 3) seems not to be violated. However, we do see a positive trend in the data, signalling that the observations are not independent from each other, and we find a non-normal distribution of the errors. It looks as if the data contain a pattern of little groupings of datapoints. The positive trend may indicate that the difference between observation and regression (y–y') becomes more and more positive when we extend the number of observations into the future. This means that the regression model will under estimate more and more the real operational costs. The positive serial correlation could be caused by a time dependent (linear) cost increasing component, for instance general price

[9] Standardised error terms are the absolute error terms (y–y') divided by the standard deviation of the error terms. This will not change the distribution of the error terms in the scatterplot, but it changes the y-axis: in stead of absolute differences between observations and the regression line the y-axis represents the errors in number of standard deviations from the mean.

inflation. Suppose we find that in these 48 monthly periods we had an annual price inflation of 12% (which is 1% monthly), we could try to correct the "nominal" data for general price fluctuations by taking out the price inflation. Deflating cost figures is done by multiplying nominal operational costs in order to get 'real' costs:

$$Real\ costs_t = \frac{([Nominal\ costs)]_t}{(1 + i)^{t-1}}$$

where

i = monthly percentage inflation

t = accumulated number of periods

Adjusting the cost data leads to the following regression output (see Figure 6.9).

Micropower Computers						
Regression Statistics						
Mulitple R	0.708340254					
R Square	0.501745916					
Adjusted R Square	0.490914306					
Standard Error	46983.98724					
Observations	48					
ANOVA						
	df	*SS*	*MS*	*F*	*Significance F*	
Regression	1	1.02256E+11	1.02256E+11	46.32237423	1.78135E-08	
Residual	46	1.01545E+11	2207495057			
Totaal	47	2.03801E+11				
	Coefficients	*Standard Error*	*t Stat*	*P-value*	*Lower 95%*	*Upper 95%*
Intercept	68187.32667	63348.3968	1.076385988	0.2873677	-59326.38045	195701.0338
Machine hours	43.2987724	6.361802435	6.806054234	1.78135E-08	30.49312848	56.10441632

Figure 6.9 Regression for inflation corrected operational costs

Deflating the cost data has led to an improvement of the model (compare the F-values, and (adjusted) r^2 of Figure 6.6 and Figure 6.9). At the same time, the model has now rendered the intercept insignificant, which means that operational costs are dependent on variation in machine hours (and other factors not included in the model).

This may not appeal to the intuition of the operational managers. Part of the operational costs is the labour cost of operators. Generally speaking, their hours do not vary with machine hours directly, but with inspection and maintenance activities. Not all products require the same level of quality control, so the inspection activities vary per product and per production run. A review of the actual data reveals that monthly labour inspection hours vary between 13 and 106 hours.

6.5 Multivariate regression

6.5.1 Multiple independent variables

Expanding the model from one independent variable (machine hours) to more than one independent variable (e.g. by adding inspection hours) in the model leads to a change from univariate to multivariate regression analysis. Adding variables to a model is mostly expected to lead to a better fit between the model and observations, and following this logic it would mean that adding a large number of variables is 'better' than having only a few variables.

However, adding variables to an equation does not necessarily mean that we will have a better model: some of the additional variables may not add much explanation to the model. This would make the model less efficient. The adjusted r^2 takes the model efficiency also into account.

The regression output is presented in Figure 6.10.

Micropower Computers

Regression Statistics	
Mulitple R	0.759322044
R Square	0.576569966
Adjusted R Square	0.557750854
Standard Error	43791.30876
Observations	48

ANOVA

	df	*SS*	*MS*	*F*	*Significance F*
Regression	2	1.17506E+11	58752821096	30.6374683	4.00486E–09
Residual	45	86295542538	1917678723		
Total	47	2.03801E+11			

	Coefficients	*Standard Error*	*t Stat*	*P-value*	*Lower 95%*	*Upper 95%*
Intercept	51482.0789	59340.15912	0.86757568	0.390229736	–68035.13492	170999.2927
Machine hours	41.40860471	5.967268053	6.939290198	1.25378E-08	29.38991008	53.42729934
Inspection hours	645.6876156	228.974133	2.819915102	0.007119054	184.5100452	1106.865186

Figure 6.10 Multiple regression operational costs explained by machine hours and inspection hours

The adjusted r^2 is a measure that controls for the number of independent variables k (excluding the intercept) and for the number of observations n used to estimate the regression equation:

$$Adjusted\ r^2 = 1 - \frac{\dfrac{SSE}{n-k-1}}{\dfrac{SST}{n-1}} = 1 - \frac{n-1}{n-k-1}\left(\frac{SSE}{SST}\right) = 1 - \frac{n-1}{(n-k-1)}(1-r^2)$$

The more variables and the less observations, the more the adjusted r^2 will be adjusted downward. In our example:

$$Adj\ r^2 = 1 - \frac{48-1}{48-2} * (1 - 0.5765) = 0.5577$$

A higher percentage of the variation in operational costs has been explained by the new model, but the F-value is lower. Here we see the penalty of including more variables in the model: the regression degrees of freedom have increased by one, which reduces the numerator of the F-function more than the denominator, leading to a lower F-value (which is still significant in our example). The coefficient of the number of inspections is significant, which shows that the operational managers' intuition was right: the number of inspection hours adds to operational costs at an average of €645 per inspection hour.

Including more than one independent variable in the model introduces an additional specification test: the independent variables may not be highly correlated with each other. A high correlation of independent variables is called 'multicollinearity' or 'collinearity'. Variables are related to each other, when variation in one independent variable not only leads to variation in the dependent variable, but also to changes in another independent variable, which in turn also influences the dependent variable. Multicollinearity does not affect the explanatory power (r^2) of the regression, but it leads to unreliable coefficient estimates. So if one is only interested in the prediction of operational costs, multicollinearity should not be a major problem. However, if we also want to interpret the role of each of the separate independent terms in the prediction of operational costs, then multicollinearity may lead to erroneous interpretations. The coefficients of the independent variables are commonly interpreted as marginal effects of the independent variable on operational costs. So, for instance, one additional inspection hour will lead to an additional operational cost of €645. This is only true in a *ceteris paribus* condition: holding all other conditions constant. As a rule of thumb: mulitcollinearity is expected to cause a major problem when the independent variables have a correlation coefficient that exceeds the value of 0.8.[10] Another test is the Klein's Rule: multicollinearity is not a problem if the correlation between the independent variables is less than the multiple correlation coefficient R of the regression.

After these two improvements (deflating cost data and adding a second independent variable), it would be wise to do another check on the error terms. The multiple regression output in Figure 6.10 also generated the following plot of the error terms (see Figure 6.11).

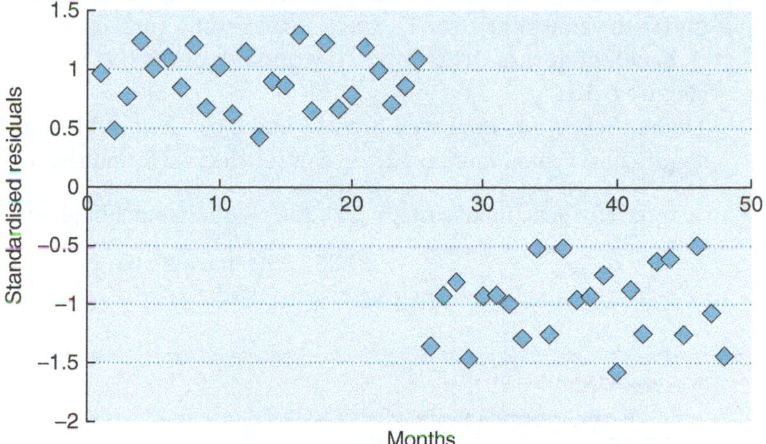

Figure 6.11 Plot of standardised error terms of the multiple regression model

Figure 6.11 shows that deflating the cost data has indeed taken out the positive trend in the error terms. But now a completely other phenomenon has become visible: a sudden systematic and lasting change in the cost data has occurred in Month 25. This phenomenon has always been in the data, but other variables' impact on operational costs have obscured this effect in our earlier analyses. Figure 6.11 reveals that, in the first 24 months, the regression model consistently underestimates operational costs and, in the second 24 months, it consistently overestimates operational costs.

6.5.2 Indicator variables

The change in month 25 has apparently changed the conditions under which the production system of Micropower Computer operates: it leads to a completely different cost function. One way of dealing with this situation is to estimate two different cost functions: one for the

[10] Correlation analysis is available in Excel under the Data-analysis menu.

first 24 month and another for the next 24 months. This solution has two disadvantages: taking only half of the observations reduces the **power** of each of the two cost functions, which will reduce the F-value and the significance of the model. Another disadvantage is that it will not be possible to estimate the **impact** of the systematic change on operational costs. A way to include a shift in conditions in the regression model is to use an 'indicator variable', also knows as a 'dummy'. An indicator variable takes on a value of 1 or 0 denoting the presence or absence of a specific condition. Suppose we knew that in Month 25 Micropower Computers has installed a new production machine. The new technology could have caused a sudden shift in fixed costs, incurring a 'step-function'. We could include an indicator variable in the model by inserting a new column in the datasheet with the heading 'New Machine' and with the value 0 for Month 1 to 24 and the value 1 for the remaining months.[11] We then estimate the following function:

$$y_t = a + bx_t + cz_t + zd_t + e_t$$

where x_t is the number of machine hours, z_t the number of inspection hours and d_t the indicator (with value either 0 or 1), and e_t is the error term.

Excel generates the following model output (Figure 6.12) and residual plot (Figure 6.13).

The model fit has improved greatly, and also all variables in the model are statistically significant. From Figure 6.12 you can see that we found the following model:

$$\text{Estimated operational costs} = 115232 + 38.29 \text{ machine hours} + 766 \text{ inspection hours}$$
$$-82393 \text{ new machine hours}$$

Micropower Computers

Regression Statistics	
Mulitple R	0.985355647
R Square	0.970925752
Adjusted R Square	0.968943417
Standard Error	11604.62902
Observations	48

ANOVA

	df	SS	MS	F	Significance F
Regression	3	1.97876E+11	65958606160	489.788909	8.35644E-34
Residual	44	5925366250	134667414.8		
Total	47	2.03801E+11			

	Coefficients	Standard Error	t Stat	P-value	Lower 95%	Upper 95%
Intercept	115232.2739	15940.10503	7.22907871	5.28382E-09	83107.10355	147357.4443
Machine hours	38.28676072	1.586471856	24.13327446	5.22208E-27	35.08943683	41.48408462
Inspections	766.6936204	60.87962736	12.5935991	3.45369E-16	643.9987951	889.3884456
New machine	−82393.85194	3372.706952	−24.42959116	3.16585E-27	−89191.09608	−75596.60781

Figure 6.12 Multiple regression using machine hours, inspection hours and an indicator variable

[11] Make sure that you position all independent variables side by side to each other in the Excel sheet, so that you can select a block instead of a single column when defining the independent variables for regression.

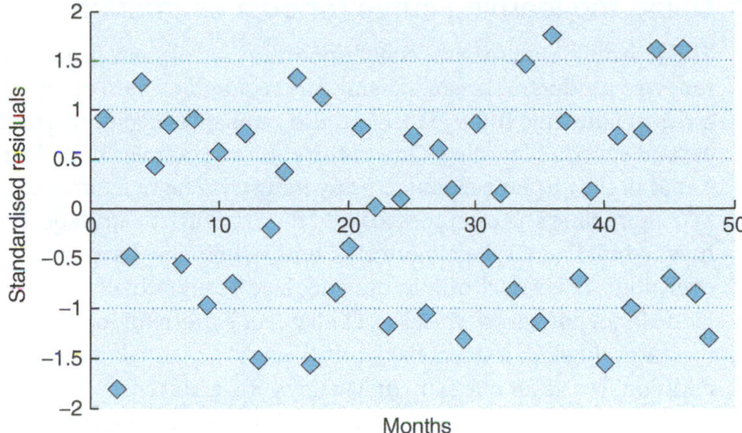

Figure 6.13 Residual plot

Inspection of the residual plot shows an equal distribution of the error terms around 0. This image does not show any systematic distortion of the data after applying the last regression model.

6.6 Modelling for learning

6.6.1 The basic economics of organisations

Products and services can be bought on the market or produced within organisations. Bringing production activities within organisational boundaries has two main advantages: it makes it possible for individuals and groups to specialise, which may eventually lead to learning effects. A learning effect is a time and cost saving effect from the ability to learn to do production tasks more efficiently. Organisations also facilitate individuals and groups to work together and to coordinate their efforts towards common goals. This may lead to economies of scale and scope. Economies of scale effects are cost savings resulting from a larger scale of operation and economies of scope are cost savings derived from producing multiple types of products. When production capacity can be used to produce a higher number of products, so will fixed costs be spread over more products, which in turn will lead to a lower average product cost. We find a similar effect when organisations try to combine different production facilities to produce a more diverse set of products or services. Also here production capacity can be used to generate more products and services, leading to lower average unit costs. Economies of scale and scope do not always lead to lower total or average costs. Sometimes increasing volume and scope may also lead to diseconomies of scale and scope. These effects dominate when a larger scale of operations leads to control problems and to excessive additional costs when production facilities need to be adjusted.

Most of the learning, and of the (dis)economies of scale and scope effects are *non-linear:* they only start appearing after a while, gradually changing the average costs per unit. In this section, we will show how to analyse learning effects.

6.6.2 Using the learning curve for cost estimation

The learning effect is especially important for organisations regularly producing new or renewed products. These companies are required to learn new production techniques within a reasonable time frame. Most of these companies could, therefore, also try to budget for a certain speed of learning. One of the earliest examples of budgeting for learning has been found in the airplane manufacturing industry. The first airplane of a new series will mostly take more time and resources to build than the fiftieth airplane. People within the firm learn how to build an airplane more efficiently when they have accumulated enough experience over time. This effect will, in the end, lead to a gradually lower average cost per airplane. Figure 6.14 portrays a typical cost behaviour pattern for total costs when production quantity increases: higher production quantity leads to a gradual reduction of marginal unit costs (the additional costs for one extra unit) and average unit costs, which give the cost curve the typical flattening effect for higher unit numbers (see left hand figure–note the non-linear scale of this chart's X-axis, which economises on space and illustrates the potential for building a mathematical model of learning effects). The learning effect leads to lower average costs per product as production accumulates (see right hand figure).

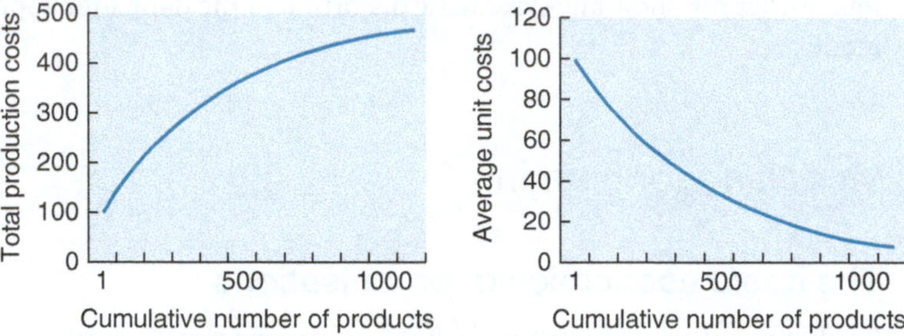

Figure 6.14 The learning effect: total cost with decreasing marginal cost (left figure) and decreasing average unit costs (right figure)

Budgeting for cost reduction because of the learning effect may help organise and control the learning experience. Having reliable information about the impact the learning effect may have on unit costs also helps setting a good price in a bidding process. When the airplane producer takes part in a competitive bidding with other producers, not taking into account the learning effect will result in setting higher selling prices, which may lead to losing the bidding to competitors.

6.6.3 Basic forms and estimation techniques

A new production process always starts with the first unit (or batch) to be produced. When the second product has been finished, the production has doubled. This doubling of production numbers is used as the basis for expressing learning performance. It is common practice to express learning performance in learning models in terms of the value to which cumulative marginal or average time (or cost) declines when production doubles. For example, when total production has been doubled from one unit to two and the average production time is reduced by 20%, the so-called **learning ratio** is 80%. The learning ratio defines the learning curve and expresses the relative average time needed for production when total production numbers have doubled. The exact definition of the learning ratio is dependent on the method used for estimating the learning effect. In the 'marginal learning curve model', the learning ratio stands for the relative time needed for producing the **additional** units. In our example, if we double production from one to two units, under the marginal learning curve model the learning ratio of 80% means that the second unit is produced in 80% of the time of the first unit. In the 'cumulative average learning curve model' a learning ratio of 80% relates to the cumulative average costs of **all** units produced after doubling the production. Going back to our example, after doubling from one to two products, an 80% learning ratio relates to the reduction of average costs of the two products in total. Since the historic costs of the first unit will not change any more after doubling the production, this means that all efficiency improvement has to come from the second product. Both models work exactly the same, but the definition of the variables is slightly different. Each approach has its specific pros and cons, depending on the intended use of the data. We will show how these two approaches work.

The marginal model

The airplane manufacturer *Softwings* has decided to introduce a new, ultralight and energy efficient small airplane for short distances. One of the newly designed parts is a small rear propeller blade that requires manual production. The first blade will require 100 production hours, but as experience accumulates, airplane designers and work analysts expect a learning ratio of 80%. The marginal model states that the *marginal* time for last product after doubling production will be 80% of the last product before doubling. This approach generates the following numbers (see Table 6.4):

Table 6.4 The marginal model

Cumulative Units produced	Marginal time for the last unit	Cumulative time
1	100 hours	100 hours
2	80 hours	180 hours
4	64 hours	? hours
8	51.2 hours	? hours
16	40.96 hours	? hours

The marginal model predicts the reduced time needed for a specific unit: the last after doubling the production. This approach makes estimation of the total production time somewhat complicated. The production time for the first product is given and equal to 100 hours. The marginal time for the last product after doubling the production is 80 hours for the second product. Total production time is the marginal time for the first and second product added together (which makes 180 hours in total for two units produced). After doubling the production again, we estimate the marginal time for Product 4 at 64 hours. We no longer are able to estimate total production time with this simple doubling approach because we do not have the marginal time needed for Product 3. If one can reliably expect consistent learning, one can mathematically estimate marginal and total production time for any level of cumulative production.

The estimated marginal time per unit (reflected in the second column of Table 6.4) is an exponential function like the left hand graph of Figure 6.14 shows. The mathematical notation is an exponential function of the following basic form:

$$y_x = ax^b$$

Where the parameters of the marginal learning curve are:

y = marginal time for the xth unit

a = time for the first unit

x = cumulative number of units produced

b = the learning exponent

The exponential function, which is non-linear in a plot on metric scales, appears to be linear in a plot on logarithmic scales (see Figure 6.15: the left figure is on metric scales, the right figure is a presentation of the same data but now on logarithmic scales). The difference between consecutive data points on a metric scale is always identical (in Figure 6.15 left figure the difference on the y-axis is always 20), while the difference between consecutive data points on logarithmic scales is a constant relative difference (in our example the next datapoint is double the previous one).

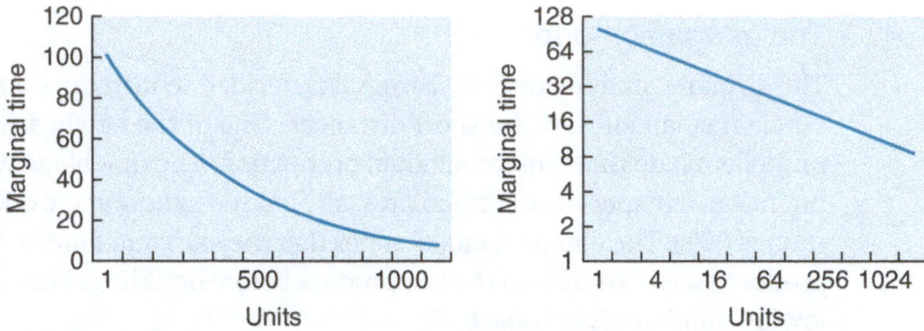

Figure 6.15 Marginal time per unit in metric and logarithmic scales

Logarithmic scales are defined by the natural logarithm or logarithms based on another log base (like for instance log base 10). It does not make a difference which one you choose, as long as you systematically use the same logarithm for all variables.

As we can see, the 'a' value of the function is given: it is the marginal time for the first unit produced (which is 100 in our example). This can also easily be seen from the function: if we use for x the first unit, then the term 1^b will always be 1, irrespective of the exact value of b. Estimating the learning exponent b can be easily done when we use the logarithmic scales. Translating metric data into logarithmic data requires the use of logarithmic calculations. We use the natural logarithm *ln*. The exponential function can be rewritten as follows:

$$\ln y_x = \ln a + b \ln x$$

Using the high-low method yields:

$$b = \frac{\Delta \ln y}{\Delta \ln x} = \frac{\ln y_2 - \ln y_1}{\ln x_2 - \ln x_1} = \frac{\ln\left(\frac{y_2}{y_1}\right)}{\ln\left(\frac{x_2}{x_1}\right)} = \frac{\ln(\textit{learning ratio})}{\ln 2}$$

In our example the b coefficient is calculated as follows:

$$b = \frac{\ln 0.80}{\ln 2} = \frac{-0.22314}{0.693147} = -0.32193$$

This leads to the following model, which is easily calculated in Excel for any X value:

$$\text{Estimated marginal labor hours} = 100.\ x^{-0.32193}$$

Table 6.5 The cumulative average model

Units produced	Cumulative average time	Cumulative time
1	100 hours	100 hours
2	80	160
4	64	256
8	51.2	409.6
16	40.96	655.36

The cumulative average model

In this model, the learning effect is not defined as the marginal time needed for the last unit after doubling the production, but now the learning effect is calculated over the cumulative production volume. This makes it easier to calculate total accumulated production time. The cumulative average model follows the same calculation rules as the marginal model, only the definitions used are different. Look at Table 6.5.

The cumulative time is now the cumulative average time multiplied by the cumulative number of units produced. The marginal model enables us to calculate quickly the production time of a specific unit, whereas the cumulative average model helps us to calculate total production time for a given total number of units.[12] The cumulative average model also works with the same equation, but the estimated y_x does not stand for the marginal production time of unit x, but for the average time of the accumulated total number of x units. The total cumulative time for the whole production of x units is:

$$xy = (x)(ax^b) = ax^{b+1}$$

6.6.4 Estimating learning models using OLS regression

The airplane company *Softwings* has actually started the production of the lightweight aircraft, and the direct production hours for the first 220 airplanes are the following (see first two columns on the left hand side of Table 6.6).

The learning curve can be estimated by a simple linear OLS regression between the first two columns, which shows a good model fit and high r^2 (0.98). However, looking at the error plot against number of units produced reveals a non linear distribution of error terms, which is exactly the learning effect that has not been captured by linear regression (see Figure 6.16).

Figure 6.16 shows that the linear regression model overestimates the costs of the first couple of units, then underestimates actual costs and finally overestimates actual costs. As you can see, the linear model will persist in overestimating production hours for units beyond the number that has been included in the current database, making the estimation error for future units consistently larger as production expands.

Estimating a non-linear learning curve can also be done by transforming number of units and production hours from ratio scales into logarithmic scales (for instance by using the

[12] One can also compute marginal cost by computing the total cumulative costs at any production level and then at one more unit, and then subtracting the smaller from the larger. This facility might explain the more common use of the cumulative average cost model in practice.

Table 6.6 Direct production time Softwings Company

Cumulative units	Cumulative hours	ln(cumulative units)	ln(cumulative hours)
1	100	0.0000	4.6052
10	480	2.3026	6.1738
20	740	2.9957	6.6067
30	1 020	3.4012	6.9276
40	1 200	3.6889	7.0901
50	1 380	3.9120	7.2298
60	1 640	4.0943	7.4025
70	1 790	4.2485	7.4900
80	1 930	4.3820	7.5653
90	2 000	4.4998	7.6009
100	2 310	4.6052	7.7450
110	2 500	4.7005	7.8240
120	2 540	4.7875	7.8399
130	2 800	4.8675	7.9374
140	2 840	4.9416	7.9516
150	2 960	5.0106	7.9929
160	3 200	5.0752	8.0709
170	3 200	5.1358	8.0709
180	3 440	5.1930	8.1432
190	3 600	5.2470	8.1887
200	3 630	5.2983	8.1970
210	3 860	5.3471	8.2584
220	3 868	5.3936	8.2605

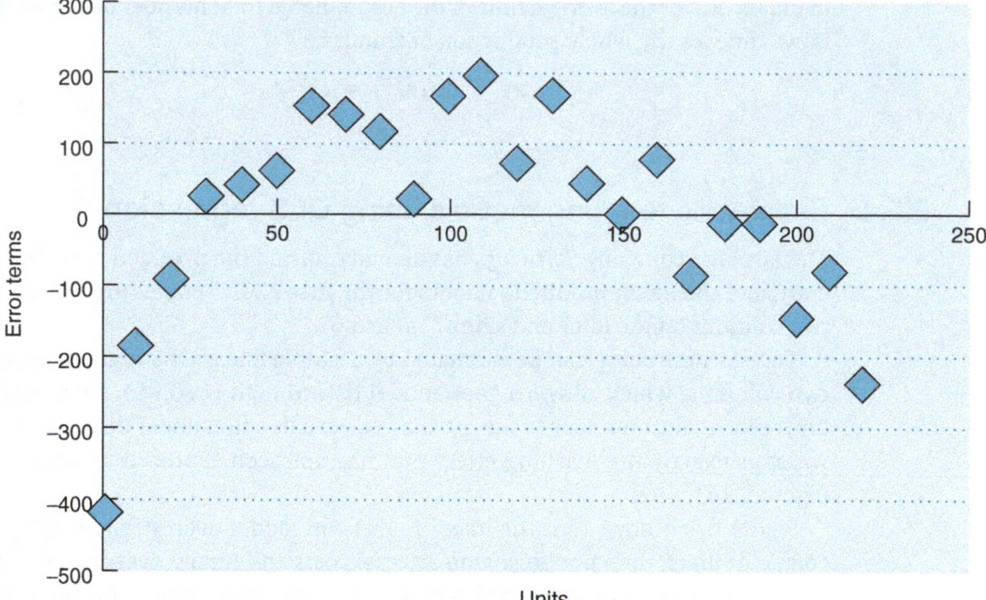

Figure 6.16 Error terms against number of units produced

natural logarithm of unit numbers and hours[13], see the two columns on the right in Table 6.6). If exponential learning exists, this transformation generates a linear function between cumulative unit numbers and hours. We can use OLS regression to estimate the coefficients. Excel returns in our example the following results:

[13]This can be done in Excel by using the LN-function.

$$\ln(\text{cumulative hours}) = 4.5933 + 0.6811 \ln(\text{cumulative units})$$

Putting this back into metric variables, we need to take the antilogarithm of the variables[14]. The antilogarithm of 4.5933 is 98.82, which gives the following equation:

$$\text{Cumulative production time} = 98.8 * (\text{Cumulative units})^{0.6811}$$

Note that we estimate total production time for the cumulative production of X units. If we want to estimate the cumulative average time per unit, we need to subtract 1 from the b-coefficient, which gives us the following equation:

$$\text{Cumulative average production time} = 98.8 * (\text{units})^{-0.3188}$$

6.6.5 Learning in practice

Learning is expected to take place in conditions where new tasks are introduced which need to be executed in a similar way, which are not completely preplanned, and which are executed at least partly by human labour. Learning is important for companies that regularly introduce new or revised products on the market while competing on cost and efficiency. For each new or revised product, some room for improvement needs to exist. Completely preplanned production systems might not offer much opportunity for learning, because technical specialists have already absorbed the learning capacity by designing an optimised production system at the start of production. In cases where learning needs to take place during production, operational managers may try to plan for efficiency improvements and include efficiency improvement targets in operational budgets. When evaluating the operational departments' performance in efficiency improvement the 'labour efficiency variance' can be a useful indicator. This variance is calculated as the difference between the planned labour hours and the realised number of hours, multiplied by the standard hourly wages of the production personnel.

Learning rates may be different for separate activities or functions that contribute to the production of products and services. The different learning ratios can be combined in a cost budget that is set up using the 'engineering method' (refer to the second section of this chapter). Learning ratios may be derived from similar experiences somewhere else inside or from outside the company, or from initial experiences working with prototype products or production systems. Table 6.7 displays an example in which different learning ratios are applied to different cost items, based on the experience using a prototype. For planning actual production activities, the product cost for the first product is based on the prototype cost data (in other words: the a-coefficient for every cost item is based on the prototype cost). The learning ratio estimates may be derived from similar innovation projects, they may come

Table 6.7 Three-year budgets based on learning predictions

Production numbers	Prototype	Learning ratio	Learning coefficient	Year 1 1-64	Year 2 65-256	Year 3 257-612
Direct material use	€1000	90%	−0.1520	€34 012	€76 187	€120 558
Direct labour use	4000	80%	−0.3219	67 109	104 690	138 427
Energy use	800	85%	−0.2345	19 310	36 496	52 948
Maintenance	100	88%	−0.1844	2 972	6 234	9 535
Administrative support	500	82%	−0.2863	9 728	16 437	22 572
Total product costs	€6400			€133 132	€240 044	€344 041

[14] In Excel the antilogarithm of the natural logarithm can be found by using the EXP-function.

from expectations of future price movements on the market (a target setting approach) or efficiency improvements targets required by management or shareholders.

We have expected in our examples that learning always takes place at the same rate throughout the whole production history. This means that, as long as learning continues, production time will drop at the same rate. In practice, however, this constant rate may appear to be variable. For instance, most learning is done at the beginning of the process and the marginal efficiency improvements become smaller when production is expanded. This can be represented by an 'asymptotic learning curve'. Learning models also presume that learning goes on forever: marginal cost differences will become smaller as production experience grows, but we still expect to see improvements. In practice, learning at a certain point in time might cease, at which point marginal time remains constant. This might reflect efficiency limits and the effects of replacement of experienced workers with less experienced, or a change in the mix of employees. Expansion of production volume may lead to lower costs, only because a larger volume leads to lower average costs when a fixed (direct or indirect) cost is present.

6.7 Data requirements

Cost estimation and analysis can only be done when the underlying knowledge or data are relevant and reliable. This means that the bookkeeping system (for financial data) and operational data systems (for non financial data on, for instance, production numbers, other cost drivers and quality indicators) need to provide accurate data. Before entering in statistical packages, the basic data should be tested on the following aspects:

- **Be aware of outliers.** Outliers are datapoints that have strongly different values than the other datapoints. This may be due to exceptional conditions, which make these datapoints less useful for estimating most probable cost figures. Moreover, extreme datapoints have a more than average impact on the estimation of the cost function. Remember that the ordinary least squares method uses squared differences between the overall mean and the observed value to estimate the regression coefficients. Large distances will have excessively large impact on the model estimates. Outliers should first be evaluated whether they represent the production setting well, or whether they are influenced by extreme disturbances. Only if the latter condition prevails can these data be left out of the analysis.
- **Match costs with cost drivers in the appropriate time frame.** Some costs are reported in a monthly period (for instance overhead costs), while some production data may be reported daily or weekly. It is important to define the appropriate time frame in which costs can be meaningfully analysed. In most cases, this will be the largest time frame reported by all relevant systems (in our example: the monthly period).
- **Ensure proper accrual.** Sometimes, costs are incurred in Month 1, but reported in Month 2 due to late billing or time consuming administrative procedures. When we want to ensure a good match of periods (which is called 'proper accrual'), the costs reported in Month 2 that relate to production numbers in Month 1 should be added to the costs of Month 1. Note that this correction means that *two* datapoints need to be changed: the Month 2 cost figure and the Month 1 cost figure.
- **Correct for confusing indirect cost allocations.** The data used in cost analysis should only include data for which a cause and effect relationship is expected. Flat fee cost allocations may lead to higher fixed cost estimates, while variable cost allocations may disturb

the marginal coefficient estimates. Arbitrary cost allocation practices disturb cost functions, and it is advisable to correct for allocated costs before the cost model is estimated.

Analysing cost behaviour helps managers in taking business decisions and assists in managing and controlling costs. It provides helpful means to make projections into the future and to understand current cost behaviour. We have a large number of different cost analysis techniques available to do this. The choice depends on the level of accuracy required and the availability of reliable and appropriate data. In many cases, improvements in both areas are required to generate useful cost estimates: better data and more sophisticated data analysis techniques.

EXERCISES

Exercise 6.1 Skylight Airlines

The dataset includes nine years of quarterly data about costs on two different cost drivers of an airline company. The dataset includes the operational costs in thousands of dollars in each quarter from 1994 until 2003, the number of passengers transported, and the tons of cargo shipped in the quarters. As a controller you should analyse the cost structure of this airline company.

Dataset for Skylight Airlines

Year	Quarter	Operating costs	Passengers	Cargo	Year	Quarter	Operating costs	Passengers	Cargo
1994	1	3137	2709	168	1999	1	3053	3118	138
1994	2	3107	2897	177	1999	2	3086	3669	141
1994	3	3016	2942	129	1999	3	3250	3487	139
1994	4	3197	2742	206	1999	4	3128	3135	150
1995	1	3010	2691	187	2000	1	3148	3203	134
1995	2	3585	2941	247	2000	2	3201	3860	134
1995	3	3003	2933	138	2000	3	3493	3593	140
1995	4	2901	2688	154	2000	4	3723	3293	153
1996	1	2862	2685	134	2001	1	3605	3589	141
1996	2	2767	3013	139	2001	2	3779	4401	145
1996	3	2802	2977	129	2001	3	3835	4050	141
1996	4	2775	2731	135	2001	4	3885	3617	156
1997	1	3351	2774	126	2002	1	3957	3598	140
1997	2	3064	3134	131	2002	2	3890	3537	131
1997	3	2994	3170	124	2002	3	3649	3190	116
1997	4	2970	2925	145	2002	4	3985	2639	119
1998	1	3074	3160	142	2003	1	3538	2878	111
1998	2	3022	3250	143	2003	2	3601	3217	109
1998	3	3122	3260	143	2003	3	3805	3165	112
1998	4	3102	3133	160	2003	4	3670	3061	126

1. Plot the data, do you see a clear relationship between the cost drivers and the operational costs?[15]
2. Test whether the number of passengers and the number of cargo shipped are reliable cost drivers for the firm. Which part of the costs are fixed cost and which part are variable costs when these two cost drivers are used?

[15]It might be helpful to change the axis of the graphs to see the pattern. This is possible by simply clicking on the axis and then formatting it.

3. Reflect on the quality of the regression equation. Does the regression meet its assumptions? Where do you see problems? Hint: Also plot the residuals against time, and against the predicted values of the operational costs.
4. The airplane industry was hit very hard by the attacks on the World Trade Centre in the 3rd quarter of 2001. This led to a decrease in both passengers and cargo shipped. Since Skylight Airlines had problems to adjust their costs downwards very rapidly they ran into problems. How do you model such a sudden shift in these time series? Assess the impact of this crisis on the airlines's costs.
5. Is there a seasonal pattern in the costs that is unrelated to the cost drivers? Examine what the impact of seasonality is on the cost pattern.

Exercise 6.2 Bethesda Hospital

The management accountant of Bethesda Hospital is reviewing the Daycare department's financial results. The Daycare department is the unit in the hospital that takes care of patients having minor injuries. People come to the hospital, get first aid treatment and go home again. In his review, the management accountant uses Daycare's monthly total operational cost figures for the last three years. He notices that the monthly costs vary considerable from month to month and he wonders why this is. In order to answer this question, he also collected monthly data about average income of patients, number of patients attended, average severity of the patients (using a ten point Severity index from 1-10) and the patients' average age. The table represents all data available for analysis.

Bethesda's Daycare department, monthly data

Months	Costs	Income	Patients	Severity	Age	Patients
1	329974	40404	1416	6	43	1416
2	275895	41792	1102	1	33	1102
3	379197	40174	1639	9	43	1639
4	336073	41408	1514	7	40	1514
5	348117	40329	1226	8	43	1226
6	360956	41349	1530	6	39	1530
7	330036	39362	2140	9	38	2140
8	335764	41047	1962	5	32	1962
9	289466	41607	948	9	42	948
10	323309	39131	1074	7	42	1074
11	236471	37422	800	1	32	800
12	252089	37832	1150	1	32	1150
13	314470	40965	1910	5	39	1910
14	243207	40715	612	6	37	612
15	277702	40105	920	10	41	920
16	312624	41000	1376	9	39	1376
17	264239	39988	1010	7	41	1010
18	260516	42164	988	6	37	988
19	257583	39594	1064	2	33	1064
20	301896	40681	1526	3	37	1526
21	265538	40484	1280	3	34	1280
22	369462	38436	1964	5	36	1964
23	299188	41498	1766	3	38	1766
24	352578	39438	2128	4	35	2128
25	322422	41506	1927	5	34	1927
26	289756	39891	1286	3	35	1286
27	319211	39231	1276	5	40	1276

Months	Costs	Income	Patients	Severity	Age	Patients
28	331680	39332	1575	5	40	1575
29	273327	40592	1278	7	36	1278
30	300798	40031	1488	2	34	1488
31	309026	39609	1702	6	35	1702
32	299330	39462	1186	2	33	1186
33	378554	39743	1978	6	42	1978
34	317952	40947	1570	6	36	1570
35	303689	38692	1928	5	38	1928
36	367118	40872	1674	8	41	1674

Required:

1. What variable(s) explain Daycare department's monthly costs best? Please explain why.
2. Suppose the average severity index would increase by 0.5 unit, how much additional costs would this incur?

Exercise 6.3 Red Cross laboratory

The Red Cross hospital has a laboratory where blood tests are conducted. Monthly costs are given, as well as the number of blood monsters (samples) examined each month (see data, also available in the datasheet).

Red Cross Lab, monthly data

Months	Costs	Samples	Months	Costs	Samples
1	101778	1459	19	98015	1035
2	79067	1056	20	114508	1685
3	109718	1752	21	105218	1230
4	98769	1477	22	122193	1986
5	102785	1462	23	123118	1864
6	97066	1566	24	125283	2356
7	109736	2034	25	119263	1952
8	91900	1653	26	117736	1453
9	90322	1054	27	112746	1681
10	93524	1157	28	121277	1933
11	67887	800	29	107819	1234
12	74587	1025	30	110048	1685
13	105675	1837	31	117167	1864
14	74132	712	32	101291	1122
15	85745	1020	33	133851	2486
16	93657	1466	34	114635	1684
17	88520	1055	35	125692	2403
18	81923	954	36	125801	2438

Required:

1. Analyse the cost data. Comment on the quality of the regression results. Are they reliable?
2. Additional information conveyed that in Month 19 new equipment was installed in the lab. Please estimate the impact of the new machine on the lab's total costs and on its cost components.

Exercise 6.4 CD-R disk toaster

A firm in Ireland produces compact disks, using a highly automated system. Unit costs depend heavily on volume and materials used per disk. The following operational costs have been recorded during the last 50 months (see data table).

Monthly production data

Month	Costs	Units	Month	Costs	Units
1	1 111 050	9582	26	1 337 996	8930
2	907 276	6587	27	1 301 138	9523
3	964 251	7476	28	1 233 975	7486
4	1 095 168	7317	29	1 259 107	9369
5	1 142 588	7988	30	1 254 780	8999
6	1 010 434	7599	31	1 221 303	6875
7	899 632	6900	32	1 274 383	7548
8	1 148 963	8792	33	1 200 426	8025
9	1 053 706	8334	34	1 220 104	7706
10	1 129 612	9061	35	1 244 227	8326
11	1 019 736	8612	36	1 206 917	8077
12	991 070	8564	37	1 268 244	8590
13	957 888	7894	38	1 182 817	6749
14	989 510	8144	39	1 190 218	6580
15	1 051 335	9274	40	1 236 386	8756
16	1 026 693	7248	41	1 221 166	8222
17	1 035 433	7432	42	1 159 764	6854
18	983 009	7555	43	1 189 390	6863
19	1 071 943	8164	44	1 199 527	6916
20	913 553	7209	45	1 243 826	7919
21	1 122 878	8854	46	1 065 796	6825
22	935 338	6578	47	1 199 060	7360
23	1 180 295	8427	48	1 202 430	8196
24	1 037 337	8815	49	1 341 998	9372
25	944 171	7254	50	1 214 140	6595

Required:

1. Prepare a regression analysis and comment on the results.

It appears that in Month 26 a new production system has been installed.

2. Make a regression analysis, taking into account the impact of the new equipment on production costs. What conclusion do you reach, looking at the result of the regressions?
3. It turns out that the new technology, installed in Month 26, was meant to make the production system more efficient, lowering variable unit cost. Please construct a model that makes it possible to check whether the new equipment actually did bring down variable operational costs. What is your conclusion?

Exercise 6.5 Consulting Services plc

Consulting Services is an advisory firm for small and medium sized companies in Ireland. It is a small company itself, employing around 12 consultants. The market is volatile and oscilates between a low 1026 and a high 1663 monthly consulting hours sold. A monthly overview of consulting hours sold and corresponding Consulting Services' operational costs is given in the following table.

Consulting Services direct monthly costs and sales over the last four years

Month	Costs	Contract-hrs	Month	Costs	Contract-hrs
1	220844	1663	25	202322	1178
2	199034	1037	26	209302	1527
3	188994	1220	27	217870	1650
4	186314	1180	28	202512	1228
5	197388	1331	29	213792	1610
6	191912	1260	30	212202	1542
7	185726	1104	31	192766	1099
8	204736	1503	32	188582	1239
9	200926	1403	33	195624	1368
10	212492	1558	34	194922	1272
11	205586	1461	35	199236	1420
12	202238	1451	36	194952	1350
13	198664	1312	37	201968	1486
14	200482	1368	38	189770	1072
15	214430	1599	39	177256	1026
16	201770	1186	40	204762	1491
17	188604	1215	41	203554	1380
18	189476	1238	42	190714	1099
19	198638	1368	43	179808	1094
20	188328	1165	44	176428	1108
21	210350	1523	45	196678	1318
22	193620	1037	46	188108	1088
23	200366	1422	47	187854	1200
24	210010	1503	48	199580	1378

Required:

1. Analyse Consulting Services' direct cost function. Please pay special attention to the error terms. What do the different error term displays suggest?
2. Try to improve Consulting Services' cost function.
3. Is it possible to come up with a model that predicts percentual changes in costs as a result of changes in volume? (This is the cost-elasticity of contract hours.)
4. What would you recommend Consulting Services management to do, based on your regression analysis found under 2 and 3?

Exercise 6.6 Archaeology Inc.

The firm Archaeology Inc. is specialised in performing archaeological excavations in geographical areas that are designated to be developed for new construction works. In the last few years, the excavation business has become increasingly competitive. Most project developers select the archaeological company for doing the excavation in their site mostly based on lowest price offers. Mrs. Abinta, the controller of Archaeology Inc., has become increasingly aware of the importance of gaining sufficient economies of scale in her company. During busy times, employees in Archaeology Inc. become flexible and perform many different tasks when required. Even back-office personnel sometimes join in to help in the excavation sites. Mrs. Abinta wonders whether it is possible to gain economies of scale in her company. She decides to analyse the average cost of archaeological excavation per hectare in the last year (50 weeks), which are the following:

Excavation costs

Weeks	Hectares	Average cost per hectare	Weeks	Hectares	Average cost per hectare
1	30	€945	26	53	€1730
2	46	€1559	27	48	€1425
3	62	€1735	28	31	€1109
4	69	€1933	29	47	€1884
5	44	€1387	30	58	€1710
6	57	€1782	31	60	€1809
7	48	€1671	32	52	€1743
8	66	€1789	33	44	€1595
9	36	€1332	34	34	€1084
10	53	€1600	35	46	€1441
11	62	€1794	36	50	€1497
12	47	€1646	37	54	€1563
13	70	€1710	38	37	€1186
14	32	€872	39	65	€1811
15	39	€1206	40	42	€1407
16	59	€1716	41	51	€1591
17	50	€1700	42	57	€1792
18	36	€1030	43	53	€1790
19	71	€1811	44	49	€1618
20	50	€1650	45	68	€1833
21	46	€1480	46	47	€1648
22	57	€1760	47	36	€1153
23	66	€1678	48	45	€1293
24	42	€1276	49	64	€1869
25	47	€1344	50	48	€1675

Required:

1. Estimate a simple regression model for the average costs per hectare.
2. Comment on the quality of the relationship you found.
3. Adapt the regression function in order to capture the economies of scale effect.
4. Try to do the same as under '3' using Excel's line fitting possibilities. Which line fitting option should be choosen and why?

Exercise 6.7 Hybrid Cars

A car manufacturer started the production of a new hybrid car. The operational costs for the first 64 cars are as follows:

Cumulative average production costs

Number of cars produced	Cumulative average cost
1	80000
2	76000
4	72200
8	68590
16	65161
32	61902
64	58807

Required:

1. What are the total operational cost of the first 100 cars produced?.
2. Car 32 is a special car and needs additional features. For an exact cost specification, we need to know the operational costs for Car 32. What are the operational costs for the production of Car 32?
3. The company just received an order for the delivery of cars 33–64 (so a total number of 32 cars) from a government agency. The variable overhead costs are €20 000 per car and the fixed overhead costs are €250 000. The company wants to earn a margin of 12% of the sales. The government agency is willing to pay a fixed amount of €3 000 000 for the whole order of 32 cars. Given the learning rate, the overhead costs and the required profit margin, should the company agree to the listed price? Give your calculations.

A small part of the car is sepearately produced. It is also new and follows a similar learning curve as the full car. Using regression on transformed CumAvCost and production volume data (to natural logarithmic scales), management accountants found the following regression results:

	Coefficients	Standard error	t Stat	P-value
Intercept	3.2581	0.005136466	2447.918241	7.95903E-41
ln(parts)	−0.1625	0.002489004	−122.3140844	1.30824E-22

4. What is the total operational production costs of the first 100 parts?
5. What is the learning ratio for these parts?

Exercise 6.8 Leidsche Rijn Vinex project

The housing project developer Van Dijk has started to build in the north west corner of the Leidsche Rijn project near Utrecht. His contract defines the building of homes for middle class owners with two to five children. In order to remain competitive Van Dijk decided to build standard houses. These houses are newly designed and have not been built before. The first 16 houses have recently been finished and the following cost summary has just been presented to Van Dijk:

Production costs

Houses	CumAvCost
1	300000
2	240000
3	216000
4	201600
5	198000
6	182000
7	179000
8	177408
9	174000
10	172000
11	168000
12	168000
13	167000
14	166000
15	164000
16	163215

The term CumAvCost stands for 'Cumulative Average Cost'.

Required:

1. What is the learning ratio of this project?
2. What is the cost function when we apply the learning rate formula? Plot the results and comment on them.
3. Use Excel's linear regression function on appropriately transformed data to determine the project's cost function. Add the result to the plot and comment.
4. Does learning take place at a steady pace? If not, what does the learning pattern look like? Please explain.
5. Van Dijk wants to double the production. What will be the average cost of a home when the total of 32 homes has been produced?

Exercise 9 Van Doorne horse trailers

Van Doorne is a family business, specialised in the production of horse trailers. The engineering department of Van Doorne Trailers has estimated 100 direct labour hours for the assembly of the first trailer of a new horse trailer line. The standard labour rate is €10 per hour. In the previous month, the new horse trailer has been taken into production for the first time. During this month, the production department produced 10 trailers in 900 direct labour hours. Labour costs were a total of €9900.

Required:

1. Calculate a labour rate and a labour efficiency variance for production to this point.
2. Assume that the company has experienced a 90% learning effect on previous new trailers, using the cumulative average learning rate definition. Van Doorne's management team expects a similar learning performance for the new horse trailer. Recalculate the labour efficiency variance when the learning effect is included in the targets for the production department.
3. Prepare a complete variance report, including the change in standards when the learning effect is built into the production targets. You can label this shift in targets the *Change of efficiency standards variance.*

Van Doorne knows that the direct labour hours for the second trailer were 88 hours. He just got a telephone call from a potential customer who wants to know the price of his trailer. He made a reservation and Van Doorne sees that the customer's product will be trailer number 16. Direct material costs of each trailer are €14800, direct overhead costs per trailer are €40 per labour hour, fixed overhad costs are €3200 per trailer and the profit margin is 12%. The profit margin is defined as a percentage of the selling price.

Required:

4. What is a competitive price for the prospective customer's trailer, taking into account the learning effect and the required profit margin?

Exercise 10 Display Inc.

The Korean company *Display Inc.* produces displays for smartphones. It has just started up a new line of highresolution displays using an improved imaging technology. The company produced the first 32 batches of 100 products each and corporate accounting just received the following production and cost data:

Production and cost data

Batch	Prod. cost per batch	Batch	Prod. cost per batch
1	380	17	72
2	254	18	79
3	168	19	70
4	132	20	79
5	150	21	72
6	136	22	74
7	100	23	64
8	110	24	71
9	86	25	66
10	104	26	68
11	90	27	67
12	84	28	69
13	93	29	64
14	78	30	63
15	86	31	64
16	84	32	62

Required:

1. Estimate, by using every given datapoint in the table, the cost function of this product. (Hint: this can be done by using log or ln transformed data).
2. A very efficient little family run company offers *Display Inc.* to take over the production of displays for batches 33 to 64 at a price of €65 per batch. Should *Display Inc.* decide to outsource production beyond the first 32 batches?

References

Yoshikawa, T., Innes, J., & Mitchell, F. (1990). Cost Tables: a foundation of Japanese Cost Management. *Journal of Cost Management for the Manufacturing Industry, fall,* 30-36.

Yoshikawa, T., Innes, J., Mitchell, F., & Tanaka, M. (1993). *Contemporary Cost Management.* London: Chapman & Hall.

Chapter 7

Investment analysis

7.1 Introduction

Investment analysis is the systematic evaluation of decisions about long-term commitments of resources in return for promised future gains. These long-term commitments can include the price paid for a financial bond that promises a stated rate of return and the recovery of the face amount of the bond at a future date. Investment analysis compares the financial bond to other financial investments after controlling for risk and term differences. Likewise investment analysis compares decisions about alternative new technologies, business locations, and even higher education. Although markets and risks differ across these types of decisions, investment analysis promises to equate their financial costs and benefits.

Investment decision making is often called 'capital budgeting' because investment capital is not unlimited and must be allocated to long term decisions wisely. These decisions determine future activities, scale of operations, locations, products and programmes. In addition to the normal financial tools of budgeting and measuring profitability, decision makers need to forecast future operating costs and benefits and need to account for the 'opportunity cost' of committing financial capital for the life of a project. This chapter presents alternative methods for evaluating capital investments that include discounted cash flow (DCF) and real option analysis (RA). This chapter considers theoretical and practical issues of preparing and interpreting these analysis methods.

7.2 Management issues

Every use of funds has an alternative use, including investments. The **opportunity cost** of any investment is the expected return of the next best application of funds. The better alternatives are available, the higher the opportunity cost of the current project. The **cost of capital,** or the **discount rate,** is a measure of the opportunity cost of investing, which measures the rate of return one would forgo by choosing one investment over the next best opportunity. The debate continues in corporate and public finance about how to choose the proper discount rate for a particular investment decision. Errors in discount rates can discourage good investments if the rate is too high and encourage bad investments if the rate is too low.

The strategic view of investment analysis can describe investment as a game against nature, such a famer's decision whether to plant a particular crop based on long-term weather reports. Strategic investment also can be a game against competitors, such as whether and where to place a restaurant in anticipation of a competitor's similar decision. Of course, investment analysis can combine games against nature and competitors, such as a mobile phone maker's decision the release a new smart phone in anticipation of market changes and a key competitor's product release.

A **capital budgeting process** may be described in several steps, which can include:

1. Identification of investment alternatives (including the 'do nothing' alternative).
2. Development of project proposals and cash flow projections.
3. Selection of the best alternative project(s).
4. Implementation of the chosen project(s).
5. Evaluation (post audit) of the implemented projects and the budgeting process.

Some organisations have an elaborate screening process that may resemble a funnel, where successive screening of projects applies strategic, financial and operational criteria. Figure 7.1 illustrates a high technology company's new product investment process (see also Case 7.20).

The set of possible investment opportunities may be vast. The first screen of the alternatives should be strategic fit, which includes customers' needs, organisational capabilities, and appropriateness for the organisation's long term goals and culture. Even more targeted analysis may be necessary to reduce the possibilities to a manageable set, but this first step should not be too hasty and, if possible, should be the outcome of a group process. For example, at the company illustrated in Figure 7.1, cross-functional project teams are responsible for generating and shepherding individual projects through the entire capital budgeting process. Another cross-functional team of high level managers approves progression to each successive step. Figure 7.1 shows a very bureaucratic but thorough process, and one might question whether it can be timely and flexible.

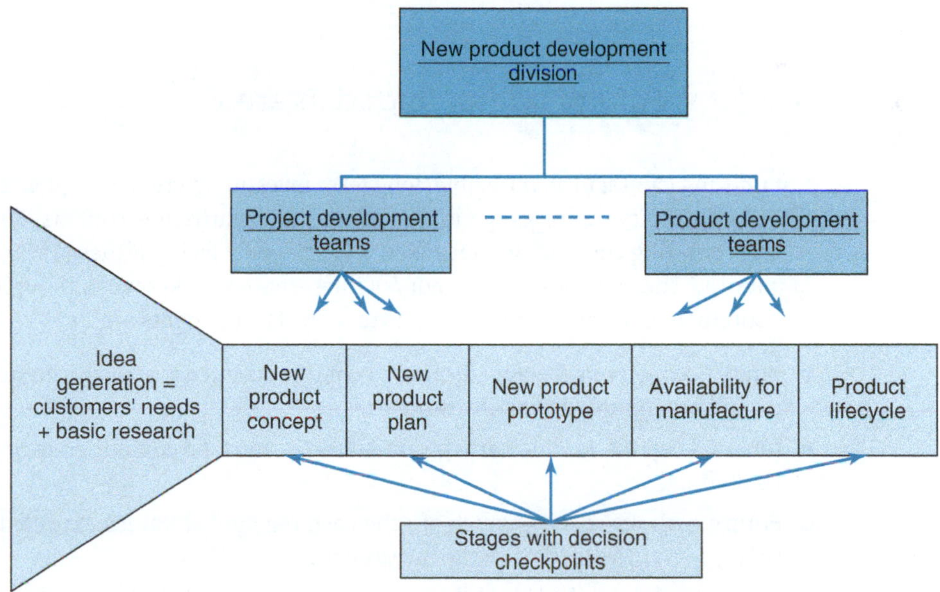

Figure 7.1 Example of a new product development investment process

An organisation implicitly evaluates new investment opportunities against its current condition, but doing so assumes that only the proposed investment changes the total expected value of the organisation. But suppose that doing nothing also comes at a cost? For example, not investing in new technology may come at a cost of reduced competitiveness. Thus, the 'do nothing' alternative should always be considered among the set of feasible investment alternatives. A practical response to applying the 'do nothing' alternative in volatile or quickly evolving markets is to use a lower opportunity cost of capital that reflects lower expected returns from 'doing nothing' while others in the market are doing 'something.' Yet another way of including the opportunity cost of doing nothing is to adjust a new project's cash flows upward for expected deteriorations in cash flows as a result of doing nothing.

All business decisions entail a) the predictions of future costs and benefits and b) subsequent aggregations of data into indices of performance, such as expected profit or return on invested capital. When commitments are short or switching costs are low, one may safely compare investments' short term profits or returns. However, when commitments are long or switching costs are high, the opportunity cost of foregone returns to tied up capital can compound rapidly (i.e. compounded interest). The DCF methods for investment analysis that are detailed in this chapter explicitly measure the compounded opportunity costs. Forecasting necessarily becomes more difficult as decision horizons lengthen. The quotes from Niels Bohr, Nobel laureate in physics[1], and, Henri Poincaré,the 'father' of chaos theory[2], quoted in Chapter 4 are equally applicable here.

Although one may never eliminate the risks of 'fortuitous' future losses or misfortunes, one may choose to structure investment decisions with inherent flexibility. That is, the flexibility to revise a commitment can add significant value to an investment. Structuring investment flexibility has become known as real option analysis (RA), which can be a significant improvement over traditional DCF methods. Financial analysts may also apply the methods of risk models discussed in Chapter 4 to investment decisions.

7.3 A brief theory of compounded interest

Committing capital to an inflexible, long term investment creates the **cost of capital,** which is the opportunity cost of foregone returns from alternative investments. This is as real a cost as any operating cost and was formulated long ago by Irving Fisher (1930) into the 'theory of interest.' The elements of the theory of interest are well known, although issues of proper measurement continue to generate controversy. The elements are:

- Time, t, which may be any discrete or continuous measure of the lifetime during which capital is committed to an investment.
- Invested capital, I_t, which are the amounts that must be committed to an investment over its lifetime.
- Future cash returns, F_t, which are the cash receipts or values expected to be earned at times, t, over the lifetime of the investment.
- Interest rate, r, which is the periodic or continuous opportunity cost of committed capital.

[1] Wikipedia. "Niels Bohr."
[2] Henri Poincaré 1903

If an amount, I_0, is invested now (end of period 0) for a single period and earns the interest rate, *r*, the invested amount will accumulate at the end of the period as follows:

$$F_1 = I_0(1 + r)$$

Reinvesting F_1 for another period is the same as committing I_0 to a two period investment:

$$F_2 = F_1(1 + r) = I_0(1 + r) \times (1 + r) = I_0(1 + r)^2$$

In general, for any investment duration, t, the single future amount, F_t, is found by:

$$F_t = I_0(1 + r)^t$$

If r is the opportunity rate of capital, committing I_0 to any investment at time t incurs the opportunity cost of the future amount (or value), F_t, and any feasible alternative must promise at least the same total value at time *t*. The compounded opportunity cost is captured in the exponential increase, *t*, of the foregone return.[3] Each period's interest is reinvested at the opportunity rate–'compound interest' is the cumulative effect of interest earning interest. Therefore, if an investment prospect promises F_t at time *t*, the most one should be willing to commit or pay for this prospect is found algebraically from the previous formula as:

$$I_0 = \frac{F_t}{(1 + r)^t} = F_t \times \frac{1}{(1 + r)^t}$$

In this formulation, I_0 is called the **present value** or **discounted value** of the future amount. The second version of the formula multiplies the future amount by a 'discount factor,' which is computed as $1/(1 + r)^t$ and is supplied by financial calculators and spreadsheet software formulas, and is sometimes still tabulated in textbooks.

The **present value** is what one would have to invest at the opportunity rate, *r*, in order to earn the future amount F_t at the end of time *t*. The theory is that one should pay no more than this amount, the present value, to own the investment. The present value of a series of future amounts is found by simply adding the discounted values of the series of future amounts.

$$I_0 = \frac{F_1}{(1 + r)^1} + \frac{F_2}{(1 + r)^2} + \ldots + \frac{F_t}{(1 + r)^t}$$

This venerable theory of interest is the foundation of investment analysis and capital budgeting, where it is operationalised as present value or discounted cash flow (DCF) analysis.

Evaluating investments in financial bonds is a relatively straight forward application of DCF analysis. A bond is a debt instrument characterised by a principal amount to be paid at the end of the investment term and contractual interest payments, based on a 'coupon' rate, paid periodically to the bondholder. Thus, all of the investing elements are nominally established by contracts. Many bonds are actively traded, and potential investors have opportunity rates that are influenced by their risk tolerances, general economic conditions and investment opportunities of similar risk. The most difficult part of valuing a financial bond is determining its risk class, which then affects its appropriate individual or market based

[3] Compounded opportunity costs are sometimes confused with the 'time value of money,' which assumes that postponing consumption confers costs. Although part of Irving Fisher's theory of interest, unless one is untrusting, literally starving for cash or unable to borrow, the notion of time value of consumption seems irrational to others (e.g. see Frank P. Ramsey 1928).

opportunity rate. Given one's opportunity cost of capital, valuing bonds is reasonably mechanical. Valuing equity securities is more complex, and valuing real assets may be just as difficult. This chapter focuses on investments in real assets, such as plant, property and equipment, but does not address investments in financial assets, which is the proper province of financial theory.[4]

7.3.1 Application of the theory to investments in real assets

Few investment decisions in real assets are straightforward because factors that affect future duration, returns and risks are numerous and usually are difficult for investors to quantify and compare. The payback criterion, which is a non-DCF method, endures partly because of the difficulties of implementing DCF methods for real asset decision making.

The **payback period** (or **time to break-even**)is the time needed to recoup an initial outlay from periodic income or cash flow. When the expected periodic future amounts received are equal, the payback period is simply the investment amount, I_0, divided by the periodic future amount, F_t.

$$\text{Payback period} = I_0 / F_t$$

When future amounts are unequal, computing the payback period is only slightly more complex: sum the future amounts until the investment amount is recovered; then interpolate between the last two periods, as shown in the following example, Investment A, in Figure 7.2. To recover the entire investment amount ($900) requires the entire Year 1 amount ($481) and a proportion of the Year 2 amount [(900 − 481)/645 = .65]; hence a payback period of 1.65 years.[5]

The payback criterion bypasses several difficult measurements (investment life and cost of capital), but not all – the future amounts are still needed. The payback criterion may seem appealing as an addition to DCF methods when general or specific market conditions are expected to change rapidly. For example, investments in high technology projects may have short but uncertain useful lives. Constraining choices of projects to those with short payback periods may shield the firm from some unspecified risk of product or process obsolescence.[6]

Investment A payback	Year, t 0	1	2	3
Investment, I_0	$ (900.00)			
Future amounts, F_t		$ 481.00	$ 645.00	$ 317.00
Cumulative recovery	$ (900.00)	$ 481.00	$ 1126.00	$ 1443.00
Years used to recover I_0		1.00	0.65	0.00
Payback period, years	1.65			

Figure 7.2 Investment A payback

[4] See financial texts such as Copeland, Weston and Shastri 2005.

[5] A less accurate but convenient approach is to divide the investment amount by the average future amount, but this requires an estimate of the investment life.

[6] For brevity, we use the term 'firm' to refer to the decision making entity, although the theory and implementations apply to other types of organisation and individuals. Gary L. Sundem 1975 is an early demonstration of the potential benefits of using a payback constraint in highly variable conditions. Also see Lefley 1996.

However, a better practice is to model the risk of specific projects more clearly rather than to rely on an inflexible payback rule. One would be prudent to use the payback period only as a complement to more formal DCF methods, not as a substitute.

7.4 Discounted cash flow methods

Discounted cash flow (DCF) methods of investment analysis are direct applications of the theory of interest to long term decision making. The primary DCF methods are net present value (NPV) and internal rate of return (IRR) methods. The NPV method computes the **net present value** of an investment as the sum of its lifetime cash inflows and outflows, which are discounted at the firm's cost of capital. Consider the previous example but now in Figure 7.3 with the context of NPV analysis and a cost of capital, r, that equals 20%.

Investment A	Year, t			
NPV at r = 20%	0	1	2	3
Future amounts, F_t	$ (900.00)	$ 481.00	$ 645.00	$ 317.00
PV factor, $1/(1+0.20)^t$	1.0000	0.8333	0.6944	0.5787
Present values	($900.00)	$400.83	$447.92	$183.45
NPV (sum of present values)	$ 132.20			

Figure 7.3 Investment A, net present value

This 'manual' approach to computing the project's NPV first multiplies each future amount by the present value factor for r = 20% for each year (or exponent, t), obtaining each amount's present value. Secondly, the NPV method sums all of the present values (including the initial investment amount) to obtain the prospect's net present value, $132.20.

Any project with a positive NPV, such as this example, promises a return of capital in excess of the firm's cost of capital. In other words, the firm could invest less than the investment cost of $900 at the opportunity cost of capital to generate the promised returns over the three-year term. By the NPV method, **one should rank all prospective investments by their estimated net present values and select from top to bottom, stopping at the project with a zero net present value or when investment funds are exhausted, whichever comes first.** A NPV of zero can result from a reduced investment cost that now equals the present values of the future amounts at the firm's cost of capital, or from an opportunity cost of capital that exactly equates the full investment cost to the present values of the future amounts.

Large projects with relatively low actual rates of return (e.g. just barely more than the discount rate) may look more promising because of their size and not because of their relative contribution to firm value. The IRR method computes the **internal rate of return,** which is the cost of capital that would exactly equate the present value of the investment costs to the present values of the future amounts to be received. One can compute the internal rate of return by trial and error, which in the current example is found to be 29.66%.[7] In other words, the example is an investment that generates a 29.66% return, which exceeds the example firm's cost of capital of 20%. By the IRR method, **one should rank prospective investments by their internal rates of return and select from the top all that exceed**

[7] Another variation of DCF methods is the NPV Index, which is the sum of present values of future amounts divided by the investment cost. It has no special features to distinguish it from the NPV method.

the cost of capital or until investment funds are exhausted. This result, in many cases, is consistent with the NPV analysis; however, the IRR method may confuse the investment analysis process. First, if projects are independent, they should be evaluated independently against the prevailing market opportunity cost of capital, not merely compared with the internal returns of individual investments, as implied by the IRR method. Second, the IRR method can find multiple rates that satisfy the zero NPV criterion, if projected cash flows change sign from positive to negative. The number of mathematical solutions is equal to the number of times that cash flows change sign during the project's lifetime. Third, the two methods can have different incentive properties, depending upon how managers are evaluated, that can affect managers' decisions in the project selection step of the process. For example, a divisional manager who is evaluated on the division's return on investment would be loath to accept a project with an internal rate of return less than the division's current return on investment, even if the new project's internal rate of return exceeds the firm's cost of capital. This important incentive issue is discussed more fully in Chapter 12. In sum, the NPV method always ranks alternative investments properly, but the IRR method might not; thus many analysts prefer to use the NPV method.

Before addressing important application issues in more detail, let us introduce spreadsheet applications of investment analysis, which we will use throughout the rest of this chapter.

7.4.1 Spreadsheet applications of DCF analysis

Many reasons account for the prevalence of spreadsheet applications for investment analysis. The power and flexibility of financial and risk modelling are certainly among the most important. Other reasons include transparency of analysis, elimination of mathematical errors, and the ability to import cash flow estimates from other sources. We briefly introduce and illustrate several Microsoft Excel formulas that perform essential DCF calculations. Consider the use of Excel to perform the DCF analysis for Investment A, as shown in Figure 7.4.

The NPV of investment A is computed two ways. The 'manual' way first computes the appropriate present value factors in row 5, secondly multiplies these factors by the amounts in row 4, and finally sums the products in cell B7. The more direct approach is to use the formula in cell B8, which adds the initial investment cost in cell B4 to the NPV formula. The

Investment A		**Year, t**		
Cost of capital, r	20%			
NPV at r = 20%	**0**	**1**	**2**	**3**
Future amounts, F_t	$ (900.00)	$ 481.00	$ 645.00	$ 317.00
PV factor, $1/(1+r)^t$	1.0000	0.8333	0.6944	0.5787
Present values	($900.00)	$400.83	$447.92	$183.45
NPV (sum of present values)	$ 132.20	=SUM(B6:E6)		
NPV	$ 132.20	=B4+NPV(B2,C4:E4)		
Investment A		**Year, t**		
IRR	**0**	**1**	**2**	**3**
Future amounts, F_t	$ (900)	$ 481	$ 645	$ 317
Internal rate of return	29.66%	=IRR(B12:E12,B11)		

Figure 7.4 DCF analysis of investment A

first argument of the NPV formula is the cost of capital in cell B2; the second argument is the range of the future amounts in cells C4 to E4.

The IRR of investment A could be found by 'manual' trial and error, but is more directly computed with the IRR formula that includes all of the initial and future amounts of the investment, cells B12 to E12 (the difference between the structure of the NPV and IRR formulas is a quirk of Excel). The second argument of the IRR formula (B2) is an optional 'guess' at the internal rate of return. The guess can be important when future amounts are highly variable because the formula (and trial and error methods) will find the 'local' IRR solution nearest to the guess, which is by default zero unless reset to the guess in the formula.

7.4.2 Investment analysis implementation issues

The use of spreadsheet software makes it easier to describe the difficulties in applying DCF analysis to evaluating investments in real assets, but does not avoid them. Difficulties in application of DCF to investments in real assets can be traced to problems of accurately modelling an investment's:

- risk and uncertainty;
- useful lifetime;
- the cost of capital;
- future cash flows.

In other words, all aspects of the real asset investment decision can be problematic.

7.5 Risk and uncertainty

Investment risk arises from the uncertain effects of future events on the stream of forecasted future cash flows. Four approaches to modelling the effects of uncertain future events include expected value analysis, sensitivity analysis, scenario analysis, and Monte Carlo analysis. These risk modelling methods are described in detail in Chapters 2 and 4, but are also briefly described and selectively applied to investment decision making here:

- **Expected value analysis** computes an average stream of future investment cash flows, wherein possible cash flow streams are driven by alternative sales forecasts (or other activities). The alternative NPVs are weighted by the probabilities or odds of the different forecasts' occurrence.
- **Sensitivity analysis** Predicts the future effects of changes in cash-flow drivers, considered individually and independently. Small changes in cash-flow drivers that predict large changes in NPV indicate likely sources of risk.
- **Scenario analysis** predicts future effects of multiple, related changes in cash-flow drivers. Analysts will typically prepare at least the best-case, worst-case and most likely case scenarios. If the scenarios each predict a positive NPV, the project probably would not

be considered risky. However, if only the best-case scenario predicts a positive NPV, the project might appear too risky to accept.

- **Monte Carlo analysis** creates randomised values of future investment cash flows to simulate a distribution of many possible investment values. One can judge the risk of the simulated NPV values by whether an investment has a sufficiently high probability of returning more than the cost of capital.

7.6 Investment lifetime

An investment's physical life might not be the same as its technological lifetime. Generally an asset's **useful lifetime** is estimated from the time of its in-service installation to its expected retirement or replacement. Times needed for installation and start-up, and retirement and removal, need to be accounted for at each end of the investment horizon. The useful lifetime of an asset generally ends when a new, comparable asset generates a higher added value than the current asset. The difference in added value may derive from higher unit revenues because of higher product quality and functionality, or lower unit costs caused by lower operating costs. The estimated useful life has direct impacts on forecasts of costs, expenses, revenues, salvage values, taxes and cash flows. One should model and assess the effects of variations in an investment's lifetime with one or more of the risk modelling methods.

Investment projects that have different time horizons or useful lives are not directly comparable. Consider the two rival investments, A and B, with expected lives of 3 and 2 years, respectively in Figure 7.5.

Although A has a higher NPV, we cannot directly compare it to B because A has an additional year of inflows and we do not know what the firm's investment opportunities are in Year 3 if it chooses B. Of course, the firm cannot know for sure, either. One may choose arbitrarily to truncate the longer investment and add a terminal salvage value, if appropriate, at the end of the second year. If the resale market could be sure of the quality of investment A at the end of the second year and, if transfer of ownership is costless, its resale value would equal the present value of the third year's inflow. The present value (at $r = 20\%$) of Year 3's

A	B	C	D	E
Cost of capital, r	20%			
Investment A		**Year, t**		
NPV at r = 20%	**0**	**1**	**2**	**3**
Investment, I_0	$ (900.00)			
Future amounts, F_t		$ 481.00	$ 645.00	$ 317.00
Net present value	$ 132.20	=B18+NPV(B15,C19:E19)		
Investment B		**Year, t**		
NPV at r = 20%	**0**	**1**	**2**	
Investment, I_0	$ (900.00)			
Future amounts, F_t		$ 555.00	$ 785.00	
Net present value	$ 107.64	=B23+NPV(B15,C24:D24)		

Figure 7.5 Investments A and B, with unequal lives

A	B	C	D	E
Cost of capital, r; PV factors	20%	0.8333	0.6944	0.5787
Investment A (truncated)		**Year, t**		
NPV at r = 20%	**0**	**1**	**2**	**3**
Investment, I_0 ; Salvage value	$ (900.00)		$ 200.00	
Future amounts, F_t		$ 481.00	$ 645.00	$ -
Net present value	$ 87.64	=B30+D30*D27+NPV(B27,C31:D31)		
Investment B		**Year, t**		
NPV at r = 20%	**0**	**1**	**2**	
Investment, I_0	$ (900.00)			
Future amounts, F_t		$ 555.00	$ 785.00	
Net present value	$ 107.64	=B35+NPV(B27,C36:D36)		

Figure 7.6 Investments A and B, with equalised lifetimes

expected $317 one year hence would be 0.833 × $317 = $264.17.[8] Assume, however, that the firm estimates the net resale value of Investment A will equal $200 at the end of Year 2, after the resale market's quality discount, relocation and setup costs. Now both investments in Figure 7.6 have equal lifetimes, but relatively different net present values – B now has a higher NPV.

Alternatively one can assume similar re-investment activities after the expected end of the shorter investment prospect. If investment lives are relatively short, one could assume multiple re-investments that result in equal length chains. Consider chaining two As and three Bs, creating two six-year series of investments, as shown in Figure 7.7.

By this second approach, both alternative investment streams have equal, comparable lives, and once again B has the relatively higher net present value. Note that the additional investment costs are themselves discounted to present values.

Both approaches to equalise investment lives are internally consistent, but as a practical matter, which should be preferred? The answer hinges on the relative difficulty and reasonableness of estimating a) the salvage or resale value of a truncated investment *versus* b)

A	B	C	D	E	F	G	H
Cost of capital, r; PV factors	20%	0.8333	0.6944	0.5787	0.4823	0.4019	0.3349
Investment A (doubled)				**Year, t**			
NPV at r = 20%	**0**	**1**	**2**	**3**	**4**	**5**	**6**
Investments, I_0, I_3	$ (900.00)			$ (900.00)			
Future amounts, F_t		$ 481.00	$ 645.00	$ 317.00	$ 481.00	$ 645.00	$ 317.00
Net present value	$ 208.70	=B42+E42*E39+NPV(B39,C43:H43)					
Investment B (tripled)				**Year, t**			
NPV at r = 20%	**0**	**1**	**2**	**3**	**4**	**5**	**6**
Investments, I_0, I_2, I_4	$ (900.00)		$ (900.00)		$(900.00)		
Future amounts, F_t		$ 555.00	$ 785.00	$ 555.00	$ 785.00	$ 555.00	$ 785.00
Net present value	$ 234.30	=B47+D47*D39+F47*F39+NPV(B39,C48:H48)					

Figure 7.7 Multiples of investments A and B

8 Note that the net present value of A is unchanged by this specific reconfiguration of cash flows.

the repeated, future investment opportunities. Both approaches are made more difficult by long useful lives and decision horizons. Estimating resale values of actively traded assets might be relatively simple and reasonably accurate for short lives. Predicting identical future investment opportunities seems justifiable only in cases where technology is relatively stable and predictable.

7.7 Cost of capital

We mentioned earlier that the choice of the discount rate or cost of capital is important for evaluating alternative investments, but the choice might not be obvious. For publicly held companies and their stockholders, some experts argue that the discount rate should be the long term market return on equity investments (historically about 8%) because that is the general opportunity for stockholders. Others argue that public firms, who act for their security holders, should use the 'risk-free' rate, adjusted upward for the expected risk of the particular project.[9] Because most firms are financed with both debt and equity, the financing decision for a particular project could affect the firm's capital structure and its cost of capital. Therefore, some argue that, because stockholders face different opportunities and risks than bondholders, the cash flows attributable to each party (e.g. earnings before interest and tax (EBIT), and tax savings and interest) should be evaluated at separate, risk appropriate discount rates.

Public or governmental organisations also have difficulty choosing the proper discount rate. If a government has many diversified projects and is unlikely to default, some public finance economists argue that the proper discount rate is the risk free rate. However, others argue that because public investment displaces private investment (by taking taxes that private parties otherwise could invest) governments should use a higher rate comparable to rates of return to private investors. These interesting topics, which are among the most important in corporate and public finance, are beyond the scope of this text. The stakes can be high depending on how these concerns are addressed, and investment selection can be very sensitive to the choice of the discount rate. For purposes of this text we assume that the different investing entities will use discount rates as follows:

Investing entity	Cost of capital
Governments and public agencies	Market risk free rate = r_f
Private debt investors.....	Risk free rate plus debt market risk premium, $r_f + \delta = r_d$
Private equity investors.....	Risk free rate plus an equity market risk premium, $r_f + \epsilon = r_e$
Publicly held firms.....	Weighted average cost of capital = WACC

These assumptions bypass many theoretical and practical controversies in the fields of finance. In general, these assumptions assume competitive capital markets where participants have full information and frictionless access to alternative investments and sources of capital.

[9] Analysts who build discount rates this way usually estimate the risk free rate as the rate of return of long term government bonds (historically about 3 to 4%) and use the Capital Asset Pricing Model (CAPM) or a variant to measure risk adjustments from the risk free rate (see Copeland et al. 2005, Chapter 6.)

Of special importance is the **weighted average cost of capital (WACC)**,which is the rate that a firm expects to pay **on average** to all its debt and equity security holders to finance its investments. Debt and equity security holders have different costs of capital and, therefore, the cash flows to them should be discounted at different rates. Because debt holders have prior claims to the firm's assets at liquidation and, because interest on debt is tax-deductible, changing the firm's capital structure or leverage by investment financing decisions can change the firm's costs of capital. The **debt to value (D/V)** ratio measures the leverage in a firm's capital structure as the proportion of debt financing relative to the value of the firm's total assets. The firm may use the WACC to discount total cash flows of alternative investments, if the firm maintains its D/V ratio by financing new investments by the same proportions of capital or by rebalancing its debt and equity balances, and if the firm's investing conditions include:

- competitive capital markets;
- choice among a set of investments comparable in risk to current assets;
- the costs of equity and debt and the corporate tax rate are constant over the life of an investment[10]

Although all of these conditions are unlikely to be consistently achieved in practice, both striving for them, and the simplicity of using a single rate for decentralised investment decision making might explain the widespread practice of firms' using the WACC to discount investment cash flows.

A firm's WACC is computed by estimating the after tax cost of each source of capital used[11] multiplied by its proportional share of the total capital used. Assume the following amounts for an example firm and its investment and financing conditions:

Market risk free rate, $r_f = 3\%$;

Debt risk premium, $\delta = 4\%$, and the before-tax cost of debt, $r_d = r_f + \delta$;

Tax rate, $\tau = 35\%$;

Equity risk premium, $\epsilon = 8\%$, and the cost of equity, $r_e = r_f + \epsilon$;

Debt to Value ratio, $D/V = 40\%$.

This firm's WACC is computed from the costs of debt (r_d) and equity (r_e) as:

$$WACC = r_d \times (1 - \tau) \times D/V + r_e \times (1 - D/V)$$

$$WACC = (.03 + .04) \times (1 - .35) \times .40 + (.03 + .08) \times (1 - .40) = .0182 + .066$$
$$= 8.42\%.$$

Given the previous assumptions (or consistent with observed practice), the firm may use its WACC of 8.42% to discount forecast future cash flows, and most likely will make appropriate investment decisions.[12]

---

[10] See Miles and Ezzell 1980.

[11] Recall that interest paid to debt holders is tax deductible for the firm but dividends to stockholders are not.

[12] Our casual observations of practice indicate that investment decisions that are nearly or barely positive NPV estimates (also known as 'knife-edge' decisions) are often made on qualitative grounds.

7.8 Forecasts of future cash flows

Analysts may forecast three types of future cash flows: investment, periodic operating, and termination cash flows.

- **Investment** cash flows include new asset costs (including installation and start-up costs) and future reinvestment or refurbishing costs. Generally all costs of acquiring and placing assets into service are considered costs of the equipment. Future reinvestment or refurbishing costs extend the life of the asset. New investment costs also can include tax effects arising from an actual loss or gain on the sale of replaced assets and tax credits offered by governments to encourage certain types of investment (e.g. clean energy). Investment tax effects can vary greatly across governmental jurisdictions and over time.
- **Periodic operating** cash flows are cash inflows and outflows that are driven by forecasted sales and production activities.[13] Periodic cash flows might not be identical to recognised revenues and expenses because of possible timing differences of revenue recognition and expense matching for financial reporting. For example, the cost of an asset is a cash outflow in the year of acquisition but asset depreciation is an operating expense that is not a cash flow in the period of expense. Depreciation does, however, reduce periodic income and the associated tax expense, which may be a cash outflow in the same period. The tax savings from asset depreciation is often called an investment's **tax shield,** equal to asset depreciation multiplied by the tax rate (the amount of income **shielded** from taxation).
- **Termination** cash flows are the expected cash flows from terminating an investment at the end of its useful life. Termination cash flows include after-tax gains or losses on sales of divested assets, employee severance costs, and physical site remediation.

Analysts note that market rates of interest contain the risk-free rate, a risk adjustment, and an expected rate of inflation. One can adjust the analysis for expected inflation[14] by either

a) Using a comparable market rate or a derived (risk-adjusted) rate plus inflation and adjusting the future cash flows for expected inflation (unless they are fixed, as in a financial bond)

b) Using a derived (risk-adjusted) rate and constant-currency cash flows, without adjusting for inflation

Either approach should lead to consistent rankings of investment projects.

[13] Sales forecasting is a difficult task, and its goal often is not absolute accuracy but relative accuracy across investment alternatives.

[14] Technically, the inflation rate and the inflation free cost of capital interact, but at low rates of interest and inflation the interaction is negligible.

Comprehensive example

Ahern Associates Ltd owns a four storey building that occupies half of a city block in the central business district of a mid-sized U.S. city. Ahern Associates has had to reduce the sales based rental rate over the past several years because of its declining state and the attractiveness of new space elsewhere in the city. Ahern Associates has learned from friends in the city planning department that several international firms are considering purchasing and renovating an adjacent building. One of the firms is rumoured to be Trumpet Properties, which is one of the largest and most successful firms of its type.

Ahern Associates is considering whether to renovate the building to make it more attractive to tenants.[15] Ahern Associates expects total rent, which is a percentage of tenant sales, will continue to decline without a renovation, but would increase after a renovation, from increased tenants' sales. The rate of rental increase would be adversely affected if Trumpet Properties competes directly by purchasing the adjacent property. However, Trumpet Properties might be less likely to purchase the adjacent property if Ahern Associates renovates the property quickly. The immediate investment decision posed is whether Ahern Associates should renovate the building? The two alternative decisions (renovate or not) must be made with two uncertain conditions (investment scenarios with or without Trumpet competition).

Relevant data values are in Figure 7.8. *Review these data before proceeding.* Assume all annual income amounts are cash flows in the same year (except for straight line depreciation).[16] Review these data and their explanatory labels carefully. In particular, note the four

Ahern Associates Data Values		
Renovation cost now	$ 1,500,000	
Renovation life	10	years
Increased salvage value at the end of renovation life	-	
General & administrative costs per year	500,000	per year
Current annual tenants' sales	$ 24,000,000	per year
Current rental rate, as a percent of tenant sales	4%	of tenant sales
Tenants' sales growth **without** renovation and:		
Without Trumpet Properties competition	-4%	per year
With Trumpet Properties competition	-8%	per year
Tenants' sales growth **with** renovation and:		
Without Trumpet Properties entry	10%	per year
With Trumpet Properties entry	4%	per year
Tenants' temporary sales decline during renovation year	-25%	per year
Cost of capital	8%	
Tax rate	35%	
Probability of Trumpet's entry if renovate now	25%	
Probability of Trumpet's entry if do not renovate now	80%	

Figure 7.8 Ahern Associates data input

15 This is a simplified description of the complete strategic investment decision that focuses on one key driver of cash flow and one potential competitor's alternative actions.

16 Each of these input data values is important to the analysis of the investment's risk. Perhaps the most important values are the estimated sales growth or decline rates because effects of errors in growth rates are compounded over the estimated lifetime.

sales (and rental) growth scenarios:(1) without and (2) with renovation and (3) without and (4) with Trumpet Properties competition.

The strategic investment decision can be illustrated with the NPV decision tree in Figure 7.9 (also see Chapter 2) with expected probabilities of Trumpet Properties' competition. The NPV analysis proceeds to fill in the blank net present values of the four scenarios and expected NPVs of Ahern Associates' two decisions. The higher expected NPV will indicate the mathematical preference.

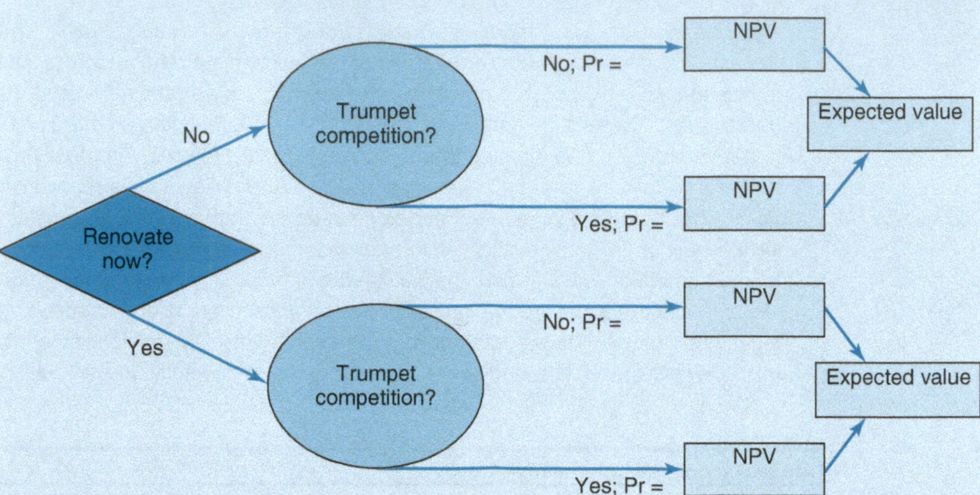

Figure 7.9 Ahern Associates NPV decision tree

After gathering the data in Figure 7.8, Ahern Associates next estimated the future cash flows of the investment alternatives. The $1.5 million renovation is expected to begin immediately, take one year, and have a ten-year life. General and administrative costs are unchanged across the four scenarios (and could be ignored for this stage of the analysis). Tenants pay rent to Ahern Associates at the rate of 4% of their sales, and this rate is not expected to change. The tenants' estimated sales revenues are currently $24 million per annum. The renovation will have an adverse effect (−25%) on tenant sales during the year of renovation. Tenant sales growth can be affected by whether there is a renovation and competition from Trumpet Properties.

The estimated cash flows of Figure 7.9's four scenarios are in Figure 7.10.[17] Each cash flow estimate begins with estimated tenant sales, which drives Ahern Associates' rental revenue over the investment lifetime. Income before tax is computed after deducting general and administrative costs and straight line depreciation. Multiplying this amount by (1 – tax rate) yields annual income after tax. Adding back depreciation gives annual net cash flow after tax. The NPV of each scenario is computed at the company's estimated cost of capital, 8%. The outcomes of the analysis are entered into Figure 7.9, which is shown now as Figure 7.11. Renovating the building has the higher expected value and appears to be the better decision from this analysis. But what if the building could be sold in its current condition for $1.8 m This amount far exceeds the expected NPV of renovating the building; perhaps Ahern Associates should sell the building now. Is this the right decision? It appears so, but we should gather more information and perform the revised 'real option analysis' to come.

[17]The complete Excel file is available to adopters of this text.

Ahern Associates NPV Solution											
A	B	C	D	E	F	G	H	I	J	K	L
Status quo: No renovation without competition by					**End of Year**						
Trumpet Properties (Probability = 20%)	0	1	2	3	4	5	6	7	8	9	10
Renovation cost	$ -										
Tenants' sales		$ 23,040,000	$ 22,118,400	$ 21,233,664	$ 20,384,317	$ 19,568,945	$ 18,786,187	$ 18,034,739	$ 17,313,350	$ 16,620,816	$ 15,955,983
Rent		921,600	884,736	849,347	815,373	782,758	751,447	721,390	692,534	664,833	638,239
General & administration costs		500,000	500,000	500,000	500,000	500,000	500,000	500,000	500,000	500,000	500,000
Depreciation on renovation		-	-	-	-	-	-	-	-	-	-
Income before tax		421,600	384,736	349,347	315,373	282,758	251,447	221,390	192,534	164,833	138,239
Income after tax		274,040	250,078	227,075	204,992	183,793	163,441	143,903	125,147	107,141	89,856
Add back depreciation		-	-	-	-	-	-	-	-	-	-
Cash flow after tax	$ -	$ 274,040	$ 250,078	$ 227,075	$ 204,992	$ 183,793	$ 163,441	$ 143,903	$ 125,147	$ 107,141	$ 89,856
NPV, years 1-10	$1,273,956										
Status quo: No renovation now with competition by					**End of Year**						
Trumpet Properties (Probability = 80%)	0	1	2	3	4	5	6	7	8	9	10
Renovation cost	$ -										
Tenants' sales		$ 22,080,000	$ 20,313,600	$ 18,688,512	$ 17,193,431	$ 15,817,957	$ 14,552,520	$ 13,388,318	$ 12,317,253	$ 11,331,873	$ 10,425,323
Rent		883,200	812,544	747,540	687,737	632,718	582,101	535,533	492,690	453,275	417,013
General & administration costs		500,000	500,000	500,000	500,000	500,000	500,000	500,000	500,000	500,000	500,000
Depreciation on renovation		-	-	-	-	-	-	-	-	-	-
Income before tax		383,200	312,544	247,540	187,737	132,718	82,101	35,533	(7,310)	(46,725)	(82,987)
Income after tax		249,080	203,154	160,901	122,029	86,267	53,366	23,096	(4,751)	(30,371)	(53,942)
Add back depreciation		-	-	-	-	-	-	-	-	-	-
Cash flow after tax	$ -	$ 249,080	$ 203,154	$ 160,901	$ 122,029	$ 86,267	$ 53,366	$ 23,096	$ (4,751)	$ (30,371)	$ (53,942)
NPV, years 1-10	$685,297										
Invest: Renovate now without competition by					**End of Year**						
Trumpet Properties (Probability = 75%)	0	1	2	3	4	5	6	7	8	9	10
Renovation cost	$ (1,500,000)										
Tenants' sales		$ 18,000,000	$ 19,800,000	$ 21,780,000	$ 23,958,000	$ 26,353,800	$ 28,989,180	$ 31,888,098	$ 35,076,908	$ 38,584,599	$ 42,443,058
Rent		720,000	792,000	871,200	958,320	1,054,152	1,159,567	1,275,524	1,403,076	1,543,384	1,697,722
General & administration costs		500,000	500,000	500,000	500,000	500,000	500,000	500,000	500,000	500,000	500,000
Depreciation on renovation		150,000	150,000	150,000	150,000	150,000	150,000	150,000	150,000	150,000	150,000
Income before tax		70,000	142,000	221,200	308,320	404,152	509,567	625,524	753,076	893,384	1,047,722
Income after tax		45,500	92,300	143,780	200,408	262,699	331,219	406,591	489,500	580,700	681,020
Add back depreciation		150,000	150,000	150,000	150,000	150,000	150,000	150,000	150,000	150,000	150,000
Cash flow after tax	$ (1,500,000)	$ 195,500	$ 242,300	$ 293,780	$ 350,408	$ 412,699	$ 481,219	$ 556,591	$ 639,500	$ 730,700	$ 831,020
NPV, years 1-10	$1,384,371										
Invest: Renovate now with competition by					**End of Year**						
Trumpet Properties (Probability = 25%)	0	1	2	3	4	5	6	7	8	9	10
Renovation cost	$ (1,500,000)										
Tenants' sales		$ 18,000,000	$ 18,720,000	$ 19,468,800	$ 20,247,552	$ 21,057,454	$ 21,899,752	$ 22,775,742	$ 23,686,772	$ 24,634,243	$ 25,619,613
Rent		720,000	748,800	778,752	809,902	842,298	875,990	911,030	947,471	985,370	1,024,785
General & administration costs		500,000	500,000	500,000	500,000	500,000	500,000	500,000	500,000	500,000	500,000
Depreciation on renovation		150,000	150,000	150,000	150,000	150,000	150,000	150,000	150,000	150,000	150,000
Income before tax		70,000	98,800	128,752	159,902	192,298	225,990	261,030	297,471	335,370	374,785
Income after tax		45,500	64,220	83,689	103,936	124,994	146,894	169,669	193,356	217,990	243,610
Add back depreciation		150,000	150,000	150,000	150,000	150,000	150,000	150,000	150,000	150,000	150,000
Cash flow after tax	$ (1,500,000)	$ 195,500	$ 214,220	$ 233,689	$ 253,936	$ 274,994	$ 296,894	$ 319,669	$ 343,356	$ 367,990	$ 393,610
NPV, years 1-10	$349,521										

Figure 7.10 Ahern Associates NPV analysis

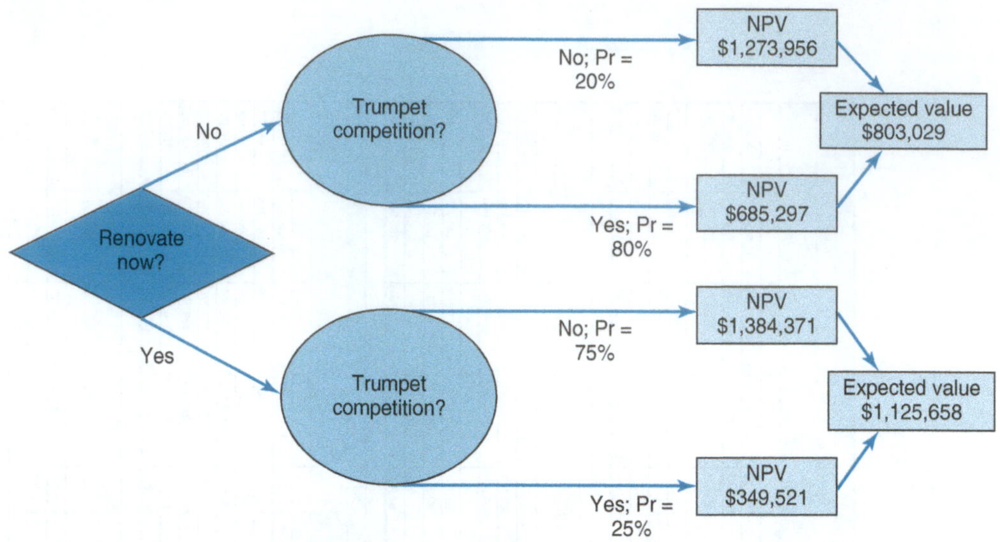

Figure 7.11 Ahern Associates completed NPV decision tree

7.9 Real options and net present value analysis

Traditional NPV analysis considers that investment decisions are made now, with currently available information. However, as time proceeds one often receives updated information that, had one known, could have changed the original investment decision. If circumstances permit, it could be quite valuable to build-in the flexibility to revise, expand, or terminate an investment upon the receipt of new information. Structuring investments as flexible decisions is known as Real-option analysis (RA). In fact, when such flexibility can be included, traditional NPV analysis can yield the wrong investment decision.

The typical steps in applying RA to investment decisions are:

1. Describe the proposed investment alternatives (e.g. invest now or defer investment) with decision trees.
2. Forecast expected cash flows and compute the NPV of each outcome of each tree, as if they were realised as expected.
3. Choose the optimal (highest NPV) outcome of each decision tree that would be chosen with perfect foresight.
4. Work backwards from NPV outcomes to make the optimal initial choice.

5. Compute the real option value of the terms of flexibility as the NPV difference between the NPV of exercising the flexibility option and the NPV of the next best choice.

We illustrate RA by returning to the building renovation example.

Ahern Associates recognises that sometimes acting quickly can prevent competitors from dominating a market. However, waiting to gather more information about the investment conditions might identify either new opportunities to take or problems to avoid. Ahern Associates is considering two alternatives: (1) renovate now or (2) defer renovation for one year. By waiting a year, Ahern Associates can convert the uncertainty whether Trumpet Properties will enter the market into a 100% probability of either having a major competitor or not. In this investment situation and in others, when the investment is irreversible and relevant information can be obtained over time, deferring a decision can be more valuable than acting immediately. In other words, if Ahern Associates can be assured that it will learn about its competitors' actions in the next year, the company perhaps should defer its investment decision. RA is the tool of choice for this type of decision.

The first decision facing Ahern Associates is whether to renovate now or wait a year. Each first choice can be represented by analysis that is similar to Figures 7.9 and 7.10, but with several differences. First, deferring the decision a year extends the investment horizon to 11 years, and to compare properly the two first choices, the cash flows associated with deciding now must be extended an additional year. Ahern Associates estimates that a $300 K reinvestment in the 10th year will extend the useful life one more year, and will not disrupt tenant sales. Second, deferring the investment decision by a year is expected to increase the renovation cost to $2 M. However, the firm strongly believes that, if it becomes known that Trumpet Properties will not be a direct competitor, Ahern Associates can raise its rental rate to 6% of sales. Figure 7.11 adds these data to the investment analysis data already presented in Figure 7.9. The new decision tree with two primary branches (decide now, defer the decision one year) and two sets of secondary branches (renovate or sell) is in Figure 7.12.

Real Option Analysis Data Values		
Net sale value of building in current condition	$ 1,800,000	
Renovation cost one year from now	$ 2,000,000	
Rental rate with **known non-entry** by Trumpet Properties	6%	of tenant sales
Cost of 11th year maintenance if renovate now	$ 300,000	in year 10

Figure 7.12 **Real option analysis data**

If Ahern Associates decides now, Trumpet Properties' competition is uncertain, but Ahern Associates expects that their immediate renovation will make the odds of direct competition only 25%. Forecasting the cash flows of this decision tree will proceed similarly as before except that we know from the previous analysis that the non-renovation alternative is an inferior solution. The revised NPV of renovation is shown as the 'Renovate now' branch. The NPVs of the two renovation scenarios (with and without Trumpet competition) shown in the upper branch are computed in Figure 7.13. The sale of the building for $1.8 M is entered as the outcome of the 'Sell now' branch of Figure 7.12. If Ahern Associates decides now, the optimal decision is to sell the building for a certain $1.8M, which is greater than the expected value of renovation.

The bottom of the decision tree in Figure 7.12 reflects flexibility in Ahern Associates' investment decision. The NPV calculations for the "Wait One Year" branch of Figure 7.12 are in Figure 7.14. Deferring the renovation a year increases the odds that Trumpet Properties will purchase the adjacent building to 80%. However, waiting a year converts that uncertainty to a certainty and, if Trumpet does enter the market, the optimal decision is to sell the building at that time (as shown in the upper branch of the tree). If it is learned that Trumpet will not enter, Ahern Associates can raise its rent, and the optimal decision is to renovate the building. The firm must decide now whether to decide or defer. At this time the expected value of the optimal deferral decisions exceeds the expected value of the optimal decide now decision, which is to sell. The difference between the two expected NPVs (defer – decide now) is the real option value of the flexibility to defer the decision one year (note that in the lower branch of Figure 7.12 the deferred value of selling is discounted one year at the cost of capital):

Expected value of deferring the decision one year	$ 1,903,340 (renovate or sell)
Expected value of deciding now	1,800,000 (sell)
Real option value of the flexibility to defer	$ 103.340

One interpretation of this value is that Ahern Associates might pay up to $103340 to learn for certain the intentions of Trumpet Properties. Because this appears to be a 'knife edge' decision, Ahern Associates would be wise to explore the sensitivity of this outcome to variations (known or random) in key assumptions of the analysis, using the risk modelling tools of Chapter 4. Note that real option values can be negative, which weighs against exercising the option.

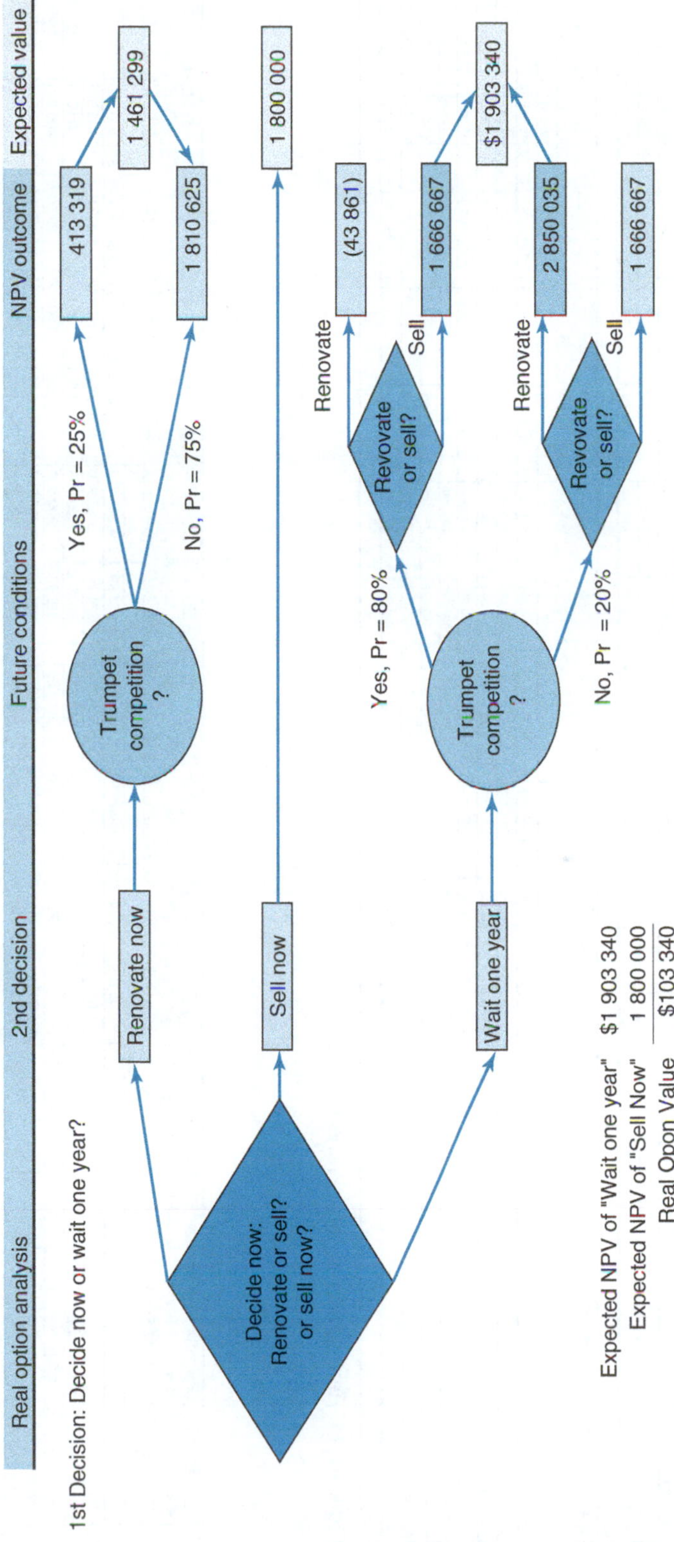

Figure 7.13 Real option analysis: decide now: renovate or sell, or wait one year

Ahern Associates RA: Decide Now												
Invest now: Renovate without competition by Trumpet Properties					End of Year							
	0	1	2	3	4	5	6	7	8	9	10	11
Renovation cost	$ (1,500,000)										$ (300,000)	$ -
Tenants' sales		$ 18,000,000	$ 19,800,000	$ 21,780,000	$ 23,958,000	$ 26,353,800	$ 28,989,180	$ 31,888,098	$ 35,076,908	$ 38,584,599	$ 42,443,058	$ 46,687,364
Rent		720,000	792,000	871,200	958,320	1,054,152	1,159,567	1,275,524	1,403,076	1,543,384	1,697,722	1,867,495
General & administration costs		500,000	500,000	500,000	500,000	500,000	500,000	500,000	500,000	500,000	500,000	500,000
Depreciation on renovation		150,000	150,000	150,000	150,000	150,000	150,000	150,000	150,000	150,000	150,000	300,000
Income before tax		70,000	142,000	221,200	308,320	404,152	509,567	625,524	753,076	893,384	1,047,722	1,067,495
Income after tax		45,500	92,300	143,780	200,408	262,699	331,219	406,591	489,500	580,700	681,020	693,871
Add back depreciation		150,000	150,000	150,000	150,000	150,000	150,000	150,000	150,000	150,000	150,000	300,000
Cash flow after tax	$ (1,500,000)	$ 195,500	$ 242,300	$ 293,780	$ 350,408	$ 412,699	$ 481,219	$ 556,591	$ 639,500	$ 730,700	$ 831,020	$ 993,871
NPV, years 1-11	$1,810,625											
Invest now: Renovate with competition by Trumpet Properties					End of Year							
	0	1	2	3	4	5	6	7	8	9	10	11
Renovation cost	$ (1,500,000)										$ (300,000)	
Tenants' sales		$ 18,000,000	$ 18,720,000	$ 19,468,800	$ 20,247,552	$ 21,057,454	$ 21,899,752	$ 22,775,742	$ 23,686,772	$ 24,634,243	$ 25,619,613	$ 26,644,397
Rent		720,000	748,800	778,752	809,902	842,298	875,990	911,030	947,471	985,370	1,024,785	1,065,776
General & administration costs		500,000	500,000	500,000	500,000	500,000	500,000	500,000	500,000	500,000	500,000	500,000
Depreciation on renovation		150,000	150,000	150,000	150,000	150,000	150,000	150,000	150,000	150,000	150,000	300,000
Income before tax		70,000	98,800	128,752	159,902	192,298	225,990	261,030	297,471	335,370	374,785	265,776
Income after tax		45,500	64,220	83,689	103,936	124,994	146,894	169,669	193,356	217,990	243,610	172,754
Add back depreciation		150,000	150,000	150,000	150,000	150,000	150,000	150,000	150,000	150,000	150,000	300,000
Cash flow after tax	$ (1,500,000)	$ 195,500	$ 214,220	$ 233,689	$ 253,936	$ 274,994	$ 296,894	$ 319,669	$ 343,356	$ 367,990	$ 93,610	$ 472,754
NPV, years 1-11	$413,319											

Figure 7.14 Real option analysis: renovate now

Ahern Associates RA: Wait one year												
Wait: In one year, learn that Trumpet Properties does not purchase adjacent property					End of Year							
	0	1	2	3	4	5	6	7	8	9	10	11
Renovation cost		$ (2,000,000)										
Tenants' sales		23,040,000	$ 16,588,800	$18,247,680	$ 20,072,448	$ 22,079,693	$24,287,662	$26,716,428	$29,388,071	$32,326,878	$35,559,566	$ 39,115,523
Rent		921,600	995,328	1,094,861	1,204,347	1,324,782	1,457,260	1,602,986	1,763,284	1,939,613	2,133,574	2,346,931
General & administration costs		500,000	500,000	500,000	500,000	500,000	500,000	500,000	500,000	500,000	500,000	500,000
Depreciation on renovation			200,000	200,000	200,000	200,000	200,000	200,000	200,000	200,000	200,000	200,000
Income before tax		421,600	295,328	394,861	504,347	624,782	757,260	902,986	1,063,284	1,239,613	1,433,574	1,646,931
Income after tax		274,040	191,963	256,660	327,825	406,108	492,219	586,941	691,135	805,748	931,823	1,070,505
Add back depreciation		-	200,000	200,000	200,000	200,000	200,000	200,000	200,000	200,000	200,000	200,000
Cash flow after tax		$ (1,725,960)	391,963	456,660	527,825	606,108	692,219	786,941	891,135	1,005,748	1,131,823	1,270,505
NPV, years 1-11	$2,850,035											
Wait: In one year, learn Trumpet Properties does purchase adjacent property					End of Year							
	0	1	2	3	4	5	6	7	8	9	10	11
Renovation cost		$ (2,000,000)										
Tenants' sales		23,040,000	$ 16,588,800	$17,252,352	$ 17,942,446	$ 18,660,144	$19,406,550	$20,182,812	$20,990,124	$21,829,729	$22,702,918	$ 23,611,035
Rent		921,600	663,552	690,094	717,698	746,406	776,262	807,312	839,605	873,189	908,117	944,441
General & administration costs		500,000	500,000	500,000	500,000	500,000	500,000	500,000	500,000	500,000	500,000	500,000
Depreciation on renovation			200,000	200,000	200,000	200,000	200,000	200,000	200,000	200,000	200,000	200,000
Income before tax		421,600	(36,448)	(9,906)	17,698	46,406	76,262	107,312	139,605	173,189	208,117	244,441
Income after tax		274,040	(23,691)	(6,439)	11,504	30,164	49,570	69,753	90,743	112,573	135,276	158,887
Add back depreciation		-	200,000	200,000	200,000	200,000	200,000	200,000	200,000	200,000	200,000	200,000
Cash flow after tax		$ (1,725,960)	$ 176,309	$ 193,561	$ 211,504	$ 230,164	$ 249,570	$ 269,753	$ 290,743	$ 312,573	$ 335,276	$ 358,887
NPV, years 1-11	($43,861)											

Figure 7.15 Real option analysis: Wait one year

7.10 Investment portfolios and capital rationing

If an organisation selects multiple investment projects, the collection of capital investments is called a **portfolio.** Most organisations have short term limits on funds available for investment; thus, capital budgeting becomes **capital rationing,** which limits capital spending on positive NPV projects to no more than the organisation's discretionary investment budget. The investment portfolio selection rule is more complicated under the rationing condition and becomes: maximise the expected value of the portfolio, subject to the constraints of a) spending no more than the capital budget and b) exposing the organisation to no more than the desired level of financial risk. The budget constraint means that the organisation may not be able to select all positive NPV projects and, if multiples of some projects may be selected, the investment rule may not be as simple as 'select all positive NPV projects until the capital budget is exhausted.' In these more complicated situations, the combinations of alternative projects may be too large to make investment decisions 'by inspection,' and one may usefully employ mathematical methods such as "linear' or 'integer programming'. These techniques are discussed in detail in Chapter 8, but this chapter will present a simplified application of these powerful methods in conjunction with some financial modelling techniques that were introduced in Chapter 4.

One of Ahern Associates' tenants serves two related markets and is planning its annual investment activity. Figure 7.16 displays the firm's opportunity cost of capital, its capital budget constraint, and cash flow characteristics of six alternative investment projects (1 through 6) that serve either Market 1 or Market 2, which offer different growth opportunities. The tenant could select none, any or all of these projects, and some are available in multiple quantities. The firm is able to estimate the first-year cash flows for each project and for simplicity we extend the cash flow over the remainders of the estimated equal lives by applying appropriate market growth rates.

7.10.1 Portfolio selection

The process of **portfolio selection** combines the requirement of positive NPV investment, constrained by a capital budget and concerns for risk. If the firm can select multiples of some or all of the available investments (e.g. one of Project 1, two of Project 3, . . .),the optimal portfolio selection decision is not readily apparent. This choice may be facilitated by using Excel's Solver tool to maximise the expected NPV of the final portfolio, **subject to** the capital budget constraint and several other constraints that might be specific to the investment opportunities. If X_i is the number of discrete projects selected, the portfolio decision may be described as:

Maximise $\Sigma_{i=1 \text{ to } n} X_i \times NPV_i$ (the portfolio NPV–the "objective" function)

Subject to: $\Sigma_{i=1 \text{ to } n} X_i \times Cost_i \leq$ Capital Budget (the sum of the initial costs must be less than the capital budget)

$X_i \geq 0$ (non-negativity–the firm cannot divest of investments not yet selected; e.g. no short selling)

$X_i \leq Q_i$ (availability–the possible multiples, Q_i, of individual investment projects)

$X_i =$ integer (only whole investments can be selected–this can be omitted when fractional ownership is possible)

A	B	C	D	E	F	G	H	I	J	K	L	M
Opportunity cost of capital		8%										
Capital budget		$ 800,000										
							Year					
Project	Market	0	1	2	3	4	5	6	7	8	9	10
Project 1	1	(100,000)	13,000	13,520	14,061	14,623	15,208	15,816	16,449	17,107	17,791	18,503
Project 2	1	(250,000)	32,500	33,800	35,152	36,558	38,020	39,541	41,123	42,768	44,478	46,258
Project 3	2	(80,000)	10,600	11,130	11,687	12,271	12,884	13,529	14,205	14,915	15,661	16,444
Project 4	2	(170,000)	22,000	23,100	24,255	25,468	26,741	28,078	29,482	30,956	32,504	34,129
Project 5	2	(180,000)	22,500	23,625	24,806	26,047	27,349	28,716	30,152	31,660	33,243	34,905
Project 6	1	(205,000)	28,600	29,744	30,934	32,171	33,458	34,796	36,188	37,636	39,141	40,707
Total cost of projects		(985,000)										

Figure 7.16 Alternative investment projects

	A	B	C	D	E	F	G
18	**Portfolio Selection**			**Project**			
19		**1**	**2**	**3**	**4**	**5**	**6**
20	Quantities available	2	1	3	1	1	1
21	Quantities Selected (initial = 0)	0	0	0	0	0	0
22	Investment costs	100,000	250,000	80,000	170,000	180,000	205,000
23	Project NPVs	2,167	5,418	6,746	10,038	4,130	19,768
24	Portfolio Cost	-					
25	**Portfolio NPV**	-					

Figure 7.17 Portfolio selection solution space

Excel's Solver is ideally suited to find the mathematical solution to this portfolio selection problem. After collecting the data in Figure 7.16, the next step is to create formulas that calculate the NPV of the portfolio (the objective function) and the constraint relationships. Figure 7.17 presents one approach to creating this 'solution space.'[18]

Row 20 of Figure 7.17 presents the availabilities of the six investment projects (i.e. the firm could select two of Project 1, only one of Project 2 and so on). Row 21 contains the portfolio selections, which initially are set to zero but for which we will direct Solver to make optimal choices. Rows 22 and 23 reflect costs and NPVs from Figure 7.17. Cell B24 computes the total cost of selected projects[19], which Solver will compare to the budget constraint in cell C7 of Figure 7.16. Cell B25 computes the NPV of the chosen portfolio, which Solver will seek to maximise. We direct Solver by filling in the dialogue 'wizard' as shown in Figure 7.18.

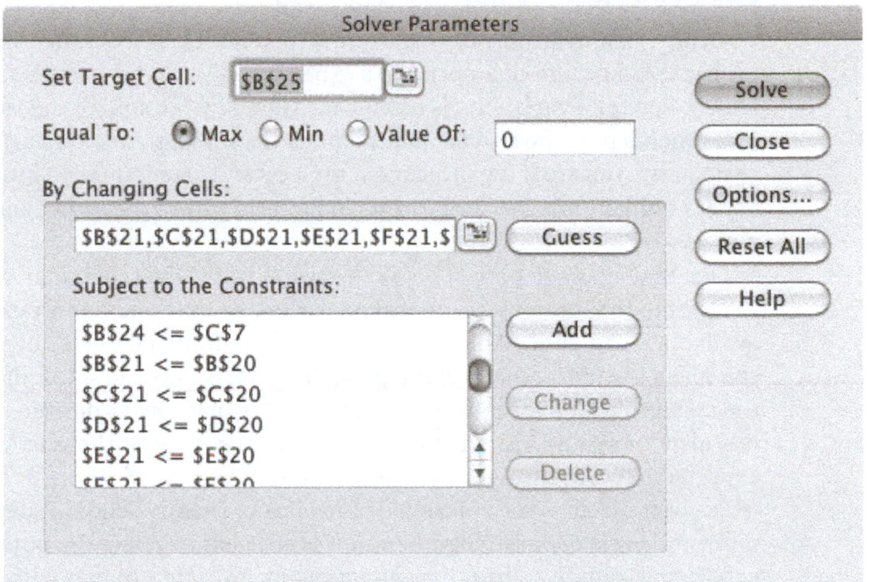

Figure 7.18 Solver parameters

[18] Nearly any systematic presentation of these formulas will work well with Solver.

[19] Cell C24 uses the SUMPRODUCT() function, which is a shortcut for multiplying two series of values. In this cell the function adds the multiples B21 × B22 + C21 × C22 + . . . + G21 × G22.

Note that more constraints would be visible by scrolling downward in the 'live' dialogue box. The first shown is the capital budget constraint. The others constrain the selection of the quantities of the projects. Not shown are the 'non-negativity' and integer-value constraints. The result of selecting 'Solve' is to revise Row 21 of Figure 7.17, as shown in the revision in Figure 7.19. The portfolio that maximises total NPV subject to the investment constraintsis: three of Project 3, one each of Projects 4, 5 and 6 and none of Projects 1 and 2.

	A	B	C	D	E	F	G
18	**Portfolio Selection**				**Project**		
19		**1**	**2**	**3**	**4**	**5**	**6**
20	Quantities available	1	1	3	1	1	1
21	Quantities Selected (initial = 0)	0	0	3	1	1	1
22	Investment costs	100,000	250,000	80,000	170,000	180,000	205,000
23	Project NPVs	2,167	5,418	6,746	10,038	4,130	19,768
24	Portfolio Cost	**795,000**					
25	**Portfolio NPV**	**54,173**					

Figure 7.19 Portfolio solution

7.10.2 Portfolio risk

Portfolio risk measures the exposure to potential loss from investment in a portfolio of projects. A measure of a portfolio's expected NPV can be a proxy for portfolio risk variability. Portfolio variability is usually measured by the sum of the variances of individual investments plus the **co-variances** among the investments. Co-variance may be positive or negative, or zero if the investment projects truly are independent. Complete independence is unlikely when a firm invests in projects within the same market or across related markets.

One may manage portfolio risk in several ways. First, one may structure investments as flexible real options, as described earlier, so that one has an exit or expansion plan available if bad or good news develops. Second, from a universe of available projects one can select the most **risk efficient** portfolio. That is, one can select the portfolio that offers the maximum NPV for a given level of risk, One may have a desired tolerance for variability (also known as 'risk attitude'), and one may choose the portfolio with the highest expected NPV for the desired level of variability or risk.[20] If one is not evaluating a 'universe' of projects, a set of feasible portfolios of (nearly) equal expected NPV might have differing levels of variability; hence, it is efficient to select the portfolio with the lowest expected variability. Firms may intentionally invest in projects with negative co-variance to reduce portfolio risk.

[20] This a common approach used by retirement investment advisors, for example.

Portfolio A	Projects					
	1	2	3	4	5	6
Quantities available	1	1	3	1	1	1
Quantities Selected (initial = 0)	0	1	2	0	0	0
Investment costs	100,000	250,000	80,000	170,000	180,000	205,000
Project NPVs	2,167	5,418	6,746	10,038	4,130	19,768
Portfolio Cost	**410,000**					
Portfolio NPV	**18,910**					
Project NPV standard deviation	-	8,002.24	9,181.63	-	-	-
		with #2	with #3	with #4	with #5	with #6
Project covariances of	#1	-	-	-	-	-
	#2		13,406,522	-	-	-
	#3			-	-	-
	#4				-	-
	#5					-
Portfolio NPV standard deviation	$ 13,234.47					

Portfolio B	Projects					
	1	2	3	4	5	6
Quantities available	0	1	2	0	0	0
Quantities Selected (initial = 0)	1	1	0	1	0	0
Investment costs	100,000	250,000	80,000	170,000	180,000	205,000
Project NPVs	2,167	5,418	6,746	10,038	4,130	19,768
Portfolio Cost	**520,000**					
Portfolio NPV	**17,623**					
Project NPV standard deviations	2,992.48	8,002.24	-	9,881.85	-	-
		with #2	with #3	with #4	with #5	with #6
Project covariances of	#1	(152,789)	-	(4,565,553)	-	-
	#2		-	(3,069,805)	-	-
	#3			-	-	-
	#4				-	-
	#5					-
Portfolio NPV standard deviation	$ 12,452.21					

Figure 7.20 Expected variability of two alternative portfolios

For example, consider the two (of many) feasible portfolios from the investment set available to Ahern's tenant shown in Figure 7.20. Portfolio A consists of one of Project 2 and two of Project 3. Portfolio B consists of one each of Projects 1, 2 and 4. The portfolios have roughly the same cost and expected NPVs.[21] However, because Portfolio B combines projects with negative co-variances, its portfolio standard deviation is much lower than that of Portfolio A, which combines positively co-varying projects. Thus, a manager who seeks to avoid risk might prefer Portfolio B to Portfolio A, despite its slightly lower expected NPV.

If the number of feasible portfolios is very great, the previous approach to managing portfolio risk will be very time consuming and might be less effective than the next method, which efficiently uses a Monte Carlo simulation method to measure portfolio risk. One may use this approach (illustrated below) to judge whether the expected variability (or risk) of the maximum NPV portfolio (selected earlier) is acceptable. Accurate forecasting of NPVs of investments and portfolios is difficult when future conditions are highly uncertain or ambiguous; that is, when historical experience might not be particularly relevant and, worse, might be misleading. One can combine Monte Carlo analysis

[21] More exact matching would be possible if fractional investments were allowed. Note that expected variability in this example was simulated using a Monte Carlo method similar to the next example. This may be the only feasible risk estimation approach for investment in unique, real assets.

from Chapter 4 with expectations about the expected, inherent variability of markets to simulate portfolio NPV variability. Furthermore, one can use the simulated distribution of portfolio NPVs to estimate the probabilities of various levels of portfolio outcome (e.g. the probability that the portfolio NPV will be less than zero). For this, we need the portfolio's estimated variance and standard deviation, which we can derive from the simulated distribution of portfolio NPVs.

Figure 7.19 presented the highest NPV portfolio of all the many possible portfolios. We can assess the risk of that portfolio choice by simulating its NPVs many times, and from that simulated distribution we can estimate and observe the probability that, for example, the portfolio NPV will be less than zero (or any other NPV hurdle).[22] The analysis steps follow the method of Chapter 4:

1. Randomise the key variables. In this case, the six projects' future cash flows were randomised based on the Ahern tenant's expectations of variability in the two market growth rates.
2. Create a Data Table for at least 1000 simulations of the selected projects' and the portfolio's NPV[23].
3. Compute the simulated portfolio NPV mean and its simulated standard deviation, which is computed as follows:

$$\text{Portfolio covariance} = \sum \text{Variances: VAR(Selected Project}_i) + \sum 2$$
$$\times \text{ Covariances:COVAR(Selected Project}_i \text{ with Selected Project}_j)$$
$$\text{Portfolio standard deviation} = \text{SQRT (Portfolio covariance)}$$

4. Using the simulated mean and standard deviation and the cumulative normal distribution (NORMDIST), estimate the probability that the portfolio NPV will be less than zero.
5. From the simulated NPV distribution compute the observed frequency that portfolio NPVs were less than zero. The summary results below indicate that this maximum NPV portfolio is not especially risky, because the theoretical and observed probabilities of a negative NPV portfolio are negligible in this hypothetical case.

Portfolio NPV simulation results	
Portfolio NPV standard deviation.....	$ 23553.93
Portfolio NPV average.....	$ 53475.68
Probability that the Portfolio NPV < 0.....	0.0115
Observed frequency that the Portfolio NPV < 0 (out of 1000)	10 times

[22] For economy of presentation, we do not present the Excel Data Table that calculates the maximum portfolio's simulated NPVs (1000 times).

[23] Warning: these simulations can dramatically slow an older generation PC and many Macs.

7.11 Evaluations and post-audits of investment analyses, decisions and outcomes

An essential management control of investment activities is a **post-audit,** which is analysis of the validity of assumptions, analyses and outcomes of an approved and implemented investment. Fortunately for practice, surveys reveal that formal post-audit controls are becoming more widely used.[24] Post-audits enable learning that can improve investment practice and success. Discrepancies or variances between expected NPV outcomes and realisations can be attributed to forecasting, implementation or operating errors that should be used to improve future decisions. Investment variances also can indicate corrective actions, particularly if the investment has been structured as a real option, with flexible post-acceptance alternatives. Importantly, the existence of a formal post-audit procedure can prevent poor quality investment analysis because analysts know that their activities will be independently reviewed. However, firms must balance sanctions for worse than expected performance by the need to encourage managers to take acceptable investment risks – all the more reason to structure investments as real options. Every investment should have exit or revision plans.

7.11.1 Pressures to avoid or bias investment post-audits

If post-audits are not conducted or not independently, individuals who analysed and approved investments can be pressured to hide or misstate post-audit information because of:

- **Escalation of commitment** Individuals have been observed in behavioural laboratory tasks and in real-life to be unwilling or unable to admit to incorrect investment decisions. Instead of correcting or terminating these faulty projects, individuals may unthinkingly increase their support, compounding the waste of resources.
- **Reputation effects** Individuals may avoid or hide bad news from a post-audit out of fear for loss of their reputation, their decision rights, or their compensation. Eventually bad news will come out, and the personal penalties may be higher than if the news were acted on earlier. The cost to the organisation is likely to be higher, and the self-interested character of the person is revealed.
- **Post-audit practices** It seems obvious that if one uses NPV analysis or RA to select investments that one also should use the same DCF approach to conduct post-audits. That is, the post-audit analysis, should look similar to the original DCF analysis, complete with periodic cash flows and the proper cost of capital. Of course, the post-audit should replace original expectations by known outcomes or revised expectations. Surprisingly, while a majority of firms report using post-audits, many of them simplify the evaluations by using accounting rates of return to assess post-audit performance–not revised DCF analyses. As indicated earlier in the discussion of the IRR method, focus on rates of return can lead to incorrect decisions and, by analogy, can lead to misleading post-audits. Because firms regularly collect and report accounting performance measures, it certainly is simpler and less time consuming to evaluate both long existing and newer investments on an accounting

[24] Azzone and Maccarrone 2001; Farragher, et al. 1999.

basis than to reconstruct a revised DCF analysis, but this appears to add to the difficulties of performing effective post-audits. There appears to be an endogeneity in practice between using accounting rates of return, which are percentages, for periodic evaluations and post-audits and IRR for investment selection. Yes, management and analysis time is short and should be used to look ahead. However, not looking as rigorously back (at least occasionally) probably inhibits investment learning and fails to exert preventive controls on investment activities.

7.12 Investment analysis summary

Investments commit capital resources for the long term, when the opportunity cost of capital compounds. Thus, discounted cash flow (DCF) analyses are important tools for screening investments and for investment post-audits. NPV analysis can misstate values when investments have, or can have, inherent features of flexibility such as termination, expansion and deferral. In such cases, real option analysis (RA) can be superior to traditional NPV analysis. Applying DCF analysis faces difficulties including modelling risk, estimating project lifetime, choosing the proper cost of capital and estimating future cash flows for individual investments and for portfolios of investments

EXERCISES

Exercise 7.1 Forecasted future cash flows.

Novelty Ltd manufactures and sells small plastic products to global wholesalers from its base in South Asia. Novelty, Ltd is evaluating a new product, with a three-year life, that will require investment in new, dedicated equipment and rental of additional space. Novelty, Ltd normally allocates sales and administrative costs as overhead for all products based on a percentage of sales revenue. Product sales of this type normally peak in the second year and drop dramatically thereafter. The following table summarises data values for the evaluation of the new product.

Novelty, Ltd data values			
Dedicated equipment	$ 650,000		
Equipment life	3	years	
Equipment salvage value	50,000	per year	
Tax rate	38%		
Discount rate	8%		
Allocated sales and administrative costs	20%	of revenue	
Existing space needed	1,000	sq meters	
Existing space cost	$ 30.00	per sq meter	
New space needed	1,200	sq meters	
New rental cost	$ 40.00	per sq meter	
Variable costs	$ 2.00	per unit	
Forecasts for the product life in year:	**1**	**2**	**3**
Unit sales (base forecast)	300,000	600,000	200,000
Sales price per unit	$ 3.00	$ 2.75	$ 2.50

Required:

Estimate after tax cash flows for the life of the new product.

Exercise 7.2 NPV and IRR Analyses.

Use the data and after tax cash flows from Exercise 7.1.

Required:

1. Compute the net present value and internal rate of return for this investment.
2. Discuss why the NPV method generally is superior to the IRR method.

Exercise 7.3 Sensitivity Analysis.

Use the data and after-tax cash flows from Exercise 7.1 and the results of 7.2.

Required:

1. Compute the annual variation in the unit sales forecast that would make this a break-even NPV product. Hint: Use Excel's Solver.
2. If the forecast of unit sales might vary plus or minus 20%, is this investment analysis sensitive to the sales forecast? Is this a risky project? Explain.
3. What unit sales variation from the base forecast (C28) will result in a favourable NPV and a payback period of 2.0 years? Hint: Use Excel's Solver.

Exercise 7.4 Forecasted future cash flows.

AllSports Ltd manufactures and sells athletic tournament products to global wholesalers from its base in south Asia. AllSports Ltd is evaluating a new product, with a three-year life, that will require investment in new, dedicated equipment and rental of additional space. AllSports Ltd will borrow the funds to purchase the dedicated equipment. Product sales of this type normally peak in the second year (the tournament year) and drop dramatically thereafter. The following table summarises data values for the evaluation of the new product, a souvenir for the Pan American Games.

AllSports Ltd data values			
Purchase of dedicated equipment	$ 800 000	purchase price	
Equipment life	3	years	
Equipment salvage value	50 000	per year	
Financing			
Working capital required for project	$ 100 000	committed at the beginning of the project and returned at the end.	
Down payment on equipment	25%	of equip. price	
Equipment loan rate	6%	per year	
Discount (opportunity) rate	8%	per year	
Tax rate	40%	on operating income	
New space needed	1 200	sq meters	
New rental cost	$ 35.00	per sq meter	
Variable costs	$ 1.80	per unit	
Forecasts for the product life in year:	**1**	**2**	**3**
Unit sales forecast	200 000	350 000	140 000
Sales price per unit	$ 3.50	$ 3.75	$ 3.00

Required:

1. Prepare a loan payment schedule for the equipment purchase using Excel's PMT() function.
2. Estimate after tax financing and operating cash flows for the life of the new product.

Exercise 7.5 NPV and IRR Analyses.

Use the data and forecasted net cash flows from Exercise 7.1.

Required:

1. Compute the net present value and internal rate of return for the new product.
2. Discuss why the NPV method generally is superior to the IRR method.

Exercise 7.6 Payback criterion.

Use the data and forecasted net cash flows from Exercise 7.1.

Required:

1. Compute the payback period of the new product.
2. Discuss why the payback criterion is inferior to DCF methods of analysis.

Exercise 7.7 Decision Trees.

You are considering an $800 investment that will pay either $50 or $150 per annum for 50 years. You may purchase the investment now, or for a fee you may defer investing in the project for one year, at which time the cash flow level, either $50 or $150 will be known with certainty. Should you invest now or wait for a year? (Adapted from Pindyck, JEL 1991).

Required:

1. Draw a decision tree that describes the NPV approach to this investment decision.
2. Draw a decision tree that describes the RA approach to this investment decision.
3. Explain the differences in these decision trees.

Exercise 7.8 NPV analysis.

Consider the information in Exercise 7.7. Additionally assume that the cost of capital is 10%. Ignore taxes.

Required:

Use the NPV approach to decide whether it is better to invest now or wait a year.

Exercise 7.9 RA.

Consider the information in Exercise 7.7. Additionally assume that the cost of capital is 10%. Ignore taxes.

Required:

1. Use RA to decide whether to invest now or wait a year to decide whether to invest.
2. How much would you be willing to pay for the option to defer the investment?

Exercise 7.10 Decision tree exercises.

Draw and label decision trees that describe the following decision situations. State feasible goals and objectives for each decision. List relevant measurable quantitative and identifiable qualitative outcomes for each alternative.

Required:

1. A student is deciding whether to live in a dormitory on campus, an apartment off campus, or at home with parents.
2. A student is deciding whether to spend Spring break (A) either (i) catching up on lost sleep and studying for three days or (ii) working for pay for three days, followed by (i) three days of mountain biking in Moab, or (ii) three days of skiing at Steamboat Springs, or (iii) three days of working for Habitat for Humanity, or (B) spending six days in Cancun, or (C) working six days for pay.

3. A student organisation is deciding how to spend its annual budget. Historically the organisation has sponsored eight monthly events (four per semester) featuring external speakers, professionalism seminars, student presentations, and community service. Student and faculty participation has been high in the autumn semester when students are interviewing for jobs and internships, but participation has been much lower in the spring. The group could sponsor more or fewer events and a different mix of events.
4. A student and faculty group is deciding how to spend a recent gift from ConocoPhillips. Future gifts depend on how the money is spent and the effectiveness of the supported activities. The group identified alternative uses that include scholarships, faculty research support, hiring teaching assistants to support large classes, student case competitions, and remodelling classrooms.
5. A ski resort is deciding whether to continue its local skier programme which this year offered season passes to individuals for $300 and families for $500. Daily passes bought at the resort cost adults $70 and children $40. The discounted season pass programme increased this season's skier days by 20% over the previous season when season passes cost $700 for individuals and $1000 for families. Food, ski lesson and rental revenues and some operating costs increase with the number of skier days. Some destination skiers, who pay full price for lift tickets, have objected to the crowding caused by increased numbers of local skiers

Exercise 7.11 **Sensitivity analysis**

Consider the data in Exercise 7.4 and the solution to Exercise 7.5. Sales forecasts could vary each year by plus or minus 20%. Sales prices could vary by plus or minus 10%, as could variable costs per unit.

Required:

Compute the sensitivity of the project's net present value to each of these three factors at their high and low values.

Exercise 7.12 **Scenario analysis**

Consider the data in Exercise 7.4 and the solution to Exercise 7.5. The data in Exercise 7.4 represent the most likely scenario. A best case scenario would be 15% increases in forecasted annual sales and 5% increases in forecasted sales price, with variable cost per unit constant. A worst case scenario would be 20% decreases in forecasted annual sales, 10% decreases in forecasted sales price and, and 15% increases in variable cost per unit. The probabilities of each scenario are 25% worst case, 20% best case, 55% most likely case.

Required:

1. Prepare NPV analyses for the three scenarios.
2. Compute the expected value of the project NPV.

Exercise 7.13 **Monte Carlo analysis**

Consider the data in Exercise 7.1 and the solution to Exercise 7.2. Sales are expected to vary randomly and uniformly between plus and minus 20% of the forecasted values.

Required:

1. Prepare a Monte Carlo analysis of the project's NPV with at least 1000 simulated values.
2. What is the estimated probability that the project will have a positive NPV?

Exercise 7.14 Monte Carlo analysis

Consider the data in Exercise 7.4 and the solution to Exercise 7.5. Sales are expected to vary randomly and uniformly between plus and minus 25% of the forecasted values.

Required:

1. Prepare a Monte Carlo analysis of the project's NPV with at least 1000 simulated values.
2. What is the estimated probability that the project will have a positive NPV?

Exercise 7.15 Post-audits

Find a recent article in an academic journal that describes the practice of investment post-audits in private industry. Summarise the findings of this article.

Exercise 7.16 Post-audits

Find a recent article in an academic journal that describes the practice of investment post-audits in government agencies. Summarise the findings of this article.

Exercise 7.17 Portfolio selection and capital rationing

Fronzak Ltd serves two related markets and is budgeting its capital expenditures for next year. Each of Fronzak's three department heads contributed two investment projects anonymously to the capital budgeting committee (CBC) for final selection decisions. The CBC has gathered information about the annual investment conditions and constraints. The firm's opportunity cost of capital is 8% per annum, and its annual capital budget is €400000. Details about the six proposed investment projects are shown below.

Data Input	
Opportunity cost of capital per annum	8%
Capital budget Euros	€ 400 000

			Cash Flows In Year								
Project	**Market**	**Available**	**0**	**1**	**2**	**3**	**4**	**5**	**6**	**7**	**8**
Project 1	A	2	(72 000)	11 000	11 770	12 594	13 475	14 419	15 428	16 508	17 664
Project 2	A	1	(157 000)	22 500	24 075	25 760	27 563	29 493	31 557	33 766	36 130
Project 3	A	3	(59 000)	8 600	9 202	9 846	10 535	11 273	12 062	12 906	13 810
Project 4	B	1	(70 000)	12 000	12 600	13 230	13 892	14 586	15 315	16 081	16 885
Project 5	B	2	(78 000)	11 750	12 338	12 954	13 602	14 282	14 996	15 746	16 533
Project 6	B	1	(110 000)	18 600	19 530	20 507	21 532	22 608	23 739	24 926	26 172

Required:

1. Compute the net present values of the six investment projects.
2. Use Excel's Solver to select the optimal portfolio of available projects. Only whole projects may be purchased.
3. Fronzak's CBC required anonymous contribution of capital projects because the committee wanted to review the projects objectively. What might be gained, what might be lost by this policy? What would you recommend?

CASES

Case 7.1 Forecast cash flows and NPV: Wind energy

The pressures of inevitably rising oil prices, concerns about climate change and improvements in alternative energy technologies indicate a growing demand for alternative energy sources, such as wind power. The coastal and north-central parts of North America feature reliable wind patterns (**http://www.windpoweringamerica.gov/wind_maps.asp**). Although many wind farms already have sprouted in these regions, the vast spaces and reliable wind can support many more installations. However, the blizzard of land use and tax regulations and the negotiating skills of energy companies, providers of capital and owners of land deter all but the most capable and patient deal makers.

Lynn Browne, a lawyer acquaintance of yours, has put together successful easement, access, and water use deals with ranchers and local government officials, and has built a reputation as an honest broker. Ms. Browne has recognised the need for professionals who can structure deals between capital providers, energy distribution companies and land owners to site wind farms. She is structuring a deal for a large Wyoming USA wind farm. If successful, the deal will compensate her with 'success royalties' that are paid as 1% of gross energy sales revenue in every year that WindSource Capital, the sponsoring capital provider, earns at least a 10% return (net income after tax) on average net assets (RONA). Ms. Browne may accept annual royalty payments for 20 years, or she may choose a lump sum pay off based on a mutually agreed upon forecast over the expected 20-year life of the installed assets. She has hired you to estimate annual sales and expenses, including her 'success royalties,' and a lump sum price she could use in her negotiations with WindSource Capital.

Required:

1. Build a 20-year model of sales, expenses and return on assets for the planned wind farm based on the assumptions of the case shown below that you have gathered from various sources.
2. Compute a lump sum value of the stream of 'success royalties.'
3. Prepare a short memorandum that explains the sources of uncertainty in computing Lynn Browne's success royalties from this deal.

Project parameters				
Wind plant size, Megawatts (MW)	300.00	megawatts		
Available hours of operation, per year	8,760	total annual hours (ignore leap years)		
Expected wind energy production time	32.00%	a factor based on the wind farm's location		
Sales price per MW-hour	$ 60.00	market price for one megawatt, supplied for one hour		
Energy price growth, per year	5.00%			
Success royalty rate, up to	1.00%	of gross sales revenue		
WindSource's required after-tax return on assets	10.00%	of RONA		
Lynn Browne's discount rate	8.00%			
WindSource's effective income tax rate	35%			
Renewable energy tax credit	$ 21.00	per MWh produced		
Life of renewable energy tax credit	10	years		
Operating expenses	**Base**	**Annual growth**		
Operations & maintenance per MW-hour	$ 4.00	2.50%	paid to WindSource employees	
Electricity cost per MW-hour	0.25	4.00%	paid to electrical distribution utility company	
Administration per MW-hour	0.25	4.00%	paid to WindSource employees	
Transmission per MW-hour	0.25	4.00%	paid to electrical distribution utility company	
Contingency per MW-hour	0.25	4.00%	paid to a contingency reserve	
Land royalties per MW-hour	1.00	0.00%	paid to ranchers, land owners	
Insurance per year, $ millions	1.40	3.00%	paid to WindSource's insurance company	
Project management per year, $ millions	1.60	0.00%	paid to WindSource employees	
Property tax per year, $ millions	1.00	0.00%	paid to county government	
Plant investment cost breakout	**Outlay**	**Life**		
20-year equipment (SL depr)	$ 400.00	20		SL depr expense, zero salvage value
10-year equipment (SL depr)	165.00	10		SL depr expense, zero salvage value
5-year equipment (2 x SL depr)	35.00	5		SL depr expense, zero salvage value
Total investment costs	$ 600.00	assume financed solely with equity capital		

Case 7.2 Real option analysis: Invest now or wait and see?

Private investors are considering whether to open a mid priced restaurant within a new condominium complex that is also located near a shopping district. The 'Peloton Café' investors expect that their café will capture 30% of this locale's dining market. The investors are concerned that a national chain restaurant might open nearby and reduce Peleton's share by half. The investors believe there is a 50:50 chance that the chain restaurant may decide to locate nearby. They do not believe the existence of the Peloton Café will affect the chain's decision. They may wish to wait one year before deciding to determine whether the chain restaurant decides to locate nearby. Whenever the decision is made, the investors expect to be able to terminate their investment after the first year of operation, probably at a loss. The following table contains data that are relevant to this investment decision.

Required:

1. Evaluate the Peloton Café investment as a real option. Should the investors act now or wait? Up to what amount would the investors be willing to pay for an option on this restaurant space. Explain.
2. Explain and describe the sources and impacts of risk in this decision.

Café investment data values	
First year's market	$ 4,000,000
Annual market growth	6%
Market share without Chain	30%
Market share with Chain	15%
Gross margin ratio	40%
Discount rate	8%
Investment cost	$ 800,000
Investment life, years	4
Salvage value at end of life	0
Tax rate	35%
Depreciation (straight line)	200,000
Sales and administrative costs	160,000
Probability of Chain entry	50%
Sale on early termination	400,000
Reinvestment cost (to extend life 1 year)	$ (300,000)

Case 7.3 NPV and RA analyses: new product development

New product development processes typically involve a multi-year, sequential set of milestones and 'go' or 'no go' decisions. The following table contains data relevant to a specific new product project. Consider the prospects for a new product that must proceed through the following representative milestones and decisions:

- Step 1. Invest in R&D (yes or no).
- Step 2. If yes, evaluate success of R&D, typically after two years. If no, earn the cost of capital on funds not invested.
- Step 3. If R&D is unsuccessful, terminate the project. If the R&D is successful, commercialise the product or conduct market research (a test market). Commercialisation or test marketing typically takes one year of activity.
- Step 4. If commercialisation is the outcome of the previous decision, observe annual net cash flows from sales. If market research is the decision, evaluate the results of the

test market (good news - a high probability of high sales, or bad news - a high probability of low sales)

- Step 5. Observe the annual cash flows after the market research.

Required:

1. Prepare decision trees for the new product development process.
2. Evaluate this new product prospect as a net present value project.
3. Evaluate this new product prospect as a real option.
4. What is the value of the option of waiting for market research before commercialisation?

New product development data (dollar amounts in $million)		
R&D investment cost now	$ 180.00	million
R&D phase	2	years
Probability of R&D success	70%	
Product life	8.00	years
Discount rate	14%	
Cost of commercialisation (year 3 or 4)	$ 700.00	million
Commercialise year 3:		
CF/yr 4-11=	$ 620.00	40%
CF/yr 4-11=	$(100.00)	60%
Additional market research cost, year 3	$ 50.00	million
Market research & Commercialise year 4		
Good news	50%	
CF/yr 5-12 =	$ 620.00	60%
CF/yr 5-12 =	$(100.00)	40%
Bad news	50%	
CF/yr 5-12 =	$ 620.00	40%
CF/yr 5-12 =	$(100.00)	60%

Case 7.4 Net cash flows and Islamic investment alternative to NPV analysis:

Safwan plans to open a store that sells Middle East food, housewares, and decorative arts in a Western city. He feels that returning travellers and former Mideastern residents who have relocated to this city will provide a growing customer base. Currently the only local competition for these goods is on the Internet, and Safwan believes that the ambience of the store, tentatively named *The Olive Traders,* will be an important aspect of the shopping experience.

He will finance the enterprise with a) his and family contributions and b) external financing known as Musharaka (see note) from the Islamic business division of One World Bank. As in the case of conventional business loans, Safwan must make a persuasive business case to the bank. The difference, of course, is that traditional DCF methods, which involve interest that is disallowed by Islamic law, should not be used to structure the bank financing.

Consider *The Olive Traders* to be a partnership between Safwan (and family) and One World Bank, wherein Safwan pays to the bank a share of profits in proportion to its capital contribution that will retire the bank's share of the partnership over a period of 10 years. He also will make an annual payment to compensate the bank for sharing the store's risks. Assume that any store losses also are shared in proportion to capital contributions and are not accumulated, carried forward or carried back. The following table contains other relevant information for *The Olive Traders.*

NOTE: Musharaka - the Islamic mortgage alternative.

Musharaka is an Islamic alternative to a conventional mortgage and has been adopted by several banks and building societies. Musharaka means profit and loss sharing. It is a partnership where the profits are shared in pre-arranged proportions and any losses are shared in proportion to each partners' capital or investment. In Musharakah, all the partners to the commercial undertaking contribute funds and have the right, but without the obligation, to exercise executive powers in that undertaking. It is a similar concept to a conventional partnership and the holding of voting stock in a limited company. Musharakah is regarded as the purest form of Islamic financing.

Example of housing purchase: Under this Islamic financial concept, the bank buys the house and legally becomes its owner. Then throughout the pre-agreed period, say 25 years, a monthly payment is made. Each monthly payment includes a charge for rent and a charge that buys a small proportion of the house itself. It is a form of variable shared equity plan with the proportion of the house being owned by the purchaser, steadily increasing as payments are made. Once the final payment has been made, the house is owned outright. Importantly, in case of default, the Islamic bank shares proportionately in any losses; the purchaser is not solely responsible. (Adapted from **http://www.whatprice.co.uk/advice/islamic-mortgages.htm**l retrieved 21June 2010.)

It is possible that acceptable Musharaka practices differ across the Islamic world. Also note that Islamic financing has been criticised by some observers as being disguised conventional financing. However, a key element of Islamic financing, such as Musharaka, is partnership risk sharing, including the sharing of losses. In concept, one could compare a Musharaka with a conventional NPV equivalent.

Required:

1. Prepare a profit sharing plan that incorporates annual retirement of the bank's share of the partnership over no more than a 10-year period.
2. Compute a schedule of planned net cash flows to Safwan and family.
3. How would you advise Safwan for his upcoming negotiations with the bank?

Case data values							
Initial store investment							
Building	€ 350,000	40	year life, zero salvage				
Equipment	30,000	10	year life, zero salvage				
Fixtures and décor	120,000	10	year life, zero salvage				
Inventory	20%	of first-year's sales					
Marketing cost	10%	of next-year's sales					
Cash reserve	10%	of next-year's cash operating expenses					
Safwan and family's capital contribution	€ 100,000						
Risk fee paid to One World Bank	€ 18,000	per year					
Safwan's federal and local income tax rate	30%	of net operating income					
Safwan's current annual living expenses	€ 40,000						
Expected change in cost of living	3%	per year					
First-year sales forecasts and annual growth		**Year 1**	**Year 2**	**Year 3**	**Year 4**	**Year 5**	**Years 6-10**
Food cost of sales (wholesale, freight-in cost)		€ 60,000	100%	15%	10%	8%	5%
Sales price markup over cost		50%	50%	50%	50%	50%	50%
Housewares cost of sales (ditto)		€ 10,000	80%	10%	15%	10%	5%
Sales price markup over cost		100%	100%	100%	100%	100%	100%
Decorative Art, cost of sales (ditto)		€ 15,000	60%	8%	16%	8%	5%
Sales price markup over cost		100%	100%	100%	100%	100%	

Case 7.5 **Forecast cash flows: Microcredit analysis**

Shanoun is a successful entrepreneur who has reached the point in his life where his family's modest material needs are secure. He now wishes to use his 'excess' wealth to nurture would be entrepreneurs in parts of the world that are starved for capital, particularly where individuals, who have no substantial assets or loan collateral, also have no opportunities. He further wishes to have an impact in the poorest parts of the Islamic world, where the need is acute. He has chosen Indonesia, where most citizens adhere to Islam, as his locus of operations. Islamic law places special requirements on financial activities (see Note), and Shanoun has determined to help create a small, mutually owned credit union to provide a reliable source of capital to entrepreneurs.[25] First, he must help build a village wealth base to sustain the credit union. To do so, he will personally support the education, equipment and marketing costs of the business ventures for a period of three years, with the expectation that all participants will save an agreed proportion of their profits with a local Islamic bank. The proposed business activities include one convenience store per village and home based manufacturing of tourist trade items such as textiles, folk art and baskets, which Shanoun commits to market for three years. Second, at the end of three years and assuming a sufficient accumulation of capital, participants will pool their savings and the village will form a mutually owned, credit union that will take over the practice of making micro-credit loans to credit union members in the village, and perhaps surrounding areas. Shanoun commits to make capital contributions and to cover losses from credit union operations for its first four years. The following table contains data relevant to this venture.

NOTE: Islamic law (Sharia) forbids the practice of gaining from financial activities unless the financial capital is at risk; this includes the prohibition of charging interest on borrowed money where the borrower assumes all responsibility for repayment. An exception seems possible when the risks of gains and losses from the use of financial capital are shared by both the provider and user of the capital. This can be accomplished by a profit/loss sharing plan that shares the interest charged to the user among the providers. One suggested solution to providing small amounts (micro-credit) is by creation of credit unions, which by nature are owned by the users and are structured to share profits and losses among the owners/users. Thus, these entities might provide micro-credit loans while ahering to Islamic law.

Adapted from 'An Inside look at Microfinance and Islamic Banking - Limitation and Possibilities,' Working Paper, May 2000, Sousan Urroz-Korori, Director, Center for World Banking and Finance, The Economics Institute, Boulder, Colorado USA

Case data values per village	*Currency in thousands of Indonesian Rupiyahs (IDR)*		
Business education cost per person, per annum	8,900	Credit union facilities and equipment, per annum	2,800
Business managers (1 year education beyond HS)	3	Credit union employees (2 years education beyond HS)	1
Retail store growth, per annum	5%	Credit union employee salary, per annum	3,800
Retail store markup over cost of sales	100%	Average microcredit loan amount	465
First year cost of sales	22,400	Capital reserve, percentage of capital	20%
Store facilities and equipment rent	11,200	Capital contribution by Shanoun, 4 years	9,300
Manufactured goods growth, per annum	10%	Loan payback period, years	4
Manufactured goods markup over materials cost	200%	Annual interest rate charged, per annum	30%
First year materials cost of manufactured goods	9,300	Loan and interest default rate, per annum	5%
Manufactured goods first year equipment	23,250	Shanoun's opportunity rate, per annum	8%
Equipment replacement, per annum	20%		
Marketing costs, next year's sales, beginning in year 0	15%		
Percentage of business profits saved	10%		

[25]This abstracts away from the legalities and regulations surrounding the creation of such an entity, which may be significant

Required:

1. Build a planning model that describes the features of this case (ignore reinvestment of distributed profits, taxes and inflation).
2. What amount of capital should Shanoun reserve now for the support of this venture.
3. How would you advise Shanoun about the sustainability of this project?

Case 7.6 NPV and scenario analysis: deep-water natural gas development

This case requires preparation of a DCF analysis, given a successful development natural gas well (deepwater, offshore). Data are drawn from a U.S. Department of Energy source and additional assumptions are listed below. Three scenarios include Pessimistic, Most Likely and Optimistic, but not all data values differ across scenarios. Adapted from:**www.eia.doe.gov/pub/oil_gas/natural_gas/analysis_publications/natural_gas_1998_issues_trends/pdf/Appc.pdf**

Project well case input	Pessimistic	Most Likely	Optimistic	Notes
Development well		1		well, assumed to be successful
Production wells		10		wells, drill half each year for two years after development
Development period		2		years (accommodate this in hard coding, because of complexity)
Success rate		80%		of production wells drilled given successful development well
Royalty rate	2%	2%	2%	of revenues
Initial well flow rate	4,000.00	5,000.00	6,000.00	thousand cu ft per well per year
Flow rate - initial period		2		years (accommodate this in hard coding, because of complexity)
Flow rate - long term decline	-6.00%	-5.00%	-4.00%	per annum
Water saturation point	78.75%	75.00%	70.00%	flow relative to initial rate
Output sales price		$ 6.00		$ per thousand cu ft
Operating costs	$ 1.50	$ 1.50	$ 1.50	$ per thousand cu ft
Initial capital investment	$ 380.00	$ 380.00	$ 380.00	$ million per project, depreciate straight line over life of project
Drilling costs	$ 12.00	$ 12.00	$ 12.00	$ million per well, depreciate straight line over life of wells
Termination cost	$ 1.80	$ 1.80	$ 1.80	$ million per well, cash flow and expense 1 year after life of wells
Income tax rate	35%	35%	35%	of operating income
Discount rate		15%		per annum
Probability	20%	60%	20%	

Additional assumptions:

- *Development period:* assume that production wells are drilled evenly over a two year period, after the development well.
- *Royalty rate:* the royalty rate is somewhat controllable by lobbying efforts. Currently US offshore drilling is subject to no federal or state royalties. This is controversial and may change.
- *Water saturation point:* assume that further natural gas is not recoverable after water saturation point reached.
- *Termination cost:* assume that termination activities occur after last year of production
- *Income tax rate:* assume that the project is part of continuing business.

Required:

1. Model the natural gas output and net cash flows.
2. Compute the NPVs for each scenario

Case 7.7 Forecast costs, present value analysis, Monte-Carlo analysis: Carbon emission tax

Consumption of fossil fuels creates emissions of carbon dioxide, which is implicated in pollution and global warming. Some advocate a tax on CO_2 emissions equal to the 'social cost of carbon' (SSC) to create incentives to reduce emissions. In theory, a tax equal to the true SSC would result in the economically optimal amount of CO_2 emissions. However, there is great controversy regarding the measurement of the SSC, with estimates ranging from $1 per ton of carbon (tC) to $1500/tC. Researchers report a mean value of $43/tC across peer reviewed academic studies. Note: One tC is roughly equivalent to 4 tCO_2.

Another dimension of controversy centres on responsibility, equity and ability to pay any carbon taxes that might be levied. For example, emitters in countries that are less developed and emerging economically may be hard pressed to pay significant carbon taxes, which also could stifle normal economic development. Kazakhstan is a former Soviet republic that is seeking to improve its economic position through the production and consumption of fossil fuels.

'Kazakhstan has the second largest oil reserves among the former Soviet republics, after Russia, as well as the second largest oil production. The country also has large reserves of natural gas and steadily increasing production. Full development of its major oilfields could make Kazakhstan one of the world's top five oil producers in the next decade. . . . .Steadily rising natural gas production is turning Kazakhstan from a net importer to a net exporter in the near term. Natural gas development has lagged behind oil due to the lack of domestic pipeline infrastructure linking the western producing region with the eastern industrial region. Kazakhstan exports most of its produced fossil fuel, but the lack of access to a seaport makes the country dependent on pipelines to transport its hydrocarbons to world markets. Neighbours China and Russia are key economic partners, providing sources of export demand and government project financing. Kazakhstan's continued growth in oil and natural gas production depends on further development of its resources together with the construction of additional export routes. '(U.S. Department of Energy)

Consider the available data on Kazakhstan's production and internal consumption of fossil fuels and CO_2 emissions from internal consumption (see the table below - at this writing these are the most complete data available). If Kazakhstan were to levy a carbon tax to encourage reductions of CO_2 emissions, how would the country proceed?

Required:

1. Predicting CO_2 emissions is quite difficult, particularly for the future (i.e. Niels Bohr). However, be bold and assume that one can extend past trends gleaned from historical data. Use the tabulated data in statistical analyses (of your design) to predict Kazakhstan's CO_2 emissions for the next 10 years, 2007 - 2016. Build the model using the tabulated data from 1992 - 2005 (plus additional data if you can find it), and test the accuracy of your model with the 2006 and 2007 data.
2. Given the reported mean estimate of $43/tC for the SSC, compute the present value of the social costs of Kazakhstan's predicted decade of emissions (you will have to choose the proper discount rate or rates). Interpret this amount.
3. Use Monte Carlo analysis to simulate the present value of the SSC of the decade of forecasted emissions. You will have to assume probability distributions for the input variables you wish to randomise. Create a histogram of simulated present values with at least 10 'bins.' Interpret this distribution of present values.
4. Kazakhstan uses most of its coal consumption to generate electricity, which also creates 60% of the country's CO_2 emissions. The Kazakhstan central government has been offered an opportunity to co-develop Russian CO_2 sequestration technology that reportedly will reduce an electrical power plant's CO_2 emissions by 75%. The technology's currently estimated cost to remove one million tons of carbon is $150/tC, but the target cost is $50/tC or less. The co-development's initial cost of $20 million and $5 million operating cost would be financed by both countries by fossil fuel exports. If Kazakhstan joins the venture as an equal partner, the country could deploy the technology domestically and share royalties equally on the Russian technology adopted by

other countries. Kazakhstan can opt to wait one year for the results of a Russian pilot test of the technology that would be financed jointly (50:50) or solely by Russia. The pilot project will be judged to be successful, if the expected average cost per ton of carbon is estimated to be no more than \$50/tC at Kazakhstan's 2006 levels of CO_2 emissions, assuming an exponential (e.g. learning curve) rate of cost reduction. If Kazakhstan does not participate in the pilot project, it may purchase the Russian technology but will not share royalties on other countries' adoptions. Prepare a decision tree of this investment opportunity.

5. What would be the average cost per tC after sequestering 2 million tC that would indicate that the pilot project in part d is successful? What royalty rate per tC would make this an attractive initial investment opportunity for Kazakhstan?

	Production			Consumption			Total CO_2
	Oil	Coal	Natural Gas	Oil	Coal	Natural Gas	Emissions
1992	442.60	139.49	286.05	404.14	100.87	709.83	265.09
1993	406.73	123.32	236.61	341.39	91.51	522.66	227.54
1994	416.47	115.329	158.92	297.62	87.64	529.72	168.18
1995	414.79	93.139	169.17	269.19	72.36	383.43	140.11
1996	458.77	85.956	149.74	245.24	64.72	509.95	142.34
1997	522.03	80.08	215.42	217.52	54.23	494.41	120.10
1998	526.90	78.07	194.23	196.64	54.36	473.22	116.28
1999	604.92	65.91	162.45	171.23	50.99	480.28	133.39
2000	725.63	81.65	314.30	194.75	55.40	490.88	143.45
2001	835.97	87.17	355.98	210.45	56.96	505.00	147.69
2002	967.51	81.27	462.63	217.16	58.58	526.19	153.77
2003	1,061.97	93.59	490.17	206.98	66.62	557.27	165.91
2004	1,245.87	95.76	723.60	221.25	68.99	811.89	185.37
2005	1,337.17	95.44	934.79	228.98	70.40	1,075.34	203.30
2006	1,387.22	106.08	905.83	234.20	75.88	1,096.53	213.50
2007	1,444.23	95.24	984.58	240.00	74.31	1,079.90	?
	Thousand BBL/day	Million short tons/yr	Billion cu-ft/yr	Thousand BBL/day	Million short tons/yr	Billion cu-ft/yr	Million metric tons/yr

Sources: (retrieved 18 June 2010)
http://www.eia.doe.gov/country/country_energy_data.cfm?fips=KZ
http://www.eia.doe.gov/cabs/Kazakhstan/Background.html
http://en.wikipedia.org/wiki/Carbon_tax

References

Azzone, Giovanni and Paolo Maccarrone. (2001).The design of the investment post-audit process in large organisations: Evidence from a survey. *European Journal of Innovation Management.* Vol. 4, Iss. 2; pg. 73–85.

Bengtsson, Jens. (2001). "Manufacturing flexibility and real options: A review," *International Journal of Production Economics,* v 74: 213-224.

Bowman, Edward H. and Gary T. Moskowitz. (2001). Real Options Analysis and Strategic Decision Making *Organization Science,* Vol. 12, No. 6, pp. 772–777.

Copeland, Weston, and Shastri, (2005), *Financial Theory and Corporate Policy.*

Edward H. Bowman Gary T. Moskowitz. (2001). Real Options Analysis and Strategic Decision Making Organization Science, Vol. 12, No. 6, pp. 772–777.

Edward J. , Kleiman, Robert T. and Sahu, Anandi P. (1999) 'Current Capital Investment Practices', *The Engineering Economist,* 44: 2, 137 -150.

Fisher, Irving (1930). *The Theory of Interest.* New York: The MacMillan Co. also available at http://www.econlib.org/library/YPDBooks/Fisher/fshToICover.html.

Lefley, Frank. (1996). The payback method of investment appraisal: A review and synthesis *Int. J. Production Economics* 44: 207–224.

Miles, James A. and John R. Ezzell. (1980). The weighted average cost of capital, perfect capital markets and project life: A clarification. *Journal of Financial and Quantitative Analysis.* Volume XV, No. 3: 719-730.

Poincaré, Henri. (1903) "Science and Method" retrieved from http://www.chaos.umd.edu/misc/poincare.html#NewtonClock .

Ramsey, Frank P. (1928), "A Mathematical Theory of Saving," *Economic Journal,* Vol. 38, No 152, pp. 543 559).

Robert L. McDonald. (2006). The Role of Real Options in Capital Budgeting: Theory and Practice. Journal of Applied Corporate Finance Volume 18 | Number 2 | Spring

Stanley Block (2007). ARE "Real Options" Actually Used In The Real World? *The Engineering Economist,* 52: 255–267.

Sundem, Gary L. (1975) Evaluating capital budgeting models in simulated environments. *The Journal of Finance,* 30(4): 976.992.

Wikipedia. Niels Bohr. http://en.wikipedia.org/wiki/Niels_Bohr.

Chapter 8

Management of operational performance

8.1 Introduction

8.1.1 Operational management

Operational management is concerned with the execution of company objectives at the operational level, or shop floor level, of the firm. At this level, managers directly plan, coordinate and control operational activities. The scope of issues operational managers handle is dependent on the responsibilities that they have been assigned. Managers of *cost centres* are mainly responsible for costs, and thus for the efficiency and productivity of operations. **Profit centre** managers are responsible for costs and revenues, which add up to the profitability of operations. Operational managers, who also have the responsibility for capital investments, are **investment centre** managers. They have the means to change the installed capacity by adding, replacing, reducing or altering the production capacity. It is not the responsibilities that define whether management is operational, but management's direct relation to operational activities. Because a cost centre's installed capacity is not easily changed, its managers have fewer alternative solutions to operational problems than investment centre managers have. The basic task of operational managers is to take operational decisions that most effectively contribute to the realisation of the organisation's strategic objectives, given installed capacity.

Generic organisational strategies are considered to be either **low cost** or **differentiation** strategies (Porter, 1985). A low cost strategy aims at lowering costs in order to become a cost leader in the market place. Low costs facilitate low pricing strategies that attract a larger number of customers, leading to higher sales and, hopefully, returns. Organisations following a differentiation strategy try to produce unique attributes that are highly valued by buyers. This enables the firm to ask a premium price for its products and services. There are many ways to make a product uniquely attractive: for instance, by improving functionality, product reliability, innovativeness and quality. When describing the way Japanese companies compete, Cooper (1995) used the 'survival triplet': in order to survive competition, companies are supposed to compete successfully in three dimensions simultaneously: price, quality and functionality. Recent research has demonstrated that most companies focus on several strategic objectives simultaneously, most importantly costs, quality and innovativeness.

In this chapter, we focus mainly on operational management. Operational managers influence costs, which may in turn influence pricing decisions and quality. By improving production processes, operational managers may also contribute to improvements in product functionality and innovativeness. We will, however, focus mainly at the standard operational responsibilities for cost and quality. Managing costs means that unit costs should be minimised, under the restrictions of a required quality level while securing a sufficient capability of improvement. Operational managers need to optimise process measures, like **efficiency** (minimising resource use per unit output) and **productivity** (maximising output per unit resource consumed). At the same time, they also try to commit a minimum of company resources, expressed in the value of assets employed or in **working capital** (defined by current assets **minus** current liabilities). **Optimisation** requires simultaneously meeting customers' value and quality expectations.

Effective operational management starts with a production plan in which company resources are allocated to activities and products in such a way that they generate the highest net added value[1] to the organisation. We discuss the production plan in Section 8.2. In Section 8.3 we extend the production capacity plan by looking at sequential production steps and how to optimise the different production flows. Instead of producing a single optimal production schedule, it is also possible to follow an incremental approach of optimising the use of production capacity by removing or expanding the most constraining resource. This approach is also known as the Theory of Constraints. This approach is presented in Section 8.4.

Quality issues are discussed in Section 8.5. Important operational management decisions include the selection of the required quality levels and of the methods to monitor and control quality performance. Some new developments, like Six Sigma, are also discussed. In the final Section 8.6, we take a closer look at the dilemmas and problems that firms face when operating in a value chain. The performance requirements in value chains are diverse and we will see how management accounting information can help in optimising the operations in the value chain and solving some of the most important operational management dilemmas.

8.2 Defining the production plan

8.2.1 Use of installed capacity

Operational planning decisions focus on production activities and deal with the allocation of resources to alternative uses in the short term when capacities are limited. Some managerial decisions fall outside the scope of operational planning. For instance, the focus on production activities means that fixed costs fall outside the scope of operational decision making. The short term orientation of operational planning excludes decisions about changing, expanding and reducing the installed production capacity. Whatever operational decisions managers make, they will not directly affect or alter fixed costs. This leaves us with two important elements for operational decision making: the revenues and the variable costs of production.

Revenues are determined by the selling price of products and services, including price discounts and service credits given and the quantities sold.[2] Variable costs may include direct and indirect variable costs. Indirect variable costs are overhead charges that vary in proportion to the number of products or services produced. Direct and indirect variable costs can influence the decisions local managers take to optimise the use of installed production

[1] Net added value is the gross value the production plan generates for the company minus its costs.

[2] We will not discuss pricing and marketing decisions at length in this chapter, but leave these topics to Marketing textbooks.

capacity.[3] A useful measure to use for short term decision-making is the **contribution margin,** which is the difference between revenues and variable costs–per unit or in total. Since operational decision making deals with maximising value and minimising cost, the contribution margin per **unit** is a useful monetary input in the operational planning decision to allocate resources to individual products, services or activities.[4]

Let us have a look at a mid sized company Bicycle Industries (BI), which produces two types of bicycles: Cruizer (standard bicycles) and ATB (all terrain bikes). BI buys frames at the market and processes them into bikes ready for the customer market. The contribution margins of the two bicycle types are the following:

- Cruizer contribution margin: €200 per unit;
- ATB contribution margin: €300 per unit.

The ATB clearly has a better contribution margin per unit than the Cruizer. If the market would buy all the bikes BI produces and the company would have unlimited production capabilities, BI would choose to dedicate all resources to the production of only ATB's, because an ATB generates €100 more than a Cruizer. This is an acceptable solution ignoring any resource constraints. In practice, however, production always takes place under resource constraints: companies have limited production time determined by machine capacity constraints, labour arrangements, work schedules and the fact that a day does not have more than 24 hours. Suppose the bicycles are processed by an **assembly department** that needs 30 minutes production time for each Cruizer frame and one hour for each ATB frame. For each hour the company's assembly department is in operation each bicycle type would generate the following contribution margin:

- Cruizer: 2 bicycles per hour = €400/hour;
- ATB: 1 bicylce per hour = €300/hour.

Now shifting the production schedule to exclusively producing Cruizers leads to a higher total contribution margin. Different numbers of total production hours available do not make much difference: if BI only produced ATB's it would generate €100 less in each hour than when it chose Cruizers to produce. The product with the lower contribution margin per unit now turns out to be the more profitable one to produce. This apparently confusing result can be explained by the fact that optimising the use of installed capacity means taking into account two different elements simultaneously: each product's contribution margin and the firm's production capabilities. The way to consider both simultaneously is to use the contribution margin **per unit of the scarce resource,** which is the contribution margin per unit divided by the amount of the constrained resource per unit.

Under a single constraint condition, the choice of which product to produce has become a relatively simple calculation. In practice however, most production systems generate several different products and services and they operate under many different constraints. A simple contribution margin calculation per unit of scarce resource does not longer suffice, and it becomes difficult to identify the right mix of products and to ascertain the economic consequences of alternative production plans. We can use the technique of **linear programming** (LP) to come to a solution. Linear programming is a mathematical technique that optimises an

[3] Some authors, like Eli Goldratt (1990) argue that **all** indirect cost allocations should be excluded because they distort operational information. In our view, if ABC analyses show that resource use in operations has variable usage, these costs should also be considered.

[4] The 'contribution margin' represents the amount that **contributes** to recovering fixed costs.

objective function under the presence of **constrained resources.** The objective function is mostly cast in monetary terms, and can be the maximisation of operating profit or the minimisation of costs. The linear programming model tries to find a solution within the possibilities of the constraining resources. In searching for a solution, it simultaneously takes the possibilities of the constraining resources into account, as we did by looking at the contribution margin per unit of the scarce resource.[5] Linear programming techniques can be used to solve different operational decisions, like the short term planning of production activities (use of resources, scheduling of production activities and the optimal composition of the product portfolio), planning the optimal mix of resources in process industries (think of oil and agro industry where different combinations of inputs lead to different end products), optimising work schedules in service industries (route planning in public transport, and composition of work teams in hospitals and schools), and selecting optimal investment portfolios (compositions of different investments, taking into account the investor's risk profile and required total returns).

In this section, we will look at optimising short-term production activities in Bicycle Industries. Let us therefore extend the BI example somewhat so that we can algebraically and graphically explain how linear programming works. We can then explore more complicated settings, which is where linear programming adds most value.

8.2.2 The basic LP model

The LP model aims at optimising the **objective function.** An objective function is a linear combination of units and their attributes (operating profit or contribution margin) that needs to be **maximised** (when the attribute adds to firm value) or **minimised** (when it decreases firm value, like cost). For BI the objective function is the following:

$$\text{Max CM} = €200 \times Q_{\text{Cruizer}} + €300 \times Q_{\text{ATB}}$$

We already had one constraint, defined by the time needed for each bicycle in the assembly department. Suppose the maximum hours of available production time in the assembly department is 4000 hours. Each bicycle also needs to be painted in the 'painting department'. Each bike will take 36 minutes (= 0.6 hours) to be painted, irrespective whether it is a Cruizer or an ATB bicycle. The maximum time time available in the painting department is 3600 hours. Each bicycle needs both assembly and painting and will therefore pass through both departments. However, the order in which each bicycle goes through the assembly and painting processes does not matter. Each bike can first be painted and then assembled, or first assembled and afterwards painted. BI's production system is reproduced in Figure 8.1. We now can define the constraints as follows:

$$\begin{array}{lll} \text{Assembly:} & 0.5 \times Q_{\text{Cruizer}} + 1.0 \times Q_{\text{ATB}} & \leq 4{,}000 \text{ hours} \\ \text{Painting:} & 0.6 \times Q_{\text{Cruizer}} + 0.6 \times Q_{\text{ATB}} & \leq 3{,}600 \text{ hours} \end{array}$$

We should also add so-called *non-negativity constraints,* because the number of bicycles we try to find are positive numbers:

$$Q_{\text{Cruizer}} \geq 0$$
$$Q_{\text{ATB}} \geq 0$$

[5] Linear programming models use different optimisation rules to solve linear programming problems, of which the Simplex method is most widely known. This method follows an iterative procedure that improves a feasible solution until the optimal solution is obtained (see for more details Riahi-Belkaoui, 2001). Excel's Solver permits the use of alternative optimisation rules.

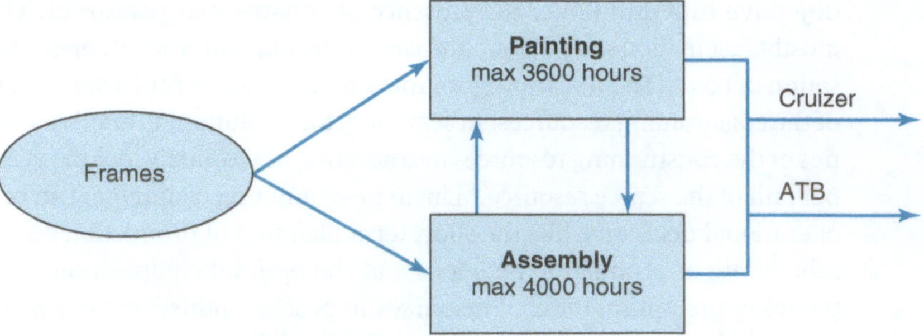

Figure 8.1 BI's production system

The production constraints can be represented graphically as shown in Figure 8.2. For instance, the capacity constraint for assembly is a linear combination of all possible combinations of Cruizer and ATB bicycles assembled when the department works at maximum capacity. If we used all capacity to produce ATB's and no Cruizers, the production output of the assembly department would be 4000 ATB's (this is the maximum value at the *y*-axis in Figure 8.2). And conversely, if only Cruizers were assembled, the maximum output would be 8000 Cruizers (and no ATB's). This is the point at the *x*-axis. The line connecting both points represents all full capacity combinations of Cruizers and ATB's. One could also decide not to use the assembly department at full capacity: this would lead to a combination of bicycles that falls below the production line.

Since both departments are used to produce both bicycle types, the surface below both capacity constraints contains all the possible combinations of bicycles that can be produced by both departments. It is the **production possibilities area** and it shows the feasible set of production plans. Going beyond this area would violate one or more of the production contraints. We now need to confront the production possibilities with the objective function: the installed capacity will be filled with a production plan in which the attractiveness of each of the products is weighted by its relative contribution margin (i.e. in comparison with the

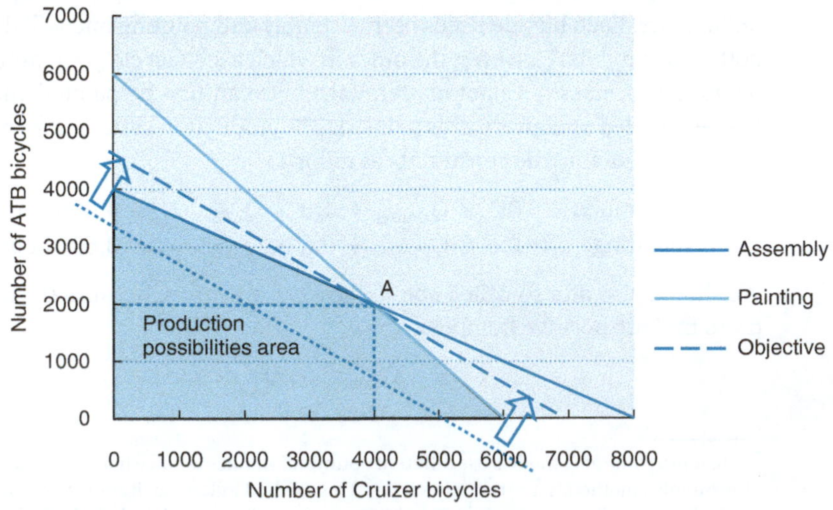

Figure 8.2 Bicycle Industries: graphic LP solution

other product's contribution margin). The relative contribution margin is the inclination of the objective line in Figure 8.2. The simplex method is designed to shift the objective line as far away from the intercept as possible, without exceeding the installed capacity. The optimum is found at point A, representing the production of 4000 Cruizer bikes and 2000 ATB's.

For relatively simple operational problems the graphic LP solution may be feasible. However, most capacity use problems are more complicated than the current example, which has only two products and two constraints. The use of Excel's Solver program may be helpful for many more complex capacity use problems. Before using the Solver, the spreadsheet must contain the necessary data and relationship information, as is shown in Figure 8.3.[6]

The Solver is located under the main menu's Data option. The Solver's drop down menu asks to identify the cell containing the objective function's value that needs to be optimised, labelled the 'target cell', which is cell D5 in our Excel sheet in Figure 8.3. Next, it requires the cells that need to be adjusted (the Changing cells) to attain the optimal solution. In our example, these are the number of Cruizer and ATB bicycles, which have been set at the minimum value of 1 in our LP model.[7] The constraints can be inserted in the lower part of the menu in two parts: the linear combination of resource use for each constraint and the capacity available. The two non-linearity constraints do not appear in the LP model, because they can be defined in the Solver's Options section by selecting the 'assume non-negative' option.

Solver generates three reports: the *Answer Report,* the *Sensitivity Report* and the *Limits Report.* The *Answer Report* (See Figure 8.4a) shows the final solution: a total contribution margin of €1 40 0000 is reached by producing 4000 Cruizer bikes and 2000 ATB's. All available capacity is fully used, which means both departments are a binding condition for the final solution and none of them has unused or slack capacity. The *Limits Report* (Figure 8.4b)

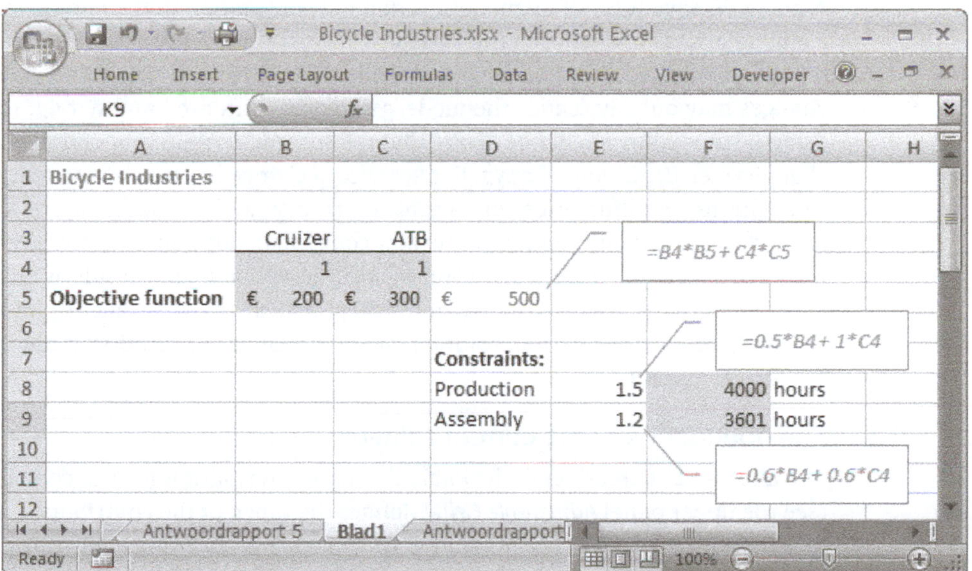

Figure 8.3 LP model for Bicycle Industries' production planning decision

[6] There is no need to copy exactly the layout of Figure 9.2, as long as the necessary data are included in the spreadsheet. Note that one might have to 'add in' Solver to Excel if it has not been used before.

[7] It is possible to use another start value, like 0, since it does not alter the final solution. We favour the value of 1 because it allows you to check the value of the objective function.

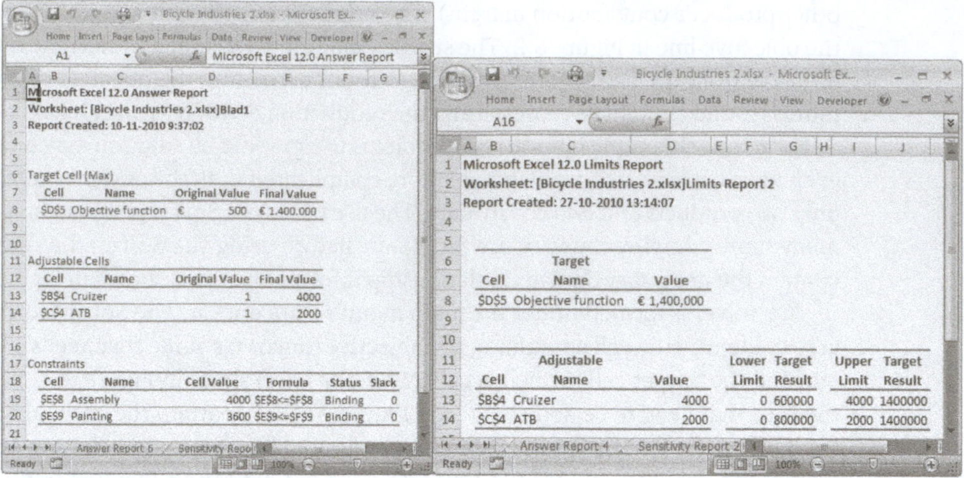

Microsoft Excel 12.0 Answer Report
Worksheet: [Bicycle Industries 2.xlsx]Blad1
Report Created: 10-11-2010 9:37:02

Target Cell (Max)

Cell	Name	Original Value	Final Value
$D$5	Objective function	€ 500	€ 1.400.000

Adjustable Cells

Cell	Name	Original Value	Final Value
$B$4	Cruizer	1	4000
$C$4	ATB	1	2000

Constraints

Cell	Name	Cell Value	Formula	Status	Slack
$E$8	Assembly	4000	$E$8<=$F$8	Binding	0
$E$9	Painting	3600	$E$9<=$F$9	Binding	0

Figure 8.4a Answer report

Microsoft Excel 12.0 Limits Report
Worksheet: [Bicycle Industries 2.xlsx]Limits Report 2
Report Created: 27-10-2010 13:14:07

Cell	Target Name	Value
$D$5	Objective function	€ 1,400,000

Cell	Adjustable Name	Value	Lower Limit	Target Result	Upper Limit	Target Result
$B$4	Cruizer	4000	0	600000	4000	1400000
$C$4	ATB	2000	0	800000	2000	1400000

Figure 8.4b Limits report

presents the relative contribution of each product: it no Cruizers were be produced but only ATB's, the contribution margin would be €600 000. When only Cruizers are be choosen and no ATB's, the contribution margin would be €800 000. Producing both at maximum capacity yields a total contribution margin of €1 400 000.

8.2.3 Sensitivity analysis

A major disadvantage of LP models, is that they are static. All the parameters used, as well as the relationships between the variables, are assumed to be known ('deterministic') and remain unchanged. However, in practice all values used in the model may change and these changes may quickly render the model's outcomes outdated and wrong. Decision makers using LP modelling should be aware that the current model's production plan may need to change when conditions change. For instance, a change in contribution margins, because of fluctuations in selling prices or variable costs, may make it necessary to rerun the model using the updated information (Excel now comes in handy: since we already have a previous model specification, the additional time and effort to obtain new results is relatively modest). Excel's *Sensitivity Report* (refer to Figure 8.5) provides some assistance by informing us about the boundaries of the current solution and how changes in certain variables will impact on the objective value.[8]

8.2.3.1 The boundaries of the current solution

The allowable increase and allowable decrease information for the contribution margins (see the upper panel *Adjustable Cells)* defines the range of the contribution margin for each product within which the final solution will not change, **holding everything else constant.** So, for instance, when the contribution margin of the Cruizer bicycle (which is currently set at €200) falls between €150 (the current objective coefficient of €200 minus the allowable decrease of €50) and €300 (the current €200 plus allowable increase of €100). This can be

[8] The Sensitivity Report will only be generated when the *Assume Linear Model* option is activated (which can be found under *Options* in the Solver's main menu).

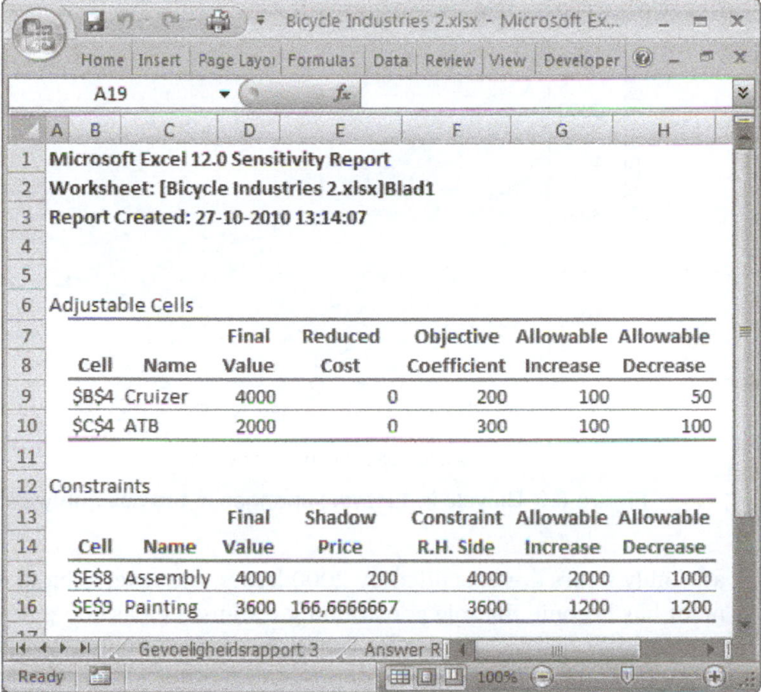

Bicycle Industries 2.xlsx - Microsoft Ex...

Home | Insert | Page Layou | Formulas | Data | Review | View | Developer

A19

Microsoft Excel 12.0 Sensitivity Report
Worksheet: [Bicycle Industries 2.xlsx]Blad1
Report Created: 27-10-2010 13:14:07

Adjustable Cells

Cell	Name	Final Value	Reduced Cost	Objective Coefficient	Allowable Increase	Allowable Decrease
$B$4	Cruizer	4000	0	200	100	50
$C$4	ATB	2000	0	300	100	100

Constraints

Cell	Name	Final Value	Shadow Price	Constraint R.H. Side	Allowable Increase	Allowable Decrease
$E$8	Assembly	4000	200	4000	2000	1000
$E$9	Painting	3600	166,6666667	3600	1200	1200

Gevoeligheidsrapport 3 | Answer R

Ready 100%

Figure 8.5 Sensitivity report on Bicycle Industries production plan

verified by looking at Figure 8.2 again. Suppose the production costs of Cruizer bicycles would dropped €100 per unit, leading to a contribution margin that is €100 higher. This would lead to the following revised objective function:

$$\text{Max CM} = €300\ \text{Cruizer} + €300\ \text{ATB}$$

This new function affects the objective line in Figure 8.2 and makes the negative inclination larger (the inclination of the objective function in Figure 8.2 becomes 'steeper'), putting the objective line exactly on top of the assembly constraint curve. This also invokes a new set of alternative solutions: between 4000 and 6000 Cruizers in combination with corresponding numbers ATB's in the range of 0 to 2000. When the contribution margin of Cruizers improves even more, then the optimal operational plan becomes the production of 6000 units of Cruizer bicycles and no ATB's.

The margins for the constraints that are similarly defined by the allowable increase and decrease values should be interpreted differently. They indicate when a constraint stops being a constraint anymore (the allowable increase) and when a constraint becomes the sole constraint, driving the other constraint(s) out of the solution (the allowable decrease). When capacity constraints are changed, the capacity constraint curves will change parallel to their original curves' position, expanding or reducing the production of both bicycles in the proportion of their resource consumption. In Figure 8.6 the solid lines represent the original constraints and the dotted lines indicate the allowable increase and allowable decrease limits for the assembly department.

When the assembly department capacity is reduced by 1000 hours, the assembly department becomes the sole constraining resource. The optimal production quantity decision is now made independent of the assembly department's capacity constraint. When the

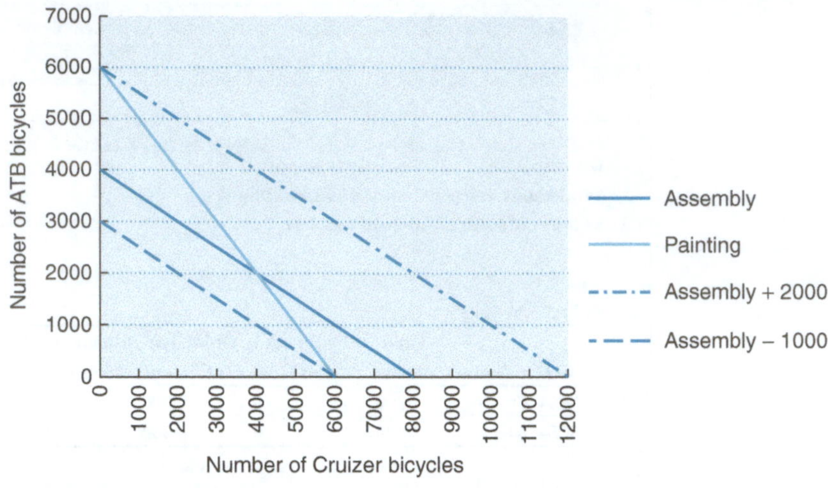

Figure 8.6 Bicycle Industries: changes in the assembly constraint

assembly hours are expanded by 2000 hours, the reverse happens: the painting department has become the sole constraining resource. Please note that the meaning of allowable increase/decrease range for constraints is fundamentally different from the meaning of the allowable increase/decrease range for the objective function. The objective function's allowable increase/decrease limits define the range within the final solution will not change (*ceteris paribus*), whereas the constraints' allowable increase/decrease limits indicate when a constraint becomes a sole constraint (the lower limit) or when it stops being a constraint at all (the upper limit).

8.2.3.2 Consequences of marginal changes

Let us return to our discussion of the contribution margins' ranges within which the current solution holds. We have seen from Figure 8.5 that when the Cruizer's contribution margin increased to more than €300, the current solution needs to be reconsidered. This means in practical terms that the model should be rerun. Now suppose that Bicycle Industries turns out to be very successful in their cost reduction program, and that a Cruizer's contribution margin of €310 has been attained. From Figure 8.2 we can see that under this condition, the optimal solution would be only to produce Cruizer bicycles and no ATB bicycles. The corresponding sensitivity report is reproduced in Figure 8.7.

We have indeed a new solution: the production of 6000 Cruizers and no ATB's. Now the ATB has been given a value for **reduced costs.** Reduced costs is a factor that indicates how much the contribution for that product has to be improved in order to make that product attractive enough to appear in the final solution (in our terms: to be produced). An increase of €10 would raise ATB's contribution margin from the current €300 to €310 which brings it to the same value as Cruizer's contribution margin. Remember that under equal contribution margins the objective line would partly overlap the production capacity constraint curve, which makes the production of different combinations of Cruizers and ATB's possible. This is also reflected in the allowable increase margin: when the additional €10 contribution margin improvement is reached, the sensitivity report predicts a different final solution.

A similar marginal change analysis can also be done for the constraints in the model. Let us return to our original solution and its sensitivity report as shown in Figure 8.5. The

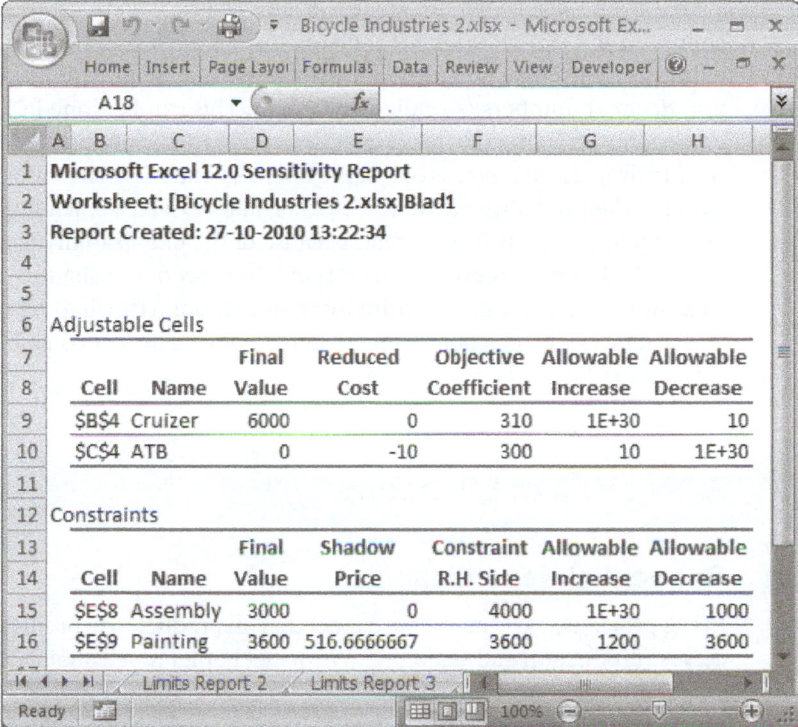

Bicycle Industries 2.xlsx - Microsoft Ex...

Home | Insert | Page Layout | Formulas | Data | Review | View | Developer

A18

Microsoft Excel 12.0 Sensitivity Report
Worksheet: [Bicycle Industries 2.xlsx]Blad1
Report Created: 27-10-2010 13:22:34

Adjustable Cells

Cell	Name	Final Value	Reduced Cost	Objective Coefficient	Allowable Increase	Allowable Decrease
$B$4	Cruizer	6000	0	310	1E+30	10
$C$4	ATB	0	-10	300	10	1E+30

Constraints

Cell	Name	Final Value	Shadow Price	Constraint R.H. Side	Allowable Increase	Allowable Decrease
$E$8	Assembly	3000	0	4000	1E+30	1000
$E$9	Painting	3600	516.6666667	3600	1200	3600

Limits Report 2 | Limits Report 3

Ready 100%

Figure 8.7 **Sensitivity report for a new contribution margin**

capacity of both constraints is fully used: the Answer report has already indicated that both constraints are 'binding' and both have no slack resources. This means that expanding the capacity of each of the constraints would lead to more production. The **shadow price** (or sometimes also called **dual price**) of a constraint indicates the increase of the total contribution margin when the capacity of that resource is expanded by one unit. It is the opportunity cost of an additional unit of production capacity. If we rerun the model using a capacity of 4001 hours for assembly, the new solution calls for the production of 3998 Cruizers and 2002 ATB's: two ATB's **more** and two Cruizers **less.**[9] The new total contribution margin is (3998*200) + (2002*300) = €1 400 200, which is indeed €200 more than the original solution of €1.4 million. The shadow price represents the attainable additional contribution margin when the constraining resource is expanded by one unit. It also sets the upper limit to the price Bicycle Industries' management is willing to pay to get the additional hour of assembly time. If an additional hour will cost more than the shadow price of €200, expanding the capacity of assembly will result in a marginal loss to the firm. Expansion will only become attractive when the price for an additional hour is €200 or less. This is why the shadow price also works as an opportunity cost: it indicates the maximum price decision makers are willing to pay for an additional hour assembly capacity.

If we rerun the model also for the painting constraint by adding one hour to the painting capacity, it will generate the following final solution: an additional €167 total contribution margin can be earned by producing 4003.33 Cruizers and 1998.33 ATB's. The production of

[9] This shows that an expansion of production capacity does **not** always lead to additional production numbers of all products: it only calls for a new allocation of capacity over products.

a part of a bicycle is in most situations not an option. In this particular example, one could choose to use this solution for the next three production periods (leading to round numbers). An alternative is to use **inter programming**, which is linear programming using only non-decimal numbers (so called 'integers'). This can be done in Excel by adding two new constraints, defining the target cells as 'integers' (this option can be found in the 'Add constraint' drop down menu as one of the operator options). The integer programming solution calls for the production of 4002 Cruizers and 1999 ATB's, leading to an additional contribution margin of €100. Note that, because of the indivisability of production numbers, the attained additional contribution margin falls short of the shadow price. This is because the shadow price is a marginal sensitivity analysis around the final solution, which does not take indivisibility of production numbers into account. The lost contribution margin is visible as slack in the assembly department.

8.3 Extensions of LP models

8.3.1 Sequential dependencies

In the previous, basic model we expect that all products are produced by all production processes (production and assembly). We do not bother much about the sequence in which each product passes through the different stages and about sequential dependencies between the stages in the value chain process. In most production systems, however, some production activities cannot be undertaken until a previous production activity has been finished. Suppose that Bicycle Industries cannot paint the bicycles until they are assembled, this introduces a sequential dependency in the production system. The production system may also be constrained by external conditions. In the basic model we assume that all products will automatically be absorbed by the market. This may not always be true. Suppose that Bicycle Industries started producing according to the basic optimal plan of 4000 Cruizer bicycles and 2000 ATB's. After a year, it then becomes clear that the local market does not demand more than 3500 Cruizers and 2000 ATB's. The original plan leads to inventories of unsold bicycles.

To avoid this, BI management has come up with an alternative plan to expand sales internationally. Marketing studies have shown that there is no market for Cruizers, but there may be demand for ATB's, provided that the current ATB's are upgraded to match the quality demands of foreign customers. In order to do so, BI created a new department, the 'upgrading' unit in which assembled bikes are painted and further equipped with specialised ATB features for the international market. The maximum capacity of this new department is 2400 hours. The international ATB's are expected to generate a higher contribution margin: €400 per unit. The international demand for upgraded ATB's is considered unlimited, given the size of the international ATB market. BI's new production system is graphically displayed in Figure 8.8.

Now, we need to consider some additional variables and constraints than in the basic model. For instance, the Painting department can only paint Cruizer frames that have been finished by the Assembly department. We, therefore, need, to define a new variable, Cruizer assembled bicycles, Cr. We have a similar situation for ATB bicycles: once ATB bikes are assembled (which is introduced in the model by the variable ATB), they can be allocated

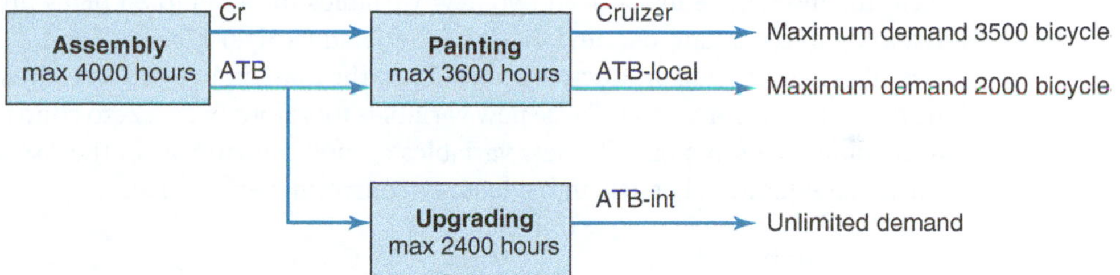

Figure 8.8 Bicycle Industries, revised production system

either to the painting department for processing for the local market (as ATB local) or to the Upgrading department for upgrading for the international market (as ATB int). The new objective function is:

$$\text{Max CM} = 0\,\text{Cr} + 0\,\text{ATB} + 1\,\text{Cruizer} + 1\,\text{ATB-local} + 1\,\text{ATB-int}$$

We have three different types of constraints in our new model:

1. **Resource constraints,** which define the availability of input factors, such as machine or department production time, labour, material, and other resources. In our example, they are the production time available in each department.
2. **Demand constraints,** which define the minimum and maximum numbers of units that can be sold or dispatched. As we know from the marketing department, the local market's demand for Cruizers is 3500 bicycles and for standard ATB's 2000 units.
3. **Balance constraints,** which define the sequential dependencies between production stages. The basic constraint here is that later production stages cannot consume more products than previous stages have produced. In our example, the painting and upgrading departments cannot process more bikes than are supplied by the assembly department.

The new model is represented in Figure 8.9.

Bicycle Industries.xlsx - Microsoft Excel

	A	B	C	D	E	F	G	H	I	J	
1	Bicycle Industries										
2											
3		Cr	ATB	Cruizer	ATB-local	ATB-int					
4		1	1	1	1	1					
5	**Objective function**	€0	€0	€ 200	€ 300	€ 400	€ 900				=B4*B5+C4*C5+D4*D5+E4*E5+F4*F5
6											
7							**Resource constraints:**				
8							Assembly	1.5	4,000	hours	=0,5*B4+1*C4≤4000
9							Painting	1.2	3,600	hours	=0,6*D4+0,6*E4≤3600
10							Upgrading	2	2,400	hours	=2*F4≤2400
11											
12							**Balance constraints:**				
13							Painting Cruizer	1	1		=D4≤B4
14							Painting & Upgr ATB	2	1		=E4+F4≤C4
15											
16							**Demand constraints:**				
17							Cruizer	1	3,500	bicycles	=D4≤3500
18							ATB-local	1	2,000	bicycles	=E4≤2000
19											

Figure 8.9 Bicycle Industries' revised production plan with sequential dependencies

In this model, we introduced two new variables for assembled bikes produced by the Assembly department, denoted *Cr* (for assembled Cruizer bicycles) and *ATB* (assembled ATB bikes). These half products are not sold on the market, but will be processed further by the two other departments. These new variables therefore have a zero contribution margin in the objective function. The new variables do not only appear in the Assembly resource constraint equation, but also in the balance constraints equations:

Painting Cruizer:	Cruizer ≤ Cr	(1)
Painting & Upgr ATB:	ATB-local + ATB-int ≤ ATB	(2)

Equation (1) determines that the number of Cruizers painted cannot exceed the number of Cruizers assembled. Equation (2) defines that the total number of ATB's produced for the local and international markets cannot be more than the number of ATB's assembled.

We only have demand constraints for the number of Cruizers and ATB's produced for the local market, since the demand in the international market is considered unlimited.

The solution calls for maximising the local Cruizers and the international ATB's which leads to lower numbers of local ATB's sold and slack resources in the painting department (see Figure 8.10). We have exclusively used number of products to reach a solution, but also resources (man hours, materials) can be introduced in the model. They appear in the objective function as negative numbers, since resource consumption is a cost to the firm.

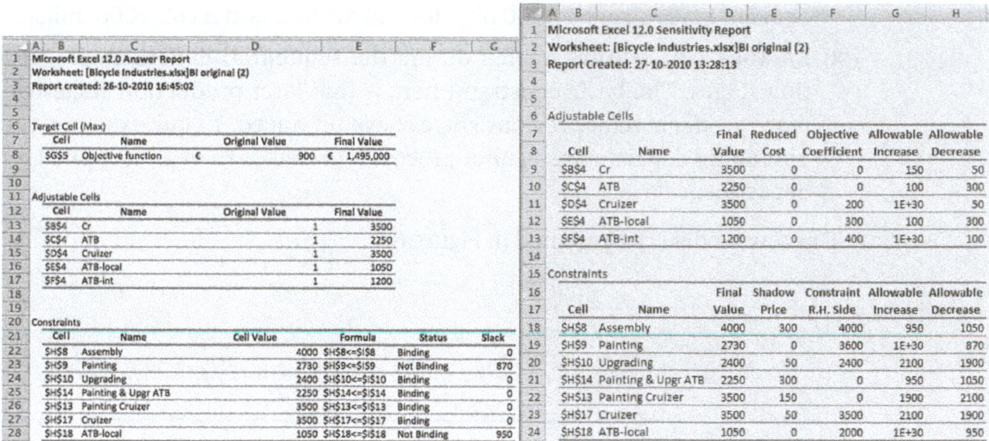

Microsoft Excel 12.0 Answer Report
Worksheet: [Bicycle Industries.xlsx]BI original (2)
Report created: 26-10-2010 16:45:02

Target Cell (Max)

Cell	Name	Original Value	Final Value
$G$5	Objective function	€ 900	€ 1,495,000

Adjustable Cells

Cell	Name	Original Value	Final Value
$B$4	Cr	1	3500
$C$4	ATB	1	2250
$D$4	Cruizer	1	3500
$E$4	ATB-local	1	1050
$F$4	ATB-int	1	1200

Constraints

Cell	Name	Cell Value	Formula	Status	Slack
$H$8	Assembly	4000	$H$8<=$I$8	Binding	0
$H$9	Painting	2730	$H$9<=$I$9	Not Binding	870
$H$10	Upgrading	2400	$H$10<=$I$10	Binding	0
$H$14	Painting & Upgr ATB	2250	$H$14<=$I$14	Binding	0
$H$13	Painting Cruizer	3500	$H$13<=$I$13	Binding	0
$H$17	Cruizer	3500	$H$17<=$I$17	Binding	0
$H$18	ATB-local	1050	$H$18<=$I$18	Not Binding	950

Microsoft Excel 12.0 Sensitivity Report
Worksheet: [Bicycle Industries.xlsx]BI original (2)
Report Created: 27-10-2010 13:28:13

Adjustable Cells

Cell	Name	Final Value	Reduced Cost	Objective Coefficient	Allowable Increase	Allowable Decrease
$B$4	Cr	3500	0	0	150	50
$C$4	ATB	2250	0	0	100	300
$D$4	Cruizer	3500	0	200	1E+30	50
$E$4	ATB-local	1050	0	300	100	300
$F$4	ATB-int	1200	0	400	1E+30	100

Constraints

Cell	Name	Final Value	Shadow Price	Constraint R.H. Side	Allowable Increase	Allowable Decrease
$H$8	Assembly	4000	300	4000	950	1050
$H$9	Painting	2730	0	3600	1E+30	870
$H$10	Upgrading	2400	50	2400	2100	1900
$H$14	Painting & Upgr ATB	2250	300	0	950	1050
$H$13	Painting Cruizer	3500	150	0	1900	2100
$H$17	Cruizer	3500	50	3500	2100	1900
$H$18	ATB-local	1050	0	2000	1E+30	950

Figure 8.10 Solution and sensitivity analysis

8.3.2 Multi-period models

Balance constraints can be used to introduce time dependent constraints. The basic idea behind a balance constraint is

Use of a resource or (half) product ≤ Availability of a resource or (half) product

Suppose we did not use all (half) products available, this would lead to inventories of (half) products. For instance, in our example we could introduce an inventory of Apn or Apx, which would impact the production plan of one period (Period 1) to the next period (Period 2). In order to model this, we introduce two inventory variables and extend the basic balance constraint in the following way:

$$\text{Ending inventory} + \text{Use} + \text{Sales} = \text{Opening inventory} + \text{Purchases} + \text{Production}$$

As you probably noticed, we have replaced the inequality operator $\leq$ by the equality sign. This is, because there are no other possibilities in making (half) products available or in consuming (half) products than the activities included in the equation. In order to link the two periods to each other, we need a new balance constraint:

$$\text{Ending inventory period 1} = \text{Opening inventory period 2}$$

In order to plan for each period independently, all variables in the objective function and in the constraints need to be period specific. The solution of this multi-period problem would determine the production level of all products in each period and the optimal inventory level between the periods. Management can also set minimum and maximum limits to these inventories. Minimum levels can be required to secure availability of products and on time delivery to clients, maximum levels may be set to reduce working capital.

8.4 Theory of constraints

8.4.1 Basic idea

The Theory Of Constraints (TOC) presented by Eli Goldratt (Goldratt & Cox, 1989; Goldratt, 1990) is not restricted to optimisation of the use of installed capacity (as we have seen in the previous paragraphs), but extends to the improvement of performance by reducing system bottlenecks in any location in the organisation's value chain. These bottlenecks may come in different forms, like market, resource, material, supplier, financial and knowledge/competencies constraints. They are not only restricted to the focal organisation, but may also be caused by other processes up-stream or down-stream the value chain. Optimising the performance of the whole system requires a process oriented view of the value chain. In this view, the production system is not a collection of discrete production processes, but a grid of interlinked value chains. The total performance of a production system is limited by its weakest link, or the 'bottleneck.'. In other words: the most economical way to improve the system's performance is to strengthen the weakest link in the system. Or, to put it differently, alleviate the bottleneck by relaxing the most constraining factor.

8.4.2 TOC and accounting measures

In the TOC, the traditional accounting measures like net profit, ROI and cash flow are translated from the company wide perspective (for which most of the accounting measures are designed) to the level of operational managers. According to Goldratt, all indirect cost allocations and other accounting allocations that are designed to calculate total (allocated) product cost figures, may lead to distorted information for operational management decisions. The basic reason for this is that full cost accounting calculations may lead to accounting information that does not reflect well how company resources are obtained to generate added value.[10] The TOC approach, therefore, has developed its own cost accounting vocabulary. Operational managers' primary task is to maximise **throughput**, maintaining appropriate levels of **inventories** and minimising **operational expenses** by actively managing internal and external constraints. The three basic elements are the following:

1. **Throughput (T)** is a TOC measure that represents the rate of generating cash by an organisation. It is a measure of **added value:** the value of outputs minus the incremental costs of inputs. For example, throughput may be calculated as revenue from sales less direct material costs for goods sold. Costs for **committed** direct labour and indirect costs are expensed and never allocated to the product.
2. **Inventory (I)** (or investment) is money tied up in the company, intended to make the production functions run efficiently. Inventory includes facilities, capital assets, equipment and materials (things purchased that the company intends to sell).
3. **Operating expense (OE)** is the money needed to generate throughput. These expenses are used to sustain operational activities. Operating expenses are all the committed overhead and fixed costs of the organisation.

Taking as accumulated figures at the organisational level, these elements relate to our accounting vocabulary in a familiar fashion:

$$\text{Return on Investment } (ROI) = \frac{T - OE}{I}$$

$$\text{Net profit } (NP) = T - OE$$

$$\text{Cash flow } (CF) = T - OE \pm \Delta I$$

However, at the operational level we see some intriguing differences. In the previous section, managers were required to maximise the **contribution margin,** which equals total selling price minus total variable costs. The variable costs may contain the following cost items: direct material costs, direct labour costs, variable energy costs, and variable indirect costs. TOC excludes all but direct material costs: other costs are incurred irrespective of the use of installed production capacity. They do not change under the influence of the operation managers' production plan, but they must be taken into account when making capacity use decisions.

Let us return to Bicycle Industries. The selling prices for Cruizer, local ATB's and export ATB's are €400, €600 and €800 respectively. Direct material cost for each product is €80, €100 and €120. The international market turns out to respond reasonably well to the new export ATB's. The marketing department expects to be able to sell 1400 export ATB's in the coming year. In response to the good news, management already made the decision to expand the upgrading department's capacity from 2400 to 3000 hours. What should be done next?

TOC advocates that following an incremental (step-wise) approach, using the following basic steps, will improve the system:

1. **Identify** the constraints.
2. **Exploit** the constraints, deciding how to make the best use of the constraints.
3. **Subordinate** all other decisions to the decision in Step 2.
4. **Elevate** the capacity of the system by expanding the most constrained resource(s).
5. **Search** for new constraints (which means: go back to Step 1).

[10] Some indirect cost allocation methods, like some ABC applications, however try to fairly represent the causal use of company resources.

Table 8.1 TOC cost elements in BI production plan

Per unit	Cruizer	ATB local	ATB int
Price	400	600	800
Direct material cost	80	100	120
Throughput	320	500	680
Operating expenses	200	300	400
Net profit	120	200	280
Total production	3500	1050	1200
Total throughput	€1120000	€525000	€816000
Operating expenses	700000	315000	480000
Total net profit	€420000	€210000	€336000

Table 8.2 Constraint identification

Process	Resources demanded			Capacity	Resource need to capacity (%)
Assembly	Cruizer	0.5 × 3,500 =	1,750		
	ATB local	1 × 2,000 =	2,000		
	ATB int	1 × 1,400 =	1,400		
	Total		5,150	4,000	5,150/4,000 = 129%
Painting	Cruizer	0.6 × 3,500 =	2,100		
	ATB local	0.6 × 2,000 =	1,200		
	Total		3,300	3,600	3,300/3,600 = 92%
Upgrading	ATB int	2 × 1,400 =	2,800	3,000	2,800/3,000 = 93%

Table 8.1 shows the financial performance of each of Bicycle Industries' products, cast in TOC terms, for the current production plan (this is the plan that was determined in the final LP solution as demonstrated in Figure 8.10).

Total costs are now subdivided into two parts: the direct material cost (costs for inputs to be used in the production process) and operating expenses (all expenses necessary to generate throughput). Throughput represents the **added value** of the production system, including all remaining costs for turning inputs into outputs and profit. Suppose BI's management does not want to settle for the current production numbers, but prefers to accommodate market demand better by producing 3500 Cruizers, 2000 ATB local and 1400 ATB international. This new plan will certainly put the production system under pressure. The question now is what constraints will emerge and how should they be resolved?

- **Step 1.** Identify the constraints. Under the new demands for products and capacities of the different production processes, we can identify which resource puts constraints on the capabilities to execute the new plan (see Table 8.2).

  For each process, we calculate first how many resources are needed to fulfill customer demand for each product. Then the projected resource demands are confronted with the capacity available for each process. As we can see, both painting and upgrading processes are capable of serving the current demand, but assembly is a constraining process.

- **Step 2.** Exploit the constraints. The second question is how the use of the constrained resources can be improved under the current capacity constraints. The basic approach here

Table 8.3 Expoiting the constraints: product prioritisation

Margin per constrained resource unit			
	Cruizer	ATB local	ATB exp
Price	€400	€600	€800
Direct material cost	80	100	120
Throughput per unit	€320	€500	€680
Time on Production	0.5	1	1
Throughput per production hour	€640	€500	€680

is to select the product that generates the highest throughput per unit passing through the constraint (see Table 8.3).

The biggest improvement will be generated from prioritising production of export ATB's. Next is the production of Cruizers and local ATB's. The operational plan for the production process looks like the following (Table 8.4).

Table 8.4 Operational planning

Operational planning for the Assembly Department		Use	Capacity
Beginning capacity			4000
Maximise ATB-exp	1400 × 1 =	1400	
Production capacity for Cruizers			2600
Production of Cruizer *)	3500 × 0.5 =	1750	
Production capacity for ATB local			850
Production of ATB local	850 × 1 =	850	
Remaining production capacity			0

*): The production capacity for Cruizers is 2600 hours, which allows the production of 5200 bicycles. The market only absorbs 3500 bicycles, which means that the production of Cruizers is set at 3500 units (maximum market demand). The remaining production capacity is shifted to ATB local.

The new plan calls for the production of 200 additional export ATB's at the expense of 200 local ATB's. This change leads to an improved net profit of €16 000.

- **Step 3.** Subordinate all other decisions to the decision in Step 2. This relates to the necessity for all processes to support the shift from local to export ATB's. One of the major implications is that excess capacity in Painting will increase. One of the implications of this is the necessity to reduce the cost of excess capacity in Painting as one of the TOC follow up decisions.
- **Step 4.** Elevate the capacity of the system. The new solution shows some production systems that are at full capacity, like Assembly and Upgrading (both at 100%). It also shows market constraints, like the demand for Cruizers and Export ATB's. The following step may be to increase the capacity of one or more of these capacity constraints. For instance by investing in additional production time of Assembly and Upgrading, or by generating more customer demand, using marketing campaigns or other forms of customer loyalty.
- **Step 5.** Search for new constraints. When the old constraints have been alleviated, new constraints may emerge. This may also happen as a result of changes in markets, in customer preferences and in production technologies. The continuous search for new constraints is a way to avoid inertia: in the new production environment it can be dangerous to become complacent with actions already taken. Recent measures taken may lose their positive impact very quickly in competitive market conditions and high paced technological developments.

8.5 Quality control

8.5.1 Quality economics

Before 1980, quality of products, services and production systems were considered important, but did not have equal importance to company management as immediate improvements of short term financial performance measures such as net cash flows, return on assets and net profit. However, gradually the rules of competition on the market place changed: the emphasis on product quality, product reliability and improved functionality gained more importance. Part of this shift was the successful introduction by Japanese companies of low cost and high quality products on the world markets. This market shift caused the need for management to incorporate quality costs and benefits in corporate decision making. One of the methods to introduce quality issues in financial management is the **Cost of Quality (COQ)** approach. This approach tries to quantify costs and benefits of quality control and quality improvement activities. These costs can be classified into four categories:

1. **Prevention costs** The costs of designing, implementing and maintaining quality assurance and quality improvement systems. Here we find costs for quality enhancement programs, investments in equipment, training of personnel and costs of preventive maintenance programmes.
2. **Appraisal costs** The costs of inspection in order to ensure that materials and products meet the required quality standards. Appraisals can be done by inspecting the quality of inputs, like raw materials and purchased parts, the quality of production processes and equipment, and the quality of finished products and of services.
3. **Internal failure costs** The costs of products that fail to meet the required quality standards. These costs can be the cost of scrap, rework, production downtime and discounts on sales of substandard products and services.
4. **External failure costs** The costs of responding to customer complaints, like cost of handling customer complaints, warranty costs, product replacement costs, freight and repair costs of returned products, costs caused by liability suits and foregone sales from loss of reputation.

These cost categories can be grouped into two parts: the cost of creating quality (prevention and appraisal costs) and the cost of non-conformance (internal and external failure costs). One may have some idea about how these costs behave and a possible pattern is represented in Figure 8.11.

Prevention and Appraisal costs are considered to have increasing marginal costs when maximum quality levels are approached. Internal and external failure costs are considered to lower when quality levels rise. The total cost of quality is the summation of both quality cost curves. This approach enables management to find an economic optimum when minimising quality costs. This would lead to the selection of optimum quality level A. In reality, however, the situation is much more complicated:

1. Quality costs are not systematically recorded in companies, which makes it difficult to come up with reliable cost figures for each of the four cost categories.
2. Most cost categories are not stable in practice: prevention activities can currently be factored into production systems, which may lower both prevention and inspection costs simultaneously.

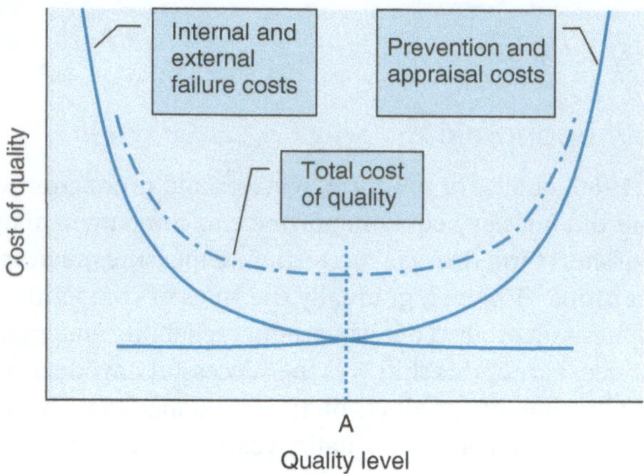

Figure 8.11 Total cost of quality

3. Our economic model almost exclusively focuses on additional, direct and tangible costs of quality performance. Quality costs cannot be considered a separate cost category. Most quality efforts are expected to also lower production costs. They result into less rework, a reduction in downtime, a better use of production time and materials, which lead to higher productivity.
4. A considerable portion of quality costs is opportunity costs: substandard products may cause customers to prefer other products, they may do harm to the brand image of the products and may put the competitive position of the firm at danger. Not only in the short term, but also in the longer term, these may add considerable amounts of quality costs (which we have labelled external failure cost).

When we take these complications together, they change drastically the quality cost curves in Figure 8.11. The net effect is that in this figure the internal and external failure costs are often underestimated, while prevention and appraisal costs are overestimated. Taken together, the adjustments may lead to a completely different picture, like the one in Figure 8.12 for instance. The economic optimum level of quality now has become to maximise quality levels. As already mentioned, the exact position and form of quality cost curves is undoubtedly very different for each company. The two examples are theoretical exercises to illustrate that the economics of quality management is heavily dependent on the assessment of costs and benefits of quality efforts.

8.5.2 Total quality management

Quality is a multi-dimensional attribute that can be defined in many ways. The American National Standards Institute (ANSI) and the American Society for Quality (ASQ) define quality as 'the totality of features and characteristics of a product or service that bears on its ability to satisfy given needs.' A more common definition is **meeting or exceeding customer expectations.** Central in this definition is the orientation on customer driven quality demands.

Quality issues emerged in the Scientific Management Movement at the start of the 19th century, when production activities were decomposed into small work tasks. In order to ensure that all production steps were executed correctly, independent 'quality control'

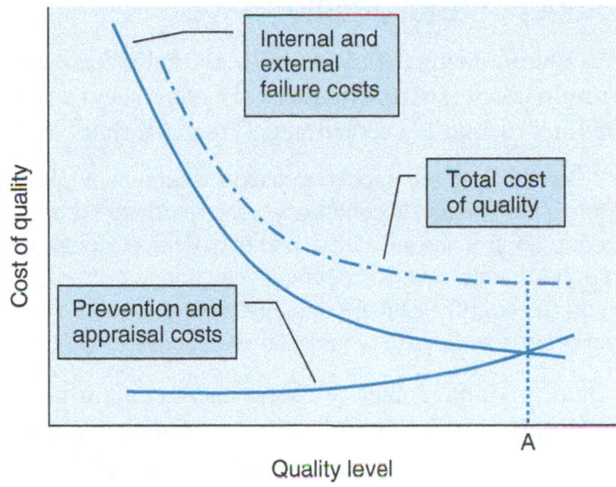

Figure 8.12 Total cost of quality revisited

departments assumed the task of inspection and quality improvement. In the 1920's, a new system of quality control emerged at the Bell Telephone Laboratories and at Western Electric. This system is based on statistical approaches to quality control, which used control charts, sampling techniques and statistical analysis tools for monitoring, analysing and improving quality performance in the work place. Especially W. Edwards Deming and Joseph M. Juran (both at Western Electric) have influenced modern quality management thinking. Mr. Deming introduced statistical quality control in Japanese companies after World War II as part of General MacArthur's rebuilding programme. His ideas were embraced by Japanese managers and introduced in their companies at a large scale. This lead to an improvement of quality levels at an unprecedented rate. Japanese products started to out perform Western products in the late 1970s and early 1980s. Deming was asked to assist US companies in their attempts to improve quality, and Ford Motor Company was the first to benefit from his advice. Within a few years, Ford had regained its strength in the automotive market and had improved profitability much more than any other car company.

The US president Ronald Reagan supported the quality movement by launching the Baldridge Award in 1987, which is designed to stimulate US companies' quality and productivity performance, to establish guidelines for improvement and evaluation, and to provide opportunities for companies to exchange experiences. The Baldridge Award is a yearly award for quality performance by companies in several categories, like manufacturing, small business, service, non-profit health care, and non-profit education. It builds on experiences with the Deming award in Japan, which was established in 1951 by the Union of Japanese Scientists and Engineers (JUSE). The Baldridge Award has currently evolved into a comprehensive National Quality Program, administered by the National Institute of Standards and Technology (NIST).[11] Other countries and regions have followed the Japanese and US example: in 1991, the European Foundation for Quality Management (EFQM), the European Commission and the European Organisation for Quality created the European Quality Award. This prize follows a similar evaluation process as the Deming Prize and Baldridge Award.

[11] For more information see the website at **http://www.quality.nist.gov.**

8.5.3 Principles of total quality

In 1992, the following definition of Total Quality has been developed by nine major US corporations in cooperation with deans of business and engineering departments of major universities and recognised consultants (Procter & Gamble, 1992):

> Total Quality (TQ) is a people-focused management system that aims at continual increase in customer satisfaction at continually lower real cost. TQ is a total system approach (not a separate area or program) and an integral part of high-level strategy; it works horizontally across functions and departments, involves all employees, top to bottom, and extends backward and forward to include the supply chain and the customer chain. TQ stresses learning and adaptation to continual change as keys to organisational success.

Total Quality Management (TQM) aims at combining six management concepts (Evans, 2005). The primary driver of TQ is the **customer and other stakeholders** of the firm. Their needs need to be understood and satisfied. Optimising processes can be done by following a **process orientation** instead of viewing the organisation as a hierarchical, or departmental organisational structure. This orientation views the organisation as a system of interdependent processes, linked laterally through a network of internal and external suppliers and customers. Because the organisation operates in a constantly changing environment, **continuous improvement and learning** is necessary to defend the firm's competitive position. In improving performance, companies need to build on the motivation, knowledge and skills of its workforce. They can do so by using **teamwork:** exchange of knowledge, ideas and capacity between internal groups and with external partners in the value chain. All these exchanges are meant to enhance **empowerment** of individuals and teams. The process of improvement is supported by objective and reliable set of **performance measures** at all organisational levels. They provide the factual information that guides behaviour and help managers to evaluate their performance. And finally, TQM requires **visionary leadership and a strategic orientation** that encourage organisational members to participate, learn, interact, measure and develop creative solutions for quality issues.

A large number of technical solutions to quality issues have recently been developed. Some of the most well-known methodologies are ISO 9000 and Six Sigma. The ISO 9000 standards are developed by the International Organisation for Standardisation (founded in 1946) in 1987 to standardise quality requirements for European countries.[12] The first edition and the revision in 1994 only required that organisations had a documented, verifiable process in place to ensure that they would consistently produce according to their previously established plans. The latest revision in 2000 sets more specific quality targets and quality procedures that align much closer to the TQ principles.

8.5.4 Six sigma

Six Sigma is a business improvement approach that focuses on outputs that are critical to customers and that have a clear financial return for the organisation. It emphasises the importance of fact based management by measuring objective performance data and using statistical techniques to analyse performance outcomes. Six Sigma is not a new idea in itself, since it follows the same quality improvement approach as Deming and Juran. In practice, however, Six Sigma turns out to be even more demanding than other statistical approaches

[12] The standards have been revised in 1994 and in 2000, leading to the ISO 9000:2000 family of standards.

that had been used before. Six Sigma was developed by Bill Smith, a reliability engineer at Motorola, during the mid-1980s. He convinced Motorola's CEO Robert Galvin to use this concept to improve final product quality testing (the current method over estimated final product quality) and to increase substantially internal quality performance. Six Sigma gained significant recognition when General Electric's CEO Jack Welch adopted the method for quality improvement in the mid-1990s. He described Six Sigma as 'the most challenging and potentially rewarding initiative we have ever undertaken at General Electric' (Lowe, 1998).

The term Six Sigma refers to six times the standard deviation as a measure of stability of a system or product characteristic: it defines the lower and upper boundaries of acceptable deviations from a production standard. Figure 8.13 represents the standard normal distribution, the x-axis represents the standard deviation. The corresponding probability density function shows that 68.27% of the observations are between -1 and $+1$ standard deviations (σ) from the mean (μ). Suppose we produced 1 million parts, and $\pm 1\sigma$ determined the boundaries of acceptable quality range, 31.73% of the parts produced would be substandard, that is 317 300 parts per million (ppm). In many cases, this is viewed as an unacceptably high defect rate: most production systems consist of multiple production stages that need to be connected, which means that the defect rate of finished products would be much higher than 317 300 ppm.

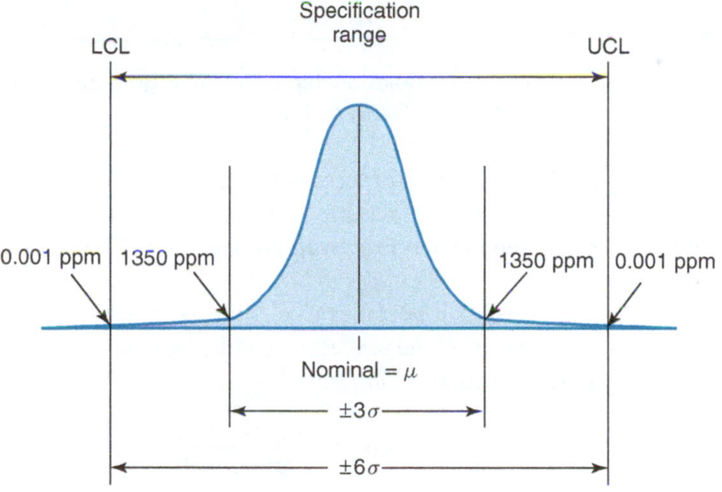

Figure 8.13 Six Sigma conformance levels (Breyfogle III, 2003, p. 13)

We could raise quality standards by looking at alternative specification limits (see Table 8.5). Six Sigma has raised the bar to $\pm 6\sigma$, which means that 99.9999998% of the products are required to be produced according to the established production standards,

Table 8.5 Different specification limits and corresponding ppm objectives

Specification limits	Percentage of products produced within limits	Defective parts per million
$\pm 1\sigma$	68.27%	317 300
$\pm 2\sigma$	95.45%	45 500
$\pm 3\sigma$	99.73%	2 700
$\pm 4\sigma$	99.9937%	63
$\pm 5\sigma$	99.999943%	0.57
$\pm 6\sigma$	99.9999998%	0.002

which leads to a required defect rate of 0.002 parts per million (ppm), or only two parts per billion units produced.

The relationship between sigma-levels and ppm is non-linear at an increasing marginal rate: at higher sigma levels it becomes more difficult to improve than at lower sigma levels (see Figure 8.14).

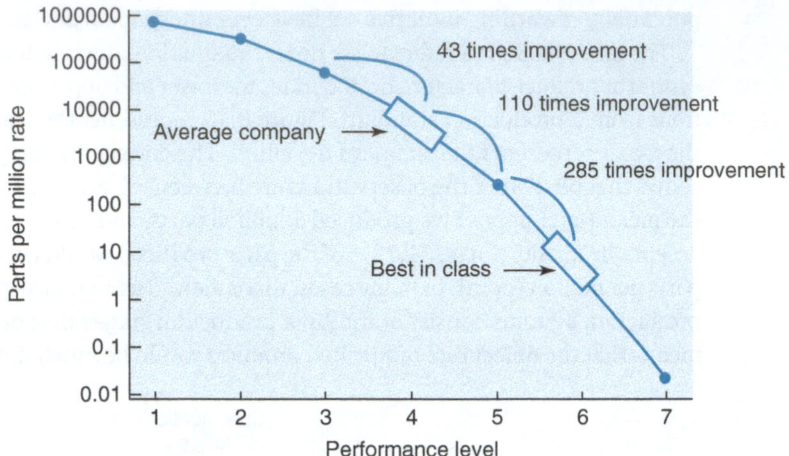

Figure 8.14 Relationship between Sigma quality levels and ppm rates (Breyfogle III, 2003, p. 13)

Consider the production process of *Coffee Delight,* a producer of coffee pads. From each production batch, five samples are taken to control the contents of each cup in grams. In one day, the company had produced 20 batches.[13] The test outcomes are represented in Table 8.6.

From these results, it becomes clear that the average weight of a sample cup is 33.55 grams. The variability of the process can be assessed by estimating the standard deviation of the sample observations as follows:

$$\hat{\sigma} = \sqrt{\sum_{i=1}^{n} \frac{(x_i - \bar{\bar{x}})^2}{n - 1}}$$

Where $\bar{\bar{x}}$ is the process mean over n samples (the mean from the test results, see Table 8.6), and $\hat{\sigma}$ is the estimated standard deviations of the whole population based on the sample observations from the tests. In our example, the standard deviation is 3.5287 grams.[14]

The process can be depicted graphically by so called $\bar{x}$ and R charts. The $\bar{x}$ chart depicts the sample means, while the R chart shows the sample's range (this is the variation between lowest and highest sample observation). Coffee Delight's $\bar{x}$ and R charts are represented in Figure 8.15.

As you can see, the $\bar{x}$ chart, which is a longitudinal representation of observations, can also be graphed using a histogram. The histogram shows the distribution of the sample means, whereas the $\bar{x}$ chart depicts the longitudinal development in sample means. This enables us to see possible trends in the data as time progresses.

---

[13] The numerical example is taken from (Breyfogle, 2003).

[14] This can easily be calculated using Excel's *standdev* function. This function is designed for sample data from a population, using the (n-1) argument. When the data comprise the full population, the function *standdevp* should be used.

Table 8.6 Coffee Delight's test results

Batch number	Weight of sample coffee pads 1	2	3	4	5	High	Low	Mean $\bar{x}$	Range R
1	36	35	34	33	32	36	32	34.0	4
2	31	31	34	32	30	34	30	31.6	4
3	30	30	32	30	32	32	30	30.8	2
4	32	33	33	32	35	35	32	33.0	3
5	32	34	37	37	35	37	32	35.0	5
6	32	32	31	33	33	33	31	32.2	2
7	33	33	36	32	31	36	31	33.0	5
8	23	33	36	35	36	36	23	32.6	13
9	43	36	35	24	31	43	24	33.8	19
10	36	35	36	41	41	41	35	37.8	6
11	34	38	35	34	38	38	34	35.8	4
12	36	38	39	39	40	40	36	38.4	4
13	36	40	35	26	33	40	26	34.0	14
14	36	35	37	34	33	37	33	35.0	4
15	30	37	33	34	35	37	30	33.8	7
16	28	31	33	33	33	33	28	31.6	5
17	33	30	34	33	35	35	30	33.0	5
18	27	28	29	27	30	30	27	28.2	3
19	35	36	29	27	32	36	27	31.8	9
20	33	35	35	39	36	39	33	35.6	6
							Totals:	671.0	124.0
							Averages:	33.55	6.2

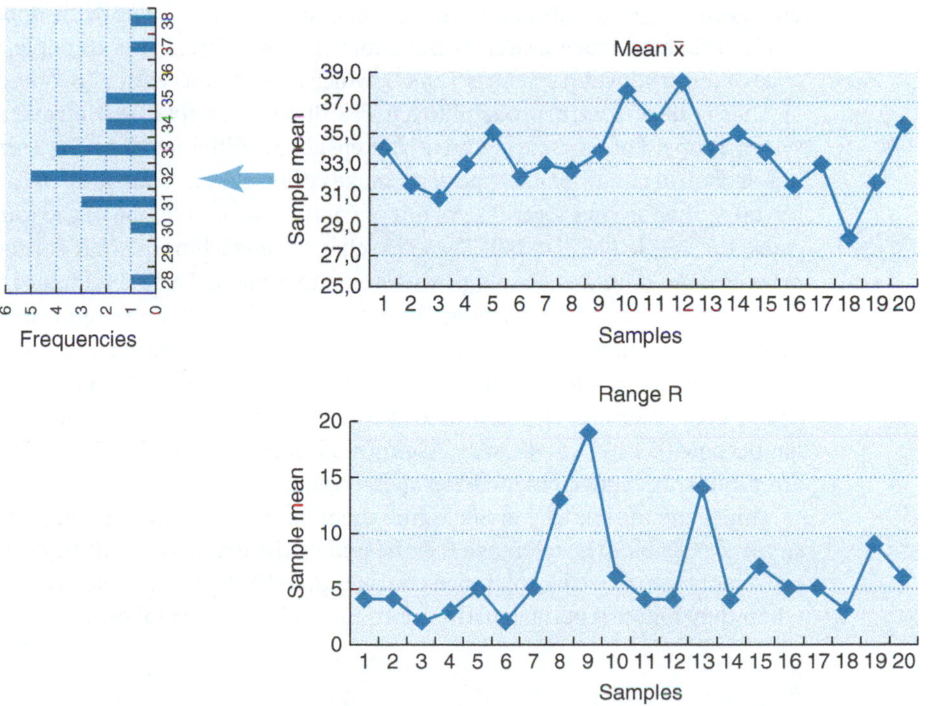

Figure 8.15 Coffee Delight's frequency chart, and $\bar{x}$ and R charts

From the histogram we see that the observations are (reasonably) normally distributed. A $\pm 3\sigma$ control interval captures 99.73% of all observations. In our example, these levels are:

$$\text{Lower control level: } 33.55 - 3*3.5287 = 22.96$$
$$\text{Upper control level: } 33.55 + 3*3.5287 = 44.13$$

This is still a reasonable large range: within these limits a cup may contain 22 grams or 44 grams (almost double). Whether this is acceptable depends on the control limits that are set by the process designers. Suppose the designers want to tolerate a minimum of 30 and a maximum of 40 grams per cup. Using the current production process, this would yield the following out of control incidents:

Surpassing the lower control level:

$$z = \frac{\mu - LCL}{\sigma} = \frac{33.55 - 30}{3.5287} = 1.0060$$

Surpassing the upper control level:

$$z = \frac{UCL - \mu}{\sigma} = \frac{40 - 33.55}{3.5287} = 1.8278$$

If we look these values up in the z-table, we obtain the chances that cups are lighter than 30 grams of 15.7% and cups that are heavier than 40 grams of 34%. This is the equivalent of 157 000 parts per million (ppm) which are too light, and 34 000 part per million that are too heavy. This makes the total number of failed products 191 000 ppm.

The inequality of chances is caused by the fact that the current average is lower than the mid-point between 30 and 40. The **tolerance** of a process is measured by the distance of the process average from specification limits. This distance is expressed in number of standard deviation units, which is the z-value. Unilateral tolerance is either the z-value of the upper or lower control level, the bilateral tolerance is the minimum of both values. In our example, the bilateral tolerance of the production system is 1.0060, which corresponds with a 15.7% out of control risk.

These out of control probabilities may still seem acceptable. However, most production systems consist of different consecutive steps. These different steps may compound the risk of out of control conditions. Suppose we make coffee blends, consisting of four different coffee flavours, that are put together. An out of control incident in one of the four coffees will also cause the whole blend to fail. The error chances in each of the four consecutive production processes are unrelated. In our previous example, we had a 19.1% chance that the blend filling is either too heavy or too light. This is the equivalent of 80.9% right sized blends. Suppose this part of the first production stage goes into the second stage and a second blend with the same error risk is added. After the second stage $(0.809)^2 = 65.44\%$ of total production is right sized. After four stages with identical error chances, the percentage right sized blends has become $(0.809)^4 = 42.83\%$. A fairly modest error chance has grown into a major problem after four consecutive production stages, causing the majority of the cups produced to fail.

This is the reason why in Six Sigma the tolerance of a production system needs to be as small as possible. The tolerance is expressed by the **process capability index C_p.** This index represents the allowable tolerance interval spread in relation to the actual spread of the data when they follow a normal distribution. C_p is calculated as follows:

$$C_p = \frac{UCL - LCL}{6\sigma}$$

When the actual mean is not in the centre of the control range, then we need a factor k that quantifies the amount by which the process is off centre:

$$k = \frac{|m - \mu|}{(UCL - LCL)/2}$$

The factor m is the mid point of the specification range, and is equal to [(UCL+LCL)/2]. The capacity index, corrected for off centre mean, then becomes:

$$C_{pk} = C_p(1 - k)$$

In our example:

$$k = \frac{35 - 33.55}{5} = \frac{1.45}{5} = 0.29$$

The capacity index for our coffee process is:

$$C_{pk} = \frac{40 - 30}{6 * 3.5287} * (1 - 0.29) = 0.3353$$

In Six Sigma terms, a process is in control when the C_{pk} capacity index is at least 2. Suppose we have a process that is perfectly mean centred, which leads to a k factor of 0. A ± 6 sigma controlled process has a total variation of 12 sigma's. Such a process would yield the following capacity index:

$$C_{pt} = \frac{UCL - LCL}{6\sigma} * 1 = 2$$

Using the Six Sigma minimum control requirements would lead to the following required standard deviation:

$$\hat{\sigma} = \frac{(UCL - LCL) * (1 - k)}{12}$$

This is a considerable reduction of variability in the system. The old and new 3σ control limits are inserted in a combined $\bar{x}$ and R chart (see Figure 8.16). Each vertical line connects the lowest and highest values in each sample. The markers indicate each sample's mean value. This chart can be created by using Excel's High-Low-End value graph facility.[15]

Under the new control requirements, 5 of the 20 mean sample values appear out of the 99% control limits and in the majority of the samples we have out of control units. If we

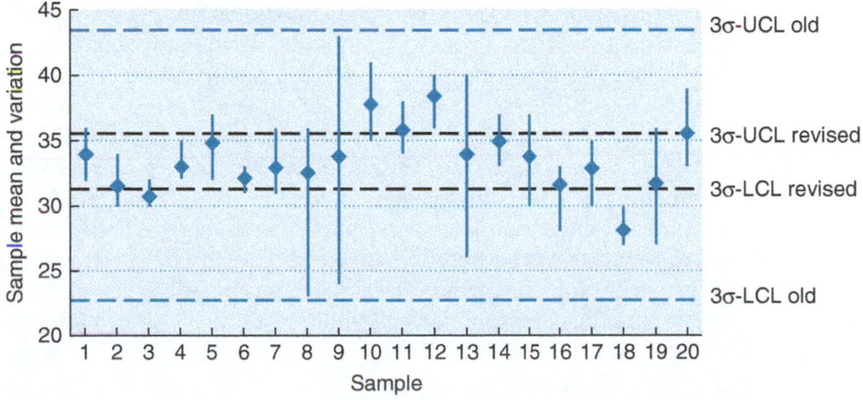

Figure 8.16 The combined $\bar{x}$ and R charts with old and revised 3σ control levels

[15] This graphing tool is originally intended to represent stock market shares movements.

manage to improve the production system up to the $\pm 6\sigma$ control requirements, the following parts per million performance will be realised:

$$LCL = \frac{33{,}55 - 30}{0.591667} = 6$$

which is a probability of 9.86588^{-10}, leading to 0.000987 failed products per million cups produced.

$$UCL = \frac{40 - 33{,}55}{0.591667} = 10.90141$$

which leads to 0 failed products per million cups produced.

Case: six sigma at Avery Dennison

The Frenchman Florian Fizaine is director of Enterprise Lean Sigma at *Avery Dennison,* a FORTUNE 500 global US based producer (NYSE:AVY) of pressure sensitive technology and materials, retail branding and information solutions, and organisation and identification products for offices and consumers. For 75 years, Avery Dennison has been a global leader in the market with sales of $6 billion in 2009, and employees in over 60 countries. Avery Dennison is based in Pasadena, California.

Avery Dennison started the Six Sigma program in 1995 mainly to reduce production costs. The consecutive phases of the program were to measure performance, to reduce variation and to improve the average value of production system performance. 'In the first years, Six Sigma has been very succesful in reducing costs and improving the use of production capacity', says Fizaine. 'In this first phase, Six Sigma was internally focused, while the complex statistics that comes with it was mainly used only by a selective group of specialists. Most of their communication with operators was by means of sample control charts.' Avery Dennison recently entered a new phase in which the company tries to involve operations managers and employees in continuous improvement activities that make the organisation leaner and that improve product quality. The firm does not exclusively use Six Sigma for this purpose, but combines it with elements of Kanban systems, Continuous Improvement programs and Lean Enterprise methods. Fizaine emphasises that the current phase intends to 'create an organisational culture of quality improvement in the value chain, cutting through functional specialisations.' This also necessarily brings together different specialists, not only from operations but also from marketing and product development. An example is Mr. Jan 't Hart, a Dutchman who works as Global Business Director Pharmaceutical Segment at Avery Dennison. He is responsible for product and market development strategies in the pharma division. 'It is important that the traditional Six Sigma internal focus on business processes is now complemented by a broader focus on external conditions, on the market and on what current and potential new customers want from us.' The current *Enterprise Lean Sigma* (ELS) program is used to reduce cost and improve service and quality in the supply chain. Performance improvement programs are not only focused on operational excellence, but also on excellence in other business functions, like human resources, information technology, finance and accounting

(Avery Dennison, *2009 Annual Report*, p. 4.)

8.6 Supply chain management

High quality demands, like we just saw under the 6 sigma approach, has led companies to specialise on specific production activities. This trend of specialisation also motivated companies to outsource parts of the production chain to other companies and to source from firms all over the world. This has brought the necessity for companies to collaborate and coordinate their activities in the **supply chain.** A supply chain is the collection of all consecutive production activities from raw material to end product delivery to the customer. Advances in information technology, new accounting measures and industry initiatives have all fostered supply-chain collaboration between companies. **Supply chain management** addresses the fundamental business problem of supplying products to meet demands in a complex and uncertain world. It looks at the supply issue at a multi-company level and aims at coordinating the activities between the participating companies to produce the products that are demanded by customers. Decision making in supply chains focuses on three main areas:

1. Strategic decisions about the structure and composition of the value chain: the number and location of production sites, the means of transportation between the sites and, for each facility, the installed capacity and technology.
2. Product decisions about the design, functionality, and quality of the products that will be produced in the supply chain.
3. Operational decisions about the use of the production and transport facilities in the supply chain, and the daily management activities to control effectively the activities in the supply chain (see also Chapter 11).

Strategic decisions about the structure of supply chains is mostly driven by the desire of the connected firms to match the quantity and quality of the supply of goods and services with customer demand. The first integrated supply chains in the 1980s were designed to attain reduced cost, faster delivery and improved quality. The basic objective was to make better use of installed capacity by reducing complexity in each step, by improving coordination across firms in the chain and by optimising the quality of each production process. The instruments we have discussed in this chapter are useful tools to optimise capacity usage, reduce costs and improve quality.

Modern supply chains are believed to have a more complex set of objectives, depending on the customers' needs they serve and on the competitive strategy choosen (Melnyk, et al., 2010). It is about combining performance on six basic dimensions:

1. **Cost,** the advanced functional specialisation between participating firms enables each firm to focus on a reduced set of tasks and to optimise efficiency of production, which may lead to cost reduction and ultimately to lower prices.
2. **Quality,** which includes security (goods should not be contaminated or otherwise unsafe) and sustainability (the products and the production processes should be "green", reducing pollution and waste, and improving the quality of the environment.
3. **Innovation,** supply chains are increasingly being used as a source for innovation: both within participating companies and between firms in the supply chain.

4. **Responsiveness,** the ability to adapt swiftly to changing customer tasts and preferences. Responsiveness requires the existence of stocks of goods and half products, and costly adaptations of production schedules. These conditions will eventually lead to higher costs.
5. **Reliability** and **Resilience,** the supply chain as a whole should be in control and should operate reliably and predictably. It should also be resilient by recovering quickly and cost effectively from disruptions caused by external factors, such as natural disasters, social factors, technological failures and economic downturns.

A supply chain needs to optimise the performance in those dimensions that are most valued by the chain's most relevant customers. The goal is to arrive at a blend of performance dimensions that differentiates a supply chain from its competitors. All chains may be successful in effectively serving their specific market segment. Some performance may not be optimised simultaneously because of possible trade offs. For instance, cost reduction may not be compatible with responsiveness or resilience, because both require additional resources enabling the company to respond and recover. A spider graph may be a helpful way to depict the specific blend chosen (refer to Figure 8.17).

Supply chains A and B have a broad area of multiple performance areas in which they excel. The main strengths in supply chain A is low cost and stable, uninterrupted business processes. Supply chain B puts its emphasis on quality, security and sustainability performance. Supply chain C is more focused on one performance area: innovation. This may be a strength, but it may also lead to an 'over-focused' supply chain that is not able to meet the other requirements of the new business environment.

Management accounting information plays an important role in the operational management of supply chains. A well-known trade off in strategic planning, product decisions and operational management of existing products is the one between inventory, flexibility and unfilled demand. Stocks can be used to buffer production numbers from demand. This may be necessary when certain production processes take longer than the maximum acceptable delivery time. Here management balances the additional cost of inventory against the opportunity cost of flexibility and the opportunity cost of unfilled demand. Flexibility costs are cost of excess production capacity that is able to absorb sudden demand fluctuations, cost of flexible production systems that, by changing to a different product type, are able to

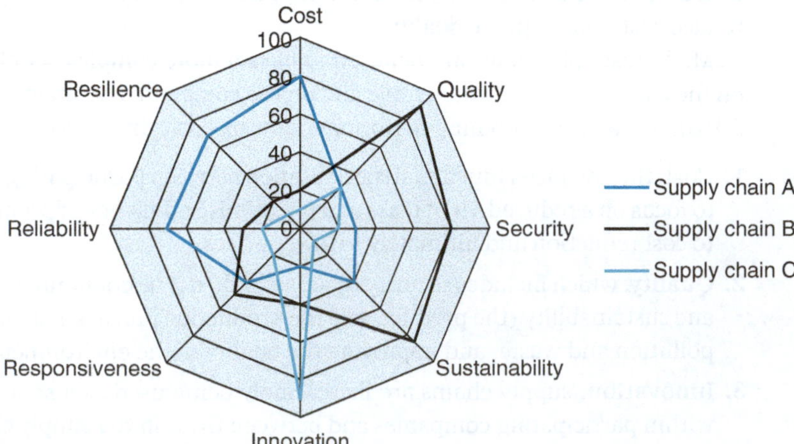

Figure 8.17 Different blending patterns in Supply chain performance

accommodate the required product mix, or costs of high speed delivery between processes in the supply chain. Some value chains have a mixed system: push-driven production systems of standardised half products in the first part produces for inventory and, in the second part, a demand driven pull system that operates on customer demand. The higher the inventory can be shifted upwards in the value chain, the more inventories can be concentrated, which may lead to lower inventory costs. However, this comes at the cost of more flexible production processes and higher speed of delivery downstream in the value chain. Linear programming models can be used to model and solve these dilemmas between inventory size, flexibility and unfilled demand.

EXERCISES

Exercise 8.1 Brunch Bakery

Brunch Bakery is a trendy sandwich shop in the centre of Amsterdam. They have a special concept in which they offer two types of sandwiches, but each with different flavours and other ingredients on it. The two types are called *Morning Star* and *Rise and Shine.* The latter consists of more exclusive ingredients. The *Morning Star* has a selling price of €3 and *Rise and Shine* sells at €5 each. Variable costs are €2 and €3.60 respectively. All sandwiches used are home made by *Brunch Bakery.* The process of making the sandwiches, consists of three steps, namely 'preparation' (kneading the dough), 'baking' and 'finishing' (slicing bread and topping sandwiches). The production time for each production step and the maximum available time are indicated in the table below:

Production data

	Preparation	Baking	Finishing
MS	4	2	1
RS	2	3	2
Available hours	900	1200	600

Required:

1. Define the optimal production plan for *Brunch Bakery,* maximising profitability.
2. Suppose Brunch Bakery wants to expand production. In which production process should they invest first?
3. Brunch Bakery has called in additional personnel and this has increased the time for Finishing from 600 to 700 hours. What is the optimal production plan? The Bakery does not produce nor sell parts of sandwiches.

Exercise 8.2 Sunshine Chairs

The small factory *Sunshine Chairs* in San Tropez, France, produces outdoor chairs and tables for use in gardens, balconies and terraces. All products are handmade and produced in sets of four chairs and one table. The company has already two different types of outdoor chairs and tables on the market: *Standard* and *Robust.* The *Standard* sets are low priced at €800 and light weight, whereas the *Robust* set is all weather proof and can be left outdoors during summer and winter. The *Robust* set sells for €1000. Cost of a *Standard* set is €700 and the *Robust* is €850.

Sunshine Chairs is considering the introduction of a new type of outdoor furniture, called *Romantic.* The chairs and tables of this type are more fancy, they should represent the good life of the French Mediterranean coast. The estimated variable cost of a *Romantic* set is estimated at €980. The company has not yet decided on the selling price, but it should be reasonable to fix it at €1200 per set.

All sets are manufactured by three production processes: Welding, Galvanising and Finishing. The technical production data are given in the following table, jointly with the maximum number of production hours available in each process.

Production hours

	Welding	Galvanising	Finishing
Standard	1	2	1
Robust	1	1	3
Romantic	1,5	3	4
Available hours	240	300	320

All data are needed to make the new production plan for the coming year. *Sunshine Chairs* is determined to introduce the new product and wants to come up with a profitable production plan for the new season.

Required:

1. Define an LP model and define the production plan for the coming year.
2. What could *Sunshine Chairs* do in order to make the production of *Romantic* garden sets an attractive alternative?
3. Suppose *Sunshine Chairs* could raise the price of Romantic sets to €1240 per set. How does the final solution look?
4. An alternative to raising the selling price is to economise on costs (restore the original selling price for Romantic). Suppose *Sunshine Chairs* is able to economise on welding hours for the Romantic from 1.5 to 1, which also brings down the variable costs to €940. Which alternative is better? Rising prices or reducing costs?

Exercise 8.3 Pedro's Italian Food Company

Pedro's Italian Food Company offers monthly service plans, providing prepared meals that are delivered to the customers' homes and that need only to be heated in a micro-wave or conventional oven. The target market for these meal plans includes double income families with no children and retired couples in the upper income brackets.

Pedro's Italian Food offers three monthly plans: *Standard Cuisine, Premier Cuisine* and *Haute Cuisine.* The Standard Cuisine plan provides frozen meals that are delivered once each month, and generates a profit of €125 for each plan sold. Premier Cuisine plan provides vacuum meals that are delivered twice each month; this plan generates a profit of €140 for each monthly plan sold. The Haute Cuisine plan provides freshly prepared meals delivered on a daily basis and generates a profit of €130 for each monthly plan sold. Pedro's Italian Food's reputation provides the company with a market that will purchase all the meals that can be prepared.

All meals go through food preparation, cooking and finishing steps in the company's kitchens. After these steps, the Standard Cuisine and Premier Cuisine meals are flash frozen. The time requirements per monthly meal plan and hours available per month are presented below.

Standard cuisine products require 2 hours of preparation, 2 hours of cooking, 2 hours of finishing and 1 hour freezing. Premier consumes 2 hours of preparation, 2 hours of cooking, 3 hours preparation and 1 hour freezing. Haute Cuisine needs 1 hour preparation, 3 hours cooking, 5 hours of finishing and no freezing. Total hours available for preparation, cooking, finishing and freezing are 80, 130, 180 and 60 respectively.

	Preparation	Cooking	Finishing	Freezing
Hours required				
Standard Cuisine	2	2	2	1
Premier Cuisine	2	2	3	1
Haute Cuisine	1	3	5	0
Total hours available	80	130	180	60

For planning purposes, Pedro's Italian Food uses linear programming to determine the most profitable number of Standard Cuisine, Premier Cuisine and Haute Cuisine monthly meal plans to produce.

Required:

1. Using the notations S = Standard Cuisine, P = Premier Cuisine and H = Haute Cuisine, state the objective function and the constraints that Pedro's Italian Food should use to maximise profits generated by the monthly meal plans.
2. We expect certain elements of the decision problem to change in the future.
   a. How would the optimal mix change if the price for Haute Cuisine were to be raised by €50 per plan sold? How would the value of the objective function be affected by the same change?
   b. How would the optimal mix change if the constraint for preparation were to be eliminated?
   c. How would the optimal mix change if the hours available for cooking were to be reduced by 30? How would this same change affect the objective function value?
   d. What would happen with the optimal mix if the profit of Standard Cuisine were increased by €10?
3. Pedro's Italian Food Company does not want to produce partial meals. Recalculate the optimal solution allowing for complete units only. What is the optimal product mix? What happened to the total profits? Why?

Exercise 8.4 Minimising costs at Petfoodies Inc.

Petfoodies Inc. produces animal food, which is delivered in packs of 10 kg each. For the production of pet food, the company mixes three different ingredients, namely Corn, Seeds and Additives. The costs of these ingredients are €0.40, €0.60 and €0.80 per kilogram respectively. Government regulation prescribes that each kilogram of pet food should contain at least 30% corn, 30% seeds and 10% additives. Additionally, each kilogram of pet food should have at least 400 Kcal in nutrition value. We know that each kilogram of corn or seed adds 400 Kcal, and each kilogram of additive adds 600 Kcal nutrition value to pet food.

For next month, the market asks for 100 000 Kg pet food, which comes down to the production of 10 000 packs of 10 Kg pet food. The price levels of ingredients on the market fluctuate considerably over time and Petfoodies wants to minimise costs as much as possible.

Required:

1. How much of each ingredient should Petfoodies buy on the market to produce the 10 000 packs of pet food required, under the condition of cost minimisation and adherence to government regulations?
2. Suppose the association of pet food producers offers to lobby for relaxing the composition and product quality constraints, which constraint would then be your favourite if your primary goal is to minimise costs?
3. The cost price of corn has risen to €0.70 eurocents per kilogram. Does this change the solution of the LP-model? How can you predict this?

Exercise 8.5 MP3 player Funky

A producer of MP3 players is currently specifying the short term production plan for the next period. The firm sells two similar types that differ somewhat in functionality and, therefore, in price but they are very close substitutes. The relevant numbers to specify the production plan are as follows;

Table 1 Basic information for Funky MP3 players

	Premium	Regular
Price	380	340
Variable cost per unit	160	140
Fixed costs for departments	800,000	1,200,000
Production time in department A	1.00	0.25
Production time in department B	0.25	1.00

The marketing department is estimating that it is able to sell a total number of 14200 products next month. Based on prior experience it is expecting that the product mix will be 1:1; thus for each product Premium it can also sell a product of Regular. The maximum production capacity of each department is 10000 hours.

Required:

1. Specify the linear program and compute the optimal production plan based on the information available. Describe the results from the answer and sensitivity report output. In which resources would you invest and why?

Top management is not satisfied with the profits and therefore asked both the marketing and production department managers to suggest improvements over this production plan. They came up with three alternatives

- to improve sales due to a decrease in price;
- to buy a new, more efficient machine;
- to influence the product mix.

Since the demand is binding, the marketing department manager is estimating whether a price cut would relax the demand constraint. Based on market research he assumes that a price cut of €40 for both Premium and Regular would increase total demand from 14200 to 16500.

2. Would this be profitable for the firm? How far could demand be increased before another restriction becomes binding?

In addition, production managers are exploring whether they are able to use other, cheaper, raw materials, or whether an investment in new machines that are more efficient would save production costs and lead to higher profits. Since cheaper material would lead to longer production times, they focus on new more efficient machines. Investing in new machines for Department A would imply that production time for Premium and Regular in Department A would decrease to 0.8 for Premium and 0.20 for Regular.

3. What would be the new optimal production in this case? (Start from Question 1 data, thus excluding the price decrease in Question 2, and the increase in demand to 16500).

The marketing department is also considering spending more effort on the most expensive product type (Premium), with the result that it is able to increase the product mix from (0.5:0.5) to (0.6:0.4) (for Premium : Regular).

4. How much would you maximum spend on this marketing campaign? (Again start from Question 1 data, thus without the impact of and Questions 2 and 3).

Exercise 8.6 Setting up an advertising plan for a new cellphone

Your company is planning a marketing campaign for the introduction of a new cellphone. Your marketing budget is €300 000 and the company wants you to optimise the use of this budget by reaching an optimal exposure for the new cellphone in the market.

You can use one, or a combination, of four marketing channels: television, radio, internet and newspapers. The following table shows for each medium what the costs are for a 'full campaign' and the resulting total audience.

Marketing costs and coverage

Channel	Full campaign	Max audience
Television	120 000	400 000
Radio	50 000	200 000
Internet	30 000	120 000
Newspaper	25 000	200 000

For each channel, a fractional campaign is possible. So if, for instance, only 50% of the full radio campaign is spent (for an amount of €25 000), around 100 000 listeners (half of the maximum audience) will be reached.

A 'full campaign' is an optimal size for the marketing campaign in a given marketing channel. When more is spent in a certain channel, the additional costs will only generate half the audience of the 'full campaign'. For example, €80 000 spent on radio commercials would lead to 50 000 * (200 000/50 000 = 4) + 30 000 * (100 000/50 000 = 2) = 200 000 + 60 000 = 260 000 listeners.

The company knows the composition of the audience in different marketing channels by sex (F = female, and M = male) and age, as follows:

The target is to reach at least 160 000 females and 210 000 males in the 20-30 year range, 160 000 females and 180 000 males in the 30-40 year range, and 130 000 females and 120 000 males over 40.

Audience composition by Sex and Age

		Age 20-30	Age 30-40	Age 40+
TV	F	0.14	0.22	0.15
	M	0.18	0.19	0.12
Radio	F	0.11	0.06	0.33
	M	0.16	0.08	0.26
Internet	F	0.34	0.18	0.02
	M	0.31	0.12	0.03
Newspaper	F	0.10	0.24	0.16
	M	0.12	0.26	0.12

Required:

1. What is the minimum marketing budget that allows the company to reach the stated marketing goals? (Hint: use as decision variables the number of people reached by each of the media, identifying in additional variables the number of people reached by extra campaigns above the number of people reached in full campaigns. The decision variable is number of people reached per Euro campaign money).
2. What does the reduced cost factor for television commercials above the full campaign numbers mean?

3. If you would like to make the additional marketing campaigns attractive, which channel is most close to becoming attractive?
4. If we would be considering to reach either more males of the age between 20 and 30 years or males between 30 and 40, which category should be chosen, if we want to do it at the lowest possible costs?

Exercise 8.7 Blue Note pharmaceutical ingredients

Blue Note produces three different ingredients for the pharmaceutical industry. In order to produce them, the company uses three departments, each one responsible for a specific production process.

- Chemical A is processed through Department 1 in batches of 100 litres. Each batch processed by Department 1 produces 70 litres of chemical B and 30 litres of chemical C. Processing costs per batch in Department 1 is €650.
- Chemical B is sold for €10 per litre. Chemical C is further processed by Department 2 to produce chemicals D and E. Department 2 processes chemical C in batches of 200 litres and total processing costs of Department 2 is €900 per batch. Each batch processed generates 100 litres of chemical D and 40 litres of chemical E.
- Chemical D is sold for €12 per litre. Chemical E can be further processed in Department 3 at a cost of €200 per batch. Chemical E is a hazardous product. Eventual surpluses of chemical E need to be disposed at a cost of €6 per litre.
- Department 3 processes chemical E in batches of 40 litres. Each batch produces 30 litres of chemical F, which is sold for €14. A complete overview of the production process is displayed in the figure:

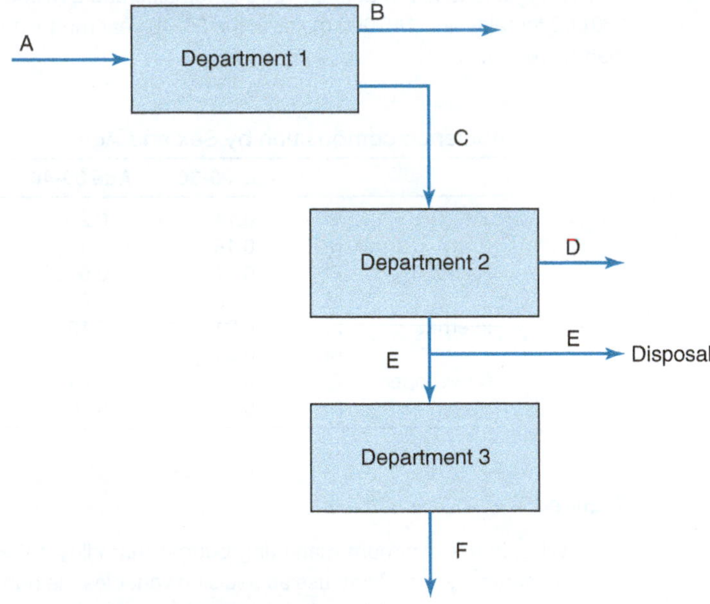

Blue Note's production process

The sales department indicates that sales of chemical B cannot exceed 35 000 litres in the coming period, the maximum demand for chemical D is estimated at 10 000 litres, and demand for chemical F is estimated at 15 000 litres maximum. Production capacity is limited in Departments 1, 2 and 3 to 600, 80 and 40 batches respectively.

Required:

1. Formulate an LP to determine the optimal production plan at Blue Note for the upcoming period.
2. Using Excel, solve the LP formulated in requirement 1 to determine the optimal plan (disable the 'assume linearity' option).
3. Which restriction should be relaxed first in order to increase profitability?

Exercise 8.8 Removing bottlenecks in operations (Goldratt)

Fruit Juicers Inc. produces three types of juicers: the basic model *Fruit Juice* (F) and two more advanced types: *Sunshine* (S) and *Cool Night* (C). The basic model is produced in two manufacturing processes: Production and Assemble. The other two products also pass through these two processes, but they require different methods of production and, therefore, consume different numbers of hours in each of the two processes. When S leaves the second process it goes through the final process Finishing 1. When C leaves the Assemble process, it goes through the final process Finishing 2. Both finishing processes are technically distinct and thus the number of production hours per unit is also different.

The standard product *Fruit Juice* requires 1.6 hour in Production and 2 hours in Assemble. *Sunshine* needs 2 production hours in Production, 1 in Assemble and 4 in Finishing 1. And finally, *Cool Night* starts with 1 hour in Production, 3 in Assemble and 2 in Finishing 2.

Total capacity of Production is 10 000 hours, of Assemble 15 000 hours, Finishing 1 is 12 500 and Finishing 2 is 8200.

Management of Fruit Juices has launched a new sales plan for the coming year in which the projected sales numbers are 2500 units of Fruit Juice, 3000 units of Sunshine, and 3500 units of Cool Night.

Required:

1. Use the TOC approach to identify the bottlenecks in Fruit Juicer's production process.
2. Follow TOC's incremental approach to accommodate the installed capacity to the projected sales numbers in the sales plan. What steps need to be taken to adjust the capacity to the plan?
3. A competitor in the upscale market has been withdrawn from the market. This leads to an additional sales volume for Sunshine, which will be increased from 3000 to 4000 units. The company is willing to invest in expansion of the production capacity in order to produce the required number of products. How much additional investment is needed?

Exercise 8.9 Improving quality performance ($\overline{x}$ and R tables, Six Sigma)

The company *Dairy Products* produces milk powder and other dairy products, like milk and butter. The milk powder is packaged in large sacks of 80 pounds each. The packing and filling machines used to put milk powder into these large sacks have not been operating well lately.

Dairy Products' management has decided to have a look at the $\overline{x}$ and R charts to see whether there are structural deficiencies that need correction. The samples are taken from the last fifteen days, one in the morning shift (a) and the other in the afternoon shift (b).

Required:

1. Make an $\overline{x}$ and R chart. Can you detect from these charts whether there are structural problems with the packing and filling machines? Which structural elements are visible in these charts?
2. The management team decides to impose a lower and upper control level. The lower control level is 70 pounds and the upper is 90 pounds. What are the chances of the existing system surpassing the upper control level? What are the chances of falling below the lower control level?
3. What is the Six Sigma capacity index for this process, if we correct the index for the mean being off-centre? Comment on the outcome.
4. Suppose management decides to apply the 12-σ distribution to the 70-90 control limits, reducing the risk of surpassing these limits. What are the new 3-σ control limits (make sure you take into account the mean being off-centre)?

Sample information (each sample contains 6 independent observations)

		Samples					
Batch		**1**	**2**	**3**	**4**	**5**	**6**
1	A	74	49	92	79	79	68
	B	65	84	76	91	71	80
2	A	65	96	78	78	79	82
	B	70	78	91	77	71	73
3	A	84	85	91	73	84	75
	B	75	71	81	77	91	81
4	A	84	94	83	85	68	70
	B	72	84	66	87	69	58
5	A	93	85	78	84	79	75
	B	82	84	77	81	86	83
6	A	83	75	83	66	66	67
	B	73	92	63	84	73	86
7	A	75	91	82	84	69	88
	B	71	92	85	86	72	80
8	A	65	97	82	87	84	68
	B	76	72	93	89	86	75
9	A	69	74	80	76	87	59
	B	92	77	68	83	74	84
10	A	71	99	77	86	73	74
	B	53	86	83	84	80	94
11	A	81	80	82	81	97	90
	B	98	68	80	90	64	83
12	A	71	93	71	95	79	74
	B	85	84	76	75	87	84
13	A	82	74	70	95	72	90
	B	67	97	91	80	76	71
14	A	79	71	68	86	71	84
	B	84	76	84	77	70	90
15	A	72	85	75	85	93	67
	B	97	70	79	81	84	85

References

Breyfogle, F. W., III (2003). *Implementing Six Sigma: Smarter Solutions using Statistical Methods.* Hoboken, New Jersey: John Wiley & Sons.

Cooper, R. (1995). *When Lean Enterprises Collide.* Boston, Masachussettes: Harvard Business School Press.

Evans, J. R. (2005). *Total Quality; Management, Organization, and Strategy.* Canada: Thomson South-Western.

Goldratt, E. (1990). *The Theory of Constraints.* Croton-on-Hudson, New York: North River Press.

Goldratt, E. M., & Cox, J. (1989). *The Goal* (revised ed.). Hants, UK: Gower Publishing Company.

Lowe, J. (1998). *Jack Welch Speaks.* New York: Wiley.

Melnyk, S. A., Davis, E. W., Spekman, R. E., & Sandor, J. (2010). Outcome-driven supply chains. *Sloan Management Review*(Winter), 33-38.

Porter, M. E. (1985). *Competitive Advantage, Creating and Sustaining Superior Performance.* New York: The Free Press.

Procter & Gamble (1992). *Report to the Total Quality Leadership Steering Committee and Working Councils.* Cincinnati, Ohio.

Riahi-Belkaoui, A. (2001). *Advanced Management Accounting.* Westport, USA: Quorum Books, Greenwood Publishing Group.

SECTION 3

Management control systems

Chapter 9

Transfer pricing for divisionalised operations

9.1 Overview

This chapter covers two related topics: management of divisionalised organisations and transfer pricing. The two are related when an organisation (firm, non-profit, etc.) divides its resources and activities among different sub-units (divisions, business units, etc.) and transfers items of value among them (goods, services, assets). The internal transactions are accompanied by bookkeeping entries to provide accountability and possibly to measure economic performance of sub-units and their managers. The bookkeeping is straightforward, but the apparently subtle addition of performance evaluation adds important emphasis to the values and meanings of the transactions. This emphasis on divisional evaluation adds the tension that creates enduring interest in the topic of transfer pricing. As a result, transfer pricing has significant implications for strategy, management control, production efficiency, international trade and taxation.

This chapter discusses:

- Alternative divisional structures that create tension between evaluations and transfer pricing;
- Quantitative and qualitative economic analysis of transfer pricing;
- International transfer pricing methods and complications.

9.2 Divisional structure, performance evaluation and transfer pricing

9.2.1 Divisionalised operations

A **divisionalised** organisation splits resources and activities among multiple sub-units or divisions[1] that have more or less operating responsibility and autonomy, along with varying degrees of direction from central management. Organisations may divisionalise for strategic advantages from distribution, differentiation and decentralisation. If designed and implemented correctly, a divisionalised organisation can be more effective and efficient than a firm that is completely centrally planned and controlled. The resources and activities of an organisation may be **distributed, differentiated, decentralised,** two of these, or all three, as indicated by strategy.

[1] We use the terms sub-units and divisions interchangeably.

Distributed organisations relocate certain resources and activities in divisions or sub-units domestically or internationally to achieve advantages of special locations. Location advantages include a) proximity to markets, suppliers, specialised or lower cost labour and materials and b) access to financial and tax incentives and tax advantages. For example, it is common for local governments to offer tax holidays or tax reductions to firms that relocate to their regions and hire local labour.

Differentiated organisations split the organisation by function, product lines, market region, or other meaningful distinctions. Differentiation allows the organisation to focus sub-units on sub-goals, such as production efficiency, product innovations, customer service or market share.

Decentralised organisations assign responsibility and authority for certain activities to relatively autonomous divisions. Whereas distributed or differentiated firms may retain central control and decision making authority, decentralised firms grant the sub-unit managers the authority to make business decisions relevant for the sub-unit's boundary of responsibility. In return, managers of sub-units are responsible and accountable for results. The benefits of decentralisation include:

1. Local managers should have better access and understanding of information about local costs, markets and new opportunities than a remote central management. They should be able to act more quickly to fix problems and seize opportunities without approval from higher management.
2. Decentralised managers can develop their capabilities to make independent decisions.
3. Decentralised firms can use incentives tied to divisional performance measures to motivate sub-unit managers to act for the overall good of the firm.

Decentralisation can have significant opportunity costs. Unknown to the firm, divisional managers might be unskilled; their information might be erroneous; and they might not fully reveal or properly act upon their information because of conflicting incentives. These are known as 'hidden action' and 'hidden information' problems that cannot be avoided completely by performance based incentives (see Chapter 12 for more on incentives). These so-called 'agency' problems may reflect managers' bounded rationality or incompatible incentives, but they are to a degree inevitable when the organisation assigns responsibility and authority to remote (unobserved) divisional managers. When the opportunity costs caused by these problems are unacceptably high, the organisation has incentive to centralise responsibility and authority.

Decentralised organisations often use performance based incentives that a) are appropriate to the boundary of the sub-unit's responsibility and autonomy and that b) will motivate and elicit efficient actions by sub-unit managers. The boundaries of decentralised autonomy and responsibility are reflected in common sub-unit types: cost, sales, profit and investment centres.

Cost centres are divisions that have autonomy and responsibility to manage their costs of operations, while meeting expectations for quality, time and innovation. Cost centres are often evaluated using the measures of operating performance described in Chapter 8, including control of costs, such as incremental, variable or full costs that are measured by traditional or ABC costing methods.

Sales centres are sub-units that have autonomy and responsibility to manage sales turnover and selling costs. Firms often evaluate their sales centres on sales levels, sales growth, market share or market share growth.

Profit centres are divisions that have autonomy and responsibility to manage costs and sales, and to meet profit expectations. Profit centres are most often evaluated on their (accounting) profit levels, achievement of profit targets in total or as a percentage of sales (also known as return on sales or net profit margin ratio).

Investment centres are sub-units that have the autonomy and responsibility to manage both profits and the assets employed to generate the profits. Both profit and investment centres may also be called 'business units' because their boundaries cover much of the decision making faced by stand alone businesses. Note that commentators may refer to a sub-unit as a 'profit center' when they really mean to say 'investment centre.' The difference is that investment centres are evaluated on measures that relate the profits earned to the assets employed. These measures include a measure of return on investment (e.g. return on investment (ROI), return on assets (ROA), return on earnings (ROE)), residual income (RI) or, its more recent form, economic value added (EVA).[2] A firm may choose to measure the performance of a profit, sales or cost centre as if it were an investment centre, because this could provide feedback on the success of the decentralised strategy. But one should take care to differentiate between the performance of the division and the performance of the division **manager**, if he or she cannot control investments. Chapter 12 discusses issues of incentives and controllability of performance.

9.2.2 Accountability for divisional results

Sometimes divisions are operationally interdependent; that is, they exchange resources (tangible or intangible) or products (goods or services).[3] In these operationally linked cases the exchanges of the items of value are accompanied by internal accounting transactions. These internal 'debits' and 'credits' firstly serve as necessary internal controls over the uses of resources. Consolidation of operating results and financial position for financial reporting, however, readily accommodate these internal transactions. Secondly, and more to the point of this chapter, these internal trades can affect decision making in the divisions. These trades can and should reflect the responsibilities of the divisions, for internal profits may be vitally important for assessment of performance and evaluation of divisions and managers. Poorly reported effects of internal trades can cause conflicts and incorrect sourcing decisions by managers who properly seek to improve their (internal) profits. The valuing and values of these internal trades comprise the topic of **transfer pricing,** and to that we now turn.

9.2.3 Basic transfer pricing

As illustrated in Figure 9.1, a firm might decentralise into a manufacturing division, **M**, that makes a product that can be sold by the sales division, **S**. If allowed, **M** might decide to sell its output to multiple buyers, including **S.** What if, for example, **M** could sell its output to an external customer at a price that is greater than what **S** is prepared to pay? Should the firm allow **M** to sell to the highest bidder, even if demand by **S** is not met? Should the firm allow **S** to purchase from other suppliers at lower cost, even if **M** has unused capacity to meet demand by **S?** If not, why not? These are questions and issues resulting from internal trade and the proper **transfer**

[2] Please refer to any intermediate level managerial or cost accounting text for descriptions of these alternative measures of performance.

[3] In other cases, however, branding and reputation link sales in one division to sales in another division, but no resources are formally exchanged. Are these divisions independent? Probably not, but valuing and charging for a brand 'externality' and the like is beyond the scope of this text.

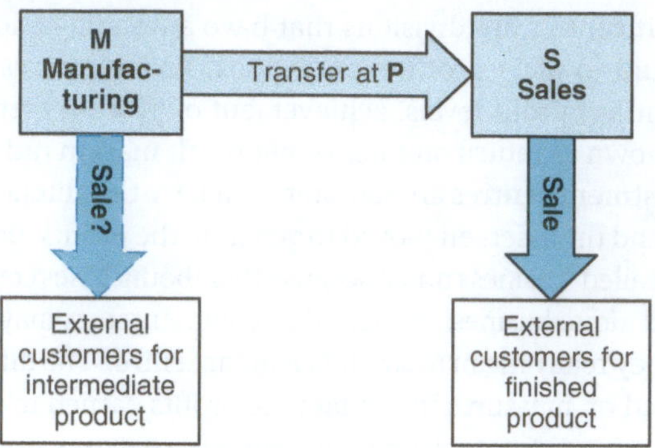

Figure 9.1 Basic decentralised, differentiated organisation

price, which is the price paid to the supplying division (M) by the buying division (S). **Transfer pricing** is the policy for how transfer prices are set and administered. Together, the transfer prices and transfer pricing policies comprise the **transfer pricing system.**

Of course, the transfer price, **P,** is not the only determinant of whether **S** buys from **M,** or whether **M** sells to **S.** Issues of strategic importance, supply alternatives and product quality, timeliness and flexibility can also be important to the sourcing decision. The transfer pricing system should strive to promote efficient product sourcing without impeding the advantages of the firm's divisional structure.

Normally, no profit is recognised by a cost centre, and transfers from a cost centre to another division are priced at cost. If **M** is a cost centre, it probably supplies its output only internally to **S,** so which measure of cost is most appropriate? Transfers at full or absorption cost at normal volumes allow **M** to recover its variable costs plus normal (fixed) capacity costs, whereas transfer volumes more (or less) than normal might require **M** to either acquire more (or idle) some capacity. Of course, transfers set by policy at variable cost avoid directly confronting **M**'s capacity cost issue but do not cover **M**'s fixed costs. Transfers 'at cost' can create some decision making ambiguity, which we will discuss in more detail later.

Transfers from profit or investment centres (e.g. **S**) normally are made to external customers at the sales price earned by the firm. The amount of profit that is recognised at the profit centre, **S,** depends on the transfer price paid to **M,** which becomes the cost transferred into the profit centre, and any selling costs incurred by **S.** If the transfer was from a cost centre (e.g. **M**), the profit centre may record all the profit (or loss). If the transfer was at some amount above cost ('cost-plus'), some profit (or loss) is recorded at the profit centre, **S,** and the remainder is recorded as the 'plus' to the supplying division, **M.** However, now the supplying division, **M,** is no longer evaluated simply on cost control, but also on an internal or pseudo profit caused by the 'plus' in the transfer price.

9.2.4 Cooperation and coordination among divisions

As just described, internal transfers can affect internal 'profits' of both selling and buying business units, even if external customers are not directly involved and perhaps without directly affecting overall profits. However, because the supplying unit's (**M**'s) revenue is an internal buyer's (**S**'s) expense, transfer prices can affect what **M** will supply and what **S** will purchase internally, which could adversely affect overall profits if the optimal amounts are not bought and sold internally. This can be a serious issue that affects divisions' decision making, their measured performance, and the firm's overall profitability. One solution to correcting sourcing decisions is for central management to require internal sales at dictated transfer prices, but this dilutes intended benefits of decentralisation. Thus, a firm may be distributed and differentiated, but not decentralised. This might be the intended implementation of the firm's strategy, but this does not create the benefits expected from decentralisation.

On the other hand, the firm might choose between a) operating **M** as a decentralised, pseudo profit centre and b) using an outsourced supplier of products to **S**, which is a true profit centre. The firm might favour using **M** as the supplier of critical inputs to the selling division, **S**, at a specific transfer price, **P**, that **emulates** the market price **S** would pay to an outsourced supplier. This transfer pricing system would retain profits otherwise sent to the outsourced supplier and would force **S** to be an efficient profit centre that consumes **M**'s output only if it can generate sufficient profit. The divisional and overall profit measures that result from internal transactions at the mandated transfer price 'at market' can signal the success or failure of this organisational strategy relative to the outsourcing alternative.[4] As we shall see, this seemingly natural arrangement may not be feasible when clear market prices are not available.

In all cases, the transfer pricing system should:

- Enhance local control;
- Facilitate resolution of internal trade disputes;[5]
- Motivate sub-units to source inputs efficiently;
- Support measurement divisions' economic performance;
- Provide an objective basis for evaluating divisional managers.

Transfer prices among interactive divisions can encourage these benefits or, if poorly designed, do great harm to the firm's strategic goals by failing to optimise on opportunities or by creating ill will through what are perceived to be unfair transfer prices. We will return to the issue of fairness later, but it should be clear that transfer pricing is very important in firms with interrelated divisions.

TRANSFER PRICING IN PRACTICE 1

Importance of transfer pricing

The global accounting and audit services firm, Ernst & Young, surveys its clients annually regarding transfer pricing practice. In 2007 Ernst & Young asked: *How important is transfer pricing to your success?* Responses by industry were as follows:

Few industry respondents (on average) indicated that transfer pricing is unimportant to their success, and most indicated that transfer pricing is very or critically important, particularly in pharmaceutical and biotechnology industries. E&Y's 2010 survey revealed increasing importance of transfer pricing over time.

[4] See also Perera et al., 2003.

[5] See Watson & Baumler, 1975.

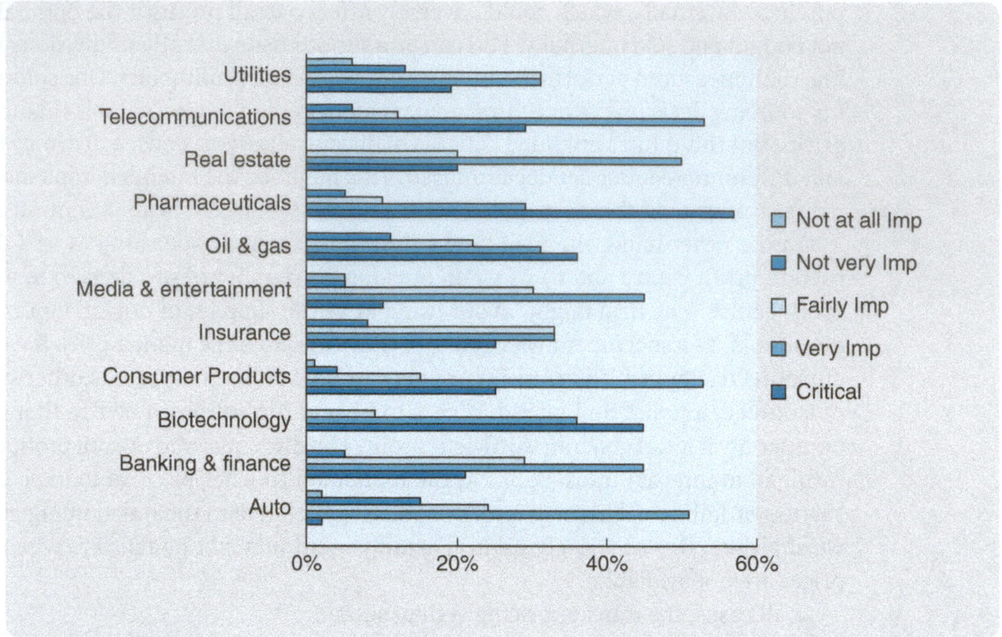

9.3 Economic efficiency

Transfer prices can affect decision making and internal trade among divisions. However, transfer pricing is not only a matter of how profit is shared among decentralised sub-units. Proper transfer prices also can lead to economic optimisation for the entire organisation and can support the expected cooperation and coordination among sub-units. Importantly, the converse is true. For example, transfer prices that are set too low in the manufacturing division, **M,** will lead to over consumption of resources by the selling division, **S,** and vice versa.

Achieving efficient transfer pricing depends on knowledge of intermediate and final product markets, internal operations and costs and, in the case of international trade that we will cover later, the rules and regulations of involved governments. Competitive markets without tax complications, our first example, permit full knowledge of all these factors. Although this appears unrealistic, it is a good and customary place to start an investigation of economic efficiency and transfer pricing. On the practical side, nearly competitive markets do exist in some cases, and as large firms continue to focus on strategic strengths, more parts of companies are spun-off, and more market prices should be observable.

9.3.1 Competitive market prices

Consider the situation where the company and its sub-units (and its competitors) have full knowledge of intermediate resource and final product markets. These markets are also perfectly competitive, which means that prices reliably portray values and scarcity of resources.[6] Further, let us illustrate transfer pricing with our simple decentralised firm that has one

[6] This is analysis of the basic transfer-pricing situation, which dates to Hirschleifer 1956.

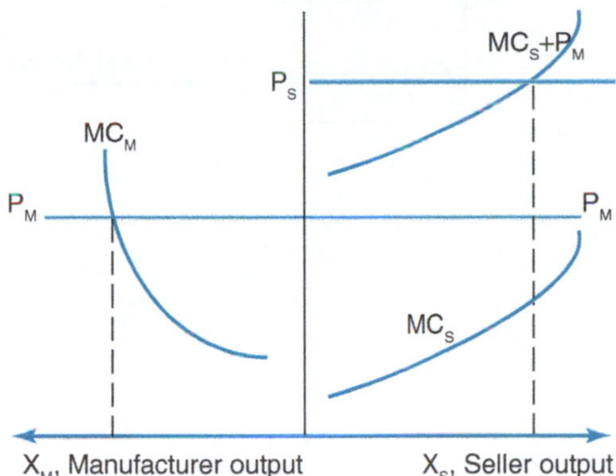

Figure 9.2 Perfectly competitive intermediate and final product markets
Note: The vertical axis is price; the horizontal axis is output.

manufacturing division, **M**, and one sales division, **S**, which also adds value to the product before a sale. This situation is displayed in the diagram of Figure 9.2, where the firm's goal is to maximise profits resulting from the sale of a final product that requires input from **M** and further processing by **S** prior to sales to external customers. Note that **M**'s output is shown reversed, to the left of the vertical axis.

M's optimisation problem is shown on the left of the vertical (price) axis. At the competitive price, P_M, for the intermediate product, **M** produces up to the quantity where the marginal cost, MC_M, equals P_M, denoted by the vertical dotted line on the left. Let us allow **M** to sell to any buyer at P_M, including to **S**, and for simplicity it sells all of its output to **S**, which pays P_M per unit transferred. If **S** is sized in a complementary manner to **M**, it processes the entire intermediate product purchased internally (note this simplification does no harm to the example because the intermediate product is widely available at the competitive price, P_M).

S' optimisation problem is on the right, where **S** adds its processing cost up to the quantity where its total marginal cost, $MC_S + P_M$, equals the competitive price for the final product, P_S, which is denoted by the dotted line on the right. Each sub-unit earns its competitive share of the profit earned by the firm, because each sub-unit operates in a competitive market. This competitive ideal demonstrates that transfer prices can promote overall efficiency. No coordination problem exists between organisational sub-units, because the market mechanism will ensure coordination through the market price.

This basic example demonstrates that, ignoring other benefits of decentralisation, it makes no difference to this company whether it acts as one organisational unit or as decentralised profit centres. Neither measurement errors nor cooperation problems will occur when all transactions are conducted at transparent market prices.

9.3.2 Absence of a competitive intermediate market

Optimal behaviour also can occur when a) no intermediate market exists for **M**'s output, b) both **M** and **S** know their cost functions, and c) **M** is considered a cost centre. The last consideration means that **M** should not be concerned with earning a profit, only with covering its costs of production (and maintaining quality, etc.). This situation is displayed in Figure 9.3, along with quantified examples of the divisions' known cost functions.

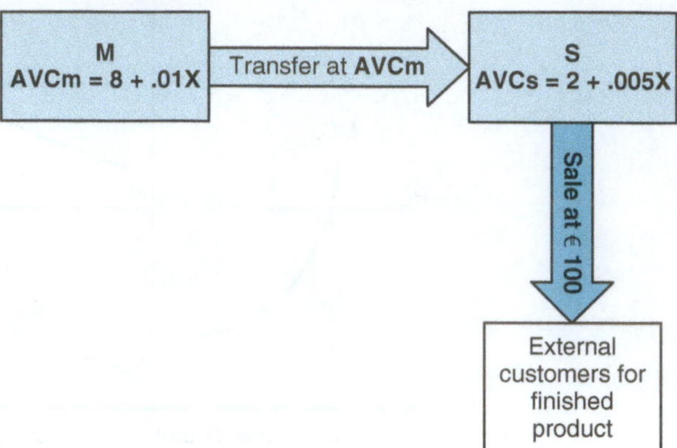

Figure 9.3 No intermediate product market, transfers at average variable cost

M's **average variable** cost, AVC_M equals $8 + 0.010X_M$, and **S' average variable** cost, AVC_S equals $2 + 0.005\ X_M$, (because **M** and **S** are sized compatibly).[7] **S** sells the firm's output at €100 per unit.

We compute the total variable costs of each division and the entire firm (f) as follows:

$$TVC_M = X(8.00 + 0.01X) = 8X + 0.010X^2$$
$$TVC_S = X(2.00 + 0.005X) = \underline{2X + 0.005X^2}$$
$$TVC_f = TVC_M + TVC_S = \underline{\underline{10X + 0.015X^2}}$$

We solve for the firm's overall marginal cost, MC_f, by differentiating TVC_f with respect to X:

$$MC_f = dTVC_f/dX = 10.00 + 0.030X$$

At firm's optimum production level, X^*, $MC_f = MR_f$:

$$10 + 0.030X^* = €100$$

Solving for X^* yields the optimal production level as computed below:

$$X^* = (100 - 10)/.030 = 3000 \text{ units}$$

The firm's total contribution margin equals:

$$TR_f - TVC_f = 100X - [10X + 0.015X^2]$$
$$= €135\,000 \text{ at } 3000 \text{ units}$$

If **M** has no other customers, the transfer price, **P,** that covers **M**'s total variable costs is sufficient to motivate and coordinate the optimal production level of 3000 units; that is:

$$TC_M = X(8 + 0.01X) = 8 \times 3000 + 0.010 \times 3000^2 = €114\,000\text{, or on average,}$$
$$\mathbf{P} = AVC_M = €114\,000 \div 3000 = €38.00$$

We now complicate this example with profit centre decentralisation.

[7] Assume that analysts discover average variable costs using a method from Chapter 5. Here we ignore fixed costs that we assume are sunk costs and do not affect the optimisation decision.

9.3.3 Incomplete markets and imperfect information, but profit centre decentralisation

Peter Drucker, management guru and originator of the profit centre concept in the 1940s and 1950s, argued for the creation of internal profit centres that simulate market settings and create market like motivations for efficiency. For example, our stylised firm that is differentiated by function (manufacturing and sales) also could be decentralised into two profit centres, even if **M** has no external customers.

Creating pseudo profit centers has had great appeal and appears to be commonly done in practice, even for divisions that have no external customers. The intent of creating so called **pseudo profit centres,** which only sell internally but really are cost centres, is to diffuse motivation caused by incentives based on profit throughout the organisation. However, simulating the power of markets to spur efficiency can have unintended, adverse consequences.

Because pseudo profit centres are evaluated on the basis of divisional profit, they may be reluctant to supply internally unless they receive sufficient 'profit' from internal sales. Without external market signals of efficiency and without the constraint of its cost function, a pseudo profit centre desires a pseudo transfer price, which may be negotiated or built by policy from average costs plus a desired (or 'reasonable') mark up that simulates profit (i.e. a 'cost-plus' transfer price).[8] Superficially, this situation resembles the example in Figure 9.2. However, the creation of the internal, pseudo market price also creates risks for opportunity losses by the firm. The 'plus' in the desired transfer prices can cause buying division(s) adversely to purchase less than the optimal level for the firm or to source inputs from outside the firm, also sending profit outside.

The pseudo-profits from internal trade can be real enough to divisional managers and can be powerful motivators. Peter Drucker (2002) later regretted applying the concept of profit centres to internal divisions that do not also sell to external customers. Drucker more recently argued that the only sale that does count, and that should count in measuring profit, is a sale to an **external** customer. If left uncontrolled, the pursuit of pseudo profits can nullify the benefits of decentralisation. Internal cooperation and coordination may be the victims of over-communicating the importance of profit to pseudo profit centres.

9.3.3.1 General problems of decentralisation without intermediate market prices

The problems of transfer pricing in firms decentralised into profit centres appear to be so pervasive that we elaborate the problems of cost-plus transfer prices:

1. The average cost as the transfer price base presumes efficient production by **M** (that is more likely in a true market setting). Enshrining the current average cost (and its inefficiencies) within the non-market transfer price provides little incentive to manage costs, particularly when **M** is guaranteed a marked-up 'plus' on its inefficient average cost.

2. The firm assumes that **M** reports its costs accurately and truthfully, when **M**'s knowledge might be imperfect and its reporting motives might be self-serving (e.g. to minimise effort while earning a guaranteed mark up on its costs).[9]

[8] Building pseudo prices from costs might seem an artificial and questionable practice. However, it can be an essential part of optimising profits **after tax**, as we shall see.

[9] This can also be a problem of outsourcing the supply of unique products to an external firm in the absence of market prices, and is a source of conflict in international transfer pricing.

3. **M**'s optimisation does not consider **S**' or the overall firm's optimisation problems. **M** will optimise to the cost based transfer prices, and its optimal quantity might differ from the optimal overall solution.
4. **M**'s guaranteed mark up might cause issues of perceived fairness and create conflicts between the sub-units. Fairness and conflicts might be resolved by allowing negotiated transfer prices, as discussed later.

9.3.3.2 Transfer price with no intermediate market

We now model a common situation wherein the firm knows the past average total costs, but the divisions have more complete and current information.[10] This example could change many choice variables to gauge the effects of departing from ideal decentralisation and transfer prices. However, simply adding to our previous example in Figure 9.3 the following reasonable changes moves the firm away from its optimal output, as calculated in Figure 9.4.

- **M** is a pseudo profit centre with an allowed mark up of 20% over accrual costs at a **normal** production volume (per *IAS 2*) of 3000 units per period. **M**'s fixed costs per period are €30 000. **M** continues accurately and truthfully to report its actual costs and accepts all orders from **S**.
- **S** is a true profit centre, with external sales, but is required to purchase M's intermediate product output at the marked up cost.

At the normal volume of 3000 units (the optimal solution in the previous example), **M** computes its transfer price, **P**, from the marked up accrual cost as follows (and in cells B7-B9 of Figure 9.4):

$$\mathbf{P} = €(8.00 + .010 \times 3000 + 30000/3000) \times 1.20 = €57.60$$

S adds this transfer price to its cost function to compute its marginal cost as follows (and in cells B11-B15):

$$MCs = \frac{d}{dX}(X(2 + 57.60 + .005X) + 12.000) = €59.60 + €.010X$$

This putative marginal cost leads S to optimise its sales level at the higher than optimal quantity of 4,040 units (as shown in cell 16). Both divisions (but especially **M** with a realised net profit margin of only 3.1%, €7168 ÷ €232 704) will be unhappy with the sub-optimal outcome, and the firm would regret the opportunity loss incurred in the amount of €16 224 (cell E26). **M**'s non-linear cost function drives costs differently than the linear accrual cost that is the basis of the transfer price, and the result is cost variances that should be expensed, because all units of the product were sold to **S**. However, the €31 616 cost variance (cells B30 and B21) could be charged to one or both of the sub-units' profit before being expensed by the firm. Neither sub-unit would want to bear the entire cost of the variance, which seems to be related to normal capacity. In reality, the cause of the variance can be traced to the profit centre strategy and transfer pricing system of the firm.

In this example, and assuming stable markets, a few order cycles might lead by trial and error to setting **M**'s transfer price at a 'normal' volume to 4000 units, which yields nearly the

[10] Activity based costing and other advanced costing methods, such as Resource Consumption Accounting likewise measure average costs, although at a finer level than traditional accrual accounting (Webber and Clinton, 2004). Although target costing has its own problems, its application here might create incentives to improve costs in the absence of true market pressures.

	A	B	C	D	E	F
1	**Pseudo-Profit Center Data**			**Per Unit**		**Per Period**
2	Sales price of final product per unit, X	€ 100.00				
3	Computed costs of mfg division, M					
4	Estimated cost function	€ 8.00	+	€ 0.010	X +	€ 30,000
5	TCm = X(8.00 + .01X) + 3,000					
6	Normal production volume, units	3,000				
7	Reported average cost per unit	€ 48.00		=(B4+D4*B6)+F4/B6		
8	Allowed markup	20%				
9	Transfer price to S	€ 57.60		=B7*(1+B8)		
10	Computed costs of sales division, S					
11	Transferred-in cost per unit	€ 57.60				
12	Estimated cost function within S	2.00	+	0.005	X +	12,000
13	S's average VC per unit, X	59.60	+	0.005	X	
14	TCs = X(60.50 + .005X) + 1,200					
15	S's marginal cost	59.60	+	0.010	X	
16	S's optimal quantity, X*, units	4,040		=(B2-B15)/D15		
17						
18	**M is a pseudo-profit center, S is a true profit center**	**Mfg Div**		**Sales Div**	**Total**	
19	Revenues	€ 232,704		€ 404,000	€ 404,000	
20	Cost of sales	193,920		101,688	$ 327,224	
21	Cost variances*	31,616				
22	Transferred cost			232,704		
23	Profit	€ 7,168	€ -	€ 69,608	€ 76,776	
24	Optimal profit if M is a cost center, S is a profit center				€ 93,000	
25	(previous example in Figure 9.3, less fixed costs)					
26	Opportunity cost				€ (16,224)	
27						
28	* Costs incurred for transferred items	225,536		=B16*(B4+D4*B16)+F4		
29	Costs of transferred items at transfer price	193,920		=B16*B7		
30	Cost variances	31,616				

Figure 9.4 No intermediate market, pseudo-profit centre, transfers at marked up cost

profit of the optimal sales of 3000 units by **S.**[11] This manipulation, however, begs the question of what normal volume means and whether accounting information should differ for internal and external reporting. This seems, rather, to be a sub-optimal outcome that is driven by a mistaken strategy to create a pseudo profit centre when a cost centre strategy (perhaps enhanced by target costing) would optimise outcomes.

The real issue for the firm is whether the opportunity costs of sub-optimisation by pseudo or true profit centres exceed the opportunity costs of a centralised structure that has noisier local information and does not infuse market like incentives throughout decision making. Because of imperfect information, this decision cannot rest solely 'on the numbers', particularly in the short-term.[12] Qualitative issues of supporting strategy by long-term negotiation, cooperation, coordination and fairness also can be important.

9.3.3.3 Negotiated transfer prices and fairness

When objective external prices are not available, some firms that use profit centres anyway choose to allow internal sub-units to negotiate their transfer prices rather than dictate the transfer price or the method. Negotiation preserves sub-unit autonomy and might be perceived as a more fair transfer pricing system by the participants than a mandated transfer price by top management. Even when external prices do exist, autonomous sub-units still

[11] Note that we have turned only one choice variable in this example. In practice divisions might also estimate their cost functions with errors, which might lead to sub-optimisation and cost variances, and divisions might not report truthfully or completely, or might avoid coordinating their activities.

[12] See Malone 2004 for an interesting discussion of this ultimately subjective decision.

might negotiate different transfer prices. This could foster communication and coordination, and result in transfer prices that are discounted from external prices, to account for saved selling and service costs that are avoided with internal sales. Eccles (1983) observed that perceptions of fairness were an interaction of the firm's decentralisation strategy and its transfer pricing policies. Mismatches of strategy and transfer pricing can be manifested as conflicts borne of perceived unfair profit distributions. Regardless, the process and outcomes of negotiation should be documented for learning and for external parties (e.g. tax and financial auditors).

Negotiation can also introduce a complication derived from division managers' relative bargaining powers and skills. Without the discipline of external market prices, the more skillful and powerful managers can appropriate most of the profits from trade, which calls into question whether the divisions should be profit centres, pseudo or real. The lesser division might feel that its share of the profits is unfair, which can lead to unproductive conflicts.[13] In contrast, negotiations between equals can lead to productive 'conflicts' that result in information sharing and a perceived fair distribution of profit. The firm may have a legitimate interest to provide transparent information to all parties and to train division managers in negotiating skills.

TRANSFER PRICING IN RESEARCH 1

Fair transfer prices

Luft and Libby (1997) assessed perceived fairness of negotiated transfer prices with a case based questionnaire. They found that respondents (executive MBA students) expected price concessions when external prices favoured one party, but not if external prices led to equal profit shares. However, respondents did not actually negotiate or face consequences of internal trade. Kachelmeier and Towry (2002) investigated two approaches to negotiated transfer prices in an experimental laboratory: computerised versus face to face negotiations. In the computerised setting, participants expected price concessions based on fairness to both parties, but concessions did not emerge during negotiations. Fairness to both parties did emerge as a main factor in the face to face negotiations. Thus, it appears that faceless, computerised negotiations tended toward efficient solutions, whereas face to face negotiations tended toward perceived more fair solutions. Should firms only conduct transfer pricing negotiations mechanically or online to increase overall efficiency? Perhaps not. Residual perceptions of unfairness might remain unresolved, unlike in face to face negotiations. Transfer pricing is a repeated process, and some inefficiency induced by concerns for fairness might be more than covered by the gains from future inter-unit cooperation and the elimination of conflicts.

9.3.3.4 Incentives and fairness of dual transfer prices in the absence of market prices

The difficulties of setting optimal transfer prices in the absence of external prices, first, might lead one to question whether pseudo profit centres are the right structural solution to optimising divisional decision making. Second, if management still desires to instill market like incentives caused by profits, some recommend the use of more than one transfer

[13] Also Chang et al. 2008 found that perceptions of transfer-price fairness differ whether a change in sub-unit profit is framed as a gain or as a loss.

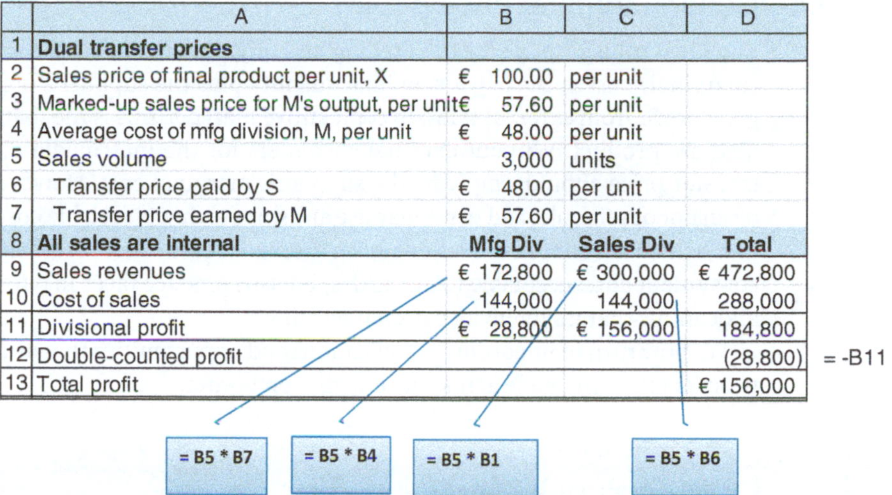

	A	B	C	D	
1	**Dual transfer prices**				
2	Sales price of final product per unit, X	€ 100.00	per unit		
3	Marked-up sales price for M's output, per unit	€ 57.60	per unit		
4	Average cost of mfg division, M, per unit	€ 48.00	per unit		
5	Sales volume	3,000	units		
6	Transfer price paid by S	€ 48.00	per unit		
7	Transfer price earned by M	€ 57.60	per unit		
8	**All sales are internal**	**Mfg Div**	**Sales Div**	**Total**	
9	Sales revenues	€ 172,800	€ 300,000	€ 472,800	
10	Cost of sales	144,000	144,000	288,000	
11	Divisional profit	€ 28,800	€ 156,000	184,800	
12	Double-counted profit			(28,800)	= -B11
13	Total profit			€ 156,000	

Figure 9.5 Dual transfer prices

price. **Dual transfer pricing** uses the transfer prices that should lead to optimisation by each party to the transaction, and simple bookkeeping to clean up residuals. For example, **M,** the supplier would be credited with a cost-plus transfer price, whereby the 'plus' generates an internal profit for **M.** However, **S,** the sales division, would be charged **M**'s marginal cost at its optimal quantity. This would induce **S** to order the optimal quantity for external sales, and **M** would earn a 'fair' profit on the exchange. Consider the following example in Figure 9.5.

This simple example shows that **M**'s €28 800 pseudo profit recognises what it would have earned, if it could sell its output externally at the marked up price of €57.60 per unit. This profit would be counted for **M**'s internal performance evaluation just as if it were true profit. The transfer price paid by **S** would be discounted by the amount of avoided internal selling costs, with no loss of profit to **M.** Because all of **M**'s sales are internal, no serious bookkeeping problems arise, and the pseudo profit is eliminated in cell D12. Eliminating **M**'s pseudo revenues and the double counted cost of sales also could accomplish this consolidation. Bookkeeping would be more complex if **M** had both internal and external sales.

Eccles (1983) observed that some firms use dual transfer prices temporarily to move the organisation to a higher level of vertical integration by stimulating internal sales. Eccles also observed problems that impeded long term use of dual transfer prices, including:

- Bookkeeping, reconciliations and performance measurement confusion often made long term use too complicated (improvements in information systems since 1983 probably have overcome this complication for most firms).
- Inaccurate sales forecasts lead to profit variances that must be allocated somewhere – no one wants unfavourable variances, and conflicts can arise.
- Because the sales sub-unit gets the intermediate product at cost, it has less incentive to monitor the efficiency of the manufacturing sub-unit.
- Unobservable costs and divisional market power create incentives to distort reported costs and prices, which impedes efficient transfer pricing (see Johnson et al. 2011).

9.3.4 General transfer pricing rules

The ideal transfer price for both selling and buying divisions is the supplier's out of pocket (marginal) cost at the buyer's optimal quantity plus the supplier's opportunity cost of foregone profit from external sales. In competitive markets, this is the market price for the intermediate product. Without external customers for the intermediate product, the optimal transfer price should simply be the supplier's marginal cost. However, marginal costs are often not observable, and firms may use an estimate that is variable cost, full cost or even ABC cost, which are short-term or long-term average measures of cost. Using 'full' costs might be convenient and acceptable to all parties, but this practice faces inevitable and arbitrary cost allocations that might invite external scrutiny.

We now turn to important complications and opportunities that arise from the scrutiny of transfers that are made across tax jurisdiction borders.

9.4 International transfer pricing

Multinational firms own and employ assets in foreign countries, and each country wants its share of taxable income derived from those assets. The taxable income in question comes in part from cross border sales via transfer prices between divisions. Firms naturally prefer to recognise as much profit as possible in low tax countries. Interestingly, firms that export items of value to sub-units in countries that charge customs duties or tariffs can expect upward pressure on transfer prices into those countries to create higher tariffs. Finding transfer prices that optimise production decisions, taxes and tariffs is a challenging task.

9.4.1 Transfer prices and income taxes

The multinational firm that transfers goods, services and intangible assets to foreign sub-units would like to recognise most of its profits in the lowest tax jurisdiction, if it is able. Consider the extension of our transfer pricing example from Figure 9.3, now as shown in Figure 9.6, where the only data change is the addition of differential tax rates for income recognised in either **M**'s or **S**' tax jurisdiction (cells B12 – B13). Assume, as shown in Panel A, that the firm optimises the production level at **M**'s marginal cost, MC_M = €68.00, and uses this as the transfer price to **S.** Panel A reflects pre-tax profit, as before, and also after-tax profit (row 21).

What if the firm optimised production with the transfer price of €68.00 but recognised intra-firm, cross border sales at a (dual) transfer price that minimised total taxes paid (or maximised profits after tax)? This is an optimisation problem (shown in Panel B) that Excel's Solver easily computes with some reasonable constraints:

- The transfer price cannot exceed the sales price (or some benchmark value, as discussed later).
- The after-tax profit of each division must not be negative.

This problem is shown in Figure 9.7, which is Solver's 'wizard' for this example. Upon completion of the optimisation problem, Solver places the tax minimising, single transfer price of €83 into cell B23 of Figure 9.6.

Note, however, that the solution in Figure 9.6 is for the optimal, pre-tax production quantity of 3000 units, which the firm would have to dictate as optimal for the firm. Perhaps the

	A	B	C	D	E
1	**Transfer Pricing with Tax Differences**				
2	Sales price of final product per unit, X	100.00			
3	Average VC of Mfg division per unit, X	8.00	+	0.010	X
4	TCm = 8X + .01 X^2				
5	Average VC of Sales division per unit, X	2.00	+	0.005	X
6	TCs = 2X + .005 X^2				
7	Total average VC per unit, X	10.00	+	0.015	X
8	Total VC = 10X + .015 X^2				
9	Total marginal cost (by differentiation)	10.00	+	0.030	X
10	Optimal quantity, units	3,000			
11	MCm = 8 + .02 X	68.00			
12	Manufacturing division tax rate	20%			
13	Sales division tax rate	40%			
14					
15	**A. Transfer Price equals Marginal Cost**	**Mfg Div**		**Sales Div**	**Total**
16	Revenues	204,000		300,000	300,000
17	Variable costs - Production	114,000		51,000	165,000
18	Transferred			204,000	
19	Profit before tax	90,000		45,000	135,000
20	Tax	18,000		18,000	36,000
21	Profit after tax	72,000		27,000	99,000
22					
23	**Tax minimising transfer price**	83.00		Found with Excel's' Solver	
24	**B. Tax-Minimising Transfer price**	**Mfg Div**		**Sales Div**	**Total**
25	Revenues	249,000		300,000	300,000
26	Variable costs - Production	114,000		51,000	165,000
27	Transferred			249,000	
28	Profit before tax	135,000		-	135,000
29	Tax	27,000		-	27,000
30	Profit after tax	108,000		-	108,000

Figure 9.6 Transfer pricing with tax differentials

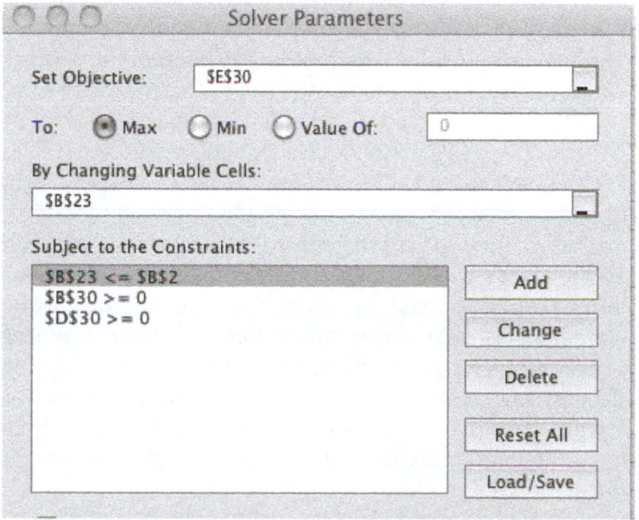

Figure 9.7 Using solver to optimise after tax profit

additional €9000 after-tax profit for the entire firm is worth an intervention in these decentralised divisions, but then the firm should consider whether profit centre decentralisation is appropriate. See also the 'research' box below for academic work on accommodating production and taxation considerations.

Left to its own optimisation, **S** would purchase fewer than 3000 units at €83, as shown below. Thus, maximising after-tax profits in this case would require the firm to encroach on the autonomy of the sub-units or to use 'two sets of books'–one for internal use and another for external use.

S's optimisation given the tax minimising transfer price.				
Tax minimising transfer price	€83.00			
S' average cost function	€2.00	+	0.005	X
S' total average cost	€85.00	+	0.005	X
S' total cost	€85.00 X	+	0.005	X^2
S' marginal cost by differentiation	€85.00	+	0.010	X
S' optimal quantity	1,500	units	= (100 − 85)/.01	

TRANSFER PRICING IN RESEARCH 2

One set of books or two?

The great majority of multinational firms (75–80%) report that they use the same transfer prices for managerial and tax purposes, presumably for simplicity and to avoid tax disputes. If considered separately, however, different transfer prices might be optimal (see Figure 9.6). It seems that firms could avoid the compromise that most likely is necessary to simultaneously accommodate tax considerations for transfer pricing. Perhaps a firm could use one set of transfer prices to motivate its interacting sub-unit managers to make optimal sourcing and production decisions that maximise profits before tax (e.g. transfers at marginal cost). The firm then could use a second set of transfer prices to minimise international tax liabilities. This practice probably requires that the internal transfer prices remain unobserved by tax authorities that might object to what appears to be duplicity.

Baldenius et al. (2004) argue that internal transfers of proprietary intermediate goods (with no external market) can be optimally priced at a single, 'weighted average' of the pre-tax marginal cost and the most favourable 'arm's length price' (as determined by methods to be discussed here later). In some conditions when the intermediate product can be sold externally, transfers at a discounted market price (arguably to reflect internal cost savings) also improves after-tax profits. Dürr and Göx (2011), demonstrate that 'two sets of books' instead can be optimal when markets are thin (few competitors) and internal transfer prices remain unobserved. In this case, the small number of competing firms could use cost based internal transfer prices (higher than marginal cost) to maximise pre-tax profits and use the most favourable arm's length prices for tax reporting. Interestingly, Springsteel (1999) reports that a majority of 'best practice' firms have used 'two sets of books' for transfer pricing. Whether the practice continues under tighter tax scrutiny is an open question at this time.

9.4.2 The arm's length principle

International tax authorities are keenly aware of firms' efforts to minimise taxes, and they might regard the example in Figure 9.6 as 'tax evasion' and intervene to reallocate profits and to insure that 'legal' taxes are collected. Many tax authorities (and customs, as we discuss later) have adopted or adapted transfer pricing rules from the OECD.[14] Simplifying and harmonising tax policies is one of the organisation's major recommendations for stimulating economic activities. Toward that end, OECD seeks to standardise the tax accounting for transfers between related entities by implementing the 'arm's length principle' as the general basis for transfer pricing. OECD defines the **arm's length principle** to mean that related party, controlled (intra-firm) transactions 'should be valued as if they had been carried out between unrelated parties, each acting in his *(sic)* own best interest.'[15] Formally, the principle is stated in Article 9 of the OECD Model Tax Convention as:

> Where conditions are made or imposed between the two enterprises in their commercial or financial relations, which differ from those which would be made between independent enterprises, then any profits which would, but for those conditions, have accrued to one of the enterprises, but, by reason of those conditions, have not so accrued, may be included in the profits of that enterprise and taxed accordingly.

Applying this principle entails determining what a comparable, uncontrolled price would have been realised for the same transaction between unrelated entities. OECD as well as non-member countries have identified multiple methods to establish and document an acceptable, arm's length transfer price.

9.4.2.1 Comparability

Many tax authorities (e.g. those in OECD countries, but also others) expect transfer prices to reflect the prices realised from **comparable**, independent trades, when available. If comparable trades are unavailable for comparison, transfer prices should yield net profit margins of comparable, independent firms. The definition of *comparable* includes many dimensions, including:

- Matching features and characteristics of products – identical products are ideal, but are rarely available for comparisons;
- Matching size, scope, industries, technologies, strategies and regions of companies on one or both sides of the trade.

Because exact matching is rarely possible, comparability may be documented as falling within a reasonable range of either prices or profit margins. Of course, one can expect some give and take between firms and tax authorities about whether proposed transfer prices achieve arm's length status.

It is interesting that companies in developing countries are reported to dislike the 'comparability' requirements imposed by OECD tax authorities because their acceptable 'comparable' firms might exist only, or mostly, in advanced countries. Such comparisons might put companies from developing countries at a disadvantage. Falcao (2012) documents that Brazil is implementing rules that do not depend on comparable firms but that place more reliance on published, stable, fixed profit margins over credible costs.

[14] The Organisation for Economic Cooperation and Development (OECD) currently has 34 member countries, and may add more in the near future. For more information see www.oecd.org.

[15] http://stats.oecd.org/glossary/detail.asp?ID=7245 and http://www.oecd.org/document/41/0,3746,en_2649_33753_37685737_1_1_1_1,00.html.

TRANSFER PRICING IN PRACTICE 2

Transfer prices and tariffs

Intra-company trade can be subject to customs tariffs as well as income taxation unless the trade takes place within trading blocks (e.g. European Union, Association of Southeast Asian Nations) or between countries with bilateral trade agreements. **Tariffs** are customs duties charged on the basis of the monetary values of imported goods, services and intangible assets. Tariffs may be levied in addition to income taxes on these items.

The objective of both the tax and customs authorities is to ensure that intra-firm trade is recorded on an arm's length basis. However, companies can experience conflicting pressures by the two authorities. The customs authority seeks higher transfer prices that maximise customs tariffs, while the tax authority seeks lower transfer prices that maximise taxable income and taxes.

In addition to the conflicting incentives of the authorities, differences exist between customs valuation rules, which are typically based on World Trade Organisation (WTO) guidelines, and the transfer pricing guidelines for measuring income from the OECD. A country's tax and customs authorities may use different rules for testing the suitability of a transaction's arm's length price. Consequently, the transfer price for purposes of a) corporate tax and b) declared value for customs purposes might differ materially. These differences exist at the country and transaction level, so there is no substitute for authoritative, local knowledge.

9.4.3 Estimating arm's length transfer prices

Multiple methods exist to determine arm's length transfer prices. Four of the most commonly used methods are:

- **Comparable uncontrolled price (CUP) pricing** The 'gold standard' because the CUP price is based on prices of documented, actual trades (transactions) between comparable, unrelated firms. This method might not be appropriate for transfers of unique, proprietary goods and services.
- **Cost-plus (C +) pricing** Transfer prices that reflect mark ups over verifiable product costs, which often are full or absorption costs because these costs can be or are verified by financial auditors. Comparable mark ups may be inferred by documenting gross profit margins of products from comparable firms. This method is most valid when the comparable firms have single or closely related product lines.
- **Transactional net margin method (TNMM) pricing** Transfer prices that reflect net profit margins (or return on sales ratios) of comparable firms. TNMM might be the least accurate because it reflects conditions when comparable single product firms', intermediate products or observable transactions do not exist. TNMM might be the easiest method to use because it is based on aggregate profitability of similar firms, not on actual transactions or similar product gross margins.
- **Advanced pricing arrangement (APA)** An APA is a negotiated transfer price between a company and the tax authorities of two or more countries in which the firm operates – the home country and one or more others. Documenting, defending and adjudicating transfer prices can be difficult, time consuming and uncertain. When a multinational firm anticipates extensive and long-term intra-firm trade between several of its operating countries,

it may seek approval of its proposed transfer prices in advance of increased trade. An APA is a contract between the firm and one or more countries' tax authorities that establishes acceptable transfer pricing and prices. Although APAs can be costly (in excess of €100 000 per agreement), they can be an attractive alternative to risking annual transfer pricing audits when arm's length prices are not readily available.

Example of cost-plus pricing

A mid sized German multinational wishes to use the cost-plus method,[16] which relies on comparable gross margins, for pricing trade between its industrial manufacturing division located in Germany and its European and North American sales divisions. After searching global databases by industry and size (in this case, with the number of employees > 1,000, but <7,000), the firm found 13 comparable companies for which sufficient, recent data are available. The final data for the 13 comparable firms, sorted by the gross profit margin, follow in Table 9.1.

The first consideration is whether these are comparable firms, but this judgment is complicated by the need for sufficient information. For example, the initial search (Hoovers.com) for industrial manufacturing firms identified more than 10 000 firms in this industry worldwide, but only 13 reported sales revenue, employment and information to compute gross profit margin ratios. Therefore, one must admit that Table 9.1 contains a sample of convenience whose statistics might not generalise to the population of industrial manufacturers. Often one must use the data at hand.

Assuming that the firms in Table 9.1 are a representative (and defensible) set of comparable firms, the next consideration is to measure the acceptable range of gross profit margins. Plesner-Rossing and Rohde (2010) report that many tax authorities rely on the 'interquartile range,' or between the 25th and 75th percentiles, of margins to benchmark proposed transfer prices. For the above sample of comparable firms, the inclusive (conservative) interquartile range is highlighted between gross profit margin ratios of 16.74% and 32.23%, which is the likely maximum allowed gross profit margin allowed, based on this set of comparable firms.[17]

The German multinational may document its product cost per unit and compute the proposed transfer price as follows.

Product cost	
Direct materials	€120.00
Direct labour	88.00
Manufacturing overhead	156.00
Total product cost	€364.00
Gross profit margin ratio	32.23%
Proposed transfer price	= Cost/(1 − GPM)
	€537.11

Of course, the company may choose to be more or less aggressive by its measures of costs, especially its allocations to manufacturing overhead, and the benchmarked gross profit margin ratio, here chosen at the top of the inclusive interquartile range.

[16] Applying the TNMM method would entail similar analysis, but using net profit margins rather than gross profit margins.

[17] Excel's PERCENTILE and QUARTILE functions (inclusive or exclusive) are easily used to measure the interquartile range. Inclusive functions use the nearest observation, while the exclusive functions interpolate to give more exact boundaries. Whether there is much difference depends on the sample size and differences in data values.

Table 9.1 Comparable Industrial Manufacturers

Company	Sales, $m	Employees	Gross profit margin	Location
Deutsche Steinzeug Cremer & Breuer AG	260.29	1372	58.42%	Germany
Actuant Corporation	1445.32	6200	36.82%	USA
Cardo AB	1175.22	5400	34.53%	Sweden
Elster Group SE	1759.34	6959	32.23%	Germany
Forbo Holding AG	1902.27	5943	32.01%	Switzerland
Deceuninck NV	739.14	2821	28.26%	Belgium
SteelisaPerma S.p.A.	908.62	1538	28.18%	Italy
FLSmidth & Co. A/S	3591.09	6862	25.81%	Denmark
PGT, Inc.	175.74	1200	23.93%	USA
Grupo Lamosa, S.A. de C.V.	707.66	5000	16.74%	Mexico
Roth & Rau AG	378.16	1209	16.28%	Germany
Samuel Manu-Tech Inc.	636.24	2969	14.68%	Canada
Cellu Tissue Holdings, Inc.	511.28	1245	11.00%	USA

TRANSFER PRICING IN PRACTICE 5

Uses of alternative methods

Many of the major accounting and consultancy firms conduct periodic surveys of their clients to capture current transfer pricing methods and trends. It appears that a) transfer price-triggered tax audits are becoming more common and more costly, b) certain methods are more common to different industries and c) preferences are moving slightly toward the use of more transactional methods. For example, Ernst & Young's 2010 survey offered these results.

1. Risk mitigation and audit defense are by far the most important priorities in preparing transfer pricing documentation efforts, which have not decreased despite adverse economic conditions.
2. The likelihood of tax audits (68%) is the major influence on choice of transfer pricing methods.
3. The definition of comparable firms is shifting to a more local basis, as local economies mature and as authorities increasingly reject documentation because of an insufficient use of local companies as comparisons.
4. The risk of transfer price audits is highest in developed, Western countries, but the risk has tripled in China and doubled in India in recent years.
5. Transfer price methods differ across types of transfers:

Methods Used	Tangible goods	Services	Intangible property
CUP	27%	21%	43%
Resale price	12%		
Cost-plus	30%	52%	
Cost		7%	
TNMM	23%	11%	21%
Profit split	3%		9%
Other	5%	8%	27%

6. The five most important transfer pricing audits (in order) involved intra-firm trade of services, tangible goods, financing, intangible property and cost sharing agreements (these also were the most common audits).
7. In response, firms are improving documentation and more importantly also making real, significant efficiency improvements to the organisations and processes for intra-firm trade.

9.4.4 Transfer pricing policies are costly, but mistakes are more costly

Faulty transfer prices can trigger large penalties and can also trigger customs fines. A U.S. pharmaceutical giant paid a $3.1 billion fine to the U.S. IRS in 2006 for faulty transfer pricing – and paid double the taxes due! Although most disputes are settled without fines (~ 80%), designing and defending practices is very costly. Globally and with good reason, transfer pricing is considered one of the most important management, tax and reporting issues by international firms.

9.4.5 Financial reporting complications

Goodwill assets can be created by business combinations (excess of purchase price over book value). IFRS 3 requires purchase price allocation (PPA) of goodwill across identifiable business units and assets. Both SFAS 142 and IAS 36 require goodwill impairment tests that can lead to revaluations of business units. Thus, write-downs may occur if business unit cash flow or profit (including transfer prices) cannot support (high) allocated fair values. Conversely, write-ups can occur if higher profit and cash flow result from transfer prices to (low) allocated fair value. Write-ups in particular could signal undervalued business units to tax authorities, who could assess withholdings for prior years that tax authorities deemed also to be undervalued. Reportedly, the complications of allocated goodwill are being flagged in transfer price audits in OECD countries. (Bjørn et al).

9.5 Summary

Financial performance measures at the division or business unit level are very important in business globally. Firms use these measures for:

- Implementing strategy;
- Keeping score;
- Divisions and managers' evaluations and compensation.

Because transfer pricing can greatly affect internal performance measures, internal profit calculations might be possible but might be unwise because motivations for private profit might impede desired cooperation among divisions. However, international transfer pricing is greatly affected by tax and customs authorities who evaluate internationally distributed divisions as if they were independent profit centres. Therefore, transfer pricing is a serious issue, affecting decisions about internal structure, location of facilities, production quantities, income recognition, taxation, tax planning and strategy, and profitability.

Tax authorities generally require arm's length transfer prices, but these are not always directly observable. Thus, multiple methods exist to estimate arm's length prices that require documentation and negotiation. Every country's regulations may differ, so local expertise may be needed to navigate transfer-pricing complexities.

EXERCISES

Exercise 9.1 Intra-firm transfer pricing

The primary product of the MaxStor Corporation is a memory device that is used in mobile phones, cameras and audio players. The MaxStor product (MSD305) is assembled in the Romania Division from components that are manufactured elsewhere. The most important component of the MSD305 is the memory cell that is manufactured in Germany under strict controls (one per MSD305) and is shipped only to the Romania Division for assembly in the MSD305. This memory cell is far superior to anything offered by competitors. Consider the following information for completing the requirements. (*Note*: Ignore taxes for parts a, b and c.)

Sales price of final product per unit, X	€32.00			
AVC of Germany memory division per unit, X	€7.50	+	0.025	X
AVC of Romania assembly division per unit, X	€2.00	+	0.006	X

Required:

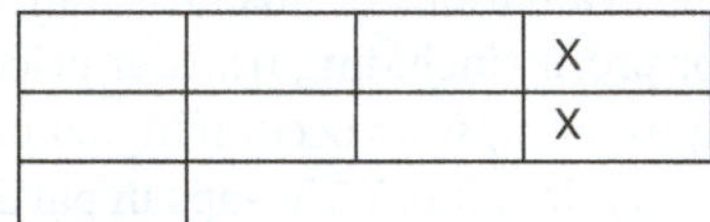

Total AVC per unit, X				X
Total marginal cost				X
Optimal quantity, units				

1. Complete the computations in the blank cells, similarly as in the example of Figure 9.3.
2. Compute by formula the optimal transfer price.

Optimal transfer price formula	Amount

3. If this transfer price is enforced, compute the contribution margins for the divisions.

	Memory div	Buying div	Total
Revenues			
Variable costs – production			
Transferred			
Contribution margin			

4. Briefly discuss complexities and managerial incentives of international transfer pricing in profit centres that sell to each other across international boundaries.

Exercise 9.2 International transfer pricing with tax differentials

Refer to Exercise 9.1. The corporate income tax rate in Romania is 16%, and in Germany it is 30%.

Required:

1. Similar to Figure 9.6, find the tax minimising transfer price for intra-company sales from the memory division in Germany to the assembly division in Romania.
2. Explain whether your belief whether this tax minimising transfer price is feasible.

Exercise 9.3 China's advanced pricing arrangements

Foreign investments and operations in China have grown dramatically in the past decade. The government of China has recently decided to administer 'advanced pricing arrangements' (APAs) for multinationals operating in China. Its first APA annual report (2009) (**http://www.chinatax.gov.cn/n8136506/n8136608/n9947993/n9948014/n10517889.files/n10518029.pdf**) has extensive information and statistics about its APA policy and current APAs.

Required:

You are a financial manager within a European electronics firm that is planning to expand its manufacturing operations in China. Review China's 2009 APA Annual report and prepare a 15 minute presentation on the APA policy and its implications for your firm's transfer pricing system, as it would apply to its Chinese manufacturing operations.

(*Note*: Several large, international accounting firms have prepared summaries of China's APA 2009 annual report. You may refer to these, but do not simply paraphrase or copy their analyses.)

Exercise 9.4 Estimate arm's length transfer price for a small firm

A small international industrial manufacturer (€20million sales turnover, 200 employees) in a developing country is preparing its proposal for the transfer price of an important, proprietary intermediate product. No comparable products are traded internationally, but a number of other small firms participate in this industry. Companies in this industry manufacture products for industrial use, including rubber and plastic products, packaging and containers, paper and paper products, and textiles. Many products in this industry are sold primarily for use by businesses rather than directly by consumers.

The company's product cost follows.

Product cost	Per unit
Direct materials	€1470
Direct labour	1650
Manufacturing overhead	4950
Total product cost	€8070

You have identified a possible set of comparable firms, as follows.

Company	Sales, €m	Employees	Gross profit margin	Location
Gruppo Ceramiche Ricchetti S.p.A.	94.59	537	64.37%	Italy
Proto Labs, Inc.	98.94	511	60.25%	USA
Alloy Steel International, Inc.	8.82	20	49.86%	Australia
Permasteelisa S.p.A.	109.08	541	28.18%	Italy
PFB Corporation	89.45	379	20.72%	Canada
WSI Industries, Inc.	24.96	76	19.80%	USA
Immediate Response Tech., Inc.	13.50	100	15.93%	USA
TreeCon Resources, Inc.	13.00	145	15.75%	USA

Required:

1. Discuss the appropriateness of the selected sample of comparable firms and what this means for defending transfer prices. *Hint:* see the discussion of transfer pricing in developing countries in the chapter and in the referenced article by Falcao (2012).
2. Measure the interquartile range of gross profit margins for these sample firms and compute an aggressive proposed transfer price for the intermediate product in question. Do you think your recommended price would be influenced by whether the company is more or less profitable than the sample of comparable firms? Explain.

CASES

Case 9.1 Transfer pricing for intellectual property

Some multinational companies have located research and development business units in India to take advantage of highly educated, relatively low cost scientific and engineering talent. The R&D activities in India often result in highly valued technologies and processes (especially in the eyes of tax authorities) that are shared with the parent companies' global operating business units. The transfers of R&D successes raise questions of identity, ownership, value added to final products and allocation of taxable income between companies' business units. The key to the last item is finding the appropriate arm's length transfer price.

Statistics cited in *Transfer pricing in Practice (page 30)* indicate that the most commonly used transfer pricing methods for intangible assets, such as intellectual property, are CUP (43%), TNMM (21%), Profit split (9%) and Other (27% - mostly royalty agreements).

Assume that you are consulting with a UK auto manufacturer, with a UK tax rate of 24%, that is considering establishing a R&D centre in India, where the corporate tax rate is 33%. The auto manufacturer's intention is that the Indian R&D centre will be focused on a) improvements to the electronic sub-systems of conventional autos and b) basic research and development for a new line of electric vehicles (EV).

Required:

1. Read the article 'Divisional performance measurement and transfer pricing for intangible assets' by Johnson.
2. Prepare a short report for the UK auto manufacturer that describes a) your judgments about the appropriate transfer price methods for the two types of products and b) how these transfer prices might be determined.

Adapted from: Arora, T., R. Mitra, and S. Gupta (2009).

Case 9.2 Estimate arm's length transfer price for a large firm

A large international industrial manufacturer (€4 billion sales turnover, 20000 employees) is preparing its proposal for the transfer price of an important, proprietary intermediate product. No comparable products are traded internationally, but a number of other large firms participate in this industry. Companies in this industry manufacture products for industrial use, including rubber and plastic products, packaging and containers, paper and paper products, and textiles. Many products in this industry are sold primarily for use by businesses rather than directly by consumers.

The company's product cost is as follows.

Product cost	Per unit
Direct materials	€2580
Direct labour	1440
Manufacturing overhead	4320
Total product cost	€8340

Required:

1. Find a set of comparable firms.
2. Measure the inter-quartile range of gross profit margins for the comparable firms.
3. Compute a 'safe' proposed transfer price for the intermediate product in question. Do you think your recommended price would be influenced by whether the company is one of the most profitable in the industry? Least profitable in the industry? Explain.

Case 9.3 International transfer pricing with tax differentials and tariffs

Tulip Technologies is a large Dutch manufacturing firm that has profit centre sub units located around the globe. Tulip Technologies is determined to harmonise and centralise its global financial services into several regional shared service centres (ssc). These SSCs are designed to provide financial services to all of Tulip's business units. The SSCs do not and will not sell financial services to independent companies. Implementation of the centralised, harmonised financial services has been complicated by the customs regulations of countries, such as Brazil, that are outside of Netherlands' trading blocks. Brazil charges multinational companies a 43% tariff on the monetary value of imported services. The intent of the Brazilian government is to create incentives for the development of local capabilities, by either multinationals or local entrepreneurs who would start independent service providers in Brazil. Consider the following data in completing the requirements.

Transfer pricing with tax differences and tariffs	
Comparable net margin (benchmark)	35%
Variable cost of services provided	€60.00
Full cost of services provided	€120.00
Cost of providing services in-country	€300.00
Cost of independent in-country services	€280.00
Arms-length transfer price	unknown
Brazil business unit operating sales revenue	€10 000.00
Brazil business unit operating costs	40%
Netherlands corporate tax rate	20%
Brazil corporate tax rate	34%
Brazil tariff on imported services	43%

Required:

Prepare a report to advise Tulip Technologies on its sourcing strategy in Brazil.

1. Consider both quantitative and qualitative issues in making your recommendation for this sourcing decision.
2. Discuss the advantages and disadvantages from using dual transfer prices in this situation.

Case 9.4 BigTime Accounting: transfer pricing and outsourcing

BigTime Accounting is an assurance services company with three autonomous divisions that are evaluated as profit centres. Consulting Division creates custom analyses and services, such as valuations and environmental compliance reports. Assurance Division provides auditing and internal control Sarbanes Oxley (SOX) services. Tax Division provides tax planning and tax compliance services. BigTime Accounting's sourcing policy is that each division may purchase and sell services internally or to external markets (subject to independence and quality restrictions), but each division is evaluated on its profits.

BigTime Accounting does not encourage its business units to discount its prices to meet competitor prices unless managers are convinced that price reductions reflect changed market conditions. However, BigTime also encourages divisions to employ its people productively to avoid large fluctuations in employment levels.

Assurance Division currently has an auditing client with operations in a part of the world where BigTime has an office that offers only consulting services. However, BigTime can work with several affiliated firms (i.e. with working relationships) in this location that offer a full range of services. Assurance Division must acquire tax liability and valuation services for its auditing client from either its own remote office or from its affiliates.

Assurance Division has received bids from BigTime's Consulting Division and two affiliates, Solo Services and Co-op Services. Consulting Division's bid for the valuation service reflected its normal pricing, which for the industry is cost plus 60%. Solo Services offered two bids – one for both tax and valuation services and one for each service separately. Co-op Services' single bid includes a price for both the tax service and co-sourcing the valuation services from BigTime's Consulting Division. Both Solo and Co-op argued that obtaining both services from the same provider will guarantee higher quality services because of the likely interactions of tax and valuation activities.

Consulting division bid	€5000		
Consulting division markup	60%	of total cost	
Consulting division variable cost	80%	of total cost	
Solo Services prices		Co-op Services prices	
Tax liability service	€6000	Tax liability and valuation services	€10 500
Valuation service	4500	Co-sourcing fee to Consulting Div.	3000`
Tax liability and valuation services	10000		

Required:

1. Identify and clearly label Assurance Division's multiple sourcing alternatives (e.g. Alternative 1, Alternative 2...) in the format shown.

Alternative 1. (label)	**(Copy and fill in for each alternative)**		
Service	**Valuation**	**Tax Liability**	**Both**
Source (label clearly)			Totals
Price to Assurance Division			
Transferred-in cost to BigTime			
Variable cost to BigTime			
Total cost to BigTime			

2. Calculate (and label) BigTime's costs of the available sourcing alternatives and identify the most profitable alternative.
3. Describe and explain the incentive and non-financial factors that might affect the sourcing decision by Assurance Division.
4. If Assurance Division obtains consulting services from BigTime's Consulting Division, what international transfer pricing complications should it expect?

References

Arora, T., R. Mitra, and S. Gupta. (2009). Transfer pricing of intellectual property in the automotive industry: A focus on India. PricewaterhouseCoopers.

Baldenius, T., N. Melumad, and S. Reichelstein, (2004). "Integrating Managerial and Tax Objectives in Transfer Pricing," *The Accounting Review,* 79, 591–615.

Bjørn. A., Lund. H., and Tseng. S. Financial reporting may create transfer pricing issues (www.kpmgvergi.com).

Borkowski, S. C. (2001). Transfer pricing of intangible property: Harmony and discord across five countries. *International Journal of Accounting* 36(3), pp. 34—374.

Borkowski, S. C. (2008). The history of PATA and its effect on advances pricing agreements and mutual agreement procedures. *Journal of International Accounting, Auditing and Taxation* 17(1), pp. 31–50.

Borkowski, S. C. (2010). Transfer pricing practices of transnational corporations in PATA countries. *Journal of International Accounting, Auditing and Taxation* 19 (1), p35–54.

Chandler, A.D. (1962). *Strategy and Structure.* MIT Press, Cambridge, Mass.

Chang, L., M. Cheng and K. Trotman (2008). The effect of framing and negotiation partner's objective on judgments about negotiated transfer prices. *Accounting, Organizations and Society* 33: 704–717.

Cools, M., Emmanuel, C. and Jorissen, A. (2008). Management Control in the transfer pricing tax compliant multinational enterprise. *Accounting, Organizations and Society* 33(6), pp. 603–628.

Cools, M., Slagmülder, R., (2009). Tax-compliant transfer pricing and responsibility accounting. *Journal of Management Accounting Research* (21), 151-178.

Deloitte (2011). *Strategy Matrix for Global Transfer Pricing.* Deloitte.com.

Drucker, Peter F. (2002). *Managing in the Next Society.* New York 10010: St. Martin's Griffin. p. 84.

Dürr, O. and R. Göx. Strategic incentives for keeping one set of books in international transfer pricing. *Journal of Economics & Management Strategy,* Volume 20, Number 1, Spring (2011): 269–298.

Eccles, R. (1983). Control with fairness in transfer pricing. *Harvard Business Review* (Nov-Dec): 149-161.

Ernst & Young (2007, 2010). *Global Transfer Pricing Trends, Practices and Analysis.* ey.com

Falcao, T. 2012. Brazil's Approach to Transfer Pricing:A Viable Alternative to the Status Quo? *Tax Management Transfer Pricing Report,* Vol. 20 No. 20, 2/23/2012.

Hirshleifer, J., (1956). "On the Economics of Transfer Pricing," *Journal of Business,* 29.

Johnson, N.B. (2006). Divisional performance measurement and transfer pricing for intangible assets. *Review of Accounting Studies* v.11: 339-365.

Johnson, N.B., E Johnson and T. Pfeiffer (2011). Dual transfer prices with unobserved cost. U.C. Berkeley working paper.

Kachelmeier, Steven J., Kristy L Towry (2002). Negotiated transfer pricing: Is fairness easier said than done? *The Accounting Review* 77(3): 571-593.

KPMG, (2011). *Compliance, efficiency, and growth in cross-border trade.* Kpmg.com

Luft, J. and R. Libby (1997). Profit comparisons, market prices and managers' judgments about negotiated transfer prices. *The Accounting Review* 72(April): 217-229.

Malone, Thomas W. (2004). *The Future of Work: How the New Order of Business Will Shape Your Organization, Your Management Style, and Your Life,* Harvard Business School Press.

McAulay, L., Tomkins, C., (1992). A review of the contemporary Transfer Pricing Literature with Recommendations for Future Research. *British Journal of Management* 3, 101-122.

OECD (2011). *Multi-Country Analysis of Existing Transfer Pricing Simplification Measures.* CENTRE FOR TAX POLICY AND ADMINISTRATION.

Plesner-Rossing, C., Rohde, C., (2010). Overhead cost allocation changes in a transfer pricing tax compliant multinational enterprise. *Management Accounting Research,* September pp199-216.

Perera, S., McKinnon, J. and Harrison, G. (2003). Diffusion of transfer pricing innovation in the context of commercialization–a longitudinal case study of a government trading enterprise. *Management Accounting Research* 14, pp. 140-164.

Springsteel, I., (1999), "Separate but Unequal—Transfer Pricing," *CFO Magazine* (August).

Watson, D. J. H., Baumler, J. V., (1975). Transfer Pricing: A Behavioral Context. *The Accounting Review* 50 (3), 466-474.

Webber, Sally and B Douglas Clinton. (2004). Resource Consumption Accounting Applied: The Clopay Case. *Management Accounting Quarterly;* Fall 6, 1; ABI/INFORM Global.

Chapter 10

Integrated financial and non-financial measures

10.1 Introduction

10.1.1 Market developments

The business environment in which organisations operate has increasingly become more turbulent and uncertain. Many countries have opened up their markets for foreign companies and lowered trade barriers. Well-known examples are China, Russia and some Latin-American countries like Brazil and Mexico. Regional and worldwide trade agreements lead to the globalisation of markets, which attracts more and new entrants in local market places who have not been there before. They sometimes introduce new products and sometimes cheaper products with the same functionality and comparable quality. Markets provide much more opportunities for niche players to become successful. In an open market, it has become easier for small companies to challenge large, established multinationals on certain offerings in which they manage to excel. For example the Ben and Jerry's ice cream started in 1978 as a small local business in a renovated gas station in downtown Burlington, Vermont. The niche they created in the ice cream market challenged market positions of Unilever and other large multinationals. Small companies can also become important players by using strategic alliances with other companies to generate sufficient funds, to acquire know-how and experience, and to gain access to markets that otherwise may have been inaccessible for them.

Lower trade barriers, open markets, and the free entry and exit of companies make markets more volatile, uncertain and competitive. The development of markets that are in constant disequilibrium and change is also stimulated by the difficulty for companies to effectively protect their technological know-how. Innovations are almost instantaneously copied by competitors and built into products that are sometimes even better than the first mover's innovative product. An historic example is the Japanese car industry that improved during the 1970s and 1980s both functionality and quality of cars that they seriously challenged the US and European car manufacturers. More recent examples are the rapid technological development of Chinese manufacturing firms and the swift imitation of Apple's iPad.

Apple's iPad

On 27 January 2010, the late Apple CEO Steve Jobs announced the Apple's highly anticipated tablet computer: the iPad. In the following 80 days, one million iPads were sold. The iPad reached this sales number in half the time the iPhone needed. Competing firms started to introduce their tablet computer versions in 2010 and mostly 2011. Archos improved their 2009 tablet computer, Hewlett-Packard introduced Slate 500 (Windows platform), Research in Motion (RIM) launched their PlayBook (Unix-type operating system), Samsung presented the Galaxy Tab, Dell the Streak (Android operating system), and Kno the Linux. During the introduction period of new competitive products, Apple already replaced the iPad by the iPad2 on 2 March 2011. The new iPad is thinner, lighter, has a faster operating system, has two cameras and sells at the same price as the original iPad.

Richard d'Aveni has coined the new market environment as 'hypercompetition'.[1] Hypercompetitive markets are created by the dynamics of strategic manoeuvering of firms, in which the frequency, boldness and aggressiveness of dynamic moves and counter moves by firms create a condition of constant disequilibrium and change. In our example, even Apple itself increases market dynamics by replacing a technology that has not yet reached the end of its lifecycle by a more advanced product.

What strategic responses should companies provide when confronted with highly competitive conditions? Michael Porter suggests adopting one of three **generic strategies:** cost leadership, differentiation or a focus strategy.[2] The basic idea behind these alternative strategies is to find a position in the market where competition is less severe and where the company can reach a reasonable profit level that is sustainable for a certain period. A cost leader can make above average returns because of cost efficiencies that are not easily attainable by competitors. In similar vein, differentiators are able to generate above average sustainable returns when they add value, for instance in improved functionality and higher quality, to their products for which customers are willing to pay a price supplement that is higher than the added value cost. Under a focus strategy, firms make a strategy choice for specific market segments, which means that they may pursue different strategies in different market segments at the same time. The more stable the market position is, the longer firms may expect to make above average returns. Porter's three generic strategies aim at bringing firms in such a position in competitive markets that their position cannot be threatened easily by their competitors. This will enable firms to generate profits that are sustainable for some time. Hypercompetitive markets however, limit the possibilities of firms to maintain a competitive advantage for a longer period. Under hypercompetitive market conditions, firms compete head-on for their share of the market by developing and exploiting **temporary** competitive advantages. Robin Cooper labelled this approach the 'confrontation strategy',[3] because firms under these conditions expect that differentiating and price dropping strategies will soon be followed by similar moves from competitors. Hypercompetitive markets make it increasingly difficult for firms to find a competitive position, which secures profits that are sustainable for a longer period. Viewed in this way, the hypercompetitive markets approach the condition of **perfect competition:** under

[1] (D'Aveni, 1994, 1995).

[2] (Porter, 1985; Porter & Linde, 1995)

[3] (Cooper, 1995)

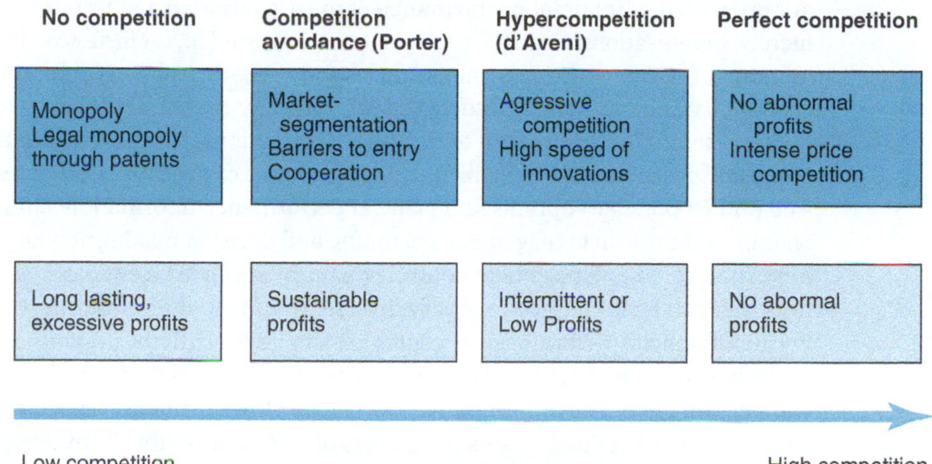

Figure 10.1 Market structures and competitive outcomes (based on D'Aveni, 1994)

perfect competition, prices are known to all competitors, and each competitor is able to adapt quickly and effectively to movements in prices and product characteristics. Under perfect competition, it is no longer possible to generate abnormal profits (see Figure 10.1).

How should firm strategy deal with increased competitive pressures? Firms should at least focus on three important competitive areas: **product characteristics, timing** and **resources.**

As Cooper shows, firms increasingly compete on basically three product characteristics: price, quality and functionality. Functionality refers to the abilities and characteristics of the product, for instance the size of cargo that can be moved by a truck, or the ease of operation of a hard-disk recorder. Products having equivalent characteristics define relevant markets. Successful companies generate products and services that are equivalent to other products, and manage to outperform them on one or more dimensions, e.g. lower prices, higher quality and functionality that customers perceive to be superior.

Important for success is not only reducing prices and improving quality and functionality, but also the timing of events. The introduction of innovations can be done by surprise, and some firms try to keep the momentum by improving their product characteristics at such a high pace that it is difficult for competitors to catch up. Both the capacity to improve product characteristics as the timing of innovations is highly dependent on the firm's resources.

Resources are assets, capabilities (like know-how and experience) and activities that are brought together (combined and re-configured) in resource bundles in such a way that they make firms outperform other firms in the marketplace.[4] The more unique and less imitable the bundles of resources are, the more sustainable the competitive advantages become.

10.1.2 Management accounting information in highly competitive industries

The use of financial performance information for decision making and control in organisations has some clear advantages. Accounting information expresses the organisation's condition and performance in monetary units (in money). In doing so, it focuses managers'

[4] See for more information literature on the Resource-based View of the firm (Wernerfelt, 1984; Barney, 1991; Wernerfelt, 1995; Makadok, 2001; Argyres & Zenger, 2009).

attention on the **financial performance** of the organisation and its business units. For commercial organisations, financial performance (expressed in, for instance, profit and return on investment) is one of the most important performance measures. It determines the financial-economic viability and independence of the company. Financial performance data even play an important role in non-profit and public organisations, because the financial budget is an important restriction within which the performance of the organisation needs to be organised and (if possible) optimised. Financial performance information should therefore play an important role in management's planning and decision making activities. It also plays an important role in management control: financial performance measures are output measures that can be used to control very diverse, routine and non-routine, business activities. Because financial performance measures are similar for both the organisation as a whole and for its business entities, they also lead to **goal congruency** within the firm. Generally, financial performance data are **objective measures** of performance, which reduces ambiguity and interpretation differences among users of this information. They are also more **precise** measures of performance, which makes it easier to determine performance differences, and thus to distinguish good performance from mediocre or bad performance. In most organisations, financial performance information can be generated at relatively **low cost,** since most companies have this information already available in their bookkeeping system for financial reporting purposes.

The use of financial performance information has however also some **disadvantages.** When financial information is used for planning purposes, managers may set clear, financial targets for the future, but these targets by themselves do not specify **how they should be realised.** By not knowing which factors drive financial performance, managers will also not be able to **actively to manage** these factors. Without any additional information, it is also very difficult to judge how **realistic** are the chosen financial targets are. Most financial information emphasises the short term and do not reflect longer term performance dimensions. These disadvantages in the planning phase also impact on the usefulness of financial performance information for controlling business performance. The exclusive use of financial information makes it difficult to understand what factors caused variations in financial performance. This makes it **difficult to evaluate and reward manager's performance.** Positive budget differences may be the result of superior management performance (either because the manager exerted more effort or because of her superior knowledge and experience) or just sheer luck. Negative budget differences may be caused by substandard management performance or just bad luck. Not being able to distinguish between the influence of external conditions and the contribution of managers may cause erroneous evaluation decisions. Bad management can be rewarded and good management punished because of the significant influence of external conditions on financial performance. This is also considered an expected cost of decentralisation (Baker, 1990).

Exclusive use of financial information for planning and control purposes may be an option in arm's length relationships between business entities, for instance in cross-holdings, financial participations and in business conglomerates. In more integrated businesses, however, managers need more information about factors that influence financial performance. They need to build a **mental model** that makes them understand what needs to be done to generate, maintain and improve performance. Building these mental models also helps management to understand the business, the working of their company's business model and the effectiveness of the planning and control systems they use. It is fair to say that when integrated businesses enter more competitive markets, the need to be able to understand the business, to focus on value drivers and to control performance becomes more and more important. This is one of the main reasons why integrated financial and non-financial measurement models have gained so much attention in recent years.

10.1.3 Choosing the right set of performance measures

Financial measures use monetary units (money) to measure an entity's condition or performance. Measures of an entity's condition are, for instance, balance sheet items (like assets and liabilities) and financial ratios (for instance debt-equity ratio, quick ratio and solvency ratio). Financial performance measures are mostly taken from the income statement (revenues, costs, net income), cash flow statements (cash inflows and outflows) or budget reports (sales and expenses). **Non-financial measures** are measures of condition or performance that are non-monetary. They can be distinguished into **objective measures** and **subjective measures.** Examples of objective non-financial performance measures are data such as market share, time-to-market, production speed, scrap and number of products failed. Subjective performance measures are responses by individuals and groups about certain characteristics of the firm or its products. Here we can think of subjective evaluations of product quality, the atmosphere on the work floor, and the appreciation of the company by the public. This information can be expressed in qualitative information, such as in written statements, or in quantitative information based on information, collected by surveys.

Managers generally use financial and non-financial measures for two distinct purposes: **decision making** and **control.** For decision making purposes, managers use information to decide what kind and how much effort they will exert, and in what direction they will be employed. One of the most crucial elements in this decision process is to have beliefs or specific information about the relationship between efforts and decisions on the one hand, and results they generate on the other. A broad scope information system, containing both financial and non-financial information, may help sorting out the relationships between investment decisions, design of production systems and production activities on the one hand and outcomes on the other. Here, the information system assists managers in making short and long term decisions. In this way it supports **learning** by reviewing previous performance data with the intention to optimise production activities in the future. The data systems used for decision making purposes may be very detailed and closely related to the managers' information needs and analysis requirements.

The other purpose of information systems is **controlling** behaviour in organisations. In small organisations, where knowledge is easily transmitted between participants, decision making can be concentrated in a single, central, decision making authority. When organisations grow, more information needs to be collected, transferred to the decision making authority and processed for decision making purposes. These activities come at a cost for the organisation. The larger the company becomes and the more specialised the know-how at the operational level is, the higher the costs for communication and decision making and the higher the risk of information quality deterioration. The alternative is to decentralise decision making authority to individuals that possess the best information to make decisions. This, however, also comes at at cost. Decentralised decision makers focus mainly on optimising the performance of their own unit, but may not be aware of the impact their decisions have on other units or on the organisation as a whole. They are also not motivated to cooperate with other units, especially when it comes at a cost. These decentralisation costs of coordination problems and private goal pursuit can be counterbalanced by installing a performance measurement and incentive system that coordinates local decision making and stimulates coordination between units (Bouwens & Speklé, 2007).

In recent years, several frameworks have been developed that help in selecting, structuring and integrating financial and non-financial performance measures. In the next section we will discuss some examples of integrated performance measurement systems (IPMS). In Section 3 we will discuss how an IPMS can be designed and put into practice.

10.2 Integrated performance measurement systems (IPMS)

In 1991, Robert Eccles published his provocative article *The Performance Measurement Manifesto* in which he predicted a performance measurement revolution in the business community (Eccles, 1991). In this article, Eccles claims that accounting performance measures do not reflect important tangible and intangible value drivers and, therefore, are obsolete at best–and more often even harmful for the business. They also do not provide the necessary information to act proactively in a business environment that is dynamic and innovative and which requires swift and immediate responses from companies. Eccles published his article at the right moment: in the eighties and nineties, companies began reconsidering their performance measurement system and to redesign them in order to make better decisions and to improve control of strategic business processes. Although accounting performance measures have maintained their important role in business information systems, it is undeniable that most companies have expanded their portfolio of performance measures significantly. It is up to the reader to consider these changes as part of a performance measurement revolution. Whatever it is, it has indeed dramatically and permanently changed the performance measurement practices in most companies.

10.2.1 The balanced scorecard

Probably the best-known integrated performance measurement system is the Balanced Scorecard (BSC).[5] This system has been developed in a series of bi-monthly meetings between representatives of 12 large companies[6] during the year 1990. These meetings were organised to study and discuss the topic of 'Measuring Performance in the Organisation of the Future.'[7]

The participating organisations envisioned that future competition would more be severe, developments in markets more be more dynamic, and companies would increasingly compete on intangible, knowledge- and experience intensive capabilities of their products, services and organisations. The current performance measurement instruments that are dominated by financial performance information, are seen as becoming obsolete, and even detrimental to the creation of future economic value (Kaplan & Norton, 1996a). The study group aimed at developing

[5] The first publications were in the Harvard Business Review (Kaplan & Norton, 1992; Kaplan & Norton, 1993, 1996b). Later on, the insights were bundled in two books (Kaplan & Norton, 1996a, 2004).

[6] These companies were: Advanced Micro Devices, American Standard, Apple Computer, Bell South, CIGNA, Conner Peripherals, Cray Research, DuPont, Electronic Data Systems, General Electric, Hewlett-Packard, and Shell Canada. It is striking that most companies are active in the high-tech industry (mostly computer and electronics) and (therefore) heavily innovation dependent for future success.

[7] The study was sponsored by the Nolan Norton Institute, KPMG's research unit. The meetings were chaired by David Norton (Nolan Norton's CEO) and Robert Kaplan served as academic consultant.

a measurement system that assists corporate management to measure effectively and control the performance of business entities in the creation of future value for the company. At the start of the study, some innovative performance measurement systems were discussed. Among them was a system developed by Analog Devices, measuring progress in continuous improvement activities that was called the Corporate Scorecard. The study group took this example and developed it further into a more generic performance measurement system that could be more widely adopted, which was called the Balanced Scorecard. The BSC thus emerged from the discussions as a common denominator of the different views of the participating companies.

The BSC is a performance measurement system that complements financial performance measures with drivers of future performance. The combination of the two leads to a performance measurement system that not only provides a picture of past performance (which is what most financial reporting systems generally do) but also allows decision makers to predict and control future outcomes by influencing performance drivers. Financial performance indicators are lagging indicators, representing the outcomes of past activities. They are in themselves not changeable, but reflect changes in performance that are driven by internal and external performance drivers, represented by leading indicators. These indicators may display the size of tangible and intangible capabilities that are available for use (like the stack of knowledge and technological know-how, the capabilities in R&D, and managerial experience), and the intensity and quality of business activities that generate future value. A common, backward looking (mostly financial) scorecard can be converted into a forward looking control device, when two things are added to the scorecard. First, managers need to know what outcomes the organisation needs to generate to become successful. And secondly, managers should possess sufficient knowledge about how these outcomes are to be produced.

The selection of measures is **driven by the vision and strategy** of the organisation. Selecting the right leading and lagging performance indicators clarifies and translates vision and strategy, it communicates strategy to other organisational units, aligns strategic initiatives and provides feedback for improvement and learning. A coherent **business model** reflects expected cause-and-effect (or 'causal') relationships among the leading and lagging performance measures. The model can be determined by empirical analysis of the relations between leading and lagging indicators, it can be inferred from ideas how managers expect the business model to work, or it can be derived from logical relations between indicators. Knowing the direction, form and strength of the relationships helps in choosing the right leading indicators proactively to control future performance outcomes. As we have seen in Section 10.1.1, the market place has become more open and dynamic, which means that timely and effective adaptation is more essential than ever before. Intangible capabilities and knowledge intensive drivers of performance determine a great deal of success. This means that the leading indicators should also reflect intangible performance drivers.

The general structure of a BSC consists of four performance dimensions: Financial, Market, Internal Business Processes and Learning and Growth (refer to Figure 10.2). These are generic dimensions that can be altered, reduced or expanded in number, or renamed depending on the organisation's characteristics and the conditions in which it operates. The choice of performance dimensions is guided by two basic questions: which stakeholder interests are important to the organisation, and what are the critical performance areas that must be explicitly monitored and controlled.

The **Financial** perspective displays the economic consequences of performance, measured by financial and accounting indicators, like return on investment and economic value added measures, and their cost and revenue components. The financial perspective is

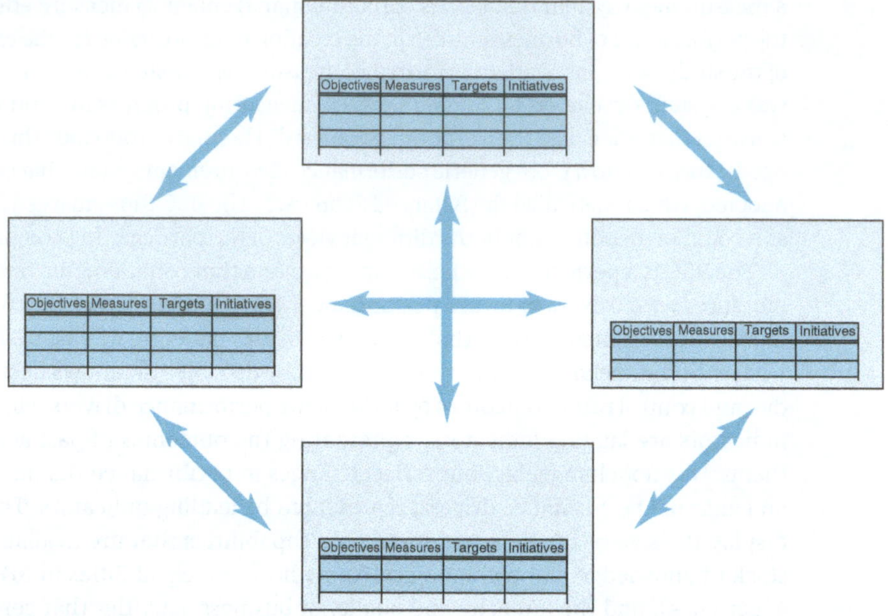

Figure 10.2 The balanced scorecard (Kaplan & Norton, 1996a, p. 9)
Source: from *The Balanced Scorecard*, Harvard Business Press (Kaplan, R.S. & Norton, D.P. 1996). Reprinted by permission of Harvard Business School Press. Copyright © 1996 by the Hardvard Business School Publishing Corporation; all rights reserved.

important in monitoring the shareholder's perspective and assuring that the shareholders' interests are sufficiently taken care of.

The **Market** perspective represents firm performance on (relevant segments of) the market where it competes with other companies. Successful competition for the customer's preference is the main source of the firm's success. This also holds for non-profit organisations competing for clients, and for government agencies competing for political support. Typical performance measures in this domain are market related indicators, like market size and product market share, and customer related measures, such as customer satisfaction and customer retention.

The **Internal Business process** perspective reports on the condition and performance of critical business functions, which are key in the value creation process. Here, most operational performance indicators can be found relating to production costs and outcomes. Outcome indicators can be focused on product quality (error reports, number of defects in parts per million (ppm), percentage of products passing quality control), product functionality (responsiveness to customers' demands), timeliness of production and delivery (percentage of products produced in time, average time to market), and process improvements (number of process improvements, efficiency improvements and reduction of waste).

The **Learning and Growth** perspective depicts the condition of the organisation's capabilities that are most critical for current and future performance. Organisations need to maintain and improve their capabilities in order to survive in today's competitive markets and to meet their long-term objectives in the future. Organisational capabilities are built on human capabilities (skills, know-how and creativity of the workforce), technical capabilities (the quality of production and information systems) as well as organisational capabilities (quality of management and of organisational procedures for decision making and control).

As already mentioned, the BSC as presented by Kaplan & Norton is a generic chart: in practice, in practice organisations may decide to use a different number or different categories of performance perspectives. For instance, a major consulting firm used the BSC for measurement of the performance of each individual consultant and identified six performance dimensions: market visibility, client satisfaction, financial performance, internal HR development, individual effectiveness (strong and weak points), and professionalism (improving know-how and experience). The first three are market performance indicators, the fourth deals with strengthening the professional team, and the last two relate to continuous learning and growth of the individual capabilities (Groot, et al., 2000).

Each dimension may contain different types of measure and the purpose of the BSC is to find the right combination of measures that jointly will lead to a coherent and complete scorecard that effectively supports decision making and control. Finding the right combination requires a balance to be struck between the relative importance of:

- the performance perspectives;
- leading and lagging indicators;
- internal and external indicators;
- subjective and objective measures;
- short-term and long-term measures.

The BSC literature as such does not provide much help in how this should be done in practice. The theoretical approaches presented in Sections 10.2.1 and 10.2.2 may offer some guidelines as to how an effective BSC should be constructed.

There are two important features that may make BSC a useful tool for managers, which are relevance and effectiveness. The BSC can become a relevant tool for steering the business when it is driven by **strategy.** Strategic choices define the outcomes the company aspires to reach and which will become its key actions and key results in obtaining the outcomes. This makes the BSC a **relevant** tool for steering the business. The BSC's effectiveness in supporting decision making and control decisions is greatly dependent on the degree of reliability with which it represents **causal relationships** between leading and lagging indicators. The strategic orientation of the BSC has always been deemed important for BSC design (Kaplan & Norton, 1992; Kaplan & Norton, 1993; Kaplan & Norton, 1996a). The combination of strategy definition and the discovery of causal relations has become a major issue in later publications about the BSC (Kaplan & Norton, 1996b; Kaplan & Norton, 2001b, 2001a, 2004). Both elements can be captured by designing **strategy maps.** A strategy map is a graphical representation of the main objectives of the organisation and of how these objectives will be attained. Building strategy maps may help the strategy development process by clarifying strategic choices and communicating strategic priorities to other participants. They may also assist in translating strategic choices into operational action by identifying the actions (represented by leading indicators) that are needed to reach the set objectives. This translation may help in assessing the achievability of set targets, in identifying weak processes in the organisation, and in the specification of concrete action plans for operational managers lower in the organisational hierarchy.

A strategy map, therefore, shows the links between performance dimensions and between performance measures. A generic strategy map may look like the one represented in Figure 10.3. This map is based on the presumption that creating economic value (for shareholders) is the ultimate goal, which is supported by performance in the other BSC dimensions. This however, is a strategic choice, which may be partly driven by the institutional conditions under which the organisation operates. Suppose we drew a strategy map for a

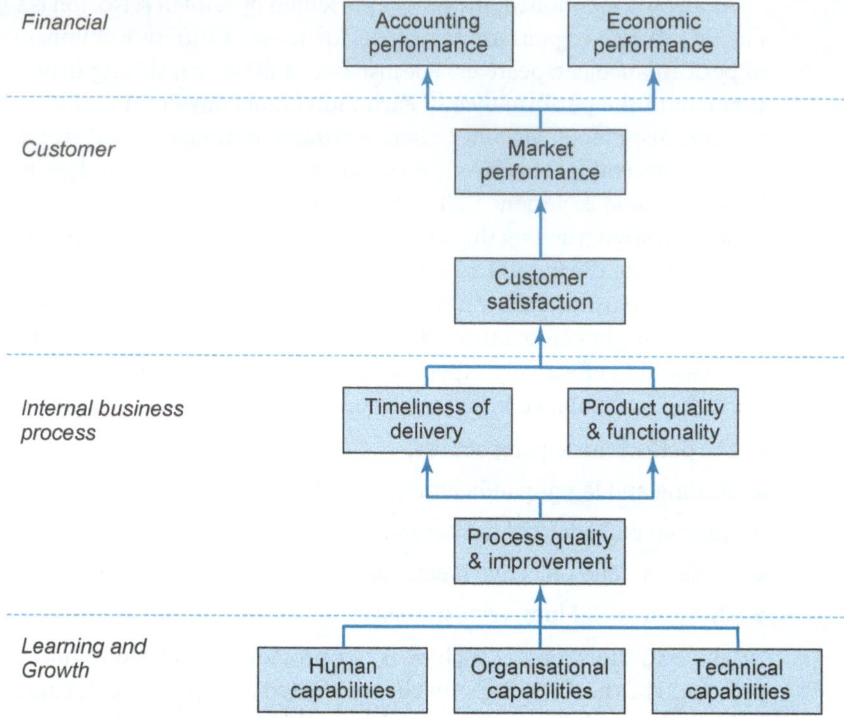

Figure 10.3 A generic strategy map

government agency or an independent non-profit organisation. The financial perspective may not be the ultimate goal, but finance may be an important condition under which the organisation operates. It may even be decisive for the development of capabilities and the performance of internal business processes. This would relocate the financial perspective from the top to the bottom of the map. The ultimate goal would then become to satisfy clients. If non-profit organisations serve clients in response a social demand, articulated by local or national politicians who supply the funding of the organisation, a new ultimate goal would then become something like satisfying a constituency.

Figure 10.3 is a simplified representation of the causal relationships that might exist in real-life organisations. An analysis of publicly available performance data of 162 large US firms from different industries for the period 1994 to 1997 reveals some of the relationships between performance dimensions as they exist in practice (see Figure 10.4). As we can see, the different performance dimensions seem to be connected to each other. But not always in a sequential fashion as was depicted in Figure 10.3. For instance, Innovation and Growth items appear to influence performance in both the customer and the internal business process dimensions simultaneously. Also reverse relations exist, for instance labour productivity in the business process perspective also impacts on the number of product introductions in the learning and growth perspective. Some items are connected with other items **within** a dimension, like the amount of R&D expenses and number of patents and production introductions. The empirically reconstructed Strategy Map in Figure 10.4 also shows that it takes some time for leading indicators to have a measurable and significant impact on the target lagging indicators. The solid lines stand for one-year lags and dotted lines represent two-year lags. Most of the lines turn out to be dotted ones: managers need to be aware that a change in leading

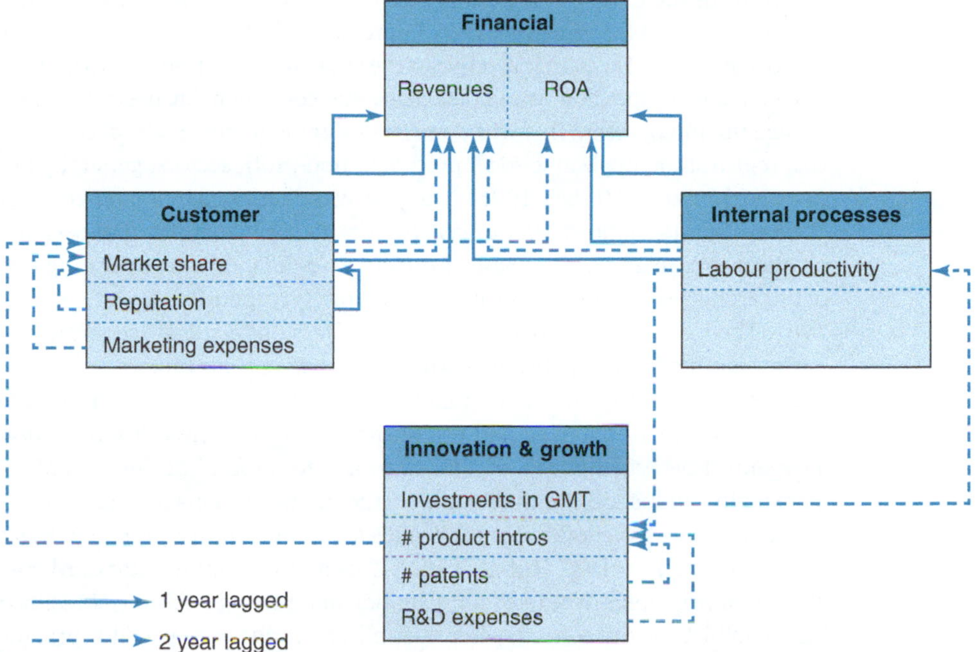

Figure 10.4 Empirical reconstruction of strategy maps in US companies (based on Bryant et al., 2004)

indicators may not immediately change the target lagging indicator, but it may take some time to become visible. Some connections, for instance between reputation and market share, have a one-year as well as a two-year time lag. Even more intriguing, some performance measures have a reinforcing impact on themselves. This is especially the case for the financial measures of performance, like revenues and return on assets (ROA). This phenomenon is also known as 'earnings persistence' (Kormendi & Lipe, 1987; Easton & Zmijewski, 1989).

The BSC in its pure form can be used for managing enterprises and business units on different hierarchical levels in organisations. The strategy maps show that, in order to effectively coordinate and manage the different parts and processes within firms, local BSC's should be interconnected with other local BSC's and with the corporate BSC. The BSC concept does not show how this should be done, other than allocating the performance measure to a local BSC where local management can effectively influence the object that is represented by the indicator.

10.2.2 The Tableau de Bord

Although the BSC has been widely used in many companies around the world, the adoption of the BSC by French companies has been remarkably low (Gehrke & Horváth, 2002; Bourguignon, et al., 2004). One of the main reasons seems to be that French enterprises already use another, similar system called the *Tableau de Bord* (which means 'dashboard') for steering and controlling business processes. The *Tableau de Bord* is basically an integrated performance measurement system and has been in use since the early 1930s. Its emergence was made possible because of the historic economic and institutional developments in France. Historically, French companies have always been heavily influenced by state intervention: about one-third of the economy is state owned or state directed since 1945. The role of the state became very visible during the Great Depression of 1929-1937, which is known in France as the 'Great Crisis.' The main objective of the state in that period was to create an environment in which fair competition would take place that could help business stay alive, grow and help reduce unemployment. This was done by designing a universally accepted single method of cost registration, applicable to all profit and non-profit sectors, generally known as the *Plan Compatable Général* (Lebas, 1996). This plan was developed by a semi-governmental body, the *Commission interministérielle de normalisation des comptabilités,* and became compulsory for all businesses in 1947. The *Conseil National de la Comptabilité,* operating under the auspices of the French Ministry of Finance and Economy, is responsible for later revisions in 1957 and 1982. The main emphasis of the *Plan Comptable* is on financial accounting.

Stimulating fair competition also meant that all organisations needed to use similar management accounting and costing methods for inventory valuation and pricing decisions. These methods were developed under the auspices of the CEGOS *(Commission Générale d'Organisation Scientifique),* organised by a federation of businesses. Members of CEGOS were mainly industrial engineers active in the Scientific Management Movement. The CEGOS developed the *Méthode des sections homogènes ou des tableaux de répartition* as early as 1927 and published it in 1937 (Lebas, 1994). This method defined standard cost pools and cost allocation principles to be used for valuation and pricing decisions. Inventory valuation was based on historic full costing, while cost-plus methods were used for pricing decisions.

Interestingly, in French companies the field of management control has been developed almost completely separated from the financial and management accounting systems. Two conditions may have caused this separate development. In France, traditionally engineers occupy a large number of leadership positions in business. Recent estimates are that around 50% of French CEO's are engineers by training. A second reason is that financial markets are not as important for the supply of capital in France as in Anglo-Saxon countries. Financial performance information may, therefore, not play a similarly important role in corporate decision making. The most important objective for most companies is to find ways to save money and increase profitability (Lebas, 1994).[8] Steering the business (or *pilotage* in French) is done based on information provided by the so called *Tableau de Bord.* This tableau monitors, as real time possible, physical and financial indicators to assess, anticipate and control performance. It is an action based tool for rapid, near time information (assessing and reporting the current status) that builds on the definition of key decision making items and the hierarchy of responsibility at a company (de Guerny, et al., 1990). The *Tableau* is primarily focused on short-term operational control, which emphasises the importance of operational, non-financial measures of performance and de-emphasises financial performance indicators. Costs, for instance, are considered to represent only 'the shadow of the business processes', as they do not adequately represent the quality of business processes and cannot be used proactively to control the business (Chiapello, et al., 2001).

Since the *Tableau de Bord* is a forward looking device, its structure is based on a causal model, linking condition and action variables to outcome variables. It is recommended that managers jointly decide on the causal model and on the selection of appropriate sets of indicators for all relevant decision makers. Indicators eligible for selection should be possible to measure, to report in a timely manner, to aid local management in taking decisions, be action oriented and it should be possible to visualise in an 'ergonomic' form that effectively

[8] This may be one of the reasons why Management Accounting is called '*Comptabilité de Rendement*', which means yield accounting or productivity accounting.

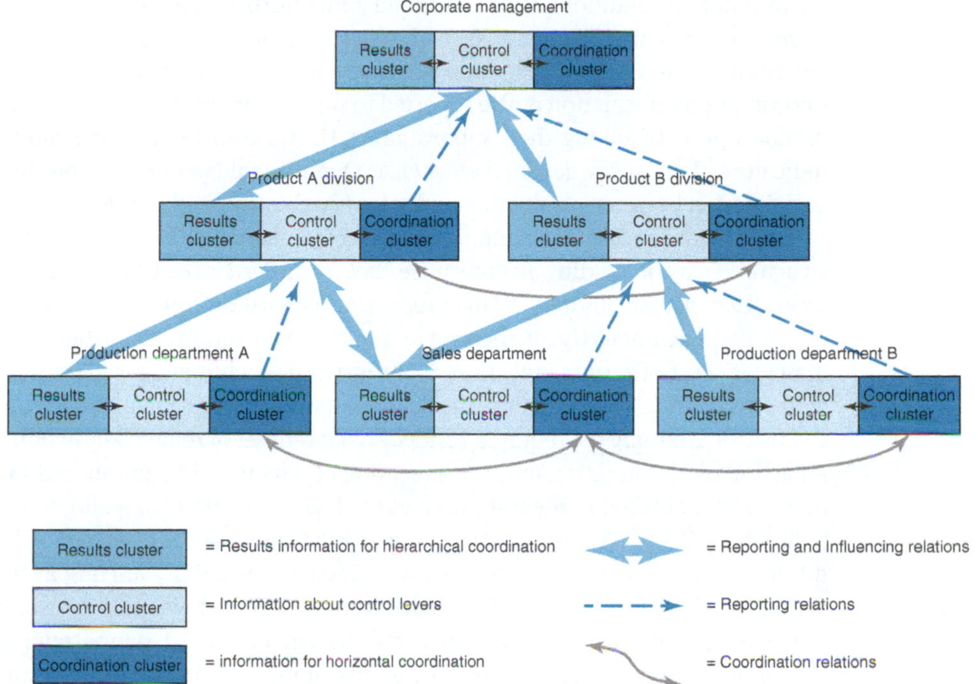

Figure 10.5 Information clusters and relations in an Enterprise *Tableau de Bord* system (based on Daum, 2005).

supports decision making. The last point is important: the *Tableau de Bord* should focus the manager on decision making, highlighting problematic areas (by alert *(clignotant)* indicators), assisting diagnostics, and helping managers to see interdependencies between variables and offsetting mechanisms.

Each operational decision maker has a *Tableau de Bord,* which is unique and tailored to the specific area of responsibility. It consists of three information clusters: the **results cluster,** the **control cluster** and the **coordination cluster** (see Figure 10.5).

Information in the **results cluster** displays each business entity's current performance in attaining the targets set out for the unit *(les résultats).* This information is relevant for the next level's management layer, since the lower level performance attained is part of the higher level managers' responsibilities that have been devolved to the operational unit. Sub-optimal unit performance may lead to operational or strategic interventions by higher level managers. The **control cluster** provides local managers with a reduced set of indicators that they need for (operational) control of their areas of responsibility. These indicators provide information about major control levers (*variables d'action* or *leviers d'action*) that enable targeted control. Information in the **coordination cluster** reflects interdependencies of the focal unit with other units within the organisation as well as with the external environment that should be monitored and managed.

An important feature of the *Tableau de Bord* is its 'nested structure': information elements are duplicated into, and linked with, *Tableaux de Bords* of other units and other organisational levels. This feature illustrates a major objective of the *Tableau de Bord* concept: to support coordination across units, functions and hierarchy levels to optimise organisational control efforts. The nesting principle is know as the *gigogne* principle, and it is designed to keep the organisation focused on corporate objectives, to keep it attuned with changing environmental conditions and to maintain joint efforts that are both hierarchically and horizontally coordinated (Daum, 2005). The coordination cluster contains information from the environment and other units upon which the performance of the focal unit is dependent. Coordination information is also reported to supervisors to enable them to monitor the coordination process among their subordinates. Useful coordination measures are 'combined indicators' *(indicateurs de convergence)* like 'Quantity sold per product produced', monitoring coordination between production and sales (de Guerny, et al., 1990).

The design process of an enterprise *Tableau de Bord* can be done in different ways. One structured way of building an enterprise *Tableau de Bord* is the OVAR method *(Objectifs, Variables d'Action, Responsable)*.[9] This process starts with defining the organisation's strategic objectives. Each objective is then related to one or several responsible managers. For each manager, a set of results indicators is put forward. Each manager identifies, based on their own causal model of production, the key action variables *(variable d'action* or *points clés)* they can use for attaining the required results. A coherent set of related key action variables makes an action plan *(plan d'action)*, the execution of which will be monitored by indicators that need to be identified in the last phase of the OVAR process (Chiapello & Lebas, 1996; Chiapello, et al., 2001). The process of formulating the enterprise *Tableau de Bord* system can done differently. Each hierarchical level may define its own OVAR, starting at the top level. The action variables at the top level are objectives one level below and the responsible managers are required to define their own action variables that are needed for attaining the objectives. This is a sequential development process that implies extensive delegation (Löning, et al., 1998; Bourguignon, et al., 2004). An alternative approach is to use an interactive process (like brainstorming sessions) in which participants try to design a coherent and integrated enterprise *Tableau de Bord* across all hierarchical levels and business functions (Daum, 2005).

10.2.3 The performance pyramid

Shortly before the BSC was made public, Lynch and Cross published their ideas about how integrated performance measurement systems should work. They developed the performance pyramid, which was based on three in-depth case studies and was further developed in many discussions with practitioners about the topic (Lynch & Cross, 1991; Lynch & Cross, 1995). Initially, their ideas were well received, but later they seem to have been somewhat overshadowed by the massive attention to the BSC. This is undeserved, because although the performance pyramid has some commonalities with the BSC, it also adds some new ideas to it. One of the most fundamental contributions of the performance pyramid is the idea that integrated performance measurement systems should be interconnected across the different organisation's hierarchical levels.

The performance pyramid (see Figure 10.6) represents the organisational hierarchy, from the corporate management level down to the level of the individual employee. Each level is supposed to contribute its own capabilities to a concerted effort to reach company wide objectives. These objectives are defined by corporate management and expressed in a corporate vision. This vision is translated for each level in the organisational hierarchy into specific and actionable targets. The level of specificity and detail of the corporate objectives increases with each lower hierarchical level.

[9] This method is developed and taught by the HEC School of Management, Paris, France.

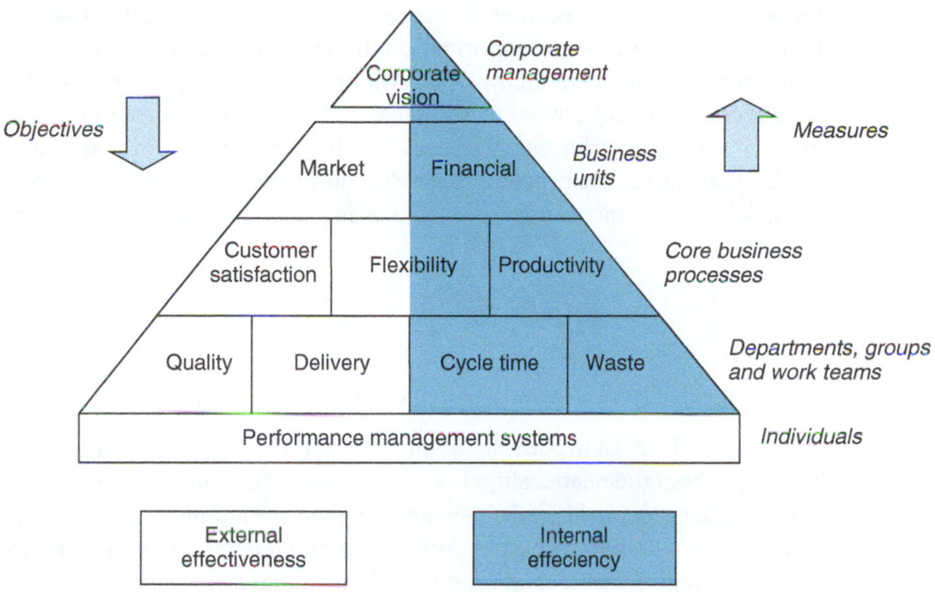

Figure 10.6 The performance pyramid (Lynch & Cross, 1991; 1995)

At the business unit level, the objectives are stated in both market and financial terms because the organisation is supposed to perform in each of these two domains. The market is the market of products and services at which the company meets the customer. The financial market is the place where financial resources are acquired and where shareholders and debt holders evaluate the company's performance.

Market performance is dependent on the ability to satisfy the customers in their current needs, but also on the flexibility of the firm to follow changing customer preferences and to also satisfy the future customer and new, potential customer groups. Financial performance is also dependent on static, current performance and dynamic, future performance. Current performance depends on productivity, which is the return corporate activities create out of each resource unit that is spent by the firm. Corporate owners and debt holders not only evaluate current performance, but also the possibilities to generate future earnings under changing conditions. In other words, the company should also be flexible in the financial domain.

Both current performance objectives can be decomposed further in the next lower hierarchical level into more operational targets. Customer satisfaction depends on the quality of the product and the way it is delivered to the customer. Delivery stands for the time it takes for the product to reach the customer, and the intensity of interaction between the firm and the customer. Reducing waste and shortening cycle times can be essential productivity goals. Both measures improve efficiency levels by producing more products for each resource unit used. The two flexibility targets, delivery and cycle time, can be seen as activities that enable the company to know the customer better and to react more swiftly to changing preferences and market conditions. Shorter cycle times, for instance, also lead to shorter time-to-market and, thus, quicker introductions of new or revised products on the market.

The objectives can be further specified for lower levels in the organisation (which are not reproduced in Figure 10.6). When the process of translation of the corporate mission to lower levels in the organisation has been completed, a measurement system can be built up that passes on performance information from the operational levels up to the higher levels in the organisational hierarchy. In this way, each level's objectives remain aligned with the overall corporate objectives and the related performance information assures coordination of organisational performance between individuals, organisational units and hierarchical levels. The market performance is mostly concerned with external effectiveness, while the financial performance is mainly created by internal efficiency of operations.

10.3 IPMS design decisions

10.3.1 Modelling causal relations for improved decision making

A strategy is a set of hypotheses about cause and effect (Kaplan & Norton, 1996a, p. 30). Thinking about the relationships between causal events and subsequent performance effects may help decision making, the development and communication of strategy, and control of task execution. In IPMS, causal events are represented by **leading indicators** and subsequent effects by **lagging indicators.** Leading indicators represent conditions or activities preceding an outcome. They can be seen as **performance drivers.** Examples of economic conditions are exchange rate movements and inflation figures, and examples of activities are speed of operations, cycle times, number of working hours and of quality assurance inspections. Lagging indicators display the outcomes attained, which can be both financial, like costs, profit, earnings per share or share price, or non-financial, as for instance quality level, on-time delivery and product functionality.

As already said, a strategy is a set of hypotheses about causal relations. This means that managers make **predictions** about what results will be attained when a specific set of actions is undertaken. These predictions may be based on knowledge about causal relations from empirical analysis of the relationships between causal events and subsequent performance effects. The empirical determination of a causal relationship is not easy, and should adhere to some very specific rules, such as logical independence, time precedence and predictive ability[10]. Causal events and effects should be logically independent, which means that effects cannot logically be inferred from causal events. They also follow a time sequence: causal events precede effects and both can be observed close to each other in time and space. The observation of a causal event necessarily implies the subsequent observation of the related effect (Edwards, 1972). Not many managers appear to perform these empirical tests (Banker et al., 2000; Ittner and Larcker, 1998). In practice, managers may also rely on guess work and common sense reasoning in determining the relationships. They may use a causal map of leading and lagging indicators to establish **finality** relations: the map expresses the desired actions and results as defined by custom, policy, or values (Arbnor and Bjerke, 1997). Finality relations are used to convince employees of the importance of leading events for final results and to establish goal and behavioural alignment[11] (Malina, Norreklit and Selto, 2004). Sometimes, causal relations are not the result of empirical causality, but of logical dependence.

[10] In theories of science this rule is also known as Hume's criteria (Cook and Campbell, 1979).

[11] The study of Malina, Nørreklit and Selto (2007) demonstrates a successful firm using causal models for managing the distribution units, while no causal relations could be convincingly confirmed by the researchers. This means that unmeasured factors may interfere in causal relations, or that causal reasoning may motivate managers to attain superior levels of performance.

Most accounting models are logical models. This may also influence relationships in the scorecard. If loyal customers are defined as the group of customers that invokes low costs and pays high prices (as is done by Reichheld and Sasser, 1990), then the relationship between sales performance and financial performance is not a causal, but mainly a logical relationship (Norreklit, 2000).

A relatively well-researched relationship is that between customer satisfaction and financial performance. The marketing literature contends that higher customer satisfaction improves financial performance by higher loyalty of existing customers, lower price elasticities, and lower marketing and transaction costs because of enhanced firm reputation and positive word of mouth advertising (Anderson, et al., 1994; Ittner & Larcker, 1998). However, improving customer satisfaction also comes at a cost and it is, therefore, uncertain whether improving customer satisfaction will always lead to improved total financial performance. Analysis in the telecom industry reveal that improved customer satisfaction is positively associated with customer retention (the possibility that current customers will return in the future). However, the relationship appears to be only strictly linear for lower values of customer satisfaction, displays a step function around average values of customer satisfaction and is capped at highest customer satisfaction levels (Ittner & Larcker, 1998). The step function can be the result of competing offerings to customers, and of customer zones of tolerance. Customers only change their behaviour when satisfaction falls below a certain low point (they leave and switch to a competitor) or exceeds a high point (more spending) (Zeithaml, et al., 1996). The zone of tolerance can be influenced by customer current expectations, past satisfaction and current product quality (Anderson, et al., 1994). The cap at the highest levels of customer satisfaction indicates that continued efforts to improve satisfaction of already very satisfied customers does not further improve customer retention and may, therefore, be a waste of money. All examples show that the causal relation between customer satisfaction, on the one hand, and customer retention or future sales on the other, may not be clear cut but may show **non-linearities** caused by changes in offerings by competitors and by customer reactions to changes in product and service offerings.

Another question is whether returning customers are able to improve profitability, because they only make it more certain that historic financial performance will be continued into the future. Data from 13 major US airlines have shown that the number of on-time flights improved customer satisfaction, while the number of ticket over-sales and number of mishandled bags reduced customer satisfaction[12]. The number of customer complaints appeared to be negatively related to the profitability ratio, expressed as operating revenues divided by operating costs. However, at the same time, improving customer satisfaction by flying more planes on time, reducing ticket over-selling, and mishandling less bags also led to lower profitability in the short term (Dresner & Xu, 1995). Improving performance thus has a direct negative effect on profitability, as well as a simultaneous positive indirect effect via the reduction of customer complaints (effectively an improvement of customer satisfaction). This may be the result of existing customers flying more frequently or the attraction of additional customers. A similar study in a bank reveals that improved customer satisfaction only indirectly leads to higher financial performance through the growth of customer numbers (Ittner & Larcker, 1998).

[12] Customer satisfaction was a proxy for the number of customer complaints.

The magnitude and the duration of both the negative direct effect and positive indirect effect of performance enhancement measures on profitability should be compared in order to judge the total effect of performance on profitability. Another study in the same industry shows that not all improvements in performance drivers lead to lower profitability. Increasing the load factor (which means selling more seats per flight) and improving market share do not lead to a significant increase in operational costs (because most costs are independent from number of customers) while they do lead to higher profitability (Behn & Riley, 1999).

Several studies have also shown that non-financial performance may also be positively related to future financial performance (Foster, et al., 1996; Banker, et al., 2000). This means that there may be a time lag between changes in the current leading non-financial indicators and the effects they have on financial performance.

As we have seen from these studies, causal relations between leading and lagging indicators may not be straightforward. The relations may be non-linear, while lagging indicators may react differently to positive and negative changes in leading indicators. The relationships between leading indicators and financial lagging indicators do not need to be direct, but may be indirect, mediated by other non-financial or financial lagging indicators. And the relationships may not be immediate, but may have time lags before changes in leading indicators become visible in financial and non-financial lagging performance information.

10.3.2 Choosing performance measures for control

When decision rights have been granted to local managers, senior management needs to set targets and use performance measures that guide local manager behaviour towards the attainment of corporate objectives. Targets set by senior management specify and communicate what the organisation expects from local managers, performance information provides feedback to senior and local management or how action choices affect both local and corporate performance, while performance related incentive compensation packages aim at aligning individual goals with the objectives of the organisation. In economic theory and, more specifically, agency theory, the 'informativeness principle' has been developed. According to this principle, non-financial measures of performance should be added to performance measurement and compensation systems (subject to their costs and risk imposed on the manager) if they provide incremental information about the manager's actions beyond that conveyed by financial measures alone (Holmström, 1979; Feltham & Xie, 1994).

However, simply adding measures to the existing set of performance measures is not enough. The IPMS effectiveness for control purposes also depends on the type of measures used. In order to become effective for control purposes, a set of performance measures needs to possess the following characteristics:

1. Performance measures need faithfully to reflect the organisation's **true objectives.** This implies that senior management has a clear idea of what the most important organisational objectives are. Based on these objectives, a set of performance measures needs to be developed that is a **fair and complete reflection** of the true organisational objectives.

2. The performance measures should be **reliable** measures of performance. Reliability relates to the measurement of financial and non-financial performance with minimal error.
3. The performance measures should be **actionable.** This means they should motivate and enable the manager to take appropriate action to change the outcome within a reasonable period of time. This also presupposes that the related conditions and events are **controllable** by the manager, which is also known as the **controllability principle.**

In the following text, we will explain more fully each requirement in turn. A graphical representation of the different performance measurement characteristics is given in Figure 10.7.

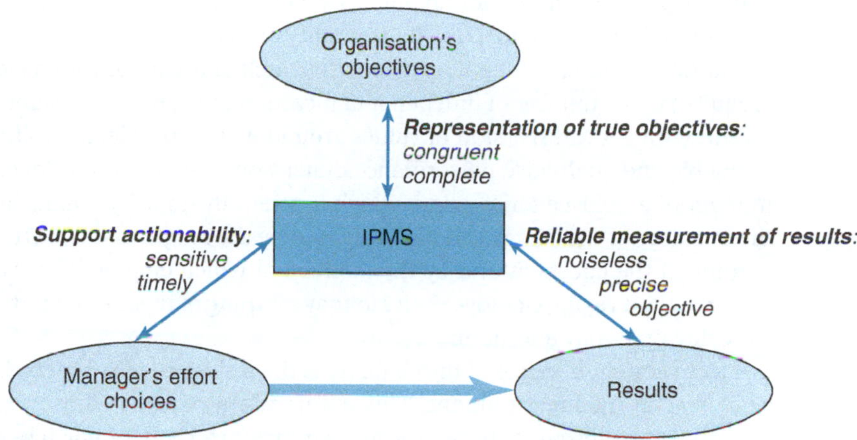

Figure 10.7 IPMS characteristics relevant for control effectiveness

Measures that do not fairly and completely capture the true desired results are called **distorted measures.** This implies that managers who perform well on the distorted measure may not contribute much to the organisation's goal achievement. An incomplete measure is, for instance, the use of a net profit measure for performance measurement purposes of a business unit manager, while also product quality is considered important. Not including a quality measure in the performance assessment of business unit managers may motivate them to maximise their score on net profit, even at the expense of product quality. In many situations, quality is difficult to measure. It means that a specific manifestation or dimension of quality is taken to which a number can be assigned. Suppose we would like to measure product quality: this can be done by taking samples of the product before shipping them to the customers and see whether they are technically fit to use. Another approach is to ask customer opinion about the product. Both may lead to different results, since the first measure focuses on technical specifications while the second measure takes fulfilment of customer needs into account. The decision on which one is a more fair representation of quality is partly dependent on the responsibilities given to the business unit manager. When they are production manager, responsible for technical quality of the products, the quality control measure may be more fair. When the BU manager has final responsibilities for the product performance on the market, the customer satisfaction measure may be more appropriate.

Measurement reliability is negatively influenced by measurement error. One of the main causes of measurement error originates from measures that do not discriminate well between results caused by the manager's efforts and performance differences caused by unrelated, external events. Such measures are called **noisy measures** because the data they provide are heavily influenced by noise coming from unrelated sources. Take for instance a business unit manager who is evaluated on the level of cost reduction achieved. Suppose that they have effectively reduced a number of cost items, but that this reduction does not surface in total cost figures because of a considerable increase in oil prices masking the successful cost reduction measures taken. A similar problem may emerge when the business unit manager is evaluated on product quality achieved. The final product quality is mostly not only dependent on the production activities of the business unit manager, but also on the quality of parts acquired from suppliers. By measuring quality when products leave the business unit, it is not possible to attribute quality problems to the one who is responsible for it.

Another source of unreliability comes from **lack of precision.** For a measure to be precise, it requires that a number of independent measurements, using the same instrument, lead to a result with a low dispersion of values around it. This problem specifically emerges when intangible and qualitative performance dimensions are measured. An example is the measurement of employee satisfaction, which is generally done by means of employee surveys. The outcome of the survey can be influenced by the length and structure of the survey, the wording of the questions and by the moment at which employees are asked to respond to the survey. Surveying employees on Monday morning may generate different responses than surveying on Friday afternoon.

A third common source of unreliability is the influence of **subjectivity.** Subjectivity may cause bias in the measurement. This occurs when persons whose performance is being measured are allowed to choose the measurement method, or participate (for instance as a resource person) in the measurement process. The freedom to choose an accounting method, for instance, may introduce subjectivity bias in the measurement. Measurement objectivity can be improved by having it done by independent people, like an external agency, or having the results verified by independent parties, for instance external or internal auditors.

The IPMS supports actionability on the part of the manager, if the measures are responsive to managerial decisions and effort. In other words the manager should be able to affect the measurement outcome. We do not use the term 'controllability' here, because in most cases outcomes are not fully controllable, but they can be influenced to a certain extent (see the example of the Groningen bridgemen).

The Groningen bridgemen

The Dutch city of Groningen (190 000 inhabitants) is an old city with a system of canals. Traffic that enters and leaves the city centre needs to cross the canals. In order to allow boats to use the canals, the city has installed swingbridges that open when a sufficient number of boats have lined up. Each swingbridge has its own bridgeman to operate the bridge. Some time ago, a severe winter made all the equipment freeze and the bridges could not be operated. Shortly after this event, the city council decided to allocate an operating budget to each of the bridgemen, while making them responsible for avoiding the severe winter conditions. Most of the bridgemen found this measure unfair, as they could not be held responsible for the weather conditions in wintertime. Nevertheless, the city council persisted in the decision and the following winter was even more severe than the previous one. Not one swingbridge was out of order this time. It turned out that the bridgemen had used the additional budget to do more maintenance during the summer to get better prepared for severe winter conditions. Although they did not control the weather, they undertook the necessary action within their ability to make sure uncontrollable events would not affect their operations.

The **sensitivity** of the measurement is important for two reasons. Sensitive measures provide meaningful feedback to the manager about the effectiveness of actions. In this way the IPMS supports local decision making and learning capacity (which is discussed in Section 10.2.1), with a special emphasis on how local decision making contributes to the attainment of an organisation's objectives. The second reason is that sensitive measures allow for making inferences about the performance of the manager, which is important for evaluation purposes. Measurement sensitivity and noise appear to be somewhat similar, because each aim at excluding irrelevant influences from the measures. In practice however, they differ. For instance, an insensitive measure may be a measure that has a too high aggregation level. Suppose a manager of a production unit is held responsible for the return on investment of the business unit. The manager is only capable of influencing the cost element in the measure but not the sales component. Fluctuations in the return measures may, therefore, be caused by factors beyond the manager's control. And yet, the return on investment ratio may be, in itself, be noiseless, which means it is not distorted by factors irrelevant to the return on investment measure.

The measure's **timeliness** is the time lag between the manager's behaviour and the moment that the outcomes of this behaviour are reported back to them. A short time lag supports actionability in three ways. It enables managers to relate cause and effect better to each other when feedback is given shortly after the action. Instant feedback also motivates managers to use the information for improvements in their behaviour, supporting experimentation, innovation and creativity. And lastly, in case of unfavourable outcomes, short feed back lags enable local managers to change their behaviour quickly. This reduces the risk of small problems growing and eventually causing great harm to the organisation.

Generally, it is a real challenge to create performance measures that perform well on all effectiveness dimensions simultaneously. One of the main reasons is that some dimensions may contradict when they are put into practice. For instance, reliably measuring performance may take some time and additional resources. This may lead to a less timely report and higher measurement costs. Making an IPMS more complete may also require the introduction of more qualitative elements in the performance measurement system that are not measurable reliably (think of the measurement of employee satisfaction, brand image or public appreciation of the company). Making the measurement system more congruent with organisation objectives may also imply that they will be less sensitive for operational performance at lower levels of the organisation. Designing IPMS requires compromising between the different effectiveness dimensions. Important decision aids that may guide the decisions in balancing the different dimensions are the cost of the IPMS and the total effect the IPMS will have on manager behaviour. A real life example of a mismatch between reliability and timeliness is given in *Low graduation rates in Dutch universities.*

Low graduation rates in Dutch universities

In the 1970s, the Dutch minister of Education had concerns about students taking too long before finishing their education. In those times, the Dutch university system did not pose any limitation to the time students could stay in the university system (which is nowadays restricted to the number of course years and one additional year for each grade). Nor did the minister have any information about the average study time. In good Dutch tradition, a committee was formed to investigate what the real average period of study of Dutch students really was. The committee took a certain cohort of students that did not start too long ago (around four years) and concluded that some 40% were still doing their studies. The committee decided to wait until a reasonable number of students eventually either graduated or finally dropped out. This took an additional four years. After this period, the committee finalised its report and concluded that, based on a reliable measurement of the average period of study, the graduation rate of Dutch students was unacceptably low. The minister took this hard evidence and confronted university officials with it. They were not very impressed. Most of the incumbent university officials were not (yet) in office when the sample students were active, and they did not feel responsible for the low graduation rates. Furthermore, since the period of observation, most programmes had changed several times and the university officials claimed that the newly created university programme did much better in terms of graduation rates. Although the minister put reliable measures on the table, they did not seem appropriate for controlling purposes and, therefore, did not have much influence on university officials' behaviour.

10.4 Integrated performance measurement systems (IPMS) in action

10.4.1 Antecedents for the use of IPMS

An important empirical question is: which organisations adopt IPMS and which organisations do not? Under what circumstances do we see firms choosing to broaden the scope of their performance measurement systems? Conditions or events that are considered to be responsible for the introduction of IPMS are 'antecedents' and 'anteceding variables' can capture their existence. As we have seen in Section 10.1, the common reasoning is that more open and competitive markets have caused the need timely, proactive corporate behaviour, focused on managing (mostly intangible) assets that greatly determine corporate success.

Empirical studies have indicated that **external conditions** may have an impact on IPMS choice. Under high environmental uncertainty conditions, performance measurement systems tend to have a broader scope and produce more timely information (Chenhall & Morris, 1986). Under uncertain conditions, business unit IPMS appear to contain more externally oriented, non-financial and *ex ante* information (Gordon & Narayanan, 1984). Another external factor is the level of government regulation in the industry. Organisations operating in regulated industries (for instance in the energy market) appear to monitor a larger set of performance indicators than organisations in non-regulated environments (Ittner, et al., 1997). Environmental uncertainty is, however, not the only condition that seems to influence IPMS adoption.

A second factor is **strategy.** Innovation strategies appear to be much more related to IPMS use than low cost strategies (Ittner, et al., 1997). A similar distinction can be made between build strategies (capturing new markets with existing or new products) and harvest strategies (exploiting existing products). Organisations following a build strategy are reported to use a broader set of performance measures than under a harvest strategy (Govindarajan & Gupta, 1985). If we look more into organisations, we find that specific types of strategy also have some impact on the performance measurement systems used. Especially strategies that involve programme for quality improvement (Ittner & Larcker, 1997), enhanced flexibility and more customer focused product offerings lead to more intense use of IPMS (Abernethy & Lillis, 1995; Perera, et al., 1997).

A third factor is **size** and **organisational structure.** Larger organisations and entities at lower organisational levels use more IPMS than small organisations and units at higher hierarchical levels (Hoque & James, 2000; Ittner & Larcker, 2002). IPMS for corporate control seem to contain relatively more financial performance measures, whereas IPMS for operational control at the work floor contain relatively more non-financial performance indicators.

A fourth factor is **product characteristics.** IPMS seems to be more widely used in product manufacturing environments and less in service firms (Mia & Chenhall, 1994; Ittner & Larcker, 2002). This is probably due to the fact that manufacturing activities provide more opportunities to specify, standardise and monitor separate production activities, whereas in service provision production is mostly done in close interaction with the client, which makes the activities difficult to specify and standardise. Also the length of the product development cycle and the product life cycle stages seem to be relevant. The longer it takes to develop a product, the more likely it is that non-financial performance measures will be used (Bushman, et al., 1996; Said, et al., 2003). A similar relation has been found for products in a mature stages of their product life cycle: more mature products are related to more intense use of IPMS (Hoque & James, 2000).

The last set of antecedent variables relates to the **production system** used. The level of automation and computerisation appears to facilitate the use of IPMS, because additional variables can be attached to the existing set of performance variables at relatively low additional costs (Perera, et al., 1997). More use of IPMS is also made when the requirements for coordination are higher. More coordination is called for when the level of interdependence between production units is high (Govindarajan & Fisher, 1990) or when they have a high level of resource sharing (Bushman, et al., 1995; Keating, 1997).

10.4.2 IPMS purpose of use

The use of IPMS appears to be diverse. A study in Finnish companies reveals that IPMS are used to steer performance by setting targets for IPMS performance dimensions and by evaluating the results. IPMS are also used as an information system for managers to see what to improve, assisting them in generating ideas and probing different strategies (Malmi, 2001).

A study among large companies in German speaking countries[13] shows that most firms use IPMS as a tool to represent financial and non-financial performance measures, grouped into categories. Around 25% of the IPMS users employ the IPMS as a tool to implement and control strategy, while 20% of the users use a sequential cause-and-effect logic to describe the company's strategy (Speckbacher, et al., 2003). A study of IPMS use in Dutch companies reveals that IPMS are mostly used as a supporting tool for (strategic) decision making and for self-monitoring, and to a lesser extent for coordination purposes (Wiersma, 2009). To summarise the results, companies in practice seem to use IPMS in the following ways:

1. a device to store, retrieve and represent a collection of financial and non-financial performance measures;
2. a mental model to develop and test alternative strategies;
3. a management control system to implement corporate strategy.

Most studies also mention that companies find it difficult empirically to verify causal relationships between IPMS performance dimensions. Most causal relations are based on expectations of how the business model works. A typical quote is the following: 'We do not know how much some factors and measures affect other factors' and 'We are not so far along yet'(Malmi, 2001).

Performance management at Philips NV

Financial performance targets are expressed in earnings before interest, taxes and amortisation EBITA which are different for each sector (healthcare, lighting and consumer lifestyle), a company wide required return on invested capital (ROIC) and a sales growth target. Targets are frequently revised as monthly results and rolling forecasts become available. Corporate financial models and benchmarking information are used to engage in discussions about local operational plans of the business units. The rolling forecasts become more important as the budget period progresses. All items on the profit and loss account, and balance sheet, are frequently reviewed as monthly performance information becomes available. Top line performance (sales) is one of the most important performance indicators. Philips uses three non-financial performance indicators as important leading indicators for future top line performance: Net Promotor Score (NPS), the Employee Engagement Score (EES) and the People Leadership Index (PLI). The NPS is a client satisfaction score indicating the willingness of current customers to recommend the product to other (potential) customers. The EES comes from an extensive employee satisfaction survey measuring employee loyalty to the company, its strategy and management. EES is considered a leading indicator for employee motivation and loyalty to the company. The PLI represents an assessment of management performance provided by subordinates in a survey covering subjects like the manager's decisiveness, effectiveness of communication, ability to inspire people, coaching and care for workers (Steens, 2010).

10.4.3 IPMS and performance evaluation

Performance measurement systems are intended to help managers evaluate performance and set out steps for future performance improvements. By increasing the number of performance variables, decision makers may get a more complete picture of past performance, but the many

[13] These are Germany, Austria and Switzerland.

different data elements also increase complexity. For instance, Kaplan and Norton suggested the use of between four and seven performance items for each dimension in the BSC (Kaplan & Norton, 1996a). This would result in between 16 and 28 different items in an entity's scorecard. The scorecard's complexity level rises when some of the indicators signal improvements in some areas while other indicators point at under performance in other areas. How would you then assess the overall performance of the entity? Single performance measures at least distinguish more unequivocally good from bad performance. The fundamental question then becomes whether human decision makers can effectively cope with IPMS complexity. Research in cognitive psychology shows that people are generally capable of processing up to seven to nine information items simultaneously (Baddeley, 1994). Human cognitive limitations may thus make it difficult to take full advantage of IPMS information. Experiments have shown that decision makers use **simplifying mechanisms** to reduce the IPMS complexities to manageable proportions.

Suppose we only have a list of randomly ordered performance indicators, a simplifying mechanism is to group the indicators into categories that are meaningful to the decision maker. In this way, the decision maker can first evaluate each category independently and then combine each category's outcome for further use. This approach is the so called **divide and conquer** strategy (Shanteau, 1988). The BSC offers a possible way of categorising multiple performance indicators, but it is certainly not the only way. Experiments have shown that when performance indicators, which show clear deviations (both positive and negative) in performance, are grouped in one BSC category, this will lead subjects to lower their importance in the overall performance assessment of the manager more than when the measures are randomly listed. This lowering of importance seems to be a way to compensate for perceived relations among indicators (Lipe & Salterio, 2002). The **divide and conquer** strategy especially seems to work when positive or negative performance variations are concentrated in specific categories. When positive and negative variations are scattered across BSC categories, the overall assessments do not appear to be significantly different from assessments using uncategorised lists of measures (Lipe & Salterio, 2002).

However, in using categorised measures, it turns out that not all categories are valued as equally important. Performance differences in the financial dimension generally have a greater impact on the overall performance evaluation than performance differences in other categories (Cardinaels & van Veen-Dirks, 2010). Using the divide and conquer strategy would then lead to over emphasis of financial performance outcomes relative to other performance dimensions. There are several reasons why decision makers would emphasise the financial dimension. One reason is the so called **outcome effect** (Mitchell & Kalb, 1981) This means that decision maker performance assessments are dominated by outcome indicators they deem most important. For instance, the assessments of qualitative dimensions of store manager performance in a retail chain appear to be dominated by whether or not the managers have attained their financial objectives (Ghosh & Lusch, 2000). Alternatively, decision makers may be more familiar with financial performance measures than with non-financial measures, because of training or experience (DeBusk, et al., 2003). Another reason may be that decision makers experience the highest performance pressures to be on the financial dimension, which come from shareholders, the board of directors or other external parties. The strong emphasis on financial results disappears when performance markers are used for instance indicating + (green), − (red) and = (yellow) signs (and colours) for above-target, below-target and on-target performance. Clear signals of performance quality seem to counteract (unconscious) importance differences attached to performance dimensions (Cardinaels & van Veen-Dirks, 2010).

Assessments of relative performance, involving comparisons between different entities within a company, may invoke another mental simplification process. IPMS generally contain two types of measures: **common measures** that are identical for every unit and **unique measures** that are only relevant for just one unit and not for other units. In practice, most common measures are financial or accounting measures, like costs, revenues and margins. Most unique measures can be found among the non-financial measures, like quality indicators, product specifications and process related metrics. When evaluators are asked to rank the performance of units based on scorecards containing both common and unique measures, they are then inclined to overweight common measures information and underweight the unique measures information in their ranking decision (Lipe & Salterio, 2000). An explanation for this result is that comparing common and unique measures across units is too complex a task for human evaluators. In order to simplify matters, evaluators start looking for common measures that allow for making easy comparisons. Unique measures may add to the final ordering of unit performance, but they are less influential than common measures. The big dilemma here is that, since common measures are predominantly accounting and financial indicators, a more complete IPMS containing more unique measures would lead evaluators to fall back to the traditional accounting and financial measures while making use of the IPMS.

Performance evaluation practice of a large multinational in consumer goods

A Dutch multinational company produces and markets 400 different brands, employing almost 180 000 workers in more than 100 countries. This very differentiated and complex multinational uses a management incentive system based on common principles, which is tailored to different local conditions. All management positions (including management trainees) receive a *Variable Play Allowance* (VPA) based on *Business Results* and *Quality of Results* performance. The Business Results part consists of two performance indicators: *Underlying Sales Growth* (USG) and *Trading Contribution* (TC). USG is calculated as a revenue growth percentage, corrected for currency exchange rate differences with the Euro, business acquisitions and business disposals. TC is a monetary amount, defined as EBIT minus an imputed cost of capital. The cost of capital is defined as the product of a company wide uniform WACC times the book value of divisional assets. The VPA *Quality of Results* part contains performance information that is especially tailored to the management position. All managers have at least one common element in the Quality of Results part, which is market share. This part will compensate USG performance that is due to total market growth when the company has lost market share to other competitors. For each manager, the Quality of Results part of VPA contains specific quantifiable items, like the successful conclusion of projects, adherence to quality norms and improvement targets. The top 150 managers also receive a bonus based on Total Shareholder Return of the total company (share price including dividend payments) and Global Performance Share Targets, which are three year performance outcomes, based on USG and operational cash flow (Groot & Van Mourik, 2010).

10.4.4 Performance implications of IPMS

Empirical research has not found a clear answer whether the use of IPMS would lead to superior economic performance (see for good overviews Ittner, 2008; Ittner & Larcker, 2009). This is partly due to the difficulty in isolating the impact of a change in the IPMS from other changes in and around organisations. Improvements in IPMS mostly facilitate or support other changes, like a strategic reorientation, the introduction of a new product or the restructuring of the organisation and its work processes.[14] Conflicting evidence may also rise because of different methods that are applied to capture IPMS use and to measure performance. IPMS use can be measured by counting the number of different performance measures used (small scope versus broad scope IPMS), the dispersion of the importance that managers place on different performance indicators (possibly classified into financial and non-financial performance measure categories), or the extent to which a specific IPMS adheres to different dimensions (as specified in the BSC or in another performance measurement framework). An even more difficult task is to measure performance implications. For corporate scorecards, accounting performance measures like net profit or ROA can be used. For listed firms, additional market information, like share price movements, can be used. However, scorecards are generally used at lower organisational levels where non-financial dimensions of performance matter most. Reliable and relevant performance information for lower level entities may not be available, and when it is, it may be heavily influenced by actions of other units in the same or related organisations.

The simplest way of measuring the effects of the use of IPMS is to ask managers how **satisfied** they are with the measurement system. Generally, most studies show a positive association between IPMS use and measurement system satisfaction (Chenhall & Langfield-Smith, 1998; Banker, et al., 2001; Rigby, 2001). Another way of measuring IPMS effects is to ask respondents how satisfied they are with the performance of their unit. Studies using this approach generally find a positive relationship between IPMS use and the respondent 'perception of organisational performance' (Lingle & Schiemann, 1996; Hoque & James, 2000; Hall, 2008). This positive relationship may, however, partly be caused by 'common method bias.' This is the tendency people have to answer all questions in a survey in a similar manner (all high, medium or low) (Ittner, 2008). There are many possibilities for respondents to answer the performance questions in different ways. A typical form of this question is 'how do you think the overall performance of your unit has been, relative to competitors?' The respondent has the possibility to choose a certain combination of different performance dimensions, leading up to overall performance, and may choose the composition of the relevant group of competitors. Both decisions involve a great deal of subjectivity, which may lead to biased outcomes.

Studies looking at financial performance generally use accounting measures, like net profit, return on assets (ROA), and return on sales (ROS). An alternative approach, which is only possible for firms listed on the stock market, is to look at economic performance, reflected by appreciation or depreciation of the firm's stock prices. Studies that use both perceptions of performance and financial performance information show that IPMS use is more strongly related to performance perceptions than to actual financial performance (Ittner, et al., 2003; Braam & Nijssen, 2004). A possible explanation is that perceptions reflect more the expectations managers have of performance improvements, whereas financial performance measures only capture the performance that has already been reached. This timing difference is clearly demonstrated in the study of Said et al. (2003) that considers the effect of executive bonus payments being based on financial performance only, or on a combination of financial and non-financial performance measures. Higher emphasis on non-financial performance dimensions appears to be positively related to current and future stock market returns and to future ROA, but not to current ROA. This result suggests that investors impound future

[14] This is also referred to as the 'endogeneity problem' the regression parameter estimates will be inconsistent, because the explanatory variables are associated with factors not included in the model, causing the variables to be, in fact, correlated with the true (but unobserved) error term (Ittner, 2008).

operating performance into the current stock price. This study is also interesting for another reason: instead of using an 'association hypothesis' between IPMS use and performance (suggesting a positive relationship between IPMS use and performance), this study uses a 'fit hypothesis'. The fit relates to an optimal level of IPMS use that is dependent on conditions (like technology, industry and strategy). The study shows that companies may have lower performance not only because of under utilising IPMS when IPMS would be beneficial, but also from over emphasising IPMS under conditions where IPMS are not supposed to work.

All previous studies suffer from the problem that it is not easy to isolate the use of IPMS from other managerial actions or external changes impacting on performance. **Quasi-experimental** studies try to overcome this problem by evaluating the effects of specific changes in the performance measurement system in a real life company. The exclusive focus on a specific company makes it possible for the researcher to monitor the chain of events, monitor additional (partly unexpected) disturbances and take measures to control their impact on performance (Cook & Campbell, 1979). This approach has also its disadvantages. The exclusive focus on a company specific situation makes it difficult to generalise the findings to other companies. It may even be difficult to generalise to similar future situations in the same company. Quasi-experimental evaluations of the introduction of IPMS show conflicting evidence. Some locations in a hotel chain that introduced non-financial measures in their incentive system (Banker, et al., 2000), and branches of a Canadian bank that implemented the BSC (Davis & Albright, 2004), show a positive impact on subsequent performance. Other studies, however, do not report significant performance improvements when IPMS were implemented (Ittner, et al., 2003; Griffith & Neely, 2009).

The evidence we discussed in this section generally shows moderate support for a positive relationship between IPMS use and performance. However, this section also shows that it is very difficult to provide methodologically convincing proof of this relationship. Evaluation studies, following a more sophisticated methodological approach, seems to produce less convincing evidence (Ittner, 2008). This calls for more, and methodologically challenging, research to learn how organisations can make optimal use of their performance measurement and reward systems.

EXERCISES

Exercise 10.1 Financial and non-financial performance measures

A popular statement from a controller's perspective is the following:

'For managing a company effectively it is better to use financial performance measures of performance in stead of non-financial measures.'

Do you agree with this statement? Provide sufficient arguments to support your position.

Exercise 10.2 Choosing the right performance measurement system

For measuring performance, three specific performance measurement systems have been proposed:

- the *Tableau de Bord;*
- the Balanced Scorecard;
- the Performance Pyramid.

Make a systematic comparison between these three systems. Provide an overview of advantages and disadvantages of each system. Which system would you prefer and why?

Exercise 10.3 Strategic positioning

You are partner of a well-known consultancy firm specialising in strategy advice. One day, you have an appointment with the CEO of a cell-phone company who is worried about the strategic choices his company has recently made. The Scandinavian company used Porter's theory and followed a low cost strategy for some time. Instead of finding a market niche where competition could be avoided, the firm finds itself attacked by competitors pursuing both low cost and high innovating strategies. They take away market share from the company in a relatively short time.

1. Characterise the market in which the cell-phone company operates.
2. Comment on the strategic choice this company has made in the past:
   a. Are the premises under which the decision was made still valid?
   b. Should the company follow one of Porter's strategy choices?
3. What is a reasonable corporate strategy for high technology companies like the cell-phone company?

Exercise 10.4 Stock price based executive evaluation systems

Many companies assess their CEO's performance on the variations in the company's share price. In most cases, rewards are also dependent on stock price performance, for instance by granting stocks, stock options and performance vested stock options.

How effective is an executive evaluation system based on stock price performance, if you use the IPMS characteristics of Figure 10.7?

Exercise 10.5 A Strategy map for schools

The generic strategy map in Figure 10.3 is designed for profit organisations, since the ultimate goal of the generic strategy map seems to be the financial performance.

What would the strategy map of a secondary school look like? What will be on the bottom half and which are the ultimate performance dimensions of the school? Which performance dimensions connect the different stages in the strategy map and how do they connect?

Exercise 10.6 Building a balanced scorecard: Big Airline, Inc

Big Airline publishes annual operating statistics, as do most airlines. Refer to the data table for an overview of all operating statistics available for the last ten years. Consider these to be key performance indicators (KPIs).

Big Airlines annual operating statistics

Operating statistics	2008	2007	2006	2005	2004	2003	2002	2001	2000	1999	1998	1997	1996
Revenue ($billions)	17.56	17.38	16.36	14.94	13.95	13.325	11.853	10.706	10.296	9.288	8.705	8.127	7.01
Passenger revenue ($billions)	15.45	15.30	14.47	13.19	12.24	11.75	10.48	9.46	8.98	8.07	7.46	6.70	5.81
Operating income ($billions)	1.478	1.259	1.158	0.889	0.521	0.263	−0.538	−0.494	−0.036	0.465	0.665	0.247	0.09
EPS. diluted	6.83	9.04	5.85	5.23	0.19	−0.66	−4.34	−3.58	1.08	3.74	5.05	−0.02	−0.63
Total assets ($billions)	18.559	15.464	12.702	11.641	11.764	12.84	12.257	9.876	7.983	7.194	6.686	8.389	6.549
Depreciation & amortisation ($billions)	0.793	0.724	0.724	0.724	0.725	0.764	0.726	0.604	0.560	0.517	0.518	0.551	0.502
Salaries ($billions)	5.341	5.018	4.719	4.526	4.679	4.76	4.562	4.057	3.55	3.158	2.838	2.778	2.558
Passengers (millions)	87	84	82	79	74	70	67	62	58	55	56	55	50
Passenger Miles (billions)	124.6	121.4	116.7	111.8	108.3	101.3	92.7	82.3	76.1	69.6	69.1	66.3	59.3
Avail seat miles (billions)	174	169.1	162.8	158.6	152.2	150.8	137.5	124.1	115	104.5	101.7	101.5	91.4
Passenger load factor	0.716	0.718	0.717	0.705	0.712	0.672	0.674	0.663	0.662	0.666	0.679	0.653	0.649
Passenger revenue per passenger mile	0.124	0.126	0.124	0.118	0.113	0.116	0.113	0.115	0.118	0.116	0.108	0.101	0.098
Price of jet fuel/gal	$ 0.590	$ 0.695	$ 0.722	$ 0.595	$ 0.588	$ 0.636	$ 0.664	$ 0.716	$ 0.804	$ 0.636	$ 0.560	$ 0.578	$ 0.562
No. aircraft	577	575	564	558	543	544	536	486	462	429	405	382	364
Employees (thousands)	91	90	86	81	78	85	84	79	74	69	66	64	59
Serious incidents (**www.airsafe.com**)	5	4	2	3	2	4	5	6	2	4	2	5	6
PL Index (GDP price deflator; **www.bea.gov**)	102.86	101.66	100	98.19	96.14	94.16	91.7	89.76	86.83	83.56	80.46	77.84	75.66
Data from annual reports unless otherwise noted													

1. Hypothesise that these operating statistics can be fashioned into a Balanced Scorecard. Draw a strategy map that displays the hypothesised linkages among the airline's KPIs.
2. Test whether the hypothesised linkages are statistically significant, as predicted.
3. Revise the strategy map with hypothesised linkages from the first requirement to a strategy map that represents the statistically significant linkages you found under the second requirement.
4. Discuss whether the original and the revised strategy maps would be reliable and useful as a balanced scorecard for Big Airline.

Exercise 10.7 Performance assessment

A French family owned food business *La Cuisine* has two locations: a children friendly family restaurant *Vacance Soleil* where large numbers of customers are served at reasonable prices for a decent meal; and a fancy restaurant *L'aigle D'or* offering exquisite food at premium prices for the upper end of the market. The family owning the restaurants has stated the following objectives for the years 2010 and 2011:

- maximise sales and profits;
- optimise customer satisfaction;
- improve quality of food and of operations.

Both restaurants have just presented the scores on the most important key performance indicators (see the data table). The owners of *La Cuisine* have a year-long tradition of granting a special reward to the best performing restaurant. To which restaurant do you think the special reward should go this year? Explain your choice.

Key performance indicators of La Cuisine restaurants

	Restaurant Vacance Soleil		Restaurant L'aigle D'or	
	2010	2011	2010	2011
Financial				
Sales	€ 250 000	€ 300 000	€ 400 000	€ 350 000
Return on sales	25%	20%	32%	40%
Customer				
Returning customer	30%	39%	60%	42%
Mystery guest rating	70	77	90	81
Internal business processes				
Waste	6%	8%	12%	9%
Cleanliness	80%	90%	96%	82%
Learning and Growth				
Hours of training per employee	100	120	200	140
Years of experience chef	20	24	25	21

Exercise 10.8 Organising scorecard information

A large international airline owns an aircraft maintenance department that services the fleet and that also services aircraft from other airlines. Performance information is depicted in the data table.

Performance information from the maintenance department over 2010-2012

Performance items	2010	2011	2012	Explanation performance items
EBIT	20	2	8	in million euros
Number of strategic projects	6	12	2	count of number of projects
On-time delivery of work	90	90	94	percentage of projects delivered on time
Productivity	150	90	140	revenues per hour labor time
Return on Capital Employed	2	0.2	0.8	in percentage
Sales to external customers	20	21	22	in million euros
Service level	70	40	100	customer satisfaction (0=very dissatisfied to 100=very satisfied)
Sick leave	5	12	8	in percentage of total work hours available
Total number of personnel	260	260	200	full-time equivalents

1. The performance items are listed in alphabetical order. Try to make sense of the performance information provided. Which year was the best year and why?

Management added a column for year 2010 of indications whether 2010 was better (upward arrow), worse (downward arrow) or equal to targets (a dot) set for 2010. See the data table.

Performance difference with target

Performance items		2010
EBIT	↗	20
Number of strategic projects	↘	6
On-time delivery of work	•	90
Productivity	•	150
Return on Capital Employed	↗	2
Sales to external customers	•	20
Service level	•	70
Sick leave	↗	5
Total number of personnel	•	260

2. Knowing this information, does it change anything you said under question 1?
3. What complexity reduction strategies (see Section 10.4.3) work best in this example?
4. What do you at least need to know in order to be able to give a good and fair judgment about this unit's performance?

CASES

Case 10.1 Improving luggage handling operations

Carl Schueller is a managing partner of Schueller Consulting Services, a company specialised in performance management systems. He is asked to advise the management of a large European airport who wants to improve the luggage handling system. When Schueller enters the office of the airport manager responsible for luggage handling, he finds him looking out of the window and down on the airport platform. 'Please join me, and look what is happening out there.' When Carl looks at the platform he sees seven planes having their cargo off-loaded. 'Now look closely what happens next' the manager warns, and he points his finger at a lorry that is returning at high speed to the terminal, carrying on it only one bag. 'That is not very economical,' Schueller comments, 'to make a ride for delivering just one bag to the terminal.'

The manager responds: 'And that is not all, it happens all the time. We want to improve our luggage handling system, by making sure we will have the luggage delivered as quickly as possible at the conveyor belt. And we want to reduce the percentage luggage that is lost, as well as the percentage luggage damaged. In order to speed up our luggage handling time and we decided to give a bonus to the team that gets the first bag of a plane to hit the conveyor belt within fifteen minutes after complete standstill of the airplane. So what happens now is that passengers see the first suitcase arriving very quickly and after that piece it takes a while before other bags start coming in. And we waste time and fuel because personnel make little rides with only one bag in their lorry.'

1. What is the fundamental problem here?
2. What causes this problem: the bonus system, the performance measurement system or the personnel's attitude? Or perhaps all three?

In the discussion that follows, Schueller suggests changing the performance measurement system: 'Perhaps you should consider not measuring the time between the plane's standstill and the first bag hitting the conveyor belt, but between the plane's standstill and the last bag delivered on the belt. In that way you assure that all bags are delivered on time.'

3. What do you think of this suggestion? What are the advantages and disadvantages of Schuller's solution?
4. Suggest a performance system that supports all luggage handling system objectives: fast delivery at the conveyor belt, a minimum number of pieces missing and luggage being treated with sufficient care.

Case 10.2 Publish or perish

Universities want their academics to be successful teachers and researchers. Teaching and research are mostly measured and evaluated separately. An important, and often intensely debated, issue is how university administrators can reliably measure the research output of academics. Please comment, using some of the IPMS characteristics mentioned in Figure 10.7, on the following alternative research output measurement instruments that have been used in universities:

1. The assessment by a committee of experts about the quality of the research programme a group of researchers intends to execute in the following four years.
2. The assessment by a committee of experts about the quality of the research publications realised in the previous four years.
3. Counting the number of journal articles and books published in the previous four years.
4. Counting the number of citations to articles published in the previous four years.
5. Counting both the number of citations and the number of articles published in the previous four years.

Case 10.3 The auditor's individual scorecard

Auditors in a big-four auditing firm are evaluated on a set of balanced scorecard information. The individual balanced scorecard (IBSC) is developed for senior auditors, who are responsible for generating sufficient profit for the firm, for managing an audit team, for training young professionals and for continuously improving the quality of their own work. The IBSC comprises information on six performance dimensions:

- Market visibility (how well-known is the auditor in the market for audit services?)
- Client orientation (what is the quality of the auditor-client relationship?)
- Team guidance (how well does the auditor coach assistant auditors?)

- Personal effectiveness (how well organised is the auditor?)
- Performance (what was the auditor's contribution to firm performance?)
- Professionalism (to what extent is the auditor capable of improving the quality of their work?)

1. Try to relate the six performance dimensions to the different task areas of the senior auditor in this firm.
   a. Are all responsibility areas sufficiently covered?
   b. Which performance measurement dimensions would you remove?
   c. What performance dimensions would you add?
2. Design two to three specific performance indicators for each of the six dimensions of the IBSC. Each indicator needs to be an objective measure of performance or conduct.
3. An audit firm generally has two main strategic priorities:
   a. Make profit for its shareholders (or partners) to secure the economic future of the firm.
   b. Exercise an independent audit of the client's financial reporting quality.

Re-evaluate the IBSC developed under requirement 2 for each of the two different roles of the auditing firm.

References

Abernethy, M.A., and Lillis, A.M. (1995). The impact of manufacturing flexibility on management control system design. *Accounting, Organizations and Society, 20*(4), 241-258.

Anderson, E.W., Fornell, C., and Lehmann, D.R. (1994). Customer satisfaction, market share and profitability: Findings from Sweden. *Journal of Marketing, 58*(July), 53-66.

Argyres, N., and Zenger, T. (2009). Capabilities, transaction costs, and firm boundaries: a dynamic perspective and integration. *Strategic Organization, forthcoming.*

Baddeley, A. (1994). The magical number seven: still magic after all these years? *Psychological Review*(April), 353-356.

Baker, G.P. (1990). Pay-For-Performance for Middle Managers: Causes and Consequences. *Journal of Applied Corporate Finance, 3*(3, Fall), 50-61.

Banker, R., Janakiraman, S., and Konstans, C. (2001). *Balanced Scorecard: Linking Strategy to Performance.* New York: Financial Executives Intenational.

Banker, R.D., Potter, G., and Srinivasan, D. (2000). An Empirical Investigation of an Incentive Plan that Includes Nonfinancial Performance Measures. *The Accounting Review, 75*(1), 65-92.

Barney, J. (1991). Firm resources and sustained competitive advantage. *Journal of Management, 17,* 771-792.

Behn, B.K., and Riley, R.A. (1999). Using non-financial information to predict financial performance: the case of the US airline industry. *Journal of Accounting, Auditing & Finance, 14*(1), 29-56.

Bourguignon, A., Malleret, V., and Nørreklit, H. (2004). The American balanced scorecard versus the French tableau de bord: the ideological dimension. *Management Accounting Research, 15*(2, June), 107-134.

Bouwens, J., and Speklé, R.F. (2007). Does EVA add value? In T. Hopper, D. Northcott & R. Scapens (Eds.), *Issues in Management Accounting* (3 ed., pp. 245-268). Edinburgh: Prentice Hall/Financial Times.

Braam, G., and Nijssen, E. (2004). Performance effects of using the balanced scorecard: the Dutch experience. *Long Range Planning, 37,* 335-349.

Bryant, L., Jones, D.A., Widener, S.K. (2004). Managing Value Creation within the Firm: An Examination of Multiple Performance Measures. *Journal of Management Accounting Research, (16),* 107-131.

Bushman, R.M., Indjejikian, R., and Smith, A. (1996). CEO compensation: the role of individual performance evaluation. *Journal of Accounting and Economics, 21,* 161-194.

Bushman, R.M., Indjejikian, R.J., and Smith, A. (1995). Aggregate Performance Measures in Business Unit Manager Compensation: The Role of Intrafirm Interdependencies. *Journal of Accounting Research, 33*(supplement), 101-128.

Cardinaels, E., and van Veen-Dirks, P.M.G. (2010). Financial versus non-financial information: The impact of information organization and presentation in a Balanced Scorecard. *Accounting, Organizations and Society, 35*(6 (August)), 565-578.

Chenhall, R.H., and Langfield-Smith, K. (1998). The relationship between strategic priorities, management techniques and management accounting: an empirical investigation using a systems approach. *Accounting, Organizations and Society, 23*(3), 243-264.

Chenhall, R.H., and Morris, D. (1986). The impact of structure, environment, and interdependence on the perceived usefulness of management accounting systems. *The Accounting Review, 61*(1, January), 16-35.

Chiapello, E., Drechsler, C., and Lebas, M. (2001). The Tableau de Bord, a French approach to management information. Unpublished paper. HEC School of Management.

Chiapello, E., and Lebas, M. (1996, May 2-4, 1996). *The 'Tableau de Bord', a French Approach to Management Information.* Paper presented at the 19th Annual Congress of the European Accounting Association, Bergen, Norway.

Cook, T.D., & Campbell, D.T. (1979). *Quasi-Experimentation:* Hougton Mifflin Company, Boston.

Cooper, R. (1995). *When Lean Enterprises Collide.* Boston, Masachussettes: Harvard Business School Press.

D'Aveni, R.A. (1994). *Hypercompetition, Managing the Dynamics of Strategic Maneuvering.* New York: The Free Press.

D'Aveni, R.A. (1995). *Hypercompetitive Rivalries, Competing in Highly Dynamic Environments.* New York: The Free Press.

Daum, J.H. (2005). Tableau de Bord: Besser als die Balanced Scorecard? *Der Controlling Berater*(7, December), 2/459-502.

Davis, S., and Albright, T. (2004). An investigation of the effect of balanced scorecard implementation on financial performance. *Management Accounting Research, 15,* 135-153.

DeBusk, G.K., Brown, R.M., & Killough, L.N. (2003). Components and relative weights in utilization of performance measurement systems like the Balanced Scorecard. *British Accounting Review, 35*(3), 215-231.

Dresner, M., and Xu, K. (1995). Customer service, customer satisfaction and corporate performance in the service sector. *Journal of Business Logistics, 16*(1), 23-40.

Easton, P.D., and Zmijewski, M.E. (1989). Cross-sectional variation in the stock market response to accounting earnings announcements. *Journal of Accounting and Economics, 11*(2), 117-141.

Eccles, R.G. (1991). The Performance Measurement Manifesto. *Harvard Business Review*(January-February), 131-137.

Feltham, G., and Xie, J. (1994). Performance measure congruity and diversity in multi-task principal/agent relations. *The Accounting Review, 69*(3), 429-453.

Foster, G., Gupta, M., and Sjoblom, L. (1996). Customer Profitability Analysis: Challenges and New Directions. *Journal of Cost Management*(Spring), 5-17.

Gehrke, I., and Horváth, P. (2002). Implementation of performance measurement: a comparative study of French and German organizations. In M.J. Epstein & J.-F. Manzoni (Eds.), *Performance measurement and management control: a compendium of research* (Vol. 12, pp. 159-180). Oxford: JAI, Elsevier Science.

Ghosh, D., and Lusch, R.F. (2000). Outcome effect, controllability and performance evaluation of managers: some field evidence from multi-outlet businesses. *Accounting, Organizations and Society, 25*(4-5), 411-425.

Gordon, L.A., and Narayanan, V.K. (1984). Management Accounting Systems, Perceived Environmental Uncertaincy and Organization Structure. *Accounting, Organizations and Society, 9*(1), 33-47.

Govindarajan, V., and Fisher, J. (1990). Strategy, Control Systems, and Resource Sharing: Effects on Business Unit Performance. *Academy of Management Journal, 33*(2), 259-285.

Govindarajan, V., and Gupta, A.K. (1985). Linking control systems to business unit strategy: impact on performance. *Accounting, Organizations and Society, 10*(1), 51-66.

Griffith, R., and Neely, A. (2009). Performance Pay and Managerial Experience in Multitask Teams: Evidence from within a Firm. *Journal of Labor Economics, 27*(1), 49-82.

Groot, T., and Van Mourik, G. (2010). International Performance Measurement and Evaluation. In W. Westerman, J. Van der Meer-Kooistra & K. Langfield-Smith (Eds.), *International Management Accounting and Control* (pp. 127-148). London: McGraw-Hill.

Groot, T.L.C.M., van Manen, J.T., Menkhorst, C.J., Roozen, F.A., and Til, G.E.A.v. (2000). *De Balanced Scorecard, Theorie, toepassingen en ervaringen* (Vol. 38). Deventer: Kluwer.

de Guerny, J., Guiriec, J.C., and Lavergne, J. (1990). *Principes et mise en place du Tableau de Bord de Gestion* (6 ed.). Paris.

Hall, M. (2008). The effect of comprehensive performance measurement systems on role clarity, psychological empowerment and managerial performance. *Accounting, Organizations and Society, 33*(2/3), 141-163.

Holmström, B. (1979). Moral Hazard and Observability. *The Bell Journal of Economics, Vol. 10, No. 1, Spring,* 74-91.

Hoque, Z., and James, W. (2000). Linking Balanced Scorecard Measures to Size and Market Factors: Impact on Organizational Performance. *Journal of Management Accounting Research, 12,* 1-17.

Ittner, C.D. (2008). Does measuring intangibles for management purposes improve performance? A review of the evidence. *Accounting and Business Research, 38*(3), 261-272.

Ittner, C.D., and Larcker, D. (2002). Determinants of performance measure choices in worker incentive plans. *Journal of Labor Economics, 20*(2), S58-S90.

Ittner, C.D., and Larcker, D.F. (1997). Quality strategy, strategic control systems, and organizational performance. *Accounting, Organizations and Society, 22,* 293-314.

Ittner, C.D., and Larcker, D.F. (1998). Are Nonfinancial Measures Leading Indicators of Financial Performance? An Analysis of Customer Satisfaction. *Journal of Accounting Research, 36*(Supplement), 1-35.

Ittner, C.D., and Larcker, D.F. (2009). Extending the Boundaries: Nonfinancial Performance Measures. In C.S. Chapman, A.G. Hopwood & M.D. Shields (Eds.), *Handbook of Management Accounting Research* (Vol. 3, pp. 1235-1251). London: Elsevier.

Ittner, C.D., Larcker, D.F., and Rajan, M.V. (1997). The Choice of Performance Measures in Annual Bonus Contracts. *The Accounting Review, 72*(2, April), 231-255.

Ittner, C.D., Larcker, D.F., and Randall, T. (2003). Performance implications of strategic performance measurement in financial services firms. *Accounting, Organizations and Society, 28*(7-8), 715-741.

Kaplan, R.S., and Norton, D.P. (1992). The Balanced Scorecard - Measures that drive performance. *Harvard Business Review*(January-February), 71-79.

Kaplan, R.S., and Norton, D.P. (1993). Putting the balanced scorecard to work. *Harvard Business Review*(September/October), 134-147.

Kaplan, R.S., and Norton, D.P. (1996a). *The Balanced Scorecard.* Boston: Harvard Business Press.

Kaplan, R.S., and Norton, D.P. (1996b). Using the Balanced Scorecard as a strategic management system. *Harvard Business Review*(January-February), 75-85.

Kaplan, R.S., and Norton, D.P. (2001a). Having trouble with your strategy? Then map it! *Harvard Business Review*(January-February).

Kaplan, R.S., and Norton, D.P. (2001b). *The Strategy-focused Organization: How balanced scorecard companies thrive in the new business environment.* Boston: Harvard Business School Press.

Kaplan, R.S., and Norton, D.P. (2004). *Strategy Maps.* Boston, Massachusetts: Harvard Business School Publishing Corporation.

Keating, A.S. (1997). Determinants of divisional performance evaluation practices. *Journal of Accounting and Economics, 24,* 243-273.

Kormendi, R., and Lipe, R. (1987). Earnings innovations, earnings persistence, and stock returns. *Journal of Business, 60*(3), 323-345.

Lebas, M. (1994). Managerial accounting in France: Overview of Past Tradition and Current Practice. *The European Accounting Review, 3*(3), 471-487.

Lebas, M. (1996). Management Accounting Practice in France. In A. Bhimani (Ed.), *Management Accounting, European Perspectives* (pp. 74-99). Oxford: Oxford University Press.

Lingle, J.H., and Schiemann, W.A. (1996). From Balanced Scorecard to Strategic Gauges: is Measurement Worth It? *Management Review*(March), 56-61.

Lipe, M.G., and Salterio, S.E. (2000). The Balanced Scorecard: Judgmental Effects of Common and Unique Performance Measures. *The Accounting Review, 75*(3, July), 283-298.

Lipe, M.G., and Salterio, S.E. (2002). A note on the judgmental effects of the balanced scorecard's information organization. *Accounting, Organizations and Society, 27*(6), 531-540.

Löning, H., Pesqueux, Y., Chiapello, E., Malleret, V., Méric, J., Michel, D., et al. (1998). *Le Contrôle de Gestion.* Paris: Dunot.

Lynch, R.L., and Cross, K.F. (1991). *Measure Up! Yardsticks for Continuous Improvement:* Basil Blackwell.

Lynch, R.L., and Cross, K.F. (1995). *Measure Up! How to measure Corporate Performance* (2nd ed.). Cambridge, USA: Basil Blackwell Business.

Makadok, R. (2001). Toward a synthesis of the resource-based and dynamic-capability views of rent creation. *Strategic Management Journal, 22,* 387-401.

Malina, M., Nørreklit, H., and Selto, F. (2007). Relations among measures, result control and performance measurement models. *Contemporary Accounting Research*(Fall), 935-982.

Malmi, T. (2001). Balanced scorecards in Finnish companies: A research note. *Management Accounting Research, 12,* 207-220.

Mia, L., and Chenhall, R. (1994). The usefulness of Management Accounting Systems, Functional Differentiation and Managerial Effectiveness. *Accounting, Organizations and Society, 19*(January), 1-13.

Mitchell, T.R., and Kalb, L.S. (1981). Effect of outcome knowledge and outcome valence on supervisors' evaluations. *Journal of Applied Psychology, 6,* 604-612.

Perera, S., Harrison, G., and Poole, M. (1997). Customer-focused manufacturing strategy and the use of operations-based non-financial performance measures: a research note. *Accounting, Organizations and Society, 22*(6), 557-572.

Pezet, A. (2006). Les "French tableaux de bord" (1885-1975), L'invention du microscope managérial. Unpublished paper. Université Paris Dauphine.

Porter, M.E. (1985). *Competitive Advantage, Creating and Sustaining Superior Performance.* New York: The Free Press.

Porter, M.E., and Linde, C.v.d. (1995). Toward a New Conception of the Environment-Competitiveness Relationship. *Journal of Economic Perspectives, 9*(4, Fall), 97-118.

Rigby, D. (2001). Management tools and techniques: a survey. *California Management Review, 43*(2), 139-160.

Said, A.A., HassabElnaby, H.R., and Wier, B. (2003). An Empirical Investigation of the Performance Consequences of Nonfinancial Measures. *Journal of Management Accounting Research, 15,* 193-223.

Shanteau, J. (1988). Psychological characteristics and strategies of expert decision makers. *Acta Psychologica, 68,* 203-215.

Speckbacher, G., Bischof, J., and Pfeiffer, T. (2003). A descriptive analysis on the implementation of Balanced Scorecards in German-speaking countries. *Management Accounting Research, 14*(4), 361-387.

Steens, H.B.A. (2010). Prestatiemanagement bij Philips: het primaat van de markt. *MCA (Management Control & Accounting), 14*(April), 8-15.

Wernerfelt, B. (1984). A resource-based view of the firm. *Strategic Management Journal, 5,* 171-180.

Wernerfelt, B. (1995). The Resource-Based View of the firm: ten years after. *Strategic Management Journal, 16*(3, March), 171-174.

Wiersma, E. (2009). For which purposes do managers use Balanced Scorecards? An empirical study. *Management Accounting Research, 20*(4), 239-251.

Zeithaml, V.A., Berry, L.L., and Parasuraman, A. (1996). The Behavioral Consequences of Service Quality. *Journal of Marketing, 60*(April), 31-46.

Chapter 11

Inter-organisational management control

11.1 Introduction

Organisations face decisions whether to own needed resources or to rent or lease them from others. At one extreme of resource use, an organisation may legally acquire all rights to a resource (e.g. buy a machine, a patent or copyright, or employ human talent) and use the resource internally. At the other extreme, an organisation may rent a resource or hire a service on a fee-for-use basis from an external party. In the latter case, the external party retains resource ownership. The hiring entity may use the external resource under the terms of a **unilateral contract**, which is a statement of fees to be paid for the promised delivery of the resource: one party pays and the other delivers the resource. As we saw in Chapter 3, the choice might be for the lower total cost option.

Therefore, the structural decision about which activities are internal or external might be viewed as an 'either–or' decision, and afterwards the boundaries of the organisation are 'bright lines.' That is not to say that the boundaries are static but, as boundaries change, different forces will regulate activities that are performed inside or outside the boundary. One premise of Chapter 3's coverage of management control systems is that organisations use bureaucratic controls, such as cultural, personnel, action and results controls, to regulate, communicate and evaluate internal resources and activities. The complementary premise in Chapter 3 is that market forces regulate externally performed activities, such as external production of materials or supply of parts or tax services performed by others. The controlling market forces include competitive pricing and service, reputation, regulation and legal enforcement of contracts. But, is the issue of control this straightforward?

The evolution of modern business organisations has made Chapter 3's stark view of the firm now too restrictive to describe many modern business relationships. The purpose of this chapter is to describe the impacts on the theory and practice of management control from resource decisions that 'blur the boundaries' of organisations.[1] These decisions that blur the boundaries include cooperative outsourcing and strategic alliances that entail more coordination than unilateral purchases of parts and materials. The purchasing and the providing entities may share ownership and decision making about resources, so it is appropriate that they coordinate management controls. It was not so long ago that many academics and professionals believed that management controls were only for internal resources and that enforceable contracts were for those used externally. Changes in resource decision

[1] e.g. Cooper and Slagmulder 2004.

making over recent years have been dramatic, and management control practice is constantly evolving to fit the management of **inter-organisational relationships (IOR)**, which are combinations of resources from otherwise independent entities to accomplish specific purposes.

11.2 Alternative IORs

IORs facilitate the combination of resources of two or more previously independent organisations. Combining resources can be done in three ways: pooling of activities (leading to organisational integration), pooling of financial resources (leading to financial integration), or both. In practice, we find many different ways in which organisations combine resources. Figure 11.1 shows some common types and degrees of integration in IORs. The most complete IOR is a merger and acquisition (M&A), wherein financial and organisational resources are pooled. The narrowest relationship perhaps is a capital investment or a franchise, which is largely independent financially and organisationally, except for agreements to follow agreed procedures and to protect the image of the brand. The point of Figure 11.1 is that much variability in IOR structure exists in practice, but we note that as organisational integration increases, *ceteris paribus*, the importance of management controls increases–and this is the focus of this chapter.

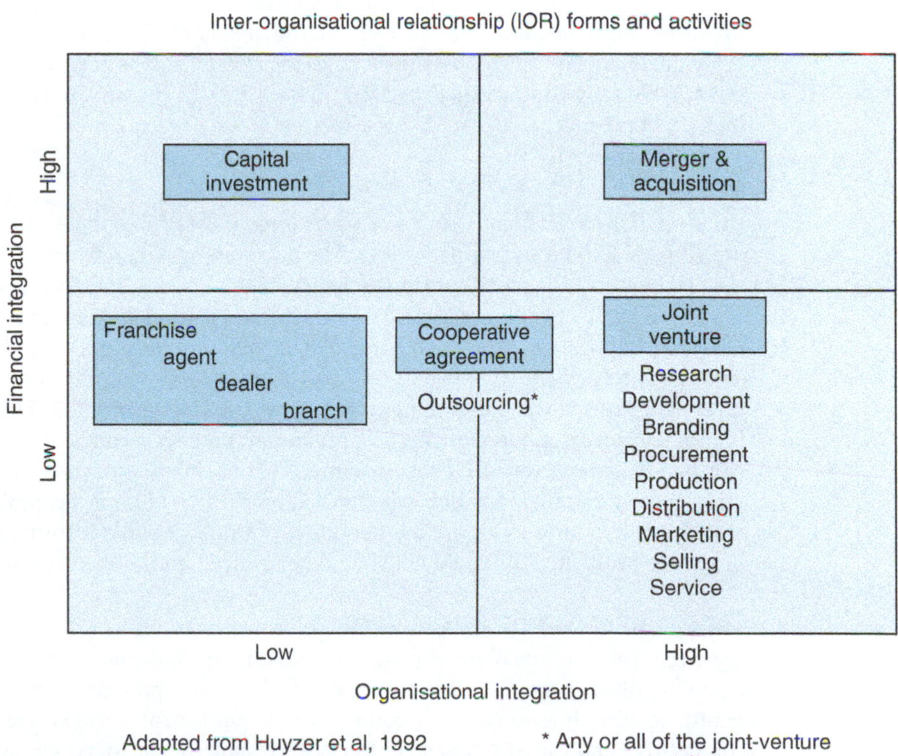

Figure 11.1 Inter-organisational relationship (IOR) forms and activities

We have observed that many different forms of IORs evolve, and control of the uses of the resources is important to both sides of the relationship. In particular, the form of IOR known as outsourcing has grown immensely over the past several decades to the point where almost every organisation outsources some activities to other entities. The management control of outsourcing IORs has been observed and analysed now for more than a decade, and we understand some of the issues, problems and solutions. While these management control opportunities are similar for all IORs, the commonality and growth of outsourcing indicate a special need to thoroughly discuss management control of outsourcing. Consider the following examples of actual outsourcing practice (gathered from public information):

EXAMPLES FROM PRACTICE

Acquisition of resources

Infosys (India) in 2007 acquired and merged three finance and accounting service centres in India, Poland and Thailand from Royal Philips Electronics (Netherlands) for approximately US$ 250 million. Infosys acquired Philips' finance and accounting facilities, knowledge and personnel. Philips' rationale for selling was to focus on its core businesses of electronics, medical imaging and lighting. Infosys' intent was to increase its global capability to provide finance and accounting services to new and existing clients. As in any merger and acquisition (M&A) transaction, Infosys assimilated and acculturated the acquired personnel and processes by careful use of management controls. Philips now outsources its global finance and accounting needs to Infosys. Because the quality of changing financial information is critically important to Philips, the outsourcing relationship is governed by a **bilateral contract,** which is a contract that specifies the fees and the reciprocal contributions promised by both parties.

Outsourcing HR resources

Unilever (UK/Netherlands) began to outsource most of its global human resource (HR) activities in 2006 to Accenture (USA). The outsourcing partnership is intended to **harmonise** Unilever's multiple HR processes, which means to unify disparate processes and procedures. Unilever's aggressive M&A transactions over several decades caused the coexistence of widely varying HR processes that Unilever could not harmonise by itself. The disparate systems surely impeded information flow, training and recognition of global talent. Unilever also expects HR outsourcing to generate cost savings of €700 million annually from improved processes and reductions of redundant processes and personnel. The seven year contract features a **service level agreement (SLA)** that details the required quality of services, fees and implementation schedules in an IOR. The SLA is a complex combination of management controls that are intended to give Unilever and Accenture advance warnings of service problems that could not wait to be resolved until the end of the contract period.

Outsourcing ground service resources

Martinair (now jointly owned by Air France and KLM) outsourced its ground activities (e.g. cargo handling, passenger processing) mostly to service providers around the globe under fee-for-service, one to two year contracts. The market for these services was reasonably competitive and the SLA based contracts were short. Thus, Martinair could easily change service providers at the end of a contract) or sooner) if it became dissatisfied with the service provider. Martinair nevertheless used management controls, which were specified in SLAs with each provider, so that it could intervene to prevent poor service that might affect its flights and customers.

Outsourcing parts manufacturing and development resources.

In 2002 Philips outsourced the global development and manufacturing of printed circuit boards (PCBs) for its electronic products to Jabil Circuit, Inc., a US based manufacturing firm. The relationship was expected to generate €5 billion turnover annually. The outsourcing relationship involved the creation of a holding company that acquired Philips' PCB facilities in Europe, North and South America and Asia. Jabil then acquired the holding company and operated the facilities. Jabil manufactures PCBs and participates in the design of PCBs for new and redesigned products. This relationship requires detailed sharing of sensitive information between Philips and Jabil regarding product design and product demand. This information sharing could not be possible without a high level of trust and effective controls to assure the timely use and protection of proprietary data.

Sources: **'Infosys Acquires Philips BPO centres,' (accessed 2 Apr 2011): http://www.offshoringtimes.com/Pages/2007/BPO_news1694.html**

'Accenture lands major HR outsourcing deal with Unilever' **http://www.cbronline.com/news/accenture_lands_major_hr_outsourcing_deal_with_unilever**.

'Jabil Announces Manufacturing Agreement With Philips,' **http://www.jabil.com/news/news_releases/2002/08282002.html.**

'Cementing the Relationship' **http://www.swissport.com/fileadmin/downloads/publications/swissreporter_2003_12.pdf**

11.3 Strategic management issues for IORs

We believe that strategic development of IORs should follow a rational, sequential process that is similar to general strategic decision making, discussed earlier in Chapter 3. Of particular interest in this chapter, this decision making process generates demand for effective management controls, which organisations draw from the portfolio of controls also presented in Chapter 3. The strategic process of building an IOR entails several phases, including:

- Goal formulation
- Partner search and selection
- Contracting
- Implementation and control
- Expansion or dissolution.

11.3.1 Goal formulation

Developing an IOR to address an important resource deficiency, in any of the forms shown in Figure 11.1, means the choice to a) not develop the resources in house and b) purchase and merge the resources from an external source, as InfoSys did when it purchased Philips finance service centres and Jabil did when it purchased Philips' PCB resources, or c) create IORs to develop and/or hire the resources from external source(s), as Martinair, Philips and Unilever did.

Discussions about forming an IOR generally begin with a recognition that the organisation is lacking the capability to perform certain activities efficiently. In our earlier examples, Jabil and Infosys chose to increase their strategic capabilities by merger and acquisition. Martinair and Philips sought to minimise their global service costs and could not do so efficiently by themselves. Because ground services and financial services were not core competencies of Martinair and Philips, respectively, the firms' strategy was to focus scarce resources on what they could do best–fly airplanes or develop new technologies. Similarly, Unilever could not harmonise its global HR processes by itself and outsourced the effort because it saw itself as primarily a marketing company, not an HR expert.

Observers of the development of IORs have commonly relied on transaction cost economics (TCE) and the resource based view of the firm (RBV) to explain the formation of IORs. TCE predicts that organisations will form an IOR when:

a. Activities and resources to be externalised are generic and do not require specific assets or knowledge,
b. Activities and resources are needed on a predictable or programmable basis.
c. Transactions are at low risk from losses because uncertainty about the opportunism and capabilities of the provider is low.

RBV explains that firms build competitive advantages on rare, valuable, inimitable resources that are not readily available from others, so they will retain and build on these internally. Alternatively, one can predict from RBV that organisations have no incentives to retain non-core resources when they can use an IOR to obtain these resources or activities at lower cost. Although TCE and RBV seek to explain the structure and performance of organisations, we regard TCE and RBV to be complementary theories. Thus, we expect firms to obtain non-core resources and activities from competitive markets. These markets feature sufficient capacity to absorb variable demands and will punish opportunistic or deceitful providers by impairing their reputations.[2] This common understanding might not be sufficient, however, to explain the organisationally integrated IORs that require more cooperation than simple market mediation of transactions for parts and services.

Organisations may begin to form relationships with IORs for value chain activities such as manufacturing or 'back office' business services. Many organisations have found that business services are relatively low valued, predictable and available in competitive markets. However, many firms are also developing IORs, even outsourcing highly valued resources and activities because they (apparently) can be controlled successfully via organisational integration across organisational boundaries. The 'smile curve' developed by Stan Shih in Figure 11.2 illustrates typical value chain activities, their relative values, and a prediction that firms will start to outsource the lower valued activities and possibly move later to higher valued activities.[3]

---

[2] Important, seminal references are Williamson 1981 and Barney 1991.

[3] **http://en.wikipedia.org/wiki/Smiling_Curve** (accessed 3 April 2011).

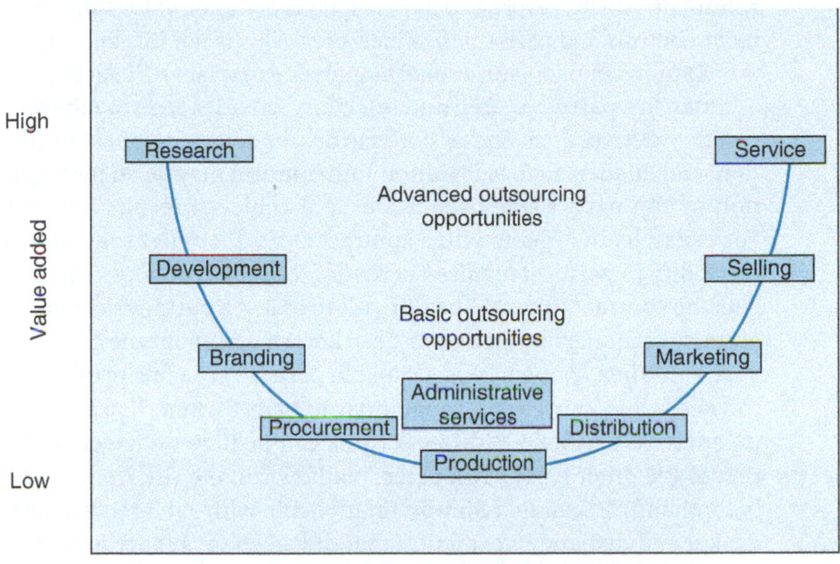

Adapted from S. Shih, Value Creation in the Knowledge Economy

Figure 11.2 Resource-value 'smile' curve

11.3.2 Partner search and choice

The difference between an IOR that requires organisational integration and the everyday actions to purchase goods and services from others, is that an integrated IOR materially affects the strategic operations of both parties and, therefore, is more sensitive to **relationship risk,** which in this context is the exposure to loss from poor performance by an IOR partner. For example, an airline like Martinair that outsources its ground services via an IOR depends on timely, error free servicing by its provider. The provider must supply sufficient capacity to meet a reasonable level of unexpected demand or variation in flight arrivals and departures. The airline must ensure that any schedule changes are determined and communicated sufficiently in advance to allow the ground services provider to react. Outsourcing critical manufacturing, finance or human resource services means that providers and purchasers likewise need to anticipate and adapt to changing needs and conditions affecting both parties. Experience and common sense reinforce that partner selection with anticipation of these types of bilateral responsibilities is critical to a successful IOR.

Partner search activities should be guided by potential partners' reputation for integrity, capability and teamwork. Assessing these attributes prior to actual experience with a partner can be difficult. It is not surprising that a common explanation for why a firm has chosen to partner with another is that: 'We have worked together successfully on other projects, and we feel comfortable that we will work well together again on the IOR'. Otherwise, a firm might rely on market reputations (evidenced by longevity in the field, impressive customer lists, experiences with peers and so on), if the information is available. When markets are 'thin,' with few participants, market reputation may be unavailable and more extensive investigations are necessary. Firms will try to assess potential partner integrity and organisational culture fit, which is expressed as perceptions of shared values and practices, such as management controls and performance measures. This is not idle speculation, for evidence exists that fit or misfit of organisational culture does explain IOR success or failure.[4]

Extensive partner search and selection activities seek to minimise *ex ante* relationship risk that derives from one or both parties' undetected opportunities for 'hidden information' and 'hidden actions.' **Hidden information** may be an incomplete or untrue description of one party's true capabilities and achieved results before or during a contract. For example, in order to win a contract a provider might say untruthfully that it has the capability to perform required activities, but really it hopes to develop capability after it gets the contract. It would be difficult to assess a partner's capabilities beforehand in the absence of market reputation or deep knowledge about the capabilities required from the partner. When shopping for a capable partner, it seems prudent to know enough about the needed resources and capabilities to detect when they are or are not available from prospective partners. **Hidden actions** can include undetected shirking and appropriation of the other party's resources, but how can the risk from hidden actions be assessed beforehand? Recall that Philips' relationship with Jabil required use of sensitive product design and demand information that, if leaked to competitors like Nokia, could damage Philips' prospects. These violations are difficult to detect after a contract is written, so a large part of the partner search and selection process assesses whether a partner can be trusted in advance.

Some amount of **trust**, which is the belief that a partner will behave as expected, is necessary in any transaction. It must be, because completely eliminating all relationship risk is impossible. The concept of trust spans several dimensions, including:

- Trust in the **competence** of the other party's capability to perform as expected
- Trust in the **benevolence** of the other party to act in the best interest of the other
- Trust in the **integrity** of the other to act and communicate truthfully
- Trust that the other will **collaborate** to resolve issues that are not specifically spelled out in the contract

These dimensions of trust may be built from the experiences of interactions of many market participants or from prior experiences between specific partners.

Selection of IOR partners invariably involves a high level of trust when partners seek a relationship for sensitive, customised products in thin markets. In such cases, both sides of the relationship may have to invest heavily to develop and support new capabilities, which necessitates long term relationships. Surely every relationship should have an exit plan. But think of the 'switching' costs a company like Unilever would incur, for example, if it decided to change global HR service providers halfway through its seven year contract with Accenture! Some observers liken these long term, blurred IORs as trust based marriages without the possibility for divorce. For example, can Accenture be trusted to partner with Unilever to identify or develop new HR executives? Careful, pre-contracting assessment of trust and a plan for verification of trust through reliable management controls seem indispensable to IOR success.

[4] Hofstede et al. (1990), Bitici et al. (2006) Pothukuchi et al. (2002).

11.3.3 Contracting

The organisation that is seeking to develop or rent resources via an IOR must decide a) with which partner and b) with what contract terms. It is possible that contract terms for the same resources might be different for different partners, but this can depend on the relative bargaining power[5] of the two (or more) parties. For example, Martinair chose to outsource ground services that were very similar everywhere (almost generic) and available competitively from multiple providers. Thus, this airline could impose many contract terms on its providers. On the other hand, Unilever sought harmonised global HR services at a time when no global HR provider existed. The market for these customised services could not be 'thinner,' and Unilever likely would not rely completely on competitive bids for specific services (that could not be fully described). Thus, choosing partners and contract terms had to be agreeable to both Unilever and Accenture, because both were taking large risks.

IOR contracting seeks to eliminate or mitigate relationship risks that can come from outside or within a relationship. External or environmental risk can come from any direction: market or industry shifts, technology breakthroughs, political changes and true environmental changes (storms, damage, etc.). These are best controlled by diversification of resources and insurance. Internal relationship risks may not be completely covered by contracts. Still the hidden action risk remains that, if the provider had the capability before, now after winning the contract it might secretly substitute inferior resources. The provider might bill for time and services not completed, or it might use its partner's resources that were contributed to the IOR for private gain. For example, the risk of a service error by an external provider that delays a Martinair cargo flight in Colombia, which affects perishable goods and that disrupts all subsequent uses of an aircraft, can be anticipated and remedies prescribed by a service contract. However, outsourcing finance and accounting activities means that Philips might not have current 'business intelligence' about its operations and customers that it would have if Philips were still performing those activities. Similarly, without internal HR personnel at the operational level, Unilever might not be able to identify its next generation of **strategic** HR managers. This type of opportunity cost based risk probably cannot be remedied by contractual terms or penalties. However, contracts can create incentives for innovation, information sharing, and initiatives not specifically required by contracts. This dynamic contracting goes beyond normal bilateral contracting that specifies reciprocal obligations and might be absolutely critical to the management control of organisationally integrated IORs.

11.3.4 Implementation and management control

Business (and life in general) would be simpler and more efficient if only trust and a handshake were needed to execute an IOR. Sadly, this is rarely the case (but fortunately for lawyers and designers of management controls!). However, just as IORs can be dynamic, the level of trust that supports an IOR can build with positive reinforcement from management controls, which reliably and repeatedly signal that the relationship is 'in control'. Thus, IOR efficiency can be implemented and improved with proper management controls.

[5] Bargaining power may be the result of knowledge, economic or political influence, or timing.

11.3.4.1 Governance

The design, use and interpretations of management controls and their signals need a framework of **governance,** which is the set of decision rights, reporting requirements and evaluation processes for a specific set of activities, such as the bilateral responsibilities of an IOR. A **governance structure** is the chosen organisational reflection of the operational, tactical and strategic responsibilities of both parties to an IOR; that is, a governance structure may specify action controls for who has which decision rights, at which level of responsibility, who reports to whom and how, and who has the authority to approve or intervene based on relevant information. We have observed governance structures that vary from detailed, daily governance activities to mostly hands off, infrequent reviews of results. We suspect that the intensity of governance reflects a) the level of strategic responsibility, b) the amount of trust in the relationship, and c) the sensitivity of parties' well-being to performance errors.

INSIGHT FROM RESEARCH 11.1

Holland Sweetener Company (HSC) was a joint venture of DSM BV (Dutch) and Tosoh Nederland BV (Japanese) that cooperated to produce and market aspartame, an artificial sweetener that competes with Nutrasweet produced by Monsanto Corporation. DSM expected to gain from production technology and shared investment costs from Tosoh. Tosoh gained access to a key raw material, which only Monsanto and DSM manufactured, to the European product and labour markets, and to DSM's advanced chemical process management tools. The joint venture's governance structure operated at a high level to inform both DSM and Tosoh about strategic plans, budgets, investments and managerial appointments. Interestingly, only a few, low level personnel were employees of the joint venture; all others were employees of either DSM or Tosoh. The joint venture contract focused on equity shares, loan approvals, profit and loss shares, dividend shares, employee training and protection of proprietary information. The contract did not clearly specify conflict resolution measures, operational performance expectations or performance measures (e.g. costs allowed). Partly as a result of this contract incompleteness, conflicts arose over such mundane items as allocations of costs of active and retired employees. Rather than renegotiate the contracts to correct for omissions, as DSM preferred, non-covered conflicts were negotiated on a costly, case-by-case basis. Fortunately, few conflicts ended in legal proceedings because employees of both national cultures appreciated the importance of saving face and compromise.

Source: Groot and Merchant (2000).

11.3.4.2 Management controls

Some have questioned whether simultaneous use of trust and management controls actually reduces trust because, they argue, the existence of management controls implies mistrust and erodes goodwill. This might be true for IORs that closely resemble market transactions for standardised products for which competitive sources exist–management controls might be redundant. In these cases markets enforce trust. However, and as discussed in Chapter 3, management controls also communicate and promote learning, both of which are likely to be important to the success of IORs that intend to deliver customised or innovative outcomes. Indeed, others theorise and find evidence that repeated and satisfactory uses of management controls build trust because continued (verifiable) conformance to desired actions confirms a party's competence and integrity.[6]

Parties to an IOR may use a portfolio of management controls from the possibilities presented in Chapter 3 (see Figure 3.12).These controls enable firms to cope with management complications of assimilating, partnering or working with previously independent organisations. The control issues of attaining goal congruence and insuring against various risks are similar for internally or externally managed resources. However, controlling people and processes across latent or continuing organisational boundaries is complicated by more cross boundary coordination, less observable activities, differences in organisational culture and history,[7] undetected misalignment of goals and incomplete contracting. All of the enhanced risks of managing an IOR might be mitigated or avoided by effective management controls that can be more complex than those used for similar, internal activities.

Internal controls typically operate within a hierarchical organisational structure, wherein sub-units report upwards on activities and outcomes that higher level stakeholders have an explicit right to observe, audit and sanction. Because of unobservability (hidden information and hidden actions), management control of delegated rights and responsibilities within an entity is not always straightforward or foolproof. When activities and reporting cross the boundaries of independent entities, as in an IOR observability can be further blurred. In response, IORs may employ so called **hybrid controls** that resemble internal management controls but structure extra adaptability and communications to inform both parties on the development and delivery of bilateral promises. Hybrid controls are intended to reduce information asymmetry between parties and to encourage cooperation and adaptation to changing conditions. Hybrid controls reflect that bilateral contracts are inherently incomplete and cannot anticipate every future state and needed response. For example, a hybrid results control might specify expectations for service quality and delivery, but recognises that customer or production changes might alter what is needed to meet performance expectations. In anticipation, parties to the IOR may schedule frequent standing meetings to discuss results, may develop 'hotlines' for fast breaking changes, and may structure incentives for both parties to act quickly and beneficially for the interests of both.[8]

The need for hybrid control of organisationally integrated IORs seems obvious, but appears to be overlooked in practice. Less than half of the M&A activities have been judged a financial success. At the purchasing end of the ownership spectrum, some observers have attributed this historically low rate of 'success' to empire building by greedy executives who anticipate larger compensation from managing a larger organisation. Still others look at the same failure rate and perceive failed assimilation and acculturation–or in this chapter's context: faulty and ineffective management controls. Many **joint ventures,** which generally are business partnerships (toward the middle of the ownership spectrum) organised for a specific purpose or project, also fail to generate the expected new technologies, products and efficiencies. Over 30% of a sample of joint ventures failed within their first 10 years.[9] Likewise many outsourcing relationships fail to deliver promised cost savings and product quality. Is this because of poor strategy? Poor choices of partners? Poor contracting? Inadequate

[6] For example, Das & Teng 1998, 2001; Neumann 2010; Vosselman and Van der Meer-Kooistra 2009.

[7] R.L. Boland et al. 2008.

[8] Speklé, 2001.

[9] Kogut, 1988.

management controls? Poor implementation? Or all of the above? This chapter's contention is that management controls, which may be used at every step of managing a resource relationship, are important determinants of the success or failure of IORs of any type.

INSIGHT FROM RESEARCH 11.2

Robin Cooper, Takeo Yoshikawa, and Regine Slagmulder have studied cooperative cost management practices of Japanese manufacturing firms and their parts suppliers.[10] These relationship tools 'blur the boundaries' of both purchasers and suppliers. They have found that deliberate, cooperative use of tools such as target costing and value engineering improves information sharing and coordination between parties. These activities of information sharing and cooperation to jointly set cost and quality goals a) increase operational efficiency, and b) allow both parties to focus on meeting customer future needs that have large implications for future products and profitability.

INSIGHT FROM RESEARCH 11.3

Netherlands Car BV (NedCar) was a joint venture between Volvo Car Company (Sweden), Mitsubishi Motor Company (Japan) and the Dutch state, which soon exited the venture. NedCar became primarily a jointly owned production facility on the mainland of Europe for the two auto companies that shared no other operations. In fact, the two auto companies shared only the factory's press and paint shops; the rest of the NedCar factory capacity was split and served Volvo and Mitsubishi separately. Transfer prices of autos delivered to each partner were set at agreed upon normal costs. Because the plant did not operate at normal capacity and was instituted as a cost centre, a major issue arose about how the partners would share unused fixed capacity costs. The management controls developed in this joint venture provide an example of how results control measures can contribute to cooperation even when parties have relatively little in common. The control mechanism was a self-termed 'solidarity principle' that enabled NedCar to recover capacity costs from Volvo and Mitsubishi and for the auto companies to share costs and information. Consider the following (disguised) example in Figure 11.3:

	A	B	C	D
1	**Hyothetical NedCar "Solidarity Principle" Example**			
2	**Capacity Costs ***	**NedCar**	**Volvo**	**Mitsubishi**
3	**Theoretical capacity, cars**	**200,000**	**100,000**	**100,000**
4	**Fixed capacity cost**	**€ 90,000,000**		
5	**Normal capacity, cars**	**180,000**	**90,000**	**90,000**
6	**Fixed cost assigned per car**	**€ 500**	**=B4/B5**	
7	**Actual production, cars**	**177,000**	**85,000**	**92,000**
8	**Fixed costs applied**	**€ 88,500,000**	**€ 42,500,000**	**€ 46,000,000**
9		**=C8+D8**	**=B6*C7**	**=B6*D7**
10	**Voume variance**	**€ 1,500,000**	**€ 2,500,000**	**€ (1,000,000)**
11		**=C10+D10**	**=(C5-C7)*B6**	**=(D5-D7)*B6**
12	**Transfers to partner's NedCar account**		**€ 1,000,000**	**€ -**
13			**=IF(D10<0,-D10,0)**	**=IF(C10<0,-C10,0)**
14	**Payments for fixed costs**	**€ 90,000,000**	**€ 44,000,000**	**€ 46,000,000**
15		**=C14+D14**	**=C8+IF(C10>0,C10,0)-C12**	**=D8+IF(D10>0,D10,0)-D12**

Figure 11.3 Hypothetical cost sharing example

[10] Cooper and Yoshikawa 1994, Cooper and Slagmulder 2004.

In this hypothetical example, Volvo produces less than the normal output, while Mitsubishi produces more (the solution is symmetrical). NedCar is owed €90 000 000 for fixed capacity costs, 50% from each partner. Because Mitsubishi has over produced, it pays the full amount of fixed overhead applied to NedCar and a payment to Volvo's NedCar account for the over applied fixed overhead. This reduces Volvo' obligation to €44 000 000. This mechanism guarantees that NedCar will recover its fixed capacity cost and encourages both auto companies to produce at normal levels. The Dutch state preferred this incentive, which acted to stabilise (variable) employment levels. This mechanism also created a monetary incentive for the more successful partner (producing more than normal) to share information and innovations with its less successful partner to help raise the latter's sales and production levels to normal.

Source: Groot and Merchant 2000.

11.3.5 Expansion or dissolution

Successful IORs may quite naturally lead to replication or expansion of current joint activities. However, this happy experience may be enabled by a contract that anticipates the option to expand an existing IOR, much like the real options discussed in Chapter 4. In this case, the 'overhead' associated with re-contracting may be minimised. Likewise, every IOR contract should have an exit plan that details:

- How dissolution may be initiated by either party
- The rights to assets and obligations of the IOR
- Procedures to be followed.

Although trust can initiate an innovation based IOR, sustaining a successful IOR of the cooperative type should include prudent uses of management controls. Anticipating the needs for change and innovation in the IOR should be reflected in a contract's action and results controls, so that it is clear that both sides should innovate and will benefit from collaborative innovation. These may include shared diagnostic and interactive controls, shared rewards and penalties for contract items, and gain sharing for true innovations.

INSIGHT FROM RESEARCH 11.4

Henri Dekker's (2003) field research provides an example of how results controls can be used for coordination, innovation and cost control. The company NMA (abbreviation of 'Nederlandse Machine fabriek Alkmaar') Railway Signalling produces safety systems to the Dutch Railway Company NS ('Nederlandse Spoorwegen'). NMA decided to form a strategic alliance for the supply and innovation of automatic half-barrier installations with Railinfrabeheer (RIB), a task organisation of the Dutch government responsible for the Dutch rail infrastructure. RIB plans and coordinates the infrastructure of the Dutch railway system and as such also defines the number of products it will demand from NMA.

To induce mutual collaborative behaviour in the innovation process, the partners NMA and RIB developed a financial incentive system, called the 'alliance fund'. This fund focuses on aligning all planned innovations, accruing their financial results and dividing the residual. As a start up capital the partners have made an equal financial contribution. Yearly, the fund forecasts cost savings that are expected from planned innovations. Cost savings come from two sources within NMA: **expected savings** from improving operations and **expected purchasing results** from parts obtained at lower than expected costs. Multiplying these by the forecasted ordering quantities delivers the expected value of the cost reductions. Figure 11.4 provides an illustration of these calculations of and contributions to the alliance fund.

The total value (TV) to be realised is determined by multiplying the realised cost reductions (RS + RPR) by the forecasted amount of sales, Q_a, which equals €145 000. The TV is used to determine the contribution each partner should make to the alliance fund. NMA contributes the **realised** cost savings, i.e. the realised cost reduction multiplied by the actual quantities ordered by RIB, which is €130 500. When actual quantities ordered are less than forecasted, as in this example, RIB contributes the unrealised savings (or 'demand variance') to the fund, here €14 500.

This mechanism guarantees profits (before cost savings) to NMA, and provides an opportunity for both parties to share the cost savings. As cost reducing innovations are successfully realised, the alliance fund increases in size. Yearly, the fund is evaluated and, when it exceeds a certain threshold, the excess is allocated to benefit both partners. When, however, the alliance fund becomes insufficient to finance further innovations, after approval of the board, the partners will make equal reinvestments. Thus, the effectiveness of this mechanism to motivate cost reductions depends on the perceived fairness of the allocations of cost savings generated by NMA.

The alliance fund also works as a 'truth inducing mechanism'. RIB has normal incentives to generate high demand, which drives high, expected total cost savings earned by NMA. NMA has incentives to accomplish cost reducing innovations because this increases the budget available for innovation. However, when purchases lag expectations, RIB must compensate for the difference, providing incentives to forecast future demand accurately and honestly. Interestingly, no extra penalties are assessed for missing cost reduction targets, nor are extra rewards given for meeting the targets. That is, ignoring these 'innovation variances' attempts to neutralise the effects of setting targets that are too easy or too difficult. However, the fact that NMA might not receive full value for its realised cost savings, might attenuate its incentives to agree to aggressive cost reductions.

	A	B	C
1	The Alliance Fund		
2	Selling price	P	€ 1,000
3	Forecasted sales units next quarter	Q_f	500
4	Expected savings per unit	ES	€ 250
5	Expected purchasing result per unit	EPR	€ 60
6	Expected value of cost reductions	$EV = Q_f \times (ES + EPR)$	€ 155,000
7	Realized savings per unit	RS	€ 210
8	Realized purchasing result per unit	RPR	€ 80
9	Actual sales units in quarter	Q_a	450
10	Total value of cost reductions	$TV = Q_f \times (RS+RPR)$	€ 145,000
11	Realized value of cost reductions	$RV = Q_a \times (RS+RPR)$	€ 130,500
12	Unrealized cost savings from demand	TV - RV	€ 14,500
13	Unrealized cost savings from innovation	EV - TV	€ 10,000

Figure 11.4 The alliance fund

We turn now to case studies of the experiences of several disguised firms that reflect differences in the management control of IORs.[11]

11.4 Case studies of inter-organisational control

CASE 1: GREENJET AIRLINE - COMPETITIVE MARKETS FOR COMMODITY GOODS AND SERVICES

GreenJet Airline was established with two aircraft, a workforce of eight, and at first operated a few round trip passenger and cargo flights from its home airport in Western Europe. GreenJet's operations and fleet expanded gradually when it initiated 'worldwide' cargo services with remote cargo establishments in Asia and two other European locations. It later expanded to serve the market in the South America by acquiring a minority equity stake in a local cargo carrier.

GreenJet was recently rated in the top-20 of the world's biggest cargo carriers. It was serving nearly 100 destinations worldwide, employing a workforce of more than 3000, and maintaining a worldwide network of 40 establishments in 25 countries. A recent difficult year for GreenJet meant an annual loss of more than €70 million, which represented the poorest results achieved in GreenJet's history. In that year, the company launched significant restructuring within the company.

Goal formulation

GreenJet implemented make-or-buy studies to determine whether resources should be retained or outsourced. It divested subsidiaries and resources that were beyond the scope of GreenJet's core business, which was scheduling and flying aircraft. In turn, GreenJet outsourced the non-core resources that it needed for operations. GreenJet typically outsourced ground operations (excluding security), including ramp handling (services to the airplane on the platform), cargo handling (logistics and storage), passenger handling and crew support (transport, hotel facilities and support services). This strategy was guided by the need for local and specialised flight operations knowledge, economies of scale, competitive service markets, low switching costs (especially avoiding severance pay in many countries), and the need for flexibility when problems arose or conditions changed. For example, it was not cost efficient for GreenJet to have its own equipment, offices and personnel in foreign locations, given its low flight frequency and short stopping times. Further, if local politics or market conditions proved too volatile, GreenJet could quickly extract its planes and few personnel without worrying about physical facilities.

Partner identification and selection

GreenJet used extensive vendor selection criteria; the most important were reputations for accessibility, good relationships, flexibility and adherence to established procedures and regulations. GreenJet obtained reputation information from peers and airport authorities. Prior experiences with a specific vendor in other locations also indicated the quality of future

[11] These realistic cases fictionalise the real world experiences of several global companies that were studied by Tom Groot, Ramiro Montealegre and Frank Selto in 2012. End of chapter exercises and case analyses also rely on these cases.

relationships. Because of the global variations in regulations and operations, a vendor's specialised knowledge was key in deciding what could be outsourced and to whom.

Established procedures and regulations were factors that varied according to national cultures. To cope with these differences GreenJet used its training, process manuals, local managers to work closely with outsourcing providers, and hired people with international experience (this last is very important for gaining and retaining cultural knowledge). Controls for variation in country regulations were perceived as more difficult than for differences in national culture.

GreenJet paid special attention to current and potential provider transparency, open discussions, constant communication, real time updates and information. Communications at the operations level were frequent and open–regularly scheduled meetings (usually weekly) discussed current operations and improvement possibilities. Good communication often led to pre-emptive and corrective actions by providers before being contacted by GreenJet. It was understood that miscommunications could cause costly delays or, worse, safety incidents. GreenJet hired good communicators and trained its new service providers to communicate according to GreenJet protocols.

This airline usually preferred global/regional service providers because of lower contracting costs for repeat contracts, better price negotiations and standardised procedures. On the other hand, large providers tended to be more rigid and charged for every extra activity they performed. Local service providers, on the other hand, were likely to have deep knowledge in a specific country, and to be more flexible in order to keep their contract with GreenJet.

GreenJet identified two key aspects of service flexibility: operational flexibility–the ability and willingness to cope with changing events (e.g. flight schedule delays) and service flexibility–the willingness to provide extra services as needed without renegotiating the contract or even without extra pay. Both dimensions of flexibility were important to choosing, renewing or cancelling a service contract and provider.

Contracting

Some of the risk factors perceived by GreenJet were:

- high turnover among knowledgeable employees;
- security and the problems of terrorism, drug trafficking and uncertainty in some countries;
- safety of their flight operations;
- losing control of ground service operations;
- the financial status of the provider that could impede their ability to remain in business.

From the outsourcing service provider perspectives, the main perceived risks were: GreenJet's changing schedules, delays and cancellations with less than 24 hours notice while still expecting normal service levels; and airline bankruptcy or non-payment after the provider had invested in the relationship and had provided billed but unpaid services.

The International Air Transport Association (IATA) played an important role controlling many operating risks in GreenJet's industry and certainly influenced the way outsourcing services were negotiated. GreenJet used the IATA contracts, which had become standard in the industry and were accepted globally. These IATA agreements were useful in establishing the operational platform, in clarifying the industry terminology and expectations, and in reducing the costs of contracting. GreenJet, however, also added unique features to the IATA contract to cover its specific service needs.

Service contracts were negotiated initially by top management from GreenJet's headquarters or by its Americas' Operations. Then, Corporate Purchasing Department was responsible for negotiating, renewing or terminating contracts with regional input. The contracts clearly identified what controls were used (results, actions, personnel, cultural). In particular, GreenJet used detailed SLAs tied to specified payments, types and quality of service. In addition, SLAs spelled out penalties for non-performance that resulted in delays, damages or safety. If the services provided were at the expected level or better, however, there were no special incentives or rewards. For GreenJet, fulfiling the agreement to the expected level or better was the way for the provider to keep the outsourcing relationship, which should be a sufficient incentive. Indeed, service providers acknowledged that all airlines seemed to use the same penalties and threats. This approach might be effective because of competitive markets in which prices were under constant downward pressure.

Governance and management control

Airline supervisors and operations managers at every station were responsible for oversight of providers' operating performance on service safety, quality and timeliness. They also audited the providers' infrastructure and equipment to assess their ongoing capability to provide effective support to GreenJet operations. SLAs spelled out required cargo and passenger procedures and were complemented by manuals (describing processes and services demanded) and operational action plans. GreenJet employees also used periodic (announced or unannounced) audits of individual flights. GreenJet understood that controlling everyone's decisions was impossible; however, establishing a clear control system was useful in creating an atmosphere of compliance to procedures.

GreenJet collected performance information for each flight from Flight Activity Reports (e.g. size of cargo handled, service time needed), and Ground Safety Reports (events and actions that have led to safety problems or may compromise safety). GreenJet prepared weekly reports for each provider's performance based on the flight activity and ground safety reports. Services were rated from zero to five, where five was outstanding. If poor ratings or other problems could not be resolved at lower levels, the Americas Management or Headquarters Management were involved.

Providers did not accept airline override of their own safety procedures (e.g., in order to turn around a flight more quickly), however. In fact, GreenJet did not encourage the outsourcing service provider to take any risks, especially if there were safety and security risks involved. Instead providers should comply with the established procedures. If there was a need to override procedures, the provider had to communicate and get permission from GreenJet before proceeding with any deviation.

GreenJet did not specify staffing levels; it was mostly concerned with results. Although airline employees did not have to directly supervise providers' employees, they needed to be present at every flight to insure that personnel acted appropriately (service aircraft, deliver cargo safely, etc.). Providers typically did not allow GreenJet to intervene or discipline their employees, except in situations where safety could be compromised. Given the high turnover of ground personnel at the providers, however, GreenJet's employees at stations were constantly monitoring the capabilities of providers' new employees; sometimes to the point of questioning qualifications or interviewing new hires. The constant needs for screening, hiring and training new employees were recognised as sources of high cost by providers. In addition, many times language was a problem (not everybody in GreenJet's Americas team spoke Spanish, for example).

The providers were responsible for providing training for their employees. GreenJet, however, trained provider ground personnel on airline specific procedures at least once a year. GreenJet was also working on standardised training for ground personnel on all procedures within a country. Providers often felt like the training ground for airlines that were offering better salaries and benefits to the providers' best employees. Indeed, GreenJet preferred to hire its employees locally, but movement of Airline personnel around the globe was also necessary to provide the knowledge required for safe and efficient operations and oversight of providers. GreenJet used bonuses and promotions to keep its key employees because their experience was so valuable.

CASE 2: INNOTECH COMPANY–THIN MARKETS FOR CUSTOMISED GOODS AND SERVICES

InnoTech Company, headquartered in Europe, manufactured diverse products for business and consumer markets in more than 60 countries on six continents, and employed more than 100 000 worldwide. Each of InnoTech's three product groups has outsourced significant activities, beginning with the manufacturing of standardised product components and proceeding to more value-added activities. Recently, InnoTech applied the 'smile curve' in Figure 11.1 to support decisions to outsource financial services(among others) that were deeply integrated with InnoTech's business processes; that is, the resources were higher on the value smile than the original curve would suggest.

Goal formulation

InnoTech's general strategy was to be 'asset-light,' but to retain the highest value-added activities of product development, marketing and branding, and manufacturing of highly proprietary products. InnoTech outsourced its lowest value-adding activities and gradually has moved up the value-adding scale. In all outsourcing relationships, InnoTech sought to be a major customer of the service provider to insure that the success of the relationship was vital to both sides.

InnoTech's outsourcing of financial services evolved over a period of five years. To InnoTech, the back office activities of financial services were fragmented, inefficient and not value-added,. International benchmarking showed InnoTech that it had functioning but high cost internal financial services–at 6% of sales InnoTech's cost was nearly double the costs of best-in-class companies. InnoTech saw service standardisation as a means of increasing quality, reducing costs and achieving a competitive advantage over its rivals. InnoTech created several financial shared service centres (SSCs) in highly educated, but low cost locations in Asia and Eastern Europe. The SSCs were partly effective by reducing wage costs (about 70% savings) and by limited streamlining of existing processes.

However, service costs remained high, in part because local managers retained existing inefficiencies that purportedly reflected local conditions. Furthermore, the morale of InnoTech's financial professionals dropped as they saw their function as clearly non-value added, with few paths to top management positions. When top managers at InnoTech saw the simultaneously impending flight of its financial professionals, stagnant service costs and quality, and maturing of the outsourcing market, they realised it was time to sell the SSCs to the right partner. InnoTech believed that building on its partially successful, internal service centres by outsourcing them to a single provider would prove the easiest and quickest route to global standardisation.

Partner identification and selection

InnoTech used a consultancy firm working with internal staff to prepare a shortlist of six potential providers, based on criteria of organisational culture, innovativeness, financial soundness and management performance. Certifications for quality, sustainability and Sarbanes-Oxley (SOX), Section 404 compliance were requirements. Closer evaluation of these criteria shortened the list to two companies, which were invited to present their business plans for the SSCs and to demonstrate their performance in similar outsourcing projects. InnoTech also visited the potential providers' clients to observe and get first hand experience on how services were being provided. In addition to objective measures of performance at these sites, InnoTech managers sought signs of trust and organisational culture. Another major issue was a provider's ability to prepare contingency plans and ensure secured and uninterrupted provision of financial services. The threat of a catastrophic event that could damage or destroy a service centre required backup service centres.

InnoTech selected FinPro for the quality of its business plan and because it offered the highest price for the SSCs. The contract between InnoTech and FinPro consisted of three parts:

- the acquisition of InnoTech's SSCs;
- an outsourcing contract specifying the financial services delivered to InnoTech;
- an exit plan.

FinPro took over the SSCs in Asia and Europe and hired more than 1000 InnoTech employees, while InnoTech retained process 'ownership' and strategic level personnel to provide what they called 'judgment-based' financial controlling and business support for its operations.

FinPro knew that its labour cost advantage in India would erode and that it must offer to clients future value on its ability to deliver transformation and automation. FinPro saw in its purchase of InnoTech's SSCs an opportunity to gain expertise, technology, scale, an excellent customer and a greater global reach. FinPro's strategy was to leverage its investments and learning from its acquisition and service relationship with InnoTech to create service standardisation tools, build best-in-class finance functions, and improve service efficiency and quality across multiple customers.

Contracting

InnoTech wanted continuous cost decreases along with improving quality, and the provider wanted to protect its profit margins. The predictable tension of these competing goals underscored the importance of contracting for planned process cost savings and creating incentives to find new cost savings. They agreed to share the cost savings. These objectives were to be achieved through predictably declining, transaction based pricing to recover the provider's largely fixed costs and gain sharing agreements for additional improvements. Aggressive cost reductions meant that FinPro had to plan productivity, cost and quality improvements consistent with its profit and growth objectives. To permit contracting for these outsourced financial services, both sides, therefore, required predictable volumes and planned standardisation and automation of services. This complex budgeting analysis was the key to negotiations and the contract between InnoTech and FinPro.

The seven year service contract specified the price reductions for each contract year, targeted to reach the desired service cost percentage of sales benchmark in year seven. The agreement set expected prices based on service volumes and costs. Contracted adjustments (within negotiated volume ranges) after each year allowed both sides to resolve pricing uncertainty. Pricing also reflected the complexity of transactions, but gain sharing gave incentives to simplify and automate transactions. Relatively more gains went to the originator of the idea. This gave incentives to both sides to improve and share knowledge. InnoTech's top managers felt that this contract broke new ground by designing in an adaptive solution to transaction based pricing.

The financial services contract contained a service level agreement (SLA) where every major step of processes was described down to fine levels of detail. InnoTech determined which steps were to be performed by the service provider and which by InnoTech. The SLA also specified approximately 30 **key performance indicators** (KPIs), which are measures of performance that are critical to an organisation's strategic success. The contract's KPIs included measures for regional and global percentages of standardisation, harmonisation and process migration, and set minimum acceptable service levels for accuracy and timeliness for such activities as invoice processing, account reconciliation, master data entries, vendor payments and fixed asset entries. Consistent under performance for more than three months caused fines for FinPro (but no rewards for exceeding required accuracy or timeliness), and continued under performance gave InnoTech the right to end the contract unilaterally.

Although FinPro was responsible for recording financial transactions, the InnoTech controller was responsible for all decisions made on the financial statements. Furthermore, only InnoTech controllers could allocate access rights to the SAP system, not FinPro. Revenue recognition and valuation decisions had to adhere to InnoTech's stringent, SOX compliant rules with no variations allowed by either InnoTech controllers or FinPro. More subtle accounting decisions (accruals, etc.) were within the local InnoTech controller's decision rights.

Governance and management control

InnoTech and FinPro created a governance structure that cascaded from strategic to operational levels of service. Both sides felt that the governance structure was critically important to managing the success and risks of the service relationship and to defuse any conflicts as early as possible. At the operational level, the process owner (e.g. an InnoTech controller) within a country met with a FinPro counterpart at least monthly, and usually more often. The tactical level governance brought together InnoTech's regional financial managers (e.g. Latin America) and FinPro's SSC and global account managers each quarter to review global problems and opportunities for improvement related to the SLA's KPIs. The strategic level involved a few, high level finance, IT and global account managers on both sides who reviewed service achievements twice per year against strategic objectives and whether the objectives should change. The governance structure was intended to insure an open, frequent communication between the partners at all levels.

A most important feature of the relationship between InnoTech and FinPro was the implementation of the gain sharing incentive for innovations in cost management. Recall that the contract included a schedule of predictable cost reductions over the life of the contract. These scheduled cost reductions were included in negotiated prices for services. However, both parties knew that innovations to lower the costs of financial services would be required as the environment of financial services evolved. Specific innovations could not be predicted, but both parities knew that they would be necessary. To accommodate the dynamic environment of certain demand but unpredictable needs, the parties fashioned a gain sharing agreement that encouraged unscheduled innovations. For example, suppose that a change in financial reporting rules was imminent. Current global reporting processes probably could be adapted to the accounting change, but at high cost. An innovation in reporting or analysis could adapt at a lower cost but, unless FinPro could benefit, its incentive would be to maintain the *status quo* and pass on the higher cost to InnoTech as a 'change order' to the contract. Both parties would benefit if FinPro could capture enough of the cost savings to make it worthwhile to develop the innovation without costly delays and negotiations.

Thus, the gain sharing incentive awarded the majority of the savings to the originator of the innovation. Results controls, tied to fairly shared mutual gains, was an efficient response to necessarily incomplete contracting in a dynamic environment.

Outsourcing financial services not only required FinPro to have expertise in accounting and information technology, but also to coordinate effectively with InnoTech's management. FinPro generated financial reports that had to be approved by InnoTech's controllers. When InnoTech's controllers did not respond quickly to FinPro's draft reports, it was increasingly difficult for FinPro to deliver the final financial reports in time to InnoTech. The outsourcing contract called for results controls that measured timeliness of reporting as well as reporting errors. These results controls were tied to financial rewards and penalties for both parties.

FinPro also needed to understand InnoTech's businesses, which varied across products and locations. Cultural differences between InnoTech's management in different countries and FinPro personnel in India were managed in various ways. For example, when the financial services in Mexico were moved to FinPro, personnel from each country lived in the other country to better understand cultural and process differences. Even so, in Mexico InnoTech personnel were not as familiar with the English spoken in India. In addition, given that all the documents were generated in Spanish, but processed in India, FinPro could not provide error correction. Although English was the shared language, it was nearly everyone's second language, and miscommunications have caused missed opportunities and mistakes.

InnoTech insisted that FinPro must adhere to strict application of its revenue and valuation accounting policies (International Financial Reporting Standards), SOX Section 404 internal controls, without deviation. Although FinPro prepared financial reports, InnoTech's site controllers were responsible for resolving any grey areas of financial reporting related to accruals and allocations. An apparently unresolved reporting issue was the dependence of internal and external auditors on InnoTech's and FinPro's self-assessments on internal control adequacy. Each quarter every InnoTech unit self-assessed internal control performance and reported to regional CFOs who reported to top management. However, the migration of financial processes to FinPro also transferred related SOX-404 controls to FinPro. Because InnoTech was the financial process owner, outsourcing parts or all of the process and related internal controls to FinPro did not outsource control responsibility.

11.5 Conclusion

Management control of IORs confronts similar challenges as management control of any internal resource. However, the degree of risk and uncertainty is increased because of the separation for strategy and operations across organisational boundaries. Management controls for IORs seek to blur these boundaries and to enable information sharing and cooperation that mitigate risks and increase trust for both parties. Research and examples from practice demonstrate that apparently successful IORs use a variety of management controls. However, it does seem clear that the roles of trust and management controls become more important as the IOR moves resource use farther from market mediated transactions of separately owned resources toward cooperatively owned and developed resources. Contracts can never be complete when demand for services is dynamic and unpredictable. Innovative uses of management controls might bridge the gap between incomplete contracting and efficient relationships. Designing effective management controls for dynamic IORs is an active and evolving area for research and practice.

EXERCISES

Exercise 11.2 Identify two examples of personnel controls used by GreenJet (See Section 11.4 Case 1).

Exercise 11.3 Identify two examples of action controls used by GreenJet (See Section 11.4 Case 1).

Exercise 11.4 Identify two examples of results controls used by GreenJet (See Section 11.4 Case 1).

Exercise 11.5 Identify two examples of cultural controls used by InnoTech (See Section 11.4 Case 2).

Exercise 11.6 Identify two examples of personnel controls used by InnoTech (See Section 11.4 Case 2).

Exercise 11.7 Identify two examples of action controls used by InnoTech (See Section 11.4 Case 2).

Exercise 11.8 Identify two examples of results controls used by InnoTech (See Section 11.4 Case 2).

Exercise 11.9 Explain why GreenJet apparently was able to use short-term, unilateral contracts with its service providers.

Exercise11.10 Explain how InnoTech found it advantageous to use a long term bilateral contract with its service provider, FinPro.

Exercise 11.11 Compare and contrast GreenJet's and InnoTech's reliance on trust in their outsourced service relationships.

CASES

Case 11.1 Theoretical research

Read the article by R.J. Boland Jr., et al (2008) that is in the list of references.

Prepare a two page report that describes this article's explanation of why creating a set of management controls for an IOR (or 'hybrid organisation'), which is a combination of two independent entities (e.g. for a joint venture or for bilateral outsourcing), is different from creating a set of management controls for a newly decentralised company. Because of this effect, was the creation of effective management controls more or less difficult for InnoTech and FinPro in Section 11.4 Case 2 Why or why not?

Case 11.2 Theoretical research

Read the article by K. Neumann (2010) that is in the list of references.

Write a two page report that describes this article's explanation of the interactions of formal management controls and trust between organisational partners. Did the use of formal management controls make trust more or less important to GreenJet and its service providers in Section 11.4 Case 1? Why or why not?

Case 11.3 Case research

Read the article by R. Cooper and T. Yoshikawa (1994) that is in the list of references.

Write a two page report that explains how the cost management systems observed in this Japanese supply chain relationship function as inter-organisational management controls.

Case 11.4 Goal setting analysis

You have interviewed an executive of a company that plans to outsource strategically important services. What key insights can you get from the following excerpt of your interview about outsourcing finance and accounting activities? Do these insights generalise to outsourcing other service or manufacturing resources? Explain.

> The main reason for us to outsource finance was focus; that is, I mean to say, finance has two main pillars. One is business controlling, and the other one is transactional accounting. We came to the conclusion that when you have so many different sites that are often small accounting transaction groups, on the one side you may lack the skills and great quality to really develop a world-class accounting process. And on the other side you also have difficulties in standardisation and harmonisation when you have your own local accounting teams spread around in so many different countries. And thirdly in the context of focus, we want to focus on the value-added thing in the finance and accounting function, which should be the role of the controller as a business partner, the colleague who understands the information, and who can analyse the information and can give good business support to the business management. While transaction accounting should be harmonised, standardised and automated, when you have that in larger centres, we expect more quality in these processes because of the size and the greater possibility to harmonise and standardise. When you have large, focused shared service centres, then you can afford to allocate leading level top professionals into these centres in order to manage world class processes in the area of procure-to-pay processes, recording and reporting processes, and order-to-cash process, this would be uneconomical without centralisation and creation of critical mass, e.g. when working with decentralised small accounting teams in 100 or more individual sites.

Case 11.5 Partner choice

You have interviewed an executive of a company that plans to outsource strategically important services.

What key insights can you get from the following excerpt of your interview about selecting IOR partners generally?

> Normally we are using a tender process where we invite at least three or more potential partners who are acting in this arena. We explain to them what our objective is, what we want to see in terms of cost and development of processes, and in terms of quality. Then these invited service providers present their proposals. Then there are a couple of critical elements very relevant to us to come to a final decision. We talk about global outsourcing, but local coverage is of essence. So being able to provide, communicate and contact all of our organisations worldwide. So time zone issues, language, skill issues are important; one of the questions therefore is, whether the potential partner we want to work together with has global presence? or is it more a regional player? The second factor would be the cost factor; so how does the cost compare with what we were able to do in-house? The third element would be quality and how to develop that moving forward. So what would be their expertise to enable and support us in improving these processes, simplifying these processes, and add more value to these processes? On the other side, can they help us in standardisation and harmonisation of the processes at various sites? Another element would be the track record of the company.

What is it that they can show us that they have done with other players in the area? These would be key critical points. We also would look at their IT infrastructure, trying to understand how their expertise with ERP systems match with what we are running? How are they connected to a backbone infrastructure so that communication from an IT perspective is working fine? So these are the four or five key KPIs that we would compare different service providers, one against the other.

Case 11.6 Partner choice

You have interviewed an executive of a company that plans to outsource strategically important products.

What key insights can you get from the following excerpt of your interview about the importance organisational culture to a successful IOR? Are these insights generally applicable to outsourcing all resources? Explain.

Also very important is the soft match: do you trust the partner's management, do you feel the right 'click', do you relate well? You enter a long-term commitment, you will have numerous meetings, and you know that you will have intense debates in which you ask your partner to stretch the limits in order to correct failures. You also know you will ask your partner to take strategic decisions and to make necessary investments. A good relationship between management teams is very important in these circumstances. Do they have a long term vision, or do they mainly care about the next quarter. Do they have a proven track record? Will the managers we meet today also be in their position in the coming year? We look at proven track records: financial performance and management performance. We have business meetings with them, but also informal meetings (drinks and dinner) in order to see whether they are partners who are not opportunistic and short term focused, but are long term focused, serious about their business and can be trusted.

Case 11.7 Provider analysis

You have interviewed an executive of a company that has outsourced strategically important services.

What key insights can you get from the following excerpt of your interview about the market determinants of outsourcing success? Do these insights also apply to manufacturing? Explain.

Our service provider was supposed to price as if they had this expertise. That is what they had sold us. Not only Company X, but I think what happened, these companies, they realised a fantastic niche in the market. But these companies first of all were consultancy companies. How consultancy companies work is they find a niche in the market, they sell the idea, and afterwards they learn how to do it. I think it happened again in the outsourcing area. The difference is that you can learn how to do what you do if it's a consultancy project. You cannot do that if your job is to deliver services. You need to know how to drive if you are sitting in the car, not just go along for the ride. I think that's a little bit of what happened in the market. When I talk to my colleagues, I've been talking to a lot of people in other companies to know what's going on, it's always the same story. And I think the outsourcing market is also learning how to do this. They are learning fast, they're buying a lot of expertise, but I think some companies that started earlier on this business, they suffered a little bit more because there was no expertise, not like now, from the providers. So the answer is, yes, we bought expertise,

> but we didn't get the expertise we thought we were buying, at least not at first. It varies a lot. In some areas, Company X and Company Y are very good, but not in all. But you know what is difficult in this equation is (cost of course is an important driver) that these providers need to cost us less than our internal organisation would cost. To cost less you can't pay a lot for very deep expertise. They need to find a mechanism where they can pay for experts but not as many experts as we would need internally. They need to have more critical mass, but I don't know what is the solution. It's a tricky equation.

Case 11.8 Goal setting analysis

You have interviewed an executive of a company that provides outsourced services.

What key insights can you get from the following excerpt of your interview about setting and communicating goals of outsourcing?

> Our strategy was not to obtain a key client and leverage the knowledge to service others. We started out with a couple of large clients, and we started out without several key analysis tools, of course, and in the course of serving those clients we found more ways that we could drive continuous improvement, and ways that we could drive out the rate of errors internally. We could be faster and more responsive to our clients. We said, for example, "You know we need a tool that is better than Excel to plan out the initial draft of the course-teaching schedule for the next sequence. If you look at University of XYZ, you will probably find that the initial planning when a professor is going to teach a class, time of day, what room, and what courses, the initial planning is probably done on Excel... And eventually somebody keys data into a system after you have agreed, after facilities have agreed, key data into a system that eventually students can enroll on. It's a nightmare because of all the issues with conflicts and coordination of changes. If you get more than one person doing the scheduling, they are at each other's throats. And within our company it could be multiple clients that we're trying to serve with the same facilities and resources. It's all about managing the facilitator's times effectively. We threw out the Excel spreadsheets, and we built a tool that has a database underneath it, and Web-style interfaces that all of our schedulers can use. We have made those investments as we have seen the need, and we have reached the scale to be able to afford it. And again there is no way an individual university or client could build a tool like that and have it be cost effective, unless you "enslaved" grad students in the IT department to do it (laughs). And then you have the problem of maintaining it.

Case 11.9 Performance analysis

You have interviewed an executive of a company that provides outsourced services.

What key insights can you get from the following excerpt of your interview about measuring performance? Build a counter argument from the client's perspective.

> How many metrics are you going to measure and report on to your client every month? . . . and potentially be accountable for from a financial point of view? 30? 50? In order to manage that many different services you can imagine how the SLA's can really spin out of control and be a huge list with a whole staff just to do all the measurement on both sides. Let me give you a really simple example, a help desk. Everyone knows what a help desk is. We've all called a help desk for a Visa card or something like that. How many metrics can you come up with to measure how you interact with that helpdesk? A whole bunch of them. How fast do they

resolve the problem? Am I happy with how they treated me? How much did it cost? How much of the information are they using that comes through the helpdesk to feed back information to improve our business processes? There are many things you could come up with to measure. For one of my most recent clients we had metrics for (and we had financial penalties if we missed, so this is serious business, often tens of thousands of euros at risk for each of these numbers every month) how many calls were resolved in five days, how many calls were resolved in 15 days, what was our caller satisfaction level, and a couple of other measures as well, just related to the help desk operations. Ideally, what you'd like to do is determine what single metric reflects the others well enough that we can just measure the one. And if we are good there, we know we are good overall. So for example, if my customer satisfaction on the helpdesk is let's say 80% or better, do I really need to measure how long they were on hold before I answer the call? Because, if I make people wait on hold for a long time, their satisfaction is going to drop; they are unhappy. So if I just measure customer satisfaction, can I skip measuring how long they waited, or how many hung up because they waited too long? Or how many people had to wait five days before their questions were answered? If I just measure that one customer satisfaction number I don't build a whole team to measure all those other things. If your client is smart, what they will say is: 'If I can hold you accountable to the end metric, which in this case might be customer satisfaction, it's not my problem about all the other stuff'. Because, if the client finds that my customer satisfaction number is dropping, I as the provider am going to be accountable to exhibit out whether it is because too many things are taking five days to solve, because too many people are waiting on hold too long, and so on. For the client as my customer it stops being 'their problem.' The smart solution when it comes to service quality and metrics is finding one metric for each service that reflects the client's business need most effectively and let your operating team manage the exceptions for all the other ones. So if I get an issue, what is the root cause of it?

Case 11.10 Partner analysis

You have interviewed an executive of a company that provides outsourced services.

What key insights can you get from the following excerpt of your interview about selecting outsourcing partners from the provider's perspective?

You must understand the client's business model enough so that the value proposition and business case that you agree on initially are things that are actually achievable. The way you define the relationship, the contract and the service. Some of our competition is saying we will to save you 20% and will exhibit it out later. Sometimes it works; sometimes it doesn't. We try to manage that particular risk very proactively during the due diligence and contract development, but that's a key one: do you understand the vagaries of the client's business model well enough to know how you really are going to achieve the things that you agree initially with the client are your **joint** results. That's probably the critical one for us. As a business, the other issues would be mostly around scale. For example, what happens if this contract shrinks down to its minimum scale? Do we still provide this service effectively? Do we still have enough staffing at that point to do it well? And will we still make any money at it? Similarly in the other direction, if the client turns out to be a lot bigger than we think, are we ready for that? Do we have a way to ramp up and be able to take care of additional callers, if we're talking about a call centre? Similarly, if it is application maintenance or service creation, do we have the capability to ramp up and respond when they have an immediate business need? So the client just acquired a new business and they want to develop a whole bunch of applications to bring the new employees up to speed on some aspects of how the business is supposed to operate now. Can we staff the team and crank out a bunch of new courseware and get some instructors trained in 90 days, or is it going to take six or eight months? Doing that kind of advance planning on both the good news and bad news sides is critical to being prepared to be successful.

Case 11.11 Change analysis

You have interviewed an executive of a company that provides outsourced services.

What key insights can you get from the following excerpt of your interview about managing the changes that result from outsourcing? Do these insights also apply to manufacturing? Explain.

I have an example of a situation where we're often dealing with senior management when we are in the contracting process, but then, when we are doing the work, we are engaged with people at much lower levels in the organisation. The senior leadership has decided to engage with us because we can help them significantly change the way they do business: better, faster, cheaper. All that great stuff! Management goes back to their organisation, and they say, 'We are contracting with [my company]. We're really excited about this; please work with them. This is going to make our business better.' Often that is about as much as the staff absorbs. . . 'better'. They don't necessarily get that it is going to be cheaper, it's going to be different, and you need to commit to change the way you're doing things. So they make their cultural assumptions about what is 'normal' and what is 'how it's done.' Then we start doing the work, and we run into these disconnects and where the change from the individual employee's point of view, let's say the department head's point of view, is a lot bigger than that person was ready for or that they understood would happen to them. And they can feel very put upon. We do a lot of work with our client's senior management around how to talk about change with their business. Proactively. And you know it's still a challenge, frankly. People don't like change. They are pretty sure they know the right way to do things, and so it's often an ongoing challenge for us to help people get their head around the idea that we're really doing it a much different way. "You mean the way I was doing that before isn't the way we want to keep doing it? Oh no!" Often in the first year of a contract there is a lot of change management that has to be done with the broader organisation of the client. To help them actually understand how much we meant it when we said 'change'! We will have a client's senior management showing back up in front of the staff meetings talking about what is 'better'. Really, I'm looking for them to say, 'The pressures of a marketplace are driving us in these directions. Our workforce is changing in these ways, and we have to be ready for that.' They really need to get a little bit more practical; so that the department heads are appreciating why it is that their world is changing.

Case 11.12 Performance analysis

In January you interviewed the Vice-President of Cargo Operations for GreenJet Airlines, Carla Scott. The company's SLAs with its ground service providers sets penalties for excessive delays at the provider's airport site, but GreenJet and its providers regularly argued about responsibility for delays. She has recently installed experimental incentives for service providers in North and South America to reduce the number of 'controllable delays'. A controllable delay is a delay of an aircraft's on-time departure from an airport that was caused by a service error that could have been prevented by better planning and execution by the service provider. An uncontrollable delay might be caused by sudden changes in weather or events that caused a late arrival.

Explain whether it appears that her experiment over the past year justifies extending the incentive program to global cargo operations.

Something I am experimenting with in the Americas' region is a 'ground time performance' program, which is the measurement and evaluation of the ground operations, when the flight arrives and departs, and during that process, how ground service performed. Did they do the job properly and mostly geared to departing on time? The key criterion is 'controllable delays.' Now in aviation there are many types of delays that are identified by IATA; it's used in the entire airline industry. We separated the delays into two different categories. We have decided some are controllable, and some are not controllable by ground operations. For example, an air traffic control delay is not controllable; an aircraft comes in late and so departs late. There's nothing you can do. If it's a maintenance issue, nothing you can do. However, if a service provider's equipment breaks down, say the loader is out of service, then that's a controllable delay because their responsibility is to be operationally ready. We established what the controllable delays are, and we found out that in the past year . . . we started this program a year ago in February . . . we started the program with a lot of controllable delays, and the graph that I am showing you, that started with a lot of uncontrollable delays, declined very steeply afterward.

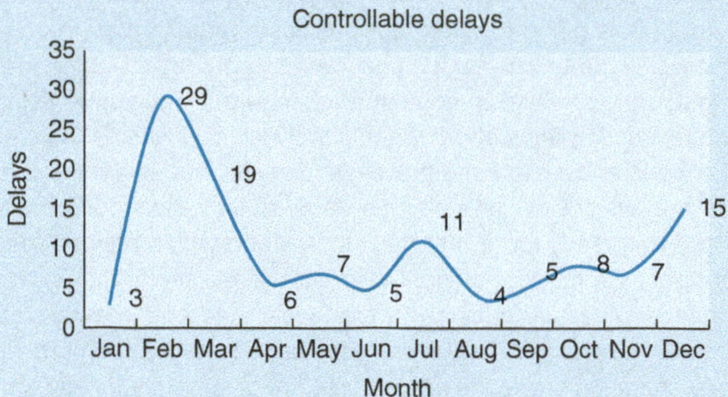

The reason was, there is another component. That was a bonus program in the Americas, which was tied into ground time. So now, all of a sudden, everybody is sensitive to ground time. I've been here for seven years, and on-time performance reports have meant nothing. There was no action, just a bunch of delays. If you can't control, there is nothing you can do. But if you focus on only the controllable delays and give people a stake in the outcome, that program is on their minds all the time. Everybody's thinking about it all the time. In December we had only 15 controllable delays and 94% ground time performance over the whole region of the Americas, and that is very, very good. I think we should deploy this incentive program worldwide. What do you think?

Case 11.13 Performance analysis

In January you interviewed the Vice-President of Cargo Operations for GreenJet Airlines, Carla Scott.

Advise her on her proposed bonus system for on-time performance.

What we can do for our providers is to make more incentives for performance, which are tied to service levels. Right now if a major problem occurs, that costs us a claim or customer ill will, we may arbitrarily deduct something from their invoice, but that always creates arguments. A better way, for example, might be if they perform to an on-time departure level of at least 95%, they could get a bonus on their invoice, or if they drop below 90%, there would be a penalty. Of course, we then have to agree on the bonus or penalty amounts, and how the on-time departure percentage is measured. Do we adjust for uncontrollable delays? This is what we're actually in the process of developing now, but we do need to provide more incentives. Look at December's Ground Performance Report, but it is not as simple as giving a monthly bonus to each provider that achieved 90% on-time performance.

GreenJet Airline ground time performance report americas region december

Station*	Flights	% On-time departure	Controllable delays	Standard ground time**	Ave actual ground time	Variance	
ABC	16	88%	2	3:07	2:12	0:55	F
BCD	8	100%	0	2:30	2:12	0:18	F
CDE	45	98%	1	2:22	1:59	0:23	F
DEF	9	100%	0	4:03	3:26	0:37	F
EFG	9	67%	3	3:03	2:57	0:06	F
FGH	49	100%	0	1:28	1:15	0:13	F
GHI	6	83%	1	1:30	1:42	0:12	U
HIJ	31	90%	3	3:14	3:26	0:12	U
IJK	19	100%	0	1:31	1:07	0:24	F
JKL	9	100%	0	1:46	1:37	0:09	F
KLM	21	95%	1	1:51	1:45	0:06	F
LMN	16	94%	1	1:30	1:38	0:08	U
MNO	4	100%	0	1:30	1:13	0:17	F
NOP	13	85%	2	2:09	3:02	0:53	U
OPQ	10	90%	1	2:36	3:55	1:19	U
Total region	265	94%	15	2:13	2:06	0:06	F

* Disguised airport codes
** Standard ground time reflects each airport's normal air & ground traffic, taxiing, and servicing times

For example, just last month (*December*) we had a situation at HIJ (*disguised Americas' regional airport code*). We had an aircraft that was very tightly scheduled for the whole rotation (*Europe–Africa–Americas–Europe*), and we were planning to use the aircraft again soon after it got back to Europe. There was a two-hour delay in HIJ, because the cargo-service provider wanted to wait for some cargo that was arriving late. So they delayed the flight two hours, and it screwed up the whole rotation and cost us a lot of money. More than the value of the cargo! Just the thing we wanted to avoid. What we gained by waiting for the cargo, we lost five times as much because of problems in the entire rotation of the fleet.

Case 11.14 Risk and national culture analysis

You have interviewed InnoTech's Americas Region Vice-President of Finance regarding national differences and risks.

What insights do you gain from this interview excerpt about risk taking and national culture? Are these insights reliable, in your opinion?

We do have differences across countries, which impact the services, and so on. There is a big difference in terms of respect for authority. For example, in Brazil we are not so much respectful of authority compared to Chile, where they have much more respect for authority. Then you go to Argentina, and again they don't have much respect for authority, and the same thing happens all over. If you go to India, they have more respect than they would have in the Netherlands. And so on. When you come with global standards or global projects, and so on, in some countries, they are immediately accepted and implemented, but in other countries they resist, and they challenge much more. So it does make a big difference. Willingness to take risks is also a big difference. If you take, for example, in Brazil, because of our economic and social and political history, we know life is unpredictable. So we're used to taking risks. Just the fact that I leave my house and I come to work, I'm taking risks. The traffic jams are awful; there can be violence on the way; so I'm taking risks all the time. You're exposed, and you need to find mechanisms to survive. So a big difference in culture makes a big difference in willingness to take risks. When you take a big part of the organisation, and you give it to someone else and you expect that it's going to be delivered, you are taking risks. It is your face as a professional that is visible. Your regional or line manager is coming to you and saying that the relationship is not working. Yes, outsourcing is risky, but so is failing to improve efficiency.

Case 11.15 Strategic outsourcing of manufacturing

You have interviewed the Senior Vice-President for Outsourcing from a company that has outsourced global production of electronic parts to a previously independent manufacturer.

1. Use the chapter's steps for strategic decision making to describe this company's production-outsourcing decisions.
2. Describe differences that you would expect if this company were outsourcing services.

Five years ago we reduced the number of outsourcing partners from dozens to five or six. We do 90% of our business with only a few partners. We had three main reasons for this: to reduce fragmentation and diversity, to maintain control, and to improve our 'leverage position'. This means we want to have a strong impact on the partner. We do not want to represent only 1 or 2% of their sales, but 10 to 20%. This makes us important to them and they important to us. It enables us to discuss strategic decisions and new investments with them on senior management level, instead of being only operationally involved with the partner.

One of our most important global suppliers is Company ABC, which has multiple plants located in Europe, Asia and North America. Although ABC also services one of our competitors, we had three main reasons to partner with ABC: first, both companies had a strategic fit. ABC wanted to strengthen its European business in one of our product sectors. We wanted to eliminate manufacturing this intermediate product, which was mainly produced in Europe. The transaction would lead to a win-win solution for both parties. Secondly, we thought the organisational cultures of both companies matched well. I think corporate culture is more important than national culture. Both companies were willing to invest in a long term relationship, and not to go for short term benefits exclusively. Both companies were trying to maintain continuity in their management. And thirdly, ABC was and is a viable and financially healthy company, which gave us confidence that the relationship can be long term.

In the end we needed to show that the strategic fit would pay off financially. How much is the partner willing to pay for our activities/business? What will be the future competitive outlook of the business on the longer term? However, we do not look further into the future than 5 to 6 years, because it is very difficult to make predictions nowadays. ABC, because of its good strategic match with us, gave us the best deal, but we agreed to evaluate the relationship after three years, with provisions for exiting the contract at that time.

We guaranteed minimum sales for the contracted years, which means we bear the risks of reduced demand, but ABC must be flexible to meet unexpected higher demands. Smoothing supply fluctuations and eliminating bottlenecks are the major concerns. We regularly monitor their input costs, product costs, on-time delivery and quality. We help them stay competitive by providing benchmarked information. We have made 'Chinese-wall' agreements for the protection of our intellectual property. So we allow them to produce even for our competitors, because we want ABC to expand and realise economies of scale that will benefit us, too. Because we are confident in ABC's governance structure, these controls should ensure ABC's performance and costs and leaks of information to competitors. This is going well, and gradually we have worked with ABC to create innovations for our products. We hope these joint innovations will increase over time.

Case 11.16 Implementation of management controls

You are the Vice President of Finance of a high technology product firm. Many but not all of your products are built for specific customer needs; other products are generic. Your responsibilities include the design and analysis of management controls for internal and external activities. Your company has decided to outsource all parts supply, manufacturing and distribution resources to external suppliers. The Director of Outsourced Logistics has described a proposed customer-order process with the flowchart that follows. The major risks to outsourcing these activities appear to be that parts supply, manufacturing or distribution could be incorrect, defective or late.

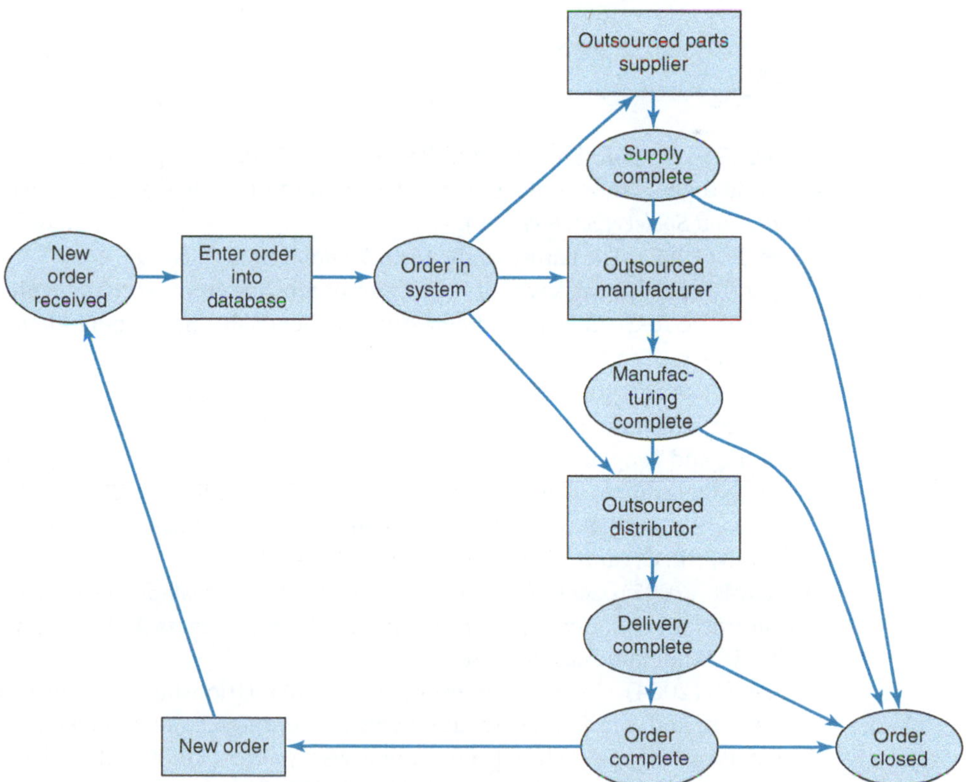

Adapted from Drizymalski and Odrey 2008, p. 731.

1. First, consider an order for a generic, general application product. Use the flow chart to choose management controls for each of the three outsource providers.
2. Next, describe what, if any differences in the order process and management controls would be appropriate for insuring the successful completion of an order for a customised product.

Case 11.17 Review the discussion of the 'solidarity principle' in the NedCar joint venture described in Insight from research 11.3

1. What were the strategic goals of the three parties (the Dutch state, Volvo and Mitsubishi)?
2. In your opinion, how well does the solidarity principle promote the goals of each of the parties?
3. What recommendations would you have to improve the management controls that guide this relationship?

Case 11.18 Review the discussion of the 'alliance fund' presented in Insight from research 11.4

1. Verify with a spreadsheet analysis that the fund payments from cost savings preserves NMA's profits at original prices and costs.
2. Evaluate the incentives for NMA to initiate or agree to aggressive cost savings. How sustainable are these incentives? Explain.
3. Contrast the "alliance fund" incentive with the gain-sharing plan between InnoTech and FinPro. Which do you prefer? Why?

Answers to Exercises–available on the text's CD

References

Boland, R.J. Jr., A.K. Sharma, and P.S. Afonso. (2008) Designing management control in hybrid organizations: The role of path creation and morphogenesis. *Accounting, Organizations and Society*, 33: 899–914.

Coase, R. (1937). The nature of the firm. *Economica,* 4, 386–405.

Cooper, R. and T. Yoshikawa (1994). Inter-organizational cost management systems: The case of the Tokyo-Yokohama-Kamakura supplier chain. *International Journal of Production Economics*, 37: 51–62.

Cooper, R., and Slagmulder, R. (2004). Inter-organizational cost management and relational context. *Accounting, Organizations and Society,* 29(1), 1–26.

Das, T. K., and Teng, B. S. (1998). Between trust and control: Developing confidence in partner cooperation in alliances. *Academy of Management Review,* 23(3), 491–512.

Das, T. K., and Teng, B. S. (2001). Trust, control and risk in strategic alliances: An integrated framework. *Organization Studies,* 22(2), 251–283.

Dekker, H. (2003). *Control of inter-organizational relationships: the effects of appropriation concerns, coordination requirements and social embeddedness* (Vol. 310). Amsterdam: Thela Thesis Academic Publishing Services.

Dekker, H. (2004). Control of inter-organizational relationships: Evidence on appropriation concerns and coordination requirements. *Accounting, Organizations and Society,* 1, 27–49.

Drzymalski, J. and N. Odrey (2008) Supervisory control of a multi-echelon supply chain. *Robotics and Computed-Integrated Mfg*, 24: 728–734.

Groot, T. and K. Merchant (2000). Control of international joint ventures. *Accounting, Organizations and Society*, 25: 579–607.

Huyzer, S.E., Luimes, W., Spitholt, M.G.M., Leest, D.J.v.d., Overloop, P.v., & Slagter, W.J. (1992). *Strategische Samenwerking, Oriëntatie en Implementatie* (2 ed.). Alphen aan den Rijn/Zaventem: Samsom BedrijfsInformatie.

Kogut, B. (1988) Joint ventures: Theoretical and empirical perspectives. *Strategic Management Journal.* 9: 319–332.

Neumann, K. (2010) Ex ante governance decisions in inter-organizational relationships: A case study in the airline industry. *Management Accounting Research*, 21 220–237

Ring, P. S., and Van de Ven, A. H. (1994). Developmental processes of cooperative interorganizational relationships. *Academy of Management Review,* 19(1), 90–118.

Ring, S. P., and Van de Ven, A. H. (1992). Structuring cooperative relationships between organizations. *Strategic Management Journal,* 13, 483–498.

Speklé, R. (2001). Explaining management control structure variety: A transaction cost economics perspective. *Accounting, Organizations and Society, 26* (4-5, May-July), 419-441.

Tomkins, C. (2001). Interdependences, trust and information in relationships, alliances and networks. *Accounting, Organizations and Society,* 26, 161–191.

Van der Meer-Kooistra, J., and Vosselman, G. J. (2000). Management control of interfirm transactional relationships: The case of industrial renovation and maintenance. *Accounting, Organizations and Society,* 25, 51–77.

Van der Meer-Kooistra, J., and Vosselman, G. J. (2006). Research on management control of interfirm transactional relationships: Whence and whither. *Management Accounting Research,* 17(3), 227–237.

Velez, Maria L., Jose, L., M. Sanchez , Concha Alvarez-Dardet, (2008) Management control systems as inter-organizational trust builders in evolving relationships: Evidence from a longitudinal case study. *Accounting, Organizations and Society*, 33: 968–994.

Williamson, O. E. (1975). Markets and hierarchies: Analysis and anti-trust implications. New York: Free Press.

Williamson, O. E. (1991). Comparative economic organization: The analysis of discrete structural alternatives. *Administrative Science Quarterly,* 36, 269–296.

Chapter 12

Incentive systems in organisations

12.1 Introduction

The past decade has witnessed dramatic events in global business and international affairs that must have shaken our confidence that we have progressed in our attempts to organise and systematise organisational performance. The world is messy, noisy and unpredictable, and important human decisions in this volatile environment have been unmasked as fraudulent, flawed and simplistic, but also in some cases as heroic and lucky. These are enduring truths about human endeavours–always have been and always will be. There is no reason to believe that the world anytime will stabilise to a comfortable equilibrium wherein rational economic actors (us, that is) can respond to clear incentives, execute rational decision making and thereby maximise utility. Expecting continued volatility, noisy information and sub-optimal decision making (whatever this might mean) seems more prudent and realistic. This means, among other things, that design of incentive systems is not likely to be straight forward.

It, therefore, seems optimistic to expect that a final textbook chapter can knit together the lessons of preceding chapters and make confident recommendations for organisational practice via the **incentive system,** which is the set of procedures and standards for awarding compensation and other benefits to employees. The key to improved decision making in the disequilibrium setting of the real world is to:

- Align individual self-interests as best as one can with that of the organisation
- 'Nudge' decision making toward organisational goals[1]
- Unleash creativity–these are not necessarily in opposition.

Describing the alternatives of incentive system design is the objective of this chapter, with the message that **incentives and incentive systems do matter, but they are not the only determinants of performance.**

12.1.1 Management control and organisational goals

Management controls (Chapter 3) by which organisations direct and help individuals to achieve the organisation's goals. The conclusion of this text is that management controls of many types may be, can be and are used by organisations to improve organisational performance (i.e. achieve the goals). Some management controls explicitly use quantitative

[1] R. Thaler and C. Sunstein 2009 have used the term, "nudge," to mean the informational and structural assistance given to decision makers to "do the right thing."

measures of performance, such as operating profit, but other controls may be qualitative, such as clan and other personnel controls. All of the controls discussed in this text may be used in incentive systems, but all encompassing incentive systems may not be feasible or desirable. Most incentive systems reflect only several key dimensions of managers' jobs and sensibly do not try to cover or 'micro-manage' every aspect. Yet narrow incentive systems have their own dangers, if decision makers are led to ignore some important aspects of organisational life.

12.1.2 Organisational setting

Organisations exist because they are more efficient means to effect some transactions than purely market mediated transactions by one person firms, or so is the message from Nobel prize winning economist Oliver Williamson.[2] As a theory, Williamson's transaction cost economics (TCE) is appealing and is reasonably descriptive of organisational behaviour. For our purposes in this chapter, TCE identifies important transactional cost drivers, including transaction frequency, asset specificity, uncertainty, limited rationality and opportunistic behaviour, that can launch our discussion of the design and use of incentive systems. These are especially pertinent to this chapter.

1. **Transaction frequency**. By TCE theory, quite frequent, repetitive transactions can create cost savings from economies of scale and are likely to be conducted within the boundary of the organisation. Likewise, less frequent, but mechanistic activities are likely to be outsourced, because they should be available from suppliers who have economies of scale. Innovation activities might be retained in many companies, for reasons related to their infrequency and uniqueness, which is considered next.
2. **Asset specificity.** Tangible and intangible assets (including **knowledge**) that are specific or unique to a transaction are likely to be retained within the organisation because of their scarcity value and competitive advantage. The opportunity cost of outsourcing specific assets can be high. In practice, organisations rely on individual specialisation and knowledge to perform valued tasks, but this leads inevitably to information asymmetry between individuals with specific knowledge and their organisations. One of the intents of management control (Chapters 3 and 11) is to motivate individuals to share their knowledge within the firm. This chapter addresses incentive systems that can motivate individuals to share private knowledge for the good of the entire organisation.
3. **Uncertainty.** Uncertainty, or the inability to foresee future events with certainty, is a fact of organisational life that increases contracting and opportunity costs. But the term, uncertainty, understates the uncontrollability, noise and unpredictability of the future. Highly uncertain activities are likely to be retained within an organisation, but internal contracting via incentive systems is still costly. An effective incentive system would discriminate between what one colloquially can call good or bad luck.
4. **Limited rationality.** Extensive behavioural research has demonstrated convincingly that almost no one possesses the hyper-rationality assumed by classical microeconomics.[3]

[2] Williamson has built TCE on a foundation of economic thought going back at least to Coase 1936. See Williamson 1981; this seminal work has launched numerous theoretical and empirical studies across many disciplines, including meaningful extensions by Williamson himself.

[3] In fact, Amos Tversky and Daniel Kahneman received the 2002 Nobel memorial prize in economics for their systematic and consistent empirical findings that humans, even famous economists, make irrational decisions.

Limited rationality exposes the firm to opportunity costs of poor decisions. In response, another important intent of management control is to help decision makers obtain the right information and use it properly.

5. **Opportunistic behaviour.** As do most economic theories of behaviour, TCE assumes that external providers and managers are opportunistic, and that they will shirk responsibilities and pursue private goals unless incentives persuade them otherwise. Although the actions of internal managers should be more observable than those of external providers, managers who are self-interested individuals might need to be 'bribed' to do what is good for the organisation. Some think this assumption is overblown or can be corrected with non-incentive management controls. We agree, but also contend that incentives do matter to promote effort, coordination, and team production over harmful shirking and internal competition.

12.1.3 Organisational outcomes

The goal of incentive systems is to promote achievement of organisational goals in the face of contrary forces. In an obviously simplified setting, one can attribute actual performance outcomes to the quality of decision making and the effects of chance, as shown in Figure 12.1.

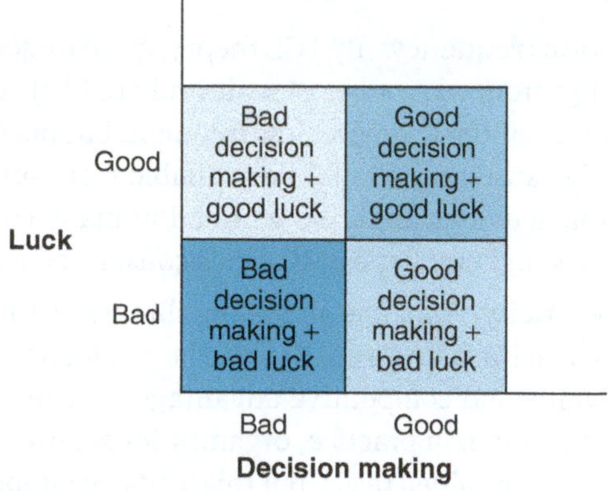

Figure 12.1 Entangled decision making and luck

Figure 12.1 illustrates a dilemma of rewarding performance. Unless everything we know about business management is wrong, one would like to reward good decision making (although having good luck, too, is a bonus) and prevent or sanction bad decision making.[4] We believe that good decision making (as discussed in Chapter 2) will result more often than not in better outcomes (e.g. closer achievement of the organisation's goals), and vice versa. However, by basing incentives on performance (outcomes), one cannot disentangle the effects of decision making and luck. Baker (1990) argues that, because decision making is unobservable, rewarding for good luck and penalising for bad luck are some of the costs of pay-for-performance and decentralised decision making. Thaler and Sunstein (2009) argue that, although incentives work to direct decision making, we can minimise bad decision making by understanding how contexts affect choices, and by providing structure to complex tasks. Ariely (2010a) is more prescriptive and argues that one should avoid basing rewards on outcomes and instead:

[4] It does appear that many banks rewarded gambling on derivative securities in the run up to the Great Recession that began in 2008. With hindsight that behaviour seems like bad decision making that should have been prevented rather than rewarded.

- Establish preferred decision making processes (an action control)
- Document that managers follow the processes
- Reward good decision making at the time that decisions are made.

Baker's application of pay for performance is common business practice, but Ariely's pay for decision making is not.[5]

It is unlikely that organisations would reward employees simply for attendance, but decentralised decision making is not fully observable (despite action controls). As a result, most organisations (perhaps wrongly) would be unlikely to ignore performance outcomes when distributing rewards. So we are here seeking guidance for designing and implementing incentive systems that reward the decision making that moves the organisation closer to meeting its goals. For that guidance, we discuss in turn the following pertinent topics:

1. Organisational goals and objectives for profit seeking, public sector and non-profit organisations from shareholder and stakeholder perspectives
2. Organisation structure effects of decentralisation and individual or group production
3. Models of motivation that describe the complexities of understanding why people do what they do and whether rewards are always important and helpful
4. Types of rewards that are available and can be deployed across organisations
5. Incentive system designs that match organisational context of goals and structure to motivation and rewards.

12.2 Organisation goals and objectives

One cannot build an effective incentive system without understanding the goals that underlay the formation of the organisation. Importantly, 'one size does not fit all' in incentive systems because goals differ. At the most basic level, organisations exist to achieve goals that individuals cannot achieve. This group context necessitates rewards that are attributable to more than each individual.

12.2.1 Private, profit seeking firms

Private, profit seeking firms seek to earn from the sale of goods and services profits that benefit owners, employees, suppliers, customers, the larger communities in which they operate and other groups. Disagreements about the nature of the relationships among these participants have produced three complementary models of firm decision making and governance: the shareholder, stewardship, and stakeholder models.

[5] The weakness of Baker's 1990 *c'est la vie* resignation is that organisations are not powerless to implement other management controls. Thaler and Sunstein and Ariely would move us to the domain of decision support systems, an important topic that is beyond the scope of this text. The weakness in Ariely's 2010 proposal is that the formation of assumptions, interpretation of data and *ex post* evaluations of them are still subjective. One could document all the analysis and overlook fundamental misinterpretations and biases (e.g. WMDs and the 2003 Iraq war). Reconstructing what should have been the best decision under historic conditions might lead to conflicting interpretations. Note, however, that auditors regularly use checklists to guide and document the audit process, as do physicians when diagnosing patient conditions. One could take this too far, however. As Hofstede 1978 observes, the systematised control system that is appropriate for cybernetic models just cannot be applied to the more complex, fluid situations that confront most business organisations and their important decisions.

12.2.1.1 Shareholder model

The venerable **shareholder model** of the firm argues that earning competitive profits is the primary objective of private business.[6] Further, the expectation of distributable profits to owners or shareholders is the only motive for founding a **business.** The shareholder model directs managers via incentives and governance mechanisms to make decisions that increase profits and thereby increase the value of the firm's shares. Any other goals are distant seconds and are achieved only if the firm is profitable. A by-product of the shareholder model is that other stakeholders benefit from the firm's profitability when they receive well-compensated employment, profitable supply businesses, high quality products and so on.

12.2.1.2 Stewardship model

The newer **stewardship model** of the firm describes managers as wanting (e.g. deriving utility) to meet owners' and shareholders' goals.[7] In this model, managers are willing stewards of the owners' resources, and they seek to safeguard and use them wisely. Thus, (properly chosen) managers see their interests as aligned with those of owners and shareholders. If so, less structure and governance is optimal than indicated by the shareholder model of the firm, because managers would view these as intrusive and detrimental to their already pro-organisational motivations. Indeed, the stewardship model prescribes delegating more discretion and decision rights to managers than the shareholder model might view as prudent. The difference between the shareholder and the stewardship models hinges on the relative roles of extrinsic and intrinsic motivations of managers, which will be discussed later in this chapter.

12.2.1.3 Stakeholder model

In the past several decades, the stakeholder model of the firm has also arisen to complement the shareholder model–normatively and descriptively, even for profit seeking firms. The **stakeholder model** of the firm argues that groups in addition to shareholders (e.g., employees, suppliers, customers, communities) should and do have interests and impacts for the firm's decision making. Some have placed the stakeholder model in a normatively superior position relative to the shareholder model, particularly compared to a version that is purported to benefit only shareholders.[8] Whether the moral values of a more inclusive model of firm decision making make the stakeholder model superior is arguable and might be appealing (to all but CEO types, perhaps).

However, lines of argument and theory also ask whether the stakeholder or stewardship approaches do describe actual practice and, if implemented, do result in higher performance and more benefits to stakeholders than would a shareholder approach. Numerous studies indicate that managers declare that their firms take an explicit stakeholder approach to management. Whether stakeholder managed firms outperform shareholder managed firms still is an open question, partly because conducting valid research on this question faces great challenges. It is quite likely that features of all three models are necessary to explain the phenomenon of management decision making.

---

[6] See M. Friedman 1970 and Jensen and Meckling 1976.

[7] See Davis et al. 1997.

[8] See Donaldson and Preston 1995, but also a critical view from *The Economist*, 22 April 2010.

EXAMPLE FROM RESEARCH: 1

What's the bottom line?

Hillman and Keim (2001) tested whether a stakeholder approach builds superior shareholder value on a non-random sub-sample of 308 of the S&P 500 firms. They tested whether the lagged annual **change** in market value added [MVA = market value of shares − (debt + capital)] of firms is associated with the leading **level** of their KLD index ratings. The KLD index is a summary measure of nine areas of corporate social performance. The study partitioned the KLD index into two sub-indices representing stakeholder management (SM) and social issue participation (SIP), and they controlled for firm size, net sales, net income, industry and firm risk. The study found that SM_{1994} is significantly correlated with $MVA_{1995-1996}$. The study also found that SM_{1994} is significant in a regression model that explains $MVA_{1995-1996}$, after controlling for sales, net income, etc. This is an interesting study that points toward validating descriptive claims of the stakeholder model. However, limited data and what appears to be a misspecified model (mismatched variable changes and levels) make for ambiguous conclusions about causality. Criticisms of this type, unfortunately, plague most empirical studies of the impacts of changes or reforms on firm level performance–it is very difficult research.

Source: Hillman and Keim 2001.

The shareholder/stewardship models and stakeholder model can be complementary, if they are considered 'duals' of the other. That is, a shareholder or stewardship model that maximises shareholder value while maintaining competitive benefits for other stakeholders might be equivalent to a stakeholder model that maximises benefits to other stakeholders while maintaining competitive returns for shareholders. A complication to this undoubtedly naïve view is that stakeholders' desired benefits very likely conflict in the real world of imperfect and incomplete markets where, for example, environmental costs and benefits are not priced, or compensation is not 'fair'. In the very long run, of course, all relevant impacts of firms' decision making should be realised in market values of the firms, but we also know that the very long run is unpredictable. In the meantime, public and non-profit organisations usually fill the market voids.

12.2.2 Public and non-profit organisations

Public and non-profit organisations seek to provide valued goods and services to stakeholders that private organisations do not provide or cannot provide profitably. These organisations are intended to reflect stakeholder goals while maintaining solvency. It appears abundantly clear from almost daily revelations about public organisations in particular that intentions might not match implementations. Public organisations respond to stakeholders through political systems, which as we all know vary widely in their institutions, procedures and effectiveness. Non-profit organisations typically respond to both immediate stakeholders (e.g., philanthropists, governmental funding agencies, employees, clients) and the public at large. It follows that the stakeholder model is more applicable to public and non-profit organisations, although its descriptiveness might be as troubled as for profit seeking firms.

12.2.3 Objectives

An effective incentive system directs employees to meet organisation goals. Both shareholder and stakeholder models are theoretically consistent with motivating managers (and other stakeholders) of all organisations to take a long term perspective.

Rewarding performance is more difficult in public and non-profit organisations and differs from profit seeking firms because of the rarity of summary measures of value produced, such as profit (or 'net revenue'). Nonetheless, many of these organisations set non-financial objectives for employees that reflect improvements in, for example, key activity levels and quality. The theories are also consistent with meeting organisational **objectives,** which are evidence of outcomes that are expected to reflect goal attainment. Objectives can be **financial** or **non-financial** in nature.

12.2.3.1 Financial objectives

Financial objectives reflect desired or targeted measures of financial performance, including growth of share price, return on investment, etc. (ROI, ROA, ROE, EVA), profits (EBIT, EBITDA, operating income net income after tax), sales revenue, and costs, as are appropriate for the level of overall and sub-unit responsibility (see Chapters 8, 9 and 10 for details). Choosing the right measures of financial performance surely is important because each can have subtle but critical incentive effects. Related difficulties have arisen when objectives are implemented as **short run** increases in profit, share values or their precursors, as exemplified by the recent (continuing) financial crisis that came to a head in 2008.

EXAMPLE FROM PRACTICE: 1

Did large banks really get such a simple thing wrong?

It is generally believed that early in this century many bank executives in developed countries invested in speculative ventures using borrowed money. *The Economist* and Andrew Haldane of the Bank of England argue that the combination of tax deductibility of interest, deposit insurance, banks 'too big to fail,' and choice of an improper financial objective, short term return on equity (ROE), contributed to reckless growth of debt and risk, while bank executives were being rewarded for increasing ROE. The growth of bank executive compensation prior to the recent financial crisis tracks closely with bank ROE. Had banks instead used return on assets (ROA: both debt and equity in the denominator) as the rewarded objective, bank executives most likely would have controlled the growth of risky debt, but they would have earned far less compensation (e.g. compensation of CEOs of US banks in 2007 might have averaged \$3.4million rather than the actual average of \$26million). It is an open question whether the choice of ROE as the financial objective was an oversight or an example of Jensen and Meckling's (1976) recipe for how self-interested managers can transfer wealth from debt holders to shareholders and themselves.

Sources: The Economist, 25 October 2011; A. Haldane 2011; Jensen and Meckling, 1976.

Financial objectives typically are less important in public and non-profit organisations because in most cases financial measures do not reflect public or non-profit goals. However, and particularly in recent times, the budget deficits of public organisations are very much in the news, although fixing direct responsibility in an effective way has always been difficult.

Likewise stakeholders and the general public generally hear about the financial performance of non-profit organisations when someone has greatly overspent or misapplied the budget, has absconded with it, or is paid unreasonable compensation.

12.2.3.2 Non-financial objectives

Non-financial objectives are targeted measures or indicators of progress toward a non-monetary goal. Pursuit of non-financial objectives is consistent with the shareholder model, if the non-financial objectives are reliable leading indicators of future financial performance. Therefore, targets such as improvements in employee capabilities, process quality and customer satisfaction can be important parts of integrated performance models, as discussed in Chapter 10. Similarly, targeting non-financial performance is consistent with a stakeholder focus, whether financial performance is the ultimate objective or not. A large social infrastructure exists to set objectives for and regulate the reporting of financial performance (e.g. the IASB for financial reporting). In contrast, largely unobservable factors determine non-financial performance, including:

- Organisational strategy, whether share- or stakeholder oriented
- Intangible assets
- Future financial performance
- Employee decision-making

Setting objectives is not an 'either–or' proposition. Many organisations–non-profit, public and private–use both financial and non-financial objectives and related performance measures. Whether organisations measure non-financial performance well is an open question.[9]

EXAMPLE FROM RESEARCH: 2

Attributes of performance measures

Recent research investigated the properties of an evolving set of financial and non-financial performance measures at an international Fortune 500 firm. The company began with a set of 29 measures (2 financial, 27 non-financial) for its distribution system. The diverse measures were designed to reflect a) objectives consistent with the company's new, more entrepreneurial strategy and b) its prescription for managing a highly competitive distributorship. However, four years later, the firm pruned the measures to 14 (5 financial, 9 non-financial). No differences between retained and dropped measures were observed on attributes of diversity, informativeness (see the later discussion), causal linkage, strategy communication, incentives or support of decision making. Retained measures were more accurate and less costly to obtain. Even measures that were thought to be crucial to the firm's strategy were dropped, if they were too costly to measure accurately. For example, market share measures (the most important of all) were dropped in favour of related sales growth, because sales growth was more easily and accurately measured–and created less conflict. This field study suggests that pragmatic concerns of ease and accuracy of measuring performance, and conflict avoidance, were more important than diversity and completeness of measurement. These concerns may favour the use of already available financial measures of performance over new, more disputable, non-financial measures.

Source: Malina and Selto 2004. Also see Gibbs et al. 2009.

[9] See C. Ittner and D. Larcker 2000, 2003.

12.3 Organisation structure

Chapters 3 and 11 discuss the implications of centralisation and decentralisation of decision making for management control and performance measurement. If incentives are based on performance, the incentive system should reflect the distribution of, and responsibility for work, in the organisation. Two structural factors have important implications for performance and related incentives: decentralised controllability **versus** informativeness and individual **versus** group.

12.3.1 Decentralised controllability versus informativeness

Controllability refers to the 'line of sight' and the uniqueness of contributions of a decision maker's (or group's) actions to performance objectives. Decision makers may not take seriously a performance measure and its proffered reward if they cannot materially affect the outcome and be recognised for it. Nevertheless, we observe that some managers are rewarded on things they cannot control, such as when they are evaluated on profits during times of market shrinkage. One explanation of such practice is that profit can be **informative** of a manager's decision making relative to the profits earned by other managers facing the same market. That is, a **relative performance measure** is informative if it distinguishes a decision maker from others that experienced similar business conditions.

Consider the example in Figure 12.3. Part A shows three identical business sub-units that sell the same product and have the same **budgeted** unit contribution margin, market size and unit sales. Part B with **actual** outcomes shows that the unit contribution margin was maintained by all at €100. However, the East market grew to 1200 units, and the West market shrank to 900 units. Units A and C met the sales budget of 100 units, while Unit B increased its sales to 120 units.

Part C compares budgeted to actual contribution margins. From this information, it appears that Unit B earned a favourable contribution margin variance of €2000 and outperformed the other two units.

Part D decomposes the budget variances in Part C into two components: **market size variances** that demonstrate effects of uncontrollable market changes that should have increased Unit A and Unit B contribution margins by €2000, if they had maintained their 10% market shares. Similarly Unit C's shrunken market should have seen a decreased contribution margin by €1000 with its expected 10% share. Additionally, the **market share variances** show that Unit A lost market share, which decreased its contribution margin by €2000. Unit B maintained its market share, but Unit C increased its share of a smaller market.

How would you rank these three business units by performance? Strictly bottom line performance (row 13 or 14) would rank Unit B at the top, and Units A and C tied for second. This perspective looks only at the 'bottom line' and ignores uncontrollable, but informative information. The more informative relative analysis separates uncontrollable performance (row 16) from controllable performance (row 17). None of the sub-unit managers can control the (exogenous) size of the product market, but top management could argue that they can control their responses to the market change. From this performance perspective Unit C's manager increased market share in a declining market, which must be far more difficult and potentially more beneficial to the firm than simply riding the rising market (Unit B) or

	A	B	C	D	E
1	**Relative Performance Measurement**	**Unit A**	**Unit B**	**Unit C**	
2	Market	East	East	West	
3	A) Annual budget				
4	Product contribution margin per unit	€ 100	€ 100	€ 100	
5	Expected market size, units per year	1,000	1,000	1,000	
6	Budgeted sales units per year	100	100	100	
7	B) Actual for the year				
8	Product unit contribution margin	€ 100	€ 100	€ 100	
9	Actual market size, units	1,200	1,200	900	
10	Actual sales units	100	120	100	
11	C) Performance report				
12	Budgeted contribution margin	€ 10,000	€ 10,000	€ 10,000	
13	Actual contribution margin	10,000	12,000	10,000	
14	Budget variance	€ -	€ 2,000	€ -	
15	D) Components of the budget variance				
16	Market size variance	€ 2,000	€ 2,000	€ (1,000)	=D4*(D6/D5)*(D9-D5)
17	Market share variance	(2,000)	-	1,000	=D4*(D10/D9-D6/D5)*D9
18	Budget variance	€ -	€ 2,000	€ (0)	

Figure 12.2 Relative performance measurement

losing market share in a rising market (Unit A). Relative performance evaluation indicates that one should rank Unit C at the top, Unit B second and Unit A last. Thus, uncontrollable but informative performance information can be a good source of information to differentiate performance.

12.3.2 Individual versus group

Organisations are made of individuals, but individual decision making affects the outcomes of sub-units and the entire organisation. Should individuals in organisations be aware of, or rewarded on, only their performance? Focusing on individual performance can impede the cooperation that might be needed for the organisation to meet its goals. After all, if only individual actions are needed, why does the organisation exist? Even when individual performance can be measured and rewarded reliably, many organisations seek to tie individual rewards to organisational outcomes to foster at least some level of teamwork. As discussed, the opaqueness of group decision making and effort can allow opportunistic freeloading and impede tying rewards to individual contributions.

EXAMPLE FROM PRACTICE: 2

Individual or group performance?

Difficulties of measuring either group or individual performance have led to widely differing approaches in practice. At one extreme, a Japanese corporation claims to only measure and reward group performance, never individual performance, instead focusing on hiring and training good employees that are highly qualified and suited to group work. A US firm, in contrast, measures and rewards individuals on a piecework basis. But to create teamwork it uses four management 'pillars': an employee management advisory board, wages based on the quality and quantity of individual worker output, annual performance based bonuses and guaranteed employment. Highly motivated, focused and capable individuals reportedly earn above average incomes for the industry and will not be laid off. Less successful employees do not last. Note that neither group performance nor individual piecework is ever the only factor in a successful incentive system.

Sources: Bylinski 1990; Taninecz 1995; Fast and Berg 1975; Tita 2010.

Group or team responsibility and production are nearly ubiquitous features of the conduct of modern business. Motivating, measuring and rewarding individuals within groups is problematic because individual preferences may differ, production is joint and efforts are largely unobservable. Further complications arise because individuals differ on dimensions of cognitive ability and socialisation.

EXAMPLE FROM RESEARCH: 3

Managing groups with freeloaders

Experimental researchers have found that groups with freeloaders (shirkers) experience differences in performance and behaviours that appear to be traced to cultural norms of cooperation. Even a single freeloader can cause a group's contributions and performance to drop dramatically. However, the outcomes are mixed when groups can punish freeloaders by withholding shares of performance rewards. Freeloaders in the US, Europe, Australia, China and Korea responded to punishment by improving their contributions and group performance. Freeloaders in Russia, Turkey, Saudi Arabia and Greece retaliated with anti-social behaviour against the 'do-gooders', with adverse effects on group performance.

Sources: Hotz 2008, Herrmann et al. 2008.

Organisations may improve the prospects for good group performance by preventive activities that improve capabilities and socialisation, and discourage freeloaders:[10]

- Team and task design that communicates common goals and methods
- Training that reinforces the impacts to all from meeting common goals
- Credible communication that frames the goals as sustainable and stable
- Individual rewards (or punishments) that actually reinforce the common goals
- Group rewards that actually reinforce the common goals.

Many have argued that individual and group incentive systems, particularly with monetary rewards, are counter productive because they essentially bribe employees and divert them from the inherent or intrinsic rewards of a job well done. Thus, the instrumentality of monetary rewards may not be sustainable and instead lead to degradations of morale and quality. For example, Kohn (1993) argues that monetary incentive pay is inherently

[10] For example, see Lindenberg and Foss 2011.

destructive of creativity, cooperation and performance. However, Gerhart and Rynes (2003) show that there is no consistent evidence that monetary rewards undermine intrinsic motivation, except in children.

Drucker, the inventor of profit centres, argued late in his career (1998) that firms should never have internal, pseudo profit centres because their internal profit incentives destroy cooperation. Baker et al. (1988) maintain that criticisms of pay-for-performance incentive systems really reflect the difficulties of **correctly specifying and objectively measuring performance objectives.** Thus, esteemed authors argue that pay-for-performance incentive systems actually might work too well when they focus employee attention and efforts on misspecified and poorly measured objectives.[11] Baker et al's solution is not to do away with incentive systems but to specify and measure their objectives better.

12.3.3 Summary of organisation structure effects

Problems abound for measuring individual, group and organisation performance. We are not going to magically improve measurement of motivations and actions that are unobservable by design (i.e. decentralisation). Abernethy et al. (2004) argue that organisational design follows unobservability of actions or results, which is reversed causation. Thus, decentralisation and control system design decisions may be complementary and simultaneous. In either case, we must depend on 'preventive' management controls and measured performance. Most organisations are not going to abandon the time honoured maxim, 'You cannot manage it if you cannot measure it.' Documenting assumptions and decision making steps, as Ariely (2010a) recommends and would seem to make decision making more structured and transparent, seems infeasible on a large scale. The complications of alternative organisational goals, objectives and structures are exacerbated by individuals' different motivations.

12.4 Models of motivation

Motivation is the driving force that causes humans to exert effort for their goals;[12] in the context of this chapter we refer to motivation for good decision making. Psychologists distinguish between **intrinsic motivation,** which is the drive that comes from within individuals (such as self-efficacy), and **extrinsic motivation,** which is the drive that is induced by external rewards (such as monetary compensation).

12.4.1 Intrinsic and extrinsic rewards

An **intrinsic reward** is the source of psychological well-being that comes from self-efficacy and self-awareness that come from succeeding at a personally meaningful task. Meaningful tasks include learning, mastering a topic or skill, and meeting difficult or interesting goals by personal ability and effort, not by luck. An **extrinsic reward** is the result of successfully completing a task that promises a tangible outcome such as money, grades, a promotion or

[11] The classic discussion of the problems of unintended consequences caused by misspecified objectives is Kerr 1975, reprinted 1995.

[12] No shortage of theories of motivation exists. By necessity, this chapter covers only a few. See: http://sites.google.com/site/motivationataglanceischool for an extensive list of motivational theories.

the avoidance of punishment. Extrinsic rewards may reinforce intrinsic motivation if the task already offers intrinsic rewards, but may also counter intrinsic motivation if it does not; that is, an extrinsic reward could be a bribe that coerces behaviour–at least in the short term.

One of organisational management's major challenges is to align goals of employees to those of the organisation by motivating them to make the right decisions. The extent of misalignment of employee and organisational goals defines the magnitude of the task to foster motivation that directs employees to achieve organisational goals. Two approaches to managing employee motivation for good decision making, then, are to a) design in motivation by hiring people with the desired intrinsic motivation and creating the conditions that foster their intrinsic rewards, and b) reinforce or induce motivation by creating significant extrinsic rewards. In both cases, money matters, because few would work for no pay for any length of time. However monetary compensation may not be always sufficient or even effective at maintaining intrinsic motivation or creating extrinsic motivation.

We search the fields of economics and psychology for sources of understanding about determinants of an individual's motivation.

12.4.2 Economic model of individual motivation

Economic theory assumes that humans are rational, goal directed and self-interested–or behave on the whole as if they were.[13] That is, humans are intrinsically motivated to increase, even maximise their own **utility**, which is a function of wealth, happiness, etc. Economists generally collapse utility into monetary wealth 'because individuals are willing to substitute non-monetary for monetary rewards and because money represents a generalised claim on resources and is, therefore, in general preferred over an equal dollar value payment in kind.'[14] Thus, when economists speak of motivation, they implicitly speak of motivation to increase (extrinsic) monetary wealth, of which more is better, despite likely declining marginal motivation for money.

The economic solution to creating motivation in organisations is not, however, simply a matter of offering more money, because employees are also assumed to have other opportunities and to be effort and risk averse. Organisations must offer sufficient (extrinsic) monetary reward to overcome employee opportunity costs of their time and efforts ('reservation wages') and aversion to taking risks. Thus, the economic solution to incentive systems is that the firm (or 'principal') offers an extrinsic reward, and the employee (or 'agent') exerts their preferred effort level, which is unobserved directly by the firm. Hence, the fundamental difficulty of the economic solution is that, even when the firm pays for performance or results, it cannot distinguish between good effort and good luck (Figure 12.1).

Economic research on motivation also focuses on alternative extrinsic rewards to attract employees with desired personal attributes for effort and risk or to induce otherwise unwilling employees to set aside their contrary effort and risk aversion and achieve the organisation's goals. Alternative rewards include no risk fixed salaries, risky cash bonuses that are contingent on meeting goals ('contingent' or 'at risk' pay), contingent promotions (with higher salaries) and, when appropriate for the type of organisation, contingent awards

[13] Or, as modified by so-called 'behavioural' theories of economics such as Transaction Cost Economics, humans are opportunistic and boundedly rational, which means we take opportunities to pursue private goals and we are intendedly rational but lack the cognitive and informational ability to be fully rational.

[14] Baker et al. 1988.

of shares or share options.[15] Share awards have been expected to be effective in aligning employee motivation to the owners of private firms, and share options are assumed to be effective in motivating risk taking because they limit downside risk.

Economic research has also investigated the motivational biases that are introduced by decentralised and group decision making. These important departures from atomised decision making units introduce problems of information asymmetry and unobservability of actions. These conditions incubate opportunities to appropriate the firm's resources (shirking, freeloading, taking perquisites–without explicitly stealing) while appearing to be aligned motivationally.

- Shirking is avoiding individual effort, which is undetected in the group setting.
- Freeloading is benefiting from the efforts of others in the group (while shirking).
- Taking perquisites is benefiting from the conditions of the job (while shirking or freeloading).

These are big problems to be sure, and economics recognises that monetary incentives (short or long term), monitoring and the use of multiple performance measures, can never overcome them completely. In other words, some loss to the firm is optimal given the impossible cost of eliminating biased motivations altogether. In fact, the unavoidable nature of these motivational losses is a consequence of why firms exist–the motivational losses are less than the opportunity costs of foregoing the operation of the firm.

12.4.3 Psychological models of individual motivation

In the broad field of psychology, personal traits and the need for physical and psychological well being[16] create intrinsic motivation and open the door to reinforcing extrinsic motivation. Physical and psychological well-being surely belong in the economist's utility, but might represent more than can be substituted for monetary wealth. Similarly, the role of 'personal traits' (other than effort or risk aversion) suggests nuanced differences from the rationality of economic motivation.

A large portion of the field of psychology reflects dissatisfaction with the descriptiveness and predictive ability of the economic model of motivation, or utility maximisation. Every dimension of the '*homo economicus*' has been challenged, often convincingly at the individual and small group level of decision making.[17] As previously noted, the assumption of rationality has received a lot of attention, and most observers now concede that individuals are not

[15] Further distinctions are compensation models that transfer relatively more risk from the employee/agent to the firm/principal:

- tenancy system (agent takes all risk);
- performance related pay (agent benefits from good luck);
- effort related pay (agent is insured against bad luck);
- salary system (principal takes all risk).

[16] Maslow's (1954/1970) hierarchy of needs is a well-known expression of individualistic human needs. The order from the most fundamental to the highest needs are physiological, safety, love, esteem and self-actualisation. Maslow theorised that we express higher needs only if lower needs are satisfied. Herzberg's Hygiene-Motivator classification is a related description of needs. Hygiene factors (pay, working conditions) are necessary but do not affect motivation except by their absence. Improvements in motivators (achievement, recognition, interesting work) do improve motivation. See Herzberg 2003.

[17] Psychology challenges to economic explanations have been less successful at the organisation and market level. It does appear, however, that 'behavioural economics' and 'behavioural finance' are moving to these larger targets by modelling the 'predictable irrationalities' that most humans exhibit. See Ariely (2010b).

consistently rational.[18] Other research challenges whether utility maximisation can explain human motivation, except tautologically. This research is difficult to pull off because straightforward tests of human decision making are joint tests of motivation, rationality, rewards, effort and risk aversion, and other personal traits. One can never vary just one of these factors in practice and retain control of the others in the field, so most of the work to isolate determinants of human motivation takes place in behavioural laboratories where experimental controls are possible (and student subjects are readily available).

To recap economic theory, individuals trade off risk, effort and reward. In a preview of psychological theories that we will soon discuss, individuals may be motivated to make trade offs that are more complex than explained by economic rationality:

- Goal difficulty–self efficacy (goal-setting theory)
- New effort–new outcome given past effort–past outcome (attribution theory)
- Effort–reward–fairness (organisational justice theory)
- Effort–outcome–reward (expectancy theory).

Briefly, we review findings from some of the most impactful efforts to test these theories.

12.4.3.1 Goal setting theory

Extensive empirical research shows that goals give direction to people's pursuits (Locke & Latham, 1990). Many laboratory studies show that **goal setting,** which is the act of setting performance targets, and **goal difficulty,** which determines the effort and ability needed, affect performance, presumably by affecting motivation. Early studies control expected effects on performance that are not directly related to motivation and typically use cognitively and physically unchallenging tasks, like sorting cards, with or without rewards. In the laboratory, motivation is varied by setting output targets, such as 'do your best' or specific targets of varying difficulty (easy, difficult and perfection). Nearly always, people just meet easy goals, are demotivated by perfection goals, and slack off when given 'do your best' goals. Studies have progressed well beyond these basic findings to investigate many moderating variables (e.g. task difficulty, risk, conflict, cheating) that can affect the impacts of goal setting. The literature on goal setting is vast and sometimes contentious, but the overwhelming laboratory evidence supports the favourable impact on **individual** performance of setting specific, difficult but attainable goals.[19] The linkage to psychological well-being is that achieving difficult goals appears to increase the high level personal needs of self-efficacy and self-esteem, with or without monetary rewards.

A laboratory study of budget goals and performance by Fisher et al (2003) reinforced goal-setting theory's prescription for setting 'moderately' difficult but attainable goals (75% of capability), rather than easy (50%) or unattainable (100%) goals. Interestingly, however, a field survey by Merchant and Manzoni (1989) found that large firms across several industries are most likely to use performance targets for sub-units that are routinely attained. This sounds suspiciously like easy goals, and one implication might be that firms employ under achieving 'satisficers' (H. Simon 1956). Merchant and Manzoni suggest that top and middle

---

[18] Efforts to improve human rationality have resulted in the growth of fields of decision support systems, artificial intelligence and creativity training. Interestingly, current research on motivation suggests that rationality and motivation are entangled to the point that rewards in isolation can impede creativity. For example, see Burroughs et al. 2011.

[19] References include Locke and Latham 1990, Locke et al. 1981, and Latham and Locke 2006. An introduction to a baffling, incredible exchange of views is Locke and Latham 2009.

managers are optimising more than operating results when they budget for easy targets that reduce transaction costs of:

- Monitoring ongoing decision making
- Changing targets between budgets
- Setting unachievable and uncontrollable goals
- Missing earnings forecasts.

EXAMPLE FROM RESEARCH: 4

Performance targets in profit seeking firms

Dekker et al. (2012) survey target setting practices by 364 Dutch firms (14% response rate). The researchers find that **target specificity** (the degree to which performance targets are clear and detailed) is related positively to contextual variables **environmental dynamism** (external sources of performance variation), **task uncertainty** (task-related knowledge and repetitiveness), and **incentive intensity** (degree to which incentives are tied to performance). Furthermore, high (low) levels of environmental uncertainty, task uncertainty and incentive intensity are tied to using estimated or benchmarked (past) targets. The survey approach permits more measurements of sources of variation on target setting than are possible in most laboratory settings, where most target setting research has been conducted. Surveys have their own challenges to validity, of course, which include sample representativeness, variable measurement and theory incompleteness.

12.4.3.2 Attribution theory

Attribution theory describes how people make inferences about the causes of their own and other people's behaviour. Attribution theory explains motivation to act is a result of how individuals attribute causes of events to their own capabilities and efforts and to the capabilities and efforts of others. Thus, attribution theory describes motivation, not just in terms of pursuit of intrinsic or extrinsic goals, but also in terms of individual self-awareness and decision making style.

Weiner (1986) describes three dimensions of attributed causes: locus, stability and controllability. Locus refers to whether one attributes the causes of outcomes to internal causes (e.g. one's talent/effort) or to external causes (e.g. task difficulty, others or luck). Stability refers to variation in the cause, or lack thereof, and controllability refers to the control one has over the cause. Thus an attributed cause may be related to effort, which is internal, unstable and controllable, or the attributed cause may be represented by any of the five other combinations of dimensions.

Numerous observations in organisations involve causal inferences about performance and the consequences of these beliefs, including the evaluation of oneself and others. The three dimensions can be internal or external to the individual, a distinction that appears to have importance for how one responds to events, such as observed performance. For example, consider the simplification of a model of motivation to reward, punish or remediate based

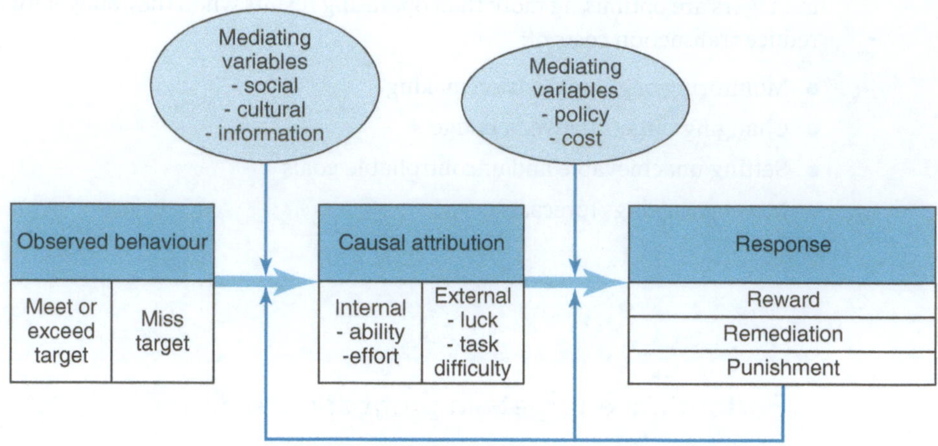

Figure 12.3 Example of the attribution model of motivation

on observed events and causal attribution in Figure 12.3 (adapted from Mitchell 1982, with a mediating cultural impact from Choi et al, 1999). Attribution theory predicts that the response matches the causal attributions of observed behaviour.

For example, a supervisor might observe that a subordinate missed targeted performance and attributes the shortfall to lack of ability. The response might be required training for the subordinate. If the shortfall is attributed to lack of effort, the superior's response might be punishment, or a change in future monetary incentives to induce extrinsic motivation for higher effort. Uncomfortable **cognitive dissonance** occurs in the subordinate, in this case, if they miss the target and make a different causal attribution, say to bad luck. People seek to reduce dissonance by achieving consonance with the information (changing attitudes, beliefs and actions), or alternatively by conflict, justifying the outcome, blaming others, or avoiding or denying the source of dissonance. The first set of responses motivated by the dissonance is beneficial to the organisation, but the second set is not.[20]

12.4.3.3 Organisational justice theory

Organisational justice is people's perceptions of the fairness of processes and distribution of rewards in organisations. The study of justice or fairness in organisations began with theories and studies of **distributive justice,** which investigates the importance of equitable distribution of rewards.[21] Distributive justice studies distinguish between equal reward allocations that promote social harmony from equitable incentive systems (such as pay for performance) that promote maximisation of performance. Equal attention has been focused on **procedural justice,** which concerns perceptions of the fairness of processes as explanations of observed behaviours of organisation members and their motivations. Perceptions of both distributive and procedural justice have been linked to dispute resolution, intended personnel turnover and dissonance. For example, perceived fairness of rewards can be a better predictor of reward satisfaction than the amount of the reward.

[20] Leon Festinger 1957 is the originator of cognitive dissonance theory, which appears to be complementary to most theories of motivation.

[21] This discussion draws from Greenberg 1990.

EXAMPLE FROM RESEARCH: 5

Management controls and organisational justice

Burney et al. (2009) found that supervisor rated employee performance in one firm is related to employee perceptions of organisational justice, which are related to employee beliefs that the management control system conforms to the firm's strategy and that its performance measures are valid. Their findings indicate that a firm's efforts to build and use a strategic and accurate management control system can result in improved performance by enhancing employee motivations that are affected by distributive and procedural justice (perhaps in addition to any direct information effects on employee decision making).

12.4.3.4 Expectancy theory

According to **expectancy** theory, developed by Vroom (1964) and Porter and Lawler (1968), the ultimate goal of action is hedonism or happiness. This state is attained by maximising benefits and minimising costs, or maximising the pleasure and minimising the pain, related to any behaviour, including decision making. Also according to expectancy theory, individuals are motivated to act by the **value** of rewards from attaining a goal, **expectation** of attaining that goal, and the **instrumentality** of actually receiving the promised reward. Value could be from intrinsic or extrinsic rewards. Expectation can derive from self-efficacy (ability plus effort), task difficulty and controllability. Instrumentality is based on controllability, processes and trust. By this theory, an individual is motivated according to how value, expectation and instrumentality interact, as depicted in Figure 12.4.

Perceived high levels of all three predict high motivation, whereas low levels of any one breaks the chain of interaction and predicts low motivation. The theory implies that, as long as two of the factors meet undefined minimal levels, increasing the third will increase motivation. This theory is also appealing, but the responsiveness and precision of these interactive effects is still very much an open question, and improvements are continuing. For example, Kominis and Emmanuel (2007) surveyed 290 middle managers in a large UK firm. To established survey questions, they added perception of the completeness and accuracy of performance measurement as representation of the instrumentality of the performance evaluation

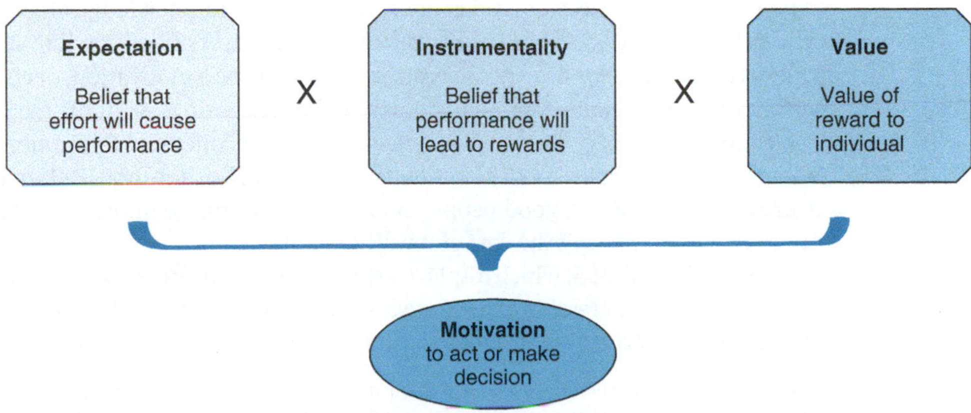

Figure 12.4 Expectancy theory of motivation

process. They found the accuracy of performance measurement particularly important for extrinsic rewards. Interestingly, they also found that extrinsic and intrinsic rewards are complementary in an actual work setting, not competing.

12.4.4 Summary of motivational theories

This has been a selective overview of theories of individual motivation. From this set of theories, we can establish a few generalisations of what matters to the motivational properties of incentive systems in organisations. Consideration of the many other theories would add nuance, we think, but not dramatically different conclusions.

1. Individuals are goal directed, whether they pursue goals rationally or not.
2. Goals may promise intrinsic or extrinsic rewards, which are complementary impacts on motivation if incentive systems are designed properly for the decision context.
3. Higher monetary (extrinsic) rewards alone might not provide sustainable motivation.
4. Specific, difficult, attainable goals provide the most motivation to succeed, but the real costs of striving for these goals must also be considered.
5. Different causal attributions of outcomes, perceived unfairness in processes and rewards, or broken links in the reward process can cause dissonance, which is unproductive and disruptive if not dealt with openly and credibly.

It does seem, however, that we can make some confident recommendations about designing effective incentive systems.

12.5 Incentive systems design

We summarise the preceding discussions by building an incentive systems tableau that should be helpful for designing or revising an organisational **reward system,** which is the collection of objectives, measures, rewards and processes to reward individuals or groups. We caution that researchers in the general field of motivation and reward typically focus on one factor (e.g. goal setting) and control or randomise the others (e.g. financial performance). Practically speaking, varying all of the important variables that we discuss would exceed the capabilities of laboratory or field experimentation. To our knowledge no one has systematically surveyed a large sample of firms to assess the diversity of possibilities. Although we believe that each factor does not operate independently on motivation, decision making and performance, we cannot confidently describe the interactions of all the factors.

We have taken as given that the incentive system is intended to promote good decision making, which makes good performance more likely than not. Related goals include attracting and retaining good people, motivating learning, reinforcing culture, reinforcing structure and optimising the cost of rewards.[22]

Consider Figure 12.5, which displays a stylised view of an organisation, its goals and structure (a simplified expression of its strategy) and many of the possible elements of its incentive system. The incentive system should be consistent with its strategic goals and structure, but

[22] For example, see Lawler 1993. More current reviews are by The International Society for Performance Improvement 2002 and Bonner and Sprinkle 2002. The impact of tangible rewards is one of the most heavily researched areas.

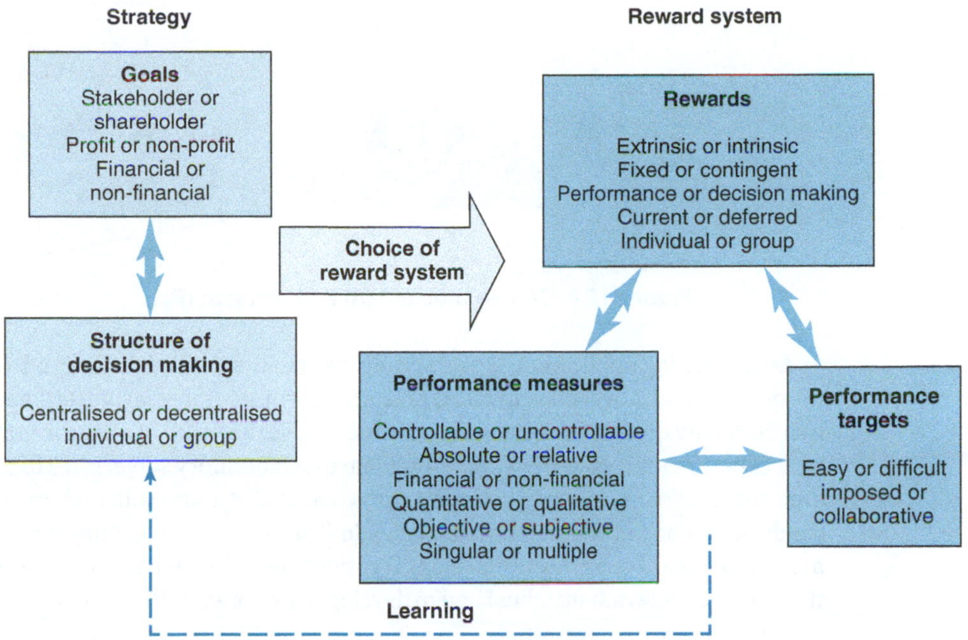

Figure 12.5 Incentive system elements and influences

the combinations of reward elements are many. Theory and evidence can help in sorting out the possibilities, but the science is not so refined as to prescribe a incentive system for any strategic situation. As is the case with most management efforts, organisations can learn and adjust as its successes with a incentive system unfold.

12.5.1 Interactive effects of performance targets, performance measures and rewards on motivation and performance

We have described each of Figure 12.5 incentive system elements. Because these elements most likely do not act in isolation, we next review the extant theory and evidence of the effects of their interactions. This discussion is far from complete because the research record is incomplete. Figure 12.5 suggests a large, interesting research agenda.

12.5.1.1 Performance targets

We have established that specific, difficult but attainable goals result in the highest performance. This is reliably so for individuals and small groups.[23] Collaboration and participation in setting goals can increase commitment to the goals, which might increase motivation, effort, and ultimate performance. However, evidence by Locke and Steele 1983 shows that participation affects performance only if participation results in a higher goal than would have been imposed. Organisational justice theory indicates that participation in setting goals increases perceived fairness, but this might not lead to improved performance. Participation might increase performance, if it increases knowledge about the task, but this appears to be an open issue.[24]

[23] See Kleingeld et al. 2011, but also recall the results of Merchant and Manzoni 1989 that many firms set easily attainable goals, perhaps to optimise a more complex definition of performance.

[24] See Erez and Arad 1986 and Parker and Kyi 2006.

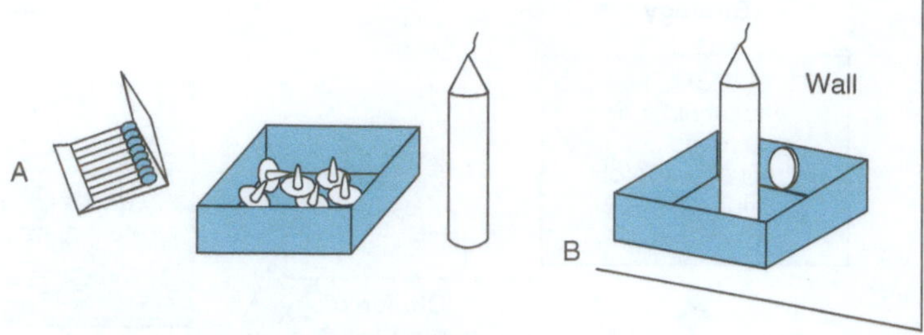

Figure 12.6 Candle problem (A) and solution (B)

An interesting application of goal setting is when the desired target is **innovation** or **creativity,** which is a novel non-financial precursor of future financial performance. Most believe that creativity derives from innate capabilities and is the result of intrinsic motivation. A common experimental test is the 'candle' problem that laboratory subjects try to solve quickly and innovatively.[25] Subjects are required to attach a candle to the wall and are given matches, a candle and a box of thumbtacks, as shown in Figure 12.6 Part A. Subjects who are offered a monetary reward consistently take longer to overcome 'functional fixedness' (e.g. tacks inside the box and irrelevant matches) and to develop the solution (Part B) than subjects who do the task without extrinsic rewards.

The evidence from this and similar experiments has been interpreted to mean that extrinsic rewards **in isolation** (e.g. contingent monetary rewards) impede creativity. The psychological mechanism might be depressed intrinsic motivation or impaired cognition from conflicting motivations. However, recent research shows that the adverse effect of isolated extrinsic motivation reverses when other, complementary personnel controls are added, such as creativity training.[26] The lesson is that none of the elements of an incentive system should be applied in isolation–another indication of why organisations use a portfolio of management controls.

12.5.1.2 Performance measures

Performance measures supply evidence that goal relevant objectives, such as profitability and gender diversity, are or are not being met. Most studies investigate the impacts of one or another of the performance measure dyads in Figure 12.5 (e.g. absolute or relative performance measures) on motivation, decision making or actual performance, while holding all, or all but one, of the other attributes constant. This is convenient for the typical 2×2 research design shown in Figure 12.7. A **research design** attempts to isolate the factors of interest while eliminating or controlling related factors that are not of primary interest. Whether these results can be generalised beyond the controlled atmosphere of a laboratory is an important issue for incentive-system design.

In a few cases, researchers have been fortunate to conduct a field experiment within a single firm wherein all but the performance measure is held constant and other factors are varied (or another variant). For example, Pritchard et al (1988) measured group level productivity (an absolute, non-financial measure) for an 8 month 'baseline' period while adding over time group feedback, group goal setting and group incentives. They reported that productivity grew steadily with each addition without adverse effects on job satisfaction, turnover intentions or morale.

[25] See Glucksberg 1962.

[26] See Burroughs et al. 2011.

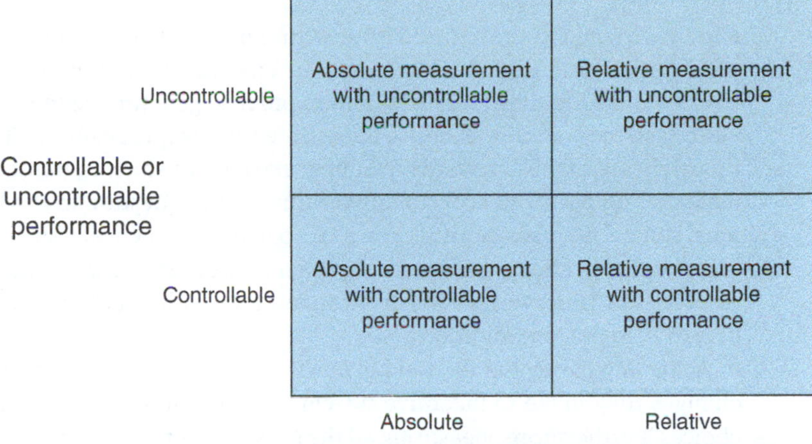

Figure 12.7 Example of a basic 2×2 research design

It is obviously difficult, unfortunately, to generalise beyond the specific research findings of these studies. But if the tests of theory are replicated in multiple settings (i.e. tasks other than the candle problem, subjects other than undergraduate college students), one's confidence in the results is increased.

We are unable to say at this time how all of the performance measurement dyads interact to affect performance, but we invite readers to search for results that are added frequently to the research record.

- **Controllable or uncontrollable performance** Most argue in favour of measuring controllable performance, but in some circumstances measuring uncontrollable performance is informative about individual ability or effort.
- **Absolute or relative performance measures** Measurement against absolute targets has the advantage of consistency with goal setting theory; however, relative performance measurement (or 'tournaments') can be informative. Internal tournaments, however, can conflict with cooperation and coordination.
- **Financial or non-financial measures** Many organisations use both types of measures, but relative weighting and trading off performance among measures is an important, unresolved issue.
- **Quantitative measures or qualitative indicators** Many organisations use both, but current research indicates more attention is paid to quantitative measures. Thus, many organisations seek to reliably quantify such outcomes as environmental performance and social impact. Whether they can be, or need to be measured, as reliably as profits for financial reporting are important issues.
- **Objective measures or subjective indicators** Similarly to the previous two dyads, research shows that organisations tend to rely formally on objective measures (e.g. accurate, reliable, non-disputable) rather than subjective indicators, because of issues related to trust, consistency and fairness.
- **Singular or multiple measures** Formally combining multiple measures for communication, planning and training is the topic of Chapter 10; whether and how these integrated systems (e.g. the balanced scorecard) can be used reliably and effectively for performance based incentive systems is an open question.

12.5.1.3 Incentives

Finally we come to the nature and structure of incentives themselves, which have received considerable attention from researchers, consultants and organisations. Similarly to the issues of performance measures, and in order to generate valid results, most research has addressed the complex incentive issues as 'either–or' propositions. That is, should organisations rely on intrinsic rewards or supply extrinsic rewards to improve motivation, decision making, and performance? To answer this type of question in the laboratory, researchers must control for all of the other effects on outcomes. Practically speaking this means controlling alternative effects and randomising subjects or measuring personal traits to avoid biased responses.[27] Thus, we almost never can test for a wide set of interaction effects that we suspect exist in real organisations.

Achieving control in the field is much more difficult because organisations choose the changes they make to incentive systems, and we do not believe that they make random choices. Furthermore, measuring all the possible traits of organisations does not ensure that they apply to individuals in the organisations. Suffice to say that many obstacles exist to understanding clearly the impact of changing rewards and incentive systems. As in the previous section, researchers, consultants and organisations are pushing the envelope of current practice to identify improvements. It is exceedingly difficult to attribute changes in an organisation's performance to a change in its incentive system (say, adoption of EVA for upper level managers), and available evidence so far is mixed.[28]

Following are a few highlights from recent research.

- **Extrinsic and intrinsic rewards** Early research indicated that these compete, such that adding extrinsic rewards diminishes intrinsic rewards to the detriment of performance. More recent research indicates that adding extrinsic rewards with other, properly matched, management controls can enhance performance.
- **Rewards based on performance or decision making (capability, process)** Pay-for-performance is a widespread practice that is criticised for impeding intrinsic motivation (see above) and rewarding luck. Current research is aimed at testing whether rewarding on the quality of decision making is a more effective system.
- **Current or deferred (long horizon, bonus bank) rewards** Current monetary rewards have been widely criticised for motivating short term, myopic decision making. In response, many firms have begun using longer horizons (e.g. three years rather than one quarter) and bonus banks. A bonus bank typically collects (or escrows) most of an annual bonus, which could be positive or negative, based on meeting or missing annual targets. Payouts are typically deferred for three years or so to avoid short termism.
- **Individual or group rewards** Rewards for small group performance can result in higher performance than individual rewards for group members. Small group incentives appear to work against freeloading better than individual awards.
- **Performance sensitivity of rewards (floors, variability and caps)** Many performance based incentive systems are structured as a **quota bonus plan** with piecework type rewards between floor and ceiling quotas. The floor appears to provide higher motivation and lower risk than simple piecework, and the ceiling limits reward costs and might temper motivation

[27] For an excellent overview of measurement and control issues see Kinney, W. 1986.

[28] For an early description of this problem, see Campbell 1969. See Ittner and Larcker 2001 for a critique of related field based research.

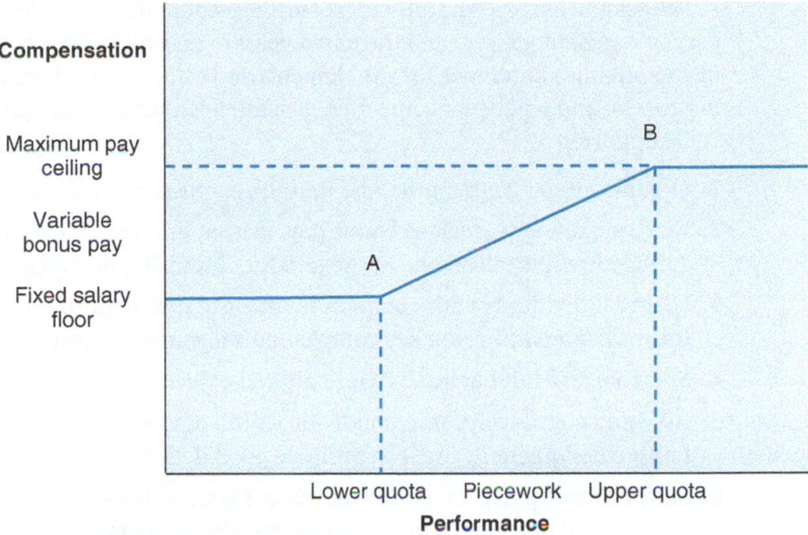

Figure 12.8 Quota bonus plan

for short termism. However, the quotas also might motivate individuals to manage the timing of outcomes to fit within the piecework reward range. Figure 12.8 illustrates the general form of this incentive structure, which is normally used for extrinsic rewards.

Performance up to the lower quota earns only the fixed salary (which might be zero). As performance based pay nears point A, the individual (or group) has an extrinsic incentive to accelerate the period's performance into the piecework range. This is precisely the intent of this reward structure, but it might also motivate cheating by recognising accomplishments (e.g. sales revenue) early or by lying. Until point B, when the upper quota is reached, the incentive is to increase performance. However, after point B, no incremental pay is earned, and extrinsic rewards cease. This controls the amount of compensation and may enhance longer term decision making, but it also creates an incentive to retard performance or delay its recognition to a future period, when it can provide a head start on bonus earning performance. This seems an inevitable impact of compensation thresholds and caps (Murphy 2001).

12.6 Summary

Incentive system design is one of the most difficult management tasks, and also one of the most important. Many reasons exist why a single reward recipe cannot work for all organisations. An effective (dare we say efficient?) incentive system must reflect the organisation's goals and objectives, which differ across organisations, even within profit seeking, public and non-profit categories. Economic and psychological models of motivation are not entirely consistent, and designers may favour straightforward economic models over more descriptive psychological models. We extrapolate from our own perceptions and great volumes of complementary research to believe that both models contribute to effective incentive system design, because both extrinsic (economic) and intrinsic (psychological) motivations are important to most individuals.

We acknowledge a) the difficulty of testing economic models in the field, b) the richness of psychological models, c) and the narrowness of feasible research. These mean that progress in completing a handbook for the elements and trade offs for incentive system design, is still in process, and will be for some time. Nonetheless, we believe that several findings are very well supported:

1. Organisational goals matter and must be expressed clearly.
2. Extrinsic rewards, such as bonus pay, matter, are important motivators but they are not sufficient, especially if one has regard for optimising overall pay levels.
3. Hiring individuals with compatible intrinsic motivation, and fostering the building of intrinsic motivation, are key complements to extrinsic rewards.
4. Specific, difficult but attainable goals and objectives are important targets.
5. Assisting cognitively limited individuals (all of us) to use the right information, and perhaps to document its use, can promote good decision making.
6. Base rewards partly on performance, but not solely on performance. Quality of decision making and duration of performance are also important.
7. Incentive system design is not a completed science, and there are many paths that might lead to success. Similarly, what works in one context might not work well in another. Beware of anyone who claims to have THE answer.

EXERCISES

Exercise 12.1 Relative performance evaluation

Absolutely! Company Ltd manufactures its products near Melbourne, Australia. The company's distribution and sales operations are decentralised by its three independent product groups (prepared foods, lighting and auto parts) and by two geographical regions (Australia-New Zealand, South Asia). A regional executive vice-president manages each geographical region. Each product group within a region has a product vice-president who reports to the regional executive. Because of free trade agreements, Absolutely! considers a product group in both regions as serving the same market, although prices might vary across regions. Fifty% of the annual evaluations of managers of the company sub-units are based on the sub-unit operating income before tax. Regional executives are evaluated on their region's total operating income before tax. Consider the following information about budgeted and actual outcomes.

	Australia-New Zealand			South Asia		
Budget and actual data	**Prepared foods**	**Lighting**	**Auto parts**	**Prepared foods**	**Lighting**	**Auto parts**
A) Annual budget						
Product contribution margin per unit, $AUD	20	100	30	18	90	25
Expected market size, units per year	100 000	10 000	30 000	100 000	10 000	30 000
Budgeted sales units per year	2 000	1 000	300	1 000	1 000	300
Budgeted fixed costs per year, $AUD	8 000	5 000	11 000	7 000	4 000	8 000

	Australia-New Zealand			South Asia		
Budget and actual data	**Prepared foods**	**Lighting**	**Auto parts**	**Prepared foods**	**Lighting**	**Auto parts**
B) Actual for the year						
Product unit contribution margin, $AUD	19	90	28	19	85	25
Actual market size, units	120 000	8 000	26 000	120 000	8 000	26 000
Actual sales units	2 500	1 200	400	900	950	290
Actual fixed costs, $AUD	8 500	5 400	12 000	6 600	3 000	7 600

Required:

1. Prepare an analysis similar to Figure 12.1 for operating income before tax for each product group and region.
2. According to your analysis, rank the managers by their operating income performance, and explain whether the results are controllable by managers and informative about managers' performance.

Exercise 12.2 Pay for performance

Scapens Corporation has hired you to develop a pay-for-performance incentive system based on its four key areas of performance. Scapens CEO ultimately wants each of the company's 20 divisions to perform at the 90th percentile level of the industry for each goal. The company reliably measures performance against each of these goals as follows:

Performance area	Performance measure	Current Scapens average	Current industry 75th percentile	Current industry 90th percentile
Employee productivity	Sales per employee	€175 000	€170 000	€200 000
Product quality	Customer-found defect rate	2.00%	1.00%	0.02%
Customer satisfaction	Customer satisfaction score (1 to 100)	72	75	89
Profitability	Return on investment	10.30%	10.00%	30.00%

For simplicity assume three types of divisions exist: low performers, average performers and high performers, with the following average frequency and performances:

Scapens performance measures	Low performers	Average performers	High performers
Number of divisions	4	10	6
Sales per employee	€137 500	€175 000	€200 000
Customer-found defect rate	4.99%	2.00%	0.01%
Customer satisfaction score (1 to 100)	42	72	92
Return on investment	−34.25%	10.30%	40%
Average salary	€150 000	€150 000	€150 000
Bonus percentage > 75th	1.00%	1.00%	1.00%
Bonus percentage > 90th	2.00%	2.00%	2.00%

Required:

Assume each division manager is paid an annual salary of €150 000. Suppose you propose an incentive plan that paid a 1% of salary bonus for exceeding the industry's 75th percentile performance on each measure and a 2% bonus for exceeding the 90th percentile on each measure.

1. What would be the average and total amounts of bonus compensation paid for the current levels of performance? What if all divisions were high performers?
2. Do you think the incentive plan is a good plan or not? Explain.
3. Propose an alternative incentive plan and estimate the bonus compensation amounts, using the current level of performance as the base.

Exercise 12.3 Quota bonus plan

The Board of Directors of Xcellerator Company plans to implement bonus compensation plans for the small company's employees, who had been compensated by salary only. The proposed plan for each member of the four-person 'C-suite' executive team has the following parameters based on annual operating profit reported to shareholders:

Bonus rate	Operating profit	Bonus compensation
0%	€0	€10 000.0
0%	€100 000	€10 000.0
10%	€100 001	€10 000.1
10%	€500 000	€50 000.0
0%	€500 001	€50 000.0
0%	€600 000	€50 000.0

Required:

1. Prepare a graph of this proposed bonus plan, and label it similarly to Figure 12.8.
2. The CEO's responsibilities include major sales contracts. Towards the end of the fiscal year, the company's operating profit stood at €90 000. At this time, the CEO was negotiating a sale with a new customer that could earn an operating profit of €25000. Discuss the CEO's incentives whether to ask the CFO to recognise the sales revenue as earned during the current fiscal year.
3. Assume that the bonus plan has been in place for several years, and the end of a fiscal year approaches, Current operating profit stands at €485 000. The CEO has completed the negotiation of a sale with an existing customer for established products that are in stock or are readily obtainable. Based on similar past sales, the expected operating profit from this sale is €60 000. Should the CEO defer completion of the sale to the next fiscal year? Why, or why not?
4. Discuss the strengths and weaknesses of extending a similar bonus plan to all employees of Xcellerator Company.

Exercise 12.4 Executive bonus plans for banks

The Business Review reported that TrustCo Bank Corp of New York reinstated its executive bonus plan that had been suspended for three years during the Great Recession.[29] The suspended plan had been based on return on equity and was a large proportion of total compensation. The revised plan means that the three top executives could receive bonuses up to 25%

[29] Barbara Pinckney 2011.

of their base salaries, which is a much smaller at-risk proportion than the suspended plan. The plan was suspended in 2008 because the board of directors felt, at the time, that it was prudent to make executive compensation less sensitive to performance standards. While the incentive plan was suspended, the bank more than doubled executive base pay. The bank will probably keep their fixed salaries at the new, higher level.

The revised plan for 2011 is based on the bank's benchmarked return on average assets, return on average equity, efficiency ratio, and the ratio of non-performing assets to total assets. To earn the maximum bonus, the bank must perform 25% better than the average of peer banks of similar size, in the same region of the US, and that also were not 'bailed out.' A spokesperson stated that, 'We think there should be an incentive program to motivate executives, but it should not be so big that it encourages risk taking and stops us from being what we are, which is sound and safe and conservative.'

Required:

1. Describe how the suspended incentive plan might have motivated TrustCo managers to take excessive risks.
2. Explain how the revised incentive plan moderates risk taking.
3. Discuss whether the new incentive plan should be pushed down into lower levels of management.

Exercise 12.5 Culture, communications and incentives

Read the Wall Street Journal article, 'CEO Broadens Vistas at LG,' 21 May 2008; URL for this article: http://online.wsj.com/article/SB121130956004907735.html

Required:

1. Explain how LG's CEO, Yong Nam, pushed profit related incentives throughout the global company. Should other international companies repeat this effort? Explain.
2. Could non-profit organisations adopt this approach for 'cost-consciousness'? Should they? Explain.

CASES

Case 12.6 Alternative incentives for pharmaceutical production and distribution

Healthcare researchers at Yale University (USA) have recently proposed an alternative incentive system for the development and distribution of medicinal drugs. The researchers argue that the current economic model is driven by patent protections and very high mark ups for proprietary drugs. One result is that pharmaceutical companies seek to develop drugs for diseases of the wealthiest of the world's population who can afford to pay for the protected, marked up drugs. Another result is that drugs are not developed for diseases that plague the majority of the world's population who cannot afford to pay high mark ups. Diseases such as tuberculosis and malaria, the researchers argue, receive scant attention from pharmaceutical companies because higher profits are available from patented, marked up drugs.

The Yale team proposes the Health Impact Fund as an alternative incentive system to motivate pharmaceutical companies to profitably target drugs for the poor's diseases. Briefly, the fund would work this way:

a. World governments would establish the Health Impact Fund (HIF) that would be the source of total compensation (approximately $6billion USD per annum) for successful introductions of impactful drugs for the majority global population.

b. Pharmaceutical firms would earn a share of the HIF from drugs that they develop and distribute at cost to fight diseases of the world's poor.
c. Each firm's proportion of the annual global health impact of its HIF drugs would determine its share of the annual HIF.

Required:

Review both sources listed below and prepare an analysis of the strengths and weaknesses of the HIF proposal for new incentives to pharmaceutical firms.

Sources: http://www.ted.com/talks/thomas_pogge_medicine_for_the_99_percent.html?utm_source=newsleter_weekly_2011-12-21&utm_campaign=newsletter_weekly&utm_medium=email

www.healthimpactfund.org

Case 12.7 Components of an executive incentive plan

Following is a disguised description of an actual executive incentive plan, taken from a publicly traded company's regulatory filing in its home country:

The 2010 Incentive Plan provides for a cash bonus calculated as a percentage of the executive officer's base salary. For fiscal 2010, the bonus target for the Chief Executive Officer ('CEO') is 100% of his base salary and the bonus targets for all other executive officers range from 60% to 75% of their respective base salaries, depending on their seniority.

Plan components

Under the 2010 Incentive Plan, the cash bonuses for the CEO and all other executive officers are determined using three different components, each with different weighting. The three components are: (1) the Company's share of revenue (the 'SOR Component'), weighted at 20%; (2) the Company's externally reported operating profit (the 'OP Component'), weighted at 30%; and (3) strategic objective goals pertaining to each officer's position and responsibilities (the 'Strategic Component'), weighted at 50%. All components are paid on a semi-annual basis.

1. **SOR Component** The SOR Component is designed to measure and reward increases in the Company's share of revenue as compared to benchmarked, similar product companies identified by the Compensation Committee of the Board of Directors. The SOR Component is subject to a minimum threshold for any payout and a multiplier that increases the payout depending on Company performance. The SOR Component multiplier is 50% if the minimum threshold percentage is reached and 100% if the target percentage is reached. After the target percentage is reached, the multiplier increases by increments of 25%, and is capped at a maximum of 200%.
2. **OP component** The OP Component is determined by a formula which measures and rewards improvements in the Company's operating profit. The OP Component is subject to a minimum threshold range for any payout and a multiplier that increases the payout depending on Company performance. For the OP Component, the threshold range of operating profit percentages is subject to a multiplier of 20%, and the multiplier increases by increments of 10% after the top of the threshold range is met. If the target range of operating profit percentage is met, the multiplier is 100%, and thereafter the multiplier increases by increments of 10%. At the discretion of the Compensation Committee, any extraordinary or one-time charges may be excluded for purposes of calculating the OP Component.

3. **Strategic component** The Strategic Component is based on a maximum of five strategic, non-financial goals for each half of the year. The minimum weighting of any one individual goal is 20% and achievement of each goal is measured on a scale of 0% achievement to 150% achievement. The threshold for any payout of the Strategic Component is 50% overall achievement and the maximum performance is capped at 150%.

Required:

1. Create a numerical example to explain how this company's three components and their multipliers work to compute an executive's bonus.
2. The same company's 2009 Incentive Plan had four, equally weighted components, including the three 2010 components and a 'growth component' that was dropped for the 2010 plan. The 2009 plan stated:

'The Growth Component is paid annually and is designed to reward year-over-year revenue growth. The Growth Component is subject to a minimum threshold for payout and a multiplier that increases the target payout as the revenue growth increases. The Growth Component multiplier increases by 20% for each percentage of revenue growth and is capped at an annual maximum of 200%.'

Explain likely reasons why the company decided to drop the 'growth component' for the next year's plan and to rebalance the weightings for the three retained components.

Case 12.8 Non-profit hospital incentive plan

Karen Garloch reported in the *Charlotte Observer* that Carolinas HealthCare System (US) paid its CEO, Michael Tarwater, $4.2 million in 2011, $523000 more than the year before. Tarwater has led the $6 billion public hospital system (30 hospitals) for 10 years and received a base salary of about $1 million, two bonuses totaling $2.5 million, and other compensation, including retirement and health benefits, of about $700000. One bonus was based on short term goals and a second was based on long term goals. 'We've had extremely good performance,' said Debra Plousha Moore, the system's chief of human resources. 'All performance goals this year were either met or exceeded.' Nine other executives at Carolinas HealthCare earned more than $1 million in 2011. More than 23000 lower level employees also received bonuses, ranging from $255 to $850 in mid January, totaling $17.6 million. The Carolinas HealthCare system is a tax exempt public hospital authority, created by state law. The system has for decades received up to $16 million dollars annually in taxpayer funds to pay for the care of indigent patients. Last year, government officials faced a severe budget crisis, observed the hospital system's increasing profitability, and they voted to end the subsidy.

Required:

Prepare a report to:

1. Develop arguments for and against the proposition that 'non-profit hospitals must offer compensation on a par with private firms to attract and retain its executives.' Be prepared to defend or attack either side in class.
2. Conduct some internet based research on hospital outcome and process quality. Describe multiple short term goals and long term goals (both financial and non-financial) that a non-profit hospital could adopt consistently for its bonus compensation plan for executives and lower level employees. Do you perceive a possibility of conflicts among these goals? Explain.

3. How would you determine target levels for the goals described in requirement 2?
4. Some incentive plans require that all targets must be met before any bonus is paid. How would you recommend that a non-profit hospital could effectively a) build a pool of bonus funds and b) distribute funds to executives and lower level employees?

Adapted from: http://www.charlotteobserver.com/2012/02/01/2974848/chs-paid-its-ceo-42m.html\#storylink=cpy

Case 12.9 Charitable organisation compensation plan

Charitable organisations compete with for-profit and other non-profit organisations for management talent. The boards of many charitable organisations realise that even intrinsically motivated managers would find it difficult to ignore higher extrinsic compensation from otherwise similar organisations. Thus, charity boards might feel the need to offer competitive financial packages to managers they would like to attract and retain. This is controversial, and it is unclear among charitable organisations whether higher compensation results in higher 'performance'. The Charity Navigator (charitynavigator.org) compiles detailed information for approximately 5000 charitable organisations, including 'top-10' lists with various characteristics. Two such lists are '10 Highly Paid CEOs at Low-Rated Charities' and '10 Highly-Rated Charities with Low Paid CEOs'.

Required:

1. How would you recommend that charities should define and measure performance?
2. Compare and contrast one charity from each list, using information from the Charity Navigator website and from the charities' websites.
3. Prepare a short, visual presentation that reflects your analysis of these two charities.
4. What is your recommendation for whether charities should seek to match higher compensation levels paid by competitors for management talent?

Case 12.10 Governmental incentive plan

Pakistan faces immense educational challenges, and appears to be falling behind other South-Asia countries in educational quality and literacy, especially among females. Although Pakistan has a goal to fulfil the country's constitutional right by 2015, observers feel there is a 0% chance of doing so within the lifetime of any living Pakistani. Remarkably, 26 countries poorer than Pakistan send a larger proportion of their children to school than does Pakistan. Only 35% of school children, aged 6-16, can read a story; while 50% cannot read a sentence. Educational observers describe Pakistan's public education system as an emergency or crisis situation for the country and its neighbours.

Although less than 1.5% of the country's annual GDP is devoted to public education, Pakistan is plagued with thousands of 'ghost schools' and many thousands of 'ghost teachers', who exist only as line items of the budget. It is little wonder that many Pakistani citizens regard corruption as another major factor in the education crisis. The rapid growth of private schools, especially in urban areas is another unsurprising outcome, as is the decline in the social status of teachers. However, low and misapplied funds appear not to be the major cause of Pakistan's poor public education performance. Rather, the major cause of the crisis appears to be public school teacher motivation to teach well.

Teachers' low job satisfaction, motivation and incentives from teaching are identified as key factors in Pakistan's education crisis. A UNESCO report, nearly ten years ago, identified non-transparent appointment practices, politicisation, poor management, lack of transport and security as major problems that are faced by Pakistani teachers. Similarly, a more recent report by T. Khan identified overall low job satisfaction among teachers that is driven by unmet higher order emotional and social needs, most notably professional self-esteem, job security, inter–personal relationships and accountability at work (among teachers, education managers, pupils and parents/communities), opportunities for career progression, the working environment, the work load and productivity/learning outcomes. Although public school teachers earn four times as much as an average parent of their students, 10 to 15% of them are absent from their teaching duties every day. Teaching quality is uneven at best and teacher attrition is high.

A recent report concluded that the following steps will improve teacher motivation:

a. Create an independent professional body of teachers that is included in decision-making for curriculum, policy and infrastructure.
b. Recruit teachers on the basis of merit.
c. Empower and hold teachers accountable with special programmes and incentives.
d. Improve compensation and working conditions, including facilities and security.
e. Focus teacher education on practical aspects of teaching.
f. Gain commitment to education from leaders at all levels in the country.

Required:

1. Describe the apparent roles of intrinsic and extrinsic rewards in the teaching profession. Do these roles vary across cultures? Explain.
2. Design and describe an incentive system that should improve public school teacher motivation in Pakistan.
3. Assume that your incentive system could be implemented. How would you define success of your new incentive system. How would you test its effectiveness?
4. Prepare a report or a PowerPoint presentation that presents your incentive system.

Sources: Education emergency Pakistan (www.dawn.com/2011/03/09/education-emeregency-pakistan.html - you may download the complete report from this site); T. Khan, Teacher job satisfaction and incentive: A case study of Pakistan (www.eldis.org/vfile/upload/1/document/0709/Teacher_motivation_Pakistan.pdf)

References

Abernethy, M.A., Bouwens, J., and van Lent, L. (2004). Determinants of control system design in divisionalized firms. *The Accounting Review 79*(3), 545-570.

Ariely, D. (2010a). Good decisions–Bad outcomes. *Harvard Business Review* December: 40.

Ariely, D. (2010b). *Predictably irrational: The hidden forces that shape our decisions.* Expanded and revised edition. Harper Perennial, New York.

Baker, G. M. Jensen, and K. Murphy. (1988). Compensation and incentives: Practice vs. theory. *The Journal of Finance* 43(3): 593-616.

Baker, G. (1990). Pay-for-performance for middle managers: Causes and consequences. *Journal of Applied Corporate Finance* 3(3): 50-61.

Bonner, S. and G. Sprinkle. (2002). The effects of monetary incentives on effort and task performance: theories, evidence, and a framework for research. *Accounting, Organizations and Society* (27): 303–345

Burney, L.L., Henle, C.A., and Widener, S.K. (2009). A path model examining the relations among strategic performance measurement system characteristics, organizational justice, and extra- and in-role performance. *Accounting, Organizations and Society,* 34(3-4): 305-321.

Burroughs, J. E., D. W. Dahl, C. P. Moreau, A. Chattopadhyay and G. J. Gorn. (2011). Facilitating and rewarding creativity during new product development. *Journal of Marketing* 75 (July): 53–67.

Bylinsky, G., (1990). The hottest high-tech company in Japan. *Fortune* 121(1), 82–88.

Campbell, D. 1969. Reforms as experiments. *American Psychologist* 24: 409-429.

Choi, I., Nisbett, R.E., and Norenzayan, A. (1999). Causal attribution across cultures: Variation and universality. *Psychological Bulletin* 125(1): 47-63.

Davis, J., Schoorman, F., and Donaldson, L. (1997). Towards a stewardship theory of management. *Academy of Management Review* 22:20-47.

Dawn.com. (2011). Education emergency Pakistan (www.dawn.com/2011/03/09/education-emeregency-pakistan.html - you may download the complete report from this site)

Dekker, H., T. Groot, and M. Schoute. (2012). Determining performance targets. *Behavioral Research in Accounting,* forthcoming.

Donaldson, T. and L. Preston. (1995). The stakeholder theory of the corporation: Concepts, evidence, and implications. *The Academy of Management Review* 20(1): 65-91.

Fast, N. and Berg, N., (1975). The Lincoln Electric Company. *Harvard Business School Case, #376-028.*

Festinger, L. (1957). *A theory of cognitive dissonance,* Evanston, IL: Row & Peterson.

Fisher, J.G., Peffer, S.A., and Sprinkle, G.B. 2003. Budget-based contracts, budget levels, and group performance. *Journal of Management Accounting Research* 15: 51-74.

Friedman, M. (1970). The social responsibility of business is to increase its profit. *The New York Times Magazine,* September 13.

Glucksberg, S. (1962). The influence of strength of drive on functional fixedness and perceptual recognition. *Journal of Experimental Psychology* 63: 36–41.

Haldane, A. (2011). Control rights (and wrongs). Wincott Annual Memorial Lecture, 24 October. www.bankofengland.co.uk/publications/speeches.

Herzberg, F. (2003). One more time: How do you motivate employees? Reprinted in *Motivating People, Harvard Business Review* January.

Hillman, A. and G. Keim. (2001). Shareholder value, stakeholder management, and social issues: What's the bottom line? *Strategic Management Journal* 22(2): 125-139.

Hotz. R.L. (2008). Revenge of the freeloaders: Study finds culture influences reaction to reward, rebuke, *Wall Street Journal.* May 30: A10.

Ittner, C. and D. Larcker. (2001). Assessing empirical research in managerial accounting: A value-based management perspective. *Journal of Accounting and Economics* 32: 349–410.

Jensen, M. and W. Meckling. (1976). Theory of the firm: Managerial behavior, agency costs and ownership structure. *Journal of Financial Economics* 3(4): 305-360.

Khan, T. (2009). Teacher job satisfaction and incentive: A case study of Pakistan (www.eldis.org/vfile/upload/1/document/0709/Teacher_motivation_Pakistan.pdf)

Kerr, S. (1995). On the folly of rewarding A, while hoping for B. *Academy of Management Executive* 9(1): 7-14.

Kinney, W. R., Jr. (1986). Empirical accounting research design for Ph. D. students. *The Accounting Review* 61(2): 338-350.

Kleingeld, A., H. van Mierlo, and L. Arends. (2011). The effect of goal setting on group performance: A meta-analysis. *Journal of Applied Psychology* 96 (6): 1289.

Kohn, A. (1993). Why incentive plans cannot work. *Harvard Business Review* Sep-Oct: 54-63.

Kominis, G. and C. Emmanuel. (2007). The expectancy-valence theory revisited: Developing an extended model of managerial motivation. *Management Accounting Research* 18: 49-75.

Latham, G and E. Locke. (2006). Enhancing the benefits and overcoming the pitfalls of goal setting. *Organizational Dynamics* 35(4): 332–340.

Lawler, E. III. (1993). Effective reward systems: Strategy, diagnosis, design and change. CEO Publication G93-5 (225). Center for Effective Organizations, Marshall School of Business, University of Southern California.

Lindenberg, S. and N. Foss. (2011). Managing joint production motivation: The role of goal framing and governance mechanisms. *Academy of Management Review* 36(3): 500–525.

Locke, E. A., and Latham, G. P. (1990). *A theory of goal setting and task performance.* Englewood Cliffs, NJ: Prentice Hall.

Locke, E., and Latham, G. (2009). Has goal setting gone wild, or have its attackers abandoned good scholarship? *Academy of Management Perspectives* February: 17-23.

Locke, E., Shaw, K. N,, Saari, L., and Latham, G. (1981). Goal setting and task performance:1969-1980. *Psychological Bulletin,* 90: 125-152.

Malina, M. and F. Selto. (2004). Choice and change of measures in performance measurement models. *Management Accounting Research* 15(4): 441-69.

Maslow, A. (1970). *Motivation and Personality* (2nd ed.) New York: Harper & Row.

Merchant, K. A. and J-F. Manzoni. (1989). The achievability of budget targets in profit centers: A field study. *The Accounting Review* 64(3): 539-558.

Mitchell, T. R. (1982). Attributions and actions: A note of caution. *Journal of Management* 8(1):65-74.

Murphy, K. (2001). Performance standards in incentive contracts. *Journal of Accounting and Economics* 30: 245-278.

Parker, R.J., and Kyj, L. (2006). Vertical information sharing in the budgeting process. *Accounting, Organizations and Society* 31(1): 27-45.

Pinckney, B. (2011). TrustCo reinstates executive incentive plan. *The Business Review.* 24 January 2011.

Porter, L. W. and Lawler, E. E. (1968). *Managerial Attitudes and Performance.* Homewood, IL: Richard D. Irwin, Inc.

Pritchard, R.D.; Jones, S. D.; Roth, P. L.; Stuebing, K. K., and Ekeberg, S. E. (1988). Effects of group feedback, goal setting, and incentives on organizational productivity. *Journal of Applied Psychology* 73(2): 337-358.

Simon, H. A. (1956). Rational choice and the structure of the environment. *Psychological Review* 63(2): 129-138.

Taninecz, G. (1995). Kyocera's amoebas. *Industry Week;* June 5: 49.

Thaler, R. and C. Sunstein. (2009). *Nudge.* London: Penguin Books.

The Economist (Buttonwood). (2011). Reforming the banks: The wrong numbers, 25 October.

The Economist. (2010). Shareholders v stakeholders: A new idolatry. 22 April.

The International Society for Performance Improvement. (2002). *Incentives, Motivation and Workplace Performance: Research & Best Practices.*

Tita, Bob. (2010). In the black, but no pink slips. *Wall Street Journal.* (Eastern edition). New York, N.Y.: Mar 1: A.23.

Vroom, V. H. (1964). *Work and Motivation.* New York: McGraw Hill.

Weiner, B. (2011). Ultimate and proximal determinants of motivation given an attribution perspective and the metaphors guiding attribution theory. *Group & Organization Management* 36(4) 526–532.

Index